ECONOMIC PROBLEMS
OF
MODERN LIFE

ECONOMIC PROBLEMS
OF
MODERN LIFE

BY

S. HOWARD PATTERSON, A. M., Ph. D.,

*Assistant Professor of Economics, Wharton School of Finance and Commerce,
University of Pennsylvania. Author of "Family Desertion and Non-
Support," and Co-author of "American Social Problems"
and "Problems of American Democracy."*

AND

KARL W. H. SCHOLZ, A. M., Ph. D.,

*Assistant Professor of Economics, Wharton School of Finance and Commerce,
University of Pennsylvania. Co-author of "Rudiments of
Business Finance" and "The Science and Practice of
Urban Land Valuation."*

FIRST EDITION
FOURTH IMPRESSION

McGRAW-HILL BOOK COMPANY, INC.
NEW YORK: 370 SEVENTH AVENUE
LONDON: 6 & 8 BOUVERIE ST.; E. C. 4
1927

THE MAPLE PRESS COMPANY, YORK, PA.

PREFACE

"Economic Problems of Modern Life" is another introductory text in economics. The authors have endeavored to prepare a book which may be used either as the basis of a course in economic problems or as supplementary problem material to the traditional first course in principles. Although there are a number of good books on economic principles, and on economic principles and problems combined, at the present time there are not many available texts, which are devoted specifically to the study of present day economic problems.

Business men, in their everyday activity, are confronted with economic problems rather than with theoretical abstractions. They are forced to learn their economic principles by contact with practical business problems. In the case of the college student, however, the situation is usually reversed. Although progression from the concrete to the abstract is an old maxim of pedagogy, most courses in economics reverse this process by beginning with a study of principles and by concluding with an analysis of as many practical economic problems as time permits. It may be, however, that a systematic study of economic theory can best be made after the student has completed a survey of some outstanding problems of our economic life. Certainly an analysis of economic principles necessitates some knowledge of the complexities of our economic organization.

Although this book is primarily concerned with economic problems, in striving to give usefulness to the text the authors have been forced, incidentally, to introduce economic principles into their discussions. Just as economic theory cannot be kept in a vacuum, so a study of economic problems would be of little educational value without an attempt to discover the underlying principles which are involved. Moreover, in order to give unity to the text, some material has been introduced which may be found in books on economic principles. Most of this is contained in the introductory chapters in Part I. The inclusion of this material is essential for those students who have not had any previous training in economic principles.

v

Since a book on economic problems, as well as one on economic principles, should be made to tell a coherent story, it was felt that, in order to avoid a truncated text, a brief survey of the general organization of economic society should also be included.

Part I, Problems of Economic Organization; Part II, Problems of Monopoly; and Part V, Problems of Labor and Industrial Unrest, are chiefly the work of Mr. Patterson. Part III, Problems of Exchange; and Part IV, Problems of Public Finance, are largely the work of Mr. Scholz. Both authors have made liberal use of the specific contributions of authorities in the various specialized fields of applied economics, and disclaim any originality as to content. Acknowledgment of particular indebtedness is made wherever possible.

Since any reading in economics is merely a start for one's own thinking, it is hoped that the questions for discussion at the end of each chapter will aid the student in assimilating his assignment. The topics for investigation are suggested by the text material, and may be found helpful for supplementary work. In the collateral reading, listed at the end of each chapter, specific assignments pertaining to materials contained in the text will be found. A certain amount of collateral reading and the systematic keeping of reading notes will be found very helpful. The student should be encouraged to obtain a broad perspective of the subject by reading other authors with different points of view. In the references are listed more advanced and specialized treatises in the various fields of applied economics, which are only surveyed in such a general text as "Economic Problems of Modern Life."

The authors desire to express their appreciation of the keen interest and helpful suggestions of many of their colleagues in the Economics Department of the University of Pennsylvania, some of whom have used sections of the present text in its earlier mimeographed form with their classes. The authors are also indebted to Mr. Frank C. Baxter and Mr. Allan G. Chester, of the English Department of the University of Pennsylvania, for reading the manuscript before its final publication.

S. H. P.

K. W. H. S.

PHILADELPHIA, PA.
January, 1927.

CONTENTS

vii

CONTENTS

PART ONE

PROBLEMS OF ECONOMIC ORGANIZATION

ECONOMIC PROBLEMS OF MODERN LIFE

CHAPTER I

THE NATURE AND EVOLUTION OF ECONOMIC PROBLEMS

1. Economics as a Social Science.—Economics may be defined as the study of business, that is, of man's wealth-getting activities. Just as biology is the science of life, chemistry the science of matter, and physics the science of force, so economics is the science of wealth. But chemistry and physics are physical sciences; economics, on the other hand, is a social science. Its subject matter is not wealth itself, but rather mankind in the production, exchange, distribution, and consumption of wealth.

The term "science" implies the inductive method of approach, rather than the deductive, although both methods may be used. Experimental proof is necessary and the collection of data imperative. Science is objective rather than subjective. Indeed, it is essentially a method, rather than a body of subject matter. Science involves the careful observation and accurate description of phenomena in some particular field. It seeks the discovery of sequence, connection, and causation. Any hypothesis or a supposed correlation must be subjected to repeated tests for confirmation into a theory. If a theory stands the test of time and further experimentation, it becomes known as a scientific law.

The theories of the social sciences are more difficult of objective and inductive proof than are those of the physical sciences. Hence, the social sciences developed later than the physical sciences. It is difficult for mankind to put itself into a test tube and to record its own reactions impassively. There are greater limitations to experiments with human beings than with guinea pigs. Again, economic conditions are so very complex that it is difficult to isolate the particular economic force which is being studied. It is often impossible to separate a given tendency from the other social forces which conceal and confuse it. Finally, economic society is dynamic rather than static, that is, it is constantly changing. Similar conditions seldom repeat themselves in exactly the same way from time to time and from place to place. The difficulty of formulating social and economic laws explains the tardy development of economics and the other social sciences. Economics has striven, however, to become a science by the utilization of the scientific method employed by the physical sciences. At present, numerous quantitative and statistical studies are being undertaken to test the validity of certain assumptions of the older economists who were philosophers rather than scientists.

Because economics is a social science, it is related to sociology, which studies especially group life and the process of association. Economic evolution and social evolution have gone on together. The higher the social organization of the group, the better able it is to adapt itself to the economic environment and to gratify more fully its economic wants. Since there is a close relationship between industrial society and other social institutions, such as the family, the church, and the school, most economic problems have important social effects. The state is also an important social institution, whose relationship to industrial society has compelled governments to assume a number of new functions, such as the regulation of public utilities and the supervision of conditions of labor. Today the institution of the state is one of the great agencies of social control. Economics is therefore related to political science as well as to sociology.

Because of the close relationship of economics to sociology and political science, it is not easy to single out certain problems of our national life and to say that they are economic, rather than social or political problems. For illustration, how would socialism be classified? Obviously, it lies in all three fields. For inclusion in this text we have merely selected from a wide range of problems those topics whose economic aspects seem to be the most striking. All of these economic problems will also have their social and political phases. Thus, monopoly is an economic problem which has important social consequences. When solutions are suggested and legislative reforms planned, we cross into the field of political science as well as sociology.

2. Pure and Applied Economics.—The aim of all science is the discovery of truth, rather than the production of effective propaganda. Furthermore, the aim of pure science is not the immediate utilization of its results, but rather the discovery of truth for its own sake. The real objective is the building up of a body of correct principles from a sound basis in fact. Thus, the pure science of economics studies the consumption, the production, the exchange, and the distribution of wealth. It endeavors to describe economic processes exactly as they take place, and not as the observer thinks that they should take place. Its prime object is to explain, rather than to justify or criticize. Moreover, ethical considerations are not involved and individual judgment is minimized. True science has no right or wrong, except merely in the sense of correctness. The "human equation" is likewise eliminated so far as possible. Thus, the pure scientist analyses a substance and pronounces it to be a powerful poison. The applied scientist seeks its uses and deliberates as to whether it shall be used in gas warfare to destroy human beings or as a tree spray to increase the world's food supply.

Applied economics differs from pure economics in the same way that applied science differs from pure science. Applied science seeks to utilize the results of pure science in some utilitarian and immediate fashion. It is confronted with particular problems, rather than with general theories. Applied science, however, is always dependent on pure science. The Industrial Revolution was made possible by the scientific renaissance which took place several centuries earlier. Numerous inventions of tremendous practical significance could never have taken place had it not been for the past research work of some theoretical scientist. The electric light, the radio and numerous coal-tar products are proof of the value of scientific research. Applied economics likewise depends on pure economics, and the solution of economic problems involves economic theory. Although there will be differences of opinion as to how the economic welfare of the group may be advanced, a common knowledge of fundamental economic principles is essential. Zeal must be tempered with knowledge.

Applied economics involves ethical and subjective elements, for here individual judgment is required. Questions of policy are involved, and the benefits of one solution must be balanced against those of another. For example, pure economics considers how the interest rate is determined and by what laws the monopoly price is established. On the other hand, applied economics considers whether or not interest should be paid and monopolies be permitted to exist. If not, what are the other alternatives and how may they be achieved? We may say that applied economics involves the social concept, but there is no general agreement as to what constitutes social welfare and how it may best be achieved. All individuals are apt to identify their own divergent points of view with the best interests of the group. History resounds with the clash of ideas of conscientious statesmen as to group welfare. Because of the introduction of this personal element, objective tests of economic welfare are difficult in the analysis of a given economic problem.[1]

3. Nature of an Economic Problem.—An economic problem differs from an algebraic problem, which has but one correct answer, in that it cannot be solved for a single unknown quantity. In an economic problem there is usually no one correct answer which excludes all others as incorrect. There are generally several ways out of a given situation, each of which has its advantages and its corresponding disadvantages. Every proposal contains the good and the bad, the desirable and the undesirable, and the student often faces a choice between conflicting and often incommensurate values. Again, economic problems are related, and what seems to be a favorable solution for one problem may cause a maladjustment in some related economic situation, even as in medicine a drug which cures one disease may induce another, and thus be of doubtful value.

A study of economic problems is very complex because it involves many things. In the first place, it is necessary to get all the facts which bear upon the problem at issue; in the second place, a careful balancing must be made between the relative advantages and disadvantages of each proposal. Indeed, training in economics does not involve so much the acquisition of a body of subject matter as it does the mental discipline of logical reasoning. Close observation and careful judgment are also imperative. There are a number of economic panaceas, which, like the widely advertised patent medicine, will cure all the ills of the body politic. The student will do well to avoid such nostrums in his search for the answers to any economic problem.

---

[1] In "Essays in Social Justice," Prof. T. N. Carver strives to outline a scientific morality in terms of its contribution to group longevity.

The good physician is a careful diagnostician and not the purveyor of cure-alls.

The study of economic problems is frequently disappointing to the beginner who is seeking predigested and carefully catalogued answers to the many questions which have been continually perplexing him. Let us make it clear at the outset that this text does not attempt any such program. It merely seeks to state the problems carefully, to break them up into their component parts, and to point out some of the many proposed solutions. After a review of some of the experiments which have been tried, the student is left free to make his own choice.

4. Origin and Development of Economic Problems.— Economic problems arise from man's attempt to secure for himself more and better economic goods, that is, those commodities or services which are not supplied free by nature and which have the ability to gratify human wants. The two primary factors in this economic drama are man and his environment. The great motivating force is found in human wants. Hence, economic problems arise from two sources: (1) out of man's struggle with his environment, and (2) out of man's competition with his fellow men to secure for himself a maximum share in the good things of life.

Nature does not supply its gifts in unlimited abundance. Economic goods are scarce because of the niggardliness of nature or because labor is necessary for their production. If we lived in some Utopia or Paradise, where all goods were supplied without effort or limit, there would be no necessity to struggle either with our environment or with our fellow men. But since ours is not a Utopian world, we find both a scarcity of goods and a need for labor. Out of a scarcity of economic goods arises a conflict of interests. Hence, economic problems exist, and society is forced to interfere in the primordial struggle for existence. Forms of competition must be regulated, for the business of getting a living cannot degenerate into predatory activities. Moreover, competition is not restricted to individuals. Primitive groups struggled for favorable pasture lands, and modern nations vie with each other for the control of foreign markets and lands rich in such natural resources as coal or petroleum. There is a conflict of interests between groups as well as within groups. Social control is just beginning to expand from national to international boundaries. International law is still in the making.

At first, human wants were very simple and limited to such bare necessities of life as food, shelter and clothing. Primitive man's efforts to make his environment supply these few wants were equally crude. One phase of the history of civilization is that of inventions and discoveries. The conquest of nature involves an increased knowledge of natural forces and an increased ability to use them in economic production. Much of this active adaptation was accomplished in the long ages of prehistoric time, before the grey dawn of history illuminated the early civilizations of the Nile and the Tigris-Euphrates. Illustrations of acquired knowledge, which is our present legacy from prehistoric times, are the discovery of fire, the domestication of plants and animals, and the invention of tools.

Man in his economic evolution has progressed from a simple undifferentiated society to a complex, highly specialized society. As our economic organization has become more intricate, new problems have arisen because of this increased complexity. A comparison of modern industrial society with that existing before the Industrial Revolution is like the comparison of a high-speed automobile with a primitive ox-cart. The latter is inferior, but far simpler. A delicate and complex machine is more apt to get out of order because of the increased possibility of error. Moreover, the consequences are apt to be far more serious. Modern economic society possesses a highly organized system of finance and credit, which makes possible a world-wide commerce and specialization, but also a world-wide interdependence. The era of barter was more primitive, and it did not have the problem of business cycles. Roundabout and capitalistic production has increased the world's wealth, but it has also enhanced the probability of misdirected production and unemployment. Progress has its costs as well as its benefits.

Increased ability to gratify human wants does not result in a decrease of economic wants. It merely means the creation of new and higher wants. The necessities of modern life include more than mere subsistence. This limitless expansibility of human wants can be seen in the evolution of economic society as a whole and also in the case of individuals whose income has increased. Material civilization is the story of increasing wants and of increasing ability to gratify old ones. The process of adjustment will be continuous so long as the stock of acquired knowledge is increasing. A dynamic society is always facing new problems of adjustment. One of the most striking characteristics of modern civilization is its fluidity; that is, old problems disappear merely to be succeeded by new ones. To hope that some day there will be no economic problems is to hope for the stagnation and lack of progress which characterize a static society. Rising standards, both ethical and material, make for social unrest and dissatisfaction with existing conditions. A progressive society has growing pains. Philosophers of antiquity approached the problem of human happiness subjectively and taught that the suppression of human wants was the philosophical ideal. Religious teachers stressed spiritual needs rather than economic wants. They subordinated the present world to the future life. Modern economists approach the problem objectively. They assume increasing material wants and give them free reign, except in so far as they are inimical to social welfare. The economic ideal is that of a constantly increasing ability to gratify human wants by superior adaptability to the physical environments and by improved social organization.

But despite the fluidity of our economic life, the economic problems of one age are often similar to those of another. Although history never repeats itself in exactly the same way, it affords many interesting analogies. Thus, agrarian problems have continued from the Roman Gracchi to the modern Henry George. The rise of constitutional democracies ended the arbitrary grants of monopoly power by absolute monarchs, but the recent concentration in industry has presented the old problem again in the form of the modern trust. One great problem of our national life disappears, only to be succeeded by an analogous problem. Problems come and go, but the stream is as continuous as Tennyson's famous brook.

5. The Industrial Revolution.—The Industrial Revolution may be defined as the changes caused by the invention of power machinery and the substitution of the factory system for the domestic system of manufacturing. Just as the Renaissance separates medieval from modern history, and as the French Revolution separates the ancient regime from the new, so the Industrial Revolution separates the old economic order from the modern. Many of the leading economic problems of today may be traced back to the Industrial Revolution, which changed the whole character and organization of industrial society. It was a tremendous period of economic adjustment which has not entirely subsided. The French Revolution, which took place at about the same time as the Industrial Revolution, was far more spectacular and attracted much more attention. Although the French Revolution produced profound social and political changes, it is doubtful if it revolutionized the lives of succeeding generations as much as did the Industrial Revolution.

Judged by a purely materialistic standard, the world of Napoleon and Washington had much more in common with that of Julius Caesar and Marcus Aurelius than it had with the world of Marconi and Edison. During the two thousand years preceding the Industrial Revolution, tremendous cultural, religious, and political changes had taken place, but progress in the arts of production, transportation, and communication was made slowly. Homespun cloth was worn by the patriots who suffered at Valley Forge, and the cumbersome hand loom was still in operation. Methods of illumination, communication and transportation had improved but slightly. Benjamin Franklin made candles by hand in the home of his father. Oil-burning lamps similar to those of ancient Rome were in general use. Modern means of communication, such as the telegraph, the telephone and the radio were undreamed of. The small sailing vessel had not been replaced by the modern steamer. Men journeyed by land on foot or by horse. The methods of travel used by the troops of Napoleon were hardly superior to those employed by the legions of Julius Caesar. Indeed, many of the old Roman roads were still in use. There had been some improvements in methods of farming, but the invention of agricultural machinery was a triumph of the nineteenth century. The population of Europe had remained almost stationary during the Middle Ages, but within a century after the Industrial Revolution it was possible for Europe to support more than twice as great a number of inhabitants. Great cities arose which were many times larger than the former medieval towns.

It is difficult to give exact dates to the Industrial Revolution. In the final analysis, it was a gradual evolution, the suddenness and rapidity of which are only relative as compared with other periods of history. One cannot say exactly when the Industrial Revolution began nor just when it ended. Perhaps it is still in progress, for the series of inventions has been fairly continuous. The process of industrialization took place at different times in different countries. It is generally conceded, however, that the

Industrial Revolution appeared first in England. Moreover, since it is generally agreed that in England the Industrial Revolution first appeared in the textile industry, we may find in the history of that industry an approximate date for the beginning of the Industrial Revolution.

Spinning had formerly been more laborious than weaving. It required a number of spinners to supply material for one weaver. Hence, inducements had been offered for improvements in the methods of spinning. The successive inventions of Hargreaves, Arkwright, and Crompton revised the situation and necessitated corresponding improvements in the methods of weaving. Under this new stimulus the first power loom was invented by an English clergyman named Edmund Cartwright. Water power was first used to run the new textile machinery, but it was later supplanted by the steam engine. In 1769, James Watt patented his single-acting pumping engine, and, in 1782, his double-acting engine for the propelling of machinery. In 1785, the latter was first used to supply power for a cotton mill, and that date represents a turning point in England's industrial history. Wood was the earliest fuel, but coal was later utilized. The early factories had developed on swift streams, but the later ones were located near deposits of coal, as the steam engine gradually supplanted water power.

The Industrial Revolution affected methods of transportation as well as methods of manufacturing. We must include as part of the same general movement Robert Fulton's invention of the steamboat in 1807 and Stephenson's invention of the locomotive in 1814. Improved methods of communication, such as the telegraph and the telephone, followed a generation later. In a general way, then, we may say that the Industrial Revolution in England began in the latter half of the eighteenth century, but continued during the nineteenth century in ever-widening aspects.

6. Effects of the Industrial Revolution.—The Industrial Revolution made manufacturing lose its etymological significance of making by hand. The substitution of expensive power machinery for the simple hand tool meant the substitution of the factory system for the domestic system. Manufacturing went outside the home and into the factory, since to use machinery economically, it was necessary to produce on a large scale. Scores and even hundreds of hands were now employed under one roof. The new machinery was too expensive to be owned by the workers themselves. Hence, they lost the ownership of their instruments of production and the control of their conditions of employment. A new group of capitalists arose who took over the balance of power from the former landed aristocracy. A different social stratification and a new class consciousness were created. Machinery did not require the skill of the former crafts- man, for it could be operated by women or children. The use of machinery involved not only large scale production, but also a rather minute division of labor, which is both monotonous and fatiguing. A sad page in the history of the Industrial Revolution is that of the exploitation of children, particularly those of pauper parents in English poorhouses. The increased use of capital made the process of production still more roundabout. The introduction of machinery created temporary unemployment and perhaps an increased likelihood of future unemployment. The craftsmen who were displaced by the new machines sometimes retaliated by wrecking the factories. For a generation, the hand weavers kept up a futile competition in their garrets and cellars against machinery and the factory system.

The location, as well as the character, of English industry was changed by the Industrial Revolution. Manufacturing sites moved northward toward the great deposits of coal, and population migrated in the same direction. There was a tend- ency toward urban concentration into great industrial centers. The fact that England was the home of the Industrial Revolution was partly responsible for her early industrial and commercial supremacy. As she became a great manufacturing nation, however, she ceased to be self-supporting. World markets were sought for the disposal of her manufactured goods and for the purchase of food and the raw material of industry. Just as the close of the Middle Ages had been a period of transition from a local economy to a national economy, so the Industrial Revolu- tion may be regarded as inaugurating a new period of inter- national or world economy. The industrialization of Germany and the United States followed several generations after that of England.

At the present time, eastern Europe and the Orient are feeling the quickening pulse of the Industrial Revolution. Machinery is being imported and factories have been founded. Cotton mills are springing up in India and within the shadow of the

Egyptian pyramids. Silk mills are being built in Japan and rail-roads in China. Oriental peoples numbering hundreds of millions are now experiencing the throes of the Industrial Revolution. In spite of the social progress of the last hundred years, a number of economic maladjustments which appeared in England during the Industrial Revolution are repeating themselves in some of the more newly industrialized sections of the world.

The Industrial Revolution was one of the greatest periods of adjustment through which economic society has passed. The process is not yet completed, and we are still suffering from many maladjustments growing out of the new conditions. Society and the individuals in it have not yet adjusted themselves to the changed economic environment. Individuals and communities have become interdependent in a sense never before known. A higher social morality is necessary and an improved social control of industry must be developed. The machine is still up on trial. Is it to be the master or the slave of society? Do its economic advantages outweigh the social costs? The machine has increased economic production and raised material standards of living, but it has created serious problems of welfare in industry.

7. Social Control of Industry.—The conflict of interests which is the source of economic problems calls for an attempt on the part of organized society to protect the interest of the group against unlimited individualism. Some rules of the game are necessary under the fiercest competition. Otherwise, certain ruthless individuals would attempt to gratify their wants and gain wealth by predatory methods. Hence, social control, which refers to the influence of society over the thought and action of the individuals who compose it, is necessary. By the exercise of social control the activities of individuals are brought into conformity with the crystallized opinion of the group. The collective mind thus restrains the individual from actions which are regarded as unsocial and impels him toward those deeds which meet with popular approval. An unsocial act is one which is regarded as inimical to the best interests and longevity of the group.

There are three stages in the evolution of social control—custom, public opinion and law. The folkways become mores, that is, custom becomes morality, as a given rite or traditional routine becomes associated with group welfare. Social evolution is the story of progress from blind tradition to rational public opinion and from mob mind to deliberative public assemblies. Written law gradually succeeds unwritten custom as history unfolds itself. Today, public opinion must first formulate itself before it crystallizes into law. Child labor laws and prohibition are examples of this development.

It must not be thought, however, that law ever supplants public opinion and custom as the sole expression of social control. The activities of modern individuals are as much influenced by the customs of the age and the public opinion of the group as by the laws of the nation. All human institutions are agencies of social control. In addition to the state, the family, the church and the school are powerful social institutions which influence our industrial life and, in turn, are influenced by it. The customs, opinions, and standards of the social groups to which we belong influence our individual thought and action as much as governmental statutes. The profession, the business, or the trade union to which an individual belongs has its own forms of social control. Thus, we speak of the professional ethics of the physician as different from those of the business world. Sabotage is condemned by one labor organization and condoned by another. The forms and strength of social control differ among various economic groups.

The type of social control as well as the necessity for it varies greatly in different stages of economic evolution. Individualism may flourish in an agricultural community, but with the advent of industrialism and the growth of cities increased social control becomes imperative. Specialization and the factory system must be accompanied by greater state control of industry. Economic interdependence necessitates a social conscience, and individual morality must broaden into a social morality. Of recent years the police power of the state has been called upon to justify the passage of social legislation which seems to encroach upon individual liberty. The police power of the state is its right to pass legislation or to enforce executive mandates when the interest of the group requires that individual liberty be sacrificed to the common safety, health, or welfare of the group. The police power of the state is now a constantly growing and expanding concept. It was submerged in the individualism or *laissez-faire* philosophy of a century or more ago, but it has been greatly extended since the Industrial Revolution and the concentration of population in congested industrial communities.

8. Local and National Control of Industry.—During the Middle Ages, what we understand by the national state was practically nonexistent. Under feudalism the manor was both the economic and the political unit. What social control of industry existed was local. The feudal barons coined their own money and made their own tariff charges.

In most cases local regulation of industry amounted merely to debasing the currency for selfish purposes and to preying upon what little commerce passed through the manors. The brighter side of the story is illustrated by such an organization as the Hanseatic League, which was organized to protect commerce and to make helpful regulations for its conduct. The guilds represented local organizations for the control of industry. They formulated and enforced the most minute regulations concerning the occupations of their members. Thus, night work was frequently prohibited, weights and measures were regulated, and the adulteration or cheapening of products forbidden.

With the decline of feudalism, the manorial system and the guilds, a new system of control developed which is known as the national system. As strong central governments developed out of the former feudal confusion, they began to regulate industry and commerce. In England, the strong monarchy of the Tudors reflected itself in economic as well as political measures. The Statute of Apprentices, for illustration, made labor compulsory and imposed on the local justices of the peace the duty of fixing wages. Monopolies were frequently granted by Queen Elizabeth to her favorites. For the carrying on of foreign trade and the development of the newly discovered land, great national trading companies were chartered. These companies often exercised political powers as well as economic functions in the exploitation of the territory specified in their charters.

The economic philosophy of this period of national economy is known as mercantilism, which reached its greatest development in the seventeenth century. Mercantilism emphasized foreign trade and measured national prosperity in terms of a favorable balance of trade. Happy was that nation whose exports exceeded its imports, and which therefore received in return a flow of the precious metals. All sorts of nationalistic regulations of commerce and industry were imposed in order to accomplish this desired result. Bounties were placed on certain exports

and duties on various imports.   In some cases the exportation of
gold was actually forbidden.   Foreign possessions were viewed
as a means of attaining the ideal of national greatness.   Colonies
were regarded as a legitimate field of exploitation, from which
the mother country could receive the raw materials of industry
and to which she could export the finished goods.   The navigation laws of the century preceding the American Revolution were
the products of a mercantilistic philosophy.

9. Reign of Laissez-faire.—A reaction finally set in against
this extreme nationalism and governmental interference with
industry.   In 1776, there appeared Adam Smith's "Wealth of
Nations," a book which had a tremendous influence on both
economic theories and practises.   The "Father of Economics"
explained in it his central principle of *laissez-faire*, or let-alone
policy.   He argued the case for free trade among nations and
strove to show that industry would flourish best when freed from
the vexatious interference of governments.   Adam Smith
regarded the functions of the state as limited to three fields—the
protection of its citizens from foreign invasion, the maintenance
of justice at home through the courts, and the establishment of
certain public works and institutions which were uneconomic
for individuals to maintain.

The economic philosophy of *laissez-faire* was gradually translated
into the actions of statesmen.   The British parliaments of the
early years of the nineteenth century removed a number of the
older restrictions on trade and industry.   Thus, the Statute
of Apprentices, which permitted wage fixing, and the Corn
Laws, which prevented the free importation of grain, were finally
repealed.   The theory of *laissez-faire* was seized upon by the
rising manufacturing class, as it opposed governmental interference with working conditions.   Indeed, the theory is sometimes called that of the Manchester School because of its
advocacy by the Manchester manufacturers.   Under such an
economic philosophy the Industrial Revolution developed.

10. New Functions of Government.—The Industrial Revolution brought about new conditions which made untenable the
former theory of *laissez-faire*, or let-alone, in industry.   Under
the dominance of a philosophy of individualism little children
and mothers toiled in factories and mines under unthinkable
conditions.   England was confronted with a condition and not
with a theory.   Labor laws and other humanitarian legislation

gradually came into existence. Moreover, a growing concentration took place in business organization, and new problems like those of the trust and the railroad called for governmental action. Monopolies became so numerous that a complacent reliance on the force of competition was no longer possible. National regulation of big business was demanded, and individual initiative was viewed with suspicion. In the case of certain public utilities, a further transition took place from governmental regulation to governmental ownership and operation. Schools of socialism developed which sought to advance all large-scale industries from the stage of governmental regulation to the ultimate goal of socialization. Europe and the United States received the dawning shock of paternalism.

The last century witnessed a tremendous growth of governmental functions and of collective economic effort. During the World War increased cooperation became imperative and governments deliberately shaped the industrial activities of their peoples. Consciously or unconsciously the former theory of *laissez-faire* has become a matter of mere historical interest. Although numerous individuals are pleading for "less government in business," a return to the *laissez-faire* of Adam Smith and Herbert Spencer is unthinkable. Whether the future will witness a further development of governmental regulation of industry, or a reaction in the other direction, remains to be seen. To the student of economic history, however, it is interesting to see how the pendulum has swung from the national system toward *laissez-faire*, and then back again from *laissez-faire* toward governmental regulation.

Numerous attempts have been made to classify the new functions of government. Some writers differentiate between the primary functions of the state, such as protection from foreign invasion and domestic disorder, and the secondary functions of the state, such as the regulation of industry. These latter functions may be subdivided according to industries which are primarily predatory, those which are primarily competitive, and those which are natural monopolies. The first type of occupation should be suppressed, and the plane of competition should be regulated in the second group of industries. Those industries in which competition is self-destructive the state should recognize as natural monopolies, to be placed under governmental operation or strict governmental regulation.

The problem of the social control of industry may be approached from still a different angle. Governmental interference with industry may be classified according to the interests of consumers, workers, investors, and the general public. Governmental interference for the protection of consumers may be illustrated by pure food laws. The state has also been forced to regulate the railroads to avoid exorbitant and discriminatory rates. In the second place, the interests of the workers have been profoundly affected by the invention of machinery and the development of the factory system. Illustrations of governmental interference with conditions of labor are factory laws to safeguard health and safety, social insurance, legislation limiting hours of work, and minimum wage laws for women. Furthermore, the state has interfered in industry to protect the investor as well as the consumer and the worker. The corporate form of business organization has divorced ownership from control and has facilitated financial manipulation. Hence, most states have passed "blue sky" laws to prevent the development of fraudulent concerns. Finally, there is a mass of miscellaneous regulations of industry which governments have initiated for the protection of the general public. The conservation of forests and the restriction of immigration illustrate this form of governmental regulation.

11. Solution of Economic Problems.—The mere increase of governmental functions and the passage of new legislation do not necessarily solve economic problems. Indeed, unwise laws and the failure of administrative machinery to function properly may merely create more serious problems. Herbert Spencer has drawn an interesting comparison between the methods of the skilled mechanic and those of the novice. He wrote as follows:[1]

You see this wrought-iron plate is not quite flat; it sticks up here a little towards the left—"cockles," as we say. How shall we flatten it? Obviously, you reply by hitting on the part that is prominent. Well, here is a hammer, and give the plate a blow as you advise. Harder, you say, still no effect. Another blow? Well, there is one, and another, and another. The prominence remains, you see; the evil is as great as ever—greater indeed. But this is not all. Look at the warp which the plate has got near the opposite edge. Where it was flat before, it is now curved. A pretty bungle we have made of it. Instead of curing the original defect, we have produced a second. Had we asked an arti-

[1] *Cf.* "The Study of Sociology," chap. **IV.**

san practiced in "planishing" as it is called, he would have told us that no good was to be done, but that only mischief, by hitting down on the projecting part. He would have taught us how to give variously adjusted blows with a hammer, elsewhere, so attacking the evil, not by direct, but by indirect actions. The required process is less simple than you thought. Even a sheet of metal is not to be successfully dealt with after those common-sense methods in which you hear so much confidence. What, then, shall we say about a society? "Do you think I am easier to be played on than a pipe?" asked Hamlet. Is humanity more readily straightened than an iron plate?

Although an economic problem like a mechanical problem may appear to be very easy of solution, it may perhaps require a very delicate adjustment. Spencer's picture of the process of adjustment should not be interpreted as an illustration of the futility of any social or governmental interference with economic maladjustments, but rather of the necessity for carefully considered methods which will not result in more harm than good.

12. Attitude of the Student.—The fact that an economic problem has no one answer, but rather a number of different solutions, makes dogmatism on the part of either the student or the teacher impossible. We shall try to make out a case for neither the open nor the closed shop, for neither free trade nor protection, but rather to present the arguments on both sides. The student should begin his study of economic problems with the scientific attitude of intellectual curiosity, and he should be prepared to follow the argument wherever it leads. All personal prejudices and preconceived opinions must be sloughed off so far as possible. Snap judgments are to be discouraged, for any decision can be made only after a careful study of the full facts in the case.

Economic problems are being discussed in modern society with the same fervor that characterized the medieval arguments on theological questions. The street corner, the club, the barber shop and the dinner table produce glib speakers if not deep thinkers. The bootblack who shines your shoes will meanwhile talk garrulously on the injustice of a higher street-car fare, although he is probably unable to answer intelligently a single question on the problem of railroad valuation and rate making. The commuter will express violent opposition to Bolshevism without any exact information concerning the nature and meaning of that movement. His imagination pictures a Bolshevik as a dangerous foreigner with long whiskers, hip boots, and a bomb in his hand: this is the extent of his knowledge in the matter, and yet he does not hesitate to express his opinion roundly. He would not dare to make such a superficial judgment in the fields of the physical or biological sciences: he would leave to the medical expert the question of a radium cure for cancer. There is just as great a need for exact knowledge and disciplined scientific thinking in the discussion of economic problems as there is in the consideration of problems in the physical or biological sciences. We must develop the scientific attitude which will impel us to suspend judgment until the facts on both sides have been secured.

If one must approach an economic problem with definite knowledge of the facts concerned, it is also true that one must approach the problem with an open mind. In its search for truth, science demands of the thinker that he be in all ways unprejudiced; on the other hand, ignorance and bias seem almost inseparable companions. The impersonal attitude is difficult to attain, however, because our feelings run high when we discuss problems associated with capitalism, private property and wages. Self-interest is apt to produce an emotional rather than an intellectual reaction. Each individual is surrounded as with a cloud by his own social environment, and one accepts the social heredity of his parents as unconsciously as he receives their physical heredity. Our "own" opinions are really a complex of those of our family circle, our church, our school, our club and our social group. The late Samuel Gompers, former president of the American Federation of Labor, and Judge Gary, of the United States Steel Corporation, were the products of two different social and economic environments. Without doubting in the least the intellectual honesty of these two men, it is easy to see how each would have analyzed differently the term "collective bargaining," and how each would have regarded differently the issue of the open and the closed shop.

In our treatment of economic problems we shall constantly be dealing with controversial questions. The vested interests, that is, selfish considerations opposing changes, are always present to conceal the underlying economic principles. It is easy to develop an economic nearsightedness which will obscure the arguments on the other side. We must strive continually and consciously to get the "other fellow's point of view." This is a difficulty which the student of the physical sciences does not have to face. The student in chemistry who drops a piece of zinc into a test tube of hydrochloric acid will obtain hydrogen in whatever university the experiment is performed: the result will be the same whether he is a Caucasian or a Negro. The human equation, however, is apt to project itself into the analysis of an economic problem.

Thus, economic problems, which have to do with wages, taxes, and the high cost of living, touch a man's personal interest very closely; he is tremendously concerned with these—for here his comfort and happiness are directly affected. Even the scientist, who seeks to investigate economic problems with an impartial detachment, must nevertheless eat, buy clothing, and keep his job. It is much easier to contemplate the production of hydrogen with a scientific aloofness than it is to contemplate the rising cost of butter or the prospect of a trolley strike. The scientific attitude seeks to eliminate this personal element so far as it is possible. Although we are on the intellectual firing line, the position of a true student should be above the smoke of battle.

13. Summary.—Economics is the science of business. The term science implies the inductive, experimental, and objective methods of approach. In its search for causation, the human equation must be reduced to a minimum. The attitude of the student must be free from prejudice and bias. Economics is a social science, that is, it does not study wealth so much as mankind in the production, consumption, exchange, and distribution of wealth. Production is usually done cooperatively today, and standards of consumption are, in general, socially determined. An attempt at the solution of economic problems involves governmental action, and economics is as closely related to political science as it is to sociology. Pure economics is analytical and seeks to describe how the industrial system operates. Applied economics studies economic problems rather than economic principles. The aim of pure economics is the discovery of truth; applied economics, on the other hand, seeks the improvement of existing conditions and the translation of knowledge into action. In the solution of economic problems, however, individual judgment is required, for a choice must be made between conflicting and often incommensurate values.

The origin of economic problems lies in natural scarcity and the conflict between man and his environment, as well as in the conflict between man and his fellows. By active adaptation to or increasing control over the environment, man has been able to gratify his ever-increasing wants. Nevertheless, a conflict of interests persists which makes necessary the social control of industry. Social control is the influence of the group over the actions of the individuals who compose it. Individual acquisition is subordinated to ideals of group welfare. Social institutions, such as the state, the church, and the family are agencies of social control. Social control has developed from unwritten custom to written law and from blind tradition to more rational forms of social control. The police power of the state is its authority to pass laws which restrict the liberty of individuals in the interests of the public safety, health, or general welfare.

As social evolution progressed the economic unit expanded. During the Middle Ages the manor was an economically self-sufficient unit, and the feudal barons were politically sovereign. Craft and trade guilds conducted manufacturing and commerce. They imposed strict regulations upon their members and occupied a monopoly position. As commerce increased towns sprang up and trade routes developed. The local economy of the Middle Ages was superseded by the national economy of modern times. Strong national governments grew up which regulated industry and trade under a system known as mercantilism. A reverse tendency put in its appearance during the period of revolutions in the eighteenth century. Individualism was temporarily in the ascendency. *Laissez-faire* represented the reduction to a minimum of governmental interference with industry.

The Industrial Revolution was brought about by the invention of power machinery and the substitution of the factory system for the domestic system. It was an important period of transition from an older economic order to modern industrial conditions. Although it increased production and raised standards of living for all classes, the Industrial Revolution created serious economic and social problems. The result has been a great increase in the functions of government and an abandonment of the former philosophy of *laissez-faire*. Social control of industry has become imperative, and a world economy has succeeded a national economy. Nevertheless, at the present time a number of American statesmen are expressing their opposition to the increasing governmental influence with business and to the increase of Federal powers at the expense of the state's rights.

Collateral Reading

BYE, R. T., "Principles of Economics," chaps. 1 and 2.

BOUCKE, F. O., "Principles of Economics," Part I.

CARVER, T. N., "Principles of Political Economy," chaps. 1, 2, 5, and 6.

CHAPIN, F. S., "An Historical Introduction to Social Economy," Parts III and IV.

CLAY, H., "Economics for the General Readers," chap. 1.

EDIE, L. D., "Economics, Principles and Problems," chaps. 1, 2 and 3.

ELY, R. T., "Outlines of Economics," chaps. 1, 3, 4, 5, and 6.

FAIRCHILD, F. R., FURNISS, E. S., and BUCK, N. S., "Elementary Economics," vol. I. chaps. 1, 2, 3, 4 and 10.

HAMILTON, W., "Current Economic Problems, " chaps. 1, 2, and 3.

MARSHALL, L. C., "Readings in Industrial Society," chaps. 1, 2, and 3.

MARSHALL, L. C., WRIGHT C. W., and FIELD, J. A., "Materials for a Study of Elementary Economics," chap. 1.

MARSHALL, L. C., and LYON, L. S., "Our Economic Organization," chaps. 1–8.

ROBINSON, J. H., and BEARD, C. A., "Development of Modern Europe," vol. II, chapter on Industrial Revolution.

SEAGER, H. R., "Principles of Economics," chap. 1.

SELIGMAN, E. R. A., "Principles of Economics," chaps. 1, 2, 3, 5, 6, and 7.

SHEARMAN, H. P., "Practical Economics," chaps. 1 and 3.

TAUSSIG, F. W., "Principles of Economics," vol. I chap. 1.

TURNER, J. R., "Introduction to Economics," chaps. 1–5.

References

ASHLEY, W., "Economic History of England."

BEARD, C., "The Industrial Revolution."

CHEYNEY, E. P., "Introduction to the Industrial and Social History of England."

DAY, C., "History of Commerce."

GRAS, H. S. B., "An Introduction to English Economic History."

HAMMOND, J. L., and B., "The Rise of Modern Industry."

HOBSON, J. A., "The Industrial System."

JENNINGS, W. W., "A History of Economic Progress in the United States."

OGG, F. A., "The Economic Development of Modern Europe." "Social Progress in Contemporary Europe."

TONYBEE, A., "The Industrial Revolution."

USHER, A. P., "Economic History of England."

VAN METRE, T. W., "Economic History of the United States."

Questions for Discussion

1. Differentiate between pure and applied economics.
2. Do you regard this distinction as valid and important?
3. In what respects is an economic problem difficult of solution?
4. How do economic problems originate?
5. Describe the medieval manor as an economic unit.
6. Trace the origin and decline of the guilds. What were their functions?

7. Name some economic changes in the transition period from medieval to modern times.

8. What is meant by the national system and mercantilism?

9. What do you understand by *laissez-faire?*

10. What was the Industrial Revolution?

11. Outline its various phases: (*a*) industrially and (*b*) geographically.

12. Outline the chief effects of the Industrial Revolution: (*a*) economically, (*b*) socially, and (*c*) politically.

Topics for Investigation

1. The scientific method of economics.
2. The claim of economics to be a science.
3. The relationship between economics and the other social sciences.
4. The Industrial Revolution and the new functions of the state.
5. The present industrialization of backward nations.
6. Social consequences of the Industrial Revolution.

CHAPTER II

FUNDAMENTAL CHARACTERISTICS OF MODERN ECONOMIC LIFE

1. Machinery and Technology.—Technology has been defined as the application of science to the problems of economic production. Power machinery is the triumph of modern technology. The machine may be defined as a tool which is operated automatically. It usually consists of a number of standardized tools, which are operated simultaneously by some natural force, such as steam or electricity. Thus, the "spinning jenny" consisted of a number of simple spindles propelled by water power.

The invention of power machinery resulted in the transition from the domestic system of manufacturing to the factory system. Manufacturing went outside the home and large-scale production succeeded small-scale production. Spinning, weaving and shoe making are now performed in factories rather than in the home. The same is true of a large portion of such other occupations as baking, preserving, dress making and laundry work. Moreover, the sewing machine and the electric vacuum cleaner have lightened the work which remains in the home. These effects of machinery and the factory system should be remembered in a discussion of the problems of women and children in industry. The farm as well as the home has been affected by machinery and modern technology. The combined harvester and reaper have come to the aid of the farmer.

It is unnecessary to write at length of the tremendous productivity of the power machine as compared with the hand tool. The manufacture of pins is a classic illustration. The invention of the printing press and the publication of books made unnecessary the laborious copying of manuscripts by scribes and monks. The process of invention has been continuous, and the modern revolving press prints hundreds of pages in the same time that it took the former hand press to make a single impression. A grinder of grain in Periclean Athens could produce a maximum of only two barrels of flour a day, but a modern Minneapolis flour mill has a daily output of seventeen thousand barrels. Many similar instances of the superior productivity of the machine might be cited, but these will be sufficient for illustration.

Modern technology and the machine have resulted in an increase of wealth, in lowered prices, in higher standards of living, and in increased leisure time. Although considerable uniformity of product is necessary in the modern system, quality has not been superseded by mere quantity. Nevertheless, our tastes as well as our daily routines have been standardized. The machine has not been an unmixed blessing. A new strain has been placed upon the worker and the producer has sometimes been sacrificed to his product. The human organism can never adjust itself perfectly to the regular rhythm and automatic movements of the machine. Moreover, industrial accidents are more likely to occur because of the use of new and powerful forces of nature, whose powers of destruction are as great as their powers of production. It is a question to what extent the disadvantages of the machine tend to balance its advantages.

The gains of modern technology and the advantages of power machinery have not been evenly distributed throughout society. Capitalism as well as the machine has been criticized. It must be remembered that the benefits of capital and capitalism are not identical. Capital is commonly defined as the product of past labor used in further production. Capital goods may be illustrated by both hand tools and power machinery. Capitalism, however, refers to an economic system of capitalistic production, in which capital is privately owned and production is conducted by individual enterprise. Critics of capitalism are not blind to the technological advantages of machinery. They seek to destroy the private ownership and operation of capital and not the capital itself.

2. Division of Labor.—A basic characteristic of modern economic life which is fundamental in a study of economic problems is division of labor. Specialization is division of labor viewed from an individual point of view and cooperation is division of labor viewed from a social point of view. There is geographical as well as individual division of labor, and minute as well as general division of labor.

A broad division of labor among various occupations is very old. The antiquity and prevalence of occupational division of labor may be illustrated by such names as Smith, Miller, Weaver and Shoemaker. Modern division of labor, however, has divided these general occupations into minute tasks. The old-fashioned itinerant shoemaker bought the leather, cut it into its proper parts, and sewed them together by hand into the finished product. The manufacture of shoes is now done largely by machinery. There are many different machines, and the manufacture of a single pair of shoes comprises a number of separate tasks. One worker merely cuts the leather, another operates a sewing machine, and another supervises the heeling of shoes. Although this minute specialization was caused by the invention of machinery, specialization makes for the further invention of machinery. When a complicated process is broken up into a number of simple tasks, it is not so difficult to devise a machine which will automatically perform a single operation.

Division of labor results in more goods, cheaper goods and increased leisure time. Its effects are similar to those of machinery, with which it is closely associated. There is a corresponding tendency to destroy the individuality of both the worker and his work. Extreme specialization resolves the working day into a continuous repetition of simple tasks. The work is monotonous and stunts the development of intelligence. There is little variety in such a task as punching holes in gloves, which are fed to the worker with ceaseless regularity and at a fatiguing rate of speed. The joy of workmanship is dulled when one performs but a single operation and is unable to carry the entire manufacturing process through to completion. Disadvantages of specialization, however, like those of machinery, are partially offset by increased leisure time and higher standards of living.

3. Roundabout Production.—Division of labor is temporal as well as geographical and individual, that is, production is divisible into stages as well as into occupations. The process of specialization is spread out over periods of time as well as among various places and individuals. Capitalistic production represents roundabout production, in which the early stages are devoted to the creation of capital goods, rather than to finished consumption goods. The roundabout method of production and division of labor are closely allied, but they are not identical. Roundabout production is indirect as well as lengthy, because it involves the use of capital. Capital goods include wealth in intermediate stages, as well as the tools which are necessary in production. The clothes we buy are made from the cloth manufactured months before from wool which was sheared from the sheeps' backs still further in the past.

The roundabout method of production has greatly increased the amount of wealth in existence, but it has also intensified the risks of production. Many capital goods are so highly specialized that they cannot be used for any other purpose than the one for which they were originally designed. The roundabout method of production requires that the productive process be carried on in anticipation of demand, rather than in response to demand. It assumes a steady, continuous demand, and sudden changes in economic wants and industrial processes are disastrous. Capital is invested in specialized machinery and in goods in process at various stages on their long journey toward consumption goods. Extreme fluctuations in consumers' demands are peculiarly unfortunate in a capitalistic and specialized society. The highly trained worker may be out of a job for the same reason that his specialized machinery is scrapped. Sudden changes in demand were not so serious in a more primitive, industrial society, in which production was carried on by individual craftsmen in response to custom orders.

The roundabout method of production makes it necessary for certain groups in society to direct the course of production and to accept the financial risks of this lengthy and expensive method of production. A socialistic society might have its capital owned collectively and the course of production determined by some central governmental agency. However, such is not the case today. We have seen that the term capitalism implies not only the existence of private property rights in capital, but also the direction of production by individual enterprisers. Numerous individual capitalists own most of the instruments of production and employ laborers to work for them. As these workers cannot wait until the products of their labor ripen into consumption goods, they must receive advances from their employers in the form of wages. Hence, the term capitalism implies the existence of a wage system. It does not necessarily infer the exploitation of labor.

4. Large-scale Production.—Division of labor reaches its greatest development under large-scale production. The use of expensive power machinery is profitable only when its products are made in large quantities. The greater the size of the industrial unit, the greater the possibility for specialization within itself. Meat packing, the manufacture of automobiles and the steel industry are good illustrations of large-scale production. Andrew Carnegie created an enormous fortune when he introduced new processes in the steel industry and made it one of large-scale production. The low price of the Ford automobile is made possible by standardization and enormous production. The packing houses of Chicago and Kansas City slaughter thousands of cattle a day and thus reduce the cost per unit of product. There is a regular routine which is followed from the swinging of a steer upon the traveling carriage to the pasting of labels on cans of corned beef.

Large-scale production makes possible the increased use not only of machinery and division of labor, but also of byproducts which were formerly wasted. The packers now boast that the only part of the hog which escapes their economic utilization is its squeal. The bristles are used for brushes, the fats for lard and soap, and the bones for buttons and fertilizer. Large industries conduct scientific investigations concerning new uses for their byproducts. Thus, the Du Pont Company and the Atlantic Refining Company maintain regular laboratories. Again, large-scale management makes possible many economies in buying, selling and general administration. Overhead, or fixed, expenses can be distributed over a greater number of products and the cost per unit reduced.

5. Exchange and Economic Interdependence.—The specialization of labor and the expansion of commerce developed simultaneously. Division of labor must be accompanied by exchange, in order that each specialist may enjoy the different products of other specialists. Commerce converts the specialization of individuals into social cooperation. Just as standardization is a result of machinery, so interdependence is a result of division of labor.

In the little pioneer groups which dotted the American frontier a century ago, each backwoodsman carried on most occupations for himself. In the last chapter we saw that the medieval manor was also an economically self-sufficient unit. However, the Crusades and other world forces stimulated commerce and tended to break down this local economy of the Middle Ages. Nations began to specialize in the production of those things for which their soil, climate, and labor forces were best adapted and to exchange them for the different products of foreign lands. The Industrial Revolution made of England and later of Germany and the United States great industrial nations. England began to specialize in manufacturing and ceased to raise most of its own food. The world of today is economically interdependent in a measure hitherto unknown. Nations starve and pestilence rages when the healing stream of commerce is interrupted. The recent embargo of western nations produced this effect on Russia.

A consideration of the various articles of food on one's dinner table will show how many distant parts of the world are represented, and how many different groups of specialists have cooperated in its production. Instead of being baked at home in the old-fashioned oven, our bread has probably been manufactured in large, electrically equipped bakeries. The flour may have been milled in Minneapolis from wheat grown in Canada. The sugar probably came from Cuba, the tea from China, and the coffee from Brazil. The canned pineapple came from the corner grocer, who purchased it from a wholesaler, who in turn purchased it from a cannery in Hawaii. A far-distant group of specialists picked the fruit which other specialists prepared, while a still different group of specialists were engaged in the work of transportation which made possible this commerce.

A number of questions suggest themselves in connection with the division of labor and the exchange of commodities which it necessitates. How can such an intricate system work smoothly and adjust itself quickly to new conditions? By refusing to cooperate, one group of specialists can impede the functioning of the entire industrial system. Again, exchange and distribution make necessary the determination of the relative importance of each factor in the wealth-creating process. If a shoemaker wishes to exchange some of his shoes for the clothes of a tailor, upon what basis shall this exchange take place? A suit of clothes is worth how many pairs of shoes? Division of labor necessitates exchange, and exchange creates a problem of value. Value has been defined as the power of one good to command another good in exchange for itself. Price is merely this value expressed in terms of money. A direct system of exchanging goods for goods is called barter. It is practiced only in very primitive communities. Civilization has been accompanied

by the utilization of some form of wealth as a medium of exchange
and as a standard of value. Money evolved as a commodity
possessing universal acceptability for exchange purposes. The
final stage in the financial evolution of society is characterized
by the development of credit, complex financial institutions and
highly organized markets.

6. Competition.—Modern industrial society is competitive as
well as cooperative. We have spoken of the conflict of interests
out of which economic problems arise. The growth of cooperation has not decreased competition, but merely changed it.
Economic competition now tends to assume peaceful rather than
violent forms. It represents group competition, moreover,
rather than the struggle of isolated individuals. During the
World War the greatest possible cooperation was sought within
the group, in order to increase its ability to compete with other
groups. Collective bargaining has similarly supplanted individual bargaining in industry.

There are many types of competition, such as the political,
social, economic, racial, and military, but we are interested
primarily in economic competition. Economic competition in
turn assumes many forms. There is competition among employers and competition among employees, as well as competition
between employers and employees. There are beneficial forms
of competition and destructive forms of competition. There is
competition among buyers and competition among sellers. The
former force tends to raise prices and the latter to lower prices.
We may also distinguish between competition among producers
and competition among consumers. The latter, which often
leads to ostentation, vulgar display, and what has been termed
"conspicuous consumption," is not so desirable as the former.
On the other hand, competition among producers is generally
regarded as making for efficiency. The lethargic enterpriser
who does not effectively satisfy the wants of consumers is not
patronized. Moreover, his costs of production will be so high
that he can be undersold by another producer.

The *laissez-faire* theorists spoke of a natural or normal price
which was fixed by the force of competition. Hence, they pleaded
for the minimum amount of governmental interference with
industry. The natural force of economic competition, they argued,
would secure the maximum group welfare. Later, the biological
struggle for existence served as an analogy for economic competi-

tion. It is interesting, but misleading. Success in economic competition does not necessarily prove superiority. It may have been attained by unfair methods of competition, or by the production of a commodity or service inimical to the best interests of society. The analogy between economic success and natural selection assumes that business success is a fair test of efficiency in the production of a socially desirable good. Such is not always the case, for business success may represent unscrupulous cleverness rather than economic productivity. Moreover, the analogy also assumes an equality of opportunity which does not exist. Riches and poverty may be more the result of different social environments than of different native capacities or economic services. There are numerous artificial handicaps in economic competition and the social struggle for success.

As economic society has grown constantly more complex, new forms of social control have been deemed necessary. The modern state has found it expedient to pass laws for the regulation of competition on which the older economists placed so much reliance. Unfair methods of competition have been legislated against, as a result of unsocial practices on the part of both labor and capital. "Combinations in restraint of trade" have been so common that economists have questioned the assumption of economic competition. Monopoly may be the rule and competition the exception, rather than the reverse. The force of competition has been challenged, moreover, not only on the grounds of its prevalence, but also on the grounds of its efficacy. The socialists contend that the present competitive system is not efficient but very wasteful. They project the advantages of large-scale production to the extreme of governmental monopoly. On the other hand, it has been contended that socialism would not eliminate competition. A conflict of interests will always exist, and socialism might merely change the character of this struggle from economic competition to less desirable forms. The competition of producers would be supplanted by the competition of politicians and "spawners."[1]

7. Individual Enterprise and Self-interest.—Enterprisers are those who direct the productive energies of economic society. The term includes all individuals, from great captains of industry to street venders, who assume the financial responsibility for

[1] *Cf.* CARVER, T. N., "Essays in Social Justice," chap. 9.

their respective ventures. If enterprisers are successful in anticipating the wants of consumers and are efficient in meeting them, they will make profits. If unsuccessful or unfortunate, they will incur losses. Industrial society is a great drama of economic success and failure. At any given moment certain individuals are achieving success and rising from one economic group into another. Other individuals are experiencing losses, and perhaps falling back into the great army of wage earners and salaried employees. America has been regarded as the land of opportunity, because of the chances which it affords to enterprising individuals to demonstrate their ability to achieve economic success.

Early economists relied on self-interest as well as on competition as the motivating forces of our economic life. Adam Smith contended that under conditions of free competition production would be guided by self-interest as "the invisible hand." Each individual knew his own interests best, and happy was that nation which interfered least with these natural forces. Price was the indicator which production would follow. The consumer would pay the highest prices for those articles which he most needed. The lure of high prices and profits would lead enterprisers into the production of the most desirable goods and services. Self-interest would prompt them to satisfy the greatest wants of consumers. The *laissez-faire* theories, however, recognized that there were some limits to self-interest as an economic motive, and that a minimum of governmental interference was necessary. Ruthless self-interest, like destructive forms of competition, must be eliminated. Hence, the state must maintain justice and order. It must repress the unsocial competition of the pirate and the predatory self-interest of the highwayman. An extension of the industrial activities of the state beyond the maintenance of peace and security was regarded with suspicion. Such were the teachings of the older economists.

Price is not a safe indicator for production to follow because of the existence of glaring economic inequalities. Demand is not the same as desire, for economic demand means effective desire, that is, desire which is accompanied by sufficient purchasing power to make itself felt. Self-interest prompts individual enterprisers to seek profits in the production of luxuries for the rich, rather than necessities for the poor. Under our system of individual enterprise, economic production will not necessarily follow the line of maximum social welfare. Modern economists are inclined, moreover, to doubt the ability of consumers to make rational choices. Ignorance, mental inertia, or susceptibility to the suggestion of clever advertisements may warp the force of self-interest as expressed in economic desires. Adulterated foods, quack medicines and shoddy clothing seem to find ready markets and to yield high profits to their manufacturers. Under a system of individual enterprise, production results in the creation of what Ruskin has termed "illth" as well as wealth.

Furthermore, it is very easy for a misdirection of production to take place, an occurrence which temporarily halts the wheels of industry. Illustrations are periods of economic depression. The socialist despairs of any economic society which is founded upon the sands of competition and self-interest. He would substitute the collective ownership and operation of the productive resources of society for individual enterprise and private property rights. He pictures a spirit of social service which will transcend the selfishness of a society dominated by self-interest and the profits motive.

On the whole, however, the present industrial system works with less friction than is often supposed. To be sure, a critic could find much to condemn in this orderly confusion which we call American business life. There is no central authority of experts to decide what goods shall be produced, in what quantities, and by what individuals. Nevertheless, our system of production by individual initiative and free enterprise works in a fairly satisfactory manner. The complex wants of countless consumers are met by the same individuals as specialized producers who exchange their commodities and services. Nevertheless, complete reliance cannot be placed on the motive of self-interest and the mechanism of price. Some social control over the direction and methods of production must be exercised.

The great interdependence of modern industrial society makes necessary the curbing of self-interest which displays itself in unsocial ways. The individualism of the frontier is no longer possible in congested industrial cities. *Caveat emptor* (let the buyer beware) was a workable arrangement when the producer was known personally to the consumer. The self-interest of the guildsman made honesty the best policy. Minute specialization and the impersonal character of our modern industrial system now separate producer and consumer. The new economic organization necessitates a quickened social conscience and improved forms of social control.

8. Institution of Private Property.—Out of the forces of self-interest and individual initiative developed the institution of private property. Private property is generally regarded as the right to acquire, to hold, to use exclusively, and to bequeath. It is important that we distinguish between the terms "wealth" and "property." Wealth is concrete and refers to a tangible good, such as a piece of land, a factory, or an automobile. Property is abstract and refers to a legal right, which is commonly embodied in some written certificate of ownership. Among the certificates of ownership of property rights in different kinds of wealth are deeds to land, mortgages on real estate, stocks, and bonds. The confusion between wealth itself and the title to wealth is responsible for such problems as that of double taxation, which will be discussed in a later chapter.

The institution of private property is the result of a long period of evolution. Early societies possessed little wealth except the natural resources by which they lived. These were sometimes so abundant as to be classed by economists as free goods. Primitive capital and consumption goods were usually scarce and individually owned, but land was sometimes regarded as belonging to the entire group. Property rights were first recognized in such personal effects as weapons, clothing, and household utensils. They were extended gradually to natural resources. Jean Jacques Rousseau wrote as follows:

The first man, who having enclosed a piece of ground, bethought himself of saying, "This is mine," and found people simple enough to believe him, was the real founder of civil society.[1]

Many theories have been advanced to explain the existence of private property. The occupation theory of private property states that this right is based on the prior claim of the one who finds wealth without an individual owner and who appropriates it. The conquest theory is similar to the occupation theory, except that it is based on force. To the victor belong the spoils. The victorious Norman soldiers of William the Conqueror were rewarded with the estates of the conquered Saxons. The legal titles to these estates were based on military conquest, but they were sustained by the English courts in the centuries which

[1] *Cf.* "A Discourse on the Origin of Inequality," Part 2.

followed. Although the occupation theory and the conquest theory of private property may explain the institution, they do not justify it. The labor theory, on the other hand, attempts to justify the institution of private property on the ground that an individual is entitled to hold and to bequeath the fruits of his own industry. The pioneer who cleared the wilderness and who braved the dangers and hardships of frontier life must have had such an inducement to leave the comforts of civilization. Again, the legal theory of private property, in brief, assumes that property exists because the law says that it shall. This legal sanction is the crystallized public opinion of past centuries. The social recognition of private property rights during past ages makes changes in the institution savor of confiscation. Another theory of private property explains the institution as a natural right. Although the political theorists of a century ago emphasized natural rights, modern thinkers are reacting from such a metaphysical concept.

The most generally accepted theory of private property today may be termed the social expediency theory. During the long ages of social evolution the institution of private property was gradually evolved. Under conditions of early group life the total amount of wealth was small and its ownership was sometimes collective. As the amount of wealth increased, private property rights developed. There seems to have been some causal relationship between these two facts. Man is an acquisitive animal and seeks to gratify this desire. It has been contended that the acquisitive motive stimulated individuals to increase production, as well as to accumulate greater wealth. The social expediency theory of private property contends that economic progress of the group was advanced by offering to individuals, as an incentive to increased production, the right to acquire, to hold, and to bequeath the wealth which they produced. Civilization and the institution of private property seem to have developed together. The state is an institution which is closely associated with the institution of private property. Indeed, one of its functions is the protection of individuals in their enjoyment of private property rights.

The fact that private property rights have a social origin must be emphasized. We must defend the institution on the grounds of social rather than individual welfare. On the other hand, any form of private property which becomes inimical to the best interests of the group must be abolished. There is no such thing as an absolute property right. Our social morality is constantly changing, and with it our ideas concerning the institution of private property. Within the memory of some persons living today, human slavery existed in this country. It required a bloody Civil War to amend the Constitution and to modify our institution of private property. Today this institution is still under fire. The single taxer contends that "The earth is the Lord's and the fullness thereof." Natural resources are the free gift of nature and not the result of any creative effort of man. Consequently, the single taxer would largely abolish the institution of private property in land. In his war against capitalism the socialist would go one step further. He objects to private property in capital as well as in land. Capital is the product of labor, he contends, and society should reward production rather than mere ownership. Consequently, the socialist would have producers' capital owned collectively. The communist opposes the institution of private property in all forms of wealth. The anarchist would destroy the political state which is the present bulwark of private property. More conservative thinkers approach the problem from a still different angle. They do not question an individual's right to acquire various forms of wealth, but they do deny his right to bequeath enormous fortunes. As the right of inheritance is the source of much economic and social inequality, these reformers propose to make each individual stand on his own feet, rather than on the shoulders of his father. Partly from social policy and partly for the sake of additional revenues, governments have turned toward the progressive taxation of large estates and inheritances.

Critics of our social system have pointed out a conflict between human and property rights. Thus, John Brown was willing to shatter by force the property rights of slave holders in favor of the human rights of slaves. It is claimed that certain vested interests, now entrenched behind legal property rights, prevent the development of our common natural resources for the equal benefit of the entire population. The speculator in land values may keep idle a fertile piece of land while other men are out of work. The speculator on the produce market may hold a large supply of wheat for a rise in price, while another individual is suffering from the lack of food. A monopolistic control of coal may force the price of fuel so high that the poor man may not enjoy the luxury of being warm. The capitalist, who owns the instruments of production of hundreds of workers, may refuse them the right to work at the only large industry within the community, unless they accept his terms of employment. There is a human right to work for a living. The world owes no man a living, but it does owe him the right to work for a living. It is contended that this human right is sometimes impaired by unrestricted property rights.

9. Summary.—A leading characteristic of modern economic life is division of labor. It necessitates an intricate system of exchange and a high degree of cooperation. Although specialization has numerous economic advantages, it also possesses certain disadvantages for the workers. The invention of power machinery and the introduction of the factory system have made for large-scale production. The machine has increased tremendously the productivity of labor, which has been reflected in higher standards of living and shorter hours of work. On the other hand, it has made the work of the machine tender monotonous and dangerous. Capitalistic production is roundabout, for it is carried on in anticipation of demand rather in response to it.

Modern economic society is competitive as well as cooperative. Competition among producers is commonly supposed to make for efficiency. Of recent years, however, competition has been questioned both as to its prevalence and as to its efficacy. Self-interest is a kindred economic concept. Although public ownership in certain industries must be considered, personal initiative and individual enterprise are still the forces behind most economic organizations. The institution of private property is of ancient origin, and there are many theories to explain its existence. It must be defended, however, on the broad grounds of social welfare rather than in terms of vested interests. We must distinguish between property rights in various kinds of wealth and between relative and absolute property rights. Among other characteristics of modern industrial society are organized exchanges or markets, risk and speculation, and the corporate form of business organization. They will be discussed in the three following chapters.

Collateral Reading

BYE, R. T., "Principles of Economics," chap. 3, 4, 5, 6, and 23.
CARVER, T. N., "Principles of Political Economy," chaps. 3, 4, 10, and 13.
CLAY, H., "Economics for the General Reader," chaps. 2, 21, and 22.

ELY, R. T., "Outlines of Economics," chaps. 2 and 8.
FAIRCHILD, F. R., FURNISS E. S., and BUCK, N. S., "Elementary Economics," vol. I, chaps. 2 and 5.
FETTER, F., "Modern Economic Problems," chap. 32.
FISHER, I., "Principles of Economics," chaps. 1 and 2.
HAMILTON, W., "Current Economic Problems," chap. 14.
MARSHALL, L. C., and LYON, L. S., "Our Economic Organization," chaps. 9–18.
SELIGMAN, E. R. A., "Principles of Economics," chaps. 9 and 10.
SHEARMAN, H. P., "Practical Economics," chaps. 4–10.
TAUSSIG, F. W., "Principles of Economics," chaps. 3–5.

References

CARVER, T. N., "Essays in Social Justice."
ELY, R. T., "Property and Contract."
MARSHALL, A., "Industry and Trade."
MARSHALL, L. C., "Readings in Industrial Society."
MARSHALL, L. C., WRIGHT, C. W., and FIELD, J. A., "'Materials for the Study of Elementary Economics."

Questions for Discussion

1. Outline the different kinds of division of labor.
2. Show the effects of machinery upon division of labor.
3. Give the advantages of division of labor.
4. Give the results of division of labor.
5. What are some dangers of extreme specialization?
6. Show the advantages of large-scale production.
7. How does a machine differ from a tool?
8. Illustrate the productivity of the machine.
9. Compare division of labor and the roundabout method of production.
10. Outline different types of competition.
11. Differentiate between wealth and property.
12. Which theory of private property do you accept and why?

Topics for Investigation

1. Economic competition and the biological struggle for existence.
2. Market value as an indicator for production to follow.
3. The benefits of the machine to the worker.
4. Theories of private property.
5. The origin and development of the institution of private property among primitive peoples.

CHAPTER III

MIDDLEMEN AND ORGANIZED MARKETS

1. Coordination of Specialists.—If division of labor is to result in cooperation, coordination in the labors of various specialists is required. Our present industrial mechanism could not operate properly without a delicate balance among its various parts— otherwise there would be friction and misdirected production. To change the figure of speech, our complex and highly differentiated organism has unconsciously evolved a very intricate nervous system, which controls the functioning of its specialized organs. This important work is done by various groups of middlemen, who are themselves specialists in organization rather than in manufacturing or agriculture.

As division of labor became more minute, commerce increased and elaborate markets developed. Production has been conducted by individual enterprise, and the motivating force has been the gain spirit. The regulating force has been that of price, and economic organization is built on the price system; hence, economists speak of the pecuniary basis of industrial society. The intangible force of price, as well as the activities of middlemen, has helped to coordinate economic production.

In a primitive economy the producer and the consumer were identical in a sense unknown today. Each individual directly satisfied most of his economic wants. A simple division of labor gradually evolved, in which each specialist bartered his products directly for those of other specialists. This stage may be illustrated by the local economy of the self-sufficient manors of the Middle Ages. As economic evolution progressed, barter was superseded by the use of money. Organized places of exchange developed and various middlemen appeared. During the Middle Ages, the handicrafts became specialized occupations, and the town markets were organized for the exchange of the products of town artisans and country peasants. The manufacturer was also a merchant, however, and the guildman sold his goods directly to the consumer.

During the later Middle Ages great fairs were held which may be regarded as the prototypes of modern organized exchanges. Wandering minstrels and friars no longer thronged the great highways; they were succeeded by peddlers, who distributed their wares along the old trade routes of Europe. The advent of capitalism took place long before the Industrial Revolution, and some of the first capitalists were these itinerant merchants. The commerce of the city states of northern Italy was very extensive, and they possessed organized markets and systems of credit. Money changers and goldsmiths became the bankers of these Lombard towns. With the decline of the guilds, specialized middlemen were necessary to coordinate the rather unorganized system of production under the domestic system.

After the Industrial Revolution specialization became more minute and commerce still more extensive. National markets broadened into world markets. New groups of middlemen developed to bridge the gaps between diverse occupations and between different stages in a given occupation. Not only were there specialized manufacturers, but also specialized wholesalers, retailers, and other types of merchants. An ever-increasing number of middlemen thrust themselves between the producer and the consumer, as production became more specialized and more roundabout.

A reverse tendency has recently put in its appearance. A number of large manufacturers are now attempting to sell their products directly to the consumer; they are conducting their own retail departments or mail-order businesses. The process of integration has succeeded that of differentiation. The new slogan is "Buy directly from the manufacturer, and save the middleman's profit." Let us see, therefore, what economic service, if any, middlemen perform in our economic organization.

2. Economic Services of Merchants.—The primary middleman is the merchant, for it is he who discovers, creates, or organizes markets. His chief function is the correlation of the diverse forces of supply and demand in an impersonal and highly specialized economy.

A common distinction is that between the merchant and the manufacturer: we are apt to say that the latter produces, but that the former merely organizes. It is essential that we recall the economist's definition of production. Production does not consist in the creation of wealth, for that is a scientific impossibility. It consists in the creation of utilities, that is, of want-gratifying qualities, rather than goods. The farmer and the manufacturer create form utilities; that is, they succeed in bringing together particles of matter into desirable economic goods. The merchant, whether wholesale or retail, creates place, time, and possession utilities. His economic service lies in the bringing of economic goods to places, times, and persons—where, when, and by whom they are most desired.

A popular tendency is to underestimate the functions of the merchant, and an oft-repeated cry is for the elimination of the middleman. It is possible to do away with middlemen, but the desirability of such action may be questioned. It is possible to eliminate the merchant, but it is impossible to eliminate the necessity of merchandizing under a system of specialization and exchange. The elimination of the middleman merely means that his functions are absorbed by the manufacturer or farmer—it results only in the restriction of specialization. Cooperative associations have been developed which seek to dispense with such middlemen as the commission merchants. An illustration is the California Cooperative Fruit Growers' Association, whose salaried agents do the work of organizing markets.

It is the task of the merchant to facilitate commerce and to lead it into the most profitable channels. He connects rather than separates the manufacturer and the consumer, and he acts both as a canal between and a reservoir for different trades and various stages of production. To be sure, he charges for his services and exacts a heavy toll from the rich flow of commodities which pass through his hands. It may be that the number of merchants is in excess of the need for such services, and that the strategic position of middlemen has resulted in excessive charges. The consumer may feel this pressure in the form of the high prices which he pays for his ultimate consumption goods. The farmer and the manufacturer also sometimes complain that the prices which they receive from the middlemen are barely sufficient to cover their costs of production. Nevertheless, it cannot be denied that the legitimate merchant does perform real economic functions. He helps the consumer to get what he wants, when he wants it, and in the desired form and quantities. He also helps the farmer and the manufacturer to dispose of the goods which they have grown or manufactured. The present industrial system is so complex that the consumer would find it difficult to purchase directly all the goods that he desires. On the other hand, the farmer and the manufacturer are so busy with their particular tasks that they have neither the time nor the ability to search out the ultimate consumers.

Another function of the middleman is the assumption of certain financial risks of production. A wholesale merchant often buys in advance the entire crop of a farmer or the output of a mill. Farmers and manufacturers are assured in advance of a certain market and sometimes of a definite price for their products. The wholesale merchant is the shock absorber in an industrial society which is characterized by production in anticipation of demand. The individual consumer buys from his retailer in accordance with his individual needs. The retailer in turn replenishes his stock from that of the wholesaler. The latter is forced to keep on hand a relatively large inventory in order to meet the continuous but changing demands of the market. Manufacturers are loath to engage in the expensive and extensive manufacture of goods without definite marketing prospects. They prefer a guarantee of the future market before making such an investment of capital; they are glad to make contracts for the future delivery of their goods at specified prices, which will cover the cost of production and provide a nominal profit. The wholesaler, jobber, or some other merchant is often willing to make such contracts. If he has estimated the market correctly and the demand is strong, he will make large profits; if his guess is inaccurate, or if prices fall, he will incur heavy losses. In a measure, the merchant may be said to insure as well as to direct the production process.

The retailer makes more attractive the goods which we buy, and thus gratifies our wants more completely. He helps to educate us as consumers, moreover, by displaying or advertising new goods, of the existence of which otherwise we might never have known. He makes the purchasing process more convenient by assembling in one store large varieties of goods. Many department stores also maintain numerous service features which transcend those of mere merchandizing, and which are designed for the comfort of their patrons. Advertising is a further specialization within the general occupation of merchandising. Its purpose is the creation of a market, rather than the organization of one.

3. Functional Middlemen.—There are other types of middlemen in addition to the merchant who organizes the market; these are sometimes referred to as functional, or technical, middlemen. Primary middlemen are the merchants who directly connect the manufacturer and the consumer, or who connect various stages in production, and it is to this class that wholesalers, retailers, and jobbers belong. Strictly speaking, the jobber is a merchant who specializes in odd lots, but the term is often used as synonymous with wholesale merchant. Functional middlemen perform certain specialized services in the general process of coordinating production. Bankers, insurance dealers, brokers, warehouse managers, and railroad companies are examples of functional middlemen. They perform such highly specialized functions as the creation of credit, the assumption of certain risks, and the storage or transportation of commodities.

The growth of commerce and the highly specialized character of our modern economic society have made marketing a very complicated process. It is a far cry back to the medieval peddler who embodied in himself many specialized occupations of today. Modern marketing involves the transportation of goods from all quarters of the globe, their assemblying and classification in great distributing centers, their storage between seasons, and, finally, their merchandising or sale to the consumer. As has already been indicated, there is considerable risk involved in marketing. There may be a loss of actual product through such physical hazards as fires and shipwrecks, or a loss in value through such economic hazards as price changes. A discussion of markets and middlemen would be incomplete without some mention of insurance companies which afford protection against loss through various physical hazards, and dealers in futures who afford protection against the economic hazards of price changes. These functional middlemen will be discussed more in detail in the following chapter on Speculation and Insurance.

The usefulness of the banker, the insurance company, and the railroad are generally acknowledged. The usefulness of brokers who handle transactions in stock or produce is more frequently questioned. We are apt to forget that they help in the organization of very intricate markets which facilitate exchange. Brokers who are members of organized exchanges strive to uphold certain rules of business by enforcing them on the floor of the exchange. The broker, as contrasted with the merchant, buys and sells not for himself, but in response to orders from his clients. The intricacy of the modern stock exchange and produce market necessitates the existence of such specialized middlemen. The banker may be said to create credit, and the broker to keep it mobile. The commission merchant performs a similar function for produce. He receives the produce from the farmer and sells it for the highest possible price, keeping for himself a certain agreed upon percentage as his commission. The merchant's knowledge of the market makes it possible to divert produce from glutted markets into more profitable ones. In addition, he performs the tasks of classification and storage. He also puts into more marketable form the various goods which pass through his hands.

4. Price as an Organizing Factor.—The price system makes the coordination of specialists almost automatic. Price is the great barometer which all economic navigators carefully study; they seek to follow, or rather to anticipate, price changes. The various and varying demands of millions of unknown consumers form the ultimate force which determines production. Our roundabout system of production makes it necessary that production be carried on in anticipation of demand. In the absence of any central authority for the guidance of production, reliance is placed upon the forces of competition and individual initiative. Can any such economic system be possessed of order, certainty, or stability? In spite of waste, temporary maladjustments, and the misdirection of production, the answer seems to be in the affirmative. The organization of production is largely accomplished by the delicate mechanism of price. A rise in the value of a given commodity will attract capital, labor, and business enterprise in that direction. A decline in its value will impel them to flow out of an unprofitable occupation and into some more productive channel. However, the fact must again be stressed that economic price is not indicative of ethical worth, and that an economically profitable venture is not necessarily one which is socially desirable. The reverse also may be true. In any case, the mechanism of price does permit the consumer to obtain what he desires, provided he has the ability to pay for it. It also tends to equilibrate supply and demand. Competition among producers tends to lower the prices and to raise the quality of the goods on the market.

The present price system is subject to two sets of forces: those which make for price changes and those which make for price stability. Changes in the demand schedule, on the one hand, and changes in the cost of production, on the other hand, tend to alter prices. Changes in the wants of consumers affect the demand schedule; and the invention of machinery, or the discovery of some new process of manufacturing affects costs of production. Both influences tend to alter prices. In addition to changes in the prices of particular commodities, there may be a rise or fall in the general level of prices. Aside from fluctuations in the individual prices of particular commodities, there may be a general increase or decrease in the purchasing power of money.

Price adjustments are in part automatic, that is, an extremely high price stimulates the production of the expensive good and in the long run its price will tend to fall. The reverse is also true. Prices are stabilized more immediately, however, by the professional activities of middlemen. The profits motive impels merchants to buy goods when and where they think they are cheap, and to sell them when and where they think they are dear. Thus, the difference of a few cents a ton will divert steel from Germany to the United States, and the difference of a few cents a bushel will hold over an elevator of wheat from May to September. Price differences in various places and price fluctuations over various periods of time are minimized by the buying and selling activities of middlemen. Although they are frequently unconscious of their broad economic functions, middlemen help to equilibrate the forces of supply and demand and thus to stabilize prices. Although actuated by the profits motive and the desire to gain by price differences and price fluctuations, middlemen serve as a kind of economic balance wheel which protects consumers and producers somewhat from the violence of price changes and price differences.

5. Nature of Markets.—The economist uses the word "market" in its exact and scientific sense, rather than in accordance with popular usage. To the average person the market place is a concrete reality, and he pictures a tradesman filling a basket with good things to eat. In its economic sense, however, the market is an abstraction. It may be defined as the equation of the forces of supply and demand: a market exists where exchanges take place, or, rather, where the forces of supply and demand are brought together. It is the meeting of minds

as to the price of some economic good of a given quality and in a given quantity. From this definition of a market there follows the law of market price, namely, that within a perfect market, at a given time, and for a given commodity or service, there can be only one price. If more than one price exists for the same commodity at the same time, there must be more than one set of supply and demand forces, and hence, more than one market. Indeed, we may define a perfect market as a place or a condition in which one price, and only one price, obtains at a given time for a given article. Due allowances must be made for transportation charges, and often a given price means a price at a certain place. Although the whole United States is one market for the Ford automobile, and its price is universally the same, this price is quoted f. o. b., which means that the consumer must add to this uniform price the varying costs of transportation from Detroit.

For such nonperishable staples as wheat and corn there are world markets. The price of a certain commodity, quoted by the Chicago Board of Trade, represents the estimates of numerous individuals who have some knowledge of demand and supply conditions for this commodity throughout the whole world. The Chicago Board of Trade price tends to dominate that of the smaller exchanges; any slight differences are immediately eliminated by the activities of middlemen, whose chief source of profits is price differences. The same is true of the market for securities, in which the New York Stock Exchange dominates. The market for such perishable commodities as milk and fresh vegetables is somewhat smaller—nevertheless, the development of refrigerator cars has widened this local market. The market for frozen meat has become a world market, similar to that for wheat and cotton.

The "given commodity" concept implies standardization of products within a market. Such standardization is often impossible or undesirable. Thus, the price of shoes will fluctuate greatly in different shops on the same street. The obvious explanation of such a situation is the existence of different kinds and grades of shoes. Although this may be true, shoes of the same quality are sometimes sold for various prices by different dealers in the same locality. This is due to the ignorance of the consumer, who cannot be an expert in all fields. He does not know to what extent price differences reflect degrees of quality. Again, there is often a prestige value attached to the goods purchased in certain exclusive shops. The same line of shoes may be stamped differently for various retailers and the individual buyers gain the impression that the goods are very different—a feeling naturally encouraged by the proprietor of the expensive shop. Although we may be specialists as producers of certain particular commodities or services, we are apt to be unspecialized as general consumers. Most consumers are consequently unskilled and are often ignorant buyers.

6. Development of Produce Exchanges.—The market place is an ancient institution which flourished in the city states of antiquity. The town markets of the Middle Ages were somewhat similar to the curb markets of small country towns, where consumers still purchase their vegetables directly from the farmers. We have noted the expansion of such local markets into national markets and finally into world markets; and again, we would particularly stress the fact that division of labor, the growth of commerce, the organization of markets, and the transition from barter to money and credit went on simultaneously.

The present markets for grain, cotton, and other kinds of produce have widened enormously because of modern improvements in transportation and communication. The invention of the telegraph and the telephone has made possible the development of an economic nervous system in the same way that the invention of the railroad and the steamboat has made possible the development of an economic circulatory system. The prices of the great staples of commerce tend to be the same in all places except for differences in transportation costs. The rapid diffusion of information and the cheapness and efficiency of modern methods of transportation have brought about world markets. The produce exchanges of our large cities are excellent illustrations of markets made possible by the new methods of transportation and communication.

The student of history traces the origins of modern produce markets to the great fairs of medieval Europe. The Antwerp Bourse was established as early as the sixteenth century, and the Royal Exchange of London was organized shortly afterward. The significant thing for us to note is that at each of these markets certificates of ownership, as well as the commodities themselves, were bought and sold. This implies the existence of credit and of responsible officers of the exchange. As produce was purchased by description rather than on sight, confidence must have been reposed in the brokers or other agents of the exchange who classified and stored the goods.

The real stimulus to the development of the produce exchanges was the existence of large stocks of agricultural staples, which exceeded local and temporary demands. Improved methods of storage as well as of transportation made possible the extension of geographical division of labor. With the development of vast new agricultural areas, enormous grain elevators and cotton warehouses became necessary, and the storage as well as the transportation of various agricultural crops became a specialized industry. Functional middlemen also began to specialize in the marketing of these products. Although a farmer is anxious to turn his harvested grain into funds as soon as possible, the miller of flour is usually unwilling to purchase a year's stock of wheat. This assumption of title is done by specialized middlemen and brokers, who buy and sell warehouse receipts of grain, cotton, and other produce. Produce exchanges developed in response to the need for promptness and convenience in the buying and selling of various commodities. Uniformity of custom, complexity of organization, and certain standards of conduct were gradually evolved.

Produce exchanges have been given various names, such as "boards of trade," "chambers of commerce," and "bourses." Their common object, nevertheless, is the standardization of conditions of exchange. The Chicago Board of Trade, organized in 1848, is perhaps the most conspicuous of all produce exchanges. It dominates the wheat market, as well as the market for numerous less important commodities. The New York Produce Exchange has also been in existence since the middle of the last century. There are also many independent exchanges, such as the New York Cotton Exchange and the New York Coffee Exchange. The Merchants' Exchange of St. Louis and the Minneapolis Chamber of Commerce are similar to the Chicago Board of Trade, but of less importance. There are numerous and important foreign exchanges, such as the Liverpool Exchange which dominates the cotton market. Other general or specialized produce exchanges, which differ greatly in character and importance, exist in all large cities of the world.

7. Nature of Produce Exchanges.—Exchanges are merely organized market places in which individuals, or rather their brokers, buy and sell various commodities. Warehouse receipts

rather than the commodities themselves change hands.   Produce
exchanges are unique in that dealings in futures take place as well
as the buying and selling of present goods.   The exchange itself
does not engage in trading, but it merely affords a convenient
place for its members to buy and sell.   It is not operated for
profit and does not regulate the prices of commodities sold on its
floor.   It merely seeks to facilitate exchange, and professes to
maintain certain standards of justice in the interests of all traders.
With these ends in view, it is commonly required that individuals
buy and sell on the exchange indirectly, rather than directly.
They must employ brokers, who are members of the exchange
and whose operations are governed by the written regulations
and the unwritten customs of the exchange.

Produce exchanges are often misunderstood by the "common
people" and they have been the target for much criticism.   These
exchanges have been held responsible for the high prices of food
and for various monopolistic tendencies.   They have been
regarded as speculative institutions in which wicked people gamble
on the prices of the necessaries of life.   Later we shall discuss some
of the dangers of organized exchanges and we shall see how their
privileges of trading are abused in spite of the efforts of the
exchange to discipline its members.   Before describing its evils,
however, it is necessary that we clearly understand the nature and
functions of produce exchanges.   Let us repeat in conclusion the
definition of the produce exchange by a close student of organized
exchanges.[1]

A produce exchange may be defined simply as an organized market
place which enables individuals to buy and sell freely certain commodities, either in person or through a broker; and which in order to facilitate such trade has for its fundamental objects the promotion of
uniformity in customs and usages, the inculcation of principles of justice,
and equity in trade, the facilitation of the speedy adjustment of business
disputes, the dissemination of valuable commercial and economic
information, and the securing to all its members all the benefits of
cooperation.   The exchange itself is not organized for the purpose of
making money, and does not fix prices or make transactions in trade as
an organized body.   It is merely instrumental in affording a convenient
market place, in regulating trade, and in disciplining the conduct of its
members.   Its members act upon their own responsibility.   They may

[1] Cf. HUEBNER, S. S., "The Function of Produce Exchanges," in the Annals
of the American Academy of Political and Social Science, vol. 38.

do as much business as they like, provided that they conform to the standards which the rules of the exchange prescribe for the regulation of the trade.

8. Classification of Produce and Warehouse Certificates.— The existence of produce exchanges depends upon several general conditions. In the first place, the produce must be one of the great agricultural staples; it must be an economic good for which there is a great demand. In the second place, the produce must be one that is easy to standardize; that is, to classify into certain general groups. This can easily be done with the great agricultural staples such as wheat, but it is hard to do with fancy fruits. The standardization of products makes it possible to sell by description and to purchase by sampling. Individuals may speculate in the price of wheat without actually seeing the produce itself, and certificates of deposit of a certain amount of cotton of a certain grade may be bought and sold in the same way that securities are bought and sold. The price may go up or down, but the quality and quantity of the goods are as stated in the certificate of deposit. These paper claims on wheat, corn, or cotton may change hands many times on the produce exchange, but the goods themselves repose undisturbed in the local elevator or in the terminal warehouse until they are ready for actual consumption.

Let us illustrate the general process. A farmer harvests his wheat crop and sends it to a local grain elevator. The wheat is both stored and classified. Thus, it is designated as "Number 1, Northern Spring Wheat," or "Number 3, Northern Spring Wheat," according to its type and quality. The farmer and other interested parties have often contended that in certain cases this classification of produce has not been fairly done: hence, state inspectors are sometimes required by law. In some states officials of the local boards of trade either perform or supervise this difficult task of classification. When the grain is moved to a terminal warehouse or purchased by a miller, it is again carefully inspected to see that it is of the stated quality as well as quantity. An entire carload may be inspected by what is known as sampling. A long, hollow tube is thrust down to the very bottom of the car, and the content of the tube is then carefully inspected. In this way it is difficult to conceal waste, dirt, or grain of inferior quality. The farmer may be paid immediately for his grain or he may receive certificates of deposits of a certain number of bushels of a given type of wheat. He can sell these paper claims on wheat to grain brokers or to specialized middlemen who are always willing to buy and sell them at what they consider favorable prices. From this group of merchants the miller buys warehouse receipts and calls for the delivery of the actual grain when he is ready to use or to store it.

9. Functions of Produce Exchanges.—Produce exchanges perform a number of very important economic functions. In the first place, they give mobility to produce. Warehouse receipts can be used as collateral against which loans may be secured. Warehouse receipts circulate in the same way that gold and silver certificates circulate instead of the bullion which is held in the Treasury at Washington. They are as negotiable as stocks and bonds, and their value may easily be read in the latest quotations from Chicago or Kansas City. Thus, the owners of produce convert their warehouse receipts into bank credit. In this way, exchange is facilitated. It is difficult to see how the harvesting and marketing of our crops could be accomplished without the use of these credit instruments. In the second place, produce exchanges furnish a continuous market. There is always a demand for these great staple crops, and there are always individuals engaged in their production. Supply and demand changes are merely relative. Consequently, there are always middlemen who are willing to buy and sell warehouse certificates and the question is merely to ascertain what is a profitable price at which to buy or to sell. The middlemen and the produce exchange furnish a continuous market to farmers on the one hand, and to millers and manufacturers on the other hand. In the third place, produce exchanges are clearing houses of information as well as of produce. They are in constant touch with conditions of supply and demand and with any influences which are apt to cause fluctuations on either side of the price equation.

The produce exchange disseminates this information, but it makes no organized effort to interpret its findings—it is the thoughts of the individual traders on the exchange that are reflected in the price quotations. Nevertheless, the following objectives are achieved: Prices are steadied from year to year by a discounting of the future, and are leveled from place to place. In this way produce exchanges—as well as the activities of legitimate middlemen—help to regulate the rate at which goods are produced and consumed. The prospect of a future scarcity of wheat is reflected in the present quotations of the exchange, and, in such a case, unless outside speculation distorts the true situation, prices rise slowly rather than jump precipitously. When the scarcity does occur, it has already been discounted by the market. The high price of wheat, moreover, has so stimulated production that a bumper crop is expected at the next harvest. This fact also has a restraining influence on price. The high price of wheat has also encouraged its importation, and discouraged its consumption. In other words, the produce market makes it possible to equate the supply and demand forces of different places and times, rather than merely of one locality and of a short period of time. In this way, price is steadied and consumption is regulated, unless unwise speculation masks the true situation. Extreme scarcity and glutted markets are rendered unlikely. Misdirected production is lessened by the accessible barometer of the produce market.

10. Organization of the New York Stock Exchange.—Stock exchanges are organized markets for the buying and selling of securities in the same way that produce exchanges are organized markets for the buying and selling of commodities. Although various large cities have their own stock exchanges, the New York Stock Exchange dominates the entire security market. Its history is almost as long as that of our young American republic, but it did not become an important financial institution until about the time of the Civil War. The growth of the stock exchange was dependent upon the growth of the corporate form of business, which stimulated the buying and selling of stocks and bonds. Nevertheless, shortly after the Revolutionary War there were a dozen men who were accustomed to meet under a buttonwood tree at 68 Wall Street for the purpose of buying and selling government bonds for themselves or for their friends.

In 1792, twenty-four such brokers signed an agreement with respect to commissions and mutual obligations. In 1817, these original street brokers took a room on Wall Street and adopted a constitution. In this original constitution fictitious sales were forbidden under pain of expulsion. In 1863, the New York Stock Exchange Building Company was organized to provide a more commodious home, which was needed because of the increase in business. Since that time a further expansion has been repeatedly necessary. Within the present twenty-two-story building, over a million shares of securities often change hands daily. In the number and value of securities listed, and in the volume of its transactions, the New York Stock Exchange exceeds the total of all other stock exchanges in this country. Although the Federal Reserve Act of 1913 provided for a number of Federal reserve banks scattered throughout the country rather than for one central bank, New York is still the financial center of the country. This national dominance of Wall Street is largely due to the importance of the New York Stock Exchange.

The New York Stock Exchange is an unincorporated association of eleven hundred members. Just as it deals in the securities of the entire nation, so its membership includes individuals or firms from all parts of the country. The large brokers of all important cities either possess a seat in the New York Stock Exchange or maintain professional relations with some New York member of the Stock Exchange. The membership of this body is deliberately limited, and a broker who desires a seat in the New York Stock Exchange can obtain it only by purchase from some present member with the permission of the general body. These seats in the New York Stock Exchange are worth large sums of money: a recent transfer cost the purchaser $300,000.[1] Many members of the New York Stock Exchange have branch offices in other important cities in the United States, Europe, and the rest of the world. Close communication is maintained by direct telephone or telegraph lines with the New York offices. The broker's ticker records the telegraphic messages from New York, and the latest quotations from the New York Stock Exchange are immediately posted on the board rooms of brokers throughout the United States and the whole civilized world. The New York Stock Exchange is not a local, but rather a national and an international institution.

The purpose of the New York Stock Exchange is to facilitate the buying and selling of securities. The new constitution adopted in 1902 states that "its objects shall be to furnish exchange rooms and other facilities for the convenient transactions of their business as brokers: to maintain high standards of commercial honor and integrity among its members; and to promote and inculcate just and equitable principles of trade and business." Only members of the New York Stock Exchange can use its facilities. All other individuals must employ some member of the exchange to act as broker for them. Investors

[1] Nov., 1927.

tell their brokers what security to buy or to sell, and in what quantity, and at what price. The broker endeavors to carry out the instructions of his client. If he is successful in making the purchase or sale at the stipulated price, he charges him the brokers' commission in accordance with an established schedule of rates. An individual may sometimes order his broker to buy or sell a security "on the market," that is, at the best current price.

The New York Stock Exchange, as we have just seen, strives to maintain the honor of the institution and the integrity of its membership. A member who is convicted of fraud is expelled, and a member who is unable to fulfill his contracts is suspended. The organization maintains a list of securities which may be bought and sold on the floor of the Exchange, and transactions in other securities are forbidden. The purpose of this is the elimination of questionable securities, and to that end, before any stock or bond may be listed on the New York Stock Exchange, it must be passed upon by a special committee. The Exchange does not guarantee the character of all securities which it lists, but it merely seeks to eliminate those which savor of fraud.

In addition to the New York Stock Exchange there is the New York Curb, which possesses its own list of securities. The securities which are bought and sold on the New York Curb are generally more speculative than those which are listed on the New York Stock Exchange. Securities which are refused admission to the New York Stock Exchange sometimes find their way to the New York Curb, although there are many securities which are not listed on either the New York Stock Exchange or the New York Curb. Application may never have been made for listing these securities—or they may be of a questionable character, or sound securities which have been issued in small amounts. Numerous conservative bonds are never listed on any exchange. Moreover, certain local corporations prefer to list their stocks and bonds on local stock exchanges rather than on the New York Stock Exchange. Thus, the Philadelphia, Chicago, and Boston exchanges possess not only their own membership of brokers, but also their own lists of securities.

11. The Stock Exchange in Action.—The New York Stock Exchange is formally opened by a chairman, who is the presiding official, at ten o'clock in the morning and closed at three o'clock in the afternoon. Fines are imposed for trading outside these regular hours. To the uninitiated the trading on the New York

Stock Exchange and the Chicago Board of Trade seems very confusing. Their apparent turmoil affords a striking contrast to the quiet, systematic operation of a large and well-ordered bank. The produce exchange has its various "pits" in which spirited trading takes place in the futures of different kinds of produce. The floor of the New York Stock Exchange is similarly specialized into different posts. Definite sections of the floor are devoted to transactions in the several types of securities, and the broker goes about from post to post in his efforts to execute the various orders of his clients. He offers to buy or to sell a certain number of shares of a given security at a named price. If he finds no taker, he moves off to execute another order and returns later in the hope of finding a taker of his original offer. He may be permitted a certain amount of latitude by his client, or he may possess several orders at different prices. Consequently, he lowers the price to sell, or raises the price to buy, until another broker accepts his offer at a given figure. The prices are raised or lowered in terms of points, each one of which represents a dollar. No fractions are recognized except eighths of a point.

Trading takes place in lots of hundred shares. Orders of less than hundred shares are ordinarily turned over to brokers who specialize in odd lots. When an offer to buy or to sell is accepted, the broker makes a note of it on a special pad which he carries for that purpose and the other broker makes a similar note: "A" records the sale to "B" of one hundred shares of XYZ preferred stock at $125\frac{3}{8}$, and "B" records the same purchase from "A" at the same price. Although no formal contracts are made other than these bids and acceptances, they are as binding as formal written contracts with affidavits attached. When there are several acceptances or offers, the first one to be heard is the one which is regarded as binding. Consequently, a premium is placed on a loud voice as well as on active legs. There are numerous telephones and stalls about the room, and each member of the exchange has immediate access to his own office. He is constantly receiving new orders to buy or to sell, and changes or cancellations of unfulfilled orders. The activities of brokers are carefully regulated by the rules of the stock exchange. The rate of commission is definitely fixed and the broker may not charge more nor less than the stipulated percentage or amount.

Promptness in the delivery of securities is insisted on by the New York Stock Exchange, a process which is facilitated by the existence of its own clearing house. For each security which changes hand there must be a buyer and a seller, represented by two brokers who are members of the Exchange. The total number of sales must balance the total number of purchases. At the close of each day's business each broker delivers and receives a certain number of shares of securities. The difference between their total values is the balance which he owes the clearing house or which the clearing house owes him.

12. **"Wash Sales," "Bucket Shops," and Buying on Margin.**— "Wash sales" are fictitious rather than legitimate sales, and hence are forbidden by the rules of the exchange. A dummy purchaser or seller is created to put through a transaction at a given figure on the floor of the New York Stock Exchange. The purpose is to inflate or to depress the value of a particular security. "Bulls" are those individuals who "have gone long" on the market; that is, they have bought securities in the hope of selling them later at a higher price. "Bears" are those individuals who "have gone short" on the market; that is, they have sold in the hope of buying later at a low price. The very fact that securities change hands so often shows the speculative character of much of the trading on the floor of the Exchange. In the course of a single year the total sales or purchases on the New York Stock Exchange exceed many fold the total of all listed securities.

"Bucket shops" as well as "wash sales" are forbidden by the stock exchange. The proprietor of a "bucket shop" receives the deposits of his "long" patrons and places them as mere bets against the deposits of his "short" patrons. He is not a legitimate broker, as he does not execute the orders of his clients on the floor of the Exchange. The broker who engages in "bucketing" is denied membership in the stock exchange. "Bucket shops" are also illegal under the laws of many states.

Stock may be bought on margin rather than outright. A conditional claim on a large number of shares is obtained instead of the absolute ownership of a smaller number. The broker furnishes the additional funds, but holds the security as collateral for his loan. The legal assumption is that the buyer on margin is obtaining his security on the instalment or credit plan. The broker is merely financing its purchase until his client is able to raise the entire amount and to pay off his remaining indebtedness. Buying a stock on margin may be gambling, but it is not bucketing. A legitimate broker actually executes the order of his client on the floor of the exchange.

Let us illustrate the general process of buying a stock on margin. "A" possesses a thousand dollars with which he desires to purchase the stock of the XYZ Company which is quoted at a hundred dollars per share. If he buys ten shares at a hundred dollars a share and the price rises to a hundred and ten dollars, he will make ten dollars per share, or a total of one hundred dollars minus his brokerage fees. Instead of buying ten shares outright, however, he may buy fifty shares on margin. He puts up twenty dollars per share and the broker lends him the remaining eighty dollars per share, or four thousand dollars out of the total five thousand dollars which is required for the purchase. If the price goes up to one hundred and ten dollars, the speculator will again make ten dollars per share, but on fifty shares rather than on ten shares. Thus, his profit on this sale is five hundred rather than one hundred dollars. He must pay to the broker, not only his brokerage fees, but also his interest on the four thousand dollars which he has borrowed. In the meantime, the speculator has also pledged his stock to the broker as collateral for the loan. The amount of margin required varies with the individual, the security purchased, and the general condition of the market. Perhaps 80 per cent of the market value of the security is a safe generalization as to the limit of a broker's loan.

Buying stocks on margin is dangerous, because the possibility of multiplying one's loss is as great as the possibility of multiplying one's gain. A fall of several points may reduce the margin to such an extent that the broker fears for his own safety. He demands more margin from the speculator. If the latter is unable to furnish this additional margin, the broker is forced to sell him out in order to save the borrowed funds and to collect his own interest and brokerage fees.

The broker obtains his loanable funds chiefly from the call money of banks, and this money must be paid on their demand. Call-money rates may fluctuate violently from day to day. There is a relationship between the prices of speculative stocks and the rate of interest on call money: low rates on call loans stimulate speculation on the exchange, but if "money is tight" the market is correspondingly depressed.

It is not the stock exchange, but the individual broker who makes possible the buying of stock on margin. He plays the part of banker as well as broker. Buying stock on margin is no better nor worse than many other forms of speculation. Real estate is often bought and sold subject to a mortgage, and a serious fall in its price can eliminate the owner's equity. Agreements of sale and options are often bought for the sole purpose of a later resale. Warehouse receipts for grain and other commodities may also be bought on margin and are frequently so purchased.

13. Functions of Stock Exchanges.—Stock exchanges give mobility to capital in the same way that produce exchanges give mobility to agricultural products, for securities, as well as warehouse receipts, may be used as collateral for loans. Bank credit is created against these securities. Stock exchanges facilitate the investment, exchange, and withdrawal of funds. They afford a continuous market for the purchase and sale of stocks and bonds. The stock exchange also throws the searchlight of publicity on its securities. One can easily follow the market values of stocks listed on the New York Stock Exchange by their latest quotations; their market prices are immediately available over "tickers," and are later published in the newspapers. The stock exchange presents a fairly accurate record of the economic success of a business venture. It lessens misdirected production and the overinvestment of capital in unfortunate enterprises. The stock exchange has a steadying effect on the prices of securities in the same way that the produce market has a stabilizing influence on the prices of commodities. The security market is a splendid barometer of business in general, as well as of particular ventures. There is the same element of future discounting by the stock exchange as by the produce exchange. Coming events influence from afar the present prices of securities—consequently, the much feared or hoped-for event has but a slightly disturbing effect on prices when it actually does occur.

The stock exchange has a rather steadying influence on the money market as well as on the security market. Banks extend their loans on securities if funds are plentiful, and they contract such loans if their reserves are low. Sudden contractions and expansions in the volume of loans are rendered unlikely because of the delicate relationship between the interest rate and the prices of securities. A rising interest rate is usually accompanied by a bullish stock market, but by a decline in the price of seasoned bonds. The reverse is also true.

The stock exchange, like the produce exchange, performs a number of economic functions, but it also presents opportunities for grave abuse. If feverish speculation prevails, the trading on the exchange disturbs rather than steadies prices, and conceals rather than reveals the true business conditions. We must differentiate, however, between the exchanges themselves and the activities of certain individuals who misuse the facilities which the various exchanges afford. Just as it is difficult for the state to make and enforce criminal legislation without interference with individual liberty, so it is difficult for the exchanges to make regulations which will restrain unsocial activities without limiting the freedom of buying and selling. The grading of produce and the issuing of warehouse receipts are designed to facilitate trade and to guarantee the quality of the product. But they also permit the outsider to speculate on the price of wheat by buying and selling paper certificates of deposit of the grain which he never sees. In the same way, a speculator on the stock market can gamble on the prices of securities to which he never expects to take final title. One would not indict the use of automobiles merely because criminals often find them helpful in carrying out their robberies, and one cannot indict produce or stock markets merely because individuals speculate on them.

14. Summary.—Improvements in transportation and storage have expanded local and temporary markets into national and permanent markets, while the modern development of commerce has expanded national markets into world markets. As economic evolution has gone on, numerous middlemen have appeared, barter has been superseded by money and credit, and organized exchanges have come into existence. The primary middleman is the merchant who organizes the market and who bridges the gap between the farmer or the manufacturer and the consumer, between various occupations, and between various stages in our roundabout system of production. Technical, or functional, middlemen are those individuals who provide certain specialized services, such as transportation, finance, and insurance. Middlemen not only coordinate the entire economic process, but also assume many of the risks of industry. Their professional activities also tend to stabilize prices over various places and times.

A market is a place or a condition in which the forces of supply and demand are brought together. Within a perfect market, at a given time, and for a given product, there can be only one price.

Price is the great organizing force of modern industry. Our economy is that of a pecuniary society. A relatively high price stimulates the production of a commodity and a low price reduces its production.

Exchanges are organized markets in which individuals or their brokers buy and sell commodities or securities. The manner and conditions of exchange are determined by their written regulations or unwritten customs; prices on the exchange, however, are the natural results of individual buying and selling. The exchange is not conducted for profit, nor does it attempt to regulate prices. Produce exchanges may be illustrated by the Chicago Board of Trade, and stock exchanges by the New York Exchange. The sale of our great agricultural staples is done on the produce exchange by description and by warehouse receipts, and the physical commodities themselves do not change hands until the purchaser who needs them cashes in his warehouse receipts. Exchanges afford a ready market for the purchase and sale of commodities and securities. They are also clearing houses of information which permit a discounting of the future. As a result, price changes are more gradual, unless feverish speculation prevails. Prices of agricultural staples are stabilized by produce exchanges, and production and consumption can consciously be directed to avoid a future scarcity or a glut in the market. The sensitivity of stock markets tends to reduce misdirected production and the overinvestment of capital in unprofitable fields. These great services of organized exchanges are in part nullified or reduced by the existence of unwise speculation. A discussion of speculation is reserved for the following chapter.

Collateral Reading

CLAY, H., "Economics for the General Reader," chap. 3.
FAIRCHILD, F. R., FURNISS, E. S., and BUCK, N. S., "Elementary Economics," vol. 1, chap. 8.
HAMILTON, W., "Current Economic Problems," pp. 141–173.
MAGEE, J. D., "Introduction to Economic Problems," chap. 3.
MARSHALL, L. C., "Readings in Industrial Society," pp. 248–266.
MARSHALL, L. C., WRIGHT, C. W., and FIELD, J. A., "Materials for the Study of Elementary Economics," chap. 8.

References

American Economic Association, *Report* on the New York Curb Exchange.
BABSON, R., "Business Barometers for Merchants, Bankers and Investors."
BOYLE, J. E., "Marketing of Agricultural Products," "The Chicago Board of Trade."

BROWN, E., JR., "Marketing."
CHERINGTON, P. T., "The Elements of Marketing."
CLARK, F. E., "Principles of Marketing."
CONVERSE, P. D., "Marketing Methods and Policies."
COPELAND, M. T., "Principles of Merchandising."
————, "Problems in Marketing."
HUBBARD, W. H., "Cotton and the Cotton Market."
HUEBNER, G. G., "Agricultural Commerce."
HUEBNER, S. S., "The Stock Market."
IVEY, P. W., "Principles of Marketing."
MARTIN, H. S., "The New York Stock Exchange."
MEEKER, J. E., "The Work of the Stock Exchange."
New York Stock Exchange Constitution and By-laws.
NYSTROM, P. H., "The Economics of Retailing."
PRATT, S. S., "The Work of Wall Street."
SMITH, J. G., "Organized Produce Markets."
WELD, L. D. H., "The Marketing of Farm Products."
WRIGHT, T., and LANDON, C. E., "Readings in Marketing Principles."

Questions for Discussion

1. Why is the merchant called the primary middleman?
2. What economic function does he perform?
3. What are functional middlemen? What functions does each perform?
4. How is price an organizing factor in production?
5. Outline the functions which organized produce exchanges perform.
6. Explain what is meant by buying on margin. Show how it differs from "bucketing."
7. Would it be possible or desirable to eliminate stock exchanges? Why or why not?
8. What do you understand by a perfect market?

Topics for Investigation

1. The modern movement to eliminate the middleman and to sell directly from producer to consumer.
2. Criticisms of price as an organizing factor of production.
3. The development of produce exchanges.
4. The constitution of the New York Stock Exchange and its regulation of trading upon the exchange.
5. "Wash" sales—their nature and purpose.
6. State laws on "bucket shops."

CHAPTER IV

SPECULATION AND INSURANCE

1. Sources and Kinds of Risks.—Risk and uncertainty are universal characteristics of modern economic organization. Life in general is fraught with numerous dangers, and industrial society is particularly hazardous. This seems to be one of the costs of economic progress. Automobiles and express trains are faster than horse-drawn vehicles, but they increase the hazards of travel. Modern technology has harnessed powerful forces of nature, whose powers of destruction are as great as their powers of production. The hazards of a worker in a modern steel mill, fitted with giant machinery and overhead cranes, far exceed those of the village blacksmith whom Longfellow has pictured in his poem.

The financial as well as the physical hazards of modern industrial society have increased. This is largely due to the growth in specialization and the consequent interdependence of modern economic life. One occupation depends on another, and goods are produced for distant markets and for individuals as yet unborn. Men invest their savings in banks and business corporations, whose officers and establishments they may never have seen. A reasonable faith, rather than an absolute certainty, is the foundation on which modern economic organization rests.

The hazards of industry may be classified as physical and financial—that is, as those causing a loss of actual product or those causing a loss of value. Fire is a physical hazard which destroys the product itself, but a fall in price will destroy values without actual loss of product. Indeed, monopolies have sometimes resorted to the device of destroying goods for the purpose of increasing their prices by creating an artificial scarcity in the supply.

The hazards of industry may also be classified as technological and marketing uncertainties. Technological risks are those which express themselves particularly in the supply schedule, that is, in the changes in the costs of production. The product

may not be so great, so good, or so cheap as had been expected.
Marketing uncertainties are those which express themselves particularly in the demand schedule. Consumers may not desire a
given economic good so strongly as had been anticipated.   Again,
their temporary purchasing power may have been reduced.
Thus, a strike in the coal regions acts as a blight on marketing
possibilities in that section.

The causes of risks in industry may be found in the physical,
the social, and the economic environments. Storms, fires, and
earthquakes are natural risks. Profits may change into losses
overnight, because of a frost or a severe storm in the citrus fruit
area. A late spring or a warm winter will reflect itself
in decreased sales in certain seasonal goods. These natural
causes of risk, which are always present in the physical environment, cannot be eliminated. However, the growth of acquired
knowledge and the progress of science has enabled man to do some
forecasting. In this way he has reduced the risks of industry due
to natural forces.

A second group of causes lies in the social environment. An
illustration of this type of risk may be seen in the changing character of human wants, Dame Fashion is a fickle mistress, and
styles change frequently and suddenly. The popular shade or
the latest cut is expensive at first, but it may be picked up from
bargain lots toward the end of the season. The merchant, who
has made his profits from early sales, prefers to sell his "left
overs" at cost, rather than run the risk of carrying them into the
next season. Extensive economic and social savings are possible
if a greater standardization and stability of human wants can be
achieved. Another cause of risk in industry, which is resident in
the social and political environment, is war, with all its disturbing
influences. The abrupt outbreak of the World War and its sudden ending caused numerous business failures. On the other
hand, great fortunes were made. During the World War, the
prices of German dyes and other scarce materials of industry
were almost impossible to forecast.

A third group of causes lies in the economic environment.
Changes in the costs of production are continuous, because of the
introduction of new processes, the obsolescence of old machinery,
and the fluctuations in the costs of raw materials. Production is
largely carried on in anticipation of demand, and changes in the
wants of consumers may reflect themselves in a scrapping

of machinery or a shutting down of industrial plants. Specialization, as previously noted, also creates economic interdependence, which enhances the hazards of industry. Labor disputes are another source of uncertainty. In addition to the competition between employers and employees, there is also competition among employers. The development of chain stores has lessened the profits and threatened the very existence of the small druggist and corner grocer.

The enterpriser himself is the source of many uncertainties of modern economic life. Human nature possesses many frailties to which economic enterprises frequently succumb. A word must also be said about the individual causes of business failures, apart from those causes of risk which are resident within our physical, social, and economic environments. According to Bradstreet Company, the preponderating majority of business failures are due to the faults of those failing. The list of causes given is interesting, but far from complete. It includes incompetence (irrespective of other causes), inexperience (without other incompetence), lack of capital, unwise credits, speculation (outside regular business), neglect of business (due to doubtful habits), personal extravagance and fraudulent disposition of property. Failures not due to the faults of those failing include specified conditions (disasters, wars, floods etc.), failure of others (apparently solvent debtors), and competition. Wherever the fault may lie, the annual number of business failures in the United States runs into the thousands. Although fluctuating from year to year, an average mortality rate of 1 per cent of all business firms seems to persist.

2. Incidence of Risks.—The enterpriser is the central figure in an economic order characterized by uncertainty. We have seen that individual enterprise and extreme speculation characterize modern economic organization. The spirit of gain lures men to take chances in the great lottery of business. The enterpriser has been defined as the individual who assumes not only responsibility, but also the financial risks of his venture. He pays fairly constant wages to his employees and fairly constant interest charges on his borrowed capital. His profits are residual—that is, the enterpriser gets what is left. In the long run, losses tend to balance profits.

It must not be thought, however, that the enterpriser bears all the risks of modern industry. A large portion of business capital is borrowed, rather than contributed entirely by enterprisers themselves. Bondholders and bankers participate somewhat in the risks of industry, although enterprisers stand as buffers between these passive capitalists and the uncertainties of business. The worker, as well as the capitalist, is not immune. On labor's shoulders fall some of the heaviest risks of modern industry, such as industrial accidents, dangerous trades, and unemployment. These human risks of industry will be discussed in Chap. XXIII. Our present problem is chiefly that of the financial risks of industry.

Although the enterpriser bears the brunt of most financial risks of industry, there are other agents in production who also participate. In addition to those whom we have just mentioned, there are functional middlemen who specialize in the bearing of certain particular risks, as for example, dealers in futures and insurance companies. There are professional speculators who deal in produce futures and who will assume the hazards of price changes. There are also insurance companies to whom the enterpriser may shift the risk of financial loss due to fire, theft, death, or shipwreck. It is with the work of these specialized risk bearers that we are chiefly concerned in this chapter.

There are four possible ways of meeting the risks of industry. They are (1) the reduction of risks, (2) the shifting of risks, (3) the diffusion of risks, and (4) the assumption of risks by the enterprisers themselves. The growth of knowledge concerning our economic and social institutions enables us to control many of the hazards of industry which material progress has created. The first task in meeting the problem of risk in industry is the reduction of these hazards so far as possible. The remaining risks of industry must either be assumed or passed on to someone else. Insurable risks are those which can be mathematically computed and allowed for in the great law of averages. It will be shown that insurance is a diffusion rather than a shifting of these financial risks. Hedging is a device by which the hazard of price changes can be shifted to specialized dealers in futures. The speculation of professional dealers in produce futures makes it possible for the enterpriser to protect himself against price fluctuations by hedging on the price of grain, cotton, or some other commodity.

3. Reduction of Risks.—Although the hazards of industry can never be entirely eliminated, nevertheless they can be reduced. Science is now studying how it can keep the genii of nature which it has enslaved from striking back at society. Modern technology must be applied not only to the process of invention, but also to the problem of safety. Such things as machinery, steam boilers, electric appliances, and giant elevators must be guarded and inspected. Railroads are striving to develop systems of mechanically perfect signals. Technological risks result in property losses as well as human suffering. Many of these can be eliminated, or at least greatly reduced, by a curbing of individual carelessness. Our annual fire losses in recent years have been averaging about five hundred million dollars. Hence, fire marshalls and insurance companies strive to educate the people of the United States in the matter of fire prevention.

Marketing uncertainties center largely about price fluctuations. Just as the physical sciences are striving to reduce the technological risks of industry, so the new sciences of business are striving to reduce marketing uncertainties. Studies of price movements and attempts to forecast them are common. Advertising has also been utilized to secure a steady as well as a wide demand for various products.

Agencies for the reduction of the risks of industry may be grouped as either public or private, and as general or particular. They must be distinguished from agencies for the bearing of risks. Many such agencies, however, not only bear risks, but also reduce them. Insurance companies, for illustration, not only pay their fire and death benefits, but also seek to educate people in the matter of fire prevention and health preservation. One of the greatest successes of workmen's compensation laws has been their stimulus to the "safety first" movement in industry. Accidents have become expensive to industry, as well as painful to the individuals affected. Modern business is likewise learning that guesswork and rule of thumb are similarly expensive.

Various departments of our national and local governments function for the protection of the lives and property of their citizens. Illustrations are municipal departments of public safety, state departments of agriculture, and the United States Weather Bureau. The latter is of tremendous aid to navigators and farmers. Both Federal and state departments of agriculture study plant and animal diseases. They are constantly seeking to eliminate those animal pests and plant blights which cause enormous annual losses to farmers. Continuous warfare is being waged against the cotton boll-weevil and the Japanese beetle. Departments of public safety labor to enforce those municipal ordinances which reduce fire and traffic hazards. Factory and building inspection is becoming a reality.

University departments, endowed societies, and private organizations are cooperating with government bureaus in the reduction of the risks of industry resident in our economic as well as physical environments. Statistical studies permit a certain amount of forecasting. Although their accuracy may be criticized in the same way as are the forecasts of the weather bureau, 100 per cent perfection is not to be expected. Careful market analyses of the general price trends of stocks and bonds are correlated with statistics of bank clearings, interest rates, freight-car loadings, and other valuable information. By combining this information in the same way that the weather man combines knowledge of temperature, atmospheric pressure, and the direction of the wind, certain general business tendencies may be discerned.

This general analysis of the state of markets helps the business man to make a particular decision in connection with a specific problem. Business cycles repeated themselves with a fair degree of regularity during the nineteenth century. They have often displayed well-defined phases. Engrossed with his own specialized work, the individual enterpriser is often unable or unwilling to make such general market analyses. Nevertheless, it is essential that he be informed of general price movements and such other economic tendencies as are discernible. Such knowledge will permit him to set his helm accordingly. It will not eliminate financial shipwrecks, but it will chart with lighthouses and buoys the rocks and shallows within the sea of inflation, expansion, and rising prices.

A number of large banking institutions employ professional economists for the study of general business conditions. They often publish periodicals which contain analyses of the markets for securities and produce. Direct telephone or telegraph communication is maintained with New York or Chicago. The broker's tape brings the New York Stock Exchange within the confines of all American cities. This rapid dissemination of market information tends to prevent wild fluctuations in prices. A rise in the price tends to introduce thousands of distant and invisible sellers, and to discourage further purchasing. A fall in the price of a commodity or a security has the reverse tendency, unless wild speculation prevails. The Chicago Board of Trade sends out a "broad tape" which may be read in the offices of produce brokers throughout the country. The "broad tape" contains more information than merely the latest prices on the exchange. It disseminates various items of news and trade gossip from all parts of the world concerning the demand and supply conditions for various kinds of produce. Bank clearings and the total volume of trade, as reflected in railroad-car loadings, are also public information. Federal reserve banks publish general information as to interest rates and bank reserves.

In addition to the informative activities of these quasi-public institutions, there are a number of private firms which collect business statistics, prepare charts, and give general business advice to their clients. An illustration is the Babson Statistical Agency. The work of Dun and of Bradstreet is somewhat different, for these companies secure information as to the financial standing of firms. Their subscribers find this information of service in determining the granting or withholding of credit. It lessens, but does not eliminate the risk of insolvent debtors.

Local chambers of commerce seek to foster local industries. The work of the National Chamber of Commerce is somewhat broader. In this connection, the United States Department of Commerce and consular service must also be mentioned. American trade, both at home and abroad, is fostered and protected. A constant effort is made by these public agencies to reduce the risks of industry and commerce. There are also numerous private associations of business men, which have been formed for the same purpose. These organizations may be either economic or geographical. An economic organization is one composed of all business men engaged in different phases of a given industry in various parts of the country. Trade journals, such as *The Iron Age*, and *The National Baker* give valuable information along their specific lines. Geographical organizations of business men may be illustrated by local boards of trade and by Rotary and Kiwanis clubs. The latter are composed of individuals representing different businesses and professions within the same community. Not only do such organizations foster commerce and reduce the risks of industry, but they also seek to raise the standards of business ethics. Thus, the slogan of the Rotary Club is "He profits most who serves best."

4. Price Uncertainties and Advance Contracts.—There are certain hazards of industry for which the enterpriser cannot obtain insurance. Chief among these uncertainties of business is the danger of loss from price changes. The profits from the manufacture of a given article may be consumed by a decline in its price in the meantime. On the other hand, the normal or estimated profit may be increased by an additional profit due to a rise in price. The enterpriser, however, is usually a specialist who does not care to speculate on price changes. He prefers to know definitely the cost of his raw materials and the price of his finished product. Just as he insures himself against loss by fire or theft, so he seeks to protect himself against price changes. He does this either by future contracts or by what is known as hedging.

Future contracts are formal agreements to buy or to sell at a specified price certain amounts of a given article at some time in the future. Let us assume that our enterpriser is a builder who is estimating on the price of a proposed home. He prepares a list of materials needed from the specifications of the architect who has drawn the plans for the house. Before submitting his bid, however, he places provisional contracts with the lumber, brick, and stone dealers to supply him with these basic building materials. If his bid on the house is accepted, the provisional contracts become final for the purchase of these goods at the contract prices. Thus, the builder or contractor is able to estimate with some degree of certainty his costs of building the house according to the specifications of the architect. Moreover, if his bid is accepted, he is guaranteed not only a market for his house, but also a definite price for his finished product. Unfortunately for the builder, however, he is unable to estimate his labor costs so exactly. The values of services as well as of commodities vary, and wages as well as prices change. Moreover, the builder has probably contracted to receive the raw materials at specified times and to finish the house by a certain date. Labor disputes may render the former undesirable and the latter impossible. Although the use of future contracts shifts the risks of industry" all along the line," the chief incidence of price changes falls upon the wholesalers and jobbers, who are the middlemen between manufacturers and consumers.

5. Speculation and Arbitrage.—Some knowledge of speculation is essential to an understanding of hedging, by which the hazards of price changes may be shifted by business men to specialized dealers in futures. Speculation is the buying and selling of goods in order to profit by price changes in the meantime. The speculator buys his land, grain, or stock at one time and sells it at another. The common form of speculation is to buy in the present market and sell in the future, but the reverse operation is also possible in both produce and stock exchanges. Selling short is a process by which a speculator contracts to sell at the present price certain produce or securities which he does not then possess, but which he will buy in the future. Unlike those speculators who profit by a rise in price, the short seller profits by a fall in price. If his estimate of the future market is incorrect and the price rises, losses will result when he is forced to buy in order to fulfil his contract, that is, to "cover" his former short sale.

Arbitrage is the simultaneous buying and selling in two different markets. Arbitrage differs from speculation in that it tends to equalize prices in two different localities, rather than over different periods of time. The arbitrager does not hold his commodity or security for a rise or fall in its price. He sells it immediately in another market. Indeed, the arbitrager places an order to buy and an order to sell simultaneously in two different places. He is the watchful hawk of markets, and his activities tend to keep price differences in various localities down to the bare minimum of transportation and insurance charges.

The judicious speculation and arbitraging of functional middlemen is economically productive. There are brokers who make a living by dealing in futures. Dealers in foreign bills of exchange and in warehouse receipts of commodities on the produce market are professional speculators. They are always willing to buy or sell their particular wares at what they consider a favorable price. The speculation of these specialized merchants or functional middlemen tends to lessen price fluctuations. Arbitrage tends to lessen price differences. The activities of functional middlemen tend to balance supply and demand forces over various times and places. In the last chapter it was shown how a restraining influence is thus exerted over both production and consumption. A future scarcity will be anticipated and reflected in rising prices in the present market. A slight rise in price will stimulate production and curtail consumption. Moreover, portions of an excessive supply can be stored away for future use and need not be dumped on the present market. The delicate mechanism of price and the activities of middlemen lessen the severities of scarcities and gluts in the market.

The accessible machinery of organized markets, such as the produce exchange and the stock market, make it possible for all individuals to gamble on the future prices of commodities or securities. There are always outsiders who are anxious to "take a flyer" on the market. The result is sometimes disastrous to themselves and often unfortunate for industrial society. These amateur speculators are ambitious enough to match their crude guesses against the careful estimates of professional speculators. As contrasted with the activities of functional middlemen, such speculation disturbs rather than balances the delicate mechanism of price. Although occasionally and temporarily successful, outside speculators invariably lose in the long run. In the meantime, their frantic buying or selling disturbs the market, usually by accentuating the prevalent price tendency, whether upward or downward.

6. Hedging.—Hedging consists of buying and selling at the same time, the one transaction in the actual present market and the other in the future speculative market. Hedging is performed by enterprisers for the purpose of protection against possible losses from price changes. By the device of hedging a loss in one market will be offset by a corresponding gain in the other. An enterpriser is thus immune to price changes, for he cannot profit by a rise in price nor can he lose by a fall in price.

A knowledge of speculative contracts and dealings in futures is essential to an understanding of hedging. In spite of the danger of tedious repetition let us illustrate the general process. "A" believes that there will be a future scarcity of wheat and that its price will advance. He therefore buys from a broker elevator receipts of wheat, which he holds until some time in the future. If his surmise is correct and the price of wheat advances, he will sell these paper claims later at a profit. If he is wrong and there is a future abundance of grain, its price will be low and losses will result from his speculation. These warehouse certificates, like stocks, may be bought on margin. This transaction is relatively simple and analogous to buying stock on margin.

The reverse process of selling short is more difficult to understand. "B" believes that the price of wheat will fall, due to a future increase in its supply. He therefore agrees to sell at the present price a quantity of wheat or warehouse receipts which he will purchase at some future time. In other words, he sells something which he does not possess, and which he hopes to purchase later at a lower price. If his expectations are true and there is a future abundance of wheat, the short seller will be able to purchase it more cheaply and to make a profit. If the reverse is true, he loses an equivalent amount. Selling short is a similar operation in both the produce and the security market. It is more justifiable in the former case, however, than in the latter, because it permits millers and cotton manufacturers to hedge on the prices of these commodities. In order to protect the other party to the contract, the one who sells short must advance a certain amount of money as evidence of his ability to make the future purchase of wheat or warehouse certificates in order to fulfil his selling short contract. If the price of wheat rises, his margin must be similarly increased, for the difficulty of meeting the contract price is increased proportionately. At the time agreed upon "B" must purchase wheat, or rather certificates of deposit, at the new price, and sell them to the other party at the contract price. In other words, he forfeits or makes the difference between the contract price to sell and the future market price at which he buys.

Let us illustrate some common protective devices used by the miller. A small manufacturer of flour has just received a large order. He is under contract to deliver a certain amount of flour at a given time for a certain price. The basis of this contract price of flour is the present price of grain. The miller may immediately order a sufficient quantity of wheat at its present price to be delivered at specified times in the future to be ground into flour. This plan of the miller is, therefore, similar to that of the builder in our previous illustration of protection against price changes by advance contracts. On the other hand, the miller may do something which is slightly different. Instead of placing orders for the actual delivery of grain, he may buy outright or on margin sufficient warehouse receipts or grain futures from a wheat broker. If the price of grain advances, he will profit by the difference between the former and the present market prices. This profit in the speculative market will permit the miller to buy grain for manufacturing into flour in the open market and at the higher price. If the price of grain falls, he loses on his speculative contract, but is compensated by being able to buy grains for manufacture into flour at a lower price than he had anticipated.

Let us now reverse the process. A large flour mill is expecting to buy a considerable quantity of grain and to store it in its warehouse. In spite of a scarcity of orders, the milling firm proposes to be ready for any emergency. If the price of grain should rise in the next few months, the concern will make a profit from its large purchase of cheap grain. If the price of grain falls, the loss will be correspondingly great. Although future orders for flour should come, the selling price of this flour will be lower because of the fall in the price of wheat. The flour concern desires to possess an ample supply of grain, and yet does not care to speculate in the grain market. The result is hedging. At the very time that the order is placed for the purchase and actual delivery of wheat, a speculative or future contract is placed for the selling short of an equivalent amount of certificates of deposit. If the price of wheat falls, the concern gains on its speculative or selling-short contract. At the same time, it loses on the sale of its flour. Its warehouses are loaded with expensive grain while the market is "easy." Its receipts from the sale of flour reflect the fall in the price of wheat, for the milling firm is forced to sell flour at a lower price than had formerly prevailed. If the price of grain should rise, the reverse would be the case. The firm can obtain a higher price for its flour than had been expected. In other words, it would have been successful in buying cheap wheat. Thus, the flour manufacturing concern would make an extra profit in its regular business, but it would receive a corresponding loss in its speculative contract. The higher prices of grain would force the milling firm to lose this margin in its contract to sell grain short.

Hedging permits a miller or a cotton manufacturer to minimize the hazards of loss from price changes. It shifts this particular uncertainty of industry to brokers or functional middlemen, just as insurance diffuses the risk of financial loss by fire or some other insurable risk. The losses of middlemen tend to balance their profits. There is some net gain, however, or they would not remain in business as professional speculators. This net profit of professional dealers in futures, like insurance charges, may be regarded as a cost of production, which the consumer pays in the prices of bread, cotton goods, and other commodities. Unless the profits of these functional middlemen are exorbitant, the ultimate consumer does not pay an excessive amount for the regularity of production and the relative stability of prices.

7. **Essentials of Insurable Risks.**—An insurable risk is one which is both calculable and common. Losses due to bad weather are insurable risks, but the losses due to price changes are generally not so regarded. They are uncertainties rather than insurable risks, and the enterpriser must seek protection against the hazard of price changes by hedging rather than by insurance. The long series of weather records, however, make it possible to estimate the mathematical chances of rain on a given date and in a given locality. Hence, rain insurance is possible. In like manner, the keeping of vital statistics has made possible the compilation of actuarial tables and thereby the development of life insurance. It is not possible to say in advance that a particular individual, John Doe, will die on some specified date. Nevertheless, it is possible to state that a given percentage of normal men and women will die at a certain age. Thus, we can estimate with mathematical exactness the chances of John Doe's living to be fifty, sixty, or seventy years of age. Some individuals will live longer than this mathematical estimate, but others will not live so long. Hence, insurance depends upon the law of averages and the insurance of a large number of individuals. A given risk may be predicted with mathematical accuracy, but it is not an insurable risk unless it is sufficiently common to permit the insurance of a large number of cases. In this way underestimates tend to balance overestimates, and profits tend to balance losses.

A final characteristic of an insurable risk is that a relatively small reserve is sufficient protection against vast possible losses. If all the houses of a certain section of a city were to take fire, the amount of fire hose and other such apparatus in the vicinity would be inadequate. If all the insured clients of a large insurance company were to die about the same time, the greatest financial reserves would be inadequate. Fire statistics and mortality tables show that such possibilities are rare in the practical experiences of life. Scientific insurance, like sound banking, merely depends on the existence of adequate reserves. If all the depositors should demand all their deposits at precisely the same time, modern banking would be impossible. A run on a sound bank would be fatal, if other banks failed to respond by loaning their reserve cash.   In a similar manner, fire companies pool their reserves in an emergency.   An experienced banker can estimate what proportion of total deposits must be kept constantly available as cash.   The banking laws of the nation and of most states specify what the reserves shall be for national and state banks.   In a similar fashion, life insurance companies and fire insurance companies are not forced to maintain sufficient funds to pay claims to all the insured at the same time.   By insuring a sufficiently large number of individuals the annual premiums or dues of the entire group will generally pay the claims of those who suffer death or fire loss during the year. Insurance companies must maintain financial reserves for emergencies, but only a small portion of these must be continually and immediately available.   The remainder of these reserves is placed in conservative investments.   Thus, most current claims are paid out of current premiums.   If the former exceed the latter, recourse must be made to cash reserves.   If a serious emergency exists, a portion of the invested reserves must be converted into cash to pay the heavy claims.   The reserve is restored by the subsequent profits of good years.

8. Nature of Insurance.—Insurance is a diffusion of risk among the insured rather than a mere shifting of the risk to an insurance company.   It has been shown that insurance requires not only the existence of a calculable risk, but also of a sufficiently large number of cases.   The result is that those individuals who do not experience the hazard against which they are insured, or who experience it at a later date or in a subaverage form, help to pay for the greater losses of other insured individuals.   One group receives protection, and the other group compensation.   Many insurance companies today are mutual, that is, policy holders automatically become stockholders.   Profits in excess of the costs of operation, the payment of benefits, and the investment of reserves are prorated and returned to the policy holders as dividends.   These dividends may take the form either of cash payments, credits to be subtracted from the premiums paid, or accumulated additions to the surrender values of the policies.   Although a given insurance company may not have mutualized, the very nature of the insurance business possesses a mutual character.   Those who suffer most from the hazard against which they are insured profit most, proportionately, by the insurance.   The reverse is also true.   Those who profit least from the insurance pay for the greater losses of the sufferers. The result is the diffusion of the risk throughout the entire group. The actual hazard is borne by the individual who suffers it, but the financial loss which it involves is diffused. Indeed, insurance may be defined as the substitution of a small but certain loss for a large but uncertain loss.

The assessment plan of insurance has been common in the past among fraternal societies. With the death, sickness, unemployment, or some other misfortune of a member of the society, all the other members contribute a specific sum agreed upon in advance. The assessment plan illustrates the mutual character of insurance and its diffusion of risks. It possesses several inherent weaknesses, however, as contrasted with scientific insurance. The latter term implies the basing of premiums on the ascertainable degrees of risk, the existence of a large number of insured individuals, and, finally, the accumulation of large financial reserves. Insurance by assessment can generally be criticized on all three of these grounds. Mutual benefit societies may prosper for a while, but the failure to take in a large number of young members soon sounds the death knell of such associations. As the charter members grow old and infirm, the assessments increase and operate still further to deter young men from joining the society.

If a business is sufficiently large it may attempt to carry its own property insurance. Let us assume, for illustration, that a certain business corporation owns a large number of buildings scattered throughout a prosperous city. Statistics as to the frequency and severity of fires make it possible to estimate the fire hazards. Consequently, the corporation may put aside a certain amount of money each year for its own fire insurance fund. It may invest these funds in other securities or it may keep them in its own business. In the latter case the transaction is merely a paper one on the company's own records. In either event, however, these yearly payments are regarded as a cost of doing business, similar to salaries or insurance premiums in outside companies. From the accumulated fund the company reimburses itself in the event of fire. The usual danger in carrying one's own insurance is the failure to estimate adequately the given hazard and to build up sufficient reserves. Again, there is not the same opportunity to diffuse the hazard over a sufficiently large number of business units. Indeed, fire insurance companies frequently reinsure themselves in other companies. This means that they in turn pool their risks and reserves to a considerable extent. In any event, insurance companies seek to scatter their risks as much as possible. No one fire insurance company likes to insure many adjoining houses. If a very large life insurance policy is desired, several life insurance companies syndicate to underwrite the risk—that is, they divide the total amount of insurance among them.

9. Types of Insurance.—The various types of insurance may be grouped into three general classes: personal insurance, property insurance, and social insurance. Life insurance is the most important illustration of personal insurance. Life insurance policies are generally made payable to the wife, mother, or some other member of the insured individual's family. Of recent years, many large industrial corporations have insured in their own favor the lives of the responsible heads of their businesses. They seek to capitalize the value of an individual's services and to compensate themselves financially for the loss of his industrial leadership. Life insurance is peculiar in that the insured individual does not receive the benefit of the insurance. It is usually carried by the head of the house to keep the wolf from the door of his potential orphans and widow. The size of the premium depends on the amount of the insurance and the age of the insured. The issuance of the policy is conditioned by a satisfactory physical examination.

In general, life insurance policies fall into two groups—straight life insurance and endowment policies. The former policy is the cheaper one to carry, but it pays only the stipulated sum at death. Endowment policies are more expensive to carry, for the premiums represent not only protection but also a form of investment. Life insurance policies may be so written that the premiums must be paid steadily until the death of the insured. On the other hand, they may take the form of twenty-year payments, after which time no more premiums are due. It is also possible to have an endowment policy written which will mature at some advanced age or on the payment of a specified number of premiums.

An annuity is a form of insurance which involves the same actuarial tables as are used in the determination of life insurance rates. The process is usually reversed, however, since the purposes are different. The payment of insurance begins on the death of the insured, but an annuity ordinarily ceases on the death of its recipient. The purchase of an annuity requires the payment of a lump sum, after which time the beneficiary receives regular payments at stipulated intervals so long as he lives. The cost of an annuity varies with the size of the benefits and with the age at which it is purchased. The older the annuitant the lower the cost of the annuity. Annuities represent old-age and income insurance. They may also be bought by the payment of regular premiums in the early years of life. It is often possible to incorporate annuity features in an ordinary life insurance policy. When the insured individual dies, or if he dies before a certain age, the face value of the policy is paid to his estate. If he lives to a certain age his premiums cease and annuity payments are made until death.

In years to come health insurance may become as important as life insurance is today. At present, however, health insurance is not very popular as a voluntary form of insurance. It is more difficult to administer than is life insurance, and the risks are harder to determine with mathematical exactness. Health insurance has developed chiefly in Europe as a type of compulsory social insurance. In addition to life and health insurance there are numerous miscellaneous types of personal insurance. Thus, a violinist may insure himself against the loss of his fingers, or an actor may insure himself against an impairment of his voice. Accident insurance is also common among traveling men who must continually subject themselves to the hazards of railroads and street traffic.

Property insurance includes protection against many types of risks and for many kinds of wealth. Fire insurance is still the most important single type, although recently numerous kinds of automobile insurance have grown in importance. Both buildings and the furniture in them may be insured against loss by fire or various other causes. It is sometimes difficult to estimate relative fire hazards and to standardize fire risks. The use of certain precautionary measures and the utilization of improved fire-fighting apparatus will often reduce the premiums. Marine insurance is designed to cover losses at sea. Automobile insurance is of various kinds, such as fire, theft, liability, and collision. The latter term is commonly used with reference to injuries to one's own automobile or self, and liability insurance to cover damage to other individuals and their property.

Liability as well as collision insurance may be written to cover personal injury or property damage or both. There are many miscellaneous types of property insurance, such as plate-glass window insurance, tornado or hail insurance, burglary insurance, etc. Credit insurance is one of the most recent types of property insurance. The object is protection against the loss resulting from insolvent debtors.

Social insurance is peculiar in that it is compulsory rather than voluntary. Large groups of individuals are automatically insured by state legislation against the hazards of accident, sickness, unemployment, or dependent old age. Social insurance is also peculiar in that it is often subsidized by the state. The human risks of industry and the problem of social insurance will be discussed in Chap. XXIII.

There are some forms of protection which are often spoken of as insurance, but which are not insurance in the strict sense of the term. These may be illustrated by guaranty and suretyship. Certain trust companies will guarantee the validity of real-estate titles, and bonding houses or surety companies will insure against loss from dishonesty of employees placed in positions of trust and responsibility. But the bonding company does not charge an insurance premium based, for example, on the hazards of a given real-estate title. It conducts its own search of court and county records and makes sure that a clear title to the particular piece of real estate exists. If so, it issues what is known as title insurance. The policy agrees to indemnify its holder and the owner of the real estate against any defect in the title. In the same way, a surety company or a bonding house does not calculate the chances that particular individuals will defraud their employers and express these hazards in a varying scale of premiums. General hazards only are usually estimated. A formal investigation is made as to the character of each individual before he is guaranteed. If there is serious doubt of his honesty, the company does not issue the bond. Varying degrees of honesty are not recognized, and consequently there is no scale of premiums based on them.

10. Insurance Compared with Gambling, Speculation, and Investment.—Insurance first developed in the form of a bet between a shipowner and some wealthy individual that the former's ship would not return. If it did so, the owner was able to pay the bet, but if it did not return he was compensated for its loss by the amount of the bet. Although the form of insurance has changed with the passage of years, it may still appear to some individuals that insurance is merely a bet which is placed under standardized conditions. The existence of calculable risks makes it possible to estimate correctly the mathematical chances of such a wager. Such a confusion between insurance and gambling ignores an important fact. In gambling, one individual's gain is another individual's loss. Insurance, however, represents a mutual gain. The actual loss may be suffered by the insured, but the financial loss is diffused throughout the group. The insured individual may never collect the insurance, but he has received protection in the meantime. Gambling is socially undesirable; on the other hand, insurance is socially desirable.

Insurance involves the existence of calculable risks and a sufficiently large number of cases to permit the law of averages to operate. Gambling may involve these two elements, but they are often absent. There are some insurance companies, however, which will issue policies against uncertainties which are neither calculable nor common. Such "insurance" is misnamed when the essentials of an insurable risk are absent. The process often savors more of gambling than of insurance, although it sometimes permits legitimate enterprisers to protect themselves against various hazards of their business. Companies which engage in this type of "insurance" make some attempt to estimate the mathematical chances involved. They seek to protect themselves by taking heavily favorable odds and by securing a variety of risks. The great English firm of Lloyds will issue insurance against almost any hazard.

Speculation, as we have noted, consists of buying or selling in the present market and performing the reverse operation in the future market. The object is profit and the source of speculation lies in price changes. On the other hand, insurance aims at protection rather than profits. Moreover, the uncertainties of speculation, that is, price changes, are not insurable risks. Hedging is analogous to insurance, however, for the professional speculation of specialized dealers in futures permits the business man to protect himself against the noninsurable hazard of price changes. Speculation, however, is subject to greater abuse than is insurance. No individual will insure himself against a risk which he does not face, but many individuals will seek to speculate in the prices of produce, securities, or land.

Investment represents the purchase of an income, but insurance represents the purchase of protection. Both insurance and investment involve saving and thrift on the part of the investor and the insured. Life insurance premiums, like savings fund deposits, are paid out of present income, and their investment represents the creation of capital goods rather than a demand for present consumption goods. It was pointed out that many insurance policies combine the elements of both investment and protection. This may be illustrated in annuities and endowment life insurance. Although an insured individual may desire protection rather than investment and hence purchases what is known as "straight life," nevertheless, the insurance company must invest some of the premiums which it receives from him. In this way an insurance company acts as middleman between the insured individual and industry, in the same way that a bank acts as a middleman between its depositors and industry. The larger portion of the assets of a commercial bank are short-term loans to business men in the form of commercial paper. The greater part of the assets of an insurance company, like those of a savings bank, are long-time loans in the form of bonds and mortgages. The interest on the invested premiums of insured individuals must be balanced against their mortality hazards as shown in actuarial tables. The return on these invested premiums tends to keep down the cost of insurance. Scientific insurance necessitates investment, because it involves the creation of reserves. The total combined assets of life insurance companies alone in 1925 represented about nine and one-half billion dollars. At that date they had almost forty-five billion dollars of life insurance in force and they received approximately two billion dollars a year in premiums. Life insurance companies alone invested millions of dollars each week.

11. Gambling, Speculation, and Investment Compared.—The universality of risk and uncertainty in industry gives rise to the common statement that "all business is a gamble." It is necessary that we attempt to distinguish between gambling and speculation and between speculation and investment. Although there are twilight zones between these terms where classification is difficult, it is possible and desirable to indicate certain marks of distinction between gambling and speculation and between speculation and investment.

The gambler creates his own hazard, but the legitimate speculator finds the element of chance in the course of his regular business. The chief distinction between gambling and speculation lies in the economic necessity for the element of chance and in the social desirability of such an assumption of risk. The risk of a poker hand is not an economic necessity, nor is betting on horse races socially desirable. Gambling does not involve cheating and the honor code among the devotees of games of chance may be quite high, nevertheless, it is economically unproductive and socially undesirable. It represents the taking of wealth without some compensating service. Gambling is based on mere chance, but speculation is based on belief or faith. The speculator should have some basis in fact for believing that the price of grain or of a given security will rise or fall. An appeal is made to reason rather than to mere luck. The speculation of professional dealers in futures is based on business experience, and their assumption of the hazards of price changes is part of their economic life.

The outside speculator invites the uncertainty of price changes instead of assuming it as part of his legitimate business. Moreover, his speculation is not always based on knowledge. It approximates gambling rather than speculation for both reasons.

Speculation on the stock exchange is less desirable than speculation on the produce exchange. There is not the same economic necessity for speculation in securities as in produce. Specialized dealers in futures on the produce exchange not only tend to balance production and consumption, but also permit entrepreneurs to hedge. There is no such necessity in the market for securities. The enormous speculation on the New York Stock Exchange is largely sterile and often disastrous from both an economic and a social point of view. Billions of dollars worth of securities pass from hand to hand in response to the desire of speculators to gamble on the market. Some are seeking to buy while others are seeking to sell the same stocks. Some speculators are expressing their belief in a future rise in prices while others are displaying an equally strong belief in a future decline in prices. Because the speculation of outsiders desiring to "take a flyer on the market" predominates rather than the professional activities of legitimate dealers in futures, such speculation frequently degen-

erates into mere gambling.   Moreover, it disturbs rather than
stabilizes prices.

The distinction between speculation and investment is as
difficult to make as that between speculation and gambling.
These various concepts gradually fade into each other like the
colors of the spectrum.   While gambling is based on chance, and
speculation on belief, investment is based primarily on knowledge
or certainty.   Speculation deals with possible or anticipated
values, but investment deals with actual or present values.
Both the risk element and the rate of return are relatively lower
in investments than in speculation.   Indeed, in speculation
the possible rate of return is usually in proportion to the risk
involved.   An investment is made to secure a permanent income,
and the investor expects to keep his purchase.   A speculation is
made in anticipation of a future sale or purchase and with
hopes of a profit from the transaction.   Wall Street draws a
very sharp line between investment and speculation.   Brokers
are inclined to use the term investment when the purchaser pays
in full and takes possession of his security.   The transaction
is termed speculation when one buys on margin or sells short.
Immediate gain rather than permanent income is desired in this
case.   A similar situation exists in the real-estate market.
The investor purchases a piece of land or a building with the
expectation of using it himself or living on the rent.   The
speculator buys the land or building with the hope of a later
resale with profit.   In some cases the land speculator does not
take title to his real estate but merely sells the agreement of
sale to someone else before its date of settlement.

12. Summary.—Risk and uncertainty are universal characteristics of modern industrial society.   Although the enterpriser
has been defined as the individual who assumes the risks of
industry, the capitalist and the laborer are not immune.   Moreover, there are certain functional middlemen who specialize in
risk bearing.   The risks of industry may be eliminated, shifted
to some one else, diffused throughout the entire group, or borne
by the enterpriser himself.

The sources of risk lie in our physical, social, and economic
environments.   Risks may be classified as physical and economic, the latter destroying values and the former actual
products.   Science and popular education are seeking to reduce
the physical hazards of modern industrial society.   Economic

uncertainties may be classified as either technological or marketing hazards. The development of the science of economics permits a certain amount of forecasting to be done and some phases of the business cycle to be anticipated.

Arbitrage is the simultaneous buying and selling of the same commodity in two different markets. Speculation is the buying or selling in the present market, and the performance of the reverse operation in a future market. Arbitrage tends to reduce price differences in various places and the legitimate speculation of professional dealers in futures tends to lessen price fluctuations over various periods of time.

Price changes are serious uncertainties but they are not insurable risks. The enterpriser may protect himself against this economic, rather than physical, hazard by making future contracts, that is, by agreeing in advance as to the prices to be charged or paid. Hedging is another device for shifting the uncertainty of price changes. Hedging consists of making a speculative or future contract at the same time that one makes an actual or present business transaction. The one is usually the exact reverse of the other. Such a transaction precludes the possibility of either gains or losses from price changes. The profit from one transaction just balances the loss from another. As hedging is made possible by the activities of professional dealers in futures, it is essentially a shifting of the uncertainties of price changes to these specialized risk bearers.

An insurable risk is one which is both common and calculable. Its mathematical chances can be estimated, and, if it is a sufficiently common occurrence, the law of averages will operate. Thus, life insurance rates are based on recognized actuarial tables, and the insurance of a large number of individuals balances gains and losses. Many insurance companies are mutual, and profits are shared by policy holders. Insurance is the diffusion rather than the shifting of a given financial loss. It represents the substitution of a small but certain loss for a large but uncertain loss. There are many types of insurance but they may be classified as personal, property, or social insurance. Guarantee and suretyship afford protection from loss, but, strictly speaking, they are not insurance.

Insurance is not gambling for it represents mutual gain. The aim of speculation is profit from price changes, but the purpose of insurance is protection. Insurance is a form of invest-

ment, for insurance companies must maintain large financial
reserves. These are placed in mortgages, bonds, or other conservative investments. The distinction between gambling,
speculation, and investment is difficult to make. Gambling
depends on mere chance, speculation on belief or faith, and
investment on knowledge or certainty. Gambling is not socially
desirable, but the legitimate speculation of specialized dealers in
futures is economically productive. Functional middlemen help
to stabilize prices and to balance production and consumption.
Speculation on the market by uninformed outsiders savors of
gambling. The aim of investment is the purchase of an income,
but the aim of speculation is a profit from the future sale or
purchase of securities or warehouse receipts which have been
purchased or sold.

Collateral Reading

BYE, R. T., "Principles of Economics," chap. 10.
CLAY, H., "Economics for the General Reader," chap. 4.
FAIRCHILD, F. R., FURNISS, E. S., and BUCK, N. S., "Elementary
    Economics," vol. 2 chap. 32.
FETTER, F., "Modern Economic Problems," chap. 12 and 13.
HAMILTON, W., "Current Economic Problems," pp. 173-183 and 545-552.
MAGEE, J. D., "Introduction to Economic Problems," chap. 9.
MARSHALL, L. C., "Readings in Industrial Society," chap. 8.
TAUSSIG, F. W., "Principles of Economics," vol. 1 chap. 11.

References

Annals of the American Academy of Political and Social Science, March,
    1917.
HARDY, C. O., "Readings in Risk and Risk-Bearing."
————, "Risk and Risk-Bearing."
HUEBNER, S. S., "Life Insurance."
————,"Property Insurance."
JORDAN, D. F., "Business Forecasting."
KNIGHT, F. H., "Risk, Uncertainty and Profit."
RIEGEL, R., and LOMAN, H. S., "Insurance Principles and Practices."
WHITE, P., "Market Analysis."
For additional references see previous chapters.

Questions for Discussion

1. Outline the chief sources of risk in industry.
2. Is the enterpriser the only risk bearer in industry? Explain.
3. How may risks be reduced?
4. Are price changes insurable risks? Why or why not?
5. Differentiate between speculation and arbitrage.
6. Differentiate between arbitrage and hedging.
7. Explain how and why a business man hedges.

8. Outline some leading types of insurance.
9. Differentiate between speculation and insurance.
10. Distinguish among gambling, speculation, and investment.

Topics for Investigation

1. Progress and the increased hazards of life.
2. Science and the reduction of risks.
3. Credit insurance or business failures as insurable risks.
4. Scientific insurance as compared with the assessment plan.
5. The growth in the volume and kinds of insurance.
6. Investment of insurance premiums.

CHAPTER V

FINANCIAL ORGANIZATION AND MANAGEMENT OF
BUSINESS CORPORATIONS

1. Nature and Kinds of Corporations.—A corporation is an association of individuals legally bound together by a certificate of incorporation and cooperating for the performance of some economic, political, or social function. A business corporation is such an association of natural or legal persons, authorized by the state in an instrument called a charter to transact business of a specified character. A corporation is a legal entity and possesses an existence apart from that of the individuals who own it. The ownership of a business corporation is expressed in shares of stock, each stockholder being a part owner of the corporate business. The corporation is authorized by the state to obtain a certain amount of capital with which to conduct its business. This entire amount of authorized capital may or may not be raised at the time of the formation of the corporation. A portion of it may be reserved for future capital issues.

Although the final control of business corporations rests with its stockholders, the actual management is delegated by them to their representatives, who are known as directors of the company. By virtue of the fact that the corporation has an existence apart from that of its owners, it is regarded by the state as a legal person. It may buy and sell property, sue and be sued in courts, and in most other respects may act like a natural person for the transaction of its business. The legal fiction of a separate corporate entity, distinct from that of its owners and officers, however, has been attacked by some recent decisions of the courts. The natural persons behind the corporate mask have been sought out, and responsibility has been placed upon them for certain offenses of the intangible corporation.

The corporate charter is the birth certificate of a corporation. It specifies the functions that have been vested in the company, and the corporation has no powers other than those expressly mentioned in the charter. If the corporation violates its privileges or exceeds its rights, it may have its charter revoked by the state which created it. Unauthorized acts or unwarranted extensions of activities are expressed in legal terminology as *ultra vires*. As long as the corporation legally performs the functions for which it was created, it may continue in existence for an indefinite period of time. Although a definite time limit is usually expressed in the charter, the corporation may apply for a new charter or for extension of the old one if it wishes to continue its existence. Under the Constitution of the United States, "Full faith and credit shall be given in each state to the public acts, records, and judicial proceedings of every other state."[1] The result is that a corporation doing an interstate business may ordinarily be chartered in any state that it desires. It may then do business in any or all of the other states. In the conduct of its business, however, it is subject to the laws of the state in which it is operating.

Corporations may be classified in a variety of ways. There are business corporations and all other corporations. There are corporations organized for economic, political, and social purposes. An ordinary business corporation and an incorporated trade union are illustrations of economic corporations. Cities and incorporated boroughs are political corporations and the creatures of their respective state legislatures. Incorporated clubs, churches, and fraternities are illustrations of social corporations. Corporations may also be classified as public and private. Incorporated political units are examples of public corporations and ordinary business corporations of private corporations. In addition, there are quasi-public corporations, such as the railroads and public utility companies. Finally, corporations may be classified as those with capital stock and those without capital stock; and as those which operate for gain and those which do not operate for gain. Public corporations, such as cities and incorporated boroughs, do not operate for gain and do not possess capital stock. It is with business corporations, organized for gain and with authorized capital stock, that we are concerned in this chapter.

2. Development of the Corporate Form of Business Enterprise. At the time of the formation of the United States, in 1789, there were only twenty-one business corporations of any kind in this country. They were primarily tollbridge and turnpike companies, water-supply companies, companies for improving inland

[1] Article IV, Sec. 1.

navigation, and insurance and banking companies. These were the most common types of business corporations until railroads began to be built during the second quarter of the nineteenth century. Industrial corporations did not develop in the United States to any pronounced extent until after the Civil War. Because of the destructiveness of this great conflict, it became a matter of considerable importance to replace what had been destroyed. Business activities developed, and the need for capital funds became pronounced. The corporate form of business enterprise was well suited to the raising of large amounts of capital, because it combined the savings of large numbers of investors.

As a result of the very rapid expansion of business activity during the last quarter of the nineteenth century, no less than 51,094 manufacturing corporations were established in the United States by 1904. The value of the products of these corporations represented 73.7 per cent of the total value of the manufactured products of all domestic concerns. From 1904 to 1919, the number of manufacturing corporations in the United States increased to 91,516—or by no less than 80 per cent. The value of the products manufactured by these corporations represented 87.8 per cent of the total of all domestic manufactured products.[1] In 1912, more than 350,000 corporations of all kinds made returns to the Federal government under the corporation tax law. Although 51.6 per cent of all manufacturing businesses in the United States in 1914 were individual enterprises, this relatively large group of establishments produced slightly less than 8 per cent of the total value of all manufactured products. Today, probably more than 90 per cent of the manufactured products of the United States is made by corporations. Thus, we get a general idea of the unusual growth of the corporate form of business enterprise during the past century. How are we to account for this economic phenomenon?

3. Advantages of the Corporation over Other Forms of Business Organization.—We may distinguish among three general types of business organization, the individual enterprise, the partnership, and the corporation. In an individual enterprise one person is the sole proprietor or owner of the business. In a partnership, two or more individuals have combined their resources and skill. The partnership form of business organization has several impor-

[1] See "Census for Manufactures."

tant disadvantages as compared with the corporation. They account to no small extent for the gradual conversion of an increasing number of partnerships into corporations.

It has already been indicated that a corporation can accumulate large amounts of capital by appealing to numerous and different investors. Its units of ownership, represented by shares of stock, are valued at different amounts, varying from a hundred dollars or more per share to less than a dollar. Consequently, a corporation can avail itself of a greater number of investors and therefore of larger funds than a small group of individuals associated in a partnership. Furthermore, each partner in a partnership is liable for the debts incurred by any associate in the name of the partnership. This liability transcends his investments in the partnership and extends to his other property. Because a creditor can attach the individual property of any one of the partners, the liability of a partnership is said to be unlimited. In a corporation, on the other hand, the liability of the stockholder is limited to the amount of his investment. Exceptions to this rule are national banks, where the stockholders' liability is double that of his investment in the bank's stock. Limited partnerships, however, are legally possible in a number of states. These usually include a managing partner, whose liability is unlimited, and one or more silent partners, who have capital in the business, but whose liability is limited by the articles of partnership to the extent of the investment.

Exchange of investment is also facilitated by the corporate form of business. A partner cannot withdraw from a partnership without the consent of all the other partners. A stockholder, on the other hand, can sell his ownership in the corporation to anyone who wishes to buy it. The corporate form of business organization possesses the final advantage of perpetuity of existence. A partnership is dissolved by the death of one of the partners, but the death of a stockholder does not impair the life of the corporate business. The corporation has an existence apart from that of the stockholders who own it. Because of these advantages of the corporation over the partnership, the corporation has become the chief form of business organization.

The problems of corporate management and control involve not only the investing public, but also all consumers. We have indicated the extent to which corporations provide us with goods in the present market. The ownership of American corporations is diffused among millions of people. There are now over fifteen million stockholders of various corporations in the United States. Of course, this does not mean that fifteen million individuals own the stock of American corporations, for one individual may be a stockholder in more than one corporation. It is impossible to determine to what extent there is a duplication in the total ownership of corporations, but it is safe to assume that at least several million separate individuals are owners of corporate stocks. When we add to this number the thousands or perhaps millions of people who own the bonds of corporations, we get an idea of the wide diffusion of investment in corporate securities.

4. Promotion of a Business Enterprise.—A promoter is an enterpriser who specializes in the organization of business projects. The substitution of the corporate form of business organization for the single enterprise and the partnership has meant the development of the profession of promoter. He is the active element who brings the passive capitalist into touch with economic opportunities. The stream of production is constantly cutting new channels, for profits may be had by gratifying new wants of consumers and improving former methods of production. The promoter discovers a business opportunity and the banker evaluates it as a sound investment. The distinction between the promoter, the capitalist, and the enterpriser, however, is often difficult to maintain. Successful business men are frequently the incarnation of all three elements. Bankers and engineers are sometimes forced to play the part of promoters as well as that of financial or technical experts.

The work of promotion may be divided into three stages— the discovery of a proposition, its assembling, and its financing. The discovery of a business opportunity means far more than the mere belief that a market exists for a given commodity or service. An analysis must be made of the probable costs of manufacture and of such technical and merchandising problems as are likely to present themselves. An unforeseen objection or difficulty may transform profits into losses. The promoter secures abundant maps, charts, and technical reports on all phases of his project. The assembling of an economic venture, moreover, is as difficult and as important as its discovery. It has been defined as "the process of getting temporary control into the hands of the promoter." The promoter seeks to fortify himself against the capture of his project by someone else. He accomplishes this by the purchase of patent rights and valuable sites. The promoter must therefore have some capital with which to do this work of assembling. He generally purchases options, or the rights to buy later, however, instead of making outright purchases.

The third stage of promotion is that of financing a project. It may be accomplished either directly or indirectly. The right to participate in a business opportunity may be sold directly to the investing public, or indirectly through brokers and investment bankers. Both methods are common, but the indirect method is generally followed in large enterprises and the direct method in small ones. The corner grocer who seeks to retire may advertise his business opportunity in the newspapers. He seeks to find a purchaser in the simplest and most direct fashion. A large corporation, which is in the process of formation or expansion, will not ordinarily attempt to do its own financing. The rights of ownership or participation, as represented by stocks and bonds, will probably be sold by some large investment house. If the total value of these securities is very great, several investment houses may combine to underwrite the issue. They guarantee to buy the securities at a certain price and strive to sell them at another. The profit of the banking syndicate lies in the margin of difference between the two prices agreed on in advance. If the market will not absorb these securities at the estimated price, the underwriters may be forced to lower the price of the security and to take the loss which such a reduction involves. The securities may be listed subsequently on the New York Stock Exchange or on some local exchange. It is interesting to see how closely the estimate of the investment banker approximates the later market price.

5. Fraudulent Securities and "Blue Sky" Laws.—Promoters are constantly seeking to sell their various projects to individuals and financial institutions with funds to invest. Many of these "business opportunities" are sound and conservative. Others are highly speculative and sometimes spurious. The promoter who peddles this type of security does not attempt to interest investment bankers. He strives to sell his "opportunity" to the small investor by means of personal solicitation and alluring letters. "Sucker lists" of gullible or wealthy individuals are part of the equipment of the illegitimate promoter. To the uninitiated, the dollar mark on a share of stock represents so much actual value. Par value is assumed by them to be the true value of the stock certificate. This magic document, like the chart of the hidden treasures on Treasure Island, will give them control over countless wealth. They dream of a comfortable future when the dollars will come rolling in from their courageous speculation. They are often disappointed, however. In spite of all efforts to educate persons of moderate means to a realization of the risks involved in investing in the common stock of new and dubious ventures, hundreds of millions of dollars are lost every year by investors in speculative securities. It has been estimated that the stupendous sum of one billion dollars is lost by the people of the United States in a single year through purchasing worthless securities. This sum is so great that our imagination can scarcely grasp it. It would buy one million motor cars, costing a thousand dollars each. It would suffice to build a city of one hundred thousand individual homes, each home costing ten thousand dollars. Such an enormous sum is said to be spent annually by the people of the United States for worthless securities. Whether the foregoing estimate of losses is an exaggeration or not, the fact remains that vast sums are lost every year by the people of the United States in unsound investments.

A number of states have endeavored by various kinds of legislation to protect investors against such "wild-cat" schemes. These laws are commonly referred to as "blue sky" laws, because the promotion of spurious enterprises is so successful that one could almost imagine that an unscrupulous promoter could capitalize the blue sky above him and sell shares of stock in it to gullible investors. The first "blue sky" law was passed by Kansas, in 1911, and it has been followed by similar legislation in practically all the states of the Union. Such legislation usually provides that a company which seeks to dispose of its securities within the state must first file with some responsible official a statement concerning the purpose of that issue. This financial statement must contain the names of the officers and directors of the corporation and specific information on the business status of the enterprise. State examination and approval must precede any attempt to sell the securities within the borders of the state. In some states it is necessary that all brokerage and investment houses be registered, and that their agents obtain licenses to sell securities. Such legislation is supplementary to the state inspection of banks, insurance companies, and other financial institutions. "Blue sky" laws, like the examinations of the New York Stock Exchange, do not guarantee the investments which pass their inspection. They merely seek to lessen the possibility of fraud and deception. In addition to state legislation and inspection, the postal authorities of the Federal government are constantly seeking to discover fraudulent uses of the mails.

6. Process of Incorporation.—The first problem in organizing a business corporation is the selection of the state in which to incorporate. State corporation laws differ widely as to costs, ease, and methods of incorporation. In selecting a state in which to incorporate, a general rule to follow is to incorporate in the state in which the chief business is to be done. This is sometimes neither desirable nor easy to determine, however. There are consulting attorneys, who are specialists in the corporation laws of various states, and whose services are often sought by organizers of corporations. After a decision has been made, an application for a charter must be presented to the secretary of state or some other official, who is charged with the duty of receiving such applications. The signatures of several incorporators must be attached, and it is commonly required that some of them be citizens of the state, as well as officers of the company.

The application must ordinarily contain the name of the proposed corporation; the purpose for which it is being formed; the place of business, the desired duration of the corporation; the names and residences of the subscribers to the capital stock; and the number, names, and method of election of the directors. The application must also state the total amount of capital stock for which state authorization is desired, and the amount of capital stock which has been actually subscribed. It is commonly required that a certain portion of the total stock be paid for at the time the application is made and that a certain amount of cash be in the hands of the treasurer of the company. The application for incorporation must be duly drawn up, and the information contained in it affirmed or sworn to in the presence of a notary public. The application must be accompanied by a fee for administrative expenses involved, and a considerable bonus, or tax, for the privilege of incorporation, is often necessary. It is commonly required that applications for incorporation be given a certain amount of advance publicity in the form of newspaper advertisements.

The authority to issue corporate charters varies somewhat in different states. In Pennsylvania applications for incorporation are made to the Secretary of State, but the governor of the state must approve and sign them. He then issues what is known as the letters patent. Letters patent is a document signed by the governor which states the fact that certain associates are incorporated under a corporate name and charter. This document and the charter, which is a more detailed certificate of incorporation, are duly registered by the proper state officials and finally become the property of the new corporation. After the receipt of a copy of the charter an organization meeting of the incorporators and subscribers to the capital stock is held. Permanent officers are elected and various by-laws are drawn up in conformity with the charter.

7. Organization of a Corporate Business.—A business corporation is an industrial democracy, which presents opportunities for liberty or corruption similar to those of our political democracies. Several distinctions, however, are very important. In a business corporation shares of stock, rather than individuals, vote. A stockholder ordinarily possesses as many votes as he has shares of stock. Moreover, his attendance at stockholders' meetings is unnecessary. Voting may be done by proxy rather than in person. A stockholder may fill in the form which he has received by mail and which authorizes a certain officer of the company to cast for him the number of votes to which he is entitled. In order to protect the interests of the minority stockholders, cumulative voting is sometimes practised. In voting for directors by this method each stockholder is allowed one vote for each share of stock he owns multiplied by the number of directors to be elected. He may cast all his votes for one director, or distribute them among the candidates for the board of directors as he sees fit. By concerted efforts in this manner, the minority interests may secure representation on the board of directors.

The ultimate source of authority in a corporation rests with the stockholders. They do not participate in the conduct

of the business, however, any more than does the voting population of a large city. Stockholders elect directors to shape
the policies of the business. The administrative officers are
sometimes elected directly by the stockholders and sometimes
indirectly by the directors after the latter have been chosen
by the stockholders. The number and respective duties of the
officers of the company are fixed in the charter and by-laws of
the corporation. The corporate democracy is a constitutional
democracy, that is, its by-laws must be made in accordance with
the general provisions of its charter. Hence, it is desirable
not to include too much plan of organization in the charter.
Conditions may change, and it is easier to alter by-laws than to
make application for a new charter.

BUSINESS ORGANIZATION OF CORPORATIONS

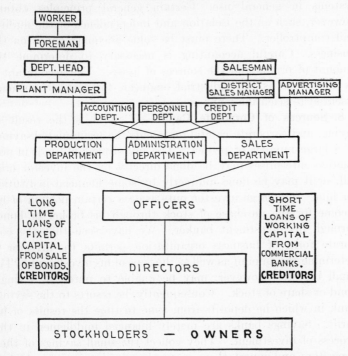

The industrial organization of a corporation, like its financial
policy, must be flexible. There is no general plan of organization for all business corporations. Indeed, one of the important
advantages of the corporate form of business organization is

flexibility. The type of corporate organization depends chiefly on the nature and size of the business. In general, we may distinguish three broad divisions of a business organization—the production department, the selling department, and the administrative department. Various vice-presidents are often utilized as heads of different departments. The possible subdivisions of the production and the selling departments are indicated in the accompanying diagram. There is sometimes no production department. Thus, a large department store is a merchandising rather than a manufacturing plant, and the expert buyer replaces the production engineer in its general plan of organization. No attempt will be made to sketch the organization of the various departments which are classified as administrative. They are as varied in nature and function as are the different accounting systems in general use. Certain general principles obtain, however, such as the isolation and independence of the auditor and comptroller. There must be some adequate check on the business. Careful accounting is necessary to determine the amount of profits and the sources of losses. The accountant is as important as the industrial engineer, for cost accounting is essential to scientific management.

8. Sources of Corporate Capital.—Capital is the result of saving, and corporate capital represents the accumulated savings of a large number of people. The investment of funds in productive enterprises may be done directly by the investor himself, or it may be done indirectly by some financial institution for him. The large investor puts aside a certain portion of his income for the purchase of stock through his broker or bonds through his investment banker. We have seen that the corporate form of business organization permits the investor to determine the amount as well as the type of his investment. The small investor, however, may be unable to purchase a single bond or share of stock. Consequently, he resorts to the savings bank in which he deposits from time to time the results of his thrift. Savings banks are merely financial middlemen in this process of investment. They collect the small savings of their depositors and invest them in productive enterprises. Out of the returns from these securities they are able to pay interest to their depositors and to maintain a margin of profit for themselves. Insurance companies likewise invest extensively the funds which they collect as premiums. In the last chapter we saw that the total reserves of insurance companies reach enormous proportions. It is sometimes contended that the investment of insurance companies represents automatic saving, but it should not be forgotten that the payment of premiums by individual investors necessitates thrift and abstinence.

There is a third form of investment which is worthy of special note. This is the investment of funds directly by the business corporation itself, rather than by the investor himself or by a financial middleman. The officers and directors of the corporation commonly reserve or reinvest earnings of the company instead of paying them all out to stockholders in the form of generous cash dividends. If the profits are reinvested in the business the term "surplus" is usually employed to explain the increase in the value of the equity of the stockholders. Improvements may be made out of reinvested earnings or a policy of expansion carried out.

9. Property Account of a Corporation.—The balance sheet of a corporation is its property account at any given time. On the one side are listed the assets of the company and on the other side its corresponding liabilities. Assets include the tangible wealth of the company and its intangible property rights against the wealth of its debtors. Liabilities are represented by the claims of other individuals against the corporation's own property. Let us examine the books of a business corporation—for illustration, those of the Progressive Book Company. Our company and its balance sheet are fictitious, for the property accounts of most large corporations would be too involved for illustrative purposes.

The Progressive Book Company begins business with a capital of $200,000. Its first statement would be as follows:

Assets		Liabilities	
Cash	$200,000	Capital stock	$200,000

It will be noted that the stock of a corporation is a liability of the company to its stockholders.

The Progressive Book Company buys a small manufacturing plant, for which it pays $100,000 cash. In order to obtain more funds, it issues first mortgage bonds of $50,000, secured by the real estate for which it has just paid twice that amount. The property account of the company now reads as follows:

Assets		Liabilities	
Cash	$150,000	Capital stock	$200,000
Plant	100,000	First-mortgage bonds	50,000

In order to conduct its business, the company must purchase equipment and raw materials. When this has been done, it begins its work of manufacturing books. The balance sheet now reads as follows:

Assets		Liabilities	
Cash	$ 25,000	Capital stock	$200,000
Plant	100,000	First-mortgage bonds	50,000
Equipment	50,000		
Raw materials	25,000	Total	$250,000
Goods in process	25,000		
Finished goods	25,000		
Total	$250,000		

In order to be successful, the printing company must not only manufacture books but also sell them. If it is to do this in the face of active competition, the company must extend credit to its customers. In turn, the Progressive Book Company need not pay cash for all its own purchases. Consequently, we must list on the balance sheet such new credit items as accounts receivable and payable and notes receivable and payable. The property account now reads as follows:

Assets		Liabilities	
Cash	$ 25,000	Capital stock	$200,000
Plant	100,000	First-mortgage bonds	50,000
Equipment	50,000	Accounts payable	50,000
Raw materials	25,000	Notes payable	75,000
Goods in process	25,000		
Finished goods	50,000	Total	$375,000
Accounts receivable	50,000		
Notes receivable	50,000		
Total	$375,000		

It is important that a certain portion of the assets be quick or liquid assets, that is, assets which may be quickly converted into cash without financial loss or serious embarrassment to the business. We shall soon see that working capital is more liquid than fixed capital. Many legitimate businesses at times suffer from frozen assets, that is, assets which cannot be easily and without loss converted into funds, although they are neither fictitious nor inflated.

Whereas the balance sheet of a corporation is a statement of its assets and its liabilities at a given time, the profit and loss statement is a record of its business over a period of time. On the one side are listed expenses, such as wages, repairs, and insurance. On the other side are listed gains, such as bank interest. The payments made for the purchase of raw materials are listed as expenses, and the proceeds from the sale of finished goods as gains. In order to make the two columns balance, the insertion of the net gain or net loss is made in the proper column. Some or all of this net gain may be paid to the stockholders at the discretion of the directors, who have the profit and loss statement before them. Some of the gains may be kept by the company as a surplus or a fund of undivided profits. If so, it appears on the next balance sheet as an increased liability of the corporation to its stockholders.

PROFIT AND LOSS STATEMENT OF PROGRESSIVE BOOK COMPANY

Losses		Profits	
Former inventory........	$250,000	Present inventory........	$300,000
Purchases of raw materials	50,000	Gross sales.............	100,000
Interest on bonds........	3,000	Bank interest............	500
Wages..................	15,000		
Repairs.................	1,000	Total................	$400,500
Insurance...............	400		
Depreciation............	5,000		
Net gain................	76,100		
Total................	$400,500		

10. Owned and Borrowed Capital—Stocks and Bonds.—The capital of a corporation may be classified as owned capital and borrowed capital. Stocks are paper certificates of ownership. The par value of a share of stock is its assumed monetary value, engraved on the face of the stock certificate. It is supposed to represent the amount of capital originally invested in a business, but frequently does not. Par value may differ considerably from the net equity of a share of stock in the assets of a corporation. The book value of a share of stock represents a careful estimate of the capital investment per share at any one time. The market value, on the other hand, represents the last selling price per share. Book value, par value and market value may all be different.

Borrowed capital is ordinarily represented by bonds, which are promissory notes, usually secured by some fixed capital of the company. A banking house commonly acts as trustee or transfer agent, and holds in its vaults the mortgage or written claim on property pledged as security for the loan. The stockholder is a member of the corporation, but the bondholder is an outside creditor. The stockholder receives dividends at the discretion of the directors, when the earnings of the business justify them. The bondholder, however, receives interest at a fixed rate and at specified times during the life time of the loan, which is also stated in the bond. The failure of a corporation to pay its interest charges means that it is insolvent, and any bondholder may petition the courts to appoint a receiver. The passing of a dividend, however, is within the power of the directors, and, in the absence of fraud, the only redress of the stockholders is an election of new officers and directors. Stocks and bonds possess this fact in common, namely, that they usually represent the fixed capital and permanent assets of the company. There are basic differences between stocks and bonds, but there is little difference in the capital goods which are represented by these different types of securities.

Stocks may be classified as common and preferred. Preferred stocks usually pay a specific rate of dividends at specified times. They are generally cumulative, that is, passed dividends must be paid before dividends can be declared on common stock. Payments to preferred stockholders take precedence over those to common stockholders, but the obligations to bondholders come before both kinds of dividends. Thus, a preferred stock is a compromise between bonds and common stock. The holders of preferred stock are part owners of the corporation and not creditors. Nevertheless, they sometimes do not possess the right to vote, or have only limited rights of voting. The margin of safety is greater in preferred stocks and bonds than in common stocks, but there is ordinarily not the same opportunity to share in profits.

Bonds may be classified according to their form, as either coupon or registered bonds. Coupon bonds have interest coupons attached to the bonds, which may be clipped by the bondholder and cashed on or after an interest-due date. The holder of registered bonds, on the other hand, receives his interest payment in the form of a check mailed by the corporation or its depository. Coupon bonds are conveniently transferred, but they are difficult to recover if lost or stolen. Bonds may also be classified according to the type of security which is pledged. Thus, there are first-mortgage bonds, secured by the company plant or other real estate, and equipment trust bonds, in which the equipment used by the company is pledged. Collateral trust bonds are those for which other securities are pledged. Debentures are usually mere certificates of indebtedness, in which there is no specific pledge of assets.

11. Fixed and Working Capital.—The distinction between fixed and working capital is as important as that between owned and borrowed capital. Fixed capital is represented by the permanent assets of the business. Illustrations are land, buildings, improvements, and machinery. Working capital within the plant is represented by goods in process and finished goods which are ready for sale. Working capital refers also to funds in the bank and to goods which can be quickly converted into funds. Solvent accounts receivable and promissory notes receivable are likewise regarded as working capital.

Although adequate working capital is just as essential to business success as is sufficient fixed capital, its importance is sometimes overlooked, and a business may fail for this reason. A corporation may easily make the mistake of investing too large a portion of its funds in fixed capital and reserving too small a portion for working capital. The result is an unfortunate expansion, which may become serious in periods of business depression. If a large portion of this fixed capital is also borrowed capital, a serious financial crisis may occur. In such an event, overhead costs in the form of fixed interest charges have become so heavy that too small a portion of the current funds is left to meet such operating expenses as the purchase of raw materials and the payment of wages. Temporary emergencies may be met by borrowing from the banks, if the business is in a sound condition, although bankers are skeptical of a business in which the fixed capital is out of all proportion to working capital. Short-term loans are obtained from banks against ordinary promissory notes or commercial paper. The purpose of such bank loans is to satisfy a temporary need for increased working capital. Funds thus obtained are not ordinarily used to increase the fixed capital of the business. Long-time loans may be obtained by an issue of bonds, which are usually secured by some of the fixed capital of the business.

12. Current Assets and the Cycle of Business Operation.— The proceeds derived from the sale of corporate stocks and bonds are as a rule converted into fixed capital, only such sums being retained for working capital as are required to meet initial operating expenditures. Those who invest their savings in corporate securities desire a certain amount of tangible evidence of the fact that their savings have been converted into fixed assets, which will endure over a relatively long period of time. After a corporation has developed its plant and equipment and is ready to begin operations, a certain fund of circulating capital is required to meet labor costs, to pay for raw materials and to provide for initial selling expenses. Unless ample provision is made for working capital out of the initial capital realized from the sale of corporate securities, the corporate management may find itself in the possession of an admirably equipped plant, but with no funds to start it operating.

Working capital or circulating capital is frequently defined as the difference between the current assets and the current liabilities of a corporation. Current assets consist of those assets which can be converted into cash in a relatively short period of time, ordinarily in less than a year. Current liabilities consist of those obligations of a corporation which fall due within a relatively short period of time. A new corporation will usually begin with its current assets in the form of cash. The replenishing of this cash fund with continued operation may be illustrated by the accompanying chart. The cash is expended in order to begin operations. Operating the plant results in production. The products are exchanged, partly for cash, but more usually in the present business world for credit, or promises to pay in the future for value received at present. When these promises ultimately fall due, they are generally paid in cash, and the revolving fund is thus replenished.

The cyclical movement of a revolving fund emphasizes the importance of keeping an enterprise operating. If cash ceases to flow out, operations cannot continue very long; without operations no new inventory will result; without sales new inventory will accumulate; and no receivables or sales will mean no replenishing of the cash fund. Each stage in the process of

production is both a cause and an effect, and a breakdown anywhere along the line will result in the curtailment of production.

MOVEMENT OF REVOLVING FUND

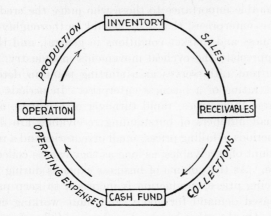

13. Current Ratios.—When at any time the cash fund cannot
be replenished sufficiently to meet operating expenditures or
cannot provide the necessary working capital to expand operations, recourse is had to other agencies for working capital.
The function of commercial banks and credit houses is primarily
to provide additional working capital for industrial enterprise.
These institutions will lend their accumulated funds to their
customers in exchange for various types of securities and
guarantees to repay the loans within a stipulated period of time,
as a rule not over one year. In this manner industries can
replenish their revolving fund of cash and thus continue
production.

It has become a maxim among credit men of commercial banks
to regard a business enterprise a fairly good credit risk whose
working capital is equal to its current liabilities. If, for example,
a business enterprise has two dollars' worth of current assets for
every dollar's worth of current liabilities, its request for commercial credit will usually be looked upon favorably. This
ratio of current assets to current liabilities is commonly referred
to as the current ratio. Too much significance, however, should
not be attached to this current ratio without at the same time
analyzing carefully the nature of the current assets and current
liabilities. A large inventory during a period of business depres-

sion, evaluated on a cost basis, may for the time being be decidedly overvalued. A large amount of outstanding accounts and notes receivable may prove worthless current assets in a period of extensive business failures. It thus becomes a matter of considerable importance to those who judge the credit rating of business enterprises, that they should be thoroughly familiar with business and market conditions in general, and that they should appreciate the cyclical movements in industry.

The current ratio serves as a starting point in determining the credit rating of a business enterprise. In periods of rising prices, large inventories, rapid turnover of products, and relatively small numbers of outstanding receivables are desirable, while in periods of falling prices, small inventories and a relatively large amount of receivables, as long as they can be collected, are preferable. As the volume of business expands during a period of advancing prices, production is increased to keep pace with the increased demand for goods, and more working capital is required. On the other hand, when demand falls off production is curtailed, and less working capital is needed.

The question is frequently asked, "What is the proper amount of working capital a corporation should have?" There is no one answer to this question. The amount of working capital required by different industries varies considerably. A business conducted on a cash basis, such as a street railway company, requires relatively little working capital, although the amount of revolving capital needed may be fairly large. The steady flow of receipts into the cash fund normally replenishes this cash fund so that extensive bank loans for working capital may be unnecessary.

Ordinarily about one and a half months' operating expenses are considered adequate for public utilities. Since operating expenses are about 70 per cent of gross revenues, another way of stating the average amount of working capital necessary for a public utility is "an amount equivalent to the revenues for one month."[1]

14. Adequate Working Capital and the Creation of a Surplus.— When a business has an adequate supply of working capital, realized primarily from the proceeds of the sale of its products, it can meet its cash obligations promptly. From a social point of view, adequate working capital in industry helps to assure a continuous flow of goods and to give steady employment to labor.

[1] *Cf.* GERSTENBERG, C. W. "Financial Organization and Management," p. 389.

It militates against stagnation in industry and aids in promoting general economic well-being. The social significance of adequate working capital cannot be overemphasized. During the period of currency inflation in Germany prior to 1924, the tendency on the part of industries was to convert their surplus earnings as quickly as possible into fixed capital, such as plant equipment, and the like. Savings available for working capital did not accumulate in the commercial banks as rapidly as in pre-war years. An important source of working capital almost dried up. The result was that German industry had its fixed assets in fairly good condition, but it lacked the necessary working capital in the form of industrial raw materials and advances to labor with which to continue production. The international loan to Germany under the Dawes Plan was intended to provide a portion of this sorely needed working capital to rehabilitate German industry.

The provision of adequate working capital is a matter of so great importance to industrial enterprises that they often create funds of undivided profits. Such a policy makes an industry independent of bank loans, but it presents very grave dangers not only to the business but also to the public. It may lead to wastefulness on the part of those controlling the working capital. Again, excess funds may be used for the manipulation of corporate securities or for investment in questionable enterprises. Federal tax legislation in recent years has encouraged the building up of large corporate surpluses. Because of the high rates of the profits tax, some corporations have withheld earnings available for distribution as cash dividends. Consequently, they have accumulated surpluses in excess of the reasonable requirements for the normal conduct of their business.

In 1923, 30,048 corporations making returns to the Federal government on 1922 incomes showed net incomes for the year of $896,254,485, with accumulated surpluses of $3,954,966,686. None of these corporations paid any dividends in 1922. On the other hand, 48,875 corporations distributed portions of their taxable net incomes, varying from 90 per cent to less than 10 per cent.[1] They had accumulated undistributed surpluses and profits of fifteen billion dollars. In view of this obvious practice of corporations to build up large surpluses, the Federal Revenue Act of 1926 provided for a 50 per cent additional tax on corporate

[1] Sixty-eighth Congress, First session, *Senate Report* 398, Part 2, p. 10.

income for each taxable year, if gains or profits are permitted to accumulate beyond the reasonable needs of business. To date, there is no court ruling as to what constitutes reasonable business needs.

15. Stock Dividends and the Management of Corporate Earnings.—When a corporation has established its earning power by the payment of all operating and overhead expenses, the net profits are available for distribution among stockholders. The directors must then decide how much of these net profits can safely be paid out in cash dividends. As was pointed out above, the practice of many corporations in recent years has been to withhold cash dividends from stockholders, and to reinvest the net earnings in whole or in part either in expansions of the business or in outside securities. In order to keep the capital in the business, stock dividends rather than cash dividends may be distributed among stockholders.

Contrary to popular belief, such stock dividends are not suddenly discovered corporate treasures. They are merely transfers from surplus or undivided profits to capital stock. If a corporation gives share for share stock dividends, the stockholder is not greatly benefited. He now has two shares of stock for every original share, but the book value of each share is now one-half its former value. The declaration of stock dividends, moreover, may embarrass the future financial policy of the company. To capitalize corporate surpluses by declaring stock dividends means that they are no longer available for the payment of cash dividends in lean years. If, for example, a corporation, having a capitalization of one million dollars, and carrying a million dollar surplus, represented by investments in marketable securities, were to capitalize this surplus by issuing a 100 per cent stock dividend, these securities could not be sold subsequently to pay cash dividends. Such a procedure would be equivalent to paying dividends out of capital and not out of income. This practice is illegal. Consequently, directors of corporations are loath to capitalize the accumulated corporate surpluses, although an attempt to collect a heavy Federal tax on such surpluses, not needed for the normal conduct of the business, would no doubt result in the declaration of additional stock dividends not taxable as income. It has often been suggested that a tax on large corporate surpluses would be a lucrative source of income to the Federal government.

The real danger in excessive corporate surpluses appears to be in the fact that they place great temptations in the paths of those who have control over these vast accumulations of capital. At present, the danger in mismanagement of corporate profits does not seem to be in the direction of too liberal a dividend policy, but rather in the direction of too conservative a dividend policy. To the extent that adequate reserves are provided for depreciation, betterments, insurance, dividends, and the like, the fiscal policy pursued by directors of corporations is sound. But profits may also be subverted. It is difficult to outline definite rules as to a safe policy to pursue in declaring dividends out of net earnings. It is generally conceded that a conservative directorate will endeavor to keep the outstanding stock of the corporation on a stable dividend-paying basis. In this manner the stock attains a settled investment value, and the credit rating of such a corporation will usually be higher than that of a corporation paying dividends irregularly both as to amounts and time intervals. In conclusion, two general rules may be given as to the dividend policy of well-managed corporations: first, to pay no dividends for some time after the company begins operations, and second, to pay out in any one year only a portion of the net profits.

16. Dangers of the Corporate Form of Business Organization. The advantages of the corporate form of business organization are partly offset by certain possibilities for abuse. The very flexibility of organization presents opportunities for financial manipulation. The increased amount of capital involved magnifies the incentive to, and the effects of, corporate mismanagement.

Overcapitalization or "stock watering" has been a serious problem in the past. At the present time its chief significance is in connection with public utilities and trust finance. Overcapitalization is the situation which occurs when the total par value of the securities of a corporation is considerably more than the fair or actual value of the capital assets which they represent. The policy of an overcapitalized corporation is just the reverse of one which has been frugally creating a surplus. Because par value is not indicative of market value or capital investment value, the practice of issuing stock without any par value has become common among industrial corporations. Stock without par value has merely its market value and its book value at any given time.

The danger of concentrated control is now of more general and practical importance than overcapitalization. The student may have noticed this problem in the previous discussion of the management of corporate earnings and the creation of surpluses. Enormous corporate investments are frequently under the control of a relatively few officers and directors. Ultimate control of corporations rests with the stockholders, who possess the right to vote for directors and in this way to express their approval or disapproval of their policy. In most large corporations, however, the secretary or some influential director may cast the votes of thousands of small stockholders who are absent from the meeting. Voting may be done by proxy, but many stockholders fail to vote at all. Active members and those who control the votes of a large number of shares dominate the situation. Concentration of control within a corporation is not difficult to achieve. It is facilitated by the existence of a large amount of borrowed capital. Bondholders do not possess even the potential power of voting for directors and policies. In addition to bonded indebtedness, or in lieu of it, large issues of nonvoting stock have been floated by numerous corporations. This practice recently attracted so much attention that a special investigating committee was appointed by the New York Stock Exchange to study the extent to which this was true of the securities listed there.

The average small stockholder knows little about the company whose securities he holds, beyond the mere fact that dividends are usually paid at certain times. So long as this takes place in a regular fashion, the investor is generally disinterested in details as to the management of the concern. The separation of ownership from control, or rather the diffusion of ownership and the concentration of control, has created the problem of "absentee capitalism." It is the modern analogy to "absentee landlordism." The great majority of the stockholders of a given company are ignorant of its general production and marketing problems. Dividend checks find their way to the bank, but financial reports to the waste basket. Investors are even more ignorant of labor policies and working conditions among the employees of the company whose securities they own. It is only after a sudden failure to meet interest payments or to declare the usual dividend that the small investor interests himself in the financial management of the corporation.

There has been a recent tendency toward the diffusion of stock ownership. Large industrial corporations have sold shares of stock to their employees on easy terms, or have engaged in profit sharing through stock distribution. In some cases, however, employees' stock has been surrounded with certain voting restrictions.

Numerous public utilities have likewise sought to convert their customers into stockholders and in this sense to "mutualize." Such stock issues have included both common and preferred stock, either with or without voting privileges. The Pennsylvania Railroad, the American Telegraph and Telephone Company, and the United States Steel Corporation have thousands of small shareholders. Thus, two different influences seem to be at work, the one making for a greater diffusion of stock ownership, but the other for a growing concentration of control.

The corporate form of business organization increases the possibility of fraud and financial manipulation. As noted before, glib salesmen still find it profitable to sell stock of fictitious value. "Blue sky" laws have been passed to make possible a governmental investigation and supervision of stock issues. However, it is sometimes as profitable to manipulate or to wreck solvent enterprises as to launch questionable ones. The stock or tangible assets may be bought cheap and the company reorganized with subsequent profits to the manipulators. The reverse is also possible and profitable. "Wash sales" and misleading information may raise artificially the price of a given security. At the opportune time "the inside ring" unloads its stock or "gets out from under." The "innocent investor" is again caught "holding the bag."

Subsidiary companies are sometimes organized for purposes of financial manipulation. Let us assume a certain corporation "A" is manufacturing automobiles for which it finds a ready and profitable market. Several directors, influential stockholders, or officers of corporation "A" become dissatisfied with their fairly substantial profits. Consequently, they organize an "independent" company known as corporation "B." The latter is formed for the manufacture, or perhaps for the mere sale, of some important parts of automobiles. Let us assume that corporation "B" manufactures automobile bodies or tops, suitable for making the automobiles manufactured by corporation "A." Because the promoters of corporation "B" are influential in corporation "A," the products of "B" are assured of a sale to "A." The prices which are paid by "A" may be somewhat higher than those prevailing in the open market or more than the cost of manufacturing the parts by corporation "A" itself. Thus, the profits of corporation "B" are made at the expense of corporation "A." The scheme is profitable to its promoters because the stock of corporation "B" is more closely held than is that of corporation "A." By the organization of a subsidiary company the promoters, or rather the manipulators, have "skimmed the milk" and appropriated the cream for themselves.

17. Social Significance of Sound Corporation Finance.— Problems of corporate finance do not concern merely the corporations themselves and their owners. They affect the welfare of many members of the community. As a rule the funds invested in corporate enterprises come from the savings of a large number of individuals, some of whom have made considerable sacrifices. The proper utilization of these funds for productive purposes affects the material well-being of all those who have invested in corporate securities. If their savings are squandered in dubious ventures or appropriated by fraudulent promoters, not only is faith in legitimate enterprise shaken, but also actual privation may result.

Most of the commodities produced today, moreover, are the products of corporations. Misdirection of production, or waste, on the part of the officers of a large corporation, is serious. Loss may injure not only investors but also the consuming public. In our highly specialized economy much capital is temporarily worthless if allowed to stand idle. In the final analysis, industrial plants have value not so much as physical units in the form of buildings and machinery, but as going concerns. Unless a sound financial policy is adopted by those in control, capital assets may not earn anything. The relative ease with which corporations can accumulate large funds may result in the uneconomic use of capital. That there is considerable waste in modern industry due to financial mismanagement was shown in the report prepared by the Hoover Commission on "Waste in Industry." Such wastefulness does not merely result in higher production costs, and therefore in higher prices; it also brings about a wasteful exploitation of our limited natural resources. Only caution and foresight on the part of those providing funds for large industrial units and a keen sense of responsibility and adequate training on the part of those in control of corporate finance can minimize the dangers inherent in the present system of "absentee capitalism" and permit us to realize the many advantages to be derived from the corporate form of business enterprise.

18. Summary.—A corporation is an association of individuals acting under a charter from the state in the capacity of a single individual for the performance of some economic, political, or social function. The corporation is a fictitious person created by law, and it has an entity apart from that of the individuals who compose it. Modern large-scale production and the use of expensive machinery have made necessary the utilization of the corporate form of business organization. Although at first limited to public utilities, the recent expansion of the business unit has been made possible by the corporate form of organization. It possesses the advantages of limited liability, perpetuity of existence, flexibility of management, and collective accumulation of large amounts of capital.

The promoter is the active element who brings the passive capitalist into touch with economic opportunities. The process of promotion may be divided into three stages—the discovery of a proposition, its assembling, and its financing. Business opportunities may be sold directly to individuals with funds to invest or indirectly through investment banking syndicates. For the protection of the "innocent investor" most states have passed so-called "blue sky" laws, which provide for governmental supervision of security issues and sales. State corporation laws differ as to the ease, costs, and methods of incorporation. A company chartered in one state may operate in all other states, but in the conduct of its business it must conform to the laws of the state in which it is operating. The organization of a corporation depends largely upon the nature of the business. In general, we may distinguish three fundamental divisions, the production department, the sales department, and the administration department.

It is important that we differentiate between fixed and working capital and between owned and borrowed capital. Stockholders are owners of the corporation and may ordinarily participate in its control. Bondholders are outside creditors who enjoy little participation except in cases of financial failure or bankruptcy. Stockholders receive dividends or shares in profits at the discretion of the directors. Bondholders receive definite interest payments at specific times during the period of the loan. Bonds are essentially promissory notes. They may be classified according to their form—that is, as coupon or registered bonds, and also according to the type of security which is pledged for their payment—that is, as first-mortgage bonds, equipment trust bonds, etc. Fixed capital, as contrasted with working capital, is not liquid—that is, it cannot be turned quickly into funds without considerable loss. Adequate working capital is just as essential to business success as sufficient fixed capital. Bonds represent long-time loans which are generally secured by fixed capital. Short-time loans for increasing working capital may be obtained by solvent business corporations from commercial banks with the aid of ordinary promissory notes or commercial paper.

The corporate form of business organization presents certain dangers of abuse, as well as the economic advantages which have been enumerated. The past evil of overcapitalization may be eliminated by the new device of issuing stock without par value. The chief significance of stock watering at the present time is in connection with public utilities and the problems of rate making. The corporate form of business organization, however, still presents the possibilities of financial manipulation and concentrated control. Although there is a wide diffusion of ownership of corporate securities, the indifference of investors and the device of nonvoting stock intensifies the possibilities of concentrated control. "Absentee capitalism" has serious social and economic aspects. Concentrated control and the devices used to secure it bring us to the problem of the trusts, which is the theme of the following chapters.

Collateral Reading

BYE, R. T., "Principles of Economics," chap. 9.
CLAY, H., "Economics for the General Reader," chap. 5.
ELY, R. T.,"Outlines of Economics," chap. 13.
MARSHALL, L. C., WRIGHT, C. W., and FIELD, J. A., "Materials for the Study of Elementary Economics," pp. 204–257.
SEAGER, H. R., "Principles of Economics," chap. 10.
TAUSSIG, F. W., "Principles of Economics," chap. 10.

References

CLEVELAND, F. A., "Funds and Their Uses."
CONYNGTON, H. R., "Financing an Enterprise."

DEWING, A. S., "Corporation Finance."
————, "The Financial Policy of Corporations."
ETTINGER, R. P., and GOLIEB, D. E., "Credits and Collections."
GERSTENBERG, C. W., "Business Organization."
————, "Financial Organization and Management."
————, "Materials of Corporate Finance."
————, "Principles of Business."
GERSTENBERG, C. W., and JOHNSON, W. S., "Organization and Control."
JORDAN, D. F., "Investments."
LINCOLN, E. E., "Applied Business Finance."
LAGERQUIST, W. E., "Investment Analysis."
LOUGH, W. H., "Business Finance."
————, "Problems in Business Finance."
MEAD, E. S., "Corporation Finance."
MEAD, E. S., and SCHOLZ, K. W. H., "Rudiments of Business Finance."
McKINSEY, J. O. and MEECH, S. P., "Controlling the Finances of a Business."
SCHLUTER, W. C., "Credit Analysis."
STOCKWELL, H. G., "How to Read a Financial Statement."

Questions for Discussion

1. What is a corporation? Outline different types of corporations.
2. Show the advantages of the corporate form of business organization.
3. Outline the steps in the promotion of a business enterprise.
4. Show how a business corporation comes into being.
5. Distinguish between the privileges of stockholders and those of bondholders.
6. Distinguish between working capital and fixed capital. Show the sources of each.
7. What is overcapitalization? Show the objectives of overcapitalization and how they may be achieved.
8. Outline some other dangers of the corporate form of business organization.
9. What is a stock dividend? Does it necessarily imply stockwatering?
10. Compare the business corporation with a political democracy in regard to the rights and duties of its members and the manner in which they are exercised.

Topics of Investigation

1. The growth of the corporate form of business organization in the United States since the Civil War.
2. "Blue sky" laws for the elimination of fraudulent enterprises and the sale of worthless securities.
3. How a business is incorporated in your own state.
4. The practise of issuing no par value stock.
5. The growth of corporate surpluses and the desirability of a Federal tax upon them.
6. The social significance of sound corporate financing.

PART TWO
PROBLEMS OF MONOPOLY

CHAPTER VI

TRUSTS AND INDUSTRIAL MONOPOLIES

1. Nature of Monopoly.—Of all the expressions which may be used to indicate the absence of competition in the economic activities of man the term "monopoly" is perhaps the most appropriate. Nevertheless, the word requires careful definition, as it is often vaguely used in popular discussion. A condition of absolute monopoly is almost as difficult of conception as one of perfect competition. Between these two extremes are numerous degrees of gradation. Under economic competition there are several sellers and several buyers, and prices are determined naturally by the free play of demand and supply forces. On the other hand, monopoly signifies a single seller, a single purchaser, or several parties who do not compete with each other. Some sort of unity of action has been achieved, as a result of which the free play of price-determining forces is interfered with. The acid test of monopoly is the power to regulate prices. It is secured by a dominant control over the supply of a commodity or service. Control over the entire supply is not necessary. An active participant[1] in the sugar trust litigation put the matter as follows:

It goes without saying that a man who produces 80 per cent of an article can control the price by not producing; the price must advance if he does not produce; and it must decline if he does produce, if he produces more than the market will take.

It is important that our definition differentiate clearly between monopoly and such kindred concepts as the corporate form of business organization and large-scale production. Although modern industrial monopolies are usually corporations, we must distinguish between the advantages and disadvantages of the corporate form of business organization and those arising from the fact of monopoly. This distinction is frequently difficult. Absentee capitalism, or the separation of ownership from control, which is apt to occur under the corporate form of business organization, facilitates the securing of concentrated control and the

[1] HAVEMEYER, H. O. *Cf.* Lexow Report, p. 111, New York, 1897.

119

development of monopoly. Hence, the common confusion between monopoly and the corporate form of business organization.

Large-scale production and monopoly are frequently confused. The economic advantages of the former are sometimes ascribed indiscriminately to the latter. Although most industrial monopolies are those of large-scale production, mere size does not of itself prove the existence of monopoly. This fact was definitely stated in a decision of the United States Supreme Court in 1921 concerning the United States Steel Corporation. The latter had been prosecuted under the Sherman Act as a combination in restraint of trade. Although large-scale production and management were demonstrated, the existence of a monopoly in the steel industry was not proven to the satisfaction of the Court. On the other hand, a small dealer may be a monopolist without possessing the advantages of large-scale production or large-scale management. The village grocer in a sparsely settled community, for illustration, may face no competition and hence may possess the power to regulate the prices of certain foodstuffs in that locality.

A monopoly also differs from a "corner." A "corner" represents a temporary scarcity which has been foreseen and taken advantage of by some individuals. The total supply of the commodity may not have been restricted in order to raise its price. The attempt to secure a "corner," however, may raise the price of the commodity temporarily by an abnormal increase in demand or decrease in supply. On the other hand, a "corner" may not increase the price beyond that which is caused by a natural scarcity of supply. An individual or a group of individuals may secure their profits merely from the successful anticipation of a temporarily high price due to natural causes. The main point of difference, however, between a monopoly and a "corner" is the temporary character of the latter.

2. Kinds of Monopoly.—Monopolies may be classified according to their extent over either time or territory. We have just distinguished between relatively permanent monopolies and such temporary control as "corners." We may also differentiate among local, national, and international monopolies. Monopolies may also be classified according to the source of their power, whether economic or social. A natural scarcity of supply gives rise to an economic monopoly, but an exclusive grant from the state gives rise to a social or political monopoly. Again, we differentiate between industrial monopolies and legal monopolies. Legal monopolies may in turn be divided into public and private monopolies.   The post office illustrates a public legal monopoly and patents and copyrights exemplify private legal monopolies.

Another distinction is that between natural monopolies and those which are sometimes stigmatized as artificial.   The term "capitalistic monopoly" is sometimes used, but it is misleading. It is not sufficiently specific, for capitalistic monopolies may be either natural or artificial.   We shall see that some industries which require great capital investments are natural monopolies. On the other hand, a great corporation, which by virtue of its enormous funds is able to control the sources of supply of a rather plentiful commodity, represents an artificial monopoly. A similar attempt has been made to distinguish between capitalistic monopolies resting on productive efficiency and those relying on superior bargaining power, that is, between the "good and the bad monopolies."   This distinction is similar to that between natural and artificial monopolies.

Natural monopolies are of two general types—those which originate because of the natural scarcity of some particular good, and those which develop because the industry is one in which competition is impossible or uneconomic.   Certain mineral waters and the wine made from grapes grown only in a small area are natural monopolies due to a scarcity of supply.   The services of a great surgeon or of a famous singer are likewise natural monopolies due to the unusual scarcity of their particular services. On the other hand, natural monopolies of organization include those industries which require a great amount of fixed capital, for example: railroads, waterworks, and electric power plants. As competition here is wasteful rather than beneficial, such monopolies are economically natural and socially desirable.   The principle of decreasing costs appears in industries which have great fixed expenses, represented by heavy interest charges and maintenance costs on the capital invested.   As the volume of business increases, the cost per unit decreases.   As competition is self-destructive and the market limited, such industries are natural monopolies of organization.   They will be discussed in Chap. VIII, which deals with public utilities in general, and also in Chaps. IX and X, which are devoted to the problems of the railroads.

The term "trust" is a popular corruption of the word trustee-ship, a device which was once used to achieve monopoly. As used here in its popular sense as the title of this chapter, the trust refers to one general type of monopoly, namely the industrial monopoly. Trusts or industrial monopolies may be illustrated by the so-called "beef trust and oil trust." Trusts should be differentiated from legal monopolies, such as the post office, and natural monopolies of organization, such as the railroads and other public utilities.

Trade unions sometimes raise the qualifications of apprentices in order to restrict the number of workers in their trades. By this regulation of the labor supply of certain skilled workers, wages in those restricted occupations are raised to higher levels. Thus there may be monopolies of labor as well as those of capital. Illustrations of such labor monopolies are the medieval craft guilds and the modern closed shop with the closed union.

3. Old and New Concepts of Monopoly.—Although the spirit of monopoly is very old, conceptions of the nature of monopoly have varied in different periods. In former times exclusive grants were regarded as the prerogatives of absolute monarchs. Queen Elizabeth rewarded her favorites with monopolistic grants, and they were later used by the Stuart monarchs as sources of royal revenue until the practice was checked by the rising tide of constitutionalism. The former concept of a monopoly is illustrated in the writings of Blackstone, who defined monopoly as "a license or privilege allowed by a king." Adam Smith, who made competition one of the main pillars of his economic philosophy, regarded monopolies as exceptional and of legal origin. He wrote as follows:

Though some exclusive privileges arise from nature, they are generally the creatures of civil law. Such are monopolies and all privileges of corporations, which though they might once be conducive to the interest of the country, are now prejudicial to it.[1]

On the other hand, the new concept of monopoly is that of an industrial concentration. It has been stated by the Supreme Court of the United States as follows:

The idea of monopoly is not now confined to a grant of privileges. It is understood to include a condition produced by the acts of mere indi-

[1] *Cf.* "Lectures on Justice, Police, Revenue and Arms," Ed. by Edwin Canaan, pp. 129–130.

viduals. Its dominant thought now is, to quote another "the notion of exclusiveness or unity;" in other words, the suppression of competition by the unification of interest or management, or it may be through agreement and concert of action. And the purpose is so definitely the control of prices that monopoly has been defined to be "unified tactics with regard to prices." It is this power to control prices which makes the inducement of combinations and their profit.[1]

Thus, modern judicial decisions have striven to express the new concept of industrial monopoly as opposed to the older idea of royal grants. The trusts have been regarded as a final step in the gradual process of industrial concentration, and the ability to regulate prices has been considered the incentive to the formation of trusts and the final test of the existence of monopoly.

4. Industrial Combination.—The modern trust is the product of an evolution which has been going on since the Industrial Revolution. It represents the last step in the tendency toward a greater concentration in the control of capital, the extensive use of which was necessitated by the economic changes which we call the Industrial Revolution. The invention of power machinery and the introduction of the factory system have made large-scale production desirable. Large-scale management and finally monopoly followed. Just as the small water power mill has been eliminated by the huge steam or electric factory, so the single enterprise has been largely supplanted by the corporate form of business organization. Capitalization in millions and even billions of dollars has succeeded that of thousands of dollars. The modern trust represents the combination of individual corporations in the same way that the corporation represents the organization of numerous individual capitalists.

The problem of capitalistic concentration did not appear in American life until sometime after the Civil War. It is perhaps safe to say that the great industrialization of the United States did not develop until then. The increased use of machinery and the introduction of new and complicated processes hastened the transition from small-scale to large-scale manufacturing. As the advantages of large-scale production demonstrated themselves the small factory gave way to the large factory. Indeed, the economical use of some of the new manufacturing processes made large-scale production imperative. In many branches of manufacturing the size and output of the industry

[1] *National Oil Company vs. Texas*, 197 U. S. 129.

increased out of all proportion to the growth in the number of individual plants. During the last half of the nineteenth century, for illustration, the number of establishments devoted to the manufacture of cotton goods and the number devoted to the manufacture of boots and shoes changed but little, although the number of employees involved and the amount of capital invested multiplied several fold. Although the number of establishments devoted to the manufacture of agricultural machinery and the number of iron and steel blast furnaces decreased to one-half of their former number, the total outputs of both industries grew to several times their former sizes.

Large-scale management followed large-scale production. The combination of plants, as well as the growth in their individual capacities, was found to be advantageous. Large-scale production made possible the economies of division of labor, the use of expensive machinery, and the utilization of byproducts. Large-scale management, in turn, reduced the expenses of buying and selling and of transportation and administration.

After 1880, the tendency toward consolidation appeared rather strikingly. Proof is found in the passage of the Interstate Commerce Act of 1887 and the Sherman Anti-Trust Act of 1890. In spite of this legislation the movement went on still more rapidly in the decade between 1890 and 1900. The "Commercial Year Book" for 1900 gives the following information concerning the formation of large capitalistic combinations:[1]

PROCESS OF COMBINATION

Decade	Number formed	Total nominal capital
1860 to 1869	2	$ 13,000,000
1870 to 1879	4	135,000,000
1880 to 1889	18	288,000,000
1890 to 1899	157	3,150,000,000

The number of combinations formed and the capital represented were seven times as great in the last decade of the nineteenth century as in the entire thirty years preceding it. The movement was especially accentuated during the last three years of the past century, when the amount of consolidation was twice that of the previous decade. This can be seen in the following table:

[1] Cf. Commercial Year Book, vol. V, pp. 564-569.

PROCESS OF COMBINATION[1]

	Years	Number of combinations	Total capitalization (stocks and bonds)
Total..............	1887 to 97	86	$1,414,293,000
	1898	20	708,600,000
	1899	87	2,243,995,000
	1900	42	831,415,000
Total..............	1898 to 1900	149	3,784,010,000
Total..............	1887 to 1900	235	5,198,303,000

Between 1901 and 1904, 127 such combinations were achieved. Shortly afterward there was a lull in the general movement of industrial combination, as numerous governmental prosecutions were vigorously pushed against the trusts. The period which followed the World War, however, was another era of industrial combination. The war on waste did not end with the signing of the Armistice, in 1918. To eliminate much of the waste of competition during the World War drastic action had been taken by many of the governmental bodies of control. This war-time experience taught many hitherto small and unorganized industries what big business had learned before the World War. Post-war consolidations and mergers took place which exceeded in number and size the industrial combinations which had taken place during the opening years of the twentieth century. Combinations were achieved in many food-producing industries. This recently revived tendency toward industrial combination may be partially explained in the changed popular attitude and governmental policy toward the trusts. In the following chapter we shall see that the possibility and the desirability of ruthless "trust busting" has been questioned by both public opinion and judicial decision.

5. Stages in the Process of Combination.—The process of growth and combination has been from small-scale production to large-scale production, then from large-scale production to large-scale management, and finally, from large-scale management to monopoly. It is as interesting to the economist to watch

[1] Prepared by Luther Conant, subsequently Commissioner of Corporations, and published by American Statistical Society, March, 1901, pp. 207–226.

the evolution of certain industries from one stage to another as it is for the biologist to study the development of the tadpole into the frog.   It goes without saying that all industries did not go through their economic evolution in the same manner nor at the same time.   The general development of industrial monopolies, however, ran somewhat as follows: The first stage was that of the small-scale production, which still prevails in the manufacture of many articles, such as cigars, butter, bricks, and ice cream.   In the manufacture of other articles, the size of the plant so increased that it passed from small-scale production to large-scale production.   The manufacture of shoes, textiles, cigarettes, and automobiles illustrate this second stage.   It must be remembered, however, that we cannot apply the same standards of size to all industries.   The capital represented by a large cotton plant would be relatively insignificant in the steel industry.

Large-scale production within a given plant, however, finally broadens into a third stage, which represents large-scale management or the combination of different plants.   A number of factories, each of which may have already increased the size of its plant to the point of maximum production efficiency, combine in order to secure the economies of large-scale management, as well as those of large-scale production.   This combination may be achieved either horizontally or vertically.

A horizontal combination is one that brings together under a single management several plants producing the same article, as, for example, a combination of fertilizer plants.   A vertical combination is one that brings together a number of plants, each of which concerns itself with a separate stage in the production of the finished product.   This is known as the integration of industry.   As an illustration, a combination of a coal mine, a blast furnace, a steel mill, and a rail steel mill, is a vertical combination.   Such a combination has its advantages, as it assures the manufacturer of steel rails of an ample supply of raw materials at a reasonable price.   The combination horizontally also has its advantages, as, for example, a saving in freight rates.   A company with one plant at New York and another at Chicago can supply the intervening market from the plant which is nearest to the point of consumption.   Because of the obvious advantages of combination in certain lines of industry, this form of organization has frequently been employed.   The American Agricultural Chemical Company is an illustration of a horizontal combination; the Bethlehem Steel Company an illustration of a vertical combination.[1]

[1] *Cf.* JONES, E., "The Trust Problem in the United States" (see introduction).

The development from large-scale management to monopoly was usually easy and sometimes unconscious. Both vertical and horizontal combinations were often formed without any thought of interfering with the force of competition, but merely to secure the economies of large-scale production and later of large-scale management. Whether the product of conscious or unconscious evolution, the fourth and final stage is that of the industrial monopoly, or trust. By this is meant the combination of a sufficient number of plants to secure control over the supply and thus over the price. Classic illustrations of huge industrial combinations are the Standard Oil Company, The American Tobacco Company, the American Sugar Refining Company, the International Harvester Company, and the United States Shoe Machinery Company.

6. Devices Used to Secure Concentrated Control.—The trust is a veritable "Old Man of the Sea," and the history of industrial monopoly has shown that it is capable of assuming many different forms. When public opinion felt that it was safely gripped in the Herculean arm of regulatory legislation, the trust assumed another form and the legal battle began all over again. Although the evolution of concentrated control did not go through the same stages in all industries, and, where it did, the stages were not simultaneous, nevertheless, there are certain well-defined stages of evolution in the growth of trusts.

There is a whole series of devices by which concentration of control has been achieved. Thus, there are price-fixing agreements, friendly understandings, called "gentlemen's agreements," trade associations, and various types of pools. Informal pools for the regulation of prices or the division of the business were, in general, the first steps toward industrial monopoly. The device of the trusteeship came next in the general evolution of concentrated control. The holding company was historically the third step in many industries. The fourth stage was often that of a merger or consolidation, which resulted in the formation of a single, giant corporation. This is perhaps the climax of our industrial drama. After the dissolution of the trusts was required by the courts, concentrated control was sought by means of interlocking directorates and a community of interests in the stock of several corporations. Thus, the legal battle of wits continued and the play still went on.

Behind these various forms of concentrated control were certain dominating spirits who became the great captains of American industry. The romance of early American life was that of the frontier and the conquest of a continent. The romance of later American life was that of high finance and the achievement of concentrated control over certain basic industries for the exploitation of the natural resources of the new world. The requirements for success were somewhat similar—courage, imagination, and a certain individualism. In the one case these qualities triumphed over the rights of the Indian, and in the other case over the rights of the "innocent investor" and the consuming public.

7. Pools and Informal Agreements.—A pool is an arrangement by which competing producers can cooperate with respect to prices and general trade conditions without the sacrifice of their individual existence. Unity of action is achieved without actual consolidation. The pool of one sort or another is the earliest and most common device for the restriction or elimination of competition. It is a blanket term and includes various sorts of informal agreements as to prices, output, sales, territory, and patent rights.

The "gentlemen's agreement" is perhaps the loosest form of pool. It is an informal understanding as to price or output without any written agreement. Such pools were very common in the early history of the iron and steel industry. The famous Gary dinners were social affairs for those interested in the steel business. "Independent" and "competing" manufacturers rubbed elbows with each other around the festive board in such a friendly manner that the new price schedules which appeared shortly after these love feasts agreed in most important points.

Another type of pool is one in which the parties agree on a limitation of output and divide it among themselves according to some prearranged scheme. It can easily be seen that such a restriction of output amounts to an upward leveling of prices. This was said to have been the situation for many years in the anthracite industry, although the agreement was made among the railroads rather than among the mining companies. The connection between the coal-carrying railroads and the coal-mining companies, however, was so close that each railroad was allotted a certain percentage of the total shipments of anthracite. In some cases these pools were so strong that penalties could be enforced in case the shipments exceeded the agreed amounts.

In the anthracite railway pool of 1873, a schedule of prices was agreed upon and authority given to a board of control to regulate them from time to time. Pools for both rate fixing and a division of the traffic became very common among other railroads after a generation of keen competition had proven the disastrous effects of severe competition in that industry.

Express companies had pools for the division of their business. Each company tended to specialize in the transportation of freight within a restricted area of the United States. The country was divided for this purpose into zones or "spheres of influence." If a given town were too small for more than one express office, a "gentlemen's agreement" kept out competing express companies. This was similar to the manner in which different religious denominations agreed on the distribution of their various foreign missionary stations. Competition among these common carriers would often have been disastrous, and pools were the first step toward a natural monopoly of organization. The subsequent success of the Federal parcels post testified to the advantage of unified control in this industry.

A pool in the meat-packing industry was organized as early as 1885. It determined the quantity of meat that each member might ship and thus exercised a considerable control over prices. In 1893, a more effective agreement was entered into by the triple alliance of Swift and Company, Armour and Company, and Morris and Company. With the addition of the Cudahy Packing Company and Hammond and Company the original "Big Five" were established. They were pictured in public opinion as the "Beef Trust." At regular meetings, each company reported on its shipments into designated territories and on the prices received.

Pools have been able to transcend lines of creed, color, and nationality. In the tobacco industry an international pool providing for the division of the field was amicably achieved. In September, 1902, the American Tobacco Company and the Imperial Tobacco Company, a British concern, entered into an agreement by which the trade of each should follow its own flag. The height of international tranquillity was reached when a new concern, the British American Tobacco Company, was organized by these two companies for the exportation of its products to the rest of the world. Some results of "absentee capitalism" may be seen in the devices proposed to stimulate a demand for tobacco in such populous countries as China, unaccustomed as yet to the civilized habits of smoking and chewing.

Pools were sometimes mere selling agencies like the Kartels of Germany.   Independent producers turned over their product to a central bureau.   The wastes of competition in selling products were avoided and the expenses of marketing reduced, but the gains of individual management in production were retained. This sort of combination, permissible in Germany, was legislated against within the United States.[1]

A frequent form of pool is the patent pool.   In 1896, the General Electric Company and the Westinghouse Company entered into a pooling agreement for the joint use of nearly all their patents.   This agreement was said to have represented the control over 90 per cent of the manufacture of electrical supplies.   It also put an end to the rivalry for the acquisition of new patents from inventors.

The pool, then, is an arrangement by which producers can secure unanimity of action with respect to output and general trade conditions without sacrificing their own existence.   It does not remove the incentive of increased profits through greater efficiency in the management of individual plants.   Although some pooling agreements have restricted the output of certain producers to the extent of preventing them from reaping the maximum advantages of large-scale production, most concerns entering into pooling agreements have been enormous corporations whose plants had long since passed the stage of small-scale production.   Pools provide flexible forms of organization, which can assume various forms and adapt themselves to the varying conditions of different industries and different periods of time. On the other hand, pools have not been able to maintain a sufficient degree of stability with regard either to prices or policies. Old pools were constantly being replaced by new ones.   These agreements were not contracts and could not be enforced by the courts.   Indeed, they were often at variance with the law. Ambitious individuals frequently broke "gentlemen's agreements" in their desire for increased business and greater gains. In crises or periods of depression pools have been unable to weather the temptation to open or secret price cutting on the part of their members.

[1] Common selling agencies were finally legalized for export trade only by the Webb-Pomerene Act.   This will be discussed in the following chapter.

Pools are most successful in businesses which require a great amount of capital and in which competition cannot arise rapidly. Again, they are most apt to be successful with a relatively small number of concerns of about the same size and strength. When any one concern is very much larger than the other members it gradually devours them. Successful pools necessitate a shrewd policy on the part of their members as well as loyalty to their agreement. Too great a restriction of output produces high prices which frequently revive competition by the stimulus of high profits. This may result in the formation of an independent concern and a new rate war. The struggle generally ends, nevertheless, with an invitation to the stranger to sit down at the common table.

8. Trusteeship Device.—The instability of pools and the difficulty of enforcing these agreements led to a search for some better device for securing concentrated control. This was temporarily found in the trusteeship, which was often the second stage in the evolution of industrial monopolies. The clipping of the word trustee gave rise to the word "trust." The first resort to this device was made by the Standard Oil Company. John D. Rockefeller and his associates had acquired a large number of oil concerns which were subordinated to the Standard Oil Company. In order to centralize more fully the control over these numerous concerns, the legal device of the trusteeship was utilized in 1879. This "trust" agreement, which was revised in 1882, included about forty companies which represented over 90 per cent of the refining plants of this country. It provided for nine trustees, who received from the stockholders of the companies concerned an assignment of their stock with voting power. The trustees gave them in return "trust certificates" of equivalent amounts. The trustees did not become the owners of the stock, but they held it in trust. Nevertheless, they possessed complete control of policy. The stockholder lost his claim on the earnings of his particular company and secured instead a proportionate interest in the common earnings. The trustees might put aside a portion of their monopoly profits as a surplus with which to purchase the securities of independent companies. In this manner they sought to secure a controlling interest in a constantly increasing number of concerns.

The success of the trustee method of securing centralized control in the oil industry resulted in the formation of similar trusteeship monopolies. The American Cotton Oil Trust was formed in 1884, the National Linseed Oil Trust in 1885, the Whiskey Trust in 1887. Seventeen sugar companies, the survivors of a number of years of keen competition, representing about three-quarters of the total refining capacity of the country, entered into a "trust" agreement in 1887. Eleven trustees constituted a board known as the Sugar Refineries company which acquired the twenty refineries of the seventeen member companies. They soon eliminated twelve of them and later consolidated the remaining eight to four. The economies of large-scale management in this industry were very apparent.

Popular indignation against the trusts gave expression to much state legislation. The national Congress in 1890 passed the Sherman Anti-Trust Act, which forbade "every contract, combination in the form of trust or otherwise, or conspiracy, in restraint of trade." Pools were often secret and unwritten agreements. Although they could not be enforced by the courts, neither could they easily be attacked by the law. As "trusts" involved written agreements of trusteeship, they could be reached by legal processes. Indeed, the new device had hardly been tried before legal proceedings were instituted against it. The state of Louisiana attacked the cotton oil "trust," the state of Nebraska the whiskey "trust," the state of New York the sugar "trust," and the state of Ohio, the oil "trust." The Circuit Court of Appeals of New York State rendered an opinion in 1890 against the North River Sugar Refining Company. It ruled that it had given over its powers to an irresponsible board—an act which was a perversion of its charter. It had also helped to create a "trust," which was a partnership of separate corporations, and therefore illegal. Other similar court decisions were handed down, and the trusteeship device was definitely held to be illegal under both common and statute law. After long and tortuous litigation the Standard Oil Company was finally forced to abandon the device which it had originated.

9. Holding Companies.—Although it has been declared illegal for individuals to act as trustees for the stockholders of allied companies, it was possible under the laws of some states for a corporation to own the stock of other corporations. The term "holding company" is applied to such security-owning corporations, as contrasted with wealth-owning or operating companies. A holding company purchases all or a majority of the stock of its

subsidiary companies either by a cash purchase or by an exchange of its own stock.   The only important changes in the transition from the trusteeship device to the holding company were the substitution of shares in the holding company for the former trust certificates and the substitution of a board of directors for a group of trustees as the agents of concentrated control.

Prior to 1889, the few holding companies that existed were the creatures of special legislation.   In 1870, for illustration, the Pennsylvania Railroad Company had been empowered to buy, hold, and sell the securities of other companies in order to control affiliated lines.   A somewhat similar arrangement was used by the Philadelphia and Reading Railroad to secure the control of the stock of certain mining companies.   Although holding companies were legal under the corporation laws of most states, special legal action was generally necessary.   No state had passed a general law permitting corporations to own, to buy, and to sell the securities of other corporations.   In 1889 and 1893, however, the state of New Jersey amended its corporation laws by a blanket provision for the legalization of holding companies. In general, a corporation might now be chartered for the purpose of holding the securities of other corporations.   Hence, the name "holding company."   Although no operating duties were required of the holding company, it could exercise nearly all the rights of ownership.   It could receive the earnings of subsidiary operating companies and distribute them as its own dividends.   As charters of incorporation are sources of taxation, other states followed the example of New Jersey.   Even if they had taken no such action, the result would have been similar.   Corporations chartered in one state can normally transact business in all others.

The secret of the popularity of the holding company is that it is a device by which concentrated control can be secured with relatively small funds.   The Atlantic Coast Line Company, for illustration, was organized with a capital of slightly over ten million dollars as a holding company for a number of southern railroads.   It secured the control of the voting stock of the Atlantic Coast Line Railroad, which was both an operating and a holding company.   In turn, it owned a controlling interest in the stock of the Louisville and Nashville Railroad Company. These two railroads, together with the Southern Railroad, controlled the Georgia Railroad and the Chicago, Indianapolis, and Louisville Railroad.   This entire system represented 11,000 miles of railroad and a capital (including both bonds and stock) of almost three-quarters of a billion dollars.   It was controlled by a holding company with a capital of only ten and a half million dollars.   Concentrated control of little over five millions of this amount would assure control over the entire system.[1]

The holding company is an artificial device representing financial wheels within wheels.   The rights of independent stockholders in subsidiary companies are often ignored, as the company's policy is determined by the interests of the group in control.   The device of the holding company intensifies the problem of absentee capitalism and the separation of ownership from control.   The public as well as the investor often suffers. The existence of puppet companies makes an evasion of the law easier and often serves to conceal the presence of monopoly. The flexibility of this monopoly device is a great source of power. Through the existence of individual concerns in various states, compliance with the divergent state laws is rendered less difficult. Although the gains of monopoly are achieved, the "independent" companies can preserve their own firm names, franchises, and good will.   On the other hand, the holding company makes necessary the maintenance of separate companies, offices, and officers.

10. Single Giant Corporations.—Holding companies were often permanent organizations, but sometimes they were mere transitional stages in the formation of a single giant corporation. In such cases the holding company continued to secure the stock of its subsidiaries to such an extent that it passed from partial to complete ownership.   A reorganization then frequently took place which substituted one giant corporation for a system of allied corporations.   Overcapitalization was common in the process of reorganization, for the par value of the securities of the new company often exceeded the value of its tangible assets and the total capitalization of the original companies.   Indeed, a motive for the change from the convenient device of holding and operating companies to a single giant corporation sometimes lay in the desire to capitalize anticipated monopoly profits. Nevertheless, the formation of a single corporation in the place

[1] *Cf.* "Intercorporate Relations of Railways in the United States as of June 30, 1906." *Interstate Commerce Commission Special Report* No. 1, pp. 15–16.

of a system of holding and operating companies simplified the financial organization and resulted in the substitution of a corporation, owning tangible wealth for a corporation owning securities.

Single giant corporations sometimes evolved without passing through the holding company stage. When the trustee device was declared illegal, the member corporations of such organizations often decided to unite into a single corporation without resorting to the device of the holding company. A consolidation is the union into another corporate body of two or more existing corporations. The assent of the legislature is necessary, as well as the consent of the stockholders. Combination can be effected by the purchase and sale of the tangible wealth or the securities of one corporation by another. A merger may be effected by an exchange of the physical assets of one company for the stock of another. In this way, one company is absorbed by another. Such a contingency was expressly provided for in the law passed by the state of New Jersey in 1889. It empowered the directors of a corporation chartered under this act to purchase a business by the issuance of stock. A powerful incentive was thus furnished to incorporate and combine within the hospitable bounds of New Jersey. The business of the incorporated company might extend anywhere within the United States. This opportunity was soon taken advantage of. The American Tobacco Company, incorporated in 1890 in the state of New Jersey, illustrates a wealth-owning company as distinct from a security-holding company. The American Sugar Refining Company, incorporated in New Jersey in 1891, is another early wealth-owning monopoly. Trust certificates were directly exchanged for the stock of the new company.

11. Monopoly Prices and Profits.—Monopoly price has been defined as that price which yields the greatest net returns to the monopoly. Costs of production are more apt to be directly expressed in competitive prices than in monopoly prices. Competition will prevent prices from remaining very far above the costs of production, for the lure of high profits will attract other producers into that industry. As the supply of a commodity or a service is thus increased, its price will tend to fall. In the case of monopoly, however, costs of production merely represent a minimum and not a maximum price level. Although a monopoly price is apt to be higher than a corresponding competitive price, such is not always the case. A monopoly may so utilize the economies of large-scale production and management that its cost of production per unit of product may be smaller than if the competition of small enterprisers prevailed. A monopoly price is also restrained by the refusal of consumers to purchase at a high price. Trusts may find that maximum net profits are to be secured by a large volume of sales at a low price, rather than by a small volume of sales at a higher price. If the monopolized commodity or service is a necessity of life, however, the consumer has little opportunity to substitute something else or to refrain from purchasing. Whether higher or lower than a corresponding competitive price, monopoly price has the advantage of greater stability. By its very definition a monopoly possesses the power to regulate the supply which is placed on the market. The fluctuations of a competitive price are due in part to the constantly changing conditions of supply. By its adjustment of the supply of a given commodity or service a monopoly stabilizes its price, although the process of stabilization is often upward to a higher price level.

There are social as well as economic, and artificial as well as natural, limits to the power of monopoly. Artificial or social limits are represented by governmental interference. State action is exemplified by attempts to dissolve a monopoly or to eliminate unfair methods of competition. Price fixing is "the gun behind the door," or the weapon of last resort. Natural or economic limitations on monopoly have just been illustrated by the power of substitution and the possibility of competition. An exorbitant price may result in a buyers' strike. High prices with excessive profits may also revive competition, as well as inhibit consumption. This is shown by the history of the sugar industry, where competition and monopoly have alternated.

Although monopolies have been careful to avoid breaking the home market, they have not always been so scrupulous about foreign markets. American trusts have frequently employed the device of "dumping" their surplus products on European countries. The same American product has been found to sell at a lower price in the foreign than in the home market. Numerous large industries operate under the principle of decreasing costs. Because of their great "overhead" or fixed expenses, the cost per unit of product decreases as the volume of output increases. In order to enjoy the full advantages of large-scale production, they have been forced to produce continuously and to maximum capacity. Thus, a surplus has been created which the home market could not absorb without breaking the monopoly price. Monopolies have found it profitable to sell this surplus in foreign markets at any price greater than bare operating expenses. Lower prices often prevailed abroad because of foreign competition. The American tariff excluded this competition in the home market. Hence, the differences in the prices at home and abroad of the same American-made product.

The monopoly profits of many American trusts have been excessive. Moreover, these monopoly profits have not been widely distributed, but have found their way into comparatively few hands. Although smaller investors have shared somewhat in monopoly profits, the lion's share generally went to the promoters and the magnates. The American Tobacco Company, for illustration, was organized in 1890 by five leading manufacturers of cigarettes. The capitalization of the company was $25,000,000, of which $15,000,000 represented common and the remaining $10,000,000 preferred stock. The Report of the Commissioner of Corporations on the Tobacco Industry showed that the value of the assets acquired, good will included, did not exceed $14,400,-000. Thus, there was overcapitalization by the addition of nearly one half "water." Nevertheless, the establishment of monopoly control made it possible for the company to earn 20 per cent on its common stock. Enormous promoters' profits were also realized in the formation of the United States Steel Corporation and the American Can Company. The reports of the Commissioner of Corporations on various trusts reveal numerous similar cases. Private fortunes have been made by the successful promotion of monopolies.

12. Trust Practices and Unfair Competition.—Monopoly is not only a problem of the consumer, but also of the producer. In addition to excessive prices and profits, another frequent charge against the trusts is that of unfair methods of competition. A common allegation has been that the trusts cut prices in local markets where competition prevailed, while maintaining higher prices in markets where there was no competition. In 1901, the United States Industrial Commission made a study of the wholesale and retail prices paid in different parts of the country for sugar, baking powder, and petroleum products. With regard to the latter commodities, it established the fact that the former Standard

Oil Company charged different prices for the same product in different places, the local price depending on the amount of competition. This practice appeared to be common in a number of businesses, and it was regarded by many individuals as legitimate. In the second place, it was alleged that some trusts influenced the local dealers to boycott other products in favor of their own. In the third place, trusts were charged with having obtained from the railroads discriminatory rates. The large shipper was favored at the expense of the small one. Discriminatory freight rates as well as prices have been proven against the former Standard Oil Company and the Sugar Trust.

A number of miscellaneous practices which are manifestly unfair must also be mentioned. They may be illustrated by the charges brought against the National Cash Register Company in 1912, when the court fined and even imposed jail sentences on some of the officers of the company. The legal indictment made the following claims. The trust had hired the employees of competitors to reveal the secrets of their business. It had bribed the employees of railroads and express companies to give information with regard to the shipment of cash registers. It had used its influence with the banks to lessen the credit of competing companies. Among the various ingenious devices employed was that of manufacturing "knockers." These were imitations of competing machines and sold for lower prices. When the competition was removed the use of that particular "knocker" was discontinued. It was sometimes advantageous to manufacture these "knockers" with weak or defective mechanism. Again, the trust bought or took in exchange the machines of other companies which it later displayed in show windows as "junk" or "For Sale Cheap." The company threatened its competitors with suits for the infringment of patent rights when no patent rights existed. It applied for patents on the processes and inventions of competing companies merely for the sake of harassing them. It induced the employees of competing companies to leave their places of employment and to come with the National Cash Register Company. Lastly, it organized supposedly competing cash register companies as puppets for many convenient purposes.[1]

[1] *Cf. Petition in United States vs. National Cash Register Company*, pp. 31–38, and "Decrees and Judgments," in Federal Anti-Trust Cases, pp. 795–798.

In addition to unfair methods of competition, it is charged that the trusts have influenced tariff legislation, and, in turn, that the protective tariff has been the "mother of the trusts." There seems to be a reciprocal relationship, however, and it is doubtful which is the mother and which is the child. It is contended that the high duties charged in the tariffs of 1883, 1890, and 1897 permitted a margin of profit to domestic producers which encouraged the duplication of plants. Trusts were formed to escape the ruinous competition which otherwise would have followed. These vested interests then sought immunity from foreign competition by higher protective tariffs. Although trusts were favored by our high protective tariff, and some of them would not otherwise have developed, other trusts prospered without tariff protection. The Standard Oil Company grew up in an unprotected industry. Free-trade England experienced a development of monopolies, but not to such an enormous extent as the United States. It is further contended that the trusts have had a corrupting influence on our political life. This allegation is made against certain legal monopolies, such as public utilities, as well as against the trusts or industrial monopolies. Attempts at the regulation of monopoly and the removal of existing evils have been met with legislative intrigue and political chicanery. Trusts have been pictured as the "power behind the throne" in the "invisible empire" of big business.

13. Advantages and Disadvantages of Monopoly.—In spite of these unfair practices of the trusts, there are certain legitimate economic advantages of monopoly which must be considered. They are more conspicuous in some types of monopoly than in others. The wastes of competition are so great in such natural monopolies of organization as public utilities, that the latter have been sanctioned as legal monopolies in the form of either exclusive franchises or public ownership. Trusts or industrial monopolies sometimes possess to a smaller degree similar economic advantages. In the main, they are merely an extension of the economies of large-scale management as well as large-scale production. The advantages of large-scale production were described in Chap. II. The advantages of large-scale management are still more conspicuous in the case of monopolies. Economies of selling are achieved by a reduction in the great expenses of competing salesmen and competitive advertising. Economies of marketing are achieved by the elimination of cross freights which are necessary under a competitive regime. The American Steel and Wire Company estimated that it saved a half million dollars in one year alone from this source. Economies in bargaining may be illustrated by the savings which result from buying in great quantities. Monopolies can also better adjust the output of their plants to the iregularities of the market. It has already been stated that a monopoly price is more stable than a corresponding competitive price.

It is argued that monopoly is inevitable in an industry which operates under the principle of decreasing costs. In such industries the extensive investment of capital and its continued maintenance create great "overhead" or fixed charges, such as heavy interest payments and replacement charges. Quantity production is necessary and competition is ruinous. The socialists claim to see this principle of decreasing costs in most modern industries because of the large amount of capital which is necessary. For this reason they regard most industrial monopolies as natural. Competition is economically wasteful and private monopoly socially undesirable. Therefore, their answer to the problem of monopoly is the governmental ownership and operation of industry.

Is it not, however, somewhat of an assumption to say that all industries are those of decreasing cost? Moreover, does this principle continue to operate indefinitely as the size of the industry increases? Is it not possible that large-scale production and large-scale management may be carried beyond the point of maximum efficiency? There is a limit to the managerial capacity of most individuals as well as to the size of most industries. Great geniuses of organization, such as Andrew Carnegie, are rare. Again, the burden of highly centralized administrative machinery may become great enough to counterbalance the economic advantages of monopoly. The point of maximum efficiency varies in different industries, but combination beyond this point spells loss of efficiency. It is claimed that this very thing has happened today in many trusts. From an economic point of view they have been likened to the famous colossus with feet of clay.

The possession of enormous capital has made it possible for some monopolies to stifle their competitors. They have retarded economic progress rather than reduced the wastes of competition. In his early political career in New Jersey, Woodrow Wilson attempted to differentiate between those monopolies which rested on productive efficiency and those which made their gains through superior bargaining power. Such a distinction between natural and artificial monopolies is difficult to make. It remains true, however, that many American trusts have reached their powerful monopoly position by unfair methods of competition. Trusts do not necessarily represent the fittest form of industrial organization merely because they have been successful in the economic struggle for existence. Many trusts are artificial monopolies which have resulted from the financial strategy and economic profiteering of certain dominant personalities. Colossal fortunes and great inequalities of wealth have resulted. Enormous power in the hands of a few individuals has produced a tremendous concentration of power as well as of wealth. Industrial democracy is a problem of the present century just as political democracy was of the past century. A plutocracy is as undesirable as an aristocracy, and an economic despotism as dangerous as a political absolutism.

14. Summary.—Monopoly implies the absence of competition and may be defined as sufficient control over the supply of a commodity or service to fix its price. There are numerous kinds of monopolies and various ways of classifying them. Although one group gradually fades into another, the distinction between legal monopolies and industrial monopolies is important. The former is the older concept, for monopoly was originally a legal grant from a sovereign. The trust represents monopolies which have gradually grown up by the process of industrial combination. Growth in size has been accompanied by concentrated control and large-scale production has been succeeded by large-scale management. Trusts may be regarded as the outcome of large-scale production and the corporate form of business organization, although monopoly must be distinguished from both.

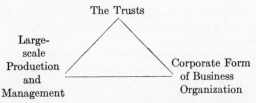

The development of the trusts followed the industrialization of the United States after the Civil War. A great period of consolidation was in the closing years of the nineteenth century and the opening years of the twentieth century. Various methods have been used to secure monopoly, and, in general, the evolution of the trusts may be divided into different stages. Thus, we have pools for price fixing or a division of the output, the device of trusteeship, holding companies, single giant corporations, and interlocking directorates.

Monopoly price is generally the price at which the greatest net profits will accrue to the monopoly. This is not always an excessive price, because maximum net profits may be achieved by large sales at a low price, rather than by fewer sales at high prices. Natural or economic limitations on monopoly price are represented by the ability of consumers to substitute something else for the monopolized article and by the possible revival of competition. Other producers may be attracted by the lure of high profits. Artificial or social limits on monopoly are represented by governmental interference. In the next chapter we shall sketch the attempt of the government to regulate the trusts.

In the formation of trusts overcapitalization has often accompanied consolidation. Thus, future monopoly profits have been capitalized. The size of monopoly profits may be seen by a study of the high rates of earnings of many trusts in spite of their overcapitalization. The consumer has complained of the high prices of monopolized articles. The producer has complained of unfair methods of competition. Democracy itself has been threatened by political corruption on the part of certain trusts. Against these dangers and disadvantages of concentrated control must be balanced the advantages which arise from an extension of the economies of large-scale production and large-scale management. The latter include economies of production, selling, marketing, and bargaining.

Collateral Reading

ELY, R. T., "Outlines of Economics," chap. 12.
FAIRCHILD, F. R., FURNISS, E. S., and BUCK, N. S., "Elementary Economics," chap. 31.
FETTER, F., "Modern Economic Problems," chap. 30.
HAMILTON, W., "Current Economic Problems," pp. 429–459.
MARSHALL, L. C., "Readings in Industrial Society," pp. 709–765.
————, WRIGHT, C. W., and FIELD, J. A., "Materials for the Study of Elementary Economics," pp. 299–323.
TAUSSIG, F. W., "Principles of Economics," chaps. 15, 45 and 65.

References

BROWN, W. J., "The Prevention and Control of Monopolies."

CARTER, G. R., "The Tendency toward Industrial Combination."

DURAND, E. D., "The Trust Problem."

ELY, R. T., "Monopolies and Trusts."

HALLE, E., "Trusts or Industrial Combinations and Coalitions in the United States."

HANEY, L. H., "Business Organization and Combination."

JENKS, J. W., and CLARK, W. E., "The Trust Problem."

JONES, E., "The Trust Problem in the United States."

————, "The Anthracite Coal Combination in the United States."

LE ROSSIGNOL, J. E., "Monopolies, Past and Present."

LEVY, H., "Monopoly and Competition."

MARSHALL, A., "Industry and Trade."

MEAD, E. S., "Trust Finance."

MOODY, J., "The Truth about Trusts."

RIPLEY, W. Z., "Trusts, Pools and Combinations."

ROOSEVELT, T., "Progressive Principles."

STEVENS, W. S., "Industrial Combinations and Trusts."

————, "Unfair Competition."

STOCKING, G. W., "The Oil Industry and the Competitive System."

TARBELL, I., "The History of the Standard Oil Company."

THOMPSON, M. R., "Trust Dissolution."

United States Census (especially Twelfth Census, 1900, vol. 7).

United States Commissioner of Corporations, *Annual Reports*, and series of reports on various industries.

United States Supreme Court *Decisions*.

United States Congressional Investigations and Committee *Reports*.

United States Federal Trade Commission, *Annual and Special Reports*.

WILSON, W., "The New Freedom."

WYMAN, B., "The Control of the Market, a Legal Solution for the Trust Problem."

Questions for Discussion

1. What is monopoly and what is the test of monopoly?

2. Distinguish between the old concept and the new concept of monopoly.

3. Make a classification of the different kinds of monopoly.

4. Outline the social and economic limitations upon monopoly.

5. Contrast the advantages and disadvantages of monopoly.

6. Outline the four stages of industrial consolidation and distinguish between horizontal and vertical combinations.

7. Outline the various devices used to secure concentrated control.

8. What is a pool? Name similar devices. State advantages and disadvantages.

9. Explain the trusteeship device for securing monopoly.

10. What is a holding company? Show its advantages and disadvantages.

Topics of Investigation

1. The amount and significance of industrial consolidation in the United States toward the close of the nineteenth century.
2. The holding company as a device for securing concentrated control with a relatively small amount of capital. Illustrations.
3. The capitalization of anticipated monopoly profits. Illustrations.
4. Unfair monopoly practices.
5. The history of the Standard Oil Company.
6. The formation of the United States Steel Company and its effects.
7. The story of the International Harvester Company.
8. Monopoly and competition in the packing industry.
9. The history of the American Tobacco Company.
10. Recent tendencies toward consolidation.

CHAPTER VII

THE REGULATION OF THE TRUSTS

1. Regulation by the States.—As economic or social problems appear in our national life, public opinion gradually formulates itself about them. Public opinion finally crystallizes into laws attempting to cope with the situation. As our industrial society is extremely dynamic, it is difficult to keep the guns of legislation trained effectively upon a given issue. The movement toward the concentration of capital made considerable progress in our economic life before any regulatory legislation was passed. The organization of effective administrative machinery came still later. For generations the common law of both England and America had opposed monopolies and had attempted to uphold the freedom of competition. Statute laws also forbade monopolies, but the legislators had in mind the older concept of monopoly. It took years for the courts to expand their definition of monopoly from that of a governmental grant to that of the modern trust. It was not until the later years of the nineteenth century that laws were passed against this new industrial monopoly:

State anti-trust laws appeared before any Federal legislation on the subject. The Kansas law of 1889 may be taken as typical. It provided:

. . . that all arrangements, contracts, agreements, trusts or combinations between persons or corporations made with a view to, or which tend to prevent full and free competition in the importation, transportation, or sale of articles into this state or in the production, manufacture, or sale of articles of domestic growth or product of domestic raw material, or in the loan or use of money, or to fix attorneys' or doctors' fees, and all arrangements, contracts, agreements, trusts or combinations between persons or corporations designed or which tend to advance, reduce or control the price or cost to the producer or to the consumer of any such products or articles, . . . are hereby declared to be against public policy, unlawful and void.

Penalties of fines and imprisonments were provided for violations. By 1894, twenty states had passed similar anti-trust legislation.

The attempts of individual states to cope with the problem of the trusts were futile. Uniform legislation in all states was impossible. The problem of the trusts, moreover, was a national one. State regulation was hampered by the fact that a trust could incorporate in a state where the laws were lenient and then do business in other states.

2. Constitutional Basis of Federal Regulation.—The Federal regulation of the trusts included the legal problem of the constitutional powers of Congress. Like other problems of our industrial life, the trusts presented the conflict of authority between the Federal and the state governments. The Constitution declares that Congress shall have the power to "regulate commerce with foreign nations and among the several states, and with the Indian tribes."[1] Fortunately, judicial interpretation of the word "commerce" has been very broad. Chief Justice Marshall, as early as 1827, declared commerce to be all intercourse.[2] The legal status of later inventions such as the telegraph, the telephone, and the railroads was defined before they were in existence. The Supreme Court has defined interstate commerce to include "not only the transportation of persons and property and the navigation of public waters for that purpose, but also the purchase, sale, and exchange of commodities." On the other hand, the Supreme Court of the United States also declared that commerce did not include manufacturing. Industry changed the form, and commerce the place, of goods.[3] This distinction, however, is of less importance than it would seem. Every large manufacturing concern is obliged to import its raw materials from other states and to ship its finished goods outside the state borders. Thus, it must engage in interstate commerce. It is safe to say that every large industry is subject to the interstate regulations of Congress. Upon this constitutional power rests the authority of the national government to cope with the trusts.

At first trusts were regarded as closely related to the railroads. Their origin seemed to be in railroad discriminations and rebates. Hence, the Interstate Commerce Act of 1887 may be regarded as a trust measure. A discussion of this law, however, will be

---

[1] Article 1, sec. 8.

[2] In the case of *Brown vs. Maryland*, 12 Wheaton 419, 1827.

[3] In the case of *E. C. Knight Sugar Refining Co. vs. United States*, 156 U. S. 1, 1895.

reserved for the chapter on railroads, because it is primarily a piece of railroad legislation. The first Federal law devoted specifically to the trusts was the Sherman Anti-trust Act of 1890.

3. Sherman Anti-trust Act.—In the platforms of both political parties frequent references had been made to the trusts. Federal aid had been promised in this matter as well as in the railroad problem. A bill was finally introduced in the national Senate by Senator Sherman, in December, 1889. After the usual course of amendments and compromises it was passed by both houses and signed by President Harrison, July 2, 1890. The most significant features of this law may be found in its first few sections:

An act to protect trade and commerce against unlawful restraints and monopolies.

Be it enacted by the Senate and House of Representatives of the United States of America in Congress assembled,

Section 1. Every contract, combination in the form of trust or otherwise, or conspiracy, in restraint of trade or commerce among the several States, or with foreign nations, is hereby declared to be illegal. Every person who shall make such a contract or engage in any such combination or conspiracy, shall be deemed guilty of a misdemeanor, and, on conviction thereof, shall be punished by fine not exceeding five thousand dollars, or by imprisonment not exceeding one year, or by both said punishments, in the discretion of the court.

Section 2. Every person who shall monopolize, or attempt to monopolize, or combine or conspire with any other person or persons, to monopolize any part of the trade or commerce among the several States, or with foreign nations, shall be deemed guilty of a misdemeanor, and, on conviction thereof, shall be punished by fine not exceeding five thousand dollars, or by imprisonment not exceeding one year, or by both said punishments, in the discretion of the court.

Section 4 gives the circuit courts of the United States jurisdiction to enforce the law, and provides that the Federal government may institute proceedings in equity to prevent and restrain any violations thereof.

Section 7 confers upon persons injured by trusts the right to sue the offending party for triple damages and the cost of the suit.

Section 8 contains a very important provision, namely, that the word person be construed to include corporations and associations.

4. Judicial Interpretation of the Sherman Act.—For a number of years after its passage in 1890 the Sherman Anti-trust Act remained almost a dead letter. This was partially due to its sweeping character and indefinite wording. Doubt existed as to the real meaning and legal significance of the statute. The effectiveness of the law was also impaired by a decision of the Supreme Court in the case of the E. C. Knight Sugar Refining Company, in 1895. As previously stated, the court contended that the Sherman Act was designed to apply to commerce and not to manufacturing. It further held that the combination of sugar refiners did not constitute a violation of the new law unless the combination attempted to monopolize interstate commerce in sugar. The Knight case differentiated not only between commerce and manufacturing, but also between interstate and intrastate commerce. This Supreme Court decision was commonly construed as a judicial interpretation of the weakness of the Sherman Act in particular and of Federal regulation of trusts in general. However, it did not imply that a manufacturing company which sells its products in other states is exempt from the provisions of the law.

The first real victory for the Federal government came in 1899, when the dissolution of the Addyston Pipe and Steel Company was ordered. This court decision demonstrated the fact that the Sherman Anti-trust Act was possessed of teeth. Another important case was that of Swift and Company, meat-packers, decided in 1905. The government accused a number of Chicago meat-packing concerns of being combinations in restraint of trade and asked the Federal court to grant an injunction against the combine. A lower court granted the injunction, but the packers appealed the case. The Supreme Court sustained the injunction and the principle that combinations which conspired to impose oppressive terms on buyer or seller were contrary to the Sherman Act.

We have seen how effectively holding companies can be utilized to form monopolies. What solution did the Sherman Act offer to this problem? The question first came up in connection with the formation of the Northern Securities Company, which was to be a holding company for a number of railway lines, among which were the Great Northern and the Northern Pacific companies. This consolidation was declared illegal by the Supreme Court, in 1904, as it suppressed competition between those two companies. The question as to the legality of a holding company again presented itself in the case of the Standard Oil Company. The Standard Oil Company of New Jersey was a holding company which owned the stock control of nineteen subordinate companies. In 1906, a government suit was brought against this combine as a violation of the Sherman Act. The Circuit Court held the company to be a combination in restraint of trade, but the case was appealed. In 1911, the Supreme Court gave its decision and upheld the view of the lower court. It ordered the Standard Oil Company to dissolve the combination with its subsidiary companies within six months.

This decision is also of peculiar interest because it introduced the adjective "reasonable" into the discussion of restraints on trade. The Court declared that the mere existence of a combination in commerce was not illegal. There must be involved a clearly proven plan to restrain trade and competition. Moreover, the courts must decide in each case, "in the light of reason," whether the combination is making use of illegitimate means of increasing its business or whether it is a legitimate attempt to introduce the economies of large-scale production. In the latter case only such restraint of trade is involved as is natural and reasonable. The Supreme Court also rendered in the same year a somewhat similar decision against the American Tobacco Company. The Court ordered a reorganization of the companies involved in this combination, but it again went on record as being not hostile to the formation of combinations based on greater productive efficiency. This point is important in the case of railroads, where both the law and the courts formerly sought to stimulate competition. On the other hand, these decisions of 1911 forbade the formation and existence of destructive or extortionate combinations, whose purpose was to eliminate competition and to raise prices. The question was no longer whether a combination in restraint of trade existed, but whether the economic effects of such a combination were good or bad.

Judicial interpretation of the Sherman Act held that it was applicable to "corners."[1] The court held that the widespread purchase of an article for the purpose of withdrawing it from trade, in order artificially to increase its price, was one of the very restraints of trade within the meaning of the Sherman Act. It was held to be unthinkable that a speculator could "corner"

[1] In the case of *J. A. Patten et al vs. United States*, 1913, 226 U. S. 524.

the cotton market without restricting interstate commerce, even if his purchase were confined to one state.

A final question presented by the Sherman Act was its effect upon the relationship between labor and capital. Was a trade union a combination in restraint of trade? If so, the Sherman Act would sound the death knell to almost a century of labor organization. In spite of this very real possibility, judicial interpretation held that such a view was not the intent of the law. The Sherman Act, however, affected one of the strong weapons of organized labor. The courts held certain types of boycotts to be conspiracies in restraint of trade. Boycotts are organized refusals of the workers and their sympathizers to buy the products of hostile employers. They will be discussed in Chap. XXVI.

5. Merits and Defects of the Sherman Act.—The Sherman Act is a general statute declaratory of a public policy. It must be judged by the soundness of this policy, by the accuracy with which it expresses it, and by the mechanism which it provides for making it effective.

The public policy which the act was intended to embody is that competition should be maintained, artificial monopoly destroyed, and its growth prevented. It is clear from the debates attending its enactment that its hostility towards large industrial combinations was especially directed against (1) their supposed power over prices, and (2) their aggressive suppression of competition. Whatever the economic advantages of monopoly may be, there will be little question of the soundness of the policy which attempts to deprive it of its power for evil in these two particulars.[1]

As to accuracy of expression, we have seen that the Sherman Act possessed little precision. It is probably true that general phrases were chosen intentionally by its framers, in order that the responsibility for determining the exact scope of the law might be left to the courts. We have seen that this work of judicial interpretation progressed very slowly. The language of the statute was also inadequate because of its inclusiveness. It embraced labor boycotts and railroads as well as trusts. The effects of the Sherman Act upon the railroads will be discussed in Chap. IX. It will be sufficient here to state that railroads are natural monopolies which should not be regarded as artificial combinations in restraint of trade. Moreover, all industrial

[1] *Cf.* YOUNG, A. A., "The Sherman Act and the New Anti-trust Legislation," *Journal of Political Economy*, vol. XXIII, pp. 213–220.

monopolies cannot be grouped together as undesirable trusts. We have seen how the courts were forced to speak of reasonable and unreasonable combinations. Finally, the criminal provisions of the Sherman Act have been almost impossible to enforce because of their severity. In general, fines but not imprisonment have been imposed for violations of the statute.

6. Dissolution of the Trusts.—It must be remembered that dis olution rarely came early enough to effect the permanent destruction of the trusts. Competition was not ordinarily restored, because some other means of achieving concentrated control was found. Monopoly had crystallized to such an extent that many of the newly formed companies did not compete. Subsidiary companies, legally restored to independence, could not immediately be made economically independent. It has been facetiously said that the effort to dissolve the trusts was as futile as an attempt to unscramble an omelette. Nevertheless, a number of suits were brought against the trusts in accordance with the Sherman Act.

During the administration of President Harrison, who was in office when the Sherman Act was passed, four bills in equity and three indictments were brought under the new Anti-trust Act. During the second term of President Cleveland an equally small number of prosecutions took place. Dissolutions during the administration of President McKinley were even fewer. Although it was during this period that industrial consolidation reached its height, not a single suit was brought against a trust. There were no criminal prosecutions and only three bills in equity.

After the assumption of office by President Roosevelt, however, vigorous action against the trusts soon followed. During the seven and one-half years of his administration, about forty prosecutions were recorded. Among the trusts attacked were the Standard Oil Company, The American Tobacco Company, the powder trust, and lesser combinations. A number of railroad combinations were also assailed. The process of "trust busting" was carried on even more vigorously in the Taft administration. Almost a hundred bills in equity and indictments were entered during these four years. Suits were brought against the United States Steel Corporation, the American Sugar Refining Company, The International Harvester Company, The United States Shoe Machinery Company, The National Cash Register Company, and many other large concerns. During President Wilson's first term the number of new indictments was much smaller, but the prosecution was continued of suits previously filed. The World War created new problems and American interest shifted from domestic to international questions. During the administration of President Coolidge, however, a number of great mergers and consolidations were attempted in various basic industries. At the present time (1926) several Federal prosecutions are pending against gigantic combinations in restraint of trade.

7. Economic Effects of Dissolution of Trusts.—The first trust to be formally dissolved under the Sherman Act was the Standard Oil Company. The effects of this dissolution were carefully investigated later by the Federal Trade Commission. The economic effects of the court order on the restoration of competition are described in the Commission's "Report on the Price of Gasoline in 1915." The conclusion was that there was little, if any, competition among the former subsidiaries of the Standard Oil Company of New Jersey. These subsidiaries included the Standard Oil Companies of New York, Kentucky, Ohio, Indiana, Nebraska, California, and Louisiana, The Atlantic Refining Company, the Continential Oil Company, and the Magnolia Petroleum Company. The Commission stated with regard to gasoline that these eleven companies "maintained a complete division of territory embracing the whole country and that almost without exception each Standard marketing company occupies and supplies a distinct and arbitrarily bounded territory." Among these various spheres of influence the price of gasoline varied. If competition had prevailed, gasoline would have been shipped from the low-priced areas to the high-priced areas, until price differences were reduced to the mere costs of transportation. Although there were independent companies, such as the Texas Company, the investigation seemed to show that they followed prices fixed by the Standard companies. It was also found that there was a community of interest among these various Standard companies based on common stockholding. Leading officers and directors of one company were frequently large stockholders in several other companies. The conclusion of the Commission was that the industry remained a combination in fact if not in law.

More recent investigations[1] of the oil industry, however, give conclusions differing from those of the Federal Trade Com-

[1] *Cf.* STOCKING, G. W.. "The Oil Industry and the Competitive System."

mission's Report of 1915. They testify to the existence of competition in the oil-refining as well as in the oil-production industry. If these findings are accurate and typical, they indicate that the dissolution of the trusts by court order is possible. Nevertheless, the restoration of competition seems to be a lengthy rather than an immediate process.

8. Change of Attitude.—The failure of dissolution to restore competition immediately engendered skepticism as to the advisability of "trust busting." Moreover, public opinion began to weigh the advantages of large-scale management against the wastes of competition. Many concerns, such as the meat packers, began a process of public education along these lines. During the World War many of the wastes of competition were consciously eliminated. "Big business" was effectively utilized for the production of war materials. The former policy of suppression gradually turned to one of regulation. We have seen the change in the attitude of the Supreme Court in the Standard Oil decision of 1911. "Regulation by the axe" gave way to regulation "in the light of reason."

This gradual change of attitude may also be characterized as a transition from a negative to a positive policy, and from punitive to a preventive point of view. The reformation of criminal corporations as well as criminal human beings makes it necessary to individualize their treatment. All the facts in each case must be obtained and studied before wise action can be taken. The results of ill-considered dissolution were found to be either negligible or negative. Just as "regulation by the axe" was followed by "regulation in the light of reason," so "regulation in the light of reason" was supplemented by "regulation in the light of expediency." This new attitude seems best illustrated in a decision of the Supreme Court regarding the United States Steel Corporation. Although the suit was begun in 1911, it was not until March, 1920, that the Supreme Court gave its decision. It was against dissolution. The court declared that "We are unable to see that public interest will be served by yielding to the contention of the Government respecting the dissolution of the Company . . . and we do see in a contrary conclusion a risk of injury to the public interest, including a material disturbance of, and, it may be serious detriment to, the foreign trade."[1]

[1] *Cf. United States vs. United States Steel Corporation*, 1920, 251 U. S. 417.

9. Bureau of Corporations.—Important changes in administrative machinery had meanwhile been taking place. Public opinion regarding the trusts had finally crystallized into law, but the law required judicial interpretation. In turn, court decisions required the expert knowledge of various specialists other than those versed in the law. The enforcement of judicial decrees, moreover, required an administrative body. It soon became evident that the legislative and judicial regulation of the trusts was not sufficient. An investigating or fact-finding body of economic experts was needed to supplement the work of such legal experts as governmental attorneys. An administrative corps was necessary also for the supervision of the trusts, if regulation in the light of reason and expediency was to succeed "regulation by the axe." Such machinery was first created in the Bureau of Corporations and later vested in the Federal Trade Commission.

Publicity was discovered as a new weapon for the regulation of the trusts. Hence the efficacy of a fact-finding body of economists who might rest their case in its final analysis with the great jury of public opinion. In 1898, an Industrial Commission to investigate trusts and monopolies was appointed. In 1900, it made a report recommending a more detailed supervision over industries and corporations. President Roosevelt in his first annual message to Congress had said that the "the first essential in determining how to deal with the great industrial combinations is a knowledge of the facts—publicity." In his second annual message he continued by saying that "publicity can do no harm to the honest corporation; and we need not be overtender about sparing the dishonest corporation."

In February, 1903, Congress established in the new department of Commerce and Labor a Bureau of Corporations. The Bureau was to investigate the affairs of industrial corporations engaged in interstate or foreign commerce. The President of the United States was to decide what portions of its findings should be made public. At the head of the Bureau of Corporations was the Commissioner of Corporations appointed by the President. The Commissioner was empowered to compel the testimony of witnesses and the production of documentary evidence.

10. Federal Trade Commission.—During the three-cornered presidential campaign of 1912 the trust issue loomed large. The

Progressive Party under the leadership of Theodore Roosevelt promised the creation of a Federal commission to control the trusts in a manner similar to that in which the Interstate Commerce Commission controlled the railroads. Where competition could not be restored or was inadvisable, the Federal government should exercise strict regulation, if necessary to the extent of price fixing. The Democrats declared their hostility toward all industrial monopolies and promised new legislation to restore the efficacy of the Sherman Act. Action would be taken against holding companies, interlocking directorates, price discriminations, unfair methods of competition, and stock watering. After his election, in a personally delivered message to Congress, President Wilson declared that "private monopoly is indefensible and intolerable." On the other hand, he also stated that there was to be "nothing essential disturbed, nothing torn up by the roots, no parts rent asunder which can be left in wholesome combination."

One of the first fruits of the Democratic administration was the introduction into Congress of a number of trust measures. After the usual process of compromise and amendment, there emerged two new laws, the Trade Commission Act and the Clayton Act. They were supplementary pieces of trust legislation, for the latter outlined general policies and the former created new administrative machinery. We shall first discuss the Federal Trade Commission, which was created by the bill of that name in September, 1914.

(A) Organization.—The law of 1914 provided for the creation of a Federal Trade Commission of five members, to be appointed by the President with the advice and consent of the Senate for a term of seven years. The new Commission was designed to be a nonpartisan body, and not more than three commissioners might be members of the same political party. After the organization of this Commission and the election of its chairman, the Bureau of Corporations and the office of Commissioner of Corporations ceased to exist. The new body took over the investigations, records, property, funds, and employees of the older body. The Commission had the authority to appoint a secretary, attorneys, special experts, examiners, and clerks.

(B) Powers of Investigation.—The principal powers of the Federal Trade Commission may be classified as those of investigation and those of administration. The aim in both cases is

the elimination of unfair practices. Its chief powers of investigation are:

. . . To gather and compile information concerning, and to investigate from time to time the organization, business, conduct, practices, and management of any corporation engaged in commerce, excepting banks and common carriers subject to the Act to regulate commerce, and its relation to other corporations and to individuals, associations and partnerships.

These powers are slightly broader than those formerly possessed by the Bureau of Corporations, and the Commission is not subject to the control of the Secretaries of Commerce and of Labor.

The specific powers vested in the Federal Trade Commission for investigation and publicity are as follows:[1]

To require the corporations subject to its control to file with it "in such form as the commission may prescribe" annual or special reports. Penalties are attached for failure to make reports or for the making of false statements.

Upon the direction of the President or either House of Congress to investigate and report the facts relating to any alleged violations of the Anti-trust Acts by any corporation.

Upon the application of the Attorney General to investigate and make recommendations for the readjustment of the business of any corporation alleged to be violating the Anti-trust Acts in order that the corporation may thereby maintain its organization, management, and conduct of business in accordance with the law."

The aim here is prevention rather than punishment. An "immunity bath" by the Federal Trade Commission generally avoids suit by the Attorney General.

Whenever a final decree has been entered against any defendant corporation in any suit brought by the United States to prevent and restrain any violation of the Anti-trust Acts, to make investigation, upon its own initiative, of the manner in which the decree has been or is being carried out, and upon the application of the Attorney General it shall be its duty to make such an investigation. It shall transmit to the Attorney General a report embodying its findings and recommendations as a result of any such investigation, and the report shall be made public in the discretion of the commission.

To investigate from time to time, trade conditions in and with foreign countries where associations, combinations, or practices of manufactures, merchants, or traders, or other conditions, may affect the foreign trade of the United States and report to Congress thereon, with such recommendations as it deems advisable.

[1] *Cf.* Sec. 6.

Such information as seems desirable may be made public in the form of reports. The Commission, and no longer the President, has the power to decide what information is to be made public.

(*C*) *Powers of Administration.*—Section 5 of the Act states that "unfair methods of competition in commerce are hereby declared unlawful." The Commission is directed to prevent persons, partnerships, or corporations (except banks and common carriers, who are subject to the Federal Reserve Board and the Interstate Commerce Commission) from employing such methods. In the previous chapter were described a number of unfair methods of competition employed by the trusts. The chief administrative duty of the Federal Trade Commission is the discovery and elimination of these unfair practices.

The new Act of 1914 proscribed the following unfair practices: (1) price discriminations; (2) exclusive dealers' agreements; (3) obvious imitations of brands, which were not protected by patents or copyrights; and (4) espionage on competitors. Unfair methods of competition had been made illegal by the Sherman Act of 1890, but the Federal Trade Commission Act of 1914 was more specific in its definition of them. Moreover, it created an administrative body of economists to cooperate with the legal department under the Attorney General. Regulation was to supplement and even to supplant prosecution.

The administrative procedure of the Federal Trade Commission is somewhat as follows: The injured party may appeal to the Commission for relief, or that body may act on its own initiative. The Commission states its charge and serves notice upon the offending party, which has the right to appear at the proper time and give reasons why the Commission should not issue a restraining order against it. If the Commission finds the practice to be unfair, it puts the facts in writing and issues an order to the corporation to desist. If the order is not obeyed, the Commission may apply to the Circuit Court of the United States for its enforcement. The court shall then have the power to make an order affirming, modifying, or setting aside the order of the Federal Trade Commission. The findings of the Commission as to the facts, if supported by testimony, are conclusive.

11. The Clayton Act.—The Clayton Act was introduced into the House of Representatives on April 14, 1914. Several other bills, such as the Interlocking Directorates Bill, were later amalgamated with it. Unlike the Trade Commission Act, the Clayton Act became an omnibus measure. After a tortuous career in both houses it was finally passed by Congress and signed by President Wilson on Oct. 15, 1914. The Trade Commission Act provided new governmental machinery; the Clayton Act, on the other hand, formulated new general policies. The purpose of the Clayton Act was to prevent the development or consummation of trusts, rather than the regulation or dissolution of existing trusts. The law may be divided into three parts: (1) a set of positive prohibitions against unfair practices, (2) legal remedies for them, and (3) labor provisions.

Among the practices regulated by the Clayton Act are local price discriminations, tying agreements, holding companies and interlocking directorates.

Section 2 of the act declares that it shall be unlawful for any person engaged in commerce to discriminate in price between different purchasers of commodities, where the effect of such discrimination may be a substantial lessening of competition or a tendency to create a monopoly in any line of commerce. Discrimination based upon differences in grade, quality, or quantity of the commodity is exempt from such provisions. There is a penalty attached for discriminations, and the enforcement of this provision is placed in the hands of the Federal Trade Commission. A loophole is left in the law by the proviso that a discrimination "made in good faith to meet competition" is not to be construed as a violation of the law.

Section 3 makes tying agreements unlawful. These include sales based upon the condition that the purchaser will refrain from buying the products of competitors. It is designed to prevent exclusive contracts, the effects of which may be to "substantially lessen competition or tend to create a monopoly."

Section 7 of the act provides "That no corporation engaged in commerce shall acquire, directly or indirectly, the whole or any part of the stock or any other share capital of another corporation engaged also in commerce, where the effect of such acquisition may be to substantially lessen competition." However, the act is not retroactive and provides that nothing in the law shall be held to "affect or impair any right hereto legally acquired." Special provision was made for the railroads in this matter of holding companies.

Section 8 of the law provided that after two years no person should be at the same time a director in two or more corporations engaged in commerce, other than banks and common carriers, any one of which has a capital, surplus, and undivided profits exceeding one million dollars, if such corporations are or have been heretofore competitors.[1] Although interlocking directorates are prohibited, the law does not prevent an individual or a group of individuals from owning stock in several "competing" companies. It was this community of ownership which made possible the continuance of monopoly after its legal dissolution had taken place. It has been argued that the Clayton Act may be circumvented by the employment of dummy directors.

The Clayton Act contained legal remedies for the unfair practices previously described. It did not contain any penalties, however, and the enforcement of its provisions was placed in the hands of the Federal Trade Commission and the Interstate Commerce Commission. This brought the bill into harmony with the Trade Commission Act, which gave that body authority over unfair practices. Its administrative procedure has just been described. The Clayton Act also repeated what was contained in the Sherman Act, namely, that any individual who was injured in his business by any practice forbidden in the anti-trust laws could bring suit in any district court of the United States and recover three-fold damages and the costs of the suit. The Clayton Act amended the Sherman Act in that it placed the injured competitor in a stronger legal position and made it easier for him to prosecute his suit. It was no longer necessary for a litigant to sue a combination in the Federal district in which it had been incorporated. The former necessity of long-distance litigation explains why so few private suits were brought under the Sherman Act. Again, the plaintiff was formerly forced to bear the entire financial burden of his suit, although the government in another suit had proven that the combination was illegal. On the other hand, the Clayton Act provides that the proceedings of a court decision establishing a violation of the trust laws shall be *prima facie* evidence, and it may be used by a private suitor against the same concern. Again, the plaintiff is able to use the injunction, which formerly could be used only

[1] A special provision was also inserted to lessen financial concentration. No individual might be an officer or director in more than one large bank, unless the banks were non-competing.

if the prosecutor were the Federal government. A private person now had the right to "sue for and have injunctive relief . . . against threatened loss or damage by violation of the anti-trust laws."[1]

The Clayton Act further provided that where a corporation violated any of the penal provisions of the anti-trust laws, such a violation should be regarded as the act of the individual officers, directors, or agents of the corporation who have authorized such illegal acts. The corporation is a legal entity, and many individuals had been shifting responsibility for their acts to this intangible person, which might be fined or dissolved, but which could not be sent to jail. The Clayton Act attempted to affirm the direct liability of the officers and directors of a corporation for its unfair practices.

The third purpose of the Clayton Act was to legalize the boycott and to limit the use of the injunction in labor disputes. It forms a part of labor legislation rather than trust legislation and will be treated as such.

12. Results of Trust Legislation.—The Clayton Act attempted to remedy some of the defects of the Sherman Act and to define more specifically unfair practices. The Federal Trade Commission Act created a new body for the regulation of the trusts, similar to the Interstate Commerce Commission for the regulation of the railroads and the Federal Reserve Board for the regulation of our national banking system. The Federal Trade Commission was created to regulate corporations engaged in interstate commerce, other than common carriers and banking institutions. The law provided new governmental machinery to supplement the work of Congress and the Courts. The trust legislation of 1914 marked the change from legislative and judicial control to administrative control. It permitted more individualized treatment, and at the same time attempted to remove the trust problem from politics. It succeeded in relieving the courts of a mass of litigation and attempted to expedite judicial action. It brought into existence a corps of administrative officials who were economic experts rather than legal authorities. It exemplified a recent tendency of governments to utilize the trained specialist. The trust legislation of 1914 did not attempt to enforce

[1] An injunction is a court order compelling a party to perform or to refrain from performing some specific act. Failure to comply implies a contempt of court.

competition where combination seemed beneficial. It permitted combination, so long as it did not proceed by unfair methods or result in extortion. Again, it was preventive, rather than punitive. It represented reasonable regulation rather than blind dissolution. The acts of 1914 sought to crystallize into law the change of attitude toward the trusts which has been previously described.

13. Webb-Pomerene Act.—During the early part of the twentieth century it was predicted that American trusts would capture the markets of the world. Not many years later the opposite view was expressed because of the vigorous governmental action against our great industrial combinations. American manufacturers had to meet the keen rivalry of powerful foreign combinations which were sometimes international in scope and often aided by their respective governments. Germany, for illustration, had effectively organized her shipping and banking facilities for the sale of her manufactures in foreign ports. Kartels, or common selling associations with powers to regulate prices and pool profits, were permitted. Powerful American corporations, such as the United States Steel, the Standard Oil, and the International Harvester were strong enough for foreign competition, but our smaller concerns, especially in competitive industries, were at a disadvantage.

A report of the Merchants Association of New York, in 1916, advocated the formation of single selling associations for all American export firms in particular industries. In the same year, the Federal Trade Commission issued an important report on "Cooperation in American Export Trade," in which it favored the withdrawal of the prohibition of combinations so far as export trade was concerned. On the recommendation of President Wilson, Congress embodied this suggestion in the Webb-Pomerene Act of 1918.

Section 2 of the Webb-Pomerene Act provides that nothing in the Sherman Act of 1890

. . . shall be construed as declaring to be illegal an association entered into for the sole purpose of engaging in export trade and actually engaged solely in such export trade, or an agreement made or act done in the course of export trade by such association, provided such association, agreement, or act is not in restraint of trade within the United States, and is not in restraint of trade of any domestic competitor or such association. And provided further, that such association does not, either in the United States or elsewhere, enter into any agreement, understanding, or conspiracy, or do any act which artificially or intentionally enhances or depresses prices within the United States of commodities of the class exported by such associations, or which substantially lessens competition within the United States, or otherwise restrains trade therein.

Under the Webb-Pomerene Act, the associations that may be formed through the combination of American exporters must file their annual reports with the Federal Trade Commission. Within a few years after the passage of the Act, a number of such associations had been formed. They now represent a membership of thousands of plants throughout the United States.

The Webb-Pomerene Act recognizes the advantages of large-scale management and expressly permits combinations in foreign trade, although at the same time it forbids them in interstate commerce. Its purpose is to permit a number of small companies, not having a sufficiently large capital or volume of business to justify the carrying on of export trade, single handed, to cooperate for this purpose in an export association. They distribute the overhead charges of such an association over their combined foreign sales and thus bring down costs. Other advantages are the securing of better credit information, the better financing of foreign business, the ability to give longer credits, which are essential in some export trades, the greater ease with which initial losses can be carried, a larger assortment of goods, and a helpful exchange of ideas among the members of the association.

One of the chief objections to the Webb-Pomerene Act is that these export associations may be used for restricting competition in the home market. In spite of the prohibitions in the law, the advantages of harmonious action in foreign trade cannot help but be carried over into the domestic market. A second possibility is that the Webb-Pomerene Act will promote international combinations. Even prior to its enactment there were international combinations in steel rails, gunpowder, thread, and other products. At the present time an international organization is taking place in the French and German steel industry. A third result of the Webb-Pomerene Act may be a further extension of foreign combinations. Monopoly, like the protective tariff, is a game at which two can play. Finally, there is the danger that the pursuit of trade by such methods may lead to strained international relations which may upset the peace of the world. The House Committee on the Judiciary, in advocating the passage of the Webb Act, stated that because of the methods adopted by other leading countries, foreign trade has become "largely a matter of competition between nations."

14. Proposal of Federal Incorporation.—In spite of the future possibility of international monopolies, the problem of the American trusts is still regarded as a national one. Indeed, it cannot be said to have passed completely from the stage of state regulation to that of national regulation. We have seen the constitutional limitations upon the Federal regulation of the trusts, due to the fact that the national government merely possesses the power to regulate interstate commerce. Individual states not only issue charters of incorporation, but also regulate corporations doing business within their borders. In this chapter the development of Federal regulation of the trusts has been traced. In conclusion, two remedial possibilities must also be pointed out, namely, Federal incorporation of large business concerns and Federal authority to fix prices.

It has been suggested that all corporations hereafter organized be required to secure Federal charters if they desire to engage in interstate commerce. In the case of existing corporations Federal licenses might be required. We have seen that many evils of the trusts are those of the corporate form of business organization rather than of monopoly. At the present time the corporation laws of many states are not only very lax, but also widely divergent. Moreover, a corporation chartered in one state can do business in all others. Federal incorporation and Federal licensing would be a step toward uniformly better corporation finance. General standards could be enforced as to periodic reports, uniform accounting systems, and the relation between nominal and real capital and between ownership and control. Such a procedure would simplify very much the work of the Federal Trade Commission and make it far more effective. It would represent preventive rather than curative treatment. Trust evils, such as overcapitalization and financial manipulation, have often been attacked too late. State legislatures have made a chaos of corporation laws and regulations. If big business has become national in its scope, is not complete national regulation imperative?

At the present time, Congress can pass a law compelling the Federal incorporation and licensing only of those corporations which are subject to Federal regulation, that is, which are engaged in interstate commerce. A constitutional amendment is not necessary to make possible the Federal incorporation and licensing of companies engaged in interstate commerce. This could be done simply by an act of Congress, but such a measure would not be drastic enough. There would still be the confusion between corporations engaged in interstate commerce and intrastate commerce. Simplicity, uniformity, and effective regulation can be secured only by the Federal incorporation and licensing of all large corporations. Such a measure would require an amendment to the Constitution, which at the present time does not give Congress power over intrastate commerce. Such a Constitutional amendment or Congressional act would be bitterly opposed, not only by those selfish interests which flourish in a condition of administrative confusion, but also by those sincere students of the problem who are strongly attached to the Federal type of government, which rests on the existence and preservation of state rights.

15. Control over Prices—A Final Resort.—Most evils of the trusts arise from unfair methods of competition and the power of monopolies to fix prices. In the past, governmental regulation has been directed chiefly toward the elimination of unfair methods of competition. Monopoly has been attacked in the pious hope that competition might be restored. However, the dissolution of the trusts is always difficult and often undesirable. The gains of combination are so great in certain industrial organizations that monopoly seems reasonable and expedient. If such is the case, a sound public policy must decree that the advantages of monopoly be shared by all consumers and not privately appropriated by the trusts. We are forced to the conclusion that if the state permits private industrial monopolies to exist, it must reserve the power to regulate the prices of their products. When the monopoly character of the railroads became apparent, the Interstate Commerce Commission acquired the power to fix railroad rates. State public service commissions have a similar power over other public utilities to make valuations, to study costs of production, and to determine "fair rates." It seems that the effective regulation of industrial monopoly presents a somewhat similar problem. Should not the Federal Trade

Commission have the same power to prescribe prices for the products of industrial monopolies as the Interstate Commerce Commission has to prescribe railroad rates? It is understood that this price-fixing power should be utilized only after a verdict as to the existence and the desirability of a given industrial monopoly.

It would seem that there are two courses open to the Federal Trade Commission in its regulation of trusts. The first possibility is the elimination of any unfair methods of competition and the restoration of a competitive price. If the dissolution of a given monopoly is either impossible or undesirable, the only alternative is a frank recognition of this monopoly. A Federal administrative body should then possess the power to determine the prices of the monopoly's products. This policy need not necessarily be followed in the case of all industries. Moreover, this price-fixing power should be regarded only as a final resort, as "the gun behind the door."

At present the Federal Trade Commission is without this power to prescribe prices and is attacking the problem of monopoly unarmed and barehanded. It regulates the trusts along the old lines of attempting to eliminate unfair practices. In the future we may hear less of the dissolution of monopolies and the destruction of unfair methods of competition, and more of this price-fixing power. At the present time, there seems to be a strong public opinion against governmental price fixing. We had numerous experiments of this sort during the late war, many of which were of doubtful success. Price fixing in the case of industrial monopolies, however, is a different problem from price fixing in the case of wheat, which is produced by small farmers. In conclusion, we may say that the problem is not "Shall we fix prices?" but rather, "Who shall fix the prices?" The choice lies often between a private monopoly and a governmental commission.

16. Summary.—The trust presents a difficult problem in the social control of industry. Public policy may pursue any one of four different courses. In the first place, there is a possibility of *laissez-faire* or hands off. Such a negative policy of inaction is quite unthinkable today. At the other extreme, there is the possibility of governmental ownership of monopolized industries. This is receiving thoughtful consideration in the case of public utilities, but it would probably be stigmatized as socialistic in the case of industrial monopolies. A third possibility is dissolution, and Federal action first took this form after the passage of the Sherman Act of 1890. The enforcement of this piece of legislation has made us dubious about both the possibility and the desirability of the dissolution of many trusts. The fourth alternative is regulation, and we may safely say that trust legislation has passed from the former attitude of favoring dissolution to the new attitude of favoring regulation. From "regulation by the axe" we have passed to "regulation in the light of reason and expediency." Administrative machinery for the regulation of the trusts has been provided in the Federal Trade Commission, which succeeded the former Bureau of Corporations. It now possesses the powers of investigation, prosecution, and publicity, but not the right to fix prices.

The government is today the silent partner in all big business. It seeks to protect the interests of the consumer, the producer, and the investor. It was formerly held that the best government was that which interfered least with the economic order. Competition was then regarded as prevalent and as tending to keep prices down to a cost of production level. The development of the modern trust, however, has made such an assumption a mere fiction in many cases. Numerous industries have gone from small-scale production to large-scale production, and from large-scale production to large-scale management. Monopoly has been the final step. In some cases this evolution of concentrated control has passed from the stage of national monopoly to that of international monopoly. Nevertheless, governmental control in the United States is still divided between the state and the national government. Big business has been economically, but not legally, nationalized.

Collateral Reading

FETTER, F., "Modern Economic Problems," chap. 31.
HAMILTON, W., "Current Economic Problems," pp. 459–478.
MARSHALL, L. C., "Readings in Industrial Society," pp. 765–781.
————, WRIGHT C. W., and FIELD, J. A., "Materials for the Study of Elementary Economics," pp. 323–340.
SEAGER, H. R., "Principles of Economics," chap. 25.
WILLIAMSON, T. R., "Readings in Economics," chap. 18.
YOUNG, J. T., "The American Government and Its Work," chaps. 7 and 8.

References

See those of preceding chapter.

Questions for Discussion

1. Why was state regulation of the trusts ineffective?

2. By what constitutional authority can the Federal government legislate upon the trust problem?

3. Outline the leading provisions of the Sherman Act.

4. Show how it was modified by judicial interpretation.

5. Has our policy of "trust busting" been successful? Why or why not?

6. Show how our attitude toward the regulation of the trusts has passed through a process of evolution.

7. Explain the organization, purpose, and powers of the Federal Trade Commission.

8. How did the Clayton Act affect the trusts?

9. What was the purpose of the Webb-Pomerene Act?

10. Do you favor Federal incorporation? Why or why not?

11. Should the Federal Trade Commission be given the power to fix prices? Why or why not? If so, how and to what extent?

Topics for Investigation

1. The strength and weakness of the Sherman Act.

2. Dissolutions under the Sherman Act.

3. The success of the Clayton Act as a piece of trust legislation.

4. The operation and success of the Webb-Pomerene Act.

5. Past experience in price fixing by Federal commissions or legislation with the exception of the railroad industry.

CHAPTER VIII

LEGAL MONOPOLIES AND PUBLIC UTILITIES

1. Legal Monopolies.—Legal monopolies are creations of law and originate either from some exclusive governmental grant to private parties or by an assumption of some industrial function by the government itself. Legal monopolies may be classified as public or private. Patents and copyrights, as well as exclusive franchises, illustrate private legal monopolies. Public legal monopolies represent the governmental ownership and operation of certain industries. Public ownership may be Federal, state, or local.

Public legal monopolies have been established for different reasons in various places and times. The tobacco industry in France and the salt industry in Saxony are governmental monopolies, established because of the lucrative revenue which they yield. Moral considerations led to the establishment of the Gothenburg system in Scandinavia, which made the sale of distilled liquors a governmental monopoly. It was hoped that the elimination of private profits would remove the incentive to an increased consumption of strong drink. In Germany, the government made a public monopoly of the railroads and telegraph lines. Although in this case there were a number of motives, the dominating one was that of national security. During the World War troops were transported with remarkable facility between the eastern and the western fronts. In the United States, the classic illustration of a public legal monopoly is the post office. The aims here seem to be not only increased efficiency, but also the sense of nationalism which is engendered by the government mails. Local public monopolies are illustrated by municipal waterworks, gas plants, and transportation systems. The governmental ownership of certain public utilities is justified by the impossibility of competition in these industries and by the essential nature of their services.

2. Patents and Copyrights.—Patents and copyrights are justified today on the broad grounds of social expediency and not as sources of private gain. The argument is that they are necessary incentives to the inventive genius of individuals and that they make for the economic progress of the entire group. Although the fathers of the nation had a background in English experience with arbitrary monopolies, the Constitution gave to Congress the power to "promote the progress of science and useful arts by securing, for limited times, to authors and inventors, exclusive rights to their respective writings and discoveries."[1] The granting of patents is a power of the Federal government, and the Patent Office is a bureau of the Department of the Interior. A patent gives to the inventor of a machine or a new process the exclusive right to the use of his invention for seventeen years. Copyrights on books and works of art are granted for twenty-eight years, and they may be renewed for fourteen years longer.

Patents have been a considerable source of monopoly profits in the United States. It has been charged, moreover, that instead of stimulating progress, they have often retarded it. Patents may be bought lest business competitors obtain them. The purchasers may then "pigeonhole" them indefinitely, because of the immediate expense of installing the new machinery necessary to develop them. It is also true that the individual who makes the invention is not always the one who profits most financially by the patent. It has been proposed to reduce the time on patents from seventeen to ten years, and to permit renewals for five or ten years, if the public interest seems to warrant it. Such is the policy of Great Britain.

3. Natural Monopolies of Organization.—Natural monopolies of organization are industries in which competition is self-destructive. This may be due either to the physical impossibility of competition or to the operation of the principle of decreasing costs. It would be physically impossible to run several competing lines of street cars on several sets of track on the same street. However, it is possible to have several independent traction companies operating in different sections of the city. Most metropolitan traction companies have originated by the consolidation of numerous small and independent lines. Public convenience and transportation efficiency demanded a unified system. It is physically possible, but highly undesirable, for several competing gas companies to lay different sets

[1] Article I, sec. 8, par. 8.

of pipes and conduits under the same street. Such a procedure would not only be uneconomic and wasteful, but it would also become an intolerable public nuisance, as each company in turn dug up the public highways. Hence, the supplying of gas and water, as well as transportation service, is a natural monopoly. The telephone and the telegraph industries are similarly natural monopolies of organization. It has been contended that the telephone industry is not one of decreasing costs. Perhaps it is more correct to say that it is not continuously one of decreasing costs. Nevertheless, whether increasing or decreasing costs prevail, the telephone and the telegraph industries are natural monopolies of organization. An enormous duplication of equipment would be necessary under competition. Moreover, each business man would be forced to subscribe to two or more telephone services in order to reach all other subscribers.

An industry of decreasing costs is one in which there has been a considerable investment of capital. The interest payments on the capital investment necessitate heavy fixed charges, irrespective of the volume of business done. Other fixed charges are the maintenance of equipment, taxes, and insurance charges. Operating expenses vary with the volume of the business, but fixed charges do not. Operating expenses are relatively constant per unit of product, but fixed expenses are not. In an industry in which there is a considerable investment of capital and heavy fixed charges, it is desirable to increase the volume of business up to a certain point of maximum capacity, in order to spread the fixed charges over a greater area of production. In this way the costs per unit of product will decrease. Hence, we call such an industry one of decreasing costs. In industries where fixed charges are relatively great, because of the large capital investment necessary, competition is ruinous. Such industries are natural monopolies of organization.

The railroad is a typical industry of decreasing costs. The interest on the capital investment, as well as the proper upkeep of bridges, tunnels, and miles of track, is a fixed charge. The greater the amount of traffic, the greater the number of units among which to divide these heavy fixed charges. When an individual purchases a railroad ticket, he not only pays for his own transportation, but he also makes some contribution to the expenses of building and maintaining the road. Like other public utilities, the railroad illustrates how the principle of decreasing costs makes it a natural monopoly. The wastes of duplicating equipment by competitive lines are apparent.

4. Ruinous Effects of Competition among Natural Monopolies. Public opinion has been slow to recognize the fact that most public utilities are natural monopolies. Competition has been invited, and in some cases insisted on, when its effects were bound to be disastrous. The desire for more business, in order to benefit by the principle of decreasing costs, made for a generation of severe competition among the railroads. Rate wars led to the cutting of rates almost to bare operating expenses and to a neglect of "overhead" which in some cases "carried them under." This was intensified by the excessive amount of railroad building which followed the Civil War. The weaker roads succumbed and were usually taken over by the stronger. The consolidated company found itself saddled with lines which were not planned as a system and which presented the wastes of duplication. In order to meet operating expenses and make a fair allowance for "overhead," the new system was forced to raise its rates. It was not until the World War that the monopoly nature of the railroad was recognized.

The story of the railroads can be paralleled by the history of local public utilities, such as street-car lines, and gas and electric plants. Competition was regarded as the life of trade. Public spirited councilmen demonstrated their freedom from the political control of corporations by issuing franchises to competing public service corporations. Competition was severe, and rate wars followed which delighted the hearts of the consuming public. Such a condition, however, did not long endure. Either one company failed and was absorbed by the other, or the competing companies came to some sort of agreement. In both cases rates went up, and the second state of the community was worse than the first. A duplication of equipment, necessitating higher rates in order to earn a fair return on the capital investment, could have been avoided if the monopoly character of public utilities had been foreseen. Today, legislatures and councils are hesitant about issuing franchises to new gas, electric and street-car companies, when others are already in existence.

5. Characteristics of Public Utilities.—Public utilities are generally natural monopolies of organization which produce commodities or services that are essential. Substitution on the part of the consumers is as difficult as competition on the part of other producers.   Every one must have water, light, heat, and transportation service.   There is a great dependence of the public on public utilities, because of the essential nature of their products, as well as because of their monopoly character.   Their products or services must be had at any price, and competition cannot be relied upon to fix a just price, in the sense of a cost of production price.

Public utilities are closely related to the problems of community health and safety.   An impure water supply jeopardizes the public health and an insufficient water pressure may be costly in case of fire.   Cheap water rates are regarded as so essential to cleanliness and health that many municipalities have hesitated to make the use of water meters compulsory in private homes. This element of public health in the problem is so important in the case of the water supply that most American cities have municipally owned and operated waterworks.   It exists to a less degree in other public utilities.   City planning is dependent on improved transportation facilities.   Congestion and bad housing are lessened by cheap and rapid transportation.   Certain British cities have developed workingmen's suburbs through municipally owned tramways.

Another feature of public utilities is the uniformity of their product or service.   Competition seems desirable where there is a great range of choice open to the consumer.   Differences of quality may be found in the pastries of various bake shops and in the services of different barbers.   Public service companies, however, do not put out a variety of products, but only one fairly uniform product, such as pure water or gas of a given quality.

Furthermore, public utilities are peculiar because of their legal, as well as their economic and social nature.   Thus, railroads are quasi-public industries, not only for the foregoing reasons, but also because of their power of eminent domain.   Local public service companies frequently enjoy the same power to condemn private property for their own use.   Finally, public service companies require a special legal grant which is known as a franchise. This is a recognition of their exceptional economic position.

6. Importance of Franchises.—A charter of incorporation is the legal right to existence which every business corporation must possess.   A franchise is the right to do business which is quasi-public in character and which involves the interests of all citizens. The problem of the franchise is more serious in the United States than in Europe, where franchises are more easily revoked. Across the Atlantic, a franchise is merely a license or privilege revokable at the discretion of the franchise-granting body. The English Parliament makes and repeals laws without any problem of their constitutionality, because no written constitution exists. Under our political system there are a number of constitutional provisions which prevent public authorities from revoking franchises which have once been granted. The Federal Constitution forbids any state to impair the obligation of contracts or to deprive any person of life, liberty, or property without due process of law. The property right has been held to include freedom of contract.

Franchises once granted are contracts between the municipality and the corporation. An attempt on the part of the municipality to change the provisions of such a franchise might be interpreted as an unconstitutional attempt to impair the existing contract. American municipalities and states have given away valuable privileges belonging to the entire community. Franchises have been written for ninety-nine years and nine hundred and ninety-nine years. Conditions have changed, but succeeding generations have been hampered by franchises granted years before by "responsible" bodies. This dead hand of the past has its hold on many modern municipalities.

Most states now have inserted provisions in their constitutions which give to state legislatures the power to amend and repeal all charters granted to private corporations. Such power has been upheld by the courts with regard to public service corporations. The Supreme Court of the United States said:

When one devotes his property to a use in which the public has an interest, he in effect grants to the public an interest in that use, and must submit to be controlled by the public for the common good to the extent of the interest that he has thus created.[1]

Such regulations, however, must be reasonable, and the regulation of charges cannot be carried so far that the practical result is confiscation of the property of the corporation. Moreover, when the franchise specifically states the right of the corporation to charge a certain rate, in return for which privilege the corporation pays a stated fee or agrees to perform certain services, such as the repairing of streets, a contractual relationship arises

[1] *Munn vs. Illinois*, 94 U. S. 113.

between the company and the public authority granting the franchise. As such it cannot be impaired by future legislation.

7. Capitalization of Exclusive Franchises.—Huge monopoly profits, concealed by overcapitalization, have been common among public utilities. The reorganizations of railroads and other public service companies have often been occasions for stock watering. The object has been to conceal high profits which were the actual or anticipated result of monopolistic control. The promoters "milked" the enterprise at the expense of both subsequent investors, and the general public. The value of a stock depends primarily on its earning power, rather than on the tangible assets which its securities represent. Numerous monopolies are not making excessive profits, if one accepts the paper value of their securities. Nevertheless, their rate of return on invested capital may be excessive. On the other hand, an attempt to squeeze out the water and to make the value of the securities correspond to the physical value of the wealth which they represent would be an injustice to the "innocent investors" who bought the stock after the "promotion" had taken place.

The preferred stock of some corporations represents the value of the tangible physical assets, and the common stock the water or capitalized monopoly profits. A sad commentary is the fact that the return on such common stock has sometimes been greater than that on the preferred stock. Great blocks of common stock often went to the promoters, who planned the consolidations, as rewards for their financial engineering. This stock generally passed through other hands, for it was subsequently bought and sold by conservative investors.

Numerous public utilities were capitalized at from two to three times the value of their actual capital. The discrepancy in accounting was avoided by placing a high value on patents or by the fiction of "good will." Public utilities sometimes secured exclusive and long-term franchises from state legislatures or municipal councils. They subsequently capitalized their free-gift franchises, and then justified their high prices as necessary to earn a "fair" rate of return on the "capital invested." The Philadelphia Union Traction Company, which was organized in 1895, and which acquired the control of all the street railroads in that city, obligated itself by the terms of its lease to pay rentals equivalent to 5 per cent interest on the capitalization of the original companies. This amounted to approximately one hundred and ten million dollars.[1] The figure of thirty-five million dollars has been taken as representative of the actual capital invested. The remaining seventy-five millions, on which 5 per cent interest was paid by the Union Traction Company, represented the capitalized value of the franchises which the underlying companies held. According to a report of the Civic Federation of Chicago, in 1901, on the street railways of that city, seventy-five million dollars, out of a total capitalization of one hundred and twenty million dollars, represented the value of the traction franchises, or the capitalized value of the Chicago street railroad monopoly.

8. Safeguarding Public Interests in Granting Franchises.—The granting of franchises to public service companies presents two aspects—the fiscal and the social. Both have been frequently ignored in the past. Franchises may be regarded as a lucrative source of public revenue. Cities can sometimes avoid raising their tax rates by a rigorous taxation of major highway privileges, which are enjoyed by public service companies. On the other hand, the social aspect may be considered as more important than the fiscal. It may be more desirable to guarantee to the community a cheap and satisfactory supply of some necessary commodity or service than to obtain increased revenue.

It is necessary to have some public service board with power to pass on the quality of the product and the rates charged the consumer by public utilities. Consequently, it is necessary to determine a fair rate of return and the value of the capital invested. Public service bodies have found these problems extremely difficult. One of the first tasks of any such regulatory body has generally been the valuation of all the physical assets of the public utilities. This information is essential before a profit and loss statement can be interpreted. To make an accurate valuation there must be free access to the books of all public service companies on the part of the legitimate investigator. A flexible policy of rate fixing by a public service commission is far more desirable than to prescribe in the franchise the exact charges to be made. Conditions change and the general price level rises and falls. A reasonable price at one time may be far from reasonable some years later. Full publicity, however, should be given to the accounts of public service corporations.

---

[1] According to Professor Spiers in "The Street Railway System of Philadelphia," p. 45.

Moreover, franchises should grant the community the option of taking over the industry at the expiration of the franchise period at a price based on a fair appraisal of its physical assets.

The duration of the franchise is a vexed question. It is certain, however, that the day of the perpetual franchise is doomed. The time limit varies with the industry and with the locality. It is hard to justify a franchise which extends over a generation, that is, for more than twenty-five or thirty years. Massachusetts devised a plan in which franchises were granted for indefinite periods, but revokable at any time. It is doubtful, however, whether investors would seek investment in industries in which they had no more protection than that given them by such a franchise. The best interests of the community are served by short-time franchises with periodic renewals. On the other hand, there seems to be no objection to the granting of exclusive franchises, if the industry is a natural monopoly. Such an exclusive franchise, however, should not be capitalized nor should the public be forced to pay a high return on a privilege which they have freely given a corporation. Overcapitalization by stock dividends has been common in the past history of public utilities. Modern public service commissions are not very favorable toward the issuance of stock dividends, and in some cases they are forbidden by the terms of the franchise.

9. Development of Public Ownership.—Governmental ownership is not new, and public industries are as old as the pyramids of Egypt and the aqueducts of ancient Rome. Some public ownership has been necessary for the performance of the political functions of government. The coinage of money has usually been a public monopoly. The post office has recently assumed the function of carrying parcels as well as letters. Indeed, it has added some banking functions through the establishment of postal savings banks. The public ownership of parks is desirable as a means of promoting public health, and the public ownership of the water supply is but an extension of the same idea. Public markets are as old as the city states of Greece, and some governments are still in the business of collecting tolls with which to keep the highways in repair.

Public ownership is both a national and a community problem. Railroads illustrate the former and most other public utilities the latter. The individual states in the Union also possess problems of public ownership. States as well as the Federal government have acquired great holdings of forest land. The conservation movement has brought back the problem of public ownership of land, which loomed so large in the pioneer days of our country. Indeed, it was with the states that the first great movement in public ownership began in the period before the Civil War. Numerous states engaged extensively in turnpike building, in the construction of canals, and later in the building of railroads. In many cases the projects were economically impossible, and in other cases political interests wrecked them. This episode in American history belongs to the period of state banks and wildcat banking. In recent years the problem of public ownership has been more important in our national than in the state life. During the World War America experienced governmental operation of the railroads but not governmental ownership. Although the railroads were returned to private management, this may not be their final status. Again, great coal strikes have occurred so frequently that the nationalization of the coal mines frequently has been suggested.

It is in our municipalities, however, that the greatest development of public ownership is apt to occur. This has already taken place with the water supply, and the movement is well on its way with regard to gas. The importance of the gas industry, however, has been overshadowed by the recent development of electricity. In the early days of electricity there were numerous small municipally owned and operated power plants. It has been found more economical, however, to manufacture electricity on a large scale and to transport it for great distances. Moreover, the industrial uses of electricity have so increased that giant power companies have come into existence all over the country. Communities as well as industries have found it more economical to purchase their current from one of these great power companies than to manufacture it. The development of the electric power industry in this country has been under private initiative rather than under public control. What the future may produce is hard to prophesy. There may be the extensive substitution of hydro-electric power for coal as a source of power. The consolidation of existing electric plants and transmission lines into great unified systems is now taking place. The industry is one of decreasing costs and a natural monopoly. The development of hydroelectric power is so closely connected with the conservation movement that eventual public ownership is not unlikely. In

the meantime, it behooves the state to be extremely watchful of
the terms under which franchises are granted to electric power
plants. Many excellent hydroelectric sites are natural monopolies, which should be socially developed rather than privately
exploited. Their conservation requires state and national action.
It is not a local or community problem.

Municipal ownership and operation of street-car companies is
very common in Europe, but rare in the United States. It is
not uncommon in American cities, however, to find public ownership and private operation. This is especially true in the case of
high-speed lines, such as subways and elevated railroads. Thus,
the city of Philadelphia has built an elevated railroad and is now
building a subway. It has leased the new Frankford elevated
road to the Philadelphia Rapid Transit Company for operation
and proposes to do the same for the Broad Street Subway.
Municipal ownership with private operation was effected with the
Philadelphia Gas Works. For a number of years the gas works
were municipally owned and operated. The experiment was far
from successful, and in 1897 the gas works were leased to a private
company. It cannot be said, however, that municipal ownership
in the United States has had much of a trial. The greatest single
illustration of municipal ownership and operation is the waterworks. Here the dominating motive is not so much economy as
the securing of a pure and adequate water supply. In recent years
there has been a development in some seaport cities toward municipally owned wharves and piers. It has been advocated as a
method of relieving the congestion of shipping, rather than as a
conscious effort toward municipal ownership.

**10. Municipal Ownership in Europe Compared with That in the
United States.**—The story of the development of public ownership on the continent of Europe is vastly different from that in
the United States. In Europe, State ownership of railroads,
telegraph and telephone lines is the rule rather than the exception. The municipal aspect of governmental ownership and
operation is even more significant than the national. Before the
World War nearly every large town or city in Germany had municipal ownership of not only the water supply, but also of lighting
service, and means of communication and transportation.
Municipal slaughter houses and milk depots were not uncommon. The development of electric street railroads was largely
under public ownership and operation. Since the Revolution in

Germany and the triumph of the moderate Socialists, public ownership, whether national or municipal, has had a tremendous impetus. All over the world the war kindled ideals of the community and greater cooperation within the group. The revolution in Russia was accompanied by the public ownership and operation not merely of public utilities, but also of almost all industries. There has been a recent reaction in that nation, however. The new democracies of Europe have been favorably disposed toward programs of nationalization. Italy and other older countries of Europe have also displayed the same tendencies.

Public ownership in Great Britain has been as significant as in Germany. Before the War and the subsequent triumph of the Labor party the municipalization of public utilities had taken place upon a large scale.

In so far as experience may serve as a guide, the results accomplished in the cities of Great Britain demonstrate not only the possibility of offering efficient service, but the actual superiority of municipal over private management, especially in accomplishing those larger social purposes which constitute the highest functions of communal life. The contribution which the British cities have made to social and industrial progress is the brightest chapter in the history of modern city development. In lowering street railway fares, in fostering the extension of the gas service, in striving constantly to improve the water service, the British cities have given to the world a valuable lesson in the possibilities of organized action in improving social conditions. All the indictments against municipal ownership and operation in Great Britain must be quashed when tested by the services which these municipalities have performed in improving the city environment, in making city life more healthful, in removing many of the causes of disease and of reduced vitality, and in opening a new horizon of the possibilities of communal action in raising the plane of city life.

There is a widespread belief that the lessons of European experience in general, and British experience in particular, are of little or no value to our American cities. The tremendous social significance of the movement for the municipalization of public utilities is dismissed with the statement that the conditions in the United States are totally different from those in Europe. That there are important differences in social organization, in the attitude of the population toward government, and in the traditions of public service, no one will deny; but in spite of these differences the fact remains that the municipalities of Great Britain and of Germany have become positive factors in the betterment of social conditions. Sooner or later American municipalities must place themselves in the same vital relation to the life of the community.

In fact, the people have a right to demand that the street railway, the gas, the electric light, and the water services shall be so performed as to further the larger ends of social welfare.[1]

11. Advantages and Disadvantages of Public Ownership.—

The arguments concerning public ownership center about costs and service. It is contended by the advocates of public ownership that the elimination of private profits would reduce the cost of the commodity or service to the consumer. We have seen that public utilities, like industrial trusts, have often reaped huge monopoly profits. Public ownership would prevent this and reduce the cost to the consumer to operating expenses and to a minimum allowance for interest charges on the capital invested. The rate of interest on municipal or state bonds is low as compared with that on the securities of private corporations. These savings should reduce the cost to the consumer. On the other hand, it is contended that private ownership and operation of public utilities may be had without enormous monopoly profits. Under an effective system of regulation, costs can be ascertained and prices fixed accordingly. Today, public utilities have passed the experimental stage. The lure of great profits is no longer necessary to attract capital. The rate of interest on the bonded indebtedness of legitimate public service corporations is not greatly in excess of that on municipal bonds.

In addition to the arguments concerning costs and profits, there is the highly controversial argument that public ownership gives superior service. A private company would not ordinarily make extensions of tracks or mains unless it expected a reasonable profit in return. Again, the community spirit and public pride are enlisted in the interests of greater efficiency. The municipalization of public utilities has given many European cities superior service as well as lower rates. It would seem, however, that American experience has not been so favorable toward public ownership. It is contended that public service in this country is decidedly inferior to that of private management. The public receives from a publicly owned plant a grade of water and gas service which it would not tolerate from a company organized for private profit. Again, the general inefficiency of public operation may result in waste and extravagance, which will show themselves in increased operating expenses.

[1] *Cf.* Rowe, L. C., "Problems of City Government," pp. 272–273.

This factor may be more than sufficient to offset any financial savings due to lower interest charges. It may result in the consumers paying higher rates or receiving poorer service than in the case of private corporations. These arguments based upon cost and efficiency of service are closely connected.

A third argument concerning public ownership may be termed the political. It has been pointed out that public service corporations have had as corrupting an influence on municipal politics as the trusts have had on state and national politics. It is argued that public ownership would remove from our public life this sinister influence of the "state within the state." The corrupting influences of private corporations seeking public franchises would be eliminated. On the other hand, it is contended that public ownership would create a far graver political problem than it would eliminate. It would bring the "spoils system" into existence to a far greater degree. The Civil Service at present is a serious governmental problem, which public ownership would only increase. Viscount Bryce called the city the failure of American democracy. The professional politician or ward boss often owes his power to the political patronage at his disposal, that is, to the number of public jobs which he can distribute to those who "vote right." The municipalization or nationalization of public utilities would increase the number of political dependents. Moreover, it might bring serious labor problems to our governmental authorities. A new and critical situation was created some years ago when the policemen of Boston went on a strike. Would the workers in municipalized gas plants, water works, or street-car lines be permitted to strike, or would such a movement of governmental employees be regarded with similar popular disfavor?

The importance of the political aspect of public ownership in our national life is well illustrated by the railroads, which employ nearly two million persons. Their votes at election would form an important item in the calculations of any candidate for office. With the public ownership and operation of the railroads the national government could not escape responsibility for the adjudication of labor disputes. The French government was once confronted with the serious economic and political problem of a strike of its railroad employees. It met the embarrassing situation by employing the rather arbitrary device of ordering the workers into military service with specific instructions to run the trains. It was possible to do this in France because of the existence of universal military service.

Numerous other arguments are advanced for and against public ownership. It is alleged that better working conditions prevail under public ownership. Both sides put forward the claim of higher wages. It would seem, however, that many public service occupations, such as those of letter carriers and school teachers, have been notoriously underpaid. Public salary schedules often indicate relative political importance, rather than relative civic needs or differences in qualifications. It is also claimed that the extension of public ownership would attract a better type of citizen to the new profession of public service. At the present time, the great executives in America are to be found in business rather than in politics. The tone of political life is higher in Europe, where public service attracts a better type of man for certain administrative positions.

Public ownership would also eliminate the problem of overcapitalization and the issuance of stock against franchise privileges, which have been given away by public authorities. On the other hand, it is contended that private management is more progressive than public ownership and operation. The resultant gains of private management more than balance its costly evils. Again, the defenders of public ownership point out the impossibility of competition in public utilities and the essential nature of the commodity or service produced. From these two premises they reach the conclusion that only public ownership and operation will be able to secure that degree of control necessary for the safeguarding of public interests. Opponents of public ownership admit these two premises, but contend that public ownership is not a satisfactory solution. They believe that sufficient regulatory power over prices and quality of service should be given to public service commissions to permit the effective regulation of private companies.

Both sides constantly appeal to the "argument from experience" to prove their views, and much concrete evidence can be gathered both in favor of and against public ownership. On the whole, it would seem that European experience has been more favorable than American. The question of public ownership, however, cannot be settled as a general proposition for all communities, for all public utilities, and for all time. We may say that it is, like the tariff, a "local issue." If there is a strong community spirit, public ownership will probably succeed. If there is political apathy and a dearth of executive ability in public life, it will fail. The same community may have the successful public ownership of one public utility and not of another. Public ownership may be favored for the water supply of a city, but not for its transportation system. National ownership of the mines does not follow from national operation of the railroads, especially during a war-time emergency. The problem should be settled only for the present generation, for we live in a dynamic society. We should not be influenced by a desire to bring about governmental ownership in general nor by a desire to eliminate it.

Socialism means the collective ownership of all agencies of production, and it has been alleged that the public ownership of public utilities is but a step in that direction. Selfish interests have often used this effective "scarecrow" to drive off the timid friends of public ownership. To stigmatize a proposal with an unpopular name is much easier than to advance rational arguments against it. Public ownership should be debated with particular emphasis on the individual features of every issue. Local issues are often clouded by attempts to generalize concerning "an inevitable trend" either toward or against public ownership.

12. Summary.—Legal monopolies are of two kinds, public and private. Patents and copyrights are private legal monopolies, while the post office is a public legal monopoly. Natural monopolies of organization are those industries in which competition is impossible or self-destructive. Public utilities are natural monopolies which produce essential commodities or services. American experience has demonstrated the failure of competition in this field of our economic life. Legal monopolies are such by virtue of public ownership or by the granting of exclusive franchises to corporations. During the past century, important franchises have been granted rather promiscuously to public service corporations. Care must be exercised in the future to protect public interests. The difficulties of effective governmental regulation of public utilities have led to a demand for the governmental ownership and operation of natural monopolies of organization. The nationalization or municipalization of public utilities is now a vital problem. A compromise solution is that

of public ownership and private operation. This experiment
has been tried in a number of American cities.

Collateral Reading

FAIRCHILD, F. R., FURNISS, E. S., and BUCK, N. S., "Elementary
Economics," chap. 50.
SEAGER, H. R., "Principles of Economics," chap. 23.
TAUSSIG, F. W., "Principles of Economics," chap. 64.

References

BARKER, H., "Public Utility Rates."
BAUER, J., "Effective Regulation of Utilities."
COOKE, M. L., "Public Utility Regulation."
GRAYSON, T. J., "Public Utilities from the Utilities Viewpoint."
————, "Evolution of Blue Sky Legislation and the Effect on Public
Utilities."
HARTMAN, H. H., "Fair Value."
HAYES, H. U., "Public Utilities."
HOWE, F. C., "The City, the Hope of Democracy."
IGNATIUS, M. B., "Financing of Public Service Corporations."
KERN, R. R., "The Super City."
MEYER, H. R., "Municipal Ownership in Great Britain."
NASH, L. R., "The Economics of Public Utilities."
RAYMOND, W. G., "The Public and Its Utilities."
ROWE, L. S., "Problems of City Government."
THOMPSON, C. D., "Public Ownership."

Questions for Discussion

1. Differentiate between legal and industrial monopolies.
2. What are natural monopolies of organization? Why is competition
self-destructive?
3. What are some essential characteristics of public utilities?
4. What considerations should govern the issue of franchises and what
fundamental provisions should be embodied in them?
5. Make out a case for the municipal ownership of the gasworks in your
community.
6. Make out a case for the private ownership and operation of the
waterworks.
7. Do you regard the compromise of public ownership and private
operation as satisfactory? Why or why not?

Topics for Investigation

1. Proposed changes in patent and copyright law.
2. Municipal ownership of public utilities in Europe.
3. Capitalization of free-gift franchises in American economic life.
4. The movement for greater municipal efficiency.
5. Nationalization of the electric power industry—advantages and
disadvantages.

CHAPTER IX

THE RAILROADS AND OUR ECONOMIC LIFE

1. Invention of the Railroad.—The Industrial Revolution completely changed methods of transportation and communication, as well as methods of manufacturing. The application of steam power to the problems of land and water transportation enormously increased commerce and intensified geographical division of labor. At the opening of the nineteenth century, land travel was on foot, on horseback or by the stage coach. Travel on water was by the old-fashioned sailing vessel or the animal-drawn canal boat. During the early years of our national existence a great impetus was given to the construction of turnpikes and canals by the desire to settle the West. The building of toll roads began about 1790, and various turnpike companies were chartered by the individual states. The relatively modern invention of the automobile has revived an interest in road building, and travel has again sought out some of the almost forgotten highways of a century ago. Turnpike construction was paralleled by the building of artificial waterways. The early part of the nineteenth century was also the era of canals. The most conspicuous example was the Erie Canal, which was begun in 1817 and finished in 1825. The invention of the steam engine and its application to both land and water transportation soon brought to an end the fever of canal building and turnpike construction. The fact that progress travels in cycles is also demonstrated by the recently revived interest in our inland waterways.

The earliest railroads were merely improved and specialized roads. Crude tracks were laid on which horse-drawn cars could run. The Quincy tramway, built in Massachusetts in 1826, was used to transport building stone for the Bunker Hill Monument. The rails used on most of the early railroads consisted of wooden beams with straps of iron nailed to the upper surface. The really distinctive feature of the railroad was the substitution of mechanical for animal power. The first successful locomotive dates from 1829, when Stephenson, an Englishman, produced

185

the famous Rockett. On its trial test on the Liverpool and
Manchester Railroad the Rockett attained a speed of twenty-
nine miles an hour. The pioneer railroad of this country was
the Baltimore and Ohio, the first rail of which was laid on July
4, 1828 by Charles Carroll, who was then, the only surviving
signer of the Declaration of Independence.

2. Growth and Present Size.—In 1830, there were but twenty-
three miles of railroad in use in the United States. During the
next ten years the total mileage reached almost three thousand,
by 1850 over nine thousand, and by the time of the Civil War
about forty thousand miles. Most of the lines ran between the
eastern seaport towns. Railroad building made but slow headway in the South, and the greater portion of the West was an
uncharted wilderness. After the Civil War the construction of
railroads proceeded at an unprecedented rate. In 1869, the first
transcontinental road was completed, when the Union Pacific
Railroad and the Central Pacific Railroad met. The period from
1867 to 1873 witnessed the construction of 33,000 miles of railroads.

Unfortunately, many of these roads were built too far in
advance of the necessity for them. As insufficient returns were
earned on these enormous investments, their securities depreciated. This orgy of railroad building was in no small measure
responsible for the financial panic of 1873. Indeed, it was precipitated by the failure of the Jay Cooke banking house of
Philadelphia, which had underwritten a large issue of the bonds
of the Northern Pacific Company. By 1880, however, the
country had recovered and the building of railroads again
assumed enormous proportions. From 1880 to 1890 the railroad
mileage of the country increased from 93,000 to 163,000 miles.
This net increase of 70,000 miles in a single decade is unparal-
leled in the economic history of any country. It was done not
only by the investment of private capital, but also by generous
governmental aid. At the outbreak of the World War in 1914,
the United States possessed 252,000 miles of railroads, as compared with 218,000 miles for all the nations of Europe combined,
and as compared with 691,000 miles for the entire world. Thus,
more than one-third of the railroad mileage of the entire world
is in the United States. According to the Census of 1920, the total
railroad mileage in operation in the United States was 259,941
miles.

The present size of the industry can be illustrated in other ways than by a mere recital of railroad mileage. The par value of the capital stock and bonds of the railroads of this country on Dec. 31, 1918 amounted to over twenty billion dollars. During the period of governmental operation from December, 1918 to March, 1920, the yearly rental paid to railroad corporations by the government was $918,000,000. If we capitalize this sum at 6 per cent, we will get a valuation of over fifteen billion dollars.

In 1913 Congress passed a law authorizing the Interstate Commerce Commission to make a valuation of all the railroads of the country. This had not been completed at the time of the passage of the Transportation Act of 1920, which restored the roads to private ownership. For purposes of rate fixing at that time, however, the Commission placed a valuation of $18,000,-000,000 on the railroads, which was over a billion dollars less than the valuation which the companies had requested. Interesting comparisons can be made to show the magnitude of the railroad industry. The capital stock and surplus of the eight thousand national banks of the United States in 1919 amounted to slightly less than two billion dollars, which is one-tenth of the value of the railroads. The Census of Manufacturers in 1914 showed a total capital investment of but $22,500,000,000. The total wealth of the United States in 1912 was estimated by the United States Census Bureau to be $180,000,000,000 of which the railroads represented $16,000,000,000. This industry represented $8\frac{1}{2}$ per cent of the total wealth of the country. The number of employees of all the railroads is about two millions. In 1920, over a billion and a quarter passengers were carried an average journey of thirty-eight miles. During the same year almost two and a quarter billion tons of freight were carried an average distance of one hundred and eighty-one miles.

3. Public Aid in Railroad Construction.—The railroads of the United States have been built and managed largely on private initiative. Although several states built and operated a few miles of railroad in the early history of the industry, they soon disposed of them to private companies. The Federal government never engaged in the building of railroads except for military purposes during the Civil War. It does, however, operate a line across the Isthmus of Panama, and it is now undertaking the construction of a railway system in the Territory of Alaska.

Nevertheless, the Federal, state, and local governments of the United States have given very substantial aid to the private agencies which built the railroads of our country. The states began actively to aid in the building of railroads as early as 1837. The enthusiasm of state legislatures for canals and turnpikes was carried over into this new enterprise. It sometimes took the form of gifts, but more often of loans. States frequently purchased the issues of railroad stocks and bonds. Although the amount of state aid was not enormous, it was given with the same disregard for the fundamentals of finance which character- ized the era of state banking. The national government began to assist railroad construction later than did the states, but it contributed even more generously.

Although a few companies received large loans from the Federal treasury, most of the aid given by Congress consisted of grants of public land. At first, it gave the land to the individual states as trustees, who in turn passed it over to the railroad companies. The first direct grants to railroad corporations were made in 1862 to secure a road to the Pacific Coast. The grant to the Union Pacific Company was twelve million acres and that to the Central Pacific Company eight million acres. Thirty-three million acres, an area larger than the state of Pennsylvania, was offered to various corporations to induce them to build the first transcontinental railroad. The Atlantic and Pacific Company (now a part of the Atchison system) received in 1866 a grant of forty-two million acres. In 1864, the Northern Pacific obtained a much more valuable grant of about the same size. The total land grants to all railroads by the Federal government was almost equivalent in size to the state of Texas.

The companies which built the first Pacific lines were aided by a Federal loan, as well as a donation of public lands. An act of 1862 permitted the Union Pacific and the Central Pacific companies to sell United States thirty-year 6 per cent bonds to secure a part of the capital to be used in the building of their roads. For a time it seemed as if the government might not be able to collect this debt in full, and the experiment was hardly satisfactory. This lavish generosity of the Federal government can be explained only by the strong desire to settle our great West. Local aids to the railroads must also be mentioned. According to the Census of 1870 there were then outstanding $185,000,000 dollars of county and municipal bonds, which had been issued to aid railroad construction. The total investments of all governmental bodies in the stocks and bonds of various railway companies has been estimated at seven hundred million dollars.

4. Railroad Systems of the United States.—The railroad systems of the United States, like Topsy, have just grown. A far different result would have been achieved if their growth had been planned by some central agency a generation in advance. Instead, there has been a conspicuous lack of system and unity. There has been a duplication of effort and a failure to construct roads along lines of greatest industrial needs. Mismanagement and selfish manipulation have often occurred, and numerous railroads have been financial failures. Out of their consequent reorganizations a number of fairly well unified systems have gradually developed. They were often the results of the individual enterprise of great captains of industry.

When the Federal government assumed the operation of the railroads during the World War, it became responsible for the property of almost two thousand individual companies. Many of these corporations were subsidiaries of others, but according to the reports of the Interstate Commerce Commission there were eight hundred independent operating companies. These roads may be classified geographically and financially.

A territorial classification used frequently by the Interstate Commerce Commission is into three districts—the eastern, southern and western. These districts are roughly divided by the Mississippi, Ohio and Potomac rivers. A more complete classification divides the country into seven parts. The first group of railroads is that of New England, and it includes the New York, New Haven and Hartford Railroad and the Boston and Maine Railroad. The second district is west of New England, east of the great terminals of Chicago and St. Louis and north of the Ohio and Potomac rivers. The railroads of this section have the heaviest traffic of any single division and are sometimes referred to as the trunk lines. Illustrations are the Pennsylvania, the New York Central, and the Baltimore and Ohio railroads. In addition to these trunk lines there is a subdivision within this territory which is traversed by the so-called "anthracite" lines. The latter include the Philadelphia and Reading, the Lehigh Valley, and the Erie railroads. The roads going south from Washington as a center, such as the Atlantic

Coast Line, lead into the southern district which in turn is sub-divided by the Allegheny Mountains into two sections. To the west and north of Chicago and St. Louis lie the wheat states. Hence, the roads in this district are known as the "granger lines." Illustrations are the Chicago, Burlington and Quincy and the Rock Island. South and west of St. Louis lies the fifth district, which is occupied by what are still referred to as the Gould roads. Still further west are the transcontinental lines, which may be divided into two rather distinct divisions, the northern and the southern. The former includes the Great Northern, the Northern Pacific, and the Chicago, Milwaukee and St. Paul. The southern section includes the Union Pacific, the Atchison, Topeka and Santa Fé, the Southern Pacific, and the Western Pacific.

In addition to this geographical grouping of railroads, there is also a financial classification. Thus, we have the Gould, Vanderbilt, Morgan, Harriman, and Hill systems, which are named after the financiers who organized them. This classification is now of mere historical interest. It shows how certain great systems have developed out of the maze of numerous small lines. In New England, for illustration, the New York, New Haven and Hartford Railroad, under the direction of the Morgan interests, began the centralization of control over the transportation agencies in that district. It was in the South, however, that the Morgan interests were most successful. They gradually secured control of the Southern system, the Atlantic Coast Line and many other railroads. Important coastwise steamship lines were also brought under a central railroad control. By the end of the century the leading transportation interests of the South were unified. West of the Mississippi River, E. H. Harriman built up a combination of the Union Pacific and the Southern Pacific. The Northern Pacific, and Chicago, Burlington and Quincy, together with the Great Northern, came under the control of James J. Hill. The Gould interests also built up a railroad system, the most important parts of which were the Wabash, the Missouri Pacific, the Denver and Rio Grande, the Western Pacific, and the St. Louis, Iron Mountain and Southern.

5. The Railroads as a Quasi-public Industry.—The railroad is a public utility and a natural monopoly of organization. As we saw in the last chapter, such industries usually operate under the principle of decreasing costs. Additional business means a decreased cost per unit. After the track has been laid and other investments of capital have been made, it is very costly for a railroad not to do a capacity volume of business. This explains the great desire of the railroads for increased freights, which factor resulted in numerous rate wars, discriminations, and rebates. The futility of competition was shown by the gradual formation of traffic pools and rate agreements. The monopoly character of the railways was very slowly realized, and its legal recognition came still later. Furthermore, the service rendered by the railroads in the transportation of goods and passengers is essential. Modern communities are highly specialized and mutually interdependent. Such a situation is conditioned by an efficient transportation system. Otherwise, tremendous economic waste and loss of life would occur. If a complete strike of all transportation employees were to continue for any length of time, the economic, the social, and even the physical life of our people would be paralyzed.

The first railways were regarded as "rail" ways similar to highways. It was expected that each individual would run cars over them, just as he drove his own horse and carriage over the public highway. Technical difficulties soon eliminated this possibility, and a single corporation was granted the exclusive right to run on a given section. Nevertheless, the public has been protected by the legal concept of the railroad as a common carrier. It cannot refuse to carry the freight of any individual if he complies with all the necessary conditions of transportation. Hence, it is quasi-public in character. Moreover, as we have seen, the railroads grew up under a system of governmental aid. Finally, railroads possess the right of eminent domain. If a railroad corporation finds it necessary to cut through a given tract of land, it may apply for the condemnation of a portion of the private property of some individual. Although the owner may not desire to part with his land, he can be compelled to sell it, provided that a just compensation is paid.

Economic, social, and political reasons make the railroad a quasi-public industry. Legal considerations make it a public, rather than a private, corporation. The result is that the railroad is subject to very strict regulations of the government, which can prescribe not only the rates, but also the quality of service that must be maintained. In most foreign countries the railroad must obtain its charter from the central government, but in the United States each state has the power to incorporate railroad companies, just as it does any other business enterprise. Nevertheless, Federal control has been secured by the power of Congress to regulate interstate commerce. At first, this power was very sparingly used, but later it developed into effective control.

6. Stages in the Evolution of the Railroad Problem.—The gradual development of the railroad problem in the United States may be divided into five stages. The first period was that of governmental aid, rather than governmental control. Railroads were regarded as the carriers of prosperity, and their development was eagerly fostered. Although enormous state aid was rendered, little supervision was exercised over their management. The second stage, which may be dated rather arbitrarily from 1870 to 1887, was a period of suspicion and of state regulation. Public opinion discovered that the railroads might be agencies for evil as well as for good. The charges of extortionate rates, discrimination, and monopoly were voiced. Pooling and rate agreements were found to be common. The result was a fever of state regulation and state commissions. As nearly all the railroads of any importance were interstate agencies, such attempts at regulation merely proved the necessity for Federal regulation. With the passage of the Interstate Commerce Act of 1887, we pass from the stage of state regulation to that of national regulation. It may be said to stretch from 1887 to 1917, when the wartime expedient of Federal operation was tried.

The fourth stage in the evolution of the railroad problem in the United States is that of national operation. It dates from the President Wilson's war-time proclamation of Dec. 26, 1917 to March 1, 1920, when the roads were returned to their owners. The Transportation Act of 1920 inaugurates the fifth and present stage. It frankly recognizes the monopoly character of the railroads without accepting public ownership or operation. Effective regulation is sought through the Interstate Commerce Commission under a system of private ownership and operation.

At first, the railroad was regarded as a competitive industry and an effort was made to enforce competition. Railroads, however, are natural monopolies. The result of such regulation was a search for new devices for concentrated control. Pools and rate-fixing agreements were succeeded by holding companies and by a "community of interests" based on interlocking directorates and the common ownership of stock. The various devices for achieving concentration of control, which were described in the early chapters on monopoly, were successfully employed by the railroads. Effective powers of regulation were slowly acquired in the meantime by the Interstate Commerce Commission.

7. Transition from State to Federal Regulation.—Most of the early state and Federal legislation concerning the railroads was devoted to methods of aiding their development. During the seventies, however, the tide began to turn. The first charge brought against the railroads was that of excessive rates, but it was gradually modified into the charge of discriminatory rates. This change of attitude toward the railroad first appeared in the agricultural section of the Middle West. It found its earliest expression in state rather than Federal legislation. The Granger Movement was then at its height, and western farmers were seeking relief from an overexpansion of agriculture. It was a period of falling prices and general business depression. Cheap money and other economic panaceas were eagerly sought by political leaders and their numerous followers.

The railroads, which had been so zealously fostered, were now viewed with suspicion. Western statesmen vaguely indicted these newly grown monsters as the cause of many of the farmers' troubles. Instead of aiding the marketing of agricultural crops, the railroads were charging prohibitive rates. Accordingly, various western states passed what has been termed the "Granger legislation" of the early seventies. These laws usually forbade discriminations in railroad rates and sometimes sought to prevent excessive charges by arbitrarily fixing maximum rates for various crops. The railroads contested this legislation in the courts on various constitutional grounds. It finally developed that the chief legal objection was the limited authority of state laws in the matter of transportation. The chief arteries of national commerce were interstate rather than intrastate, and the Constitution had vested in the Federal Congress power over interstate commerce. If it could be shown that the common carriers were engaged solely in transportation within state borders, they remained subject to their own state legislature and public service commission. Otherwise, they came under the jurisdiction of the Federal government, which possessed the power to regulate interstate commerce. This elementary principle of constitutional law was definitely affirmed in the Wabash Case of 1886.

If the regulation of interstate commerce was so clearly the power of the Federal government, it was accordingly its manifest duty to carry it out. Consequently, the Interstate Commerce Act of 1887 was passed the following year. The era of the Federal regulation of the railroads was thus inaugurated.

This division of authority between interstate and intrastate commerce, simple though it be as a general statement, has been difficult of practical administration. Conflict and confusion between the Federal and the state governments were common for a generation in transportation matters. Interstate and intrastate commerce frequently followed the same transportation routes and passed over the same railroads. Nevertheless, two different authorities were forced to pass on matters of interstate and intrastate commerce. Such a situation led to certain injustices as well as much confusion. Differences in rates existed between the same places. The conflict between interstate and intrastate rates finally culminated in the Shreveport Rate Case of 1914. The court decided that the lower intrastate rates were prejudicial to interstate commerce. It suggested that the discriminations be removed by observing on both classes of traffic the interstate rates set by the Interstate Commerce Commission. The final step in Federal control was taken in the Transportation Act of 1920. This law states specifically that where an intrastate rate discriminates against interstate commerce, the Interstate Commerce Commission shall prescribe a rate which shall be binding on both classes of traffic.

8. Rate Discriminations.—Before tracing the development of Federal regulation of the railroads it is necessary to discuss the problem of rate discrimination, some knowledge of which is essential to an understanding of many pieces of railroad legislation. Aside from differences between interstate and intrastate rates, railroad discriminations may be of three general types: discriminations as to commodities, discriminations as to localities, and discriminations as to individuals.

Discriminations among commodities are represented by serious differences in freight rates for the transportation of various commodities under similar conditions. A good illustration of discriminations among commodities may be found in the former freight rates on wheat and flour. A large portion of the wheat of the Northwest was manufactured into flour in the mills of Minneapolis and Duluth. At one time, however, the freight rate on wheat was considerably lower than that on flour, in spite of the fact that a slight difference in the freight rates of these two commodities was sufficient to make it profitable to ship wheat rather than flour. Hence, western millers contended that their business was being deliberately ruined in favor of the flour mills of the East. In any case, it can easily be seen that freight rates influence the location of industries and that they can accomplish the life or death of existing industries. Moreover, the determination of freight rates is a very difficult matter. There must be some differences—not necessarily discriminations—between the rates charged for different commodities. The more valuable the commodity in proportion to its weight and bulk, the higher has been its freight rate. This rather common commodity discrimination of the railroads has been described by the rather misleading expression of "charging what the traffic will bear."

The second type of railroad discrimination is that between different localities. Rates on a given type of freight ordinarily vary directly with the distance that it is shipped. In many cases, however, this general principle did not apply. Railroad rates were sometimes higher for a short haul than for a long haul, due to the existence of competition in the latter case. Let us assume, for illustration, that there are three towns: A, B, and C, and that the distance between A and B is considerably greater than that between A and C. Let us further assume that several railroads run between A and B, but that only one railroad connects A and C. As the railroad is an industry of decreasing costs, there is a great desire on the part of each of these roads for as much freight as it can carry. Where competition exists, as between A and B, there is a strong temptation to cut freight rates to any point above bare operating expenses rather than to lose the business. As no railroad competition exists for the transportation of freight between A and C, freight rates for this shorter distance might be greater than that for the longer distance between A and B. Hence, the town C might well claim that it is discriminated against. Similar rate discriminations existed between seaports and inland cities, because of the possibility of cheap water transportation in the former case but not in the latter. Railroads connecting two seaports were often forced to reduce their freight rates for this route or lose the business to the steamship lines. On the other hand, the railroad was compelled to maintain higher rates for the same distance—and in some cases for even shorter distances—where no competition prevailed, in order to meet its total fixed charges as well as mere operating expenses. Hence, rate discriminations prevailed among communities, and some towns contributed to railroad overhead expenses while others did not. It has been shown that the trusts resorted to similar discriminatory practises, charging higher prices where no competition prevailed, but lowering their rates when competition threatened. Although the principle of discrimination among localities is similar, the railroads, unlike the trusts, are public utilities and common carriers. Hence, they have become more subject to governmental regulation, even to the extent of rate determination. Arbitrary discriminations in the rates of public utilities are against public policy, and even justifiable differences in railroad rates among various localities mean that one community will prosper at the expense of another.

Discrimination between persons was perhaps the worst form of railroad discrimination. For the most part it consisted in giving preferential rates to large shippers at the expense of the smaller ones. Such railroad discriminations played no small part in the formation of trusts. Most of these agreements were secret understandings and difficult to prove. Where there was outward adherence to a schedule of rates, discrimination took the form of secret rebates to the large or especially favored shippers. Some of the most conspicuous cases of discrimination have been made public by various governmental investigations of the trusts. It was shown, for illustration, that the former Standard Oil Company had an agreement with the Cincinnati and Marietta Railroad to transport its oil for ten cents a barrel from Macksburg to Marietta, although it was charging other companies thirty-five cents for the same service. In addition to this preferential rate, there was also a rebate by which the former Standard Oil Company received the excess charge of twenty-five cents a barrel which competing companies were forced to pay. Such a railroad was not a common carrier, but merely a tool of the trust. Although this illustration is one of the most flagrant cases on record, railroad discriminations played an important part in the development of other trusts besides the former Standard Oil Company. Even though discriminations had been specifically forbidden by the Interstate Commerce Act of 1887, the Interstate Commerce Commission went on record in 1898 as follows:

There is probably no one thing today which does so much to force out the small operator and to build up those monopolies against which law and public opinion alike beat in vain, as discrimination in railroad rates.

9. Interstate Commerce Act of 1887.—The evils of discrimination and the apparent connection between the railroads and the trusts led to a demand for some sort of Federal action. State regulation had been tried and found wanting. The powers of Congress over interstate commerce gave a basis in constitutional law for the Federal regulation of the railroads. As early as Grant's administration a committee of the Senate had been appointed to consider the regulation of the railroads with a view to lowering the rates charged. The second Senatorial committee report stressed the allied problem of discriminations in railroad rates. After the usual process of compromise and amendment the House of Representatives and the Senate finally agreed on a bill which passed into law as the Interstate Commerce Act of 1887. It applied to interstate and foreign freight and passenger traffic carried by the railroads or in cases of continuous shipment by railroad and water. The Interstate Commerce Act did not apply to intrastate traffic, nor to interstate or foreign traffic carried entirely by water. It is of peculiar significance as the first important piece of Federal legislation for the national regulation of common carriers. The Interstate Commerce Act may be divided into two parts; the one dealing with prohibitions against discriminations and monopoly practices, and the other providing for the establishment of the Interstate Commerce Commission.

Section 1 provided that all charges should be just and reasonable. It declared unlawful every unjust and unreasonable charge. Section 2 prohibited all unjust personal discriminations in the form of special rates, rebates, or otherwise. Section 3 forbade discriminations between localities, commodities, and connecting lines, and required reasonable and equal facilities for the interchange of traffic. Section 4 contained the famous "short and long haul" clause, making it unlawful for a common carrier to charge more for a shorter than for a longer distance over the same line and under similar circumstances. Section 5 prohibited competing railroads from pooling their freights or their net earnings. The intent of this section was to restore competition. Section 6 stipulated that all rates and fares be printed and posted for public inspection. Schedules of rates and charges were to be filed with the Interstate Commerce Commission. Section 7 made it illegal for any carrier to interrupt unnecessarily the continuous passage of freight for the purpose of changing an interstate shipment into two or more intrastate shipments. Such practices had been resorted to in order to take advantage of a more favorable intrastate rate. Section 8 rendered a carrier liable for damages for losses sustained by a violation of the law. Section 9 provided that any person claiming to be damaged by unjust discriminations or other unlawful practices of a railroad could bring action for recovery either before the Interstate Commerce Commission or in a district or circuit court. Section 10 provided a fine of not exceeding five thousand dollars for each violation of the law.

Section 11 established the Interstate Commerce Commission of five members to be appointed by the President of the United States with the consent of the Senate. The commissioners could not engage in any other business while in office, nor could they own railroad securities. The term of office was six years, and not more than three commissioners might be members of the same political party. Sections 12 to 21 outlined the powers and duties of the Interstate Commerce Commission. It was given power to inquire into the management of all common carriers. It could compel them to produce their records and give testimony. No witness could refuse to testify, although such testimony could not be used against him in criminal proceedings. Inquiries might be instituted on outside complaint or on the initiative of the Commission. When an investigation was made, the Commission was to make a report in writing of its findings and its recommendations as to reparations. If it appeared that the law had been violated, it was to serve notice on the offending railroad to desist from its illegal acts. When a common carrier refused to obey an order or a requirement of the Commission, it was the duty of the Commission to bring proceedings against it in a circuit court of the United States. The findings of the Commission as to the facts were to be regarded in the court as *prima facie* evidence. The Commission was to require from each interstate carrier an annual report concerning capitalization, receipts, equipment, expenses, etc. It included

a "complete exhibit of the financial operations of the carrier
each year, including an annual balance sheet."

Summing up the results of the Interstate Commerce Act, it
will be seen that the law still regarded the railroad as a competitive industry. The plane of competition and the practises
followed were merely subjected to governmental scrutiny.
The Interstate Commerce Commission was given power to
proscribe but not to prescribe railroad rates. It could merely
declare a given rate unreasonable. The Commission's powers
were those of investigation, prosecution, and publicity. Its
decisions were not binding on the railroads and could be enforced
only by litigation. The Supreme Court held that its powers
were only those clearly specified in the act. Again, the Federal
Courts failed to sustain the Commission in many of its railroad
suits. They rendered decisions based on their own rather than
on the Commission's interpretation of the facts. They allowed
the defendants to introduce new evidence which had not been
passed on by the Commission. The Federal courts also refused
for a number of years to compel witnesses to give testimony of
an incriminating nature. The Interstate Commerce Act,
however, did secure the publicity of railroad rates and eliminated
a number of flagrant discriminations. Although the powers of
the Interstate Commerce Commission were limited, a beginning
had been made, and a permanent Federal organization had been
created for the regulation of the railroads. As the course of
subsequent railroad legislation is traced, we shall see how the
powers of this body were gradually increased.

10. Effects of the Sherman Act on the Railroads.—The Sherman Act, which was passed three years after the Interstate
Commerce Act, applied to the railroads as well as to industrial
monopolies. The Interstate Commerce Act forbade pooling, and
the Sherman Act prohibited agreements as to rates. A generation of sad experience was necessary to show the futility of such
enforced competition among railroads. The prohibition of pools
and rate agreements merely gave a tremendous impetus to the
formation of holding companies. Competition was impossible
and unified control finally evolved in spite of opposing legislation.
In 1890, less than half the total mileage of the country was
operated by companies controlling more than a thousand miles
of road, but by 1910 more than 60 per cent was so controlled.

The formation of great railroad systems out of the wreckage of competing lines has been mentioned in an earlier paragraph. In the year 1901, for illustration, three great combinations took place. The Pennsylvania Railroad acquired a large interest in the Baltimore and Ohio, the Union Pacific acquired control of the Southern Pacific, and the Northern Securities Company combined the Great Northern and the Northern Pacific, just after these roads had acquired control over the Chicago, Burlington and Quincy. Against such tendencies of the railroads toward unity and concentration of control the law and the courts struggled in vain. The Supreme Court rendered a decision against the Northern Securities Company in 1904 and ordered that holding company dissolved as a combination in restraint of trade. Nevertheless, it was impossible to eliminate the community of interest represented by the common ownership of stock, by which the desired unity of control was continued. The lease of the Southern Pacific by the Union Pacific was likewise held to be illegal, but active competition between the two roads was not restored. Before the close of the nineteenth century the railroads had become a natural monopoly, although the law and the courts refused to sanction it.

11. Summary.—The railroad played a conspicuous part in our national history. The economic development of continental United States would have been impossible without adequate transportation facilities. The railroads made possible our great territorial specialization and expansion. The development of our railroads was on individual initiative, although generous governmental aid was given. The quasi-public character of the railroads is illustrated by their power of eminent domain. Because of the enormous investment of capital necessary for the construction and maintenance of railroads, the industry is one of decreasing costs and a natural monopoly of organization. Nevertheless, early state legislation attempted to enforce competition by the prohibition of pooling and rate agreements. Concentration of control was sought by means of holding companies and other devices. After a generation of ruinous competition among the railroads, a number of fairly unified systems developed.

The earliest problem of the railroads was that of excessive and discriminatory rates. The Interstate Commerce Act of 1887 forbade railroad discriminations and provided that railroad rates should be reasonable and just. It created the Interstate Commerce Commission to supervise the railroads and their activities. That law marked the transition from state to Federal regulation. At first, the powers of the Interstate Commerce Commission were merely those of investigation, prosecution, and publicity. The following chapter will continue the story of railroad legislation; and the gradual development of effective regulatory powers and machinery will be shown therein.

Collateral Reading

FAIRCHILD, F. R., FURNISS, E. S., and BUCK, N. S., "Elementary Economics," chaps. 9 and 29.

FETTER, F. A., "Modern Economic Problems," chap. 28.

MARSHALL, L. C., WRIGHT, C. W., and FIELD, J. A., "Materials for the Study of Elementary Economics," pp. 259–286.

SEAGER, H. R., "Principles of Economics," chap. 24.

TAUSSIG, F. W., "Principles of Economics," chaps. 62 and 63.

References

ACKWORTH, W. M., "The Elements of Railroad Economics."

Annals of the American Academy of Political and Social Science, March, 1918 and November, 1919.

BROWN, H. G., "Transportation Rates and Their Regulation."

BYE, R. T., "Social Welfare in Rate Making," *Political Science Quarterly,* December, 1917.

CLEVELAND, F. A., and POWELL, F. W., "Railroad Finance."

CUNNINGHAM, A. J., "American Railroads."

DIXON, F. H., "Railroads and the Government."

DUNN, S. O., "The Regulation of the Railroads."

GRUNSKY, C. E., and GRUNSKY, C. E. JR., "Valuation, Depreciation and the Rate Base."

HADLEY, A. T., "Railroad Transportation: Governmental Control and Reconstruction Policies."

HANEY, L. H., "The Business of Railroad Transportation."

HAINES, H. S., "Problems in Railroad Regulation."

JONES, E., "Principles of Railroad Transportation."

————, and VANDERBLUE, H. B., "Railroads: Cases and Selections."

JOHNSON, E. R., and HUEBNER, G. G., "Railroad Traffic and Rates."

————, and VAN METRE, T. W., "Principles of Railroad Transportation."

————, "Next Steps in Railroad Consolidation." (*Proceedings* of the American Philosophical Society, 1925.)

MACGILL, C. E., (and others), "Railroad Transportation in the United States."

MILLER, S. L., "Railroad Transportation."

MORRIS, R., "Railroad Administration."

RAPER, C. L. "Railroad Transportation."

RIPLEY, W. Z., "Railroads: Rates and Regulations."

———, "Railroads: Finance and Organization."
———, "Railroad Problems."
SHARPMAN, I. C., "American Railroad Problem."
VANDERBLUE, H. B., "Railroad Valuation."
———, and BURGESS, K. F., "Railroads: Rate Service Management."

Questions for Discussion

1. Show the growth of the railroads in the United States.
2. Show the present size and importance of the railroad industry.
3. Make a classification (with a map before you) of the different railroad systems of the United States.
4. Why is the railroad to be regarded as a quasi-public industry?
5. What was the evil of discrimination and why was it important in the economic development of the United States?
6. Outline the stages in the evolution of the railroad problem.
7. Outline the leading provisions of the Interstate Commerce Act.
8. How did the Sherman Anti-trust Act affect the railroads?

Topics for Investigation

1. The railroads and the settlement of the West.
2. The era of canals and turnpikes.
3. Public aid in railroad construction.
4. State regulation of the railroads.
5. Judicial interpretation of the Interstate Commerce Act of 1887.

CHAPTER X

FEDERAL REGULATION AND RAILROAD RATES

1. Elkins Act.—The Elkins Act of 1903 was the first important piece of railroad legislation after the passage of the Interstate Commerce Act of 1887. It dealt almost exclusively with the problem of personal discriminations and was designed to prevent the fostering of the trusts by preferential treatment on the part of the railroads. The specific aim was the elimination of secret rebates. The Elkins Act made corporations as well as their agents responsible for violations of the law. The penalty of imprisonment, provided by the Interstate Commerce Act, was eliminated, because it was found difficult to secure convictions with this penalty attached to a verdict. Fines of $1,000 to $20,000 were substituted. The test of discrimination was to be any deviation from the published schedule of rates. Moreover, the receiver of rebates as well as the giver was to be regarded as violating the law. A writ of injunction might also be used to prevent discriminations.

2. Hepburn Act of 1906 and the Era of Effective Railroad Regulation.—The Hepburn Act of 1906 may be said to mark the beginning of effective regulation of railroad rates by the Federal government. The law extended the scope of the Interstate Commerce Act to express companies, sleeping-car companies and pipe lines for the transportation of petroleum. The legal definition of railroads was broadened to include "switches, spurs, tracks and terminal facilities," and the term "transportation" to include "cars and other vehicles and all instrumentalities and facilities of shipment and carriage irrespective of ownership." The Hepburn Act provided that no road should transport over its lines:

. . . any article or commodity, other than timber and the manufactured products thereof, manufactured, mined, or produced by it, or under its authority—except as may be necessary for its use in the conduct of its business as a common carrier.

This provision was aimed specifically at the discriminations practised by the coal-carrying railroads, some of whom were directly or indirectly interested in the marketing of coal. Publicity of rates was insured by the prohibition of any common carrier from engaging in transportation without first filing its schedule of rates with the Interstate Commerce Commission. No deviations could be made, except after thirty days' notice to the public and to the Commission. Free transportation of passengers and free passes, except in a few specified cases, were forbidden. Any shipper receiving a rebate of any kind from a common carrier should forfeit to the Federal government a sum equal to three times the amount of rebates received during the previous six years. The offering, soliciting, accepting, or granting of rebates was made a misdemeanor. In addition to the fines provided in the Elkins Act, the Hepburn Bill provided that any person, whether officer or director, agent or employee, convicted of such misdemeanor

shall be liable to imprisonment in the penitentiary for a term not exceeding two years, or both fine and imprisonment in the discretion of the court.

Important provisions were contained in the Hepburn Amendment with respect to the Interstate Commerce Commission. Its membership was increased from five to seven, with the provision that not more than four members might be of the same political party. The term of office was changed from six to seven years, and the annual salary was raised to $10,000. The powers and duties of the Commission were greatly increased. It had formerly been permitted to declare a given rate unreasonable, but not to state what it considered a reasonable one. The Hepburn Amendment to the Interstate Commerce Act permitted the Commission to determine just and reasonable rates, regulations, and practices. It could prescribe as well as proscribe railroad rates. These orders of the Interstate Commerce Commission fixing maximum rates were to take effect within a reasonable time, unless later set aside by the Commission or the courts. As a fine was provided for the failure to comply with these orders, railroads could no longer ignore them. The burden of initiating litigation to test the validity of its orders was shifted from the Commission to the railroads. Another great advance was made by granting the Interstate Commerce Commission power to prescribe a uniform system of accounting for all railroads engaged in interstate commerce. Special agents and examiners were to be employed to inspect all the accounts and records of common carriers. In addition to the customary annual reports, monthly reports of earnings and expenses were now required, as well as other special reports which might give greater publicity to the railroad industry. It was an offense for the railroads to mutilate, falsify, or destroy their records.

The efficacy of the Interstate Commerce Act had been impaired by the slowness with which litigation proceeded and by the power of the courts to review the orders of the Interstate Commerce Commission. An Expediting Act had been passed in 1903. It was now further provided that in case of an appeal from a decree of the circuit court the case should take precedence in the Supreme Court over all other matters except criminal cases. Although the Hepburn Amendment did not limit or specify the grounds on which the Federal courts could annul the orders of the Commission, in practice they have confined their activities to a consideration of the law, leaving unquestioned the findings of the Commission as to the facts. It became apparent that the intent of Congress was that the Interstate Commerce Commission should be considered as a competent and effective administrative board. The orders of the Commission were not to be set aside by the courts except where it had exceeded its statutory powers or violated constitutional guarantees. The Supreme Court ceased to review and interpret the facts of the case. It continued to pass on the legality of the orders of the Commission, but not on their wisdom or expediency.

3. Mann-Elkins Act.—The Mann-Elkins Act of 1910 contained among others the following three provisions. In the first place, it gave to the Interstate Commerce Commission the power to suspend changes in railroad rates. Whenever a carrier should file a schedule of new and increased rates the Commission was to make an investigation of the reasonableness of such an increase. Pending such an investigation the new schedule might be suspended for a period of time. Thus, the burden of proof for an increase in rates rested with the railroads. Under this provision the railroads of the East were prevented from raising their rates in 1910 and again in 1913. A second provision of the Mann-Elkins Act increased the effectiveness of the "short and long haul" clause of the Interstate Commerce Act of 1887. It will be remembered that this provision was designed to eliminate discriminations and particularly the charging of a higher rate for a short distance than for a longer distance. The amendment removed the words "under substantially similar conditions," which had afforded a basis for exemptions from the application of the original law. In the third place, the Mann-Elkins Act created a special Commerce Court for cases against common carriers. It was hoped to expedite litigation and also to bring about a greater specialization within the Federal courts. Unfortunately this Commerce Court met with public disfavor and was very short lived. It was abolished in 1912 by the failure of Congress to make financial provision for its continued support. It was legally abolished in 1913 and its duties assigned to the Federal district courts.

4. The Panama Canal Act.—The Panama Canal Act of 1912 made it unlawful, after July 1, 1914, for any railroad company, or any other common carrier, to have any interest in common carriers by water operating through the Panama Canal, or elsewhere, "with which said railroad or other common carrier aforesaid does or may compete for traffic." The Interstate Commerce Commission was to pass on the facts as to competition and the possibility of competition. Railroad ownership of competing vessel lines operated elsewhere than through the Panama Canal might be permitted, if the service was being operated in the interests of the public. By this law the leading eastern trunk railroads were required to dispose of their vessel lines on the Great Lakes. The law also provided that the Commission might require the connection of rail and water carriers to establish through routes. In such cases the Interstate Commerce Commission might fix the maximum joint rates to be charged. This legal provision was inserted to prevent the railroads from retarding the development of water transportation by the practise of discrimination.

5. Effects of the Clayton Act on the Railroads.—The Sherman Anti-trust Act of 1890 was considerably modified by the Clayton Act of 1914. It will be remembered from Chap. VII that an important provision of this new law was its limitations on holding companies. Under the Clayton Act all corporations engaged in commerce were forbidden to

. . . acquire directly or indirectly the whole or any part of the capital stock of another corporation engaged also in commerce, where the effect of such acquisition may be to substantially lessen competition.

It was provided, however, that this law should not prohibit carriers from purchasing or aiding in the construction of short branch lines, nor prevent them from extending any lines through stock acquisition in cases where there was no substantial competition between the purchasing and the selling companies. Common carriers were also forbidden by the Clayton Act to have any dealings in large amounts of securities and supplies, or to make contracts for construction or maintenance with another corporation, if a director, manager, purchasing or selling agent had any substantial interest in the other corporation. An exception was made where the transaction takes place as a result of competitive bidding under regulations prescribed by the Interstate Commerce Commission. This provision was designed to prevent the prostitution of weak corporations by powerful ones through a collusion of their officers. The close connection between certain railroads and the coal, oil, and timber interests, which resulted in the practice of "milking" one corporation at the expense of another, has been noted.

6. Safety and Labor Legislation for Railroads.—In order to complete the summary of railroad legislation before the World War, it is necessary to mention certain safety and labor measures that were passed. As an illustration of the former type of railroad legislation may be cited the Safety Appliance Acts, the first of which was passed in 1893, and which made compulsory the use of automatic couplers. An Act of 1907 forbade carriers except under unusual circumstances from permitting their employees to remain on continuous duty for more than sixteen hours. Railroads were also required to make monthly reports of accidents to the Interstate Commerce Commission.

The Eardman Act of 1898 was designed to prevent railroad strikes through mediation and voluntary arbitration. The Chairman of the Interstate Commerce Commission and the Commissioner of Labor should attempt mediation on the application of either party. If their mediation was unsuccessful a resort might be made to a board of arbitration. The Newlands Act of 1913 changed this machinery somewhat. It provided for a Federal Commissioner of Mediation and Conciliation, appointed by the President with the consent of the Senate. A final resort might be made to a regularly appointed Board of Arbitration. Mediation and arbitration were used successfully several times by these officers and boards to avert threatened rail strikes.

A serious labor crisis was reached in 1916. The four great railroad labor organizations had been demanding a basic eight-

hour day and overtime pay at the rate of time and a half. This
demand was for increased pay rather than shorter hours. Conferences between employees and employers failed, and the
railroad managers offered to submit the matter to arbitration.
President Wilson proposed a conference at Washington and
recommended that the eight-hour day be adopted with pro ra⁺a
pay for overtime. The managers felt that railroad earnings
refused to justify increased wages. Thereupon, union leaders
called a country-wide strike for Sept. 4, 1916. On Sept. 2,
Congress hastily enacted the Adamson Eight-Hour Act, which
provided that the basic eight-hour day become effective on Jan.
1, 1917. Railroad managers sought an injunction against the
law, and a United States District Court declared it unconstitutional. The Supreme Court, however, upheld the constitutionality of the Adamson Act and the employees were granted their
back pay from Jan. 1. A serious railroad strike was thus averted,
but the administrative boards established for the regulation of
the railroads suffered a serious loss of prestige.

7. Governmental Operation of the Railroads.—The declaration of war with Germany was not unforeseen by the railroad
officials of the country. As early as Feb. 16, 1917, the American
Railroad Association created a special committee on National
Defense, consisting of railroad officials from various parts of the
country. Five members of the body were later chosen by the
President to serve on what was known as the Railroad War
Board. Plans were laid for the cooperation of the railroads with
the military officials of the country and for greater expedition in
the moving of freight. Because great congestion existed in the
railroad terminals of the eastern seaports, the national emergency
produced plans for the greater cooperation of various roads into
what was known as the "Continental Railroad System."
Demands on the railroads were enormous, but the board was
without legal authority to compel the observance of its recommendations. There was a serious lack of equipment caused by
the failure of the railroads to obtain substantial increases in
rates. Moreover, the employees were demanding increases in
wages to meet increased costs of living. Another great obstacle
to transportation efficiency was the diversified system of governmental control. Each civil or military board was seeking priority in its shipments and the railroad administration was in serious
danger of breaking down under their varied and insistent

demands. On Dec. 1, 1917, the Interstate Commerce Commission in a special report requested that the President assume control of the railroads during the war. It further requested that whatever legal obstacles prevented unified operation by the carriers be immediately removed and that the government give the roads financial assistance.

The Army Appropriation Act of August, 1916 had authorized the President in time of war to assume control of the transportation systems of the United States. Acting under this authority from Congress, President Wilson, on Dec. 26, 1917, issued his proclamation for the assumption of control of the railroads of the country by the Federal government. He named Secretary of the Treasury, William G. McAdoo, as Director General of the Railroads, and under his centralized control the organization of the individual railroad companies was gradually changed. A central administrative bureau was established in Washington, and the country was divided into great operating districts, each in charge of an experienced railroad official. Railroad presidents disappeared and Federal managers took their places. The identity of individual lines was often lost. Express companies were likewise required to consolidate into a single company, control over which was likewise assumed by the government.

On Mar. 21, 1918, the Railroad Control Act was passed to deal with the problems which arose out of the President's war-time proclamation concerning the railroads. This law guaranteed to each railroad corporation an annual payment not exceeding its average net operating income for the three years ending June 30, 1917. The government was to provide for the maintenance and repair of equipment and a revolving fund of four hundred million dollars was created to pay the expenses of Federal control. The President was authorized to initiate all charges, classifications, regulations and practices by filing them with the Interstate Commerce Commission. The roads were to be returned to their owners within a year and nine months after the ratification of the treaty of peace.

The Federal railroad administration made a number of important changes. There was the joint use of terminals, cars, equipment, repair shops, and other facilities of the individual roads. The central control of the routing and distribution of the traffic relieved somewhat the severe congestion. Duplicate service was eliminated and economy effected by the use of standardized equipment. The railroad administration organized a number of regional and district rate committees, which took the place of the former traffic associations. The principle of collective bargaining was recognized and a nonpartisan Railway Wage Commission appointed. The eight-hour day was adopted and wages were standardized and substantially increased. As increased revenues were necessary, freight rates were advanced 25 per cent and passenger fares to three cents a mile in May, 1918. Unfortunately this financial relief did not come until a serious deficit threatened. Railroad earnings during these years showed a marked contrast to war profits in other industries.

8. Results of War-time Experiment.—The general arguments for and against governmental ownership and operation of public utilities were outlined in Chap. VIII. The student is asked to review these arguments and to make his own application to the railroad industry. He is reminded that we had governmental operation, but not governmental ownership of the railroads during the World War. Moreover, the experiment was only for a very brief period and should not be taken as typical. The success or failure of what was primarily a war measure offers little proof of either side of the argument concerning the advantages and disadvantages of public ownership.

For our own appraisal of the war-time experiment with the railroads we shall substitute the opinion of a leading authority on transportation problems.[1] Their verdict is as follows:

From the standpoint of operating results the management of the railroads by the government was on the whole satisfactory. Arbitrary measures were necessary to obtain the movement of essential traffic, and such arbitrary measures as were desirable the Railroad Administration could and did put into effect. The unification of the physical facilities of the railroads and the redistribution of traffic made it possible to relieve the congestion which existed when Federal control began, and throughout the twenty-six months of government operation the record of traffic movement was good. There were numerous complaints on the part of individual travelers and shippers, and there was unquestionably much reason for complaint, but in nearly all cases inconveniences suffered by individuals were the necessary result of making the military activities of the Government the matter of paramount consideration.

[1] *Cf.* JOHNSON and VAN METRE, "Principles of Railroad Transportation," p. 510.

From a financial standpoint the results of Federal control were not so satisfactory. The advances in rates initiated by the Railroad Administration were insufficient to meet the greatly increased costs of operation, and throughout the period of Federal control there was a deficit. The excess of operating expenses and rentals over operating revenues for the twenty-six months' period amounted to approximately $900,000,000. It is possible that several million dollars must be paid in taxes before the obligations of the government are met. Some railroad companies will unquestionably present large claims on account of the undermaintenance of their properties. On the other hand the Government has large sums due from the carriers on account of additions, betterments, and loans.

9. The Transportation Act of 1920.—Various plans for unscrambling the railroad omelette were suggested in the year which followed the signing of the armistice. The Plumb Plan proposed the conversion of governmental operation into governmental ownership, by the Federal purchase of the railroads. Control was to be vested in a board of directors in which the railroad employees had the controlling votes. Although this plan had the backing of the American Federation of Labor, it was not adopted. The return of the railroads to private ownership was embodied in the bill which Congress finally passed. This was known as the Transportation Act of 1920 or the Esch-Cummins Act. The Transportation Act of 1920 contained provisions for (1) the return of the railroads to their private owners on Mar. 1, 1920, (2) a method of fixing railroad earnings, (3) the consolidation of the railroads, (4) an increase in the membership and powers of the Interstate Commerce Commission, and (5) new machinery for the settlement of labor disputes.

Certain financial provisions were also included for the transfer of the railroads to private operation. The law guaranteed to the railroads for the following six months a net return equal to the rentals paid during governmental operation. They had the option, however, of assuming complete financial independence after Mar. 1. If a railroad elected to continue its guaranteed rentals, any excess in its earnings were to be returned to the Federal government. An appropriation of three hundred million dollars was held as a fund from which the railroads might secure loans during the next two years. The equipment of many roads was so depreciated that their demands for new rolling stock and other capital outlays were imperative. Those railroads which were indebted to the government because of expenditures for equipment were permitted to fund their obligations for a period of ten years with interest at 6 per cent. Fares and rates in existence at the end of Federal control should not be reduced during the guaranteed six months' period except with the approval of the Interstate Commerce Commission. Furthermore, it was stipulated that no reductions in wages or salaries were to be made within the same period. The financial position of the railroads at the end of the war was deplorable, and it was held by many authorities that these provisions were not sufficiently generous.

The Commission was authorized to divide the country into rate districts and to prescribe a rate for each district, which under efficient management would yield a net income sufficient to pay a "fair" rate of return upon the capital invested. The Commission should make a valuation of the railroads from time to time to determine the amount of their investments. A "fair" rate of return was fixed at $5\frac{1}{2}$ per cent for the two years following Mar. 1, 1920. It was provided, however, that an additional one-half of 1 per cent might be allowed for capital investments in the nature of additions and betterments. It was obvious that all the railroads in a given rate district were not on the same financial basis. On the other hand, rates must be uniform, for the Commission had no intention of restoring the former competition and discrimination. A given rate might be more than sufficient for a strong railroad, but not enough for a weak road. Therefore, the government introduced into the Transportation Act of 1920 the principle of profit sharing. All profits in excess of this statutory rate of 6 per cent were to be divided into two equal parts. One-half of the excess profits was to be kept in reserve by the road earning it, and the other half to be turned over to the Commission as "a general railroad contingent fund." This fund was to be used for making loans to weaker railroads and for the purpose of acquiring railroad property by the Commission to be leased to operating companies. This statutory definition of a fair rate of return expired two years after Mar. 1, 1920, after which date the Interstate Commerce Commission was empowered to define it from time to time. At present it is fixed at $5\frac{3}{4}$ per cent of the railroad's capital investment.

The Interstate Commerce Commission was directed to prepare and adopt a plan for the consolidation of the railroad properties of continental United States into a limited number of systems. Nevertheless, the pious hope was expressed that competition should be preserved as fully as possible. It was evident, however, that the only possible competition among the railroads was in the service and not in the rates. The new law provided that the several systems be so arranged that the cost of transportation, as between competitive systems and as related to the value of railway property, should be the same. The systems could employ uniform rates on competitive traffic and could earn substantially the same rate of return. Some consolidation has taken place since 1920, but not as much as had been anticipated. Consequently, there has been some agitation in favor of compulsory consolidation, for the combination of individual railroads into integrated systems is imperative. A reactionary tendency was disclosed when the Interstate Commmerce Commission refused its permission to the proposed Nickel Plate Railroad Consolidation. It objected to the methods of finance, but failed to show how these defects might be removed and the gains of consolidation achieved.

The Transportation Act of 1920 increased the membership of the Interstate Commerce Commission to eleven and the salary of each member to $12,000. It strengthened still further the powers of the Commission. The law sought to preserve the gains of cooperation which the war had engendered. The Commission was authorized to regulate the capitalization of railroads. In the last chapter we saw how the Transportation Act of 1920 also gave it greater measure of control over intrastate rates. Furthermore, the Commission was now given the authority to name minimum as well as maximum rates. The problem of railroad rates has shifted from excessive to inadequate rates. Moreover, in cases of emergency the Interstate Commerce Commission can exercise control over the car service of the railroads. The Commission's consent was also made necessary before a railroad could undertake the construction of extensions or branch lines. The railroad development of the future, if not of the past, was to be planned as a unit. Moreover, the Commission was given the power to require the joint use of railroad terminals and other facilities where it seemed necessary, and under terms prescribed by the Commission. Finally, the law now permitted the pooling of traffic and earnings, although such devices were no longer necessary. The monopoly character of the railroad was finally written into law.

It was proposed to insert clauses into the Esch-Cummins Act to provide for compulsory arbitration in the railroad industry. Instead, the law authorized the creation of railroad boards of labor adjustment. A central Railroad Labor Board was created consisting of nine members—three representing the employers, three the employees, and three the general public. They were appointed by the President with the consent of the Senate. This body heard all cases referred to it by the subsidiary bodies concerning wages and working conditions. Its decisions, however, had no binding effect upon either party and there was no penalty for disregarding them. Consequently, its opinions were ignored by both capital and labor, and the board suffered a constant loss of prestige. It was finally abolished in May 1926 by an act of Congress which restored the former method of direct negotiations between the workers and the railroads. Provision was made for mediation and voluntary arbitration and for local boards of adjustment. The Railroad Labor Board like the Commerce Court passed into history. The compulsory arbitration of labor disputes within the railroad industry is still a dream of the future.

10. Decline of Railroad Earnings.—By an act of Congress in March, 1913, the Interstate Commerce Commission was required to make a valuation of all railroads. The Commission was also directed to prepare a classified inventory of the physical assets of the railroads and to ascertain their original cost, the cost of reproduction, and the original cost less depreciation. In order to fix railroad rates, which power had been given to the Commission by the Hepburn Act, it was necessary to know the value of the capital invested in the railroad industry. A reasonable rate must be one which is fair to the owners of railroad securities as well as to the users of railroad services.

With the background of a generation of struggle against excessive and discriminatory rates, the coveted power of rate fixing was at first used negatively by the Interstate Commerce Commission for the prevention or limitation of increases in railroad rates. The decline of railroad earnings became rather serious in the period following the Hepburn Act of 1906. The last generation of the nineteenth century had been one of falling prices, but the first two decades of the twentieth century were characterized by rising prices.   In spite of the decline of railroad earnings, however, the Interstate Commerce Commission steadily refused increases in railroad rates.   The rise of prices began after 1897 and was attended by increased costs for repairs, equipment, and labor.   Railroads which were just beginning to recover from a period of ruinous competition now faced the problem of declining earnings.   Even before 1914 it had become apparent that increases in railroad rates were necessary.   Consequently, the Interstate Commerce Commission granted in July, 1914, a portion of what was known as the "5 per cent demand." Further increases were granted in the following December, but prices continued to rise in 1915 and 1916.   When the government took over the operation of the railroads it guaranteed earnings to railroads upon the basis of those of the previous three years. Because of the rise in the general price level and labor costs the net earnings of the railroads fell below this guaranteed amount.   In May, 1918, rates for both passengers and freight were sharply advanced, the latter by a flat 25 per cent increase.   This granted a temporary relief which lasted until after the War.   The business depression of 1920, however, reflected itself in railroad earnings. Railroads which had formerly suffered from freight congestion and from a shortage of rolling stock now faced the problem of idle cars.   The Interstate Commerce Commission granted a large increase in both passenger and freight rates to become effective in September, 1920.   Meanwhile, the Transportation Act of 1920 had put into effect its statutory rule for rate fixing.

Railroad earnings since the passage of the Transportation Act of 1920 are reported as follows by the Federal Bureau of Railway Economics.   Although the figures are merely for 189 Class I railroads, they represent most of the railroad mileage of the country.   Two rates of earnings are given, one based on the valuation of the Interstate Commerce Commission and the other on the valuation by the railroad themselves.

RAILROAD EARNINGS

Years	Earnings	Per cent on Interstate Commerce Commission valuation	Per cent on railroad valuation
1921............	$ 600,937,356	3.33	2.92
1922............	760,187,319	4.41	3.61
1923............	961,955,457	5.22	4.48
1924............	986,744,996	5.01	4.33
1925............	1,136,973,477	5.63	4.83

The "net" earnings for 1925 were the largest in American history, and continued to increase during the first ten months of 1926. But because of increased investment the rate of return was not so large as in the pre-war year of 1916. In spite of these large totals, however, the rate of profits in the railroad industry is small. According to the valuation of the Interstate Commerce Commission the 1925 earnings represent a profit of $5\frac{1}{2}$ per cent. If the greater book valuation of the railroads themselves is accepted their earnings represent a profit of less than 5 per cent. In either case the average rate of return is low. A number of important railroads in years of industrial prosperity were actually running at a loss. In 1925, fourteen Class I railroads suffered losses. Five of these roads were in the east, eight in the west and one in the south. In spite of the apparent inadequacy of railroad earnings, some grounds for optimism may be found in the gradual increase of earnings over this short period. Although no proof of the superiority of private operation, it must be admitted that the total profits and rate of profits of the railroads increased considerably after their return to private operation.

11. Ideal of a "Fair Rate."—The economic wastes of competition among the railroads finally resulted in the concept of this industry as a natural monopoly of organization. In the absence of a competitive price, governmental regulation is necessary to protect the public against exorbitant monopoly prices. We have traced the development of the Interstate Commerce Commission as an administrative board of the Federal government for the regulation of railroad rates and railroad policies. In the absence of competition and of complete monopoly the determination of prices is social rather than economic, that is, they are fixed by an administration or governmental body.

The legal concept of a fair or reasonable rate has gradually developed within the railroad industry. It finally became apparent that not only must the public be granted protection against discriminatory and excessive rates, but also that the investor must be given some security in his quasi-public investment. Moreover, the concept of a reasonable or fair railroad rate also involves labor. The enthusiastic reception of the Plumb Plan by the railroad workers testified to the fact that they also considered themselves partners in the railroad industry. The effect of railroad rates on wages in that industry and the reciprocal effect of wages on railroad rates are important. Not only must the consumer receive reasonable rates and the investor a fair rate of return on his capital, but the worker must also receive a living wage. There are three parties interested in the problem of railroad rates, whose interests are sometimes in harmony but often in conflict.

12. Difficulties in the Determination of Fair Rates and the Allocation of Transportation Charges.—Although the term "fair rate" is very vague, and exact definition is difficult, one of its most common interpretations is that a fair railroad rate is one which yields a fair rate of return on the capital invested. This so-called cost of production interpretation is reflected in the Transportation Act of 1920. Such an interpretation does not nor cannot evaluate the services of labor. The return on capital investment is stressed, but the return on the human investment is assumed. Moreover, several problems are involved in fixing railroads rates at that point which will yield a fair rate of return on invested capital. In the first place, what arithmetical rate of return on the investment should be regarded as a "fair rate" of return? In the second place, what value should be placed on the capital investment which is to be used as the basis for such a computation? In the third place, what set of railroad rates will yield that desired rate of return on the computed value of the capital investment? The Transportation Act of 1920 fixed the rather arbitrary rate of $5\frac{1}{2}$ per cent with an additional one-half of 1 per cent allowance as a fair rate of return. Some students of the problem claim that this percentage is too low, and a few that it is too high. Again, can there be any such thing as a flat rate of return for all roads and for all years? On the other hand, to differentiate between the strong and the weak roads would place a premium on inefficiency. To vary this fair rate of return with the progress of the business cycle might lead to general confusion and certain injustices. To vary this fair rate of return from time to time according to the prevailing interest rate might be neither practical nor just.

Assuming a given percentage as constituting a "fair rate" of return, on what valuation should it be based? The Interstate Commerce Commission has been wrestling with the problem of railroad valuation since 1913. It is not clear what constitutes the fairest method of appraising the railroad investment. Should our railroad valuation be limited merely to the physical assets of the railroads or should it include such intangible assets as good will and franchise privileges? If we exclude these intangible assets, which are difficult to measure, our problem is still far from solved. What is the proper basis for the valuation of the physical capital investment of the railroad? A fairly good case may be made out for any one of the following methods: the original cost, the original cost less depreciation, the cost of present reproduction, or the probable cost of reproduction in the near future.

Assuming a given rate of return and a given valuation as fair, how can railroad rates be fixed in order to secure the desired earnings? With these two factors constant it is still difficult to determine a "fair rate" because the railroad is an industry of decreasing costs. As an abstract proposition, it seems just that a certain freight rate should be proportionate to the cost of rendering its particular service. The practical application of this principle, however, is extremely difficult. Railroad costs consist of both operating expenses and fixed charges on the investment. What share of the overhead expenses of a railroad system should be charged against the cost of moving a particular piece of freight a certain distance? Operating expenses can be fairly definitely measured, and railroad officials can speak of "train-mile" costs, that is, the expense of running a given train a mile. Such information, however is insufficient. It does not enable us definitely to allocate the cost of moving a particular piece of freight for a particular distance. How can we arrive at what might be termed "unit costs?" It seems obvious that the charge for transportation should be proportionate to the weight or bulk of the freight and the distance that it is to be carried. The very nature of the railroad industry, however, is such that costs of transportation do not increase proportionately with either of these two factors. The cost is less per ton to transport train-loads than car loads, and disproportionately less per ton for car loads than for still smaller loads. Likewise, expenses per mile grow less as the distance increases, because terminal expenses and other fixed costs of train movements can be spread over a longer haul.

The railroad is an industry of joint costs as well as one of decreasing costs. Joint costs are those expenses which are involved in the simultaneous production of two or more commodities or services. An illustration is the refining of crude petroleum into paraffin, kerosene, and gasoline. It is impossible to apportion these combined expenses of refining petroleum among its various products. The producer can only arbitrarily divide the joint costs of production and add a portion to the price of each of the different products of one common origin. The capital invested in railroad tracks, bridges, and tunnels is similarly devoted to the transportation of both freight and passengers. The cargo of a single freight train, in turn, consists of many different products. The movement of a train adds place utilities simultaneously to numerous different products. To divide the common costs of production among the different commodities represented is a difficult matter. The fact that the railroads operate under the principle of joint costs, as well as of decreasing costs, renders difficult the application of the cost of production theory to the determination of fair railroad rates.

13. Theories of Rate Making.—Another theory of railroad rate determination is to make the value of the service rendered the basis of the railroad rate. This method seeks to fix railroad rates according to the values added to articles by their transportation from one place to another. All other things being equal, if a bushel of grain is worth ten cents more in an Eastern city than in the Dakotas, that increase in value may be attributed to the place utility which the railroad has created. Value of service, however, is difficult to determine for freight, and still more difficult to determine for passenger transportation. A rough approximation of this value of service has been the chief basis of railroad charges as fixed in the past by railroad officials. "Charging what the traffic will bear" has been a guiding policy in rate making, which has sometimes been sanctioned by the Interstate Com-

merce Commission.   If this theory is carried to the limit and the
railroads attempt to appropriate the entire value of the service
rendered, their rates may be regarded as unreasonable and monopolistic.   Such a policy would ignore the element of costs in rate
making.   A modifying factor in railroad rate making has been
the intrinsic value of the commodities themselves.   Increases in
the values of cheap, bulky articles, which are attributed to transportation, are discounted, and the losses made up by higher
charges on more expensive articles.   Although such a policy
savors of discrimination among goods, it is probably socially
beneficial.   It operates like a luxury tax and helps to distribute
the burden of transportation charges among consumers where
they can best be borne.   "Charging what the traffic will bear" is
generally used to refer to such price discriminations in rate
making rather than to attempts to absorb all the increases
in place utilities on all articles transported.

   In the practical determination of railroad rates there seems to
be an upper and a lower limit.   The rates charged for any service
must at least equal the costs incurred in performing that service,
or, stated negatively must equal the expenses which would have
been avoided had the service not been rendered.   Moreover,
no railroad charge can be greater than the value of the transportation service to the shipper or traveler.   To determine between
those upper and lower limits what constitutes a reasonable and
fair charge is the task of governmental regulation.   As time goes
on, increasing importance will be attached to the factors of social
expediency and industrial progress.   The socialization of railroad rates will call for the fixing of freight rates largely with
reference to the values of commodities, and for the fixing of the
fares so that they will correspond more nearly with the abilities
of different consumers to pay.

   14. Summary.—The present chapter continued the story of
railway legislation from the passage of the Interstate Commerce
Act.   In reviewing the various pieces of amendatory legislation
we stressed the increase in the powers of the Interstate Commerce
Commission.   The Hepburn Act was particularly important for
it gave to the Commission the power to prescribe as well as to
proscribe railroad rates.   The concept of the railroad industry as
a natural monopoly of organization has gradually taken root in
both public opinion and Federal legislation.   The Interstate
Commerce Commission now has almost complete power over

railroad rates and services. This involves some plan of railroad valuation and some theory of rate making.

The determination of a "fair rate" is important to the consuming public, to the railroad employees, and to the holders of railroad securities. The statutory determination of a "fair rate" does not solve the problem, for railroads present individual differences. Moreover, it merely raises the question as to whether the valuation should be on the basis of original costs, reproduction costs, or some compromise plan. The apportionment of transportation charges among different commodities, services, and distances is also a vexed question. There seems to be an upper and a lower limit to railroad rates. The lower limit is represented by the costs of rendering the service and the upper limit by the increase in value which the service of transportation renders.

The governmental operation of the railroads must be regarded primarily as a war measure. The short length of time and the critical period which it covered makes us hesitate about drawing any conclusions from it as to the general problem of governmental ownership and operation. The rise of the general price level and the decline of railroad earnings had been taking place some time before the war-time experiment was necessitated. The passage of the Transportation Act of 1920 secured the return of the railroads to their private owners but provided for strict Federal regulation and integration. If this arrangement fails to secure adequate transportation facilities and the elimination of past evils, there remains the alternative of governmental ownership and operation.

Collateral Reading

FAIRCHILD, F. R., FURNISS, E. S., and BUCK, N. S., "Elementary Economics," chap. 30.
FETTER, F., "Modern Economic Problems," chap. 29.
HAMILTON, W., "Current Economic Problems," chap. 8.
MAGEE, F. D., "Introduction to Economic Problems," chaps. 11 and 12.
MARSHALL, L. C., WRIGHT, C. W., and FIELD, J. A., "Materials for the Elementary Study of Economics," pp. 286–299.
WILLIAMSON, T. R., "Readings in Economics," pp. 417–425.
YOUNG, J. T., "The New American Government and Its Work," chap. 6.

References

See those for the last chapter.

Questions for Discussion

1. What was the purpose of the Elkins Act?
2. Why was the Hepburn Act of great importance?
3. What were the chief provisions of the Mann-Elkins Act?
4. How did the Panama Canal Act affect the railroads?
5. How did the Clayton Act affect the railroads?
6. What tests of success would you apply to the period of governmental operation of the railroads and with what conclusions?
7. Outline the leading provisions of the Transportation Act of 1920.
8. Trace the gradual evolution in legislation of the concept of the railroad as a natural monopoly of organization.
9. Show why the determination of a "fair rate" is difficult.
10. What economic considerations must guide the Interstate Commerce Commission in the determination of railroad rates?

Topics for Investigation

1. The Federal administration of the railroads during the World War.
2. The condition of the railroads upon their return to private ownership.
3. The proposed Plumb Plan for the reorganization of the railroads.
4. Railroad consolidations since 1920.
5. A proper basis for the valuation of the railroads.
6. Social considerations in the determination of railroad rates.

PART THREE
PROBLEMS OF EXCHANGE

CHAPTER XI

PROBLEMS OF MONEY AND PRICES

1. Nature and Characteristics of Money.—An analysis of monetary problems necessitates a clear understanding of the nature and characteristics of money. So many popular misconceptions exist concerning the significance of money in our economic organization, that it is impossible to discuss monetary problems intelligently without first removing some common errors. The fact that money will buy things has led to the common belief that human welfare and happiness depend upon the possession of plenty of money. Indeed, a certain moral significance is popularly attached to its possession. A person is said to be worth so many million dollars, because he happens to have control over funds to that extent. Business success, material progress, good fortune, "worth"—these are measured alike by most persons in monetary terms. Because of the pecuniary character of modern economic life, it is essential at the outset that the true nature and characteristics of money be clearly understood.

Money is a convenient tool, a device which man has developed to facilitate the exchange of economic goods. It is a go-between, a medium of exchange, which makes possible the obtaining of economic goods to gratify human desires. If there were no economic goods over which to obtain control, there would be no medium of exchange or money. A person stranded on a desolate island with barrels of money in his possession would soon discover that all this meant nothing, if it could not get him food to keep him from starving. Therefore, we should have clearly in mind that it is not the possession of money, but that which it will buy, which ultimately determines the extent to which human desires will be gratified.

In order adequately to serve its purpose as a medium of exchange, money must possess general acceptability. Unless people are willing to give economic goods in exchange for it, the possession of money will have no economic significance.   This was well illustrated in post-war years in certain European countries, where money depreciated until it was practically worthless as a medium of exchange.   Furthermore, to enjoy general accepta-bility, money must possess certain qualities which will induce traders to accept it in exchange.   These desirable qualities of a generally acceptable medium of exchange are commonly referred to as the characteristics of a good money.   They include porta-bility, durability, homogeneity, divisibility, cognizability, and stability of value.   The significance of some of these charac-teristics will be amplified in the subsequent discussion of mone-tary problems.

Money does not serve merely as a convenient medium of exchange.   It is also the standard or measure of value, in terms of which the values of all economic goods can be expressed. When the value of an economic good is thus expressed in terms of money, this value is called price.   Price is therefore value expressed in terms of money.   Money performs another very important function in modern industrial society, which is really a corollary of its function as a standard of value.   It is employed as a standard of deferred payments, since it has become custom-ary to express credit transactions in monetary terms.   The debtor and creditor relationship, which has been so extensively developed in modern industrial society, emphasizes the importance of this third function of money, *viz.* that of a standard of deferred payment.

We thus see that money performs three functions in our ex-change economy.   It serves (1) as the generally accepted medium of exchange, (2) as the standard of value, and (3) as the standard of deferred payments.   Monetary problems arise whenever it fails to perform any or all of these functions adequately.   Before analysing some of our monetary problems, let us first note the kinds of money in circulation in the United States today.

2. Kinds of Money in Circulation in the United States.—In addition to standard gold money, a number of other kinds of money circulate freely in the United States and are readily accepted in payment of obligations.   For all practical purposes they are the equivalent of standard gold coin.   Their exchange value is the same as that of our standard money, not because they possess the same use value or commodity value as gold, but because they are readily redeemable in gold.

According to the monthly statement of the Treasury Department, the different kinds and amounts of money in the United States on Nov. 1, 1926 were as follows:

KINDS AND QUANTITIES OF MONEY IN THE UNITED STATES[1]

Kind of money	Stock of money in the United States
Gold coin and bullion............................	$4,491,121,596
Gold certificates.................................	(1,685,760,779)*
Standard silver dollars...........................	534,991,184
Silver certificates...............................	(464,497,150)*
Treasury notes of 1890............................	(1,346,804)*
Subsidiary silver.................................	292,552,453
Greenbacks—United States notes...................	346,681,016
Federal reserve notes.............................	2,066,792,800
Federal reserve bank notes........................	5,282,658
National bank notes...............................	700,714,532
Total, Nov. 1, 1926..........................	8,438,136,239

* These amounts are not included in the total since the money held in trust against gold and silver certificates and Treasury Notes of 1890, is included under gold coin and bullion and standard silver dollars, respectively.

The circulation of so many different kinds of money in the United States raises several interesting and pertinent questions. How did these different kinds of money come into existence? Are all of them necessary to facilitate exchange? How may our monetary system be simplified?

3. Development of Our Monetary System.—In 1792, the Congress of the United States passed a coinage law adopting both gold and silver as standards of value. Both metals were made full legal tender, *i.e.* they had to be accepted in payment of public and private debts. The Secretary of the Treasury was instructed to coin both metals freely for all applicants. The mint or coinage ratio, established between silver and gold by the Act of 1792, was fifteen to one. This means that a silver dollar weighed fifteen times as much as a gold dollar. Gold and silver circulated side by side for a period of time, being freely exchangeable at the mint in the above ratio. A person presenting fifteen ounces of silver of standard fineness at the mint could

[1] Circulation statement, Treasury Department, November 1, 1926.

obtain one ounce of standard gold or its equivalent in coined money.

Some time after the Act of 1792 went into effect, however, the market ratio between silver and gold became nearer fifteen and a half to one. In the markets of the world a person could purchase approximately fifteen and one-half ounces of silver for one ounce of gold, but for fifteen ounces of silver he could obtain one ounce of gold at the mint. He would thus profit to the extent of about one-half an ounce of silver on such a transaction. Under these conditions silver would be brought to the mint to be coined, and gold would be converted into bullion to be used in the markets of the world, either to buy more silver or to make foreign payments for other goods. As more silver came into circulation, gold slowly disappeared, and a monometallic, rather than a bimetallic, standard of value developed. Silver, overvalued at the mint, was driving the undervalued gold from circulation. This tendency of a legally overvalued money to displace a legally undervalued money is commonly referred to as Gresham's law. It is named after Sir Thomas Gresham, an advisor to Queen Elizabeth, who first formulated the principle.

Realizing that silver was slowly displacing gold, Congress, in 1834, attempted to change the situation in order to bring gold back into monetary circulation. Under the Acts of 1834 and 1837 a new mint ratio was adopted, which was 15.988 to 1, or, as it is commonly spoken of, sixteen to one. According to this newly adopted ratio, the standard silver dollar was to contain 371.25 grains of pure silver and the standard gold dollar 23.22 grains of pure gold. As a result of the adoption of this new coinage ratio, silver was now undervalued, for the market ratio continued about fifteen and a half to one. Silver gradually disappeared from circulation, and gold became the standard of value of the country. This situation continued until the Civil War.

During the Civil War, under the Act of 1862, United States notes, popularly referred to as "Greenbacks," were issued in excessive quantities by the Federal government. Consequently, both gold and silver slowly disappeared from circulation. When these paper dollars were no longer redeemable, dollar for dollar in gold or silver, the bimetallic standard no longer existed in the United States. We had been brought to an inconvertible paper standard. In 1879, however, the United States was able to resume specie payment and ceased to be on an inconvertible paper basis.

The Act of Congress of Feb. 12, 1873 omitted the standard silver dollar from the list of authorized coins and established the gold dollar as the unit of value. The act stated that 25.8 grains of gold nine-tenths fine, or 23.22 grains of pure gold, bearing the required stamp and impress of the government was a dollar. The monometallic standard temporarily triumphed over bimetallism.

Under the Bland-Allison Act of 1878, Congress reintroduced the silver dollar and required the Secretary of the Treasury to purchase monthly from two to four million dollars worth of silver bullion in the markets of the world and to coin it into standard silver dollars. Under the operation of this act, about three hundred million silver dollars were coined during the next twelve years. These silver dollars were largely deposited with the United States Treasury, and silver certificates, redeemable on demand, were issued therefor. In spite of the fact that the ratio of silver to gold (*i.e.*, its gold price) continued to fall, even after the purchase of large amounts of silver by the government, agitation for cheap silver money continued. The Sherman Act of 1890 required the Secretary of the Treasury to purchase four and a half million ounces of silver monthly at the market price. They were to be paid for in treasury notes. These notes were made full legal tender and were redeemable in either gold or silver coin. The silver thus purchased was to be coined into standard silver dollars as rapidly as the notes were presented for redemption. The Sherman Act also provided that the notes, when redeemed, might be reissued. As a result of the operation of the Bland-Allison Act and the Sherman Act, the Federal government accumulated over 576,000,000 standard silver dollars. Only a small number of these, however, were ever in actual circulation, because of the inconvenience of handling them. They were kept in the Treasury, and silver certificates redeemable in silver on demand, as well as the Treasury Notes of 1890, were circulated in their stead.

In October, 1893, the Sherman Silver Purchase Act was repealed, because the increasing influx of silver coin was resulting in a proportionate withdrawal of gold from circulation. On Mar. 14, 1900, Congress passed a law, definitely making the gold dollar the single standard of value of the United States. The Act provided that all forms of money coined or issued by the United States should be maintained at par with gold. It further provided for the redemption of legal tender notes in gold on demand, and required that a reserve of $150,000,000 be kept in the Treasury for this purpose. If the fund at any time falls below $100,000,000 the treasury is required to restore it to $150,000,000 by selling bonds. The legal tender notes thus redeemed may be reissued, but only for gold. Because of the danger of loss in the weight of gold coins in circulation due to abrasion, Congress as early as 1863 authorized the issue of gold certificates against gold coins and bullion deposited in the Treasury of the United States.

The monetary stock of the United States also contains over a quarter of a billion dollars of subsidiary coins, used for small change and coined from time to time in limited quantities to meet the general needs for such coins. These subsidiary coins are decidedly overvalued at the mint, but do not drive gold from circulation in accordance with Gresham's law, because their circulation is definitely restricted and they are legal tender only to a very limited extent, as prescribed by law.

4. Development of Bank Currency in the United States.— Under the Act of 1863, establishing our National Banking System, national banks were required to buy government bonds, against which they could issue their circulating notes up to 90 per cent of the par value or market value of these bonds,[1] whichever was smaller. As an incentive to state banks to become members of the National Banking System, Congress passed a law in 1865, imposing a tax of 10 per cent on all notes issued by state banks. This made it unprofitable for state banks to continue to issue bank notes.

National bank notes are issued and redeemed under the direction of the Comptroller of Currency. The government bonds, against which security national bank notes are now issued, are deposited with the United States Treasurer, together with a 5 per cent gold reserve for redemption purposes. The Secretary of the Treasury is ultimately responsible for the payment of all national bank notes. Although these national bank notes enjoy wide circulation, over $700,000,000 being outstanding on Nov. 1, 1926, their relative importance as a circulating medium is decreasing with the increasing circulation of Federal reserve notes. The Federal Reserve Act of 1913 was so shaped as to pro-

[1] Since 1900 these notes may be issued up to the par value of the bonds.

vide for the gradual retirement of the national bank notes. As these circulating notes are retired, the Federal Reserve Board may require the Federal reserve banks to purchase the bonds which had secured the national bank notes, to an amount not "to exceed $25,000,000 of such bonds in any one year." Upon the deposit of these bonds with the Treasurer of the United States, Federal reserve banks may receive circulating notes equal in amount to the par value of the bonds so deposited. These Federal reserve bank notes are thus issued and redeemed under practically "the same terms and conditions as national bank notes." At present, however, Federal reserve bank notes form a relatively insignificant part of our currency system. They have not replaced the national bank notes, as was expected.

5. Federal Reserve Notes.—Because of the inelasticity of national bank notes, which can be issued only against the security of United States government bonds, and which cannot be expanded or contracted to meet business requirements, the Federal Reserve Act of 1913 also provided for the circulation of a new type of currency, namely, the Federal reserve notes. These notes are a direct obligation of the Federal government, and are not bank currency in the sense that they are issued by a Federal reserve bank, although the act is not explicit on this point. It says that they are "to be issued at the discretion of the Federal Reserve Board" and that they "shall be obligations of the United States."[1] Again it speaks of them as "issued to the bank," but not by a Federal reserve bank. On the other hand, the act contains such phrases as "Every Federal reserve bank shall maintain reserves in gold . . . of not less than forty per centum against its Federal Reserve notes in actual circulation" and "Federal reserve notes issued through one Federal reserve bank," etc. Federal reserve notes are technically issued by the United States government, but not as ordinary political or fiat[2] money, as were the United States notes under the Act of 1863. They are really in the nature of bank currency issued by the Federal reserve banks, which apply to the Federal reserve agents for the amount of notes they require and which furnish the collateral security.

[1] Section 16, Federal Reserve Act of 1913.

[2] Money which is made legal tender by legislative decree and which possesses no commodity value or specific security behind it other than the government's promise.

The law provides that Federal reserve notes shall normally be secured by a minimum gold reserve equal to 40 per cent of their face value, although, as will be shown later, this reserve requirement is not rigid. The notes are redeemable on demand at the United States Treasury or at any reserve bank in gold or other lawful money. On Nov. 1, 1926, Federal reserve notes formed over 24 per cent of the stock of money in the United States.

6. Maintaining the Gold Parity of Our Different Kinds of Money.—In the preceding pages the development of the different kinds of money enjoying general acceptability in the United States today has been traced. It is the monetary policy of the United States government to maintain the gold parity in value between gold coin and gold bullion in the markets of the world, as well as between standard gold money and the other kinds of money in circulation.

The parity between gold coin and gold bullion is maintained automatically by the free convertibility of one into the other. If the gold dollar tends to become worth more than 23.22 grains of pure gold, gold will, under our system of free coinage, be brought to the mint and coined until the tendency is checked. If, on the other hand, gold in the markets of the world is worth more as bullion than the dollar into which it is coined, gold coins will be used as bullion until the mint and market values of gold are once more approximately the same. Thus, the gold standard is maintained as far as gold coin and bullion are concerned.

The parity between gold and the nine other forms of money in circulation is likewise maintained by virtue of their ready convertibility into gold. So long as the issue of various kinds of money is definitely restricted by law, there is little reason for anxiety concerning the maintenance of the gold standard. If, however, a national crisis should arise, the question of priority in the redemption of different kinds of money would become one of decided importance. Gold certificates are the first direct claim on the gold for which they stand. No law expressly requires the redemption of silver dollars in gold, although it has become the established policy of the government to do so in order to maintain their gold parity. For the redemption of the United States notes, of which $346,681,016 are included in our stock of money today, a special gold reserve fund of $150,000,000 has been set aside since 1900. The redeemed notes are reissued and help to maintain the gold reserve by again exchanging for gold. Thus, the volume of United States notes in circulation remains the same from year to year, since the redeemed notes are constantly reissued. The two kinds of bank currency, national bank notes and Federal reserve bank notes, are kept at a parity with gold by being redeemable on demand in gold or lawful money, both at the Treasury and over the counter of the issuing bank. As we have noted before, however, they are secured by only a limited gold reserve. Federal reserve notes are likewise kept on a par with gold by being readily redeemable in gold upon demand.

7. Simplification of Our Monetary System.—The many kinds of money in circulation in the United States today, with different provisions for gold redemption, suggest certain defects in our monetary system. It is not necessary that we have the great variety of currencies which have been developed from time to time in the past. A simplification of our monetary system seems desirable. Even as many business corporations have reorganized in order to simplify their financial plans and to include a number of outstanding obligations with different priorities under the equity of a single mortgage, so the government may simplify our monetary system in order to eliminate those forms of money which are superfluous, and to substitute a simpler type of credit currency based on standard gold to meet the needs of business. How may this be accomplished?

The stock of money in the United States includes over a half billion silver dollars, of which amount only about 15 per cent was in actual circulation on Oct. 1, 1926. The remainder is stored in the United States Treasury, as security for the silver certificates in actual circulation. It is not this large amount of silver, however, which gives the silver certificates their general acceptability. It is ultimate faith in the government's redemption of the certificates in gold on demand which preserves their gold parity. Not only is this large silver accumulation unnecessary for monetary purposes, but it is also an actual expense to the government, since it must be counted, together with the other assets of the government, with every change in administration.

This large hoard of silver might be disposed of in several ways. In the first place, the silver certificates may be slowly withdrawn from circulation as they are received in payment of obligations to the government, and an equal amount of silver disposed of in the open market. Secondly, the silver certificates may be replaced by United States notes and the silver sold for gold. This gold may be added to the $150,000,000 redemption fund. The percentage of gold reserve against the outstanding United States notes would thus tend to increase, since the silver would probably sell for considerably more than one-third of its monetary value. Furthermore, the likelihood of a demand for the redemption of small bills would not be great, since small monetary units are constantly required in every-day trade. The gold reserve would be more than adequate for the outstanding liability in the form of United States notes. Some of the silver might also be retained for subsequent conversion into subsidiary coin. If large amounts of silver were suddenly offered for sale by the government, violent protests would probably be voiced by the silver-mining industry. In order not to injure this industry unduly, the process of withdrawing the superfluous silver supply from our stock of money could be spread over a number of years. There appears to be no sound reason for continuing the silver certificates in circulation, if they can be replaced by small bills in the form of United States notes, adequately secured by a gold reserve large enough to stand the test of any great emergency.

By any of the foregoing plans our monetary system can be freed of its superfluous silver. The loss sustained by the government from the sale of silver dollars as bullion would be a relatively small item. Let us assume that the total stock of silver were to be sold over a period of ten years, at one-half its coin value. The net loss to the government would be only about $25,000,000 per year, or less than twenty cents annually per capita for the population of the United States. Moreover, it is merely writing off the books of the government a depreciation which has in reality already taken place.

The Federal reserve notes, as previously stated, were adopted to provide an elastic credit currency, a currency which could be expanded and contracted to meet business needs. This elastic credit currency has rendered the national bank notes superfluous in our monetary system. One of the chief defects of these national bank notes was their inelasticity. A discussion of the present significance of national bank notes and of Federal reserve notes in our monetary system today will be included in an analysis of banking problems in the following chapter.

8. Defects of the Gold Standard.—More significant than the problems due to the complexity of our system are those resulting from changes in the value of standard gold money. These changes are reflected in fluctuations in the general level of the gold prices of commodities over a period of time. Numerous studies of the changes in the purchasing power of the dollar are being made by compiling index numbers. These compare the levels of either wholesale or retail prices of selected groups of commodities at one time with another time. Such index numbers reveal the fact that the standard gold dollar of the United States is an accurate measure of value at any one time, but over a period of time its value in terms of commodities changes. This is shown in the following index numbers of wholesale prices, compiled by the Department of Labor in Washington and published in the *Monthly Labor Review*.[1]

INDEX NUMBERS OF WHOLESALE PRICES OF 404 COMMODITIES

Year	Index number
1913	100.00
1914	98.1
1915	100.8
1916	126.8
1917	177.2
1918	194.3
1919	206.4
1920	226.2
1921	146.9
1922	148.8
1923	153.7
1924	149.7
June 1925	157.4
June 1926	152.3
July 1926	150.7

An examination of the foregoing index numbers of wholesale prices in the United States reveals the fact that from 1913 to 1920 the general level of wholesale prices rose by 126 per cent above its former level. In other words, the level of wholesale prices more than doubled. It required $2.26 in 1920 to purchase wholesale approximately the same amount of commodities that could

[1] September, 1926.

be bought for one dollar in 1913. Since 1920, the general price level has fluctuated slightly from year to year. From July 1925 to July 1926 it fell no less than $5\frac{3}{4}$ per cent.

This "dance of the dollar" can be seen by a study of retail price indices as well as of wholesale price indices. The instability of the purchasing power of the gold dollar in the United States is paralleled by fluctuations in the value of the monetary units of other countries employing the gold standard. Since we are concerned primarily with the monetary problems of the United States, this discussion is limited to an analysis of the defects of our standard money, and to suggested remedies for them.

The continuous changes in the level of gold prices, as revealed in index numbers, indicate the extent to which the purchasing power of the gold dollar varies from time to time. Gold lacks one of the chief characteristics of a good money, namely, stability of value. Our monetary unit is an elastic standard of value. It is a flexible and not a fixed measure, such as the yard, the foot, the pound, and the gallon. Although fixed as to gold content or weight (23.22 grains of pure gold), the gold dollar is not fixed as to value. But fluctuations in the value of the dollar are serious, because value is the very thing that the gold dollar seeks to measure.

9. Effects of Changes in the Level of Prices.—Periods of rising and of falling prices affect all economic classes, whether wage earners, enterprisers, or capitalists. The most marked effect of changes in price levels, however, can be observed between the debtor and the creditor classes. A rise in the purchasing power of money, that is, a general fall of prices, benefits creditors, while a fall in purchasing power of money, that is, a general rise of prices, benefits debtors. When prices fall between the time of contracting an obligation and the time for its payment, the debtor returns an amount of money to the creditor which will purchase more economic goods than he received; when prices rise, the debtor returns the monetary equivalent of less economic goods than he received. Over a short period of time, with but a slight change in the general level of prices, the losses thus sustained by either debtors or creditors may be insignificant; but with such extensive changes in the level of gold prices as were experienced in the United States during the past decade, the losses incurred by the debtor and the creditor classes attain considerable importance. Moreover, modern industries frequently contract debts maturing many years hence. Even a gradual change in the level of prices during the interval between incurring the obligations and their final payment may mean considerable loss to either the debtors or the creditors.

Not only the debtor and the creditor classes are affected by changes in price levels. In general, periods of rising prices mean increasing business profits, since many of the production costs, such as wages, rentals, and interest on capital, tend to lag behind the advancing selling prices of products. Salaries likewise usually advance more slowly than does the general price level. On the other hand, in a period of falling prices the wage-earner and the salaried man may be benefited, because wages usually do not fall as soon as the level of prices begins to recede. But at the same time the workers are subjected to the risk of unemployment. Those who are dependent on a fixed monetary income in the form of rentals, interest, or annuities will lose in their control over economic goods as prices advance and gain as prices fall. The serious effects of changes in the purchasing power of our money upon all economic classes emphasize the desirability of a stabilized currency.

10. Why the Value of the Gold Dollar Fluctuates.—Under our system of free and gratuitous coinage of gold, the value of gold money, for reasons previously explained, tends to be the same as the value of gold bullion. Consequently, the ordinary supply and demand forces which cause the value of gold bullion to change in the market will also cause its monetary value, that is, its purchasing power, to change correspondingly. A decline in the value of gold means a rise in the general price level, and an increase in the value of gold is the same as a fall in the general price level. Therefore, the problem which confronts us is to explain the reasons for the changes in the value of gold.

The value of gold is determined in the same manner as is the value of any other commodity, *i.e.*, by the interaction of the forces of demand and supply. An increase in the demand for gold without a corresponding increase in its supply will tend to raise its value, and a decrease in the demand for gold without a corresponding decrease in supply will tend to lower its value. The demand for gold is not a simple but a composite demand. Gold is demanded for industrial purposes in the arts of production, for monetary purposes as a medium of exchange, and for secondary monetary purposes as reserves for outstanding credit currency. The demand for gold in the arts of production is fairly elastic, but it cannot be measured with any degree of accuracy.

At present it is believed to absorb between one-fourth and one-third of the annual production, and in the future it may be depended upon to increase with the growth of the world's population and wealth.[1]

The monetary demand for gold depends upon the extent to which it is used directly in exchange for goods. The use of gold coin in exchange transactions in the United States today is relatively insignificant since the large majority of exchanges are consummated by employing credit instruments in one form or another. The demand for gold as a reserve for both government and bank credit currency in the United States has increased rapidly from year to year. It has been estimated that over 90 per cent of all exchange transactions are now made by using credit rather than standard money as the medium of exchange. Gold or standard money has been called the foundation of our monetary system, and credit its superstructure.

In view of the constantly increasing importance of credit currency as a medium of exchange, the opinion has frequently been voiced that the problem of stabilizing the purchasing power of the dollar is a banking rather than a money problem. With adequate control of our credit currency it is believed prices can be stabilized. The gold reserve behind our credit currency today is practically meaningless. Little importance is attached, moreover, to the fact that between 1915 and 1917 an unprecedented flood of gold came to the United States in payment of foreign obligations. Today, the United States has over 40 per cent of the world's monetary supply of gold.

But the constantly increasing demand for credit currency with expansion of industrial activity implies an increased demand for gold reserves on the part of the government and the banks, if the gold standard is to be maintained. It is, therefore, safe to assume that the importance of gold as the basis of our credit structure will tend to increase rather than to decrease in the future. Credit currency today enjoys general acceptability in place of standard money because people have faith in its continued general acceptability. As long as this faith lasts, the importance of gold reserves behind credit currency, no matter how large or how

[1] *Cf.* Seager, "Practical Problems in Economics," p. 387f.

small, will be relatively unimportant. However, any influence which will undermine this faith will stimulate a sudden demand for actual commodity money.

The problem of stabilizing the value of our standard gold dollar resolves itself into a question of regulating our circulating currency, so that this regulation will counteract any changes in the composite demand for gold. Other things being equal, as the value of the dollar tends to rise, an increased amount of dollar currency put into circulation will cause its value to decline, and as the value of the dollar tends to decrease, a curtailment of dollar currency in circulation will cause its value to rise. Various ways of stabilizing the purchasing power of the dollar by regulating the monetary supply have been suggested. Those pertaining to regulating the supply of standard money or of credit currency issued by the government will be discussed in this chapter, while those which deal with regulating bank currency will be outlined in the following chapter.

11. The Compensated Gold Dollar.—According to this plan of stabilizing the dollar, the legal weight of the gold dollar will be made to vary from time to time to conform with changes of commodity prices as shown by index numbers. In other words, the content of the gold dollar is to be changed directly with the movement of prices. When the accepted index numbers show that prices are rising, the gold content of the dollar is to be increased, as a result of which the number of dollars in a given quantity of gold bullion will become less. As prices go down, the gold content of the dollar is to be decreased, and the number of dollars thereby increased. This plan, known as "the compensated dollar," is commonly associated with the name of its sponsor, Prof. Irving Fisher.

The plan of changing the weight of the gold dollar to conform to changes in price levels means the complete withdrawal of gold coin from circulation, and the substitution of gold certificates in full. These gold certificates would represent a claim on the gold deposited in the Treasury of the United States, but the quantity of gold received for a gold certificate would be heavier or lighter according as prices were high or low. Additional gold coming into the Treasury would necessitate the issue of new gold certificates. The quantity of dollars which the additional gold represented would depend on the index number at the time. Gold certificates would always circulate in place of gold, and individuals who demanded actual gold for them would get varying weights of the metal, depending upon variations in the index numbers.   The general public receiving and paying paper dollars would hardly be aware of the changes in the gold content of their money.   Nevertheless, they would be benefited by the constant value of the dollar, that is, by the elimination of serious changes in the general price level.

The critics of the compensated gold dollar have expressed serious doubts as to its effectiveness in stabilizing the purchasing power of the dollar.   They contend that a lessening of the gold content of the nominal dollar would not have any immediate effect on the general price level.   Even if the level of prices were to rise, there is no reason to believe that the number of gold certificates in circulation would be diminished, unless they were actually presented for gold, either for export or for use in industry. Moreover, a rise in the general price level here does not necessarily mean an exportation of gold in settlement of adverse trade balances unless the prices of those commodities which enter into export have actually risen.   Nor is it likely that a sudden increase in the purchase of gold to be used in the arts of production would be stimulated by a rise in the level of prices. Over a short period of time the compensated dollar would probably not be effective as a means of stabilizing the purchasing power of the dollar, but it might do so in the long run, or act as a restraining tendency on present prices.   Professor Taussig puts it as follows:

The only thing clear is that a force would begin to come into operation, which *if* left at work for a sufficient period, would bring a change in the basis of the currency system, then in the total of currency, eventually in the total of outstanding purchasing power, of such a kind as to check long-continued swings of prices one way or the other.[1]

12. Inconvertible Paper Standard of Value.—Inconvertible paper money has been called political money, government money, or fiat money, because its use as money depends on the political authority issuing it.   Its monetary value is not derived from a commodity of general serviceability, such as gold.   When people have become habituated to the use of a paper medium of exchange, it is usually not difficult to make pieces of paper serve as money by a mere government decree.   This has been amply illustrated in most countries during the past decade.   If such

[1] *Cf.* "Principles of Economics," vol. 1., p. 440, third revised edition.

paper money is made full legal tender for debts, and is receivable
at its face value for all public dues, it will normally perform the
monetary functions as well as metallic or commodity money.
The value of paper money, like that of gold, will be determined
by the interaction of the forces of demand and supply. However, its supply will not be determined by costs of production,
as in case of gold, but by governmental policy. Moreover, its
demand will not be a composite demand, but only a monetary
demand. If fiat money is issued by the government in the same
quantity as the specie previously in circulation, completely
replacing such specie, the level of prices will be the same as
before, assuming there is no change in the rapidity of circulation,
in the quantity of traded goods, and in the method of trading.
If it is issued in twice the quantity of the specie, prices under the
assumed conditions will be doubled, and the value of the fiat
money reduced correspondingly.

As long as the issue of such an inconvertible paper currency
can be rigorously controlled, and people are willing to accept it,
fiat money can undoubtedly perform the monetary functions
performed by metallic currency. In the long run, prices can be
stabilized by regulating the supply of fiat money in accordance
with changes in accepted index numbers, increasing the quantity
of the circulating medium as prices decline and decreasing it as
prices advance. But experience has amply demonstrated that
few governments have been able adequately to control the issue
of an inconvertible paper currency. Advancing prices, resulting
from an overissue of money, will stimulate business activity and
spell prosperity in the minds of most people. A government
which contracts the quantity of circulating medium in order to
bring about a reduction of prices soon finds itself very unpopular.
As Professor Taussig has so aptly expressed it:

Most people have only vague notions of what money is, what are its
functions, how it affects prosperity. Their instinctive attitude is almost
always that of welcoming an increase in the money supply. Especially
during and after periods of rising prices, the panacea of ever plentiful
money has many ardent advocates.[1]

Furthermore, there is always the grave danger of following the
line of least resistance on the part of governments having absolute
control over the issue of money. Taxes are never popular, and

[1] *Cf.* "Principles of Economics," vol. 1, p. 309.

if a government can reduce direct taxes by issuing paper currency, this may be a far easier and more convenient method on the part of the government to obtain purchasing power than to levy direct taxes.   If the obligations thus created by the government cannot be met, new obligations in the form of additional currency issues are commonly created.   The process of currency inflation develops, money depreciates in value, prices rise accordingly, and with the rise in prices we experience all the consequent effects upon various economic classes.

The danger of an overissue of fiat money on the part of governments is the fundamental objection to political money.   Unless the issue of an inconvertible paper currency can be rigorously controlled with a view to stabilizing the level of prices, fiat money would prove a very hazardous substitute for our present metallic currency.   To substitute a money depending for its value upon governmental decree rather than on production costs is placing enormous powers in the hands of a government.   The frequent abuse of this power by governments in the past makes possible the acceptance of a plan to substitute an inconvertible paper currency for a commodity money very doubtful.

13. The Multiple or Tabular Standard of Value.—A third proposal for monetary reform, intended to stabilize the purchasing power of money, would eliminate gold coin as the standard of deferred payments.   Rapid changes in price levels, such as were experienced during the past ten years, result in gross injustices between debtors and creditors.   The multiple or tabular standard of deferred payments has been suggested as a remedy for these injustices.   This proposal is briefly as follows: Debtors shall be required to pay creditors an amount of control over commodities equal to the amount they have borrowed.   In order to determine this amount, accurate index numbers must be prepared to indicate from time to time the changes in the general price levels.   The amount of money to be repaid by the debtor will be determined by these general index numbers.   For example, if the level of prices of the tabulated commodities has advanced 10 per cent between the time of making a loan and its payment, 10 per cent more in money is paid by the debtor to the creditor.   The payment of this larger sum will give the creditor as much of commodities as he loaned.   On the other hand, if the level of prices fell 10 per cent between the time of making a loan and its payment, the debtor would pay back only 90 per cent of the money borrowed. Interest payments would be adjusted in like manner. Thus, a single commodity money would no longer be the standard of deferred payment, for the index number of a tabulated group of commodities would take its place.

Certain objections may be raised to the policy of substituting a multiple for a single standard of deferred payments. In the first place, there is much uncertainty about the best way to compute the index numbers. What weight shall be given to the different commodities? Shall wholesale or retail prices be taken? How shall actual changes in prices be recorded? These are only a few of the many problems arising in connection with the preparation of index numbers. Furthermore, the multiple standard injects a new element of uncertainty into credit transactions. The debtor would not know how much money he has to repay when his debt falls due. To be sure, there is an element of uncertainty in present credit transactions, due to price fluctuations, but a multiple standard of deferred payment would not eliminate this, but merely introduce a new type of uncertainty.

14. Adequacy of the Present Gold Standard.—At present, the monetary situation throughout the entire world is still in a somewhat chaotic condition. France and Italy are among the important European countries, which before the World War maintained the gold standard, but which today employ inconvertible paper currencies as their media of exchange.[1] Some governments are exercising a rigorous control over the further issue of fiat money, while others are resorting to a continued inflation of their currencies. Again, some countries have practically repudiated their obligations by substituting a new currency for their debased political money, and are making every effort to retain the gold parity of their new money. This is particularly true of Germany, which has repudiated its paper mark issues and adopted a new monetary unit based on gold by redeeming one trillion paper marks for one of the new Reichsmarks. On the other hand, Great Britain was the first important nation engaged in the World War to return to the gold standard by recognizing and redeeming

[1] On Oct. 25, 1926, the Belgian government created a new monetary unit, the Belga, having a fixed relationship to the paper Belgian franc at the ratio of 5 to 1. Thus the value of the Belgian franc will be 2.78 cents, or about 14.4 per cent of its original gold par.

its paper obligations at par. The United States retained the gold standard in spite of the monetary disturbances throughout the world arising from the European conflict.

The disorganization of monetary systems has emphasized the importance of a stabilized standard of value, not only as a medium of exchange, but also as a standard of deferred payments. Because of the violent price fluctuations experienced in recent years, particularly in those countries which had abandoned the gold standard, with all the resultant injustices to various economics classes, efforts to stabilize the purchasing power of money have become almost universal. Realizing that the best workable monetary device that has thus far been perfected by man is the gold standard, most countries are at present striving to reëstablish this standard. The fluctuations in gold prices are relatively insignificant as compared with the price fluctuations in those countries which have departed from the gold standard. As time goes on, the more rigorous control of credit currency, based on gold coin, will in all probability tend still further to eliminate gold price fluctuations. The methods developed to control the issue of such credit currency in the United States will be analyzed in the following chapter.

15. Summary.—Money performs three distinct functions in our exchange economy. It serves as the generally accepted medium of exchange, the standard of value, and the standard of deferred payments. There are ten different kinds of money in circulation in the United States today. They include (1) gold coin, (2) gold certificates, (3) standard silver dollars, (4) silver certificates, (5) Treasury Notes of 1890, (6) subsidiary coins, (7) "greenbacks" or United States notes, (8) Federal reserve notes, (9) Federal reserve bank notes, and (10) national bank notes. These different kinds of money have come into existence from time to time since the establishment of the United States. In 1792, a bimetallic standard of value was adopted, both silver and gold being coined freely at the mint in the ratio of fifteen to one. Because of the divergence between the mint and the market ratios of silver and gold, first gold and then silver slowly passed out of circulation, in accordance with the operation of Gresham's Law. In 1863, "greenbacks" or United States notes and national bank notes came into existence. In 1873, the gold dollar was made the standard of value of the United States. The acts of 1878 and 1890 authorized the extensive purchase and coinage of silver, as a result of which more than half a billion silver dollars came into circulation. The Federal Reserve Act of 1913 provided for an elastic credit currency in the form of Federal reserve notes. It also authorized the issue of Federal reserve bank notes intended to replace national bank notes.

The parity between gold coins and gold bullion is maintained automatically by the free convertibility of the one into the other, while the nine other kinds of money in circulation in the United States are kept on a par with gold coin by virtue of their ready convertibility into gold. Gold reserves of varying amounts are provided for the redemption of United States notes, national bank notes, Federal reserve notes, and Federal reserve bank notes. Our monetary system may be simplified by removing the superfluous kinds of currency, such as the silver dollars and the national bank notes from circulation, replacing them with United States notes and Federal reserve notes, respectively.

More important than the simplification of our monetary system is the problem of stabilizing the purchasing power of the gold dollar. The instability of the dollar is reflected in index numbers, indicating changes in price levels from time to time. These changes in the purchasing power of the dollar affect all economic classes—wage earners, enterprisers, capitalists, creditors, and debtors.

The value of the gold dollar fluctuates because of changes in the demand for and the supply of gold. The demand for gold is a composite demand, since gold is used not only in the arts of production, but also for monetary purposes. It has been suggested that the value of the gold dollar be stabilized by regulating the supply of gold coin to conform to changes in demand as reflected in index numbers. The compensated dollar would be made equal to either a larger or smaller amount of gold, according to whether the level of prices was rising or falling. This plan of stabilizing the purchasing power of the dollar has been objected to by those who hold that there is no close relationship between the supply of gold dollars and the general price level, and who believe that the problem of stabilizing prices is one of controlling credit currency rather than one of regulating the supply of standard gold money.

A second plan to stabilize prices is to abolish entirely a commodity standard, such as the gold standard, and to substitute an inconvertible paper currency, deriving its value from governmental decree. The chief objection to such fiat or political money is that governments ordinarily do not or cannot exercise a rigorous control over the issues of government money. Prices invariably begin to rise with excessive issues. Finally, it has been suggested that a new standard of deferred payment be adopted, based on the index number of a selected group of commodities, rather than on the gold dollar. Such a multiple standard would introduce a new element of uncertainty into financial activities in place of the present uncertainties due to price fluctuations. In general, the countries which have abandoned the gold standard for inconvertible paper money have experienced greater price fluctuations than those maintaining the gold standard. Consequently, most countries are today striving to reëstablish the gold standard, which has been found to be as satisfactory and workable a standard of value as has yet been devised.

Collateral Reading

EDIE, L. D., "Economics, Principles and Problems," chaps. 25 and 26.
ELY, R. T., "Outlines of Economics," chap. 14.
FAIRCHILD, F. R., FURNISS, E. S., and BUCK, N. S., "Elementary Economics," chap. 24.
FETTER, F. A., "Modern Economic Problems," chap. 6.
HOLDSWORTH, J. T., "Money and Banking," chap. 6.
TAUSSIG, F. W., "Principles of Economics," chap. 31.

References

BELLERBY, J. R., "Monetary Stability."
CASSEL, G., "Money and Foreign Exchange after 1924."
CLEVELAND, F. A., "Funds and Their Uses."
DEWEY, D. R., "Financial History of the United States."
FISHER, I., "Stabilizing the Dollar."
FOSTER, W. T., and CATCHINGS, W., "Money."
GRAHAM, M. K., "An Essay on Gold."
HEPBURN, A. B., "A History of Currency in the United States."
House of Representatives Committee on Banking and Currency. *Hearings on Stabilization of Purchasing Power of Money*, Dec., 1922, Jan., 1923, Feb., 1924.
JACK, D. W., "The Economics of the Gold Standard."
KEYNES, J. M., "Monetary Reform."
————,"The Economic Consequences of Sterling Parity."
KNAPP, G. T., "The State Theory of Money."
MOULTON, H. G., "The Financial Organization of Society."
PHILLIPS, C. A., "Readings in Money and Banking."
WALKER, F. A., "Money and Banking."

Questions for Discussion

1. What is money?
2. What are the characteristics of a good money?
3. Enumerate the different kinds of money in the United States.
4. Outline the monetary developments in the United States prior to the Civil War.
5. What is meant by bimetallism? What are the objections to bimetallism?
6. How did United States notes or "greenbacks" come into existence?
7. Account for the large number of silver dollars in our monetary system.
8. Explain the origin of national bank notes.
9. Are Federal reserve notes bank notes? Give reasons for your answer.
10. How is the gold parity maintained between gold and other types of currency?
11. Show how our monetary system can be simplified.
12. What are the chief defects of the gold standard?
13. Show how changes in the level of prices affect different groups.
14. Why does the value of the gold dollar fluctuate?
15. What is meant by the compensated dollar? What objections are there to it?
16. What is meant by an inconvertible paper standard?
17. Do you think that fiat money could serve all monetary functions satisfactorily? Give reasons for your answer.
18. Explain the multiple or tabular standard of value.
19. What effect do you think a multiple standard of value would have upon the volume of saving? Reasons?
20. How may the adequacy of the gold standard be defended on the basis of recent monetary experience throughout the world?

Topics for Investigation

1. Economic significance of the return to the gold standard by Great Britain.
2. Causes and effects of currency inflation in Germany, 1919 to 1923.
3. The present French currency problem.
4. Analysis of the distribution of the world's monetary supply of gold.
5. Effect of a stabilized dollar upon the volume of saving.
6. Speculative activity and changing price levels.

CHAPTER XII

SOME PROBLEMS OF OUR MODERN BANKING SYSTEM

1. Functions of Commercial Banks.—Banks, as institutions which deal in money and credit, commonly spoken of as funds, may be divided into two general classes: (1) commercial banks, and (2) investment banks. Commercial banks obtain their funds primarily by purchasing the deposits of their customers. They sell funds by making loans to their customers. The business of commercial banks thus consists chiefly in receiving deposits and making loans.

Deposits are obtained from many sources. Private persons who have a personal bank account deposit their "cash items," in the form of money, checks, drafts, and other credit instruments, and receive credit for these deposits on their pass books. In accepting deposits, banks agree to repay them, in whole or in part, on demand, or in case of time deposits, on or after a stipulated time. In addition to personal deposits, commercial banks also receive deposits from business enterprises, which make extensive use of banking facilities. In our financial centers, furthermore, banks obtain a large volume of deposits from banks in smaller cities and rural districts. Finally, many banks carry deposits of Federal, state, and local governmental agencies.

Funds deposited in banks are derived largely from loans made by the banks to their customers. When a customer gets a loan from his bank he will ordinarily receive deposit credit on his pass book for the amount of the loan, less the discount which is deducted by the bank at the time the borrower gives his promissory note for the full amount of the loan. Thus, commercial banks create deposits out of loans, and thereby provide funds for their customers. These funds, circulated in the form of deposit currency, enjoy ever wider acceptability in our modern industrial society, and serve as a convenient substitute for actual money as media of exchange.

248

Commercial banks receive deposits and make loans extensively to business enterprises by discounting "paper" or documents arising out of commercial transactions. These include trade or bankers' acceptances, warehouse receipts, and the like, commonly spoken of as commercial paper. The loans made by commercial banks are usually short-term loans, intended primarily to furnish industry with working capital, which is employed to purchase industrial materials and to meet various current operating expenses.

Loans made by commercial banks differ not only as to the security accepted, but also as to the conditions of payment. They may be either unsecured loans on personal notes (one-name paper) or loans on endorsed notes (two-name paper). On the other hand, loans may be secured by collateral, in the form of stocks or bonds, warehouse receipts or other types of security. Again, they may be either call loans, payable at any time at the will of either borrower or lender, or time loans, payable within a stipulated period of time.

Since commercial banks provide industry with temporary funds to be used as working capital, the prudent commercial banker strives to have a continual flow of funds available for loans. This can be realized by building up deposits and by making loans which will be self-liquidating over relatively short periods of time. Furthermore, ready funds may be obtained by commercial banks from other banks, if the collateral which they hold is acceptable for rediscount. This factor will be stressed later in this chapter.

The security behind the deposit liabilities of a bank consists of loans and discounts based on personal credit, securities hypothecated for loans, personal liability of stockholders (in case of national banks and of some state banks to the extent of the face value of their stock), the bank's deposits of its funds in other banks, the bank's stock of money, and finally, its tangible property (building, etc.). Although these bank assets may have a nominal value far in excess of the value of deposit liabilities, they do not suffice to maintain the solvency of a bank, unless they can readily be converted into cash. Demand deposits are in the nature of call loans, and are subject to withdrawal on the part of the depositors at any time. If a depositor wants to withdraw his deposits, not by drawing a check on his bank, but by demanding money, the bank must be in a position to meet his demand. To do so, it must keep enough ready cash on hand or be able to obtain sufficient cash to enable it to meet all demands made by depositors for actual money. A bank's reserves against deposits consist of the amount of ready money it has available to meet demands for cash payments. The amount of such bank reserves is usually expressed as a certain percentage of the deposits, and varies in different commercial banks from as low as 5 per cent or less to 25 per cent or more. These reserves against deposit liabilities may be held in the bank's own vaults, or, as will be pointed out later, they may be deposited in other banks.

In addition to the functions of making loans, creating deposits, and accepting deposits, some commercial banks provide a medium of exchange by issuing their own circulating notes. Thus, the national banks of the United States make extensive use of the privilege of bank-note issue. On Nov. 1, 1926, there were over seven hundred million dollars in national bank notes in circulation, representing 8.3 per cent of the total stock of currency in the United States on that date. State banks no longer issue circulating notes, but confine their activities largely to accepting deposits and making loans.

Many minor functions are also performed by commercial banks. They provide a safe place for valuable articles in their safe deposit vaults, renting such depositories to their customers. Again, many commercial banks have savings departments, where time deposits are kept, on which a fixed rate of interest is allowed. In our large cities commercial banks have extensive dealings in foreign exchange and issue letters of credit to settle foreign obligations. Some large commercial banks have recently entered the field of investment banking, so that the functions of both commercial and investment banks are often performed by the same institution.

2. Functions of Investment Banks.—Investment banks are financial institutions intended primarily to aid in providing industry with fixed capital. They perform this function by financing the purchase and sale of securities, by organizing underwriting syndicates to facilitate the marketing of long-term investments, and in general, by acting as functional middlemen between investors and investment opportunities. With the aid of the investment banker, industries and governmental agencies obtain funds through long-time loans. Whereas the primary function of the commercial banker is to provide industry with working capital, the function of the investment banker is to provide industry with fixed capital.

The functions of the two types of banking institutions are more or less interrelated today. When an investment banking syndicate has underwritten an issue of industrial securities, it will often pledge these securities, in whole or in part, as collateral for a loan from a commercial bank. The funds thus borrowed are then advanced to the enterprise, whose security issue has been underwritten. They will ordinarily be converted into fixed assets in the form of plant extensions, betterments, etc. In this manner, the commercial bank loan is employed to provide industry with fixed rather than with working capital. When the securities are sold subsequently by the underwriting syndicate to investors, the proceeds are applied to the repayment of the commercial bank loan, and the collateral is withdrawn. Therefore the deposits of commercial banks may also aid in the development of the fixed assets of industrial enterprises, and not serve merely as sources of working capital. In spite of their interrelationship, however, the functions of commercial and investment banks may be fairly well differentiated.

3. Development of the Commercial Banking System in the United States—1791 to 1863.—The First Bank of the United States was chartered by Congress in 1791 for a period of twenty years, along lines laid down in a report on the financial situation of the newly established republic by Alexander Hamilton, first Secretary of the Treasury. The government subscribed to only a small part of the capital stock of the new institution, while the balance was obtained from private subscriptions. The bank was under private management. It soon established branches in different parts of the country and issued bank notes, which circulated freely without depreciation. It acted as the chief depository of governmental funds, made loans to the government when requested, and transferred funds at the order of the Treasury. In general, the First Bank of the United States was eminently successful. In 1809, however, when the stockholders petitioned Congress for a renewal of their charter which expired in 1811, the question of its renewal was made a political issue. Strong opposition to the national bank was developed on the grounds that it was interfering with state banks and that it was largely dominated by foreign influence. Congress did not renew the charter in 1811. The assets of the bank were sold to Stephen

Girard of Philadelphia, who organized the Girard Bank with a capital of $1,200,000. The stockholders of the First Bank of the United States received $434 for each $400 share of stock they held in the bank.

With the dissolution of the First Bank of the United States in 1811, state banks sprang up in great numbers. In many instances they were poorly supervised and managed. In 1814, many of these state banks suspended specie payment, and the Federal government, whose funds were largely deposited in them, defaulted on the interest on the public debt. This chaotic banking condition aroused sentiment in favor of another national bank, which was finally chartered by Congress in 1816, again for a period of twenty years. The Second Bank of the United States was modelled after the First National Bank. It soon restored financial order, brought about the resumption of specie payment and generally was as successful as the First Bank of the United States. When its charter was about to expire in 1836, however, political rivalry once more manifested itself. The bank was looked upon as the embodiment of plutocratic interests, and was charged with a too pronounced development of centralized power. Its charter was permitted to expire in 1836 and was not renewed by Congress.

The period from 1836 to 1863 was characterized by another period of uncoordinated and often poorly regulated state banking. The funds of the Federal government, which had previously been deposited in the United States banks and in state banks, were withdrawn and placed in the "independent treasury," established in 1840, abolished in 1841, and reestablished in 1846. The "independent treasury" was continued until 1921, when the Federal Reserve Board took over its nine offices and subtreasury branches.

4. The National Banking System.—The national banking system grew largely out of the financial difficulties of the Federal government during the Civil War. The Act of 1863, authorizing the chartering of national banks, revised in many respects in 1864, and notably modified by the Federal Reserve Act of 1913, is still the basis of our national banking system.

At the outbreak of the Civil War the circulating medium of the United States consisted of metallic currency and state bank notes, issued by some sixteen hundred banks operating under state laws. As a rule these state bank notes had only local circulation, and in some instances were nearly worthless. In order to provide a sound national currency, as well as to find a market for United States bonds, the sale of which was of vital importance for the prosecution of the war, the national banking system was established.

The Act of 1863 provided that banks taking out a national charter must buy government bonds and deposit them with the Treasurer of the United States. When bonds had been thus deposited, the national banks were entitled to receive currency notes up to 90 per cent of the par or market value of the bonds, whichever was the lower. However, no bank was allowed to issue an amount of notes exceeding its paid-up capital.[1] Since the obligation to redeem national bank notes is shared by the United States government, note-issuing banks are required to maintain a redemption fund of "lawful money" with the Treasurer of the United States, equal to 5 per cent of the value of their outstanding notes. Thus, the issue of $100 in national bank notes today entails the investment of $105 of the resources of the bank of issue. National bank notes issued against government bonds ultimately rest more on the credit of the government than on the credit of the issuing bank. They are secured by a government promise to pay, dollar for dollar, by virtue of the security in government bonds; by a 5 per cent redemption fund; by a first lien upon the assets of the issuing bank; and by the personal liability of the stockholders of the national bank which issues them.

In addition to the issue of bank notes against government bonds, national banks perform the general functions of commercial banks, namely, to make loans and to accept deposits. In order to insure prompt payment of deposit liabilities, national banks were required under the Act of 1863 to keep a reserve of "lawful money" (including gold and silver coin, gold and silver certificates, and United States notes), against their deposits. Banking centers were divided into three classes, central reserve cities, reserve cities and non-reserve centers, commonly known as "country banks". Banks in central reserve cities had to keep a 25 per cent "lawful money" reserve against deposits in their own vaults. Reserve city banks were also required to carry a 25 per cent reserve, one-half of which or less, could be

---

[1] As previously indicated in Chap. XI, since 1900 national bank notes may be issued to the full amount of the par value of the bonds.

kept on deposit in central reserve cities. Country banks had to keep a 15 per cent reserve against deposits, three-fifths or less of which could be deposited with central reserve or reserve city banks. In other words, country banks had to keep an actual cash reserve of 6 per cent in their own vaults, and reserve cities 12½ per cent. On the other hand, central reserve city banks had to keep a reserve against deposits of at least 25 per cent of lawful money.

5. Defects of the National Banking System Prior to 1913.— The foregoing brief survey of the legally prescribed powers and privileges of national banks suggests certain outstanding defects of our national banking system prior to 1913. They were, primarily: (1) lack of coordination and of centralized control; (2) inelasticity of credit; (3) pyramiding of reserves.

Strictly speaking, the national banking system was no system at all. One bank could not legally establish branches in another city. The banks in the different cities were so many individual units, each looking after its own interests. Clearing house associations were established in the larger cities only by voluntary agreements among the member banks. They made possible a slight degree of cooperation, but were unable to prevent suspension of cash payments when an emergency arose.

As a means of self-protection in times of financial stress, each bank withdrew its deposits from other banks. This decreased the possibility of extending further loans, particularly on the part of central reserve banks, at the very time when extension of credit was most necessary. The maintenance of the independent treasury of the United States added to the difficulties of the national banks by causing irregular withdrawals of money from circulation when obligations to the government had to be paid. Bank reserves were depleted when large governmental revenues flowed into the treasury, and these funds did not come into circulation again until some time later.

Banks, moreover, could not expand their lending power readily to meet business needs. The inelasticity of credit resulted not only from the rigid legal reserve requirements against deposits (25 per cent and 15 per cent), but also from the inability to rediscount commercial paper, in order to obtain a further extension of credit. There was no general rediscounting agency under the national banking system prior to 1913. Reserves against deposits in national banks could not legally be employed to extend further credit, at the very time when these funds were sorely needed. The rigid reserve requirement of the national banking act of 1863 has been likened to a possible legal requirement that for safety sake a 25 per cent police reserve shall at all times be kept in the city hall. When a riot call is issued in an emergency, these policemen cannot legally perform any function except to remain in the city hall for "safety's sake." The folly of such a legal provision is obvious.

Furthermore, national bank notes were perversely elastic, for at the time when their circulation should have been expanded to meet increased business requirements, it contracted. This was illustrated during the period from 1880 to 1891. During this interval, the volume of outstanding national bank notes declined 51 per cent from $345,000,000 to $169,000,000. Nevertheless, this period was one of industrial expansion and of growth in population and national wealth. The reason for this contraction of national bank note currency was the fact that the Federal government was using its large surplus revenue to pay off its debts. In the eleven years under consideration the Treasury of the United States paid over one billion dollars for the reduction of the national debt. This retirement of our public debt very materially decreased the number of outstanding government bonds, against the security of which bank notes could be issued. Furthermore, the bond-secured currency notes did not expand to meet the varying seasonal demands for funds, primarily in agricultural districts.

The National Banking system prior to 1913 was also defective in that it permitted the pyramiding of bank reserves in large financial centers. No bank will keep any more money idle in its own vaults than is absolutely necessary. Since country banks were permitted to deposit three-fifths of their reserves with central reserve and reserve city banks, and these reserve city banks, in turn, could deposit one-half of their lawful reserves with central reserve city banks, the tendency was for idle funds to drift to the large banking centers, primarily New York, where they would yield from 2 to 3 per cent interest and yet be subject to call at any time. In order to keep these deposits as liquid as possible, central reserve city banks preferred to invest their surplus funds in call loans, made chiefly to stock brokers against the security of listed stocks and bonds.

In times of financial stress "country banks" would withdraw their deposits from reserve city banks, and these in turn would demand their deposits from the central reserve city banks. In order to meet their obligations, central reserve banks were forced to call their loans. Hence, prices on the stock market collapsed under a wild wave of selling, in order to realize funds. In the absence of any adequate source of credit currency or any rediscounting agency to tide over such periods of financial distress, suspension of payments of demand obligations on the part of many banks all over the country was inevitable. Every bank sought to build up its own reserves in order to remain solvent, while the further extension of bank credit was practically suspended for the time being.

In the absence of any powerful central or regional banks, mobilizing at the points of weakness, thus upholding the whole structure of credit and giving confidence and support to all sound banks, the accumulated reserves in New York and other reserve cities were torn down and scattered among thousands of individual banks each scrambling for all the gold it could get. Under every great strain this individual reserve system has completely broken down.[1]

6. Events Leading to the Adoption of the Federal Reserve System.—After the last severe financial panic in the United States, that of 1907, definite steps were taken by Congress to remedy the glaring defects of the national banking system. The Aldrich-Vreeland Act of 1908 permitted national banks to organize national currency associations for the purpose of issuing emergency currency against commercial paper and certain types of securities other than government bonds. The Act of 1908 was a form of emergency legislation, and it was to expire in 1914; but pending the establishment of the new Federal reserve banking system, it was extended to June 30, 1915.

The Aldrich-Vreeland Act also created the National Monetary Commission, composed of members of the Senate and the House of Representatives, charged with making an investigation into the monetary and banking systems of the leading commercial countries of the world. Their painstaking report, representing studies, investigations, and collections of materials over a period of four years and filling nearly fifty volumes, constitutes the most exhaustive study of the subject ever made.

[1] *Cf.* HOLDSWORTH, "Money and Banking," p. 349.

With its report the commission also submitted a constructive plan, known as the "Aldrich plan," named after the Chairman of the Commission.   The plan provided for a National Reserve Association, a banker's bank, and in many of its details indicated an effort to remedy every one of the outstanding defects of the national banking system.   Because of the impending presidential election in 1912, Congress took no action on the "Aldrich Plan."   The Democratic party was specifically opposed to any plan involving a central bank.   With the advent of the Wilson administration and a Democratic majority in Congress, the matter of banking reform was one of the first objects on the program of the special session of Congress, which began Mar. 5, 1913.   A new banking plan was drawn up, known as the Owen-Glass Bill, which embodied many of the features of the "Aldrich Plan."   The bill was introduced in the House of Representatives, June 26, 1913.   After many weeks of active discussion inside and outside the halls of Congress, and after numerous amendments in details, the bill was finally enacted into law, December 23, 1913, as the Federal Reserve Act of 1913.

7. Organization of the Federal Reserve System.—The Federal Reserve Act provided for the division of the country into from eight to twelve districts with a Federal reserve bank in each district.[1]

The capital stock of each Federal reserve bank is to be not less than four million dollars.   National banks are required, and state banks and trust companies are permitted to subscribe to the capital stock of the Federal reserve bank in their district and thus to become members of the Federal reserve system.   The amount of such subscriptions is equal to 6 per cent of their own capital and surplus.   One-half of this amount must be paid in three equal instalments, and the other half remains subject to call.

Each Federal reserve bank is supervised by a board of nine directors, holding office for a period of three years.   Three of these directors are appointed by the Federal Reserve Board, and six are chosen by member banks.   Of these six, three represent the member banks and three must "be actively engaged in their

---

[1] There are now twelve Federal reserve districts.   The centers of these districts are (1) Boston, (2) New York, (3) Philadelphia, (4) Cleveland, (5) Richmond, (6) Atlanta, (7) Chicago, (8) St. Louis, (9) Minneapolis, (10) Kansas City, (11) Dallas, and (12) San Francisco.

district in commerce, agriculture or some other industrial pursuit." The chairman of the board of directors of a Federal reserve bank is appointed by the Federal Reserve Board and is known as the "Federal Reserve agent." At the suggestion of the Federal Reserve Board, moreover, the board of directors of each Federal reserve bank names one of its members governor. He performs administrative duties similar to those of a bank president.

Although privately owned and managed, the Federal reserve banks are under strict centralized, governmental supervision and control. Supervisory powers are vested in the Federal Reserve Board, composed of eight members, two of whom, the Secretary of the Treasury and the Comptroller of the Currency, are members *ex-officio*. The remaining six members are appointed by the President of the United States, by and with the advice and consent of the Senate. One of the appointive members of the Federal Reserve Board is designated governor of the board, another vice-governor, and the Secretary of the Treasury is *ex-officio* chairman of the board. The board has its headquarters in Washington.

8. Powers of the Federal Reserve Board.—Broad, sweeping powers are given to the Federal Reserve Board. They include, among others, the power (1) to supervise generally all Federal reserve banks; (2) to appoint three directors of each Federal reserve bank and to suspend any of its officers or directors; (3) to rearrange Federal reserve districts as it sees fit; (4) to examine accounts and affairs of reserve banks and member banks, and to require such statements and reports as are necessary; (5) to determine classes of commercial paper eligible for rediscount and to exercise general supervision over rediscounting rates charged by Federal reserve banks; (6) to require the reserve bank of one district to rediscount the discounted paper held by a reserve bank in another district; (7) to suspend reserve requirements of reserve banks and of member banks; (8) to supervise and regulate through the office of the Comptroller of the Currency the issue and retirement of Federal reserve notes; (9) to give consent to reserve banks to establish foreign branches and agencies; and (10) to supervise open-market operations of the member banks.

This summary of the powers of the Federal Reserve Board, although incomplete, indicates in a general way, the extent to which the board supervises and directs the activities of the

Federal reserve banks. To advise and consult with the Federal Reserve Board and to keep it in touch with economic and financial conditions throughout the country, the Federal Reserve Act also creates a Federal Advisory Council, composed of one representative of each Federal reserve bank, elected annually by its board of directors. This council meets in Washington at least four times each year to confer with the Federal Reserve Board.

9. Operation of the Federal Reserve System.—Federal reserve banks have been called "bankers' banks," since they deal primarily with member banks and with the government, and not with the general public, except for certain open-market operations explained below. Their chief functions are set forth in the preamble to the Federal Reserve Act of 1913 as follows:

To furnish an elastic currency, to afford means of rediscounting commercial paper, to establish a more effective supervision of banking in the United States, and for other purposes.

In order to provide an elastic currency, the Federal reserve banks must be able to expand and contract the volume of circulating medium to meet business requirements. To expand credit currency, they must have control over funds which they can lend to member banks when required. They obtain their funds from three main sources: (1) capital stock subscriptions of member banks; (2) deposits of member banks; and (3) government deposits. In addition to the funds realized on the subscriptions to the capital of the Federal reserve banks (one-half of which subscriptions have been paid to date, Nov., 1926), member banks are also required to keep the reserves against their own demand and time deposits with the Federal reserve banks in their respective districts. Central reserve city banks are required to have reserves of "lawful money" equal to not less than 13 per cent, reserve city banks not less than 10 per cent, and other banks not less than 7 per cent of their demand deposit liabilities. These reserves of member banks, as well as a 3 per cent reserve against time deposits, are reserve balances held by the Federal reserve banks. The amount of cash which each member bank keeps in its own vault is left to the discretion of the individual bank. The reserve balances of member banks with Federal reserve banks may be built up either by actual cash deposits or by rediscounting eligible commercial paper. Finally, Federal reserve banks obtain funds from governmental deposits. The Federal

Reserve Act of 1913 provides that moneys held in the general fund of the Treasury, with certain exceptions, may,

. . . upon the direction of the Secretary of the Treasury, be deposited in the Federal reserve banks, which banks, when required by the Secretary of the Treasury, shall act as fiscal agents of the United States.[1]

These three main sources of funds form the basis for the extension of deposit credit on the part of Federal reserve banks. The Federal reserve banks are normally required to maintain reserves against deposits equal to 35 per cent. These reserve requirements, however, are not rigid, but may be suspended by the Federal Reserve Board for definite periods of time, on payment by the Federal reserve bank of a graduated rate of taxes on increasing deficiencies.

Thus, the Federal reserve system provides for an elastic bank credit (1) by establishing a rediscounting agency for member banks, (2) by centralizing reserves by member banks in the Federal reserve banks, and (3) by materially reducing the reserve requirements against deposit liabilities. Whereas central reserve city banks under the national banking system prior to 1913 were required to have a rigid minimum of 25 per cent reserve against demand deposits, today these banks need have a reserve of only 10 per cent. This reserve, in turn, may be made the basis of a further extension of credit by the Federal reserve bank, which normally is required to have only 35 per cent reserve of actual gold against its net deposit liabilities.

10. Federal Reserve Notes.—Not only may Federal reserve banks lend their deposit credit to member banks, but they, in turn, can obtain credit currency in the form of Federal reserve notes, when such credit currency is required. The Federal Reserve Act of 1913[2] authorizes the issue of Federal reserve notes at the discretion of the Federal reserve banks through the Federal reserve agent. These currency notes are not issued solely against the security of government bonds, as are national bank notes, but may be issued against collateral security arising out of sound commercial transactions, such as drafts, bills of exchange, bankers' acceptances, trade acceptances and the like. Any Federal reserve bank may make application to its Federal reserve

[1] Section 15.
[2] Section 16.

agent for such amounts of the Federal reserve notes "as it may require." These Federal reserve notes are obligations of the United States, are "receivable by all national and member banks and Federal reserve banks for all taxes, customs, and other public dues," and are redeemable in gold on demand at the Treasury of the United States. Federal reserve banks to which these notes are issued are required to maintain at least a 40 per cent gold reserve against the notes in actual circulation. Of this gold reserve fund, at least 5 per cent must be deposited as a redemption fund with the Secretary of the Treasury, and the remainder is held by the Federal reserve agent, together with the other collateral security. Federal reserve notes may also be issued to Federal reserve banks against the security of either gold or gold certificates, dollar for dollar. When thus issued against a 100 per cent gold reserve, they are the equivalent of gold certificates.

Federal reserve notes provide an elastic credit currency, which was lacking under the national banking system before 1913. National bank notes, as we have seen, could be issued only against the security of certain government bonds. Federal reserve notes, on the other hand, can be issued against the security of commercial paper, arising out of business transactions. As business expands, further credit can be obtained to finance the needs of industry by making commercial bank loans. Commercial banks, in turn, can take their acceptable commercial paper for rediscount to their Federal reserve bank and the Federal reserve bank can, if needed, obtain credit currency in the form of Federal reserve notes by depositing sound commercial paper with its Federal reserve agent, against which he will issue these currency notes.

The provision that in normal times a 40 per cent gold reserve must be held against Federal reserve notes in actual circulation is not rigid. The percentage may be allowed to fall below 40 per cent, on condition that the Federal Reserve Board establish a progressive annual tax on further note issues, varying directly with the deficiencies in the reserves. This tax must be paid by the Federal reserve bank to which the notes are issued, but it must be added to the rates of interest and discount charged to member banks. Consequently, in times of emergency, Federal reserve notes may be issued even beyond the 40 per cent legal reserve requirement. Nevertheless, the graduated tax acts as a deterrent to further inflation.

Elasticity of currency does not involve merely the ability to expand in accordance with business requirements, but also the ability to contract. The Federal Reserve Act of 1913 provides for the retirement of Federal reserve notes when they are no longer needed. When the demand for these notes on the part of individuals and industrial units falls off, the surplus notes will normally find their way into banks, either as deposits or as repaid loans. Since member banks must keep their legal reserves on deposit with the Federal reserve banks, the Federal reserve notes will tend to return to the reserve banks through which they were issued, as deposits of member banks. These notes can then be withdrawn from circulation. The provision that the Federal Reserve Board may charge interest on Federal reserve notes not covered by a 100 per cent gold reserve is a device calculated to encourage the retirement of redundant Federal reserve notes.

The Federal Reserve Act also provides the necessary machinery for the contraction of deposit currency. The pressure of high discount rates, the progressive tax on increasing deficiencies in the legal reserves against deposits, as well as other restrictions by Federal reserve banks on rediscounts, tend to discourage further borrowing and to induce borrowers to pay off their loans. Consequently, the circulation of deposit-currency tends to contract.

11. Open-market Operations of Federal Reserve Banks.— Anticipating that the rediscounting function of member banks may not keep all the funds of the Federal reserve banks actively employed, the Federal Reserve Act also provides for certain open-market transactions of the banks. Reserve banks may deal in government securities and in state and municipal obligations maturing within six months, as well as in bankers' acceptances and bills of exchange arising out of commercial transactions. These open-market operations of Federal reserve banks exercise a measure of control over money market conditions, since the active competition of the Federal reserve banks with commercial banks for acceptable commercial paper and government securities in the open market will affect the money rates charged by these banks. On Oct. 20, 1926, the combined total resources of the twelve Federal reserve banks amounted to $5,080,560,000, of which total, bills bought in the open market aggregated $292,-824,000 and United States government securities, $323,805,000.

These United States government securities bought in the open market by the Federal reserve banks did not include the bills discounted, secured by United States government obligations.[1]

12. Post-war Inflation and the Federal Reserve Policy.— Although the Federal Reserve system is still comparatively new, the war-time and post-war policy pursued by the Federal Reserve Board has won much favorable comment. In only a few instances has it been open to question. In September, 1917, perhaps moved by a mistaken fear, the Federal Reserve Board showed a mercantilistic bias when it imposed an embargo on the exportation of gold from the United States. This gold embargo was continued until June, 1919. The large flood of gold[2] which had poured into this country from July, 1915, to June, 1917, and which, in turn, had made possible the extensive expansion of our credit currency, stimulated an inflation of prices. By keeping rediscount rates relatively low between 1917 and 1919, the Board further encouraged the use of credit at a time when credit contraction would have retarded the rapid upward movement of prices. The Board appears to have been influenced in its discount policy more by the amount of legal reserves available for an extension of credit than by the effect of such an overexpansion of credit on the level of prices. At the conclusion of the war, however, it promptly warned people against the dangers of inflation and wisely counseled the banks to limit their further expansion of credit. Still, prices continued their upward swing after February, 1919, until they reached a peak in May, 1920, and then fell rapidly. In the meantime, the ratio of gold reserves to circulating Federal reserve notes fell until it reached nearly 40 per cent in the early months of 1920, when prices were highest. The reserves of some banks actually fell some points below 40 per cent. Much of this post-war inflation might have been averted, it is contended, if a more drastic rediscount policy had been adopted and put in force earlier by the Federal Reserve Board.

13. Present Significance of the Federal Reserve System.— The war-time and post-war lessons, taught by the effects of the banking policies of the Federal Reserve Board and the Federal reserve banks, have been invaluable. The Federal reserve system has demonstrated its value, and today is an indispensable

---

[1] *Cf. Federal Reserve Bulletin*, Nov., 1926, p. 806*f.*

[2] About one and a quarter billion dollars, net.

part of our banking system. Some of the provisions of the Federal Reserve Act of 1913, however, are relatively insignificant today. Gold reserves, as a basis for credit extension, have become practically meaningless for the time being. The large increase in bank deposits in recent years and the high ratio of legal reserves to Federal reserve notes and net deposits in Federal reserve banks afford a wide legal margin for credit expansion. If these reserves are used as a basis for credit expansion the nation may easily be led into another period of inflation, with all its distressing consequences. In September, 1920, the percentage of reserves to net deposits of Federal reserve banks and Federal reserve notes in circulation was 43.3, but in September, 1926, it was 73.6. Additional Federal reserve notes of over five billion dollars could be issued on rediscounted paper to member banks on the basis of our present gold reserves. In the absence of heavy gold exportations, the Federal reserve banks would still be within their legal reserve requirements. Commercial banks could expand deposits by making loans on the basis of the credit currency secured through rediscounts. In other words, there are billions of dollars of unused bank credit available in the United States today. We have all the machinery of credit inflation on hand, "but due to the caution of some of our able bankers, inspired and stimulated by the experience of some years ago, we have not used it."[1]

The present reserves of gold and of gold certificates held by the Federal reserve banks have no direct bearing on the volume of bank deposits subject to check and the volume of Federal reserve notes in circulation. The volume of available credit currency today does not vary directly with the volume of gold coin or gold certificates in the Federal reserve banks. Consequently, changing the weight of the gold dollar in order to stabilize the level of prices, as suggested in Chap. XI, would probably not produce the desired results under present conditions. The price level is affected by every dollar in circulation, whether in the form of standard money or in the form of representative currency. It is affected by checks and drafts, just as well as by Federal reserve notes, bank notes, United States notes, and other money in circulation. Since bank credit in the form of

[1] *Cf.* WILLIS, H. PARKER, "The Present Relationship between Credit and Prices," *Proceedings of American Academy of Political Science*, Jan., 1925, pp. 111–121.

demand deposits constitutes the primary circulating medium in the United States today, careful control over the extension of bank credit, based on analyses of business requirements and of industrial activity, would probably bring about a greater stability of the price level than control over the supply of gold and of gold certificates.

The Federal Reserve Board seems to be the logical agency to exercise this control as far as it is able. Strangely enough, responsible officers of banks and even members of the Board have at times asserted that they are not concerned with price movements, and that in the determination of discount policies the price situation is not a definite factor. But the movement of prices should be a fundamental factor in determining the discount and open-market policies of the Federal Reserve Board.

There is no service the Federal Reserve Board could render to this country—or, indeed, to the distracted countries of Europe—that would be comparable to its utmost efforts to stabilize the price-level in the United States.[1]

Stabilization of prices cannot be brought about solely by the control of discount rates and the open market activities of Federal reserve banks. As long as commercial banks have plenty of funds to lend, demand deposits may be expanded considerably before use is made of the rediscounting privilege offered by the Federal reserve banks. Even if the Federal Reserve Board, in regulating discount rates, were guided largely by price movements, fluctuations in the volume of bank deposits and in the volume of Federal reserve notes in circulation would be determined to a considerable extent by the acts of individual bankers. Their loan policy would be a controlling factor in regulating price movements.

It has been a well-established observation in the past that bank credit tends to expand with rising prices and to contract with falling prices. In anticipation of larger profits in periods of rising prices, business men will increase their borrowings from banks and so expand deposit currency. Although the rediscount rate may act as a moderating influence, it is able to curb inflation only if it can check the expansion of commercial credit beyond the requirements of legitimate business activity. To accomplish this objective, the rediscount rate must be such that

[1] *Cf.* FOSTER and CATCHINGS, "Money," p. 357.

there is no profit in borrowing from Federal reserve banks. On the other hand, to curb deflation, the rediscount rate must be an incentive to borrow. Prompt action on the part of bankers cooperating with the Federal reserve banks is important in order to guide business men in their commitments.

Much educational work still remains to be done before bankers fully realize the cumulative effect of their individual loan policies. Classification of paper eligible for rediscount is an invaluable guide to commercial bankers. More significant, however, is a thorough understanding of the interrelationship between bank credit, price movements, methods of production and marketing, and general productive activity at home and abroad. The careful compilation of statistical data on commodity movements, industrial output, crop estimates, as well as on banking and financial activity, gold movements, and the like, contained in the *Monthly Federal Reserve Bulletins* issued by the Federal Reserve Board, reflect the importance attached to such data. Federal reserve banks in the various districts and many commercial banks are likewise issuing periodical bulletins, which survey industrial and financial conditions in their respective localities. As such data are made available and their significance is carefully weighed, they will serve as valuable guides, not only to the business man but also to commercial bankers.

14. Simplification of Bank Currency.—In view of the fact that Federal reserve notes have provided the elastic credit currency which was lacking under the national banking system before 1913, bond-secured bank notes, whether national bank notes or Federal reserve bank notes, are superfluous in our currency system today. As indicated in Chap. XI, Federal reserve bank notes were authorized under the Act of 1913 as a convenient means of displacing national bank notes. Both of these forms of bond-secured bank notes, however, are defective in that they cannot be expanded or contracted in accordance with business needs. With the present possibility of expanding deposit currency, based on legal reserve requirements, there appears to be no valid reason for continuing these bank notes in circulation. The requirements as to the purchase of the outstanding 2 per cent government bonds, carrying bank-note privilege, might be altered by suitable legislation. This might allow the purchase or exchange of these bonds by the Federal reserve banks or the United States government for new bonds bearing a somewhat higher rate of interest, but without any bank-note privilege attached. In this manner our present superfluous bank notes could gradually be retired. We would then have only two forms of credit currency in circulation, namely, United States notes and Federal reserve notes. The latter provide an adequately elastic currency to meet any emergency, and furnish

. . . more perfect means for adjusting the supply of currency to the legitimate business needs of the country than we can hope to obtain so long as we continue in circulation the ten different kinds of money that are now outstanding.[1]

15. Summary.—Banks are institutions dealing in funds, that is, in money and credit. They obtain funds in the form of deposits, derived from personal accounts, business enterprises, other banks, and governmental agencies. These deposits are obligations of the banks to depositors. Deposits arise largely out of loans made to depositors. Commercial banks provide industry primarily with temporary working capital. Investment banks aid in providing fixed capital by marketing long-term securities. By means of temporary loans on securities to be sold to investors commercial banks also help investment banks to provide funds for permanent investments.

The first Bank of the United States, chartered by the Federal government for a period of twenty years, was established in Philadelphia, in 1791. In spite of its success as a banking institution, its charter was allowed to expire in 1811. The chaotic banking conditions in the United States, following the abolition of the First Bank of the United States, led to the chartering by Congress of the Second United States Bank in 1816. Although very successful, political antagonism again prevented its continuation after a second life of twenty years. From 1836 to 1863, the commercial banking functions of the country were performed chiefly by state banks. In 1840, the independent United States treasury was established. Although abolished in 1841, it was reestablished in 1846 and continued until 1921, when it was incorporated in the Federal Reserve System.

Our national banking system grew out of the financial difficulties of the Federal government during the Civil War. It was established primarily to provide a market for the sale of government bonds. National banks had to subscribe to United States

[1] *Cf.* SEAGER, "Practical Problems in Economics," p. 373.

bonds, but they were permitted to issue their circulating notes against them. Rigid reserve requirements against deposits were also provided in the National Banking Association Act of 1863. These reserves were largely pyramided in the central reserve cities.

The national banking system before 1913 was defective in three main respects: (1) a lack of coordination and of centralized control; (2) an inelasticity of credit; and (3) a pyramiding of reserves. The Federal reserve system, established under the Act of 1913, remedied these defects. The system is composed of twelve district banks, which are owned by the member banks. National banks must become members of the Federal reserve system, and state and private banks are permitted to join.

Federal reserve banks are supervised by boards of directors, chosen in part by the member banks and in part by the central supervisory board. This supervisory body is the Federal Reserve Board, composed of six appointive members and two *ex-officio* members—the Secretary of the Treasury and the Comptroller of the Currency. It has broad supervisory powers over the Federal reserve system, chief among which powers are (1) to determine what commercial paper is acceptable for rediscount; (2) to establish rediscount rates; (3) to require rediscounting between Federal reserve banks; (4) to supervise the issue and retirement of Federal reserve notes; and (5) to supervise open-market operations of Federal reserve banks. The Federal Advisory Council consists of one representative of each Federal reserve bank. It meets at least four times a year with the Federal Reserve Board, primarily to keep the Board in touch with the general financial and economic conditions throughout the country.

Federal reserve banks make possible an elastic credit currency, not only because of the relatively low reserve requirements against deposits and the flexibility of reserves, but also because of their ability to obtain credit currency, not merely against government obligations, but also against ordinary commercial paper. Furthermore, they exercise a degree of control over the money market by virtue of their sales and purchases of commercial paper and securities in the open market.

Because of the large influx of gold into the United States during and since the World War, the possibilities of credit expansion, based on gold reserves, is now enormous. There are billions of dollars of unused credit currency in the United States, which can easily be employed to inaugurate a new era of inflation, with all its consequent evils, if the extension of credit by bankers is not wisely controlled.   Gold reserves are no adequate guide to bank credit policy today.   The Federal Reserve Board is the logical agency to supervise and control the banking policy of the country, in order to prevent a new period of rapidly rising prices. It cannot accomplish the desired results without the hearty cooperation of bankers, who have control of huge funds in the form of bank deposits.   A better understanding of the significance of business statistics in their relation to price movements, not only on the part of bankers, but also on the part of business men, is greatly desired.

Since the Federal reserve notes provide a sufficiently elastic currency, the national bank notes and the Federal reserve bank notes are now superfluous in our currency.   Our monetary system would be considerably simplified if they were gradually retired. This could be done by refunding the present low-interest-bearing bonds, against which they are issued, with other bonds yielding a somewhat higher rate of interest.

Collateral Readings

EDIE, L. D., "Economics, Principles and Problems," chap. 27.
ELY, R. T., "Outlines of Economics," chap. 15.
FAIRCHILD, F. R., FURNISS, E. S., and BUCK, N. S., "Elementary Economics," vol. 1., chap. 23.
FETTER, F. A., "Modern Economic Problems," chap. 9.
MAGEE, J. D., "Introduction to Economic Problems," chap. 5.
SEAGER, H. R., "Practical Problems in Economics," chap. 20.
WILLIAMSON, T. R., "Readings in Economics," chap. 21.

References

DUNBAR, C. F., "The Theory and History of Banking."
Federal Reserve Bulletin, issued monthly by the Federal Reserve Board.
GOLDENWEISER, E. A., "The Federal Reserve System in Operation."
HOLDSWORTH, J. T., "Money and Banking."
KEMMERER, E. W., "The A B C of the Federal Reserve System."
MOULTON, H. G., "The Financial Organization of Society."
PHILLIPS, C. A., "Readings in Money and Banking."
Reports of the Aldrich Currency Commission, 1910 to 1912.
SCROGGS, W. O., "A Century of Banking Progress."
"The Federal Reserve System—Its Purposes and Work," Annals of the American Academy of Political and Social Science, January, 1922.
WILLIS, H. P., "The Federal Reserve System."
————., and EDWARDS, G. W., "Banking and Business."

Questions for Discussion

1. What is a bank?
2. How do bank deposits originate?
3. Distinguish between the functions performed by commercial banks and by investment banks.
4. Trace the development of commercial banks in the United States prior to 1863.
5. What were the reasons for establishing the National Banking Association?
6. What is the security behind national bank notes?
7. Outline the chief defects of the National Banking System prior to 1913.
8. What events led to the adoption of the Federal reserve system?
9. "Federal reserve banks are essentially bankers' banks." Explain.
10. How is the Federal reserve system organized?
11. What are the chief powers of the Federal Reserve Board?
12. Show how the Federal reserve system remedied the main defects of the National banking system.
13. How do Federal reserve notes come into circulation? How are they retired?
14. What is meant by the "open market operations" of Federal reserve banks?
15. Show how the Federal reserve rediscount policy may result in credit inflation.
16. "Gold reserves as a basis for credit extension are insignificant today." Do you agree? Reasons.
17. What, in your opinion, should be a fundamental factor in determining the discount policy of the Federal Reserve Board at present? Give reasons for your answer.
18. How may our bank currency be simplified?

Topics for Investigation

1. Advisability of regulating the discount rate on the basis of index numbers rather than on the basis of legal gold reserves.
2. Extent and significance of open-market operations of the Federal reserve banks.
3. Services of Federal reserve banks to member banks.
4. Analysis of recent proposals for changes in the Federal reserve system.
5. What has the Federal reserve system accomplished to date?

CHAPTER XIII

THE PROBLEM OF THE BUSINESS CYCLE

1. Nature of the Business Cycle.—The continuity of industrial activity in modern countries has been intermittently interrupted by economic disturbances, accompanied at times by more or less pronounced changes in price levels, in industrial output, and in conditions of employment. The recurrence of periods of business activity, followed by periods of business stagnation, has been so persistent that these apparently rhythmical movements have come to be spoken of as business cycles. A business cycle may therefore be defined as a series of changes in business activity, commonly characterized by periods of alternating prosperity and depression. These fluctuations in business activity have been particularly pronounced since the advent of our modern industrial age of machine production.

No two business cycles have been alike, either in intensity or in duration, although every cycle is ordinarily composed of a complete upward and downward swing in business activity. Furthermore, no two cycles have revealed precisely the same upward and downward movements of prices, although at times pronounced changes in the general level of prices have accompanied periods of prosperity and of depression.

Shortly after the Industrial Revolution, in 1793, England experienced her first general regressive movement of prices and of industrial activity. The United States witnessed during the nineteenth century many periods of business stagnation, during which industrial activity was decidedly curtailed and large numbers of workers were without employment.

2. Business Crises in the United States.—The phase of the business cycle which first attracted the attention of writers was the crisis or turning point, when, over a relatively short period of time, industrial prosperity ceased and business stagnation set in. Historians have long since observed these recurring crises, and have, therefore, come to measure business cycles from one crisis to another. The first notable crisis in the United States occurred

271

in 1817, brought about largely by violent trade adjustments after the War of 1812.   In 1837, the first crisis which was international in scope was experienced.   This was followed two years later by another business reverse in the United States.   These crises were brought on largely by the rapid westward expansion, overspeculation in land, inflation of state bank-note issues, and the financial disorganization due to the discontinuance of the Second Bank of the United States.

The next pronounced business disturbance, which also affected European countries, came in 1847.   This was followed ten years later by the crisis of 1857, which in turn had superseded an extended period of prosperity and of rising prices, traceable largely to the discovery of gold in California.   In 1860, just before the outbreak of the Civil War, there was a slight business disturbance in the United States.   It was in 1873, however, that this country experienced, what was possibly the severest crisis in its history.   It followed a wave of wild speculation, especially in the direction of railroad expansion.   In 1884, another crisis was experienced in the United States, followed by a year of business depression.   The crisis of 1890, precipitated by the failure of a large banking house in London, was only slightly felt in the United States, but in 1893 a very pronounced crisis set in, which was superseded by a period of business depression lasting for four years.   The rapid industrial expansion in the United States was again partially checked in 1900, when Europe also passed through a severe crisis.   In 1903, money became so tight in New York and in other financial centers, that the rapid liquidation of securities precipitated what has been called the "rich man's panic."   This financial panic, however, caused only a slight retardation of business activity.   In 1907, another severe crisis occurred, inaugurated by the failure of the Knickerbocker Trust Company in New York.   This business disturbance was international in scope, and it was followed by a marked industrial depression which lasted through 1908.

After a period of business recovery the outbreak of the European conflict brought on another crisis, which was due to the sudden withdrawal of funds from New York on the part of European countries.   In the post-war crisis of 1920, the United States experienced the most violent collapse of prices in its history.   The average wholesale price indices between 1920 and 1921 fell from 272 to 151.

3. General Characteristics of the Phases of the Business Cycle.—For purposes of analysis, business cycles are commonly divided into a number of distinct phases, designated as (1) the period of prosperity, (2) the crisis (period of liquidation), (3) the period of depression, and (4) the period of gradual recovery. Let us note the outstanding characteristics of each one of these phases.

During the period of prosperity, prospects for business profits are bright. Caution on the part of the enterpriser is gradually superseded by bold action. Worn out industrial equipment is replaced by new tools and machinery. New industries are extensively established, while old industrial plants are improved and expanded. The demand for industrial raw materials and producers' goods increases more rapidly in period of time than the demand for consumers' goods. Thus, the prices of these commodities tend to advance faster than the prices of consumers' goods.

In order to aid in the financing of industrial enterprises, new securities are marketed. Stocks in industrial corporations prove particularly attractive, because of anticipated larger dividends with increasing profits, while outstanding bonds, yielding a fixed rate of interest, tend to decline in market value. New bond issues, on the other hand, can be sold only by raising the interest rate on the investment. Wages gradually rise, as the shortage of labor increases and the demand for still higher wages becomes increasingly persistent. There is relatively little unemployment. Everyone is spending freely, and the accentuated demand tends to raise the prices of various commodities. The wave of prosperity becomes cumulative. The increased demand for consumers' goods, in turn, increases the demand for producers' goods.

In anticipation of further profits, speculation, not only in securities but also in land and in commodities, becomes the order of the day. As a result of intensive industrial, as well as speculative activity, the volume of bank loans and deposits increases rapidly. Business men borrow heavily from banks in order to obtain their necessary working capital, while speculators borrow to take advantage of the rising market. As bank reserves against deposits slowly decrease, interest on short-term loans tends to advance. Gradually the intensive utilization of labor power diminishes its efficiency, capital costs and rates on loans advance, business expenses increase steadily until the aggregate production costs slowly overtake the selling prices, and the margin of profits dwindles. Railroads are unable to handle their congested traffic. Speculation, however, continues. Finally, discontentment with the high prices of various products induces criticism, at first sporadic, and then more general. People buy only those goods which are absolutely essential to their livelihood. Manufacturers, therefore, begin to curtail any further expansion of industrial equipment. Thus, the demand for producers' capital and for raw materials declines, even as the demand for consumers' goods diminishes, and the period of prosperity comes to an end.

With the increasing difficulty of obtaining further extensions of credit, since banks are approaching the legal limits to their lending capacity, holders of goods are forced to sell. Furthermore, in order to obtain funds to meet maturing obligations and to stimulate buying, manufacturers and merchants begin price cutting. "Bargain sales" and "reduction sales" are advertised far and wide. Unable to continue profitable production, some industries are forced to shut down and others to work on part time. Unemployment increases and wages drop. The prices of industrial securities, primarily stocks, decline rapidly. Banks are very cautious in making further loans, and interest rates on short-term loans tend to advance. Money is "tight," and business enterprises, which are unable to obtain further extension of credit, fail in increasing numbers. Many industries which are not forced into actual bankruptcy incur heavy losses.

The curtailment of industrial output and the partial liquidation of stocks of commodities gradually diminish the amount of outstanding bank loans and discounts. Bank reserves thus tend to increase and the conditions in the money market slowly improve. Meanwhile business men become discouraged, timid, and pessimistic. The former bustling activity is converted into business stagnation, as the period of liquidation ends and the period of depression sets in. The pronounced decline in the physical volume of production during the period of liquidation becomes less accentuated during the period of depression. Trade is below normal and uncertain. Many industries are shut down entirely, while thousands of unemployed are idly walking the streets of our industrial centers.

The consumption of a certain quantity of goods goes on, even though production is curtailed. Although the standards of living of some individuals may be lowered because of the reduction in their income, a moderate demand for goods continues. As the consumption of many commodities, for the time being, exceeds production, the surplus stock of goods is gradually used up, and eventually a shortage of essential commodities manifests itself. Meanwhile, the abundant labor supply tends to force down the wages of labor, and bank loans can be obtained by the enterpriser at lower interest rates. Production costs will also tend toward a lower level because of greater efficiency developed in the management of business. With the scale of production costs reduced, goods can once more be produced profitably, but at a relatively lower level of prices.

During the period of business depression the financial situation improves considerably. At the time of the crisis there may be some bank failures, but as loans are gradually repaid and further loans and discounts decline, deposits tend to become less and reserves greater. Interest rates on short-term loans are gradually lowered as funds become more abundant. The prices of securities yielding a fixed rate of interest tend to advance, while the market prices of shares of stock remain low. Imports decline while the prevailing low prices of many products stimulate exports. New enterprises and industrial expansions are not undertaken to any great extent during the period of depression, since the possibility of profits is too uncertain. The shortage of some basic commodities, however, eventually inaugurates a slow upward movement in the prices of these products. This, in turn, stimulates an effective demand for other commodities, and so the physical volume of production tends to increase again. Trade expands more and more, as is reflected in increased bank clearings, the larger volume of railroad traffic, and similar indices. Unemployment decreases, as factories which have been shut down or working on part time take on new help.

During the period of recovery, bank loans and discounts slowly increase with the expanding volume of production and trade. But interest rates on commercial loans are low because of the abundance of loanable bank credit. Activity in the security market is gradually resumed, stock prices, which are low, slowly begin to rise, while bond prices remain fairly high for the time being. With better prospects of profits, the activity in the stock market increases, as is evidenced by the increased volume of securities traded.

The characteristic conditions prevailing in each phase of the business cycle may be summarized in tabular form as follows:

CHARACTERISTIC ECONOMIC CONDITIONS IN THE PHASES OF THE BUSINESS CYCLE

Characteristic conditions	Period of prosperity	Crisis and period of liquidation	Period of depression	Period of recovery
Industrial output.......	High	Decreasing	Low	Slowly recovering
Industrial expansions...	Rapid	Discontinuing	Very little	Slowly resumed
Commerce and trade....	Extensive	Declining	Limited	Expanding
Employment..........	Abundant	Decreasing	Scarce	Increasing
Money wages..........	Rising rapidly	Declining	Low	Slowly rising
Bank loans and discounts..............	Extensive	Restricted	Small in volume	Gradually expanding
Bank reserves..........	Decreasing	Increasing	Large	Slowly decreasing
Discount rates.........	Rising	High	Low	Fairly low
Level of prices.........	Relatively high	Usually declining	Lower	Slowly advancing
Prices of old bonds with fixed yields..........	Fairly low	Slowly advancing	Fairly high	Slowly declining
Prices of stocks........	High	Falling rapidly	Low	Low, then recovering
Dividends and business profits..............	Large	Decreasing	Small	Slowly increasing
Interest rates on new investments.........	Rising	High	Fairly low, few issues	Gradually advancing
Speculation in commodities and securities................	Extensive	Diminishing	Very little	Slowly increasing
Bank clearings.........	Large in volume	Shrinking in volume	Low	Gradually increasing in volume
Business failures.......	Few	Rapidly increasing	Fairly large in number	Less and less
Psychological factor....	Bold action and optimism	Fear	Pessimism	Caution and timidity

4. Price Levels and the Business Cycle.—The cyclical movements in business activity are often accompanied by more or less pronounced changes in the level of prices. During the period of business recovery prices tend to advance, reaching a high point during the period of prosperity, then declining until they fall to a relatively low level during the period of industrial depression. These cyclical price changes should be differentiated not only from seasonal variations in the prices of various commodities, but also from the gradual, long-run, changes in the level of prices, known as the secular trend.

The cyclical price changes are not the same for all commodities. The prices of some commodities and services advance more rapidly than the prices of others during the periods of recovery and prosperity, not only because of the habitual aversion of the consuming public to higher prices, but also because of public control exercised over prices charged by public service enterprises.

In order to measure the cyclical price fluctuations, Prof. Warren M. Persons has prepared a special price index, based upon the prices of a selected group of ten commodities, which are particularly sensitive to cyclical price changes. The commodities used in this index are cotton-seed oil, coke, pig iron, bar iron, pig zinc, mess pork, hides, print cloths, sheetings, and worsted yarns. The accompanying chart of the price changes between 1898 and 1914 shows distinctly cyclical movements in the prices of these ten commodities.

CYCLICAL MOVEMENTS IN PRICES OF TEN COMMODITIES 1898-1914

But, as we shall see later, price changes and cyclical movements in industrial activity are not necessarily correlated phenomena. The business cycle is much more than a series of price changes. Every phase of industrial life—the physical volume of production, business profits, investments, wages, interest, etc.—is affected in one way or another in the course of the business cycle. Some of the explanations of business cycles will next be considered.

5. Explanations of Business Cycles.—(A) *Natural Phenomena or Physical Cause Theories.*—Many attempts have been made by students of the rhythmical movements in business activity to discover the reasons for, or possibly the ultimate cause of, the periodic recurrence of prosperity and depression. Some writers have sought the cause in phenomena of nature. The first of these theorists was the English economist, Jevons, who advanced the theory that the disturbances on the sun, known as sun-spots, occurred in ten-year cycles, and that these cyclical recurrences caused corresponding cycles of climatic conditions on the earth. These atmospheric disturbances, in turn, affected crops, causing periods of business prosperity and depression, due to the interdependence of agriculture and industry. This theory, however, assumes a regularity of recurrent phases of the business cycle which does not exist. More recently, H. L. Moore has shown that rainfall in the Ohio Valley occurs in eight-year cycles, and has combined his observation with the cyclical movement of business. He holds that the eight-year cycles of rainfall generate crop cycles, which in turn cause cyclical activity in industry. Both the "sun spot" and the "rainfall" theories of business cycles are open to the objection that they exaggerate the regularity of recurring phases of prosperity and depression. Even though these natural phenomena theories are not given much credence today, further observation and study may show that a higher degree of correlation exists between natural phenomena and the cyclical movements in business activity than is generally believed at present.

(B) *Overproduction Theories.*—Some theorists have attempted to trace the ultimate cause of the business cycle to some inherent defect in our present competitive system of capitalistic production. The Marxian Socialists, for example, hold that the search for profits causes periodic overproduction. The inability to consume all the goods produced causes periodic gluts of the markets, when production has to stop to allow consumption to catch up. The overproduction and the underconsumption theories are two different aspects of the same idea. The overproduction theorists see that factories and warehouses are overstocked from time to time with goods which can no longer be sold profitably. Consequently, they contend that industrial activity is suspended for the time being and men are thrown out of work, because their productive capacity has grown too great. Too much production, in other words, necessitates recurring periods of idleness. On the other hand, the proponents of the underconsumption explanation of business cycles hold that consumption cannot keep pace with production, since those who would like to have the goods which have been produced do not have the necessary purchasing power with which to buy them.

Both the overproduction and the underconsumption explanations of business cycles are based on fallacious reasoning. They make the erroneous assumption that the total demand for products, *i.e.* money incomes, is essentially different from the total net value of these products. They do not maintain that there is misdirected production or unequal distribution, but that there is a general excess of product over total purchasing power. They appear to overlook the fact that realized income, no matter in what form or by whom obtained, is employed either for direct gratification or for further indirect use in durable form. There may be misdirected production and unequal distribution of income, but there is no possibility of having too much of everything. The place where every human want is permanently satisfied is visualized as somewhere in the Great Beyond. It is true that in misdirected production we may discover an explanation of periodic "gluts" of the market with certain economic goods, but this does not mean that periodically our industrial system breaks down because we have produced too much of everything. It may be, moreover, that business cycles are caused in part by a recurrent maladjustment in the balance between producers' and consumers' goods. Again this is misdirected production rather than overproduction.

(C) *Self-generating Theories.*—The advocates of these theories maintain that each phase of the business cycle is generated by conditions which have been developed in preceding phases. As long as sufficient credit is available, it is inevitable that a period of prosperity will follow a period of recovery; and when the supply of credit is exhausted, a crisis will follow a period of prosperity, which will in turn introduce the liquidation phase. The proponents[1] of the self-generating explanation of business cycles, notably Mitchell, Hansen, and Foster and Catchings, begin their explanation of the business cycle with an analysis of conditions prevailing in one of the phases of the cycle, and indicate how these conditions inevitably generate the following phase.

Mitchell does not appear to stress credit conditions as a generating influence as much as do Hansen and Foster and Catchings, but all agree that each phase is generated by conditions which have developed in preceding phases. In the words of Mitchell:

The recurrent phases presented by economic activity, wherever it is dominated by the quest of profits, grow out of and grow into another.

[1] *Cf.* MITCHELL, "Business Cycles," HANSEN, "Cycles of Prosperity and Depression in the United States, Great Britain and Germany," and FOSTER and CATCHINGS, "Money."

An incipient revival of activity, for example, develops into full prosperity, prosperity gradually breeds a crisis, the crisis merges into depression, depression becomes deeper for a while, but ultimately engenders a fresh revival of activity, which is the beginning of another cycle.[1]

Thus, the self-generating theorists regard the explanation of the business cycle as a descriptive analysis of cumulative changes, by which one set of business conditions grows into another.

In his recent lucid study[2] of business cycles, A. B. Adams concludes that the self-generating theorists are correct in holding that a period of prosperity generates a crisis, a crisis grows into depression, which in turn grows into recovery. But he does not believe that, assuming the availability of abundant credit, recovery necessarily "generates a period of prosperity, or that prosperity grows out of conditions developed in recovery."[3] He contends that business cycles are not without beginning or end, but that "each business cycle has a definite beginning and a definite ending—each begins with a cumulative upward movement designated as prosperity, and if not interrupted by war or some major happening originating outside of the business system, ends with a subsequent readjustment of value harmonies designed as recovery."[4] He bases his conclusion on the following line of reasoning. A period of prosperity, as reflected in consistent increases in prices of consumers' goods, must have been preceded by an extensive expansion of capital equipment. Unless this expansion has already taken place under a peace-time condition of recovery, or, in the absence of a large favorable trade balance, consumers' money incomes would not be sufficient to buy currently offered consumers' goods at prices high enough to afford a sufficiently large profit to producers to induce them to make extensive expansions of present capital equipment.

Unless producers see new opportunities for larger profits they will not employ bank credit to increase capital equipment necessary to give consumers large enough money incomes to sustain rising prices of consumers' goods. Therefore, if new physical forces, such as new kinds of consumers' goods, new machinery, possibilities of exploiting rich natural resources, and large crops are not extensively introduced in the period of recovery, it will not generate prosperity. The nature of and the extent to which

[1] Cf. "Business Cycles," p. 449.
[2] Cf. "Economics of Business Cycles," 1925.
[3] Cf. Op. cit. p. 212.
[4] Cf. Op. cit. p. 213.

such forces are developed in each period of recovery will in turn condition the subsequent phase of the business cycle. Each period of recovery, therefore, is unique. It is not generated by preceding phases, and therefore marks the beginning of a new cycle. This explanation, developed by A. B. Adams, may be considered a modified or limited self-generating theory of business cycles.

(D) *Unequal Distribution Theories.*—Some theorists have attempted to discover the causes of business crises in the changes in the percentage of net product value going to different agents of production in various phases of the cycle. In the unequal distribution of money income is to be found the chief cause of the business cycle. Some hold that it is the "lag" of interest rates behind advancing prices which stimulates prosperity and brings on the crisis; others believe that the increase in profits brings on prosperity and eventually leads to the crisis; while still others subscribe to the theory that in times of rising prices wages lag behind and consequently cause cyclical fluctuations. The leading sponsors of the unequal distribution theories of business cycles are the American economists, Irving Fisher and T. N. Carver, and the British economist, J. A. Hobson.

(E) *Capitalization Theories.*—It has been suggested by some writers that business crises are brought about by the mistaken capitalization of the productive agents. In our present capitalistic system production is carried on largely in anticipation of demand, and the value of durable capital goods, industrial plants, and equipment is built up, in part, on anticipated rather than on actual income. The amount of this anticipated income is largely a matter of conjecture. Because of mistaken estimates of these future values, as reflected in maladjustments of industrial capitalization, constant revaluations of sources of income are necessary. As long as private investment continues, and men are guided in their investment activities, not so much by their own judgment, as by the example set by others, the "hypnotism of the masses" will continue to be an important psychological factor in determining the capitalization of industry. The recurring maladjustments in the capitalization of industrial enterprises have constantly necessitated readjustments in values, which have often undermined confidence and precipitated industrial crises.

The foregoing explanations of the causes of business cycles by no means exhaust the entire list. Misdirected saving and investing, maladjustments in the relationship between fixed and working capital, tariff revisions, "consumers' strikes" and other phenomena have been found to influence general business conditions and have consequently been considered by some writers as basic causes of business crises.

It is doubtful whether any one factor can be singled out as being the sole generating or primal cause of the rhythmical recurrence of periods of business prosperity and depression. Economists are inclined to accept the causal sequence or self-generating explanation of the business cycle, which discovers in each phase the essential conditions out of which the following phase develops.

6. Remedying the Effects of Business Depressions.—Many remedies have been proposed to alleviate the distressing conditions brought about by recurrent business depressions. Some of these proposals have been exceedingly fantastic, as for example, the suggestion that prosperity can be perpetuated by furnishing an unlimited supply of cheap money. The advocates of such a plan would have the government issue inconvertible legal tender paper currency. The folly of any such cheap money proposal is apparent to anyone familiar with the functions of money in our exchange system.

Those who hold that the cyclical movements in business activity are inherent in our present economic organization have suggested various methods of alleviating the suffering due to unemployment in periods of depression. Some have suggested that purchasing power be supplied directly to the involuntary idle out of an employment fund. A kind of industrial workers' insurance fund may be set up out of excess business earnings in periods of prosperity, which may be used to pay laborers when production is curtailed. The purchasing power thus received by the workers would create a demand for products and keep many industries operating which would otherwise be idle.

Others would give employment in periods of depression by expanding public works. During the depression of 1921, for example, many cities and counties expanded public works and so provided a large amount of employment for the idle. Again, it has been suggested that the distress during a business depression may be alleviated by having public utilities adopt a program of expansion. It would be difficult, however, to induce railroads to expand at a time when part of their available equipment is standing idle. Other utilities would undoubtedly voice similar objections to a program of industrial expansion in a period of depression. Moreover, so long as profits afford the fundamental stimulus to industrial activity, it is doubtful whether many enterprisers can be induced to adopt an extensive program of industrial expansion when their products cannot be profitably marketed, even though they could obtain labor services, materials, and bank credit at a much lower cost than in a period of prosperity.

Not only have many measures been proposed to remedy the evil effects of business depressions, but suggestions have also been made from time to time to regulate and control business activity, with a view to making our industrial system work more smoothly and uniformly.

7. Public Control of Business Cycles.—Cumulative prosperity may be controlled both publicly and privately. Public control may be exercised by public supervision of the issuance of industrial securities with a view to establishing a proper relationship between commercial credit and fixed capital investments. If a governmental agency were given the power to supervise and regulate the issuance of industrial securities, better direction could be given to capital investment than under a system of unregulated private industrial development. During the World War a Capital Issues Committee was assigned the task of controlling the issues of new securities, with a view to preventing the expansion of nonessential industries. A similar public commission could permanently supervise and guide the investment of funds in new enterprises and so diminish the possibility of misdirected capitalization in industry, a procedure which would tend to bring about greater industrial stability.

The possibility of controlling commercial credit by the Federal reserve banks under the supervision of the Federal Reserve Board has been discussed in the preceding chapter. If the Federal Reserve Act were so amended as to require the Board to regulate the extension of loans and discounts in times of peace with a view to regulating general business activity, using price and business indices, rather than legal gold reserves as the basis, this would tend to serve as a stabilizing force and facilitate the orderly production and movement of economic goods.

8. Private Control of Business Cycles.—In cooperation with governmental agencies, business men themselves may aid in alleviating periods of business depression and unemployment. To avoid cumulative business prosperity leading to a crisis, enterprisers should regulate conditions in their own industry with a view to preventing an overexpansion of inventories, both of raw materials and of finished goods; an overexpansion of customers' credit; an overexpansion of commercial borrowing; and an overexpansion of capital equipment. Furthermore, they should adopt conservative dividend policies and strive to reduce unit costs of production by eliminating inefficiency and waste. To understand the significance and the effects of their own individual business policies, enterprisers should also become more familiar with general business statistics and analyses of business trends, which are invaluable guides to modern industrial activity.

9. Are Rising Prices Necessary for Genuine Economic Prosperity?—The fact that in the past advancing prices and industrial prosperity have frequently gone hand in hand has led many to believe that the two phenomena are one and inseparable. A periodic rise in the general level of prices has come to be accepted as an indicator of improvement in business conditions. Price movements and business trends are correlated in the minds of many students of the business cycle.

Rapidly rising prices in Germany between 1919 and 1923 stimulated business activity considerably. Although factories worked overtime and there was little unemployment, closer observation soon revealed the fact that this industrial prosperity was artificially stimulated and exceedingly unwholesome. History has repeatedly demonstrated that business prosperity which is stimulated by rising prices is of comparatively short duration, and is followed by a wave of industrial depression and falling prices. Such prosperity is artificial and transitory.

During the year 1926 the United States has been in the midst of a period of industrial prosperity. The wheels of industry and commerce are still humming busily, optimism seems to prevail, there is little unemployment, and prospects for an extended period of good business are unusually bright. Abundant evidence of this happy state of affairs can be obtained from the statistical data published in various commercial and financial journals, which reflect the trend of business. Statistics on the volume of industrial output, on unfilled orders in basic industries, on conditions of employment, on accumulation of stocks of goods, on bank loans, deposits, reserves and discount rates indicate the extent of business activity in the United States in 1926.[1]

---

[1] The *Statistical Bulletins of the Standard Daily Trade Service* give an excellent statistical survey of general economic conditions throughout the country.

To be sure, the familiar phenomenon of excessive speculation, in the past commonly identified with a wave of prosperity, has not been lacking. Never in the history of the New York Stock Exchange has there been greater speculative activity than during the year 1925 and the early months of 1926, when the market prices of many shares of stock advanced by leaps and bounds. Advances in the prices of stocks from thirty to forty points were common.[1] The climax of this speculative wave in the stock market came in March, 1926, when the prices of many securities fell precipitously. But in spite of this collapse in the stock market, there has been no general business crisis or depression in the United States during the year 1926. The phenomenal rise and fall of prices on the stock exchange appears to have had little effect upon industrial conditions and upon the general business outlook.

Coincident with this wave of speculation in the stock market there has also been a series of unusual land booms in Florida, along the South Jersey coast and in a number of large cities throughout the country. Stories of the increases in the selling prices of land often sounded more fabulous than the imaginative tales in the Arabian Nights.

In spite of this speculative activity on the one hand, and the legal possibility of extending bank credit based on our large gold reserves, on the other, the wholesale price levels of commodities have not advanced, but rather declined during the past year. This is illustrated in the following monthly index numbers prepared by the Department of Labor:

UNITED STATES BUREAU OF LABOR STATISTICS[2]

Wholesale commodity price index (1913 base = 100)

1925—September	160	1926—April	151
October	158	May	152
November	158	June	152
December	156	July	151
1926—January	156	August	149
February	155	September	151
March	152		

[1] In some instances the market prices advanced over one hundred points. By way of illustration, United States Cast Iron Pipe in 1923 sold at $20, but in 1925 it sold as high as $250 per share. Hudson Motors stock, which early in 1925 sold for $33.75, reached a market price of $139.50 before the end of the year. American Can shares could be bought for $33 in 1921, while in 1925 they reached the high point of $297.

[2] *Cf. Federal Reserve Bulletin*, p. 803, Nov., 1926.

Some observers, to be sure, see in the wild speculative activity of recent years and in the large amount of available bank credit a real menace to continued industrial stability. They seem to fear that we are laying the foundation for a new period of price inflation. Much of this fear can undoubtedly be traced to past experience, for, as has been observed, business prosperity and rising prices have frequently gone hand in hand. Consequently, there are those who believe that without the artificial stimulus of excessive expansion of bank credit and the resultant advances in price levels, we cannot have continued economic prosperity.

We should, however, distinguish between two kinds of economic prosperity. The one may be called artificial, the other real. The former is stimulated by an overexpansion of circulating media, largely in the form of deposit currency, and the resultant advance in the price levels. The latter is brought about by increased production and greater industrial efficiency, so that a larger volume of economic goods may be available to gratify human desires. Real economic prosperity is not identified with quantities of money in one's possession, but with an abundance of economic goods.

The type of prosperity enjoyed by the United States in 1926 was undoubtedly stimulated by the same acquisitive motives which have prompted industrial activity in the past. But there are various ways of gratifying these acquisitive desires of man. Increasing profits, over a period of time, are measured by the spread between aggregate production costs (prime and overhead) and selling prices, times the volume of business transacted. In the past, profits have frequently been realized because the selling prices of many commodities advanced more rapidly than combined production costs. In recent years, industrial activity in the United States has undergone many very interesting changes. The margin between aggregate costs and selling prices has widened and increasing profits have served to stimulate business enterprise. But where formerly selling prices, over a period of time, tended to advance more rapidly than aggregate costs of production, in recent years those costs were decreasing in many industries, while their selling prices were remaining fairly constant, or in some cases actually declining.

A number of reasons have been given for the present large industrial output in the United States without the artificial stimulus of advancing prices. In the first place, it is contended that the increased tendency toward employee ownership of industry is helping to develop a spirit of cooperation between employer and employee which is conducive to greater industrial efficiency. A recent survey revealed the fact that fifty large American corporations, each having a capitalization of over one hundred million dollars, have effective plans for employee ownership. This modern tendency is believed to be a powerful antidote to industrial disputes and labor unrest, which have often proved so costly in the past. Secondly, the introduction of scientific and personnel management in many industries has eliminated much waste and industrial inefficiency. Third, many industries which expanded their industrial equipment extensively during the wartime and post-war periods have been able to utilize this equipment more intensively and extensively during the past years without being compelled to expand their fixed assets. As this equipment is gradually used to capacity it is believed by some observers that further plant extensions will necessitate new financing, which will tend to bring about an expansion of credit currency.

The extensive integration which is going on in industry and the simplification of marketing processes are said to be further factors in the present reduction of production costs. As ever larger industrial units are developed, overhead costs become increasingly great. Hence the incentive to divide these fixed charges over a larger number of units of product, thus making the total costs per unit lower. The margin of profit per unit in such industries may decrease, but the increased volume of output makes the aggregate profits greater. Fifth, modern merchandising methods, instalment sales and cooperative marketing systems appear to have facilitated the marketing of industrial output and to have made possible an increased volume of consumption. Sixth, the spirit of cooperation between banking interests and business men, which appears to be developing rapidly, is conducive to a better understanding of the interrelated problems of these two important branches of our modern economic life. Seventh, the compilation and analysis of business statistics by public and private agencies serve as invaluable guides to modern business enterprisers. Finally, industrial research, carried on by many large corporations, as well as by private organizations and institutions of learning, has brought forth much valuable information which has been employed by the modern business enterpriser to increase industrial efficiency and lower production costs.

These various factors have been recently noted as being conducive to increasing industrial efficiency, eliminating waste and lowering production costs in many of our basic American industries, although statistical data cannot always be furnished to corroborate these contentions. So long as large profits can be realized by practicing economies in production, however, the stimulus of rising prices to promote industrial activity does not seem necessary. How long further economies in production costs will continue is a subject for speculation, but eventually the point of increasing costs or of diminishing returns will set in. There are those who predict that when that point has been reached, continued prosperity can be had only through the stimulus of advancing selling prices which will lead ultimately to another crisis and depression.

10. Summary.—Business cycles are series of changes in business activity commonly characterized by alternating periods of prosperity and depression. Since business crises first attracted the attention of writers on business cycles, it has become customary to measure cycles from one crisis to another. The United States has experienced a number of more or less severe crises since the beginning of the last century, notably those of 1817, 1837, 1847, 1857, 1873, 1884, 1893, 1907, 1914, and most recently that of 1920.

For purposes of analysis, business cycles have been divided into four phases: the period of prosperity, the crisis (period of liquidation), the period of depression, and the period of recovery. Each phase of the business cycle is set off by characteristic economic conditions. The period of prosperity is characterized by extended industrial activity and general business optimism. The period of liquidation frequently reveals declining prices of many commodities, calling of bank loans, increasing unemployment, and gradually leads to the period of depression, when many industries have suspended production in whole or in part, while credit conditions slowly improve. The shortage of certain economic goods finally makes possible the resumption of profitable productive activity on a larger scale, and business recovery sets in once more.

Many explanations of business cycles have been suggested from time to time. Some of the theories connect the cyclical movement in industry with natural phenomena, such as sun spots and the amount of rainfall.   Others ascribe business depressions to an inherent defect in our industrial system, motivated largely by acquisitiveness.   The stimulus of profits, they contend, causes periodic overproduction, when industrial activity has to be suspended in order to give consumption a chance to overtake production.   Some theorists hold to the belief that the business cycle is a self-generating phenomenon.   In each phase of the cycle, they contend, conditions develop, which grow into the next phase, even as these conditions have grown out of conditions in the preceding phases.   Again, it has been argued that the business cycle is caused chiefly by defects in our system of distribution. Finally, the contention has been voiced that business cycles are due to mistaken estimates of future values, reflected in a misdirected capitalization of industry.

The evil effects of business depressions may be alleviated by providing a fund in periods of prosperity out of which to pay the involuntarily idle in periods of depression.   The purchasing power thus distributed would keep many industries operating that would otherwise be idle.   It has also been suggested that public works should be expanded in periods of depression, and that public utilities and private industrial enterprises should adopt a program of expansion when business is dull.   But it is doubtful whether enterprisers could be made to see the expediency and economy of such a program of expansion.

Business may be controlled both publicly and privately, with a view to minimizing recurrent business depressions.   The issue of industrial securities may be supervised by a public commission, while the extension of commercial credit, based chiefly on price indices, may be regulated by the Federal Reserve Board. Cooperating with public agencies, business men can also aid in preventing recurrent periods of depression, by avoiding overexpansion of their enterprise in a period of prosperity, and by adopting a conservative financial policy.

The United States, during the year 1926, was in the midst of a period of economic prosperity.   But the general level of commodity prices has been declining rather than advancing for some time, although the legal possibilities of extending still further bank credit are very large.   It has been suggested that large profits in many industries are not due to the advances of selling prices over production costs, but rather to the many economies in production. Increased efficiency has lowered aggregate production costs and has thus resulted in large profits without rises in the selling prices of commodities. How much longer production costs can be lowered is a matter of speculation. There are those who believe that when no further economies in production can be realized, the era of prosperity will continue only if stimulated by an expansion of credit. In this fashion artificial prosperity will be created by a rising price level, but it will ultimately bring on another crisis.

Collateral Reading

FETTER, F. A., "Modern Economic Problems," chap. 10.
FISHER, IRVING, "Purchasing Power of Money," chaps. 4 and 11.
ADAMS, A. B., "Economics of the Business Cycle," chap. 11.
MAGEE, J. D., "Introduction to Economic Problems," chap. 4.

References

ADAMS, A. B., "Economics of the Business Cycle."
EDIE, L. D., and others, "The Stabilization of Business."
FISHER, IRVING, "The Business Cycle Largely a 'Dance of the Dollar.'"
FOSTER, W. T. and CACTHINGS, W., "Business Conditions and Currency Control," *Harvard Business Review*, vol. II, No. 3, April, 1924.
——, "Money."
——,"' Profits."
HANSEN, A. H., "Cycles of Prosperity and Depression in the United States, Great Britain and Germany."
HASTINGS, H. B., "Costs and Profits; Their Relations to Business Cycles."
HEXTER, M. B., "Social Consequences of Business Cycles."
HOBSON, J. A., "Economics of Unemployment."
MITCHELL, W. C., "Business Cycles."
MOORE, H. C., "Economic Cycles; Their Law and Cause."
——, "Generating Economic Cycles."
National Bureau of Economic Research, "Business Cycles and Unemployment."
PERSONS, WARREN M., and others, "The Problem of Business Forecasting." Quarterly Publications of the American Statistical Society, Dec. 1923.
SCHLUTER, W. C., "The Pre-war Business Cycle," "Studies in History, Economics, and Public Law," vol. 108, No. I.
SCHUMPETER, J., "*Die Wellenbewegung des Wirtschaftslebens*."
SPRAGUE, O. M. W., "History of Crises under the National Banking System," *Senate Document* No. 538, Sixty-first Congress.

Questions for Discussion

1. What is the nature of the business cycle?
2. "The business cycle is a phenomenon identified with our present industrial organization." Explain.
3. Outline the phases of the business cycle.
4. What are the characteristic conditions of each phase?

5. Explain and criticise the natural phenomena theories of the business cycle.

6. "The overproduction theories of business cycles are based on unsound reasoning." Do you agree? Reasons.

7. What is meant by the self-generating theories of the business cycle? Do you consider these logical explanations?

8. How can unequal distribution cause periods of prosperity and of depression?

9. Explain what is meant by the capitalization theories of business cycles.

10. What remedial proposals have been made to alleviate the effects of business depressions? Criticise these proposals.

11. Outline a program for public control of business cycles.

12. How may private interests aid in controlling business movements?

13. Are advancing prices necessary for business prosperity?

14. How do you account for the recent wave of prosperity in the United States?

Topics for Investigation

1. Commodity speculation and the business cycle.
2. Is continuous economic prosperity possible?
3. The psychological basis of business depressions.
4. "Consumers' strikes."
5. Public control of business cycles.
6. Business depressions as insurable risks.

CHAPTER XIV

INTERNATIONAL TRADE AND FOREIGN EXCHANGE

1. What is International Trade?—International trade or foreign trade is the exchange of commodities and services between private persons or business units located in different sovereign countries. Only infrequently do the governments of such countries carry on trade directly. During the World War the United States government made extensive loans to the Ally governments, with the proceeds of which these governments purchased materials from private business units in the United States. Such transactions, however, are the exceptions and not the rule. International trade is carried on primarily by private persons and industrial enterprises located in different countries.

2. Peculiarities of International Trade.—International trade and domestic trade are essentially the same. Both consist of an exchange of commodities and services for commodities and services. At the basis of the exchange of goods, whether domestic or foreign, is division of labor or specialization. Furthermore, both domestic and foreign trade are carried on for mutual gain and benefit. We produce and sell goods, whether at home or abroad, in order that we may buy other goods. The extent to which we are able to sell will depend not merely on our productivity, but also on our ability to find others who will buy that which we have produced. On the other hand, we will be able to buy products to gratify our desires to the extent that we are able to sell our own products. We produce in order that we may consume, and the volume of available consumable goods will be limited by the amount we produce. We cannot buy unless we sell, and we cannot sell unless we buy, for, strictly speaking, we sell funds, whether money or credit, whenever we employ them to buy economic goods. This principle of exchange is fundamental in both foreign and domestic exchange.

The grouping of peoples into sovereign states and nations, each politically independent of the other, has led to the popular misconception that economic interests and political boundaries are coextensive. As a result, international trade has come to be regarded as essentially different from domestic trade. It is popularly believed that a nation benefits by its export trade, while imports are often viewed with apprehension and concern. This misunderstanding can be clarified only by realizing that in every exchange transaction, whether domestic or foreign, he who buys also sells, and he who sells, also buys. Furthermore, each exchange is made with a view to realizing mutual benefits.

There are, however, several differences between domestic and foreign trade which should not be overlooked. They are differences in degree rather than differences in kind. In the first place, different countries have their own monetary units, in terms of which the values of different goods are expressed, and the monetary units of most countries differ. The problem of converting the value of goods, expressed in terms of the monetary unit of one country, into the monetary unit of another country makes the process of international trade somewhat more complicated than that of domestic trade. Secondly, domestic trade is usually free from such obstructions as customs inspection, varying commercial laws, and strange languages, which are frequently of considerable significance in international trade. Furthermore, tariff regulations and other artificial obstacles which may hamper international trade, are usually absent in domestic trade. Finally, there are differences in race, nationality, and political affiliation, which affect man's economic conduct, while the relative immobility of labor and capital plays a more important part in shaping a nation's foreign trade than its domestic trade.

3. Reasons for International Trade.—As previously stated, all trade, whether domestic or foreign, is based on specialization and exchange. One nation may have an advantage over another nation in the production of certain goods, because of its control over natural resources, its favorable climatic conditions, its abundant and efficient labor supply, or because of the impetus of an early start. These differences in the productive capacity of the laborers of various countries will persist; they cannot be overcome by political decrees or legislative enactments. The fact that bananas can be grown more readily in tropical than in temperate nations cannot be altered by placing an import duty on bananas brought into a temperate nation, in order to stimulate the raising of bananas there. The fact that highly skilled labor, gifted with painstaking care, can create artistic products in one country cannot be set aside by arbitrarily enacting laws, which prevent the sale of such products in other lands, with a view to developing similarly skilled labor there. In spite of restrictions and legal barriers, the relative advantages due to the causes cited above will persist. These relative advantages of different countries, like those of different groups within a country in the production of certain commodities, make exchange mutually profitable. They suggest the guiding principle which controls foreign trade and which is commonly spoken of as the law of comparative advantage. It may be stated as follows: *Each country will produce for export those goods which it can produce most cheaply and will import those goods which other countries can produce most cheaply.* Applied to domestic production and exchange, the same doctrine can be stated thus; *each individual or industrial group within a country will produce and sell those products which it can produce most cheaply and buy those products which others can produce most cheaply.*

Thus, we see the close similarity in the underlying principles which control both foreign and domestic trade under competitive conditions. In the absence of trade restrictions and of hampering legislation, the capital and labor force in each country will tend to be applied to those branches of production where they will yield the maximum product. We have pointed out that, because of home ties, linguistic barriers, political insecurity and hampering legislation, labor and capital tend to be less mobile among countries than within a country. Therefore, differences in "real" production costs of a large variety of commodities persist among nations. With the same amount of labor and capital applied to the production of a great number of products, the United States may have an absolute advantage over China. Such an absolute advantage, based on greater labor efficiency, better utilization of capital, and more abundant natural resources, however, does not preclude the possibility of mutually profitable trade between the two countries. Only if the absolute advantage of the United States over China in the production of all commodities were exactly the same would trade between China and the United States cease to be mutually profitable. An equal advantage of one nation over another in the production of all commodities is practically impossible. When one country has a relative or comparative advantage over another country in the production of some commodity, and the other country enjoys a comparative advantage in producing something else, both countries will benefit by exchanging these products.

The importing country may be able to produce the imported product more cheaply than the exporting country, but it is more profitable for the importing country not to produce that product for itself. It is more advantageous for it to specialize in the production of some other commodity in which it possesses a still greater advantage. The exporting country similarly specializes in the production of that commodity in which it has relatively the least disadvantage. Its exportation of that commodity will enable it to import in exchange some other commodity which it could produce still less advantageously, if at all. The question may arise as to why the less fortunate country should export anything. The exports of a nation pay for its imports, and the less favored nation must produce some goods with which to buy the products of the more favored nations. Immigration laws, ignorance and the immobility of labor and capital prevent the distribution of the labor supply and productive enterprises of the world in accordance with the geographical and economic opportunities of various parts of the globe. Hence, absolute as well as relative differences in productive efficiency persist among nations. If such were not the case, nations would continue to have relative advantages and disadvantages in the production of certain particular goods, but not absolute productive advantages and disadvantages.

A simple illustration will make clear the working of the principle of comparative advantage. Let us assume that one day's unskilled labor in the United States will either yield twenty bushels of wheat or extract five tons of coal. In England, on the other hand, we will assume that one day's unskilled labor can produce either twelve bushels of wheat or four tons of coal. Under the assumed conditions, the United States would have an absolute advantage in the production of both wheat and coal. Nevertheless, it would not produce both, but merely that one of the two commodities in which it had the greater advantage, namely wheat. If no trade in these two products existed outside of the countries here considered, twenty bushels of wheat in the United States would tend to exchange for five tons of coal, and in England twelve bushels of wheat would exchange for four tons of coal. The United States has a comparative advantage over

England in the growing of wheat, but England has a comparative advantage or a relatively smaller disadvantage over the United States in the mining of coal. Let us assume the United States were to exchange twenty-two bushels of wheat for six tons of coal in England. The United States would gain one-half ton of coal on the transaction, since at home it could get only five and one-half tons of coal for the twenty-two bushels of wheat (assuming, for the sake of simplicity, that transportation costs will be identical in both cases). On the other hand, at home England could obtain but eighteen bushels of wheat, but in America a possible maximum of twenty-four bushels of wheat for six tons of coal, depending upon the bargaining powers of the traders in the two countries. If it received twenty-two bushels of wheat in exchange for six tons of coal it would gain four bushels of wheat on the transaction, since at home six tons of coal, (one and one-half day's labor) would exchange for only eighteen bushels of wheat under the assumed conditions. Thus, as a result of the exchange with the United States it has gained four bushels of wheat. It would therefore be of advantage for labor in this country to concentrate on the production of wheat and for England to apply its labor power to the mining of coal. Such an exchange is of mutual advantage to both countries, if the gains of geographical specialization are greater than the costs of transportation.

The foregoing hypothetical example indicates in a general way that it is not absolute but comparative advantages which determine the direction and nature of trade between two countries. The price at which the exchange of commodities and services is actually consummated will depend upon the interaction of the forces of supply and demand as reflected in the mutual bargaining powers of the traders.

4. The Mechanism of International Trade.—Since international trade is usually not conducted by governmental agencies, but by private persons and business units in search of profits, the question of making international payments is one of paramount importance to those who buy and sell in the markets of the world. When an American manufacturer has discovered a market abroad for his products, he cannot profitably consummate the trade unless he can get something from his customer in exchange that will be worth more to him than that which he is selling. His customer abroad will normally not have the exact goods which the American manufacturer wants to barter for the goods he intends to buy. He has purchasing power in terms of monetary units which have general acceptability in his country, but which are not generally acceptable in America. The American manufacturer, selling his goods abroad, wants dollars in payment, and not pounds sterling, francs, or marks. On the other hand, if his foreign customer is unable to pay him in terms of dollars, but only in the currency of his own country, the American manufacturer and exporter usually wants to be certain that he will be able to obtain a definite number of dollars for the payment he is receiving in foreign currency. Furthermore, the American trader can ordinarily not wait for weeks or months until his product has been delivered at a distant port to his foreign customer, and then have the contractual consideration sent to him. He wants payment in terms of dollars after he has shipped his goods.

To meet the need of the international trader, a third party has been interjected between buyers and sellers in the two countries, who assumes "the exporter's right against his foreign customer"[1] and who pays the exporter either at once or at a stipulated future time the amount owed him by his foreign customer. This third party is the banker or dealer in foreign exchange. The instrument, by means of which the foreign exchange banker gives effect to the transfer of goods, is a bill of exchange, which may be defined as an order drawn by one party on another, signed by the party giving it, requiring the person to whom it is addressed to pay a fixed sum of money to the bearer of the order at a stipulated time. The person who writes out the order is the drawer, the person to whom it is addressed is the drawee, and the recipient of the money is the payee.

5. How Bills of Exchange Originate.—Orders drawn by Americans against foreigners to pay a definite sum of money originate by selling either commodities or services to foreigners. In other words, demands on a foreigner residing abroad to pay a definite sum of money to an American can ordinarily be made only if something has been sold abroad by the American trader. When an American manufacturer or exporter has sold a consignment of shoes to a British customer at a stipulated price of five thousand dollars, let us say, he will draw a draft on his foreign customer, requesting that he pay his bank or its correspondent

[1] *Cf.* FURNISS, "Foreign Exchange," p. 2.

abroad five thousand dollars at a stipulated time. To this draft he attaches his bill of lading, the insurance receipt, the hypothecation slip, and other papers. By means of these documents he transfers his legal title in the shipment of shoes, or their replacement value in case of loss, to the holder of these paper instruments. This documented draft or bill of exchange he then sells to his banker who deals in foreign exchange, and receives credit on his pass book for a deposit of five thousand dollars, less the prevailing rate of discount, deducted by the banker. As far as the American manufacturer is concerned, the transaction is completed, unless the foreign customer should fail to make remittance. He has sold his shoes abroad, and has received payment in terms of dollars, even before the shipment has been delivered to his foreign customer.

The banker who has bought the bill of exchange then sends it, fully documented, to his foreign correspondent bank, which will take the bill to the foreign customer for his acceptance. When he has written his acceptance across the face of the bill, it indicates that the importer has obligated himself to pay the amount at the time and place stipulated in the draft. The document thus becomes a trade acceptance. The foreign importer has agreed to pay five thousand dollars for the consignment of shoes at a definitely set date. But he sells the shoes when he receives them, presumably in England for English currency. How can he convert these pounds sterling into American dollars, with which to meet his obligation when it falls due? He will have to buy American dollars with the proceeds of his sale of shoes at home. The banker who sells him American dollars or their equivalent in credit currency will have obtained them by buying them from British traders who received them in payment of either commodities or services. The number of dollars available for sale on the part of the British banker will depend upon the volume of sales and possible advances made in terms of American dollars.

Thus, the supply of dollar exchange available abroad with which to make dollar payments will in turn be limited by the extent to which American buyers have paid in American monetary units for commodities and services bought abroad, or have made dollar loans to foreigners.

6. Visible and Invisible Items of International Trade.—Bills of exchange on any country do not originate merely from trading in commodities between the residents in different countries. Transactions other than merchandise trades may create either a demand for or a supply of bills of exchange. All those transactions which demand international payments are known as items of international trade. They consist chiefly of commodity imports and exports, commonly referred to as visible items of international trade. In addition, there are a large number of invisible items, such as tourist expenditures, immigrant remittances, international loans, repurchases of securities held by foreigners, interest on foreign loans, merchant marine, banking, and insurance service charges, all of which require international payments, and which therefore affect the supply of and the demand for bills of exchange on various foreign countries.

For illustrative purposes, let us consider the international trade between only two countries, such as the United States and Great Britain. Which of the foregoing items of international trade would create a demand for bills of exchange on London in New York, and which would create a supply of bills of exchange on London in New York? When American importers purchase commodities in England they create a demand for British currency in exchange for their American dollars, with which to pay for their purchases. Furthermore, when American tourists travel in England they demand British currency with which to pay for their hotel accommodations, transportation expenses, and other service charges. They are, as it were, consuming British commodities and services in England, rather than here at home. This is obviously similar to an import transaction into the United States. It creates a demand for British exchange.

Furthermore, if British citizens come to the United States and sell their services here, converting the American dollars received in payment into bills of exchange on London, to remit to their friends or relatives at home, such immigrant remittances are analogous to importing transactions and create a demand for bills of exchange on London. Again, when Americans buy British securities and these securities are paid for in British currency, a further demand for bills of exchange on London is created. These illustrations serve to show how invisible as well as visible items of international trade create a demand for bills of exchange on a foreign country. Similarly, a supply of bills on London in New York will arise not merely from our commodity exports, but also from such invisible items of trade as borrowings in England, interest on investments abroad and repayment on maturing obligations to us, as well as expenditures of British subjects visiting America and merchant marine services rendered British residents by our merchant marine.

7. Multiple Exchange and the International Balance Sheet.— If only two countries, such as the United States and England, were engaged in international trade with each other, it is clear that for every claim which we established against England, a counterclaim would have been established by England against us.   If we loaned British subjects a certain amount of purchasing power by buying securities of English industries, such as industrial bonds, our foreign investments thus made would give us a claim against England; while to the extent that purchasing power was loaned to England, she could in turn claim our commodities and services.   Thus, the loan would be offset by exports from the United States.   But the claims of American traders on English traders, and of English traders on American traders may be balanced or offset against each other indirectly as well as directly.   If, for example, Americans have sold goods to Frenchmen, and have bought goods from Englishmen, American bills drawn upon Frenchmen for payments may be employed to balance English bills drawn on Americans.   In this manner a triangular exchange is set up, which is completed by the importation of French goods into England.   When a large number of nations are engaged in international trade, not merely triangular but many-sided exchanges will take place.

Under such conditions, the total estimated value of the visible and invisible items of international trade of a country will tend to balance.   They fail to balance exactly, primarily as a result of possible errors in estimates of invisible items of trade.   For example, the balance sheet of the United States, in account with the rest of the world, in 1924 and 1925, contained the following items:

THE BALANCE SHEET OF THE UNITED STATES, 1924 and 1925[1]

We sold or received credit for:	Millions of dollars		
	1925	1924	Change
Merchandise...............................	$4,934	$4,621	$+313
Silver.....................................	99	110	− 11
Gold......................................	262	62	+200
American securities (stocks, bonds, etc.)..........	411	319	+ 92
Foreign bonds (which we held for investment) paid off....................................	140	45	+ 95
United States government receipts:			
On debts of foreign nations....................	27	23	+ 4
Interest on debts of foreign nations............	160 ⎫	159 ⎫	
Services	⎬	⎬	+ 66
Use of our capital (private interest and dividends)	520 ⎭	455 ⎭	
Use of our ships............................	75	76	− 1
Service to foreign tourists.....................	100	100	
Motion-picture royalties......................	75	70	+ 5
Increase in foreigners' bank Balances in the United States.................	....	216	−216
Total exports, visible and invisible.............	$6,803	$6,256	$+547
We bought or paid for:			
Merchandise...............................	$4,268	$3,651	$+617
Silver.....................................	65	74	− 9
Gold......................................	128	320	−192
American securities (repurchased)...............	90	114	− 24
Foreign securities (exclusive of refunding).........	920	795	+125
American paper money (which foreign nations were using)....................................	62	50	+ 12
Services:			
Use of foreign capital........................	165	150	+ 15
Use of foreign ships.........................	83	68	+ 15
Services to American tourists..................	660	600	+ 60
Remittances by residents of United States to foreign relatives and for missionary and charitable purposes.......................................	360	355	+ 5
Reduction of foreigners' bank balances in United States......................................	61	....	+ 61
Expenditures abroad by United States government..	5	5	
Total imports, visibile and invisible	$6,867	$6,182	$+685
Excess of exports over imports.................	$ −64	$ +74	$+138 (net change)

8. Par of Exchange and Rate of Exchange.—When two countries employ the same commodity, such as gold, as their standard of value, but use different quantities of this commodity in their monetary unit, in terms of which they express the value of other commodities, the ratio of these unit quantities of the same standard of value to each other is called the par of exchange.

[1] Taken from statistics in *"Trade Information Bulletin* 399," compiled by the United States Department of Commerce.

The par of exchange of gold between two gold standard countries is obtained by dividing the quantity of pure gold in the monetary unit of one country by the quantity of pure gold in the monetary unit of another country. For instance, there are 113 grains of pure gold in the British pound sterling, and 23.22 grains of pure gold in the American dollar. Dividing 113 by 23.22 we obtain the quotient 4.8665 which indicates that there is 4.8665 times as much pure gold in the British monetary unit as in the American monetary unit. It means that normally one thousand pounds sterling will exchange for $4,866.50.

As a rule, people do not want actual gold in payment of obligations. They prefer to transact business with the aid of credit instruments, notes, drafts, and checks for domestic exchange, and bills of exchange for international transactions. When an American exporter can readily sell his claims against his foreign customer to make payments in a foreign currency to a banker who will give him domestic currency at or near the par of exchange, he will ordinarily prefer to do so, rather than require actual payment in gold at the par of exchange. The bankers dealing in foreign exchange will normally pay approximately the par of exchange for bills drawn by a domestic trader against a foreign customer, since they believe they will be able to resell these bills to domestic traders who have debts to pay abroad.

When, however, many more bills for payments by foreigners are offered for sale by exporters than are demanded by importers, bankers will find that it is not so profitable to buy foreign bills, whereby they are tying up their funds in currencies which are not in demand at the par of exchange. They will therefore refuse to pay the par of exchange, and will establish a rate of exchange below par which, in their opinion, will draw more buyers into the market for these foreign bills of exchange. This rate of exchange at any time signifies the price at which bills payable in the currency of one country will exchange for the currency of another country. If, for instance, the rate of exchange between England and the United States were quoted at $4.78 this means that for every claim to one pound sterling the dealers in foreign exchange will pay $4.78, less their service charges, in American money. On the other hand, it will require $4.78 (plus commission) to buy one pound sterling under the assumed conditions.

9. The Gold Points.—A dealer in foreign exchange in this country with claims on a foreign customer would not ordinarily sell his bill of exchange for $4.78 per pound sterling, but would ask his customer to pay him in gold at the par of exchange. He would estimate the time required to send his bill abroad for collection, the cost of transporting gold, together with insurance costs, and if he found it more profitable to collect his bill in gold than to sell it at a large discount, he would do so. The points at which it is found to be more profitable to send gold from one country to another, rather than to buy or sell bills of exchange at points above or below par, are known as the "gold points." They represent the points above and below the par of exchange, beyond which the rate of exchange on any country will normally not fluctuate. With reference to British bills of exchange these points are about $4.88 and $4.84 but vary somewhat from time to time. When the rate of exchange on London rises above $4.88 it may be cheaper to export gold from this country in payment of obligations in terms of pound sterling than to pay the premium on such bills. On the other hand, when the rate falls below $4.84, it may be found cheaper to import gold at $4.86 per pound sterling and to cover the costs of shipment, rather than to take payment in terms of bills of exchange at a discount. Thus, upper and lower gold points are established. The upper gold point is known as the *gold export* point, and the lower gold point the *gold import* point.

10. Gold Used Normally in International Trade to Settle Trade Balance.—We thus see that international payments for invisible and visible items of trade are made primarily by means of bills of exchange, and gold is normally shipped from one country to another in payment only if the rate of exchange varies above or below the par of exchange in excess of the actual costs of a shipment of gold. In other words, when a nation has an adverse trade balance, *i.e.* when the value of the imports (visible and invisible) exceeds the value of the exports (visible and invisible) causing bills on foreign countries to rise above the gold shipping point, gold will be sent out to settle such an adverse trade balance. On the other hand, a nation whose total exports exceed the total imports in value over a period of time will normally import gold in settlement of the trade balance in its favor. For example, with reference to England and the United States, if the total international payments due in London exceed the total payments due in New York, the difference between these two items will normally be settled by actual gold shipment from New York to London, and then, only if the rate of exchange has passed the gold shipping points.

11. Effects of Gold Shipments from One Country to Another.— When the rate of exchange on a gold standard country is such that gold flows out in payment of foreign obligations, certain forces are normally set in motion which, if unrestricted, will tend to maintain an international equilibrium in exchange rates, price levels, the distribution of the gold supply, and movements of merchandise. As gold leaves a country, it will cause the loan market there to tighten. Diminishing bank reserves will tend to reduce the available quantity of money and bank credit. This reduction in gold reserves will be reflected in rising interest and discount rates. On the other hand, the country receiving a large importation of gold will increase its gold reserves. This will tend to increase the available quantity of money and bank credit, based on such gold reserves. In order to stimulate borrowing of their augmented funds, banks will lower their interest and discount rates. In accordance with the quantity theory of money, the changes in the gold supply of the two nations will affect their price level, tending to lower it in the gold exporting country and to raise it in the gold importing country. This, in turn, will stimulate increased purchases in the country with the relatively lower prices, thus expanding its exports, while at the same time its imports will tend to decrease because of the higher prices prevailing abroad.

The movement of gold from one country to another to settle trade balances will, therefore, normally set forces in motion which will counteract its continued flow in one direction. As the country which has been exporting its gold increases its exports of merchandise and decreases its imports, it will gradually increase the number of claims it holds against foreign countries. This will tend to raise the rate of exchange on such a country once more to the par of exchange, when claims and counter claims will be settled with bills of exchange.

During the World War, however, many European countries discovered that their gold reserves were being drained because of the large demand for dollar exchange with which to make payment for goods bought in the United States to prosecute the War. Since these countries were unable to establish a corresponding number of claims against us by means of exports to the United States, the rates of exchange on these countries in New York gradually declined below the gold import point, and gold began to flow into this country. The net importation of gold into the United States from 1914 to 1919 exceeded one billion dollars, and European countries became alarmed because their gold reserves were being so heavily drained. In consequence, an embargo on gold was declared, and no further gold was permitted to be exported in payment of trade balances abroad. With the lower gold point on various foreign countries suspended in New York, the rate of exchange was no longer fixed by the actual cost of gold shipment. It declined rapidly and the currencies of most foreign countries with a former gold standard depreciated in terms of gold.

12. The Purchasing Power Par.—During the World War and the years which followed it, many European nations inflated their currencies and departed from the gold standard. Although Great Britain has returned to the gold standard and Germany has stabilized its monetary unit, the par of exchange in many continental countries today is a fiction or an ideal, rather than a reality. In those countries the exchange rates do not represent slight and temporary deviations from a par of exchange, which are caused by a shifting of trade balances and which are automatically rectified by an importation or exportation of gold. Current exchange rates represent rather the amount of inflation and the deviation from the original gold standard.

When the rate of exchange is not regulated by the par of exchange and the cost of gold shipments, *i.e.* when it no longer represents a ratio between two fixed quantites of gold or deviates from this ratio merely to cover costs of gold shipment, how is it then determined? At the beginning of 1920, for example, the pound sterling was quoted at about $3.50 (par $4.86). This meant that a certain volume of British currency in England had about as much purchasing power as did $3.50 of American money. To be more exact, it was not the general purchasing power of the pound sterling in England which was equivalent to $3.50, but only the exportable or importable commodities, which could be bought in similar quantities in England and in the United States by spending $3.50 or its equivalent, namely a pound sterling, (making due allowance for tariff and freight charges). The rate of exchange, however, did not correspond exactly from day to day to this ratio of purchasing power. It was influenced by immediate requirements for payments to be made by Americans to Englishmen, whether for visible or invisible items of trade, and vice versa, by payments Englishmen had to make to Americans. But in general, the rate of exchange did not deviate very far from the internal purchasing power.

If, however, the rate of exchange falls very rapidly, as did the rate on German marks between 1919 and 1923, an artificial stimulus is given to exports from the country with the depreciating currency, which in turn tends to increase the demand for such currency and again stabilizes the rate of exchange at approximately the internal purchase power parity. But when a government artificially creates an increased supply of exchange to offer for sale abroad in order to obtain funds to make payments of obligations due, the tendency will be for the rate of exchange not to be stabilized at the purchasing power parity for some time, but to continue to decline more rapidly than internal prices continue to move upward. The relatively higher prices in other countries, moreover, will militate against increased imports on the part of the country with the depreciating currency. This was the case in Germany from 1919 to 1922, when foreigners with their high-valued currencies in terms of marks, could purchase very advantageously in German markets. Domestic prices did not rise, i.e. the purchasing power of the mark within the country did not fall, as rapidly as the rate of exchange on marks. Not until domestic prices eventually caught up with the rate of exchange did foreigners cease to find "bargains" in Germany. In this manner, a temporary stimulus may be given to exports by means of an issue of inconvertible paper currency.

But ere long it leads to trouble, as the country with its rapidly depreciating currency experiences increasing difficulty in buying industrial raw materials abroad. Moreover, it can no longer obtain the necessary working capital at home to operate its industries, since the incentive to save is destroyed when the people realize that their purchasing power is shrinking from day to day. Under such conditions production will be curtailed, while everyone will convert his depreciating funds into commodities as quickly as possible. All this was well illustrated by the wild orgy of spending in Germany during the period of currency depreciation from 1919 to 1923, and was repeated to a certain extent in France during the year 1926.

13. World Exchange Problems.—In the preceding pages we have briefly reviewed the peculiarities of international trade, the nature of the par of exchange, the determination of the rate of exchange, the gold shipping points and the purchasing power parity. At present, a number of foreign trading countries have their currencies still on an inconvertible paper basis. England, as previously noted, has reestablished the gold standard and resumed specie payment. Germany has practically repudiated her mark debt by exchanging one trillion paper marks for its new Reichsmark, which for more than two years has been approximately on a par with gold. Various other European countries, as for example France and Italy, have not yet reestablished the gold standard, but have an inconvertible paper currency.

Exchange rates tend to fluctuate more widely in countries not on the gold basis. If the restoration of the original par of exchange by a return to the gold standard is impossible, stabilization may be secured by a revaluation of the currency. Revaluation implies a return to the gold basis, but with some other gold content for the standard of value, and hence, a new par of exchange. For illustration, if a restoration of the franc to its former value of about twenty cents is impossible, a revaluation of the franc at five or four cents might be possible. The franc would then contain one-fourth or one-fifth of the original number of grains of gold. Although revaluation involves a partial repudiation, it would help to stabilize the exchange rate. A relatively stable exchange rate seems even more important than a restoration of the original gold standard. As inflation takes place, the exchange rate falls and prices rise. However, as we have seen, prices do not rise so rapidly in the home market as abroad. Hence, an artifical stimulus is given to buying in a nation with an inflating currency. It is not so much the high or low exchange rates, but the constantly changing exchange rates that disturb the stream of international trade.

The problem of debt payment, at home and abroad, involves many serious issues. To the extent that domestic creditors are paid their debts in terms of a depreciated currency, they stand to lose. This is well illustrated in France, where the franc has depreciated to less than one-fifth of its pre-war purchasing power, and domestic prices have risen accordingly. The creditors who loaned their funds in pre-war years, whether public or private, will lose a large part of their actual principal if repaid in the present depreciated currency. On the other hand, post-war creditors would receive a decided premium on their loans if repaid in terms of pre-war gold francs. Furthermore, foreign creditors, demanding gold payments, impose a real hardship on the debtor countries with depreciated currencies.

International trade can no doubt continue to be carried on with those nations which cannot settle their adverse trade balances with gold shipments. But in order to prevent further depreciation of their currencies and further declines of their exchange rates under such conditions, they must either increase their exports or expand their foreign loans. A further extension of credits on the part of the United States, the leading creditor nation of the world, in order to stabilize foreign exchange rates at their present levels, is merely staving off the inevitable day of reckoning. Even the present purchase power parity of those countries which have abandoned the gold standard can be retained only by avoiding adverse trade balances, *i.e.* by an expansion of their exports to meet payments, not merely for current imports, but also for payments on foreign obligations. The problem of keeping foreign exchange rates at their present par and of meeting foreign obligations thus resolves itself into a problem of increased industrial output and exportation of products and services on the part of the debtor nations of the world, at the same time limiting their imports of goods so that their trade balance for years to come will be favorable. The willingness of the United States to accept largely augmented imports from abroad will be a determining factor in stabilizing the rates of exchange of various foreign countries at their present purchase power par.

14. Summary.—International trade consists of the exchange of commodities and services between private persons of two sovereign nations. It is akin to domestic trade in that it is based on specialization and exchange for mutual benefit. It differs from domestic trade, however, because of the differences in monetary units of various countries and because of custom regulations, tariff restrictions, linguistic barriers, and racial and political affiliations. International trade is carried on, even as is domestic trade, because of mutual gain. The guiding principle controlling foreign exchange is the doctrine of comparative advantage, which may be stated thus: each country will export those goods which it can produce most cheaply and will import those goods which other countries can produce most cheaply.

International trade is carried on by means of bills of exchange, which may be defined as orders drawn by one party on another, requiring the person to whom the order is addressed to pay a fixed sum of money to the bearer of the order. Bills of exchange originate not merely from international transactions in commodities but also from such invisible items of international trade as interest payments abroad, foreign loans, tourist expenditures, and service charges. All those items which create a demand for payments to be made by foreigners to us are analagous to import transactions while those items which result in demands on us for payments to foreigners are analogous to export transactions.

Various gold standard countries have differing quantities of gold in their monetary units. The par of exchange between two gold standard countries is the ratio of the gold content of the monetary units of two countries. Bills of exchange on any gold standard country will normally sell at or near the par of exchange. If such bills are at a premium exceeding the cost of gold shipment, it will be cheaper to export gold than to make foreign payments with bills of exchange, and if bills are at a discount exceeding the cost of shipment, it will be cheaper to import gold than to accept bills of exchange in payment of foreign obligations. Thus, the gold shipping points are normally determined by the cost of gold shipment. However, when a nation suspends gold shipment to settle its adverse trade balance, its rate of exchange will tend to decline, and will be established at approximately the internal purchasing power of the currency which is no longer convertible into gold. When a nation has established itself on an inconvertible paper currency basis, it can stabilize its exchange rate only by developing a favorable trade balance with which to meet its foreign obligations. Unless this is done its exchange rate will tend to decline still further and domestic prices will continue to rise—a situation which will eventually entail the same economic and social consequences as were experienced by Germany from 1919 to 1923. The world exchange problem thus resolves itself into a question of increased production and mutual willingness on the part of the debtors and creditors to buy and to sell.

The revaluation of the monetary unit would substitute a definite but a smaller number of grains of gold for the original gold content of the national monetary unit. Such revaluation would create a new par of exchange for countries with a depreciated currency.

Collateral Reading

ELY, R. T., "Outlines of Economics," chap. 17.
MAGEE, J. D., "Introduction to Economic Problems." chap. 16.
TAUSSIG, F. W., "Principles of Economics," vol. I, chap. 32.

References

BASTABLE, C. F., "The Commerce of Nations."
————, "Theory of International Trade."
BROWN, H. G., "International Trade and Exchange."
CLARE, GEORGE, "The A B C of Foreign Exchange."
DENNIS, A. P., "The Romance of World Trade."
EDWARDS, G. W., "International Trade Finance."
ESCHER, F., "Elements of Foreign Exchange."
————, "Foreign Exchange Explained."
FURNISS, E. S., "Foreign Exchange."
GRIFFIN, C. E., "Principles of Foreign Trade."
HOBSON, J. A., "International Trade."
LITMAN, S., "Essentials of International Trade."
SAVAY, N., "Principles of Foreign Trade."
WHITAKER, A. C., "Foreign Exchange."
WITHERS, H., "International Finance."
————, "Money-Changing—An Introduction to Foreign Exchange."
YORK, T., "Foreign Exchange."

Questions for Discussion

1. What is meant by international trade?

2. What is the difference between international trade and domestic trade?   In what respects are they alike?

3. "All trade is based on specialization and exchange."   Explain.

4. State and illustrate the law of comparative advantage.

5. "International trade is carried on with the aid of bills of exchange." Explain what is meant by bills of exchange.

6. Show how bills of exchange originate.

7. Define and illustrate "visible" and "invisible" items of international trade.

8. What is meant by triangular exchange?

9. Distinguish between the par of exchange and the rate of exchange.

10. "Normally the rate of exchange will fluctuate only between the gold shipping points."   Why?

11. What function is normally performed by gold in international trade?

12. Trace step by step the effect of extensive gold shipments from one country to another.

13. What caused many European countries to abandon the gold standard during the World War?

14. Explain what is meant by the purchasing power parity.

15. How does the present exchange situation affect the problem of international debt payment?

16. What is a fundamental requisite to stabilization of international exchange rates?

Topics for Investigation

1. Analysis of the "trade balance" of the United States since the World War.

2. Importance of "invisible items" in our trade balance.

3. Effects of a depreciating currency upon foreign trade and exchange rates.

4. Significance of stabilized exchanges for international trade.

5. Our foreign trade compared with our domestic trade.

6. How may our imports be stimulated?

CHAPTER XV

INTERNATIONAL TRADE AND FOREIGN INVESTMENTS

1. Relationship between International Trade and Foreign Investments.—The intimate relationship existing between international trade and foreign investments is generally recognized. It is not so much the volume of a nation's foreign trade nor the value of the exchanged commodities which affects the international ebb and flow of capital. It is rather the "balance of payments," the difference between the value of imports and of exports, both visible and invisible, which reflects either the debtor or the creditor status of a nation. When invisible items of international trade, such as immigrant remittances, tourist expenditures, as well as merchant marine and banking service charges, are relatively unimportant, and when, under such conditions, an unfavorable trade balance is not settled by specie payment, the nation with the adverse merchandise trade balance is either increasing its foreign debts or is receiving payments on previously made foreign investments. In other words, it stamps a country either as a debtor or a creditor nation.

2. Development of Foreign Investments.—During the early stages in the development of a nation's foreign investments, the lending country will normally show a favorable merchandise trade balance, while the borrowing country will have an unfavorable balance of trade. This is so because the borrowing country is receiving commodities from abroad for which it is not making immediate payments. To the extent that payments for the excess of commodity imports over exports are deferred, a nation becomes indebted to other nations. On the other hand, the creditor nation will export more commodities than it imports. Its foreign investments will normally increase by an amount measured approximately by the excess of its commodity exports over its imports. This is the case particularly when various invisible items of international trade play a relatively unimpor-

312

tant role and when specie payments are not made to settle adverse trade balances.[1]

When, after a period of time, the borrowing country begins to repay principal and pay interest, in excess of the amounts of the new loans it is making abroad, its balance of payments will normally be reversed. It will show an excess in the value of exports over the value of imports. On the other hand, the creditor country or countries will have an unfavorable trade balance, the value of their imports being greater than the value of their exports. This is so because the debtor country is compelled to make payments for that which it has previously bought abroad, if it is going to honor its obligations. On the other hand, the creditor countries, to the extent that they want payment of foreign obligations, must accept goods from abroad. The term "goods" is employed to include both commodities and services.

We may, therefore, distinguish among four groups of countries, with reference to their international trade balances and the flow of capital investments. There are (1) immature borrowing countries, (2) immature lending countries, (3) mature debtor countries, and (4) mature creditor countries.

(*A*) *Immature Borrowing Countries.*—These will normally show an excess of imports over exports, while capital investments are flowing in from abroad. Foreign investors of capital funds will lend the necessary purchasing power required to pay for the goods not paid for with exports. From 1849 to 1873 the United States was such an immature borrowing country.

(*B*) *Immature Lending Countries.*—These countries will normally show an excess of exports over imports, which excess will measure approximately their increase in foreign investments from year to year. Since 1917 the United States has been an immature lending country, its favorable trade balance roughly measuring the increase in its capital investments abroad.

(*C*) *Mature Debtor Countries.*—These countries may continue to borrow abroad, but the volume of new loans does not equal the annual interest and amortization payments on formerly contracted international obligations. Such countries will show a favorable

[1] The terms "nation" and "country" are here used figuratively rather than literally. International trade is carried on primarily by private individuals and business units. Only seldom, as we have previously noted, do governments engage in international trade directly, as did the allied governments during the World War.

trade balance, the excess of exports over imports measuring approximately the excess of interest and amortization payments over new debts incurred abroad and payments on foreign obligations due them. From 1873 to 1915 the United States was such a mature debtor country.

(D) *Mature Creditor Countries.*—These are countries which have invested heavily abroad, and which are receiving interest and sinking fund payments in amounts larger than those representing their additional foreign investments. Under these conditions they will normally show an unfavorable trade balance, the excess of imports over exports reflecting the excess of interest and sinking fund payments over new investments abroad and payments on their own foreign debts. Several years during the past century England has been a mature creditor nation.

3. The Position of the United States in International Trade and Foreign Investments.—Prior to 1850, discrepancies between commodity imports and commodity exports of the United States were settled largely by shipments of specie. Securities or foreign loans played only a negligible part in the trade balances. The period from 1849 to 1873, on the other hand, was characterized by an unusually large excess of imports over exports. This was due not merely to the increased gold production since 1849, the hampering effects of the Civil War upon our export trade, and the decline of the American merchant marine, but also to the great increase in the amounts of foreign capital funds borrowed for domestic investment. The reconstruction activities after the Civil War and railroad building in the Middle and Far West created extensive demands for capital funds. It has been estimated that one billion dollars were invested by foreigners in the United States from 1850 to 1873.

During the twenty years from 1873 to 1893, the excess of merchandise exports over imports of this country had an average annual value of $113,000,000 representing, to a large extent, interest payments on foreign debts. From 1893 to 1914, the balance of international payments was essentially the same as during the preceding period. The average annual value of commodity exports exceeded that of imports by about $485,000,-000. This large favorable trade balance was offset in part by tourist expenditures and immigrant remittances, but chiefly by increased borrowings abroad and by payments due on outstanding foreign obligations. By 1910, between five and six billion dollars worth of foreign capital was invested in the United States. Interest and sinking fund charges on this large investment exceeded $300,000,000 annually and even after making allowance for approximately $75,000,000 interest on United States investments abroad, a net interest claim of between $200,000,000 and $225,000,000 had to be met by the United States annually for several decades prior to the World War.

The war changed our status from that of a mature debtor nation to that of an immature lending country. From the summer of 1914 to December, 1918 the excess of American commodity exports over imports reached the enormous total of $11,800,000,-000, while the export balance for the fiscal year ending June 30, 1919 alone exceeded $4,000,000,000. Since 1919 our annual favorable trade balance, although not so large, has continued. For the calender year 1925, the merchandise trade balance of the United States showed an export excess valued at $666,000,000.

The large trade balances accumulated during the World War were offset primarily by repurchases of American securities held abroad, by a net import of gold, exceeding one billion dollars during the war period, and by extensive investments of American capital abroad. Not only the war-time loans of the United States government to the Allied governments, aggregating in principal and accrued interest nearly twelve billion dollars at present (Dec., 1926), but also investments of American capital on private account, estimated at eight and a half billion dollars net, have swelled the foreign debt owed to the United States to the huge total of about twenty billion dollars. According to recent statistics, compiled by the Department of Commerce, no less than $432,658,300 was invested abroad by Americans during the first half of 1926, indicating that we are still increasing the foreign indebtedness to us.

The change in our status from a mature debtor to an immature lending nation has come about in such a relatively short period of time and such enormous sums are involved, that many persons have failed to appreciate the full significance of the change.

4. Significance of Our Changed Status from Debtor to Creditor Nation.—When a person owes someone else a certain amount of money, and he expects to meet his obligation, his primary concern is to provide the necessary funds with which to pay his debts. He will ordinarily obtain the requisite means to make payments by selling his services or the products of his labors to others for money or its equivalent. The money income which he has thus obtained is made available for debt payment. But before he can utilize any of his earned income to pay his debts, he must provide for his necessities, such as food, shelter, and clothing. Not until he has earned a surplus over and above that which is necessary to maintain his industrial efficiency, can he normally hope to make debt payments. In the absence of income from other sources, a person must work and save a portion of his income to pay his debts. His ability to realize an income will ultimately be limited by his ability to sell his services. Unless he can find someone who will pay him for his labor or for the products of his labor, he cannot ordinarily provide means with which to meet his obligations. This is true, no matter whether he is indebted to a fellow citizen or to a foreigner.

Before the World War the United States was a mature debtor nation. The people of this country owed more abroad than foreign countries owed them. Their problem was, therefore, to provide the wherewithal to meet their foreign obligations. They had to work, to produce, in order to create the necessary excess of exports over imports required to meet debt payments. The proceeds derived from the sale of goods abroad which were immediately employed to buy other goods in foreign lands could not be applied toward debt payment. Only the excess value of exports over imports, resulting in a surplus of funds, was available for the payment of foreign obligations. To create such an excess, the people of the United States had to sell more goods abroad from year to year than they bought, even as earlier in their history they had bought more goods abroad than they had sold.

The foreign trade policy of our Federal government was developed with a view to facilitating and stimulating our necessary export trade. Consular service was established in the leading ports of the world. Commercial attaches in foreign cities collected much valuable information concerning market conditions abroad. Special agents of the Department of Commerce from time to time investigated trade conditions in foreign lands with a view to widening the markets for our products. Trade and commerce reports were published periodically and circulated with a view to keeping American manufacturers and exporters informed as to business conditions and business opportunities abroad. Building up our foreign trade was commonly construed to mean facilitating our exports. Little or no attention was paid to the development of our imports. They were regarded by many as a necessary evil, incidental to our export trade. Our traditional tariff policy reflects our aversion to large imports.

Prior to the World War our favorable trade balance from year to year had come to be looked upon by many as the natural order of things, as indeed it was under existing conditions. In the minds of most people it was indicative of national progress and prosperity, and few fully comprehended the real reason for our continued favorable trade balance. That is why today, with our changed status from a mature debtor to a creditor nation, they continue to view with apprehension and concern the possibility of an unfavorable balance of trade. They fail to realize the relationship between foreign trade balances and the international ebb and flow of capital investments, outlined in the preceding pages. Today, as before the War, they advocate a widening of markets for our surplus products, building up our foreign trade, and as indicative of their aversion to imports, they favor not only high rates of protection but also an American subsidized merchant marine to carry "American goods in American bottoms."

The inconsistency of such a policy, particularly under present conditions, when foreign countries owe us on public and private account approximately twenty-one billion dollars, is obvious. How can we hope to continue selling abroad, if we are going to diminish the possibility of foreign countries selling us their shipping services—by subsidizing our merchant marine—and curtail the importation of foreign products by establishing a high protective tariff? If we intend to change our status from an immature lending country, which is still investing more abroad annually than it is receiving on debt account, to that of a mature creditor nation, we must become reconciled to an unfavorable trade balance. We must shape our foreign trade policy with a view to encouraging, rather than to discouraging, our imports. At the same time, it would be advisable to inaugurate rigorous governmental supervision of further investments abroad, even though such a policy should not meet with the favor of those who are opposed to the paternalism of our Federal government.

5. Payment of Foreign Debts Owed to the United States.— We have indicated to what extent foreign countries are indebted to the United States today. Payment of interest and principal, even though extended over fifty years or more, can be made only under the following conditions: In the first place the debtor countries must be able and willing to produce an exportable surplus of goods. These goods must be marketed and the proceeds from the sales made available for payments to the United States. Let us assume all the foreign obligations, public and private, funded on a 4 per cent basis, with 1 per cent for amortization. Public debts will probably yield less than 4 per cent when and if agreements for their repayment are eventually ratified by all the separate debtor nations and the United States, while private loans abroad yield higher interest rates. An average interest rate of 4 per cent and 1 per cent for debt retirement would mean an approximate annual payment on public and private debt account of possibly one billion dollars. To receive this amount each year we must develop an adverse trade balance, if not of merchandise alone, then of commodities and services combined.

Secondly, the United States must be willing to accept these payments in the only manner in which they can be made. When payment on account of foreign debt is once begun on a large scale, it is more than likely that it will be reflected in an unfavorable merchandise trade balance, for it is doubtful whether invisible import items, with the possible exception of tourist expenditures, will increase very materially in years to come. The development of our merchant marine during and since the World War, together with the partial removal of the competition of German shipping, militates against largely increased services being rendered the people of the United States by foreign merchant marines. Immigrant restriction, on the other hand, will tend to decrease, rather than to increase, the remittances made by foreigners to their relatives and friends in their native countries. The ascendency of the United States in international finance will likewise tend to decrease the possibility of large earnings on the part of foreign banking institutions by selling their services to the people of the United States. With the development of our own marine insurance the possibility of foreign insurance companies rendering us services is also diminished.

Tourist expenditures abroad, however, may increase in the future, as traveling and living conditions in foreign lands continue to improve, and the lure and romance of overseas travel grows in this country. But the attitude prevailing among many foreigners, that most Americans traveling abroad have unlimited means and should be charged accordingly, will tend to counteract the attractiveness and popularity of foreign travel, no matter how reasonable ocean transportation rates may become. Furthermore, the time element involved in ocean travel, at least at present, will tend to limit the number of tourists abroad to the leisure class and to the relatively small group of persons enjoying extended vacations. Third, the linguistic barriers and the resultant annoyances and inconveniences incidental to traveling in foreign lands will act as a deterrent to possibly increased tourist travel abroad. Finally, the annoyance of passports, visas, inspections, customs, and all the many petty rules and regulations in various countries detract, to no small degree, from the pleasure of foreign travel. For these reasons it appears doubtful whether tourist expenditures will offset, to a much greater extent than at present, the items of principal and interest owed us from abroad.

We are therefore led to the conclusion that if foreign countries, over a long series of years, are going to repay us that which they owe, and we are willing to accept such payment, we must become reconciled to an unfavorable merchandise trade balance, possibly amounting to between a half a billion and a billion dollars annually. In other words, because of the foreign obligations owed to the United States, our trade balance must eventually become unfavorable when the debt payments made by foreign countries exceed our new investments abroad. Making new loans abroad in amounts equal to or greater than interest and amortization payments on account of existing debts is merely postponing the day when we will become a mature creditor nation with a continuously unfavorable balance of trade.

6. How Can We Acquire an Unfavorable Trade Balance?— An unfavorable merchandise balance can be acquired in one of several ways. In the first place, we may keep our exports approximately at the figures which they have attained in recent years, but increase our imports very materially. For example, the value of our merchandise exports in 1924 was $4,590,000,000, while our merchandise imports were valued at $3,609,000,000. This favorable trade balance may be converted into an unfavorable trade balance of, let us say, one billion dollars by importing commodities valued at two billion dollars more, annually, than in 1924, providing the value of our exports remains about the same. Secondly, we may increase our merchandise imports more rapidly than our merchandise exports until an unfavorable trade balance sufficiently large to allow for foreign debt payments to the United States has been realized.   Finally, we may decrease our exports very decidedly, while at the same time we continue to import commodities at approximately the same rate as at present.

Each of these means of acquiring an increasingly unfavorable merchandise trade balance, however, will encounter practical objections.   A large increase in imports will soon revive the agitation for more protection.   Industries at home which will feel the pressure of foreign competition too keenly will voice their objections to the increased importation from abroad and will bring all the time-worn arguments for a protective tariff to bear. The second means of increasing the value of our imports over the value of our exports will encounter the same objections as the first.   Not only will the continuously unfavorable trade balance be viewed with apprehension, but the increased sale of foreign goods in this country will tend to stir up further agitation for more protection, which will probably be made a popular political issue.   Finally, to decrease our exports very materially would do inestimable harm to many of our exporting industries.   Our surplus of agricultural and industrial products is constantly seeking new markets, and our governmental agencies seem to be making every effort to assist in building up rather than in diminishing our export trade.

The practical obstacles in the way of converting a favorable trade balance into an increasingly large unfavorable balance are not insurmountable.   But in the process of readjustment some domestic industries will undoubtedly suffer from growing foreign competition.   On the other hand, foreign countries, bent upon meeting their overseas obligations, will have to expand their industries and their commerce very materially, which in turn will mean keener competition for foreign markets.   This will intensify business rivalry throughout the world, and will tend to cause American exporters to seek further governmental aid to make possible their effective competition with foreign enterprises for world markets.   The Webb-Pomerene Act of 1918, legalizing the formation of combinations of American exporters for the purpose of facilitating our export trade, is an outstanding illustration of Federal legislation intended to assist our exporters in their competition with foreign exporters for the markets of the world.

In the final analysis, therefore, the problem of making extensive international debt payments resolves itself into a question of ability and willingness to produce, to buy, and to sell. If debtor nations of the world are willing to meet their obligations and increase their industrial output, with which to make payments, the problem of debt payment is not yet solved. The creditor nations must signify their willingness to buy that which the debtor nations have to sell, or make possible selling their surplus product somewhere, to provide means with which to make payments. Not until the United States, as the chief creditor nation of the world, is willing to alter its traditional trade policy so that extensive payments on account of foreign debts can eventually be made will foreign countries be able to meet their obligations to us. If we want payment we must make possible the conditions of payment. These imply, first and foremost, the ability on the part of debtor countries to produce an exportable surplus of goods. Our extensive post-war loans to foreign countries for productive purposes indicate that we have been willing to aid in their industrial recovery and development. But to date we have been too reluctant to take the second step necessary to receiving extensive payments on account of foreign debts. We have adhered tenaciously to our traditional policy of protection to American industries. The Tariff Act of 1922 has been characterized as the "highest Chinese Wall we have ever erected."

Furthermore, there are those who have in recent years ardently advocated a subsidized merchant marine, so that American goods may be carried in American bottoms. In other words, we have thus far not registered any great willingness to accept payments of foreign obligations by encouraging the augmented importation of either commodities or services. As a matter of fact, there are those who believe that the possible injury to many of our American industries resulting from largely increased imports would be far greater than the benefits to be derived from foreign debt payments. They apparently fail to realize the advantages of foreign investments to both debtor and creditor countries.

7. Benefits of Foreign Investments.—When a nation invests its surplus funds abroad, as we have done very extensively in recent years, the conditions under which the foreign loans are made are usually specified in the agreement drawn up between the debtor and the creditor or creditors. Frequently the funds, realized on the sale of foreign securities to American investors, are spent here to purchase industrial materials with which to develop a foreign public or private enterprise. When, for example, an American manufacturing concern sells its products to a Chinese railway company, accepting in payment the securities of the foreign corporation, which are marketed in whole or in part through investment bankers in this country, the proceeds of this foreign investment are spent here and have accordingly stimulated our export trade.

The effect of foreign investments upon our export trade is not so obvious when the funds are not spent directly to purchase materials in the lending country. Nevertheless, it is just as real. Let us assume a group of United States investors has made a loan of $50,000,000 to an Argentine company, with which this company purchases industrial materials in England. The British exporters, who accept dollar exchange in terms of which the loan was made, do so because they know they can sell their dollar exchange for British pound sterling. But the bankers who buy the dollar exchange do so because they, in turn, know that someone will buy it from them in order to meet obligations in the United States. These obligations have grown out of purchases made from us. Thus the dollar loan to an Argentine company has been employed, in a triangular exchange, to pay for American exports.

As a rule, the great lending countries of the world are industrial rather than purely agricultural nations. When payments of interest and repayment of principal are made, the inflow of imports increases. These imports are largely in the form of industrial materials and consumption goods. Because of this increased importation, raw materials in the country receiving payments are more abundant than would be the case otherwise, and the supply of consumers' goods is likewise increased. This will tend to decrease production costs as well as the cost of living in the creditor country. The larger imports, made possible by the returns on foreign investments, will consequently tend to raise the material standard of living in the lending country. Finally, by virtue of the loans made abroad, the borrowing countries, which will normally have applied the proceeds of these loans to develop their natural resources and industrial enterprises, will find their production costs decreasing because of the loans. This will tend to increase their prosperity and give them more purchasing power with which to buy goods abroad. Consequently, it will stimulate further exports from the creditor country. Thus, we see that not merely the original foreign investment but also the increased industrial output, stimulated by foreign investments, normally tends to increase the exports of the creditor country, while the larger imports, due to debt payment, result in lower production costs and higher standards of living.

The foregoing line of reasoning is based on the assumption that the proceeds from foreign investments are employed by industrial enterprises to stimulate production. When, however, loans are made abroad for unproductive purposes, to buy military and naval equipment, munitions, and other implements of destructive warfare, they will indeed stimulate exports, as did our huge loans made to the Ally governments during the World War; but to the extent that these implements are employed to destroy rather than to produce, they do not aid in developing foreign natural resources and industrial output which, in turn, increase the material prosperity of the borrowing countries. The purchasing power of such countries will consequently be decreased rather than increased by virtue of such loans; and debt payment, under such conditions, must inevitably involve a real hardship to the debtor nations.

8. Inter-ally Indebtedness.—The intergovernmental debts incurred by the countries allied against the Central Powers in the World War are commonly spoken of as Inter-ally debts. Much has been said and written in recent years concerning these obligations. Some writers have advocated their payment in full, others have argued for debt reduction, while still others have advocated complete cancellation.

To date (Dec. 1, 1926) Debt Funding Agreements have been drawn up between the United States, as the leading creditor nation, and thirteen of the debtor countries,[1] involving a principal sum of approximately eleven and a half billion dollars, to be paid over a period of sixty-two years from date of ratification. But this does not necessarily mean that the debt problem, so far as the United States is concerned, has been finally settled.

The debt funding agreements made to date provide for combined interest and principal payments to the United States of $210,000,000 in 1926. These amounts increase from year to year until they reach the maximum annual total of $427,000,000 in 1976.

[1] Poland, Lithuania, Hungary, Finland, Great Britain, Belgium, Latvia, Estonia, Czechoslovakia, Rumania, Italy, France, and Yugoslavia.

ESSENTIAL DETAILS OF DEBT FUNDING AGREEMENTS BETWEEN THE UNITED STATES AND THE PRINCIPAL DEBTOR COUNTRIES[1]

Country	Date of agreement	Original amount of debt	Principal of debt as funded	Accrued interest as funded	Present worth of payments (at time of funding)	Rate of interest on funded debt, per cent		Annual payments on funded debt		Total amount to be paid (principal plus interest)	Term	Percentage of debt reduction
						Initial	Final	Initial year	Peak year			
Belgium	8-18-25	$ 377,029,570.06	$ 417,780,000	$ 40,750,429.94	$ 226,020,669	0.77	3½	$ 3,840,000	$ 12,861,850	$ 727,830,500.00	62	46
Czechoslovakia	10-13-25	91,879,671.03	115,000,000	23,120,328.97	92,167,514	3	3½	3,000,000	5,884,725	312,811,433.88	62	19
Estonia	10-28-25	12,066,222.15	13,830,000	1,763,777.85	11,404,289	3	3½	483,000	548,550	33,331,140.00	62	10
Finland	5- 1-23	8,281,926.17	9,000,000	718,073.83	7,420,497	3	3½	315,000	359,185	21,695,055.00	62	18
France	4-29-26	3,340,416,043.72	4,025,000,000	685,000,000.00	2,008,122,624	1	3½	30,000,000	125,000,000	6,847,674,104.17	62	50
Great Britain	6-18-23	4,074,818,358.44	4,600,000,000	525,181,641.56	3,792,350,150	3	3½	161,000,000	187,250,000	11,105,965,000.00	62	18
Hungary	5-29-24	1,685,835.61	1,939,000	253,164.39	1,598,429	3	3½	67,770	78,885	4,693,240.00	62	20
Italy	11-14-25	1,647,869,197.96	2,042,000,000	394,130,802.04	535,312,311	0.125	2	5,000,000	80,988,000	2,407,677,500.00	62	74
Latvia	9-24-25	5,132,287.14	5,775,000	642,712.86	4,760,424	3	3½	201,250	235,980	13,958,635.00	62	18
Lithuania	9-22-24	4,981,628.03	6,030,000	1,048,371.97	4,972,364	3	3½	210,900	239,855	14,531,940.00	62	18
Poland	11-14-24	159,666,972.39	178,560,000	18,893,027.61	146,989,791	3	3½	5,916,800	9,315,000	435,687,550.00	62	18
Rumania	12- 4-25	36,128,494.94	44,590,000	8,477,878.67	35,343,429	3	3½	200,000	2,249,020	122,506,206.05	62	21
Yugoslavia	5- 2-26	51,037,866.39	62,850,000	11,819,226.00	20,236,000	0.125	3½	200,000	2,406,000	95,177,635.00	62	68
Totals		$9,810,994,094.03	$11,522,354,000	$1,711,799,435.69	$6,886,698,491			$210,434,720	$427,417,050	$22,143,539,939.10		

[1] From "European Economic and Political Survey," vol. 1, No. 19, p. 2, June 15, 1926.

9. Payments on Old Indebtedness and Creation of New Indebtedness.—Thus far, $432,000,000 have been paid to the United States government on account of principal and interest by seven of the debtor countries, in accordance with the provisions of the debt-funding agreements. These payments were in the form of either United States standard gold dollars or obligations of the United States government issued after Apr. 6, 1917 at par and accrued interest to date of payment. They constituted what may be termed *legal payments*. Many persons have been led to believe that these remittances on the part of the debtor countries furnish ample evidence of their ability to meet their obligations. We must, however, draw a careful distinction between *legal payments* and *economic payments*. If a debtor country meets its legal obligations to the United States government, and at the same time incurs other obligations abroad, equal to, or in excess of, the legal debt payments made, it has merely met one obligation by incurring another. It has not made economic payments, for it has not developed its productive resources to create an exportable surplus of economic goods.

From 1923 to 1925, inclusive, various countries indebted to the United States floated new loans in the United States, aggregating over $800,000,000, or nearly twice the amount of legal payments made by them up to Dec. 25, 1925. These new capital flotations were distributed as follows:

SUMMARY OF NEW CAPITAL FLOTATIONS OF CERTAIN DEBTOR COUNTRIES IN THE UNITED STATES, 1923–1925 INCLUSIVE[1]

Country	State loans	Municipal	Corporate	Total
Finland	$ 35,000,000	$ 7,000,000	$ 18,000,000	$ 60,000,000
Great Britain			38,225,000	38,225,000
Hungary	9,000,000	10,000,000	5,525,000	24,525,000
Poland	58,000,000		4,000,000	62,000,000
Belgium	180,000,000		12,347,500	192,247,500
Czechoslovakia	37,250,000	1,500,000	10,000,000	48,750,000
Italy	150,000,000		34,004,400	184,004,400
Rumania	15,000,000	1,500,000	400,000	16,900,000
France	108,545,000		94,030,000	202,575,000
Totals	$592,795,000	$20,000,000	$216,531,900	$829,326,900

[1] These totals do not include borrowings in the United States on the part of foreign corporations whose activites extend over two or more countries, which totaled $151,732,000 during the period under consideration.

These extensive new borrowings on the part of debtor countries in the United States during the past three years lead us to conclude that economic payments of debts to the United States government, arising out of the World War have in reality not begun as yet. In view of this fact it may be well to bear in mind the arguments which have been advanced from time to time in favor of cancellation of these obligations, either in whole or in part.

10. Cancellation or Reduction of Inter-ally Indebtedness.— The inter-ally debts were incurred largely to aid in financing the World War. They were made by various belligerent countries very extensively to purchase necessary war materials. They were utilized primarily to destroy, rather than to build up, industry; they were destructive rather than productive. This is one of the primary reasons why cancellation of these debts has frequently been urged. The proponents of debt cancellation, furthermore, emphasize the possible injury resulting from debt payment to industries in the creditor countries. Take the United States, for example. We are both an industrial and an agricultural country. The Allied countries, which are largely indebted to us, are likewise partly industrial and partly agricultural. The products which they could give us by way of economic payments for the cannon, war implements, torpedoes, munitions and other destructive machinery are not akin to those we gave to them, for we would not want them. What then can they give? Largely products which are similar to those produced by some of our own industries. To the extent that we accept these products —textiles, steel rails, motors, surgical instruments, as well as industrial raw materials—some American industry will find itself injured because of foreign competition, and the old cry for more protection will be sounded far and wide.

Again, advocates of cancellation contend that the war-time prices paid for our products were in excess of the present lower level of prices. To ask for repayment in terms of the present dollars for debts contracted in terms of inflated war-time dollars is manifestly unfair. The general level of prices in 1918 was at least 30 per cent higher than the present (1926) price level. If, therefore, payment of war debts to the United States is made in terms of the present value of the dollar, it is equivalent to paying us approximately 30 per cent more on principal account than we loaned, assuming no further pronounced change in the level of prices. They contend, therefore, that the inter-ally debts should at least be adjusted, if not cancelled entirely, to allow for the change in the price level. Furthermore, it has been argued that at least that portion of the debt incurred by various European countries to purchase supplies after the close of the War, intended to relieve distress and suffering in three countries, should be completely wiped out. The amount involved is only $141,000,000, but if canceled, would remove the entire obligations of Austria, Finland, and Hungary to the United States, as well as 40 per cent of Poland's obligation.[1]

Finally, the proponents of either total or partial inter-ally debt cancellation argue that we were jointly fighting for a cause, side by side with our Allies, and should therefore share the financial war burden jointly with them. They make a moral issue of the problem of debt cancellation, and point out the possibility of creating international good will by adopting a policy of mutual forgiveness of debts arising out of the World War.

11. Possible Adjustment of Inter-ally Debts and America's Future Debt Policy.—The essential difference between the war-time investments and foreign loans normally made to promote industrial activity abroad should not be lost sight of. The benefits of foreign investments, outlined above, cannot be realized if the proceeds derived from foreign loans are wasted and destroyed. The full realization of this fact may ultimately cause a change of attitude toward foreign payment of war-time obligations in this country. If not cancelled entirely, an adjustment of these obligations to allow for unproductive expenditures, as well as for the change in the level of prices, would result in a very material reduction of the principal sums owed us on account of the inter-ally indebtedness. The extent to which our governmental credits to the Allied governments were employed to buy implements of warfare—cannon, munitions, torpedoes and the like—can be ascertained with a fair degree of accuracy. Furthermore, fairly accurate price indices are available on the basis of which to make adjustments of the contracted obligations.

Settlement of inter-ally debts along lines here suggested in a general way would result in a decided reduction of international obligations arising out of the World War, and would once more tend to establish a normal relationship between foreign invest-

[1] This suggestion is contained in an unpublished manuscript by Ernest M. Patterson.

ments and international trade, with its resultant mutual benefits to both debtor and creditor nations. But even if a program of war-debt settlement were adopted to allow for unproductive expenditures and for changes in price levels, the United States would still remain a creditor nation to the extent of possibly twelve to fifteen billion dollars. When economic payment of interest and repayment of principal on this indebtedness are begun, in excess of our new investments abroad from year to year, it is very doubtful whether we will be able to continue our favorable merchandise trade balance. There is, however, absolutely no reason to view an unfavorable merchandise balance of trade with apprehension and alarm, as so many do at present. It will but indicate the normal relationship between a mature creditor country and its international balance of payments and must inevitably accrue to the benefit of the nation as a whole.

Our governmental policy should be so developed as to facilitate increased importation of foreign products. This may be done (1) by compilation of data on possible products which foreign countries have for sale or can produce to advantage; (2) by giving American buyers information, through commerce reports, of favorable markets throughout the world; (3) by lowering the tariff. That some American industries will be injured as a result of largely increased imports cannot be denied. Nevertheless, it would be manifestly unfair to withhold from the masses the benefits to be derived from increased products imported from abroad, for the sake of a few industries which may be affected adversely by such importation. After the period of industrial readjustment, there is every reason to believe that the people of the United States will be permanently benefited by an unfavorable merchandise trade balance, even as England has been for nearly a century.

12. Summary.—The relationship between international trade and foreign investments is reflected primarily in the merchandise trade balance of a country. We may distinguish among four groups of countries, with reference to their foreign investments and their trade balances: (1) immature borrowing countries, which will normally have an unfavorable balance of trade; (2) immature lending countries, which show a favorable balance of trade; (3) mature debtor countries, with a favorable balance of trade; and (4) mature creditor countries, having an unfavorable trade balance. Prior to 1850, the United States did not borrow abroad very extensively. From 1859 to 1873, however, our foreign obligations increased very materially. Foreign countries invested in the United States to provide funds for reconstruction after the Civil War and to aid in our railroad building. From 1873 to 1914 we were a mature debtor country, as reflected in our annual favorable trade balance. The World War changed our status from a mature debtor nation to an immature lending country.

At present (1926), foreign countries owe the United States on public and private account the huge amount of approximately twenty billion dollars net. If we expect payment of interest on this large debt as well as repayment of principal, we must eventually become reconciled to an unfavorable trade balance. It is doubtful whether the invisible items of import, with the possible exception of tourist expenditures, will increase very materially in years to come. Even tourist expenditures will probably not be much larger in the future because of the attitude of foreigners toward American tourists, the time element involved in travel, linguistic barriers, and governmental regulations. Payments of foreign obligations will therefore have to be made largely in the form of commodities.

We may acquire an increasingly unfavorable merchandise trade balance by keeping our exports at the present figure and expanding our imports very materially; by increasing our imports more rapidly than we increase our exports, until we acquire an unfavorable trade balance, sufficiently large to allow for debt payments; and by decreasing our exports, keeping our imports approximately as at present. The practical obstacles in the way of acquiring an unfavorable balance of payments are not insurmountable, but to remove them would require a change in our traditional foreign trade policy. We must realize that a nation benefits not only by the stimulus to exports, resulting from investments abroad, but also from the consequently greater imports, which in turn react upon exports. These benefits are realized from foreign investments if the proceeds of loans are employed for productive purposes.

When nations employ funds obtained by making loans abroad for destructive purposes, to buy war implements and munitions, however, the expenditures do not accrue to the benefit of the borrowing country. The inter-ally debts resulting from the World War were made largely to purchase war implements.

Those who favor cancellation of these debts, in whole or in part, contend that the loans were unproductive; that they were made at an inflated level of prices; and that the funds were expended for a common cause. A settlement of the inter-ally debts to allow for unproductive expenditures and for the change in the price level would result in a very material reduction of these large obligations, and would tend to reestablish a more normal relationship between foreign investments and international trade, with its resultant benefits to both debtors and creditors. The United States, as the leading creditor nation, must ultimately become reconciled to an unfavorable trade balance if it expects to receive payments on account of foreign debts in excess of its new investments made abroad from time to time. Such debt payments will accrue to the benefit of the people of the United States as a whole.

Collateral Readings

ALEXANDER, M. W., "The Economic Significance of the Inter-Ally Debts," pp. 51–58.

JOHNSON, ALVIN, "America as Creditor Nation," pp. 90–95.

LEFFINGWELL, R. C., "An Analysis of the International War Debt Situation," vol. 102, 1922.

MOULTON, H. G., "War Debts and International Trade Theory." *The American Economic Review*, vol. 15, No. 4, Dec., 1925.

ROBERTS, G. E., "Should the United States be Reimbursed by Debtor Countries and How?" *Annals* of the American Academy of Political and Social Science, vol. 120, pp. 23–29.

References

BOGGS, T. H., "The International Trade Balance in Theory and Practice."

CULBERTSON, W. S., "Commercial Policy in War Time and After."

———, "International Economic Policies."

DUNN, R. W., "American Foreign Investments."

FRIEDMAN, E. M., "American Problems of Reconstruction."

———, "International Finance and Its Reorganization."

HOBSON, C. K., "The Export of Capital."

International Trade Situation, "*Annals of the American Academy of Political and Social Science,*" vol. 94, Mar., 1921; vol. 102, July, 1922; vol. 108, July, 1923; and vol. 120, July, 1925.

LATANE, J. H., "America as a World Power."

VIALLATE, A., "Economic Imperialism and International Relations during the Last Fifty Years."

Questions for Discussion

1. Point out the relationship which exists between international trade and foreign investments.

2. Outline the effect upon the normal merchandise trade balance, as a nation changes from a mature debtor to a mature creditor nation.

3. What was the position of the United States before 1914 in reference to foreign investments?

4. How did this position affect its normal pre-war trade balance?

5. What significance do you attach to our changed status from a debtor to a creditor nation?

6. How should our changed status affect our trade policy?

7. What evidence have we that our foreign trade policy has not changed very materially since the war?

8. What is the extent of foreign indebtedness to the United States, both on public and private account?

9. Outline the means available for the payment of foreign debts?

10. To what extent may invisible items of international trade enter into payment of debts owed to the United States?

11. By what methods may an unfavorable merchandise trade balance be acquired by the United States?

12. Criticise each of these methods.

13. Indicate the benefits to be derived from foreign investments by both debtor and creditor nations.

14. Can these benefits be realized if the proceeds from the loans are spent unproductively? Give reasons for your answer.

15. What arguments may be advanced in favor of cancellation of inter-ally indebtedness?

16. What are the objections to such cancellation?

Topics for Investigation

1. Provisions of the debt-funding agreements.

2. Analysis of possible methods of repayment of foreign obligations to the United States.

3. The operation of the Dawes Reparation plan.

4. Analysis of trade balances of debtor nations over a period of years.

5. Validity of arguments for and against inter-ally debt cancellation in the light of existing economic conditions of both debtor and creditor nations.

6. Extent of American tourist travel in foreign countries.

7. Importance of our merchant marine services in international trade.

CHAPTER XVI

THE PROBLEM OF A PROTECTIVE TARIFF

1. What is a Protective Tariff?—A protective tariff is a duty imposed upon imported articles for the purpose of protecting home industries from foreign competition in domestic markets. The fiscal and the protective aspects of a tariff are frequently incompatible. To the extent that an imported article yields revenue the domestic producers are not protected against this article, and when they are completely protected against competition with a foreign article, the latter will not be imported. As no tariff can be collected on it, such a "protective tariff" will not yield revenue. In view of the popular usage of the term "protective tariff," however, its use will be retained in the subsequent discussion in the sense in which it has been defined above.

2. Effects of a Protective Tariff upon International Trade.— In our analysis of the benefits of international trade in Chap. XIV we assumed the free exchange of commodities and services between the citizens of two countries, based on mutual advantage and gain. Artificial restrictions upon the free exchange of economic goods eliminate or lessen the benefits of geographical division of labor. If a duty is imposed by a governmental agency upon an imported article, that article will normally not be imported unless the benefit derived from importing it exceeds the amount of duty plus the transportation charges. To the extent that the duty prevents the consummation of the trade, the importing as well as the exporting country will suffer an immediate economic loss. The citizens of the importing country can obtain the foreign article subject to duty only by paying a higher price for it. By offering more of their purchasing power for the article, they reduce the quantity of their purchasing power available to buy other goods. On the other hand, industries in the exporting country are also affected by the duty. As the sales of their products are reduced because of the import duty, foreign producers will have to lower their selling prices in order to attract new buyers, or else curtail their production. The lowering of the selling price in the exporting country will tend to force the marginal producers of the exportable article from the field of active competition, and thus work hardship upon such individuals. Industries injured by virtue of the destruction of their foreign market due to the import duties, will discontinue or curtail their production. In the process of industrial readjustment, the available purchasing power within the country will tend to be diminished, a consequence which, in turn, will react unfavorably upon the exports from the country which has restricted its imports by means of a protective tariff.

A protective tariff, moreover, diverts the productive powers of a country imposing such a duty on imports from enterprises in which its advantage is greatest to less advantageous enterprises. To the extent that fewer commodities result by thus diverting labor and capital into less productive channels, both importing and exporting countries will suffer economic loss because of the restrictions imposed upon the free exchange of goods. But social and political benefits, as well as the possible long-run economic gain derived from a policy of protection, may offset this immediate or present economic loss and cause the continuation of a protective policy. Before attempting an analysis of the benefits claimed for a protective tariff, let us briefly survey the background of the tariff policy of the United States.

3. Historical Background of the United States Protective Tariff.—Our present high protective tariff policy is the outgrowth of the Civil War, although a certain amount of protection was offered to American industries by the very first Tariff Act of Congress in 1789. The Tariff Act of 1816, in a number of cases, imposed tariff rates higher than those which had existed prior to the War of 1812. In 1824, many rates were increased still further. The rates on cotton and woolen goods, for example, were as high as $33\frac{1}{3}$ per cent of the value of these articles. Beginning in 1832, a gradual downward revision of our tariff was undertaken by Congress. Rates were still further reduced under the so-called Walker Tariff Act of 1846, named after the Secretary of the Treasury who sponsored it. In 1857, a further reduction of the tariff was made. Under this schedule the most important rates of protection ranged from 30 per cent to a level of

24 per cent ad valorem.[1]   In general, therefore, the tendency of our tariff rates prior to the Civil War was distinctly downward.

The Tariff Act of 1864 reverted again to higher rates, imposing an average rate of more than 47 per cent ad valorem on dutiable articles.   For fifteen years after the Civil War, Congress increased rather than decreased the amount of protection offered to American industries, for it gradually lowered the internal revenue duties on articles subject to heavy import duties.   By 1872, nearly all internal revenue taxes on general manufactures had been repealed.   The Tariff acts of 1883 and 1890, however, both tended in the direction of higher duties.   The slight downward revision in 1894 was superseded in 1897 by the Dingley Tariff Act, which was a distinct return to a highly protective policy.   The Payne-Aldrich Tariff Act of 1909 made many changes in rates both upward and downward, but in general effected little, if any, reduction in the average rates imposed on dutiable articles.

The Payne-Aldrich Tariff Act was superseded in 1913 by the Underwood Tariff Act, which, with the exception of the Wilson Act of 1894, provided the first genuine downward revision of our tariff in half a century.   The rates of duties under this act were lower on practically all articles, and the so-called "free list" was largely extended.   Dutiable articles were classified into fourteen schedules, and the rates ranged from 5 to 60 per cent ad valorem.   The reduction in the average rate on dutiable articles was from 42 per cent, under the Payne-Aldrich Tariff, to 33 per cent.   By extending the "free list," 63 per cent (ad valorem) of the imported articles were admitted free under the provisions of the Underwood Act, as compared with 49 per cent which were admitted free of duty under the Payne-Aldrich Act.

Finally, in September 1922, Congress adopted the Fordney-McCumber Tariff Bill, which has been called the high-water mark of our policy of protection.   In some cases this Act provides ad valorem rates as high as 400 per cent.   The rates on raw wool range from 30 to 155 per cent (ad valorem) according to the coarseness of the wool, and from 70 to 110 per cent on woolen yarns.   Furthermore, a number of articles on the free list under

[1] *Ad valorem* duties are those levied against the values of imported articles, as contrasted with *specific* duties, based on the quantities of the imported articles or *compound* duties, which are a combination of *specific* and *ad valorem* duties on the same article.

the Underwood Tariff Act were returned to the dutiable list under the Tariff Act of 1922, including such products as salt, wool, manufactures of iron and steel, and staple food products.

The present Tariff Act, moreover, gives the President of the United States the power to revise the rates of duty whenever he shall find, upon investigation by the Tariff Commission, that the difference in production costs here and in the principal competing countries abroad are not equalized by the prevailing rates of protection. The changes in rates thus made by the President may not exceed 50 per cent of the rates provided in the Tariff Act of 1922, but if this does not bring about the desired equalization of costs, the President may direct that an ad valorem duty be imposed on the selling price of the article in American markets, rather than upon the price of the article in the country of its origin.

This so-called flexibility of the tariff rates under our present Tariff Act is a distinctly new departure in tariff legislation in the United States. Acting under this "flexible provision" of the Tariff Act of 1922, President Coolidge, on Mar. 7, 1924, ordered an increase of twelve cents a bushel in the tariff rate on wheat and an increase of twenty-six cents per one hundred pounds in the duty on wheat flour, as well as a 50 per cent decrease in the ad valorem rate on mill feeds. These rates became effective within thirty days after their promulgation. The basis on which the new rates were established was "the differences in costs of production."

These new rates marked the first change in the duties provided under the Tariff Act of 1922, and the presidential proclamation of Mar. 7, 1924 was the first instance in which the President of the United States exercised the powers conferred on him to either increase or decrease rates, after investigation by the Tariff Commission.

In view of the prevailing high rates of protection in the United States today and the possibility of raising these rates still further on the part of the President, let us briefly review the many arguments which have been advanced from time to time by the advocates of a policy of protection to American industries.

4. "Infant Industry" Argument.—Admitting the possible immediate economic loss resulting from a protective tariff, protectionists point to the future economic benefits to be derived from protecting certain industries in their early stages of development against foreign competition. All countries are not in the same stages of industrialization; some have "stolen a march" on other countries, which countries possibly have equally abundant natural resources and an equally abundant and efficient labor supply. Hence, the advocates of protection contend that if an opportunity were to be given these industries to establish themselves at home, they would eventually be able to compete effectively with established industries abroad. Protection is necessary to attract the requisite capital into those enterprises which would not come into existence without protection. When such industries have once been established, it is argued, the protection will no longer be necessary.

This so-called "infant industry" argument enjoyed considerable popularity at one stage in our tariff history, and it has been revived from time to time. After the War of 1812, it was effectively employed to obtain higher protective duties for our newly developed textile industries; and again, after the World War, it was advanced as an argument for protection to our analine dye industry, which had grown up during the war.

Many "infants," which more than a century ago received protection, are unable to stand on their own feet today. That they are unhealthy "infants" is reflected in the high rates of protection afforded various textile products under the Tariff Act of 1922. Furthermore, many of the infant industries, which desired protection and still enjoy it, came into existence during war periods when domestic producers enjoyed monopolistic advantages because of the curtailment of foreign competition. Our textile industries, for example, were expanded considerably during the War of 1812 and the period of embargo and nonintercourse preceding the war. Again, our aniline dye industry was developed largely during the World War because of the absence of competition of German dyes on our domestic markets. Many "infants" are feeble children, the product of unwholesome conditions, rather than of normal industrial growth and development. The United States is an industrially developed country today, and the "infant industry" argument can no longer be applied to all industries in good faith. It has been effectively employed in the past to obtain temporary protection, but subsequently other arguments were advanced by protectionists to make this temporary protection permanent.

5. Diversity of Industries Argument.—Closely akin to the "infant industry" argument for protection is the contention that protective duties result in the diversification of industries at home, and that the benefits of such diversification in the long run will more than offset temporary economic loss. This argument, however, is based on unsound reasoning. The contention that more rather than less specialization will result in diverting labor and capital within a country from more advantageous to less advantageous enterprises is illogical. When available capital funds and labor supply within a country are employed in enterprises which do not enjoy the greatest economic advantage, economic loss is inevitable. The possibility of specialization and diversification of industry is decreased rather than increased. When capital and labor are diverted to the protected industries, they are withdrawn from other industries where they were more productive. A new industry in a country may indeed be created by means of protection against foreign competition, but only at the expense of other more profitable industries. Nothing is added to the total industries of a nation.

This conclusion can be arrived at by still another line of reasoning. When a new industry is created by shutting out a foreign product, this reduction in imports causes a corresponding reduction in exports. When foreigners cannot sell to us they will not have the wherewithal to buy from us. Some home industry, producing for export, is therefore injured as a result of diverting capital and labor to a new industry. The tariff has resulted in diverting industry into less productive channels, but has not added any industries.

Furthermore, a diversification of industries within a country will be brought about under conditions of the free and unrestricted exchange of goods. This is amply illustrated in the United States today, with its textile industries in New England and more recently in the South; with its steel industries in Pennsylvania, Ohio, and Indiana; with its automobile industries largely localized in Michigan; and its meat-packing industries mainly located in Chicago. Most of our many diversified industries within the United States have developed under conditions of freedom of trade between the citizens of the various states.

6. Economic Independence or Self-sufficiency.—A third economic argument for a protective tariff contends that the possible economic loss sustained from protective duties is more than offset by the advantages to be derived from the feeling of economic security and independence in times of war. At the outbreak of the World War, Great Britain, for example, experienced considerable difficulty in obtaining lenses and optical instruments, so essential to the conduct of modern warfare, because these articles had been imported largely from Germany prior to the War. Shortly after hostilities broke out in Europe, in 1914, the United States suffered a veritable analine dye famine, because we had imported most of our dyes from abroad before the War and had not developed any extensive dye industry of our own. A protective tariff, it is argued, would have induced capital and labor to flow into the building up of these industries and thus would have made us more self-sufficient in times of war.

In a modified form, the self-sufficiency argument for protection has been applied, particularly in post-war years, to those industries which are essential to the successful prosecution of a war. It is contended that so-called "key industries" should be established by affording domestic producers the necessary protection to encourage their development in times of peace. Thus, we may have the basic products for the conduct of modern warfare at home, in case of an emergency or of an impending national peril.

The national self-sufficiency argument, no matter in what form it is presented, is based on the assumption that war is inevitable and unavoidable, for if war were avoidable the argument would lose much of its significance and force. So long as we believe that the best safeguard against international conflict is preparedness for war, we must admit the validity of the argument for protection of "key industries" to aid in assuring national safety. The economic loss becomes a cost of national security. But in the opinion of those who believe that all international disputes can be settled by arbitration and who hold that war can be outlawed, this cost of national safety is both unnecessary and unjustifiable.

On the other hand, the idea of economic independence and national self-sufficiency in times of peace, fostered by a protective tariff, particularly under present conditions, is illogical and futile. The extensive international obligations arising out of the World War have emphasized the economic interdependence of the nations of the world rather than their self-sufficiency. This interdependence will be accentuated still further when economic payments are made in settlement of these obligations.

7. Home Market Argument.—Closely akin to the self-suffi-ciency argument is the argument advanced by Henry Clay, intended to reconcile the agricultural and manufacturing interests in the United States. It centers around the idea that the pros-perity of the American farmer depends upon a continuous market for his products, and that this can best be realized by building up manufacturing centers in this country. Foreign markets are not so dependable as domestic markets, since they may be wholly or partially destroyed by political disturbances over which we have no control. The destruction of foreign markets as a result of the World War has emphasized the importance of dependable markets to domestic producers. The home market argument, in the light of past experiences, attains a certain degree of validity. The economic loss resulting from a protective tariff intended to develop a home market again resolves itself into a cost incurred to assure our political security and self-sufficiency in times of war, as well as greater industrial stability in times of peace.

Furthermore, it is argued by the supporters of the home market argument that shipping agricultural products abroad and import-ing manufactures involve double freights for ocean transporta-tion which could be saved by manufacturing at home. The error in this line of reasoning is obvious. The payment of freights, whether for land or ocean transportation, results in real economy, if goods can be bought cheaper and on more favorable terms in a distant market than near home. If a protective tariff develops certain home manufactures, which would not come into existence without protection, another market is indeed created at home for the farmer's product. But it is not an additional market. It is a substitute for that market which was destroyed when our exports were cut off because of the restriction on imports.

8. Equalization of Costs of Production.—Much has been made in recent years of this argument in tariff controversies. The Republican Tariff Platform in 1908, for example, declared:

In all protective legislation the true principle of protection is best maintained by the imposition of such duties as will equal the difference between costs of production at home and abroad, together with a rea-sonable profit to American industries.

In 1912 the Progressive party platform contained the following confession of faith: "We believe in a protective tariff which shall equalize conditions of competition between the United States and foreign countries."[1]

The proponents of this argument for protection hold that duties equal to the differences between domestic and foreign production costs should be levied on competitive imported articles. A number of interesting and pertinent questions are raised by the "equalization of production costs" argument, which has been called the "scientific" principle of protective tariffs. In the first place, we must answer the questions: What is to be included in "costs of production?" Are we to consider the "real" costs or the "money" costs of production? Secondly, we must inquire: Whose costs of production are to be used as the basis for equalization? Different producers in competitive industries have differing production costs, as is witnessed in part by different margins of profits per unit of product in competitive industries. This is equally true of domestic and of foreign producers. Are we, therefore, to take the average money costs of the entire industry in this country as a basis for comparison, or the costs of the least efficient or marginal firm, or, possibly, the costs of the most efficiently organized firm here and abroad? In the words of Thomas Walter Page:[2]

There is, in fact, no such thing as a single "domestic cost of production" for any commodity. There are almost as many different costs as there are producers; and the question arises: which should be taken for comparison with a foreign cost to find a standard for measuring duties?

Furthermore, after we have decided what is to be included in the concept of costs, how are the costs to be ascertained; by private declaration of individual firms or by investigations on the part of governmental agencies? Even if the answer to these and many similar queries could be found, the unsoundness of the "equalization of costs" argument for protection becomes apparent upon slight scrutiny. The argument, carried to its logical conclusion, would place a premium on inefficiency. The less efficient our domestic industries became when competing with a foreign product the higher would have to be the protective duties on the products of competing foreign industries in order to equalize "costs" of production. We are thus led to the conclusion that the "equalization of production costs" argument is not only unsound in principle, but also unfit for practical application.

[1] Cf. CULBERTSON, "Tariff Policy of the United States in War Time and After," p. 127ff.

[2] Cf. "Making the Tariff in the United States," p. 92.

9. Dumping Argument.—This argument was frequently advanced by protectionists in the years immediately following the World War, when, because of currency inflation in various European countries, exchange rates dropped more rapidly than the internal prices advanced, making the countries with depreciating currencies good markets in which to buy. In other words, the countries with the low exchange rates were, for the time being, able to undersell their competitors abroad in countries with relatively high rates of exchange, such as England and the United States. Protection was urged to safeguard domestic industries against a flood of cheap foreign goods, pouring into this country.

Such an expression as "flooding" our markets with cheap imported products is both expressive and impressive. But upon investigation the dreaded "flood" turns out to be not much more than a little surface ripple. For example, the physical volume of German textile products exported to the United States in 1913 was 200,442 tons, while in 1920 it was only 14,274 tons, and still less in 1922, the year of the passage of our present tariff act.[1] The American textile industry, in general, was not severely injured by such a relatively small volume of German textiles imported in post-war years, no matter how low the price may have been. Iron and steel products imported from Germany in 1922 were likewise below the volume imported in 1913 from the present German territory. The "dumping" argument was voiced in recent years, particularly with reference to German products. Statistics of the physical volume of German post-war exports, however, do not bear out the general impression that the American market was flooded with cheap German goods in post-war years, because of which American competing enterprises needed more protection. Furthermore, the stabilization of German currency in November, 1923, and the debt burden imposed on German industry under the provisions of the Dawes Reparation Plan have caused the advantages of German producers in underselling their foreign competitors in the markets of the world to become largely a matter of history. At best, the "dumping" argument for protection, had only temporary significance, as applied to countries with rapidly depreciating currencies.

There is, however, another aspect of the "dumping" argument which has more permanent significance. Many of our large modern industrial units, controlling vast amounts of fixed capital,

[1] *Cf. Statistisches Jahrbuch*, 1921–1922, p. 175*ff.*

operate under conditions of decreasing costs. In other words, their total costs of production per unit of a product tend to decrease as the number of units produced increases. If the domestic market for their products is such that they can sell only a portion of their possible industrial output at a price sufficient to cover both constant and prime costs and a reasonable profit, any additional output, up to the full capacity of the enterprise, may be sold in foreign markets at a lower price, sufficient at least to cover the prime costs. Any margin in selling price above such prime costs will mean extra profits to the industry, since the domestic prices charged cover all the constant costs.

Consequently, many industries have from time to time resorted to selling a portion of their output abroad at prices below the domestic price of their products. If this is done permanently, and similar competitive enterprises are consequently prevented from developing aboard, it is obvious that the foreign purchasers will really be the gainers. But if the lower price is charged only temporarily abroad, until foreign competitive enterprises have been driven from the competitive field, and then monopoly prices are charged, the problem of protection to domestic industries against such practices becomes one of paramount importance and will sooner or later invite governmental interference. The extent to which an industry can resort to these practices will depend ultimately upon a variety of factors, such as the nature of the demand for the product and the possibility of substitution, as well as the possibility of governmental interference. To protect American competitors against such dumping of foreign products on our markets, the Federal government, under the provisions of the anti-dumping tariff laws of 1921 and 1922, authorized the President of the United States to penalize acts of unfair competition by imposing an extra duty of from 10 to 50 per cent ad valorem, or by forbidding the importation of offending products outright.

10. Higher Wages or Standards of Living.—One of the most popular arguments advanced by protectionists is to the effect that protective duties make wages high in America and are needed to preserve these high rates of wages. The high American wages, in the minds of many people, are caused by the protective tariff, and the American standard of living can be maintained only if goods made by cheaper foreign labor are kept out.

This popular notion that our high wages can be maintained only by means of a protective tariff rests on ignorance and misunderstanding of the underlying causes which lead to differences in money wages, price levels, and general prosperity in various countries. The products of our highly paid American labor compete effectively with the products of "pauper" labor in foreign markets. For the twelve months ending September, 1925 the value of our exported commodities was nearly five billion dollars. These goods were underselling the products of foreign labor in the markets of the world, and they were competing effectively with cheap foreign labor. Why? Because our labor was effective in the exporting industries, and so received high wages. This effectiveness of our labor and not the protective tariff, is the cause of the high wages of American labor.

To be sure, when a particular industry has come into existence because of the tariff, the high American wages could not be maintained in this industry without protection. But the price of the product of such a protected industry is likewise higher than the price which would prevail if there were no tariff. The labor in the protected industry receives a high wage because the consumers of this product pay a higher price for it than they would have to pay were there no protection.

Unfortunately, the difference between real wages and money wages is little understood by most persons. Even though money wages are higher in America than in foreign countries, unless the larger amount of money received by American labor will buy a larger amount of goods, the American laborer is no better off than the foreign workman. But if his money buys more goods, it is only because there are more goods to buy, and these goods must be produced. When labor is transferred from a more to a less productive enterprise, because of a protective tariff, an inevitable loss in product is sustained. Geographical division of labor is restricted, and as a result of diverting labor into less productive channels, its general productivity and real wages are lowered. The popular mind, however, does not comprehend this, and sees only the injurious effect upon the money wages in the protected industry, if the protection were to be partly or wholly removed. The fact that a new demand for labor would be created in our export industries as more goods were bought abroad is of little or no significance to those who feel that they would be adversely affected by the removal of protection from their particular products.

11. Employment Argument.—Closely connected with the higher wage argument is the contention that a protective tariff creates employment for American labor, and that the removal of protection would result in increased unemployment. The workingman is thoroughly convinced that protective duties increase the demand for labor, for to the extent that imports are kept out, American labor will be employed to make products formerly imported. Unfortunately, he takes only a narrow view of the problem. He does not seem to realize that, as has been stated repeatedly, less imports will also mean less exports, and therefore, while he is employed because of the protection, others, who have been working in exporting industries, will be out of work, likewise, because of the protective duties. It may indeed happen that more men will be employed to produce as many commodities as could be had before the imposition of the protective duties, *i.e.*, under conditions of unrestricted international trade. The larger amount of labor employed, however, will not result in a greater flow of consumable goods, which constitutes the real income of the community. There is in the popular employment argument for protection only a variation of the old "make-work" fallacy of production disguised under the cloak of protectionism.

Still, both of the foregoing arguments for protection were supported once more in a recent address by a high government official, when he is quoted as having said:

Protection has contributed in our country to making employment plentiful with the highest wages and the highest standards of living in the world, which is of inestimable benefit to both our agricultural and industrial population.[1]

12. Money Argument.—This argument for protection is stated in words imputed to Abraham Lincoln, but in all probability never uttered by him. One version of this frequently quoted citation is contained in the speech delivered by Congressman Randall before the National Tariff Commission Convention, as follows:

I don't know much about political economy, but I know that when we purchase a ton of steel rails from Great Britain for $100 we get the rails

[1] *Cf. New York Times*, Dec. 8, 1925, p. 8.

and Great Britain gets the money, and when we produce the rails from our own mines and in our own mills we have both the money and the rails.

The fallacy of this statement is obvious to anyone who has grasped the significance of the principles of exchange. Nevertheless, the quotation, in one form or another, appears repeatedly in protectionist literature, and consequently must be refuted once more.

In the first place, the money argument is based on the false assumption that the labor and capital, if not employed here in the manufacture of steel rails, would not be employed at all. Secondly, it assumes that dollars paid for rails in England are not going to flow back to this country to purchase other commodities, for if they did we would eventually have both the rails and the money. In the third place, it assumes that we would not buy the rails at home if we could get them more cheaply here than in England (making due allowance for transportation costs). Finally, if carried to its logical conclusions, there would be no trade at all within the country, for the best economic interests of the different parts of the United States would be served if each industrial area kept its product and its money at home in order to have both the money and the product. The money argument, no matter how stated, rests on the popular misunderstanding of the significance of money in our exchange economy. It is a survival of eighteenth century mercantilistic doctrine.

Many of the popularly voiced arguments for protective tariffs are based on fallacious reasoning. As has been previously observed, a mercantilistic bias still lingers in the minds of the masses. They think of exports as bringing money into the country and of imports as taking it out, and money to them is the desired goal of economic thinking. In the popular belief, we gain by our exports and lose by our imports. The many arguments advanced for protective duties are built up around the idea that our national material prosperity depends upon our policy of protection to American industries. If this popular illusion can be dispelled, a decided step forward in the settlement of the complex economic and financial problems arising out of the World War will have been taken. Without an understanding of the significance of foreign trade and of international exchange in connection with the settlement of foreign debts, we cannot hope for a payment of these obligations. One of the obstacles in the way of their settlement is our high protective tariff, supported largely by time-worn arguments which in many instances are fallacious and unsound.

13. Conservation of Our Natural Resources.—The proponents of free trade do not merely point out that economic loss results from trade restrictions, but also call attention to the fact that such restrictions tend to destroy or use up our important natural resources more rapidly than would be the case under conditions of unrestricted trade. For instance, certain branches of mining, such as of iron and coal, have from time to time been protected in utter disregard of the fact that this causes the United States to use up these indispensable materials, which, in the absence of the tariff, could be obtained, at least in part, from other countries. Our American forests are being destroyed at a rate far exceeding the rate of reforestation, yet the Tariff Act of 1922 imposed both specific and ad valorem duties on many kinds of wood and manufactures of wood imported from abroad.[1] Such a policy of protection against the importation of essential natural products cannot be stamped as wise or expedient. In recent tariff debates in Congress, this phase of the tariff issue has received considerable attention. Nevertheless, duties on many kinds of natural products are still levied, resulting in a more rapid consumption of our own natural resources than would be the case if no tariff restrictions were imposed.

14. Protective Tariffs and Trusts.—Our protective tariff has been referred to as "the mother of trusts." It has been pointed out that the higher duties charged on imports under the Tariff Acts of 1883, 1890, and 1897 so increased the margin of profit of domestic producers that it resulted in a reckless duplication of industrial plants at home. In order to escape ruinous competition among these many domestic industrial enterprises, trusts and monopolistic combinations were formed. It cannot be denied that our policy of protection has encouraged the formation of some of the trusts in the United States. The recent complaint of the Federal Trade Commission against the Aluminum Company of America, charging the industry with practices which tend to lessen competition and create monopoly in aluminum in the United States, is a case in question. That this industry has been tenderly treated by the tariff makers can be gleaned from the

[1] *Cf.* Schedule 4, Tariff Act of 1922.

Tariff Act of 1922, which raised the import duty on aluminum from two to five cents a pound and doubled the duty on aluminum wares. Such higher tariff rates result in lessening effective foreign competition, and in creating monopolistic advantages for the domestic industry.

15. Tariff Reform and Vested Interests.—In the preceding pages the pros and cons of the many popular arguments for a protective tariff have been briefly summarized. In view of the changed status of the United States from a world debtor to a world creditor nation during and since the great European conflict, the arguments for a protective tariff can no longer be viewed in the light of either their historical significance, or their past justification, or possibly their popular appeal. The tariff question today must be viewed from the standpoint of present expediency and future benefits to the nation as a whole. The relationship between international trade and foreign investments was pointed out in Chap. XV. Furthermore, the economic benefits accruing to the people of the United States from extensive payments on the part of debtor nations, in terms of commodities and services, were described. In order to make possible the realization of these benefits, we must shape our tariff policy with a view to encouraging rather than to discouraging the importation of goods from abroad. The development of our tariff policy must, therefore, be away from, rather than toward, trade restrictions.

It would be foolhardy to advocate the sudden removal of our protective tariff, in order to realize the benefits of free trade. "No one would propose that persons, who had in good faith made great investments in plant, on the reasonable supposition of the continuance of the protective policy, should be deprived of the protection suddenly and without notice.[1]" The problem of tariff revision cannot be solved over night. Its solution requires not only time, but also a definite program, a definite plan of action. A permanent tariff policy is necessary for the United States, one which is not based on either tradition, precedent, political alignment, or fallacious arguments, but one which has been developed with a view to conditions confronting us today. Before any permanent tariff policy can be formulated, however, a thorough understanding of the full significance of our present creditor status in its relationship to international trade and the

[1] *Cf.* TAUSSIG, "Principles of Economics," vol. I, p. 543.

tariff is necessary.   This is fundamental, if our future tariff policy is to be established on a sound scientific basis.   The problem of drawing up a permanent tariff policy requires for its solution expert knowledge and scientific training, as well as painstaking study and thorough analysis.   It will not be solved until it is removed from politics and placed in the hands of adequately trained persons, charged with establishing a permanent tariff program, which, in view of our present status, will accrue permanently to the benefit of the nation as a whole.

16. Tariff Commission and a Scientific Tariff.—The Revenue Act, approved by Congress Sept. 8, 1916, provided for the establishment of the United States Tariff Commission, composed of six members, appointed by the President, by and with the consent of the Senate, "to investigate the administration and fiscal and industrial effects of the customs laws of this country now in force or which may be hereafter enacted, the relation between the rates of duty on raw materials and finished or partly finished products," and, "in general, to investigate the operation of customs laws" and "to submit reports of its investigations" as provided in the Act.

The United States Tariff Commission today has no power to establish rates, like the power enjoyed by the Interstate Commerce Commission.   It is merely a fact-finding commission, and its existence may be terminated with any change of administration or by refusal on the part of Congress to make the necessary appropriation for it continuance.

The first step toward placing our tariff issue on a permanent, scientific basis should be to create and maintain a permanent independent tariff commission, similar in organization to the commission created under the Revenue Act of 1916.

Second, this commission should formulate a definite long-run tariff policy, developed in view of the significance of our present international status as a creditor nation.   The permanent policy should be shaped with a view to promoting the general economic welfare of the nation and not that of specific industrial groups. It should be developed to facilitate the payment of foreign obligations to the United States, and be based, not on the time-worn, fallacious arguments for protection, but on sound economic principles of production and exchange.

Third, the commission should have power, not merely to investigate the economic effects of prevailing duties, but also to establish tariff rates in accordance with its previously adopted tariff policy.

It requires time to make any fundamental change in a traditional policy. A slow process of education is a necessary prerequisite. Not until the general public can be made to understand and appreciate the close relationship between a protective tariff, foreign investments, and international trade, can we hope for a change in the popular attitude toward our traditional tariff policy. This change in attitude must eventually come, and will probably be hastened because of the changed status of the United States from a debtor to a creditor nation within the past ten years.

17. Summary.—A protective tariff, as popularly understood, is a duty imposed upon imported articles for the purpose of protecting home producers from foreign competition in the home markets. To the extent that this duty restricts trade, it results in economic loss to both importing and exporting countries. The purchasers in the importing countries must pay a higher price for the protected articles while the exporting countries will normally find exports curtailed because of the protective duty. Moreover, a protective tariff diverts the productive powers of a country, imposing the duty on imports, from more advantageous to less advantageous enterprises, resulting in economic losses.

The high protective tariff policy of the United States is the outgrowth of the Civil War, although a certain degree of protection was given to American industries by the first Tariff Act of Congress in 1789. Except for a slight downward revision of the tariff in 1894 the general tendency of rates on many imported articles from 1863 to 1913 has been distinctly upward. The Tariff Act of 1922 in many instances contains the highest duties as yet imposed on imported articles. Furthermore, it authorizes the President of the United States to revise the rates, upward or downward, if, upon investigation, the difference in costs of production here and abroad warrant such revision.

Many arguments have been advanced from time to time in favor of protection to American industries. The "infant industry" argument is advanced by those who feel that many domestic enterprises could be developed to compete effectively with foreign industries after they had once become established in this country. But most infant industries fostered by a protective tariff are unable to compete effectively after being established, unless the protective duties are continued. The argument favoring protection to domestic enterprises in order to diversify industries at home fails to take cognizance of the fact that as new industries are developed because of the tariff, others, formerly producing for export, are either injured or destroyed. The economic "self-sufficiency" argument for protective duties, carried to its logical conclusion, would stop all trade. If advanced as a plea for preparedness for war the economic loss sustained in order to develop national self-sufficiency becomes a cost of national security. The "home market" argument for protection is fallacious, even as many other arguments for protection are economically unsound, since it is based on the erroneous belief that "real" markets for goods are increased by substituting one market for another. The argument for a protective tariff, based on equalizing costs of production abroad and at home is not only unsound in principle but also unfit for practical application. The "dumping argument" attained a certain degree of validity during the currency inflation period in different European countries after the World War, but today it is largely inapplicable, except in cases where industries dump their surplus industrial output on foreign markets with a view to obtaining control of such markets. The "higher wage" or "standard of living" argument makes a popular appeal, since the difference between real wages and money wages is little understood by the average individual. American labor receives high wages, not because of high tariffs, but because of its productivity—its industrial efficiency. The "employment" argument fails to realize that protection to our industry tends to divert labor from exporting industries to the protected industries, but in reality does not create new jobs, as is popularly believed. Finally, the "money" argument for protection savors of the old mercantilistic idea that a nation's welfare depends upon the amount of money it has.

The advocates of either freer or unrestricted trade point to the fact that the protective tariff tends to accelerate the rate of destruction of our limited natural resources and encourages the development of monopolistic combinations at home.

The tariff problem of the United States can be solved eventually by dispelling the many mistaken notions concerning the benefits of a protective tariff to the country as a whole, and by a better understanding of the fundamental principles of exchange.

A permanent tariff policy should be adopted by the United States, not based on precedent or tradition, but viewed in the light of our present creditor status. The problem of perfecting and administering such a permanent tariff program should no longer be made a political issue, but should be entrusted to a permanent tariff commission without partisan affiliation, having power to establish tariff rates in conformity with a definitely adopted long-run policy.

Collateral Reading

ELY, R. T., "Outlines of Economics," chap. 18.
HAMILTON, W. H., "Current Economic Problems," Nos. 139–150 incl., pp. 319–337.
SEAGER, H. R., "Practical Problems in Economics," chap. 22.
TAUSSIG, F. W., "Principles of Economics," vol. I, chaps. 36 and 37.

References

ASHLEY, PERCY, "Modern Tariff History."
ASHLEY, W. J., "The Tariff Problem."
GREGORY, T. E. G., "Tariffs—A Study in Method."
GRUNZEL, JOSEF, "Economic Protectionism."
HIGGINSON, J., "Tariffs at Work."
HEWINS, W. A. S., "Tariffs, Trade in the Balance, Protection or Free Trade."
PAGE, W. T., "Making the Tariff in the United States."
PATTEN, S. N., "The Economic Basis of Protection."
PIERCE, FRANKLIN, "The Tariff and the Trusts."
TAUSSIG, F. W., "Selected Readings in International Trade and Tariff Problems."
———, "Tariff History of the United States."
———, "Free Trade, the Tariff and Reciprocity."
———, "State Papers and Speeches on the Tariff."
———, "Some Aspects of the Tariff Question."
United States Tariff Commission: Reciprocity and Commercial Treaties.

Questions for Discussion

1. What is meant by a protective tariff?
2. Show how a protective tariff affects international trade.
3. Trace the development of the tariff policy of the United States prior to the Civil War.
4. What has been the chief trend in the tariff legislation of the United States since the Civil War?
5. What is meant by the "flexible feature" of the Tariff Act of 1922?
6. Outline the "infant industry" argument for a protective tariff.
7. Do you consider this a sound argument for protection?
8. "A protective tariff helps to diversify our home industries." Do you agree? Give reasons for your answer.

9. What is the assumption on which the "self-sufficiency" argument for protection is based? Is this assumption sound?

10. What is meant by the "scientific" principle for a protective tariff?

11. Do you think it possible to establish a tariff for protection to home industries on a scientific basis? Why or why not?

12. "We need protection to safeguard domestic industries against a flood of cheap foreign goods." Do you agree?

13. "Our protective tariff is necessary to safeguard our high American standard of living, and to keep our labor employed." Can a protective tariff achieve these objectives?

14. How does protection affect money wages? Real wages?

15. Point out the fallacies in the "money" argument for a protective tariff.

16. Our tariff has been called "the mother of trusts." Explain and criticise.

17. What is the significance of our present creditor-nation status in relation to our future tariff policy?

18. Outline what you consider should be the underlying provisions of a permanent tariff policy for the United States.

Topics for Investigation

1. The duties and functions of the Federal Tariff Commission.

2. The arguments for and against a tariff commission with rate-fixing powers.

3. The economic significance of the "flexible" provisions of the Tariff Act of 1922.

4. Tariff revision in relation to our present creditor status.

5. The cost of "protection" and the benefits derived from it.

PART FOUR
PROBLEMS OF PUBLIC FINANCE

CHAPTER XVII

PUBLIC EXPENDITURES

1. Scope of Public Finance.—Public finance is the science which deals with governmental receipts from all sources, their expenditure, and their administration. It is a branch of the science of economics, for it deals with the gratification of human desires with the aid of economic goods. Some human desires are gratified privately, while others are gratified collectively through a governmental agency. No sharp line can be drawn between the desires which are gratified individually and those which are gratified collectively. We secure protection to person and property by carrying weapons for defensive purposes and by providing our homes with burglar alarms and safety vaults, while on the other hand we also rely upon police protection to afford us this security. We gratify our desire for an education either by employing a private tutor or by attending public schools.

In order to gratify our desires, whether individually or collectively, economic goods are necessary. Both public and private finance deal with obtaining possession of economic goods. Inasmuch as the value of these economic goods is usually measured in terms of money, the receipts and expenditures of money, whether public or private, will determine the extent of our control over economic goods, and their utilization to gratify human desires either directly or indirectly.

Public finance, moreover, is a part of economics because of its influence upon the production, distribution, and consumption of wealth. When public funds are employed either to aid private industry or to carry on public productive enterprise, definite direction is given to certain productive activities. "When the effect of securing revenues in different ways is considered from the standpoint of justice, some definite theory of distribution must be in mind."[1] When a governmental agency places a sufficiently heavy tax on a so-called "luxury" it can definitely

[1] *Cf.* HUNTER, "Outline of Public Finance," p. 5.

limit the consumption of the particular commodity. Again, the funds obtained by governmental agencies from various sources are expended for different purposes. The general direction and extent of these expenditures will in turn influence the nature of the productive activities of private business enterprises. The economic significance of public finance should therefore not be lost sight of, for economic principles form the basis of the science *of public finance.*

2. Differences between Public and Private Expenditures.— There are several basic differences between public and private expenditures. Public expenditures are made to promote the general welfare, to create legal security, to maintain peace and independence, and to aid in the development of the economic life of the people as a whole. Private expenditures, on the other hand, are usually made to gratify the desires of an individual, either directly or indirectly. Again, the services rendered by a governmental agency cannot be individualized and separately evaluated, while private expenditures are made in exchange for specific services, an appropriate payment being made for every service rendered, based on mutual gain, mutual benefit to buyer and seller. As a rule, no special payment is made for special services rendered by the government to an individual, since such special services are intended to accrue equally to the benefit of others. Moreover, public expenditures are made to render services, while in private finance expenditures are frequently made to acquire more wealth, *i.e.* to make profits. A fourth difference between public and private expenditures is that it is impossible in public finance to compare costs of production with value of the product, because of the immaterial nature of the services rendered. In private finance the costs of production in the long run will determine the value of the product, if competitive conditions prevail. Finally, governmental agencies regulate their income by their expenditures, while private individuals ordinarily regulate their expenditures by their income. Modern governments proceed to ascertain how much will be required to finance public needs and then set about to devise ways and means to obtain the necessary funds to meet these requirements.

3. Historical Development of Public Expenditures.—In early civilizations, public life was primarily identified with the family. Consequently, there was but little call for public expenditures, although at a very early date the extensive religious fêtes and the construction of shrines and temples must have required a certain pooling of resources on the part of ancient peoples. Warriors furnished their own weapons, and the reward for their services was the success of their enterprise. Funds for public enterprises were usually derived from levies upon conquered peoples, and labors for the benefit of the community were performed by the subjugated peoples. Even ancient Greece and Rome employed these methods to obtain public revenues and to develop public enterprises.

In Athens, a complex system of public expenditures was developed, when the financial burden of public construction became heavy. Again, great expenditures were incurred for public festivals and public sacrifices. Poor relief was also rendered with public funds. Since most military services were rendered voluntarily by citizens, expenditures for war were relatively small. As early as 406 B.C. Roman armies were paid, but for a long time such payment amounted to little more than a reimbursement of expenses. The courts of the Roman Emperors, however, became exceedingly extravagant and drew heavily upon public revenues. Large sums were also expended in imperial Rome for the construction of public buildings and public roads. Charities and war relief, likewise, absorbed a portion of the public funds. However, neither in early Greek nor early Roman life can we differentiate very clearly between public and private expenditures. Many citizens offered their services gratuitously to the state, and in early Roman days the emperors were supposed to live upon their own private wealth.

Under the feudal system of the Middle Ages, public funds were so directly under the control of the feudal princes that they began to regard them as their own. The lords owned the land from which they derived their revenues. As monarchial governments developed, public revenues were identified with the private purses of the rulers. Expenditures were made to gratify the desires of the kings, and their subjects benefited by such expenditures only to the extent that the interests of their ruler coincided with their own interests.

Constitutional governments have developed a new attitude toward public expenditures, characterized by the efforts on the part of the direct representatives of the people to control public finances. This concept has found expression in the Constitution of the United States, which provides that all bills for the raising of revenue for public expenditures shall originate in the House of Representatives, whose members are elected directly by the people.

4. Modern Tendencies in Public Expenditures.—With the gradual abolition of political absolutism and an increasing tendency toward constitutional government, it was believed by many that public expenditures would also decrease. Mercantilism, as a governmental policy, was rapidly being replaced by a *laissez-faire* attitude, and the idea prevailed that the government which governed least would govern best. Hence, the frequently expressed belief that governmental activities would diminish and governmental expenditures decrease. But this prediction has not come true, for one of the striking characteristics of public finance during the last century in every civilized country has been the rapid growth in public expenditures. How are we to account for this phenomenon?

In the first place, we must bear in mind the enormous economic changes wrought by the Industrial Revolution. The introduction of the factory system and the increase in specialization resulted not only in a rapid development of towns and cities, but also in the increased interdependence of man. Furthermore, the increased productivity resulting from the utilization of power machinery made possible the supporting of ever-increasing numbers of people. Population throughout the civilized world multiplied rapidly during the last century and a half. In 1790 the population of the United States was but 3,929,214; on Jan. 1, 1925 it was estimated at about 114,000,000. Europe, in 1786, had an estimated population of 167,000,000; in 1914 this number had increased to over 450,000,000. Such a rapid growth of population was made possible by the remarkable development of the arts of production and the opening up of new territories and sources of wealth during the past century and a half. With the increase in population and the increasing economic interdependence of man, as a result of the industrial development of the last one hundred fifty years, the human desires which could best be gratified collectively likewise multiplied. Increased governmental regulation of industrial activities and of private enterprise in its relationship to general welfare has become necessary. This fact, in part, accounts for the rapid growth of certain items of public expenditures during the past one hundred and fifty years.

The economic changes brought about by the introduction of the machine process reacted upon existing social and political institutions, and these in turn also underwent profound modifications. Practically all of these changes resulted in increasing the sphere of governmental activities, which were gradually enlarged "to embrace not only protection from internal disorder and foreign aggression but also public education and health, public works, provision for spiritual as well as physical advancement, and other related activities."[1]

5. Increase in Public Expenditures in the United States.—The increased governmental activities brought about by the economic, social, and political changes of the past century are reflected in the growth of the public expenditures of the Federal government of the United States, as well as in the increased state and local governmental expenditures. In 1791, the total ordinary governmental expenditures of the Federal government, paid for primarily out of revenues derived from taxation, amounted to but $4,269,027. The population of the United States in 1790 was 3,929,214. This indicates a per capita ordinary expenditure of about $1 in 1791. In 1912, on the other hand, the per capita ordinary expenditure of the Federal government was $6.84, while in 1920 it was no less than $57.72.

Although the per capita ordinary Federal expenditure shows such a remarkable increase since 1790, this does not necessarily indicate a corresponding increase in the burden of taxation imposed upon the people. Even though these expenditures have increased more rapidly than population, it is doubtful if prior to the World War they were increasing more rapidly than the estimated increase in either national wealth or national income of the people of the United States. The following table[2] shows the increase in ordinary Federal expenditures by decades since 1850, compared with the increase in population and in estimated national wealth for the corresponding periods.

[1] *Cf. Report of Natl. Indl. Conference*, "Taxation and National Income," No. 55, p. 10.

[2] The *Statistical Abstract* of the United States for 1924 and the *Report* of the Secretary of the Treasury of the United States for 1924 p. 392*ff*.

INCREASE IN FEDERAL EXPENDITURES IN THE UNITED STATES

Years	Population	Total ordinary Federal expenditures[1]	Estimated national wealth	Per capita wealth	Per capita expenditures
1850	23,191,876	$ 39,543,492	$ 7,135,780,000	$ 307.69	$ 1.77
1860	31,443,321	63,130,598	16,159,616,000	513.93	2.01
1870	38,558,371	309,653,561	30,068,518,000	779.83	7.61
1880	50,155,783	267,642,958	43,642,000,000	870.20	5.28
1890	62,947,714	318,040,711	65,037,091,000	1,035.57	4.75
1900	75,994,575	520,860,847	88,517,307,000	1,164,79	6.39
1912	95,340,000[2]	689,881,334	187,739,071,090[2]	1,965.00[2]	6.84
1920	105,710,620	6,141,745,240	290,000,000,000	2,689.34	57.72

[1] Include disbursements for War, Navy, Indians, Pensions, Interest, Civil and Miscellaneous Expenditures, exclude Panama Canal, Public Debt, and Postal Services.
[2] Estimated.

As will be noted in the foregoing table, the per capita ordinary Federal expenditures expressed in monetary terms have increased slightly more than fourfold from 1850 to 1912 while the estimated nominal value of the wealth of the United States increased more than sixfold during the period in question.

Not only Federal expenditures, but also state and municipal disbursements have grown rapidly during the past century. It is doubtful, however, whether the combined public expenditures of all governmental units in the United States increased more rapidly than the estimated value of the national wealth of the country. It has been estimated that in 1916 a lower percentage of the national wealth of the United States was being expended by governmental agencies than in 1870. "All governmental units" (other than the Federal government) "spent $15.20 per thousand of the wealth in 1890, while in 1912 the expenditure was but $13.30."[1]

We must not lose sight of the fact that during the past seventy-five years the value of money has changed from time to time. Increased public expenditures do not necessarily mean increased services rendered, and decreased expenditures do not imply curtailed governmental activities. Increased public services may be rendered with the same or even a somewhat decreased public expenditure in a period of falling prices. On the other hand, greater public expenditures in a period of rising prices do not necessarily mean more collective benefits or greater public services rendered.

[1] *Cf.* HUNTER, "Outlines of Public Finance," p. 35.

6. Increased Public Expenditures in Other Countries.— The general observations as to the increase in public expenditures in the United States during the past century apply equally to other countries. The total revenues of all European nations combined in 1786 were about five hundred and ten million dollars, while in 1880 they were approximately three billion dollars. During the same interval the combined populations of Europe increased from one hundred sixty-seven million to three hundred thirteen million, so that the per capita governmental revenues increased from three dollars in 1786 to more then nine dollars in 1880. The increase in ordinary expenditures of various governmental units may be gleaned from the following tables although allowance must be made for the changes in the value of the monetary units.

INCREASED EXPENDITURES OF EUROPEAN GOVERNMENTS[1]

Prussia...............	1849	282.3 mill. Marks
Prussia...............	1911 to 1912	3,872.2 mill. Marks
Bavaria...............	1825 to 1826	49.1 mill. Marks
Bavaria...............	1912	676.2 mill. Marks
France...............	1816 to 1828 (Average)	960 mill. Francs
France...............	1911 to 1912	4,386.5 mill. Francs
Italy.................	1861	312 mill. Lire
Italy.................	1909 to 1910	1,905.6 mill. Lire
Russia...............	1859	560.2 mill. Roubles
Russia...............	1912	2,975.3 mill. Roubles

These figures indicate the general trend of public expenditures throughout the civilized world during the past century. Caution should be exercised however, in comparing the combined public expenditures of various nations, as such comparisons may lead to erroneous conclusions, even when the comparisons are made on a per capita basis or in terms of percentages of national income. It is doubtful whether any valid conclusions can be drawn from such comparison, for the concept of "proper" governmental functions and governmental activities differs in different countries. Expenditures which in one country are public are private in another. Since public ownership of systems of transportation in some countries increases public revenues and public expenditures, it is obviously incorrect to compare such expenditures with the public expenditures of a governmental agency operating no public enterprises.

[1] *Cf.* Compiled by Eheberg *"Finanzwissenschaft,"* p. 43.

Although it is impossible to make any valid comparisons of public expenditures in various countries, it is apparent that, in general, public expenditures in all civilized countries have increased even more rapidly than population during the nineteenth century and particularly during the first two decades of the twentieth century. The per capita total expenditure of certain governments on the pre-war purchasing power basis for 1902 to 1903 and 1920 to 1921 has been estimated as follows:

INCREASE IN GOVERNMENTAL EXPENDITURES IN UNITED STATES AND EUROPE[1]

Fiscal year	United States	United Kingdom	France	Italy	Germany	Japan
1902 to 1903	$22.34	$40.62	$23.78	$13.91	$44.07*	$4.96
1920 to 1921	44.82	60.58	58.19	25.53	56.09	7.84

* Fiscal year 1903–1904.

7. Causes for Growth of Public Expenditures.—Four causes may be cited for the general upward trend in public expenditures during the past century and a half: first, costly wars and expensive peace-time military and naval equipments; second, increased density of population, tending to multiply social problems and to increase the human desires which can best be gratified collectively; third, increase in regulative activities and police powers exercised by governmental agencies; fourth, ease of governmental borrowing.

Most important among these causes of increased governmental expenditures are the outlays for war purposes. According to Professor Bullock[2] 80.7 per cent of the Federal expenditures of the United States in 1870 were due to payments for army, navy, pensions, and interest on debts arising from wars. In 1880, this item was 74 per cent of the total Federal expenditures; in 1890, 66.4 per cent; and in 1900, 72.4 per cent. Since the beginning of the twentieth century, until the outbreak of the World War, the aggregate Federal expenditures for war purposes were constantly increasing, but in relation to total Federal expenditures actually showed a slight decrease. The World War, however, has caused a very decided increase in military and naval expenditures, as is indicated in the following statistical compilation.[3]

[1] Cf. "Taxation and National Income," p. 20
[2] Cf. "Readings in Public Finance," p. 49.
[3] Cf. Statistical Abstract of the Unites States for 1921, p. 747.

DISBURSEMENTS FOR WAR PURPOSES INCLUDING PENSIONS, INTEREST ON THE PUBLIC DEBT, AND ALL OTHER ACTIVITIES RELATING TO WAR. YEARS ENDING JUNE 30, 1912 TO 1921[1]

Year ending June 30	War Department	Navy Department	Pensions and Pensions Office	Interest on public debt	War activities, other departments	Special war activities	Total disbursements for war purposes	Percentage of total ordinary disbursements
1912	$115,072,793.29	$136,389,659.75	$155,344,785.52	$22,616,300.48		$164,909.37	$429,588,448.41	62.2
1913	119,970,406.99	134,092,426.93	177,071,800.04	22,899,108.08		160,865.91	454,194,607.95	62.6
1914	125,411,183.90	140,543,059.30	175,392,464.73	22,863,956.70	$390,639.91	173,370.32	464,774,674.86	63.2
1915	127,950,545.94	142,721,524.13	166,066,633.58	22,902,897.04	1,046,015.41	2,806,513.42	463,494,129.52	60.9
1916	133,944,449.57	155,883,194.66	160,885,132.06	22,900,313.03	765,689.89	135,081.68	474,563,860.89	63.9
1917	412,076,572.48	258,148,087.10	161,818,831.59	24,742,139.42	858,958,677.92	16,076,105.49	1,731,820,414.00	83.0
1918	5,667,874,908.80	1,370,477,407.61	182,549,161.29	197,526,608.36	4,859,468,436.97	1,134,042,311.78	13,411,938,834.81	97.2
1919	9,239,471,908.60	1,915,468,272.39	222,917,744.38	615,867,337.52	3,697,323,833.20	2,434,054,933.74	18,125,104,029.83	95.6
1920	1,053,012,975.61	632,690,267.94	214,621,763.43	1,024,024,440.02	546,802,737.67	2,025,594,702.24	5,496,746,886.91	89.5
1921	504,846,579.56	647,870,645.21	261,825,335.77	996,676,803.75	395,228,508.67	938,085,160.80	3,744,533,033.76	83.5

[1] Includes, under Treasury Department "Purchase of Obligations of Foreign Goverments," as follows: 1917, $855,000 000.00; 1918, $4,739,434,750.00; 1919, $3,477,850,265.56; 1920, $421,337,028.09; 1921, $73,896,697.44.

It may be contended by some that it is wrong to refer to military and naval expenditures as disbursements "for war purposes." The advocates of preparedness hold to the doctrine that the best assurance of peace is to be prepared for war. However, this theory has not been substantiated by fact, for the World War was precipitated in spite of the ever-increasing expenditures for preparedness on the part of European countries prior to 1914. The enormous money costs of the War have upset all human calculations. The combined direct monetary costs of the important European wars of the nineteenth century have been estimated at £2,907,000,000 or approximately $14,500,000,-000,[1] while the net direct money cost of the World War has been placed at $186,000,000,000[2] or more than twelve times the money costs of the combined European wars of the nineteenth century. Even when the monetary cost of the World War is estimated in terms of the pre-war purchasing power of the gold dollar, it is found to be nearly six times as great as the costs of the European wars of the last century. The net expenditures of the United States in prosecuting the War were nearly twenty-three billion dollars. In November 1918, the month in which the Armistice was signed, military expenses averaged more than fifty-five million dollars a day.

The consequent burden imposed upon the peoples of the various nations is made even more vivid when we compare the 1918 war expenditures of the belligerent countries with their estimated national pre-war income.

NATIONAL INCOMES AND WAR EXPENDITURES OF THE PRINCIPAL BELLIGERENTS, 1918[3]

Countries	Annual national pre-war income	War expenditure, 1918
United States...................	$38,000,000,000	$18,000,000,000
Great Britain..................	10,700,000,000	13,896,505,940
France.......................	7,300,000,000	10,671,000,000
Russia.......................	6,500,000,000	9,000,000,000*
Italy.........................	3,000,000,000	3,946,920,000
Germany......................	10,500,000,000	
Austria-Hungary..............	5,500,000,000	

* 1917.

[1] Cf. GRAMMOND, E. "Cost of the War," Journal of Royal Statistical Society, May, 1915, p. 361.

[2] Cf. BOGART, E. L., "War Costs and Their Financing," p. 105.

[3] Cf. ibid., p. 106.

In emphasizing the general increase in public expenditures for war purposes and the enormous money costs of the World War, we are apt to minimize the general tendency toward increased expenditures on the part of governmental units for other purposes. The expenditures of the various state governments in the United States increased from $185,764,000 in 1903 to $1,310,332,793 in 1923 or more than sevenfold. Allowing for the depreciation of the value of the dollar during the period in question, the increased state expenditures are nevertheless very significant. The same holds true of expenditures of cities having over 30,000 population, in which the money expenditures increased from $468,638,000 in 1903 to $1,201,923,000 in 1919.[1] The major portion of these increased expenditures is the result of a multiplication of the social problems due to the increasing complexity of modern society. It includes increased expenditures for health and sanitation, education and public charities, as well as increased expenditures for different forms of regulative activities. Public regulation of various enterprises known as public utilities, governmental supervision of banking, enforcement of "blue sky" legislation, and many other forms of governmental regulative activities are making increasing demands upon public funds.

Finally, the ease of governmental borrowing, the possibility of issuing tax-exempt securities (which will be discussed subsequently), may be cited as another cause of increased governmental expenditures in recent years. The net indebtedness of the Federal government, arising primarily out of the World War, increased from $1,908,635,000 in 1917 to $24,479,302,000 in 1919. The net indebtedness of the state of New York increased from $4,494,000 in 1890 to over $320,000,000 in 1924. During the War most European Governments resorted to borrowing as well as to increased taxation to meet their increasing expenditures. Since the War, the ease of borrowing has been superceded by a loss of faith in various foreign governments, and their ease of obtaining credit has suffered correspondingly.

8. Proper Scope of Public Expenditures.—The several causes for the general upward trend in public expenditures have been noted above. An attempt to justify such increased expenditures involves an analysis of the functions of government. Different writers holding divergent views concerning the proper scope of

[1] *Cf.* "Taxation and National Income," *Research Report* No. 55, p. 14.

governmental activities have expressed themselves differently as to the "proper" amount of public expenditure. Some have attempted to fix this as a certain percentage, ranging from 5 to 25 per cent of the total annual income of a nation. Others have attempted to estimate "proper" governmental expenditures on a per capita basis. It seems doubtful, however, whether any such method of fixing a "proper" amount for public expenditures is possible. In the final analysis, all public expenditures must be justified on the basis of social expediency and political experience. We have noted above that certain human desires can be most economically gratified collectively. In the words of Professor Daniels:[1]

If we avoid the "falsehood of extremes" we shall find very general acquiescence in the belief that there are some things which state action is likely to effect with a balance of advantage in any society.

Without entering into a detailed, theoretical analysis of the functions of modern governmental agencies, we may accept as a working hypothesis that in general proper public expenditures are those which are normally made by governments today, and that all extensions of these expenditures must be judged on their own merit.

We must not lose sight of the fact that a governmental agency is a productive organism in modern society. The "proper" amount of public expenditures should therefore be gauged on the basis of the utility to the community which such expenditures create. As economic, social and political institutions increase in complexity, the number of desires which can best be gratified collectively by a public agency will also increase. This idea is expressed in the law of increasing public expenditures formulated by the late Professor Adolf Wagner.

Comparisons between different countries and different periods show regularly among progressive nations an extension of public activities. This manifests itself extensively and intensively. The state and its subordinate political units continually undertake new functions, and they perform their duties, old and new, better and better. In this way, that is, through public agency, the needs of the population, especially their common needs, are satisfied to an increasing extent; and the public services for the satisfaction of needs continually improve in quality.

[1] *Cf.* "Public Finance," p. 26*f.*

The clear proof of this is given statistically in the increased demands made by the state and the subordinate political units.[1]

9. Budget Control of Public Expenditures.—Until recent years relatively little consideration has been given to the study of public expenditures. The average citizen is concerned primarily with the burden of taxation imposed upon him, and is apt to favor that governmental agency which makes only slight demands upon his individual income and to be out of sympathy with the governmental unit which imposes heavy burdens of taxation upon him. It is essential that more attention should be given to governmental expenditures and that the citizens of any community should obtain a more intelligent grasp of the significance and purpose of public expenditures. "When the average citizen is as careful about how public funds are spent as he is about spending his private salary we will not hear any more about government extravagance."[2] Until recently it has been quite impossible for the average citizen to obtain accurate information concerning public expenditures. As a result of the adoption of budgets by various governmental agencies, however, and of the wide publicity given to such budgets, the situation has materially improved.

A budget is a plan for financing a governmental agency or an enterprise during a definite period of time. It is prepared by a responsible executive and submitted to a representative body for approval and authorization. The preparation of a budget involves a careful analysis of public expenditures, and of present as well as of anticipated receipts. A budget may be prepared either by the executive or the legislative branch of the government. A budget officer, or a bureau or commission, responsible to the executive, may be charged with drawing up the budget plan. In the case of the Federal government, the President prepares the budget estimates, but members of Congress have the power to introduce appropriation and taxation bills. In the separate states, the legislatures likewise retain the right to initiate revenue legislation. Governmental budget making in the United States is still in the experimental stage, but recent developments in budgetary control of public expenditures are decided steps in the right direction.

[1] *Cf.* WAGNER, *"Grundlegung der politischen Oekonomie,"* 3rd ed. vol. I, p. 893.

[2] *Cf.* SECRETARY MELLON, "Nation's Business," p. 14, November, 1923.

Budgeting laws have been adopted not only by the Federal government but also by a large number of state governments and municipalities, as well as by most modern foreign governments. As a result of the general publicity given to proposed governmental financing, every citizen is given an opportunity to exercise his own judgment on the proposed expenditures. He will have to be convinced of the expediency of soldiers' bonuses, railway aid, ship subsidies and the like before he gives his approval. This approval or disapproval of public expenditures can be conveyed very forcefully in democratic governments by means of the ballot.

10. Summary.—Public finance deals with governmental revenues, their expenditure and their administration. It is a branch of economics, not merely because it deals with the gratification of human desires, but because of its influence upon the production, distribution and consumption of wealth.

Public expenditures are made to promote the general welfare and not to gratify the desires of an individual. As a rule governmental agencies regulate their income according to their expenditures, while private individuals regulate their expenditures by their income. In ancient times public expenditures were relatively small, but as civilization progressed public expenditures likewise increased. This increase in public expenditures has been particularly pronounced in the last century and a half in both the United States and in European countries, because of the many economic, social and political changes since the Industrial Revolution. The increased public expenditures may be ascribed specifically to costly wars and peace-time military equipments, increased socialization of consumption, increased regulative activities of governmental agencies, and the ease of governmental borrowing.

The proper scope of public expenditures must be judged on the basis of social expediency and political experience. Public expenditures will increase, since the many human desires which can be most economically gratified collectively are increasing with the increasing interdependence of man. Not until recent years has the average citizen begun to show any interest in public expenditures. The adoption of budgetary control by most modern governmental units is offering to the general public an opportunity to observe the trend of public expenditures and to voice either its approval or disapproval of public expenditures for various purposes.

Collateral Readings

ELY, R. T., "Outlines of Economics," chap. 21.
HUNTER, M. H., "Outlines of Public Finance," chap. 2.
JENSEN, J. P., "Problems of Public Finance," chap. 3.
MARSHALL, WRIGHT, and FIELD, "Materials for the Study of Elementary Economics," chap. 19, Nos. 238–240.
SEAGER, H. R., "Practical Problems in Economics, "chap. 26.

References

ADAMS, H. C., "The Science of Finance."
BOGART, E. L., "Direct and Indirect Costs of the Great War."
BULLOCK, C. J., (editor) "Selected Readings in Public Finance."
Bureau of Census, "Wealth, Debt and Taxation."
DALTON, HUGH, "Principles of Public Finance."
DANIELS, W. M., "Public Finance."
HUNTER, M. H., "Outlines of Public Finance."
JENSEN, J. P., "Problems of Public Finance."
National Industrial Conference Board, Taxation and National Income, *Research Report* No. 55.
PLEHN, C. C., "Introduction to Public Finance."
ROBINSON, M. E., "Public Finance."
ROSA, E. B., "The Expenditures and Revenues of the Federal Government," *Annals* of the American Academy of Political and Social Science, vol. 95.
Secretary of the Treasury, *Annual Reports* on the State of Finances.
STAMP, SIR JOSIAH, "Studies in Current Problems in Finance and Government."
Statistical Abstract of the United States, 1924.

Questions for Discussion

1. Define public finance.
2. Why is public finance a part of economics?
3. Distinguish between public and private expenditures.
4. For what purposes were public funds expended in ancient times?
5. "Constitutional governments have developed a new attitude toward public expenditures." Explain.
6. Account for the increase in public expenditures since the Industrial Revolution.
7. Have our public expenditures increased more rapidly than our national wealth and our national income during the past century? What significance do you attach to your answer?
8. Do you consider it correct to include disbursements for upkeep of army and navy in times of peace among "expenditures for war purposes?" Give reasons for your point of view.
9. What is the proper scope of public expenditures?
10. Explain what is meant by budget control of public expenditures.

Topics for Investigation

1. Changes in state and local expenditures over a period of years.
2. Reasons for increased state and local expenditures during the past ten years.
3. Governmental budgets, their preparation and use.
4. The distinction between public expenditures and social expenditures.
5. Increasing collective consumption of economic goods.
6. Standardizing public expenditures.

CHAPTER XVIII

PUBLIC RECEIPTS FROM BORROWING

1. Sources of Public Receipts.—Public receipts to defray the various public expenditures discussed in the preceding chapter are derived from a variety of sources. They may be obtained by public borrowing in one form or another, or they may be derived from public revenues, such as earnings of public enterprises, sale of public properties, fees, special assessments and taxes. The nature and significance of public borrowing as a means of obtaining control over economic goods on the part of governmental agencies will be discussed in this chapter.

2. Borrowing Not a Source of Public Revenue.—As commonly understood, borrowing is not a source of public revenue. The word "revenue" is derived from the French *revenir* meaning to "come back." It implies a return or reward for something, whether for commodities or for services. In this sense of the word, public loans cannot be construed to be "public revenue," for they are not a reward or return for public services. The actual payment for such services, no matter how immaterial they may be, is made with taxes and the public revenues from other sources enumerated above.

Loans, whether public or private, are liabilities of the borrower. Revenues, on the other hand, are assets. The liabilities which a government incurs when it borrows must ultimately be paid, if they are paid at all, out of revenues. Therefore, when a governmental agency resorts to borrowing as a means of financing its present expenditures, the procedure is in reality equivalent to asking payments out of anticipated future revenues. Even a refunding operation of a public debt is not a payment for either the commodities or the services which the governmental agency has obtained with the proceeds of the original loan. Such goods can ultimately be paid for only out of public revenues.

When any government, for reasons to be discussed subsequently, is unable to meet its obligations out of current revenues, it incurs liabilities in the form of loans, which it hopes to repay with its anticipated future revenues. H. C. Adams speaks of the

371

proceeds derived from the sale of bonds and of other forms of commercial credit as well as the funds derived from the issue of treasury notes as "anticipatory revenues."[1] It would perhaps be more in accordance with everyday business usage to refer to loans as the proceeds derived from incurred obligations which are to be repaid out of anticipated future revenues. Such terminology would differentiate clearly between public loans as governmental liabilities and public revenues as governmental assets. A governmental unit can obtain funds at any one time, either by incurring liabilities or by drawing on its assets. Funds obtained in either way will hereafter be referred to as public receipts.

3. Purposes of Public Borrowing.—In recent years governments have been making increasing use of their credit to obtain funds to defray certain nonrecurring, extraordinary expenditures. Such expenditures are frequently necessitated by an unforeseen, unpreventable, or at least unpredictable event. The Japanese earthquake, a great national calamity, made it necessary for a government to float a large loan to defray a portion of the extraordinary public expenditures resulting from the catastrophe. During the World War, all the belligerent countries resorted to borrowing in one form or another, as a means of obtaining funds with which to pay for a part of their suddenly increased public disbursements.

But governments resort to borrowing also for other reasons than to meet the expenditures resulting from a great national emergency. Not infrequently they will incur debts, the proceeds of which are employed to develop certain public enterprises, which once developed, "will pay for themselves." The actual capital required for the development of such projects is advanced to the government out of the accumulated savings of the investors in governmental obligations. The government has thus incurred a capital liability which it hopes to repay, in whole or in part, with the revenues derived from the specific payments made for the services rendered by the enterprise in question. Municipal water works, Federal railways, and the like are familiar illustrations of such enterprises.

Moreover, governments frequently resort to borrowing to finance either the erection of public buildings—schools, libraries, museums, and hospitals—or the construction of roads, bridges, dams, viaducts, and the like. Such durable public improve-

[1] *Cf.* "The Science of Finance," p. 227.

ments yield up their benefits to the community at large, either directly or indirectly, over a relatively long period of time. Although the initial funds required for these constructions are usually advanced to the government in the form of loans, they are ultimately paid for primarily with revenues derived from taxes.

4. Public Borrowing to Finance Wars.—Modern governments have resorted to extensive borrowing, particularly to defray a portion of the suddenly increased public expenditures incidental to prosecuting wars. In 1861, the gross interest and noninterest-bearing debt of the United States, excluding gold, silver, and currency certificates, amounted to only $90,582,417. But in 1865, at the close of the Civil War, this item had increased to $2,677,929,021, as the result of the extensive public borrowing to finance the war. From 1917, the year the United States entered the World War, until 1919, the gross interest and noninterest-bearing public debt of the Federal government increased from $2,975,618,585 to no less than $25,482,034,419.[1]

Similar increases in the monetary value of national debts as a result of the World War may be noted in European countries as follows:

SUMMARY OF PUBLIC DEBTS OF PRINCIPAL EUROPEAN BELLIGERENT COUNTRIES IN 1913–1914 AND IN 1919 (IN MILLIONS OF DOLLARS)[2]

Countries	Population	Pre-war debts	Pre-war annual debt charges	Post-war debts	Post-war annual debts charges	Annual post-war debt charges per capita	Post-war debt—per cent of estimated pre-war wealth	Post-war debt charges in estimated per cent of pre-war income
Great Britain...	46,089,000	$ 3,458	$119	$ 37,657	$1,421	$30.83	54.10	12.92
France.........	39,700,000	6,598	252	30,494	1,930	48.61	52.13	32.17
Italy..........	36,717,000	3,031	103	15,009	577	15.71	65.83	14.43
Russia.........	182,183,000	5,092	218	54,402	766	4.20	90.67	11.78
Belgium.......	7,658,000	722	25	1,889	85	11.10	12.59	6.54
Germany.......	67,818,000	1,165	42	40,007	2,201	32.46	49.70	20.96
Austria........	30,958,000	2,631	101	17,071	622	20.09	72.64	25.92
Totals......	....	$22,697	$860	$196,529	$7,602			

[1] The noninterest-bearing debt included primarily the United States notes—obligations originating at the time of the Civil War—less the amount of the gold reserve held for their redemption since 1900. *Cf. Annual Report* of the U. S. Treasurer for 1922, p. 465 and for 1924, p. 156.

[2] Compiled from L. R. GOTTLIEB, "Debts etc.," in *Quarterly Journal of Economics*, vol. 34, November, 1919, p. 164*ff.*

Due caution should be exercised in interpreting the above data, since they are not corrected to allow for the depreciation in the value of the dollar during the period in question. One observation, however, can be made regarding the above statistics. There has been a very substantial increase in public debts of the principal European countries participating in the World War as a result of extensive borrowing on the part of these countries for purposes of war financing.

5. Borrowing versus Taxing to Finance Wars.—Many conflicting views are held as to the expediency and economy of public borrowing instead of taxing to finance a war. Some contend that such borrowing greatly increases the costs of the war. A certain force of governmental employees is required to administer the debt, pay interest, and collect the necessary revenues for debt charges in the form of taxes. These costs would not be incurred, it is contended, if the war were financed by taxing rather than by borrowing.

Furthermore, it is held that the possibility of shifting a part of the physical burden of the war to future generations by domestic borrowing is illusory and illogical. The war is fought with present goods and man power. The losses of such goods and man power, due to the destructiveness of war, are borne by the generation which fights the war and not by future generations. Those who sacrifice that which they possessed in either material wealth or labor power are the real losers as the result of wars. Future generations, it is contended, never possessed that which was destroyed during the war, and no one can lose anything which he has never had.

This line of reasoning can be illustrated by a very simple example. Let us assume that the average citizen, "A" loaned his government a thousand dollars during the war, in return for which he received a claim on the government in the form of a bond for a thousand dollars, payable, let us say, in ten years. How will the government obtain the necessary revenues, assuming that the loan was floated within the country, and no indemnities were exacted with which to repay the loan? Such revenues will in all probability be derived from taxes. If now "A," because of the governmental obligation to him, finds that he is required to pay in Federal taxes every year an amount equal to the interest he is receiving on his bond, plus the costs of either sending to him his semiannual interest check or paying his coupons and collecting the interest from him in taxes, in addition to an amount which, at the end of ten years, will be the equivalent of a thousand dollars, which will then be repaid to him, he may well ask himself what has become of the original thousand dollars which he loaned to the government.

He has in reality given the government two thousand dollars, plus the interest he has received on his loan, plus the various costs enumerated above. He ultimately received one thousand dollars from the government in payment of his bond. If the government had not been obligated to repay the thousand dollars borrowed during the war, "A" would not, under the assumed conditions, have been obliged to pay the taxes required to redeem the governmental obligation at maturity. He could have saved the amount he had to pay in taxes, and at the end of ten years would presumably have accumulated another thousand dollars. Thus, the original one thousand dollars which he "loaned" to the government during the war are lost as far as "A" is concerned. He might just as well have paid them in taxes directly to the government, and thus have saved himself, and others similarly situated, the payments of the costs of collecting revenues and administering public debts. To the extent that *these* "costs" have to be borne by future generations, we can speak of actual shifting of the burden of a war on to the future. If, however, the person who has made the loan to the government subsequently does not pay the taxes to repay the loan, he will benefit at the expense of his fellow citizens, who bear the burden of taxation for debt payment. In other words, the repayment of the loan may affect the subsequent distribution of the income of a country, but from the point of view of the nation as a whole, the burden of the war has not been shifted by means of internal loans.

If this contention is sound, the question may be asked, why do governments resort to borrowing instead of taxing to finance wars? It is sufficiently clear that the purpose of both borrowing and taxing is identical. Either method is employed to transfer immediate control over commodities and services from private individuals to the government. There are, however, certain distinct and well-recognized advantages of borrowing over taxing for war financing.

In the first place, borrowing gives the government immediate control of purchasing power, whereas taxing involves time in legislating and collecting taxes. Second, borrowing will frequently bring forth accumulated savings which might not be attached by specific taxes. Third, borrowing makes possible the social appeal which in times of a national emergency, such as the World War, is often a more potent factor in achieving results than legal compulsion. Fourth, borrowing generally leaves the time and manner of making payments to the discretion of individual lenders. During the World War, banks offered so-called "easy-payment" plans to subscribers to Liberty bonds, and thereby made lending more attractive. Lastly, there are always a certain number of individuals who make a very definite sacrifice in times of war to aid their government financially. They curtail their consumption, at times even of so-called necessities, to buy bonds "till it hurts." It is doubtful whether any system of taxation, devised under war-time conditions, would meet with the approval of the masses, if taxes were made very heavy. It is a well-established observation that human beings often make sacrifices voluntarily against which they would rebel if made under legal compulsion.

Even though we admit these general advantages of borrowing over taxing as a means of obtaining funds to finance wars, we should not overlook the disadvantages. There are undoubtedly some who in times of a great national crisis will make personal sacrifices in the form of curtailed consumption and greater productive efforts in order to provide a larger surplus to lend to their governments. There are, on the other hand, many people who will regard bonds as evidences of ability to pay and who will spend even more than formerly. They feel that they have performed their patriotic duty when they have bought a government bond and proceed to sell it immediately, if necessary even at a small loss, in order to get purchasing power. Moreover, if government bonds are accepted as collateral security for bank loans, such borrowing must sooner or later lead to credit inflation. Again it has also been contended that war loans will lead to the adoption of a tax system after the war which will be a hardship to one class of society and a benefit to another, thus tending to increase the inequalities in the distribution of wealth and of income.

In times of war, moreover, certain taxes, particularly those imposed on so-called war profits, can be collected without much difficulty, because of the general wave of patriotism which militates somewhat against a possible criticism of governmental policies in a great national crisis. This has been called capitalizing the enthusiasm of the war period on the part of the government. Again, as we have noted above, governmental borrowing requires certain subsequent expenditures for administration of public debts which would not be necessary if the funds had been obtained by taxing instead of by borrowing.

6. Sound Policy of War Financing.—The alleged advantages and disadvantages of either borrowing or taxing as a means of obtaining public receipts for war purposes have been briefly summarized above. The question now suggests itself as to the proper policy which governments should pursue in financing a war.

From the economic point of view, taxation rather than public borrowing for war purposes should be stressed, for, as we have seen, borrowing is but an illusory method of shifting the physical burden of a war upon future generations. To the extent that an individual lends his funds to the government during the war, but is able to escape subsequent taxes required for the repayment of the loan, he benefits by having lent his funds rather than having had them taken from him by taxing. But someone else must presumably pay the taxes required to repay the loan. The burden has merely been shifted from one individual to another, but not from the nation as a whole. Only if the war obligations are incurred by the people of one country to the people of another country can we speak of an actual shifting of war burdens by borrowing. In such a case the people who granted the loans are not the same as those who must repay them. The debts which the allied powers incurred to the United States during and since the World War impose a real burden on the subjects of the allied countries when payments are made.

But in spite of the deceptive nature of public borrowing as a means of war financing, it is of decided practical importance. Wars, as has been observed, require immediate, extraordinary expenditures on the part of governments. A tax program, hastily developed and enacted, may, even in times of war, defeat the very purpose for which it was adopted, namely the obtaining of revenues. Tax legislation cannot be enacted over night, as it requires time, whereas the government's requirements to prosecute a war are immediate and vital. Borrowing cannot be abolished under such conditions. Nevertheless, the fiscal experiences of various nations during the World War taught certain very unmistakable lessons. The nations which made a relatively greater use of taxation than of borrowing suffered less from credit inflation. In general, they emerged from the war financially and economically sounder than those nations which resorted more to loans and minimized the use of taxation.   Great Britain, Japan, and the United States, adopting the former policy, came out of the war with better tax systems and perhaps a greater sense of public obligation than did either Germany, Italy, or France, leaning more toward the latter policy of borrowing as a means of financing the war.   The following table shows the ratio of receipts from taxation to total expenditures during the World War on the part of the principal belligerent countries.   The same ratio for 1913–1914 is included for purposes of comparison.

RATIOS OF RECEIPTS FROM TAXATION TO TOTAL EXPENDITURES DURING AND
BEFORE THE WORLD WAR

	Ratio during war	Ratio 1913–1914
United States......................	25.9	96.0
Great Britain......................	24.7	82.7
France............................	15.4	92.1
Italy.............................	14.9	52.7
Germany..........................	11.0	81.8
Japan............................	62.2	69.7

Those countries which had a relatively small pre-war ratio of taxation to total disbursements derived considerable revenues from certain public enterprises, and did not necessarily resort to borrowing to make up the difference between revenues from taxes and expenditures.   During the war, however, all belligerent countries show a decided decrease in the ratio of taxation to total disbursements.   The higher ratios are displayed by the nations which appear to have emerged from the World War stronger financially than did the others.   We may therefore conclude that in view of the experiences of different nations during the World War, the policy of maximum taxation and minimum borrowing for purposes of war financing appears sound both in principle and in practice.

The significance of the foregoing analysis of war financing will perhaps be minimized and depreciated by those who believe that wars can be permanently abolished.   If this laudable objective can be realized, the problem of war financing will become one of historic interest rather than of either present or future importance.

7. Forms of Public Loans.—Governments sell their credit in a variety of forms, not merely to obtain as wide a market as possible for their obligations, but also to secure the maximum returns in the shortest possible time and at the lowest possible cost. With these objectives in view, the selling price of public obligations is usually established at a figure which will prove attractive to the possible purchaser. Special inducements in the form of borrowing privileges, convenient payments, tax exemption, and the like are offered to make the securities popular with the investing public. The denominations of different types of securities, as well as the maturities, are varied to suit all kinds of investors. On June 30, 1922, the interest-bearing debts of the Federal government of the United States, arising primarily out of the World War, were composed of the following obligations:

INDEBTEDNESS OF FEDERAL GOVERNMENT JUNE 30, 1922[1]

Liberty Loan bonds (varying maturities and rates).....	$15,081,611,500
Victory Liberty loan notes...........................	1,991,183,400
Treasury notes (varying maturities)..................	2,246,596,350
Treasury certificates (varying maturities).............	1,828,787,500
War savings securities.............................	619,371,842
Treasury savings securities.........................	58,947,043

Tax certificates, maturing in three months, are frequently employed by governments in anticipation of future receipts. Treasury certificates and treasury notes, having maturities of from three months to possibly four or five years, are usually issued for purposes of temporary financing, in anticipation of receipts from long-term bond issues or from revenues. At present, the Federal government of the United States will accept treasury notes and certificates in payment of Federal income taxes, while Liberty bonds may be employed in payment of Federal estate taxes. In other words, the creditors of the government, who have loaned their funds to the government to prosecute the war, may now surrender certain of their claims against the government in payment of the tax obligation imposed upon them. This serves as a further illustration of the similarity between borrowing and taxing as means of war financing.

[1] *Cf. U. S. Treasury Annual Report* 1922, p. 784.

Governments obtain immediate funds for war purposes in other ways than by issuing interest-bearing obligations of various types. When this means of obtaining receipts proves inadequate and revenues are not available, purchasing power can be obtained by issuing legal tender notes, such as the "Greenbacks" authorized by act of Congress in February, 1862. Such notes are, in reality, non-interest-bearing, compulsory loans, floated by the government and forced on the people, since they must be accepted at their face value in payment of private debts.

When governments take their promissory notes to the banks of issue and obtain credit currency, they are, to be sure, paying a rate of discount to the banks for the privilege of obtaining the bank notes. However, if at maturity the promissory notes are superseded by new promisory notes of the government, and there are no definite legal restrictions imposed on the extension of credit by the banks to the government, the effects of such operations are closely analogous to the direct issue of credit currency on the part of the government. In the former case, no interest is paid on the loan, while in the latter case, interest is paid out of further loans. In both cases, however, the government has obtained control of purchasing power with which to finance its immediate requirements. The latter method of public financing has been employed extensively by certain European countries, particularly by Germany, Austria, Russia, and Poland, and to a somewhat lesser degree by Italy, France, and Belgium during and since the World War.

If a definite fund is provided or specific collateral is pledged to insure the payment of a debt at maturity, such a debt is said to be funded or bonded. On the other hand, a debt contracted on the general credit of the borrower without providing specific funds for redemption purposes is said to be a floating debt. This distinction, however, is relatively insignificant with reference to outstanding public obligations, since the old idea of specific security has largely disappeared. In general, the chief distinction between funded and floating public debts is the time element. Debts yielding a fixed rate of interest and maturing after ten, twenty, or possibly fifty years are considered funded debts, while relatively short-term interest-bearing obligations are regarded as floating debts, even though specific receipts are pledged for their repayment. For example, the treasury certificates issued from time to time by the Federal government of the

United States during the World War in anticipation of receipts from loans and taxes were considered floating debts. Liberty bonds, on the other hand, were regarded as funded debts.

8. Economic Effects of Public Borrowing.—Having reviewed the different forms of public loans, the economic effect of public borrowing, for the several purposes enumerated above, will next be considered.

It has been noted that public borrowing is not always for productive purposes. To the extent that the borrowed funds are employed productively in the development of public enterprises of various kinds, there is a mutual gain to debtor and creditor. New productive capacity has been created with the borrowed funds which will yield a flow of benefits to the community at large. Private debts are incurred extensively to develop productive enterprises; and when governments employ their credit for similar purposes, there is no essential difference between public and private borrowing. A government does not necessarily have to depend upon the productivity of its borrowed funds for interest payments and the repayment of principal, as does private enterprise. Such payments are made by levies in the form of taxes. To the extent that the benefits derived from such payments are not commensurate with the sacrifices made, a net material loss to the community must result.

In any industrial community at any one time there is a certain fund of available liquid capital seeking investment. When the government enters the competitive money market and bids for this fund, interest rates will tend to rise. But in competing for these loanable funds the state has a certain advantage over private competitors, since, as was stated above, it is not dependent upon the productivity of the capital borrowed to meet interest and principal payments. Again, as we shall see later, a government has an advantage as borrower because of special concessions it can make to its creditors. When interest rates on public loans are raised above the normal market rates, more liquid capital will be attracted by such loans, and private industry will be required to adjust itself to the diminished supply of capital. Moreover, the higher rates of interest will tend to cause an increase in savings and a curtailment of consumption of commodities, which will lessen the demand for some of the products of industry. When private enterprises find certain of their costs increasing because of the higher rates which they must pay for this capital, and at the same time see a falling off in the demand for their products, production under private management may be very definitely curtailed. According to Professor Daniels:

> . . . some compensating effects arise from the greater energy exerted under the stimulus of necessity and the more efficient utilization of what capital remains available for private industry, but real incomes of all classes except the capitalists and the speculators are likely to fall because of the curtailed supply of necessities and comforts.[1]

Even more significant in its economic effects is the excessive expansion of credit due to heavy public borrowing. When in an emergency a government's needs are so great that the available supply of liquid capital does not suffice to meet its immediate requirements, there must be an inevitable encroachment upon past accumulations of the capital of the nation. The flow of commodities and services normally required to replace the stock of existing capital goods in a country, as that stock either depreciates or is consumed, must now be diverted in whole or in part into the public treasury. To obtain control over such goods, further purchasing power is required by the government. But when a government obtains such increased amounts of purchasing power to meet its requirements, by expanding credit currency in one form or another without a corresponding increase in exchangeable commodities, the result will be a rise in prices. Such a rise in prices will in turn increase the demand for purchasing power, not only of the individual consumers, but also of private enterprises.

The several methods of currency expansion employed by governments have been previously enumerated. However, a policy of public borrowing does not necessarily lead to inflation. Inflation of currency results from expanding the circulating media at a more rapid rate than the volume of business expands, causing in a relatively short period of time a marked rise in prices. This may be brought about not only directly by an excessive borrowing on the part of governments in one form or another, but also indirectly by making the government bonds acceptable as security for bank loans to private individuals. A very simple illustration will make this clear.

John Brown invested a thousand dollars of his accumulated savings in a Liberty bond. He then proceeded to pledge this

[1] *Cf.* "Public Finance," p. 299.

same bond as collateral for a loan from his bank for eight hundred dollars, with which he bought an automobile. His thousand dollars had thus been expanded into eighteen hundred dollars without a corresponding increase in production. His bank (assuming it to be a member of the Federal Reserve System) in turn could take its government bonds and, within certain limitations, pledge them as collateral with the Federal reserve bank in its district. By rediscounting commercial paper with government bonds as collateral, it could obtain further credit currency which it could make the basis of further loans. The effect of an excessive expansion of the circulating media beyond a certain point, no matter by what methods it may have been achieved, is the same, namely, rapidly rising prices with corresponding losses to certain classes and gains to others.

9. Significance of Issuing Tax-exempt Securities.—When governments employ their legal right to give preferential treatment to their creditors in subsequent payments of certain taxes, they have a decided competitive advantage over private enterprisers in the market for loanable funds. It has been noted above that there is always a certain amount of accumulated savings available for investment. These savings will normally seek investment in the most favorable markets. If the income derived from the securities issued by private industries is subject to various Federal, state and local taxes, whereas the income derived from certain governmental obligations is tax-exempt, it is apparent that, other things being equal, the investor will ordinarily place his funds in those securities which will yield him the largest net return. Consequently, governmental agencies issuing such tax-free securities enjoy a distinct advantage over private enterprises in the money market. Tax-exempt securities are said to be particularly popular among investors of large means, whose Federal "surtaxes" would absorb a large portion of their incomes, if such incomes were not exempt from certain taxes because they are derived from tax-exempt securities.

The effects of issuing tax-exempt securities on the part of governments have been widely discussed in recent years. Income tax returns would seem to indicate a tendency on the part of some persons to seek tax evasion by investing in such securities. In 1916, there were 1,296 persons in the United States declaring an income of over three hundred thousand dollars for Federal income tax purposes. The corresponding figures for the following years were: 1917, 1,015; 1918, 627; 1919, 679; 1920, 395. This decline in the number of individuals declaring relatively large incomes for Federal tax purposes has been ascribed, in part, to the practice of investing in tax-exempt securities. To be sure, there are other methods of tax evasion, but, in the words of the Secretary of the Treasury, Mellon:

> The most outstanding avenue of escape from the surtax exists in the form of tax-exempt securities, which under our constitutional system may be issued without restriction by the states and their political subdivisions and agencies. The Federal government may likewise issue securities wholly exempt from taxation.[1]

Recent investigations,[2] however, tend to show that the extent of investment in tax-exempt securities by persons with large incomes in order to evade high surtaxes, is not nearly as extensive as is popularly believed.

10. Recent Increase in State and Local Obligations.—The relative advantages enjoyed by governments in competing for loanable funds have perhaps resulted in a certain amount of governmental extravagance in post-war years. Loans floated by states and municipalities in recent years indicate a very decided increase, as can be gleaned from the following statistical data.[3]

NET FUNDED DEBT (GROSS DEBT LESS SINKING FUND ASSETS) OF STATES, COUNTIES, AND MUNICIPALITIES IN THE UNITED STATES, 1912 AND 1922

	1912	1912 per capita	1922	1922 per capita
States.............	$ 345,940,000	3.58	$ 935,544,000	8.64
Counties..........	371,528,000	4.33	1,272,790,000	13.18
Incorporated places and all other civil divisions........	3,104,426,000	54.27	6,481 406 000	*
Total...........	$3,821,984,000	.....	$8,699,740,000	

* Not computed.

From 1912 to 1922 the debts contracted by states, municipalities, and other civil divisions increased no less than 127 per cent.

[1] *Cf.* Annual Report, Treasury, 1922, p. 15.

[2] *Cf.* PATTERSON, E. M., in Supplement to "The New Republic," November, 1925.

[3] *Cf. Statistical Abstract of the United States,* 1924, p. 198.

By far the larger part of these obligations has been incurred since the close of the World War. Several reasons for these increased post-war borrowings have been given. In the first place, it has been asserted that many public improvements which should have been made by these governmental units from time to time during the war were postponed because of the urgency of the requirements of the Federal government for the prosecution of the War. It is also contended that the various state and local governments owed it to those who had rendered national services in one form or another to find work for them during the period of economic readjustment after the War. Valid as these arguments may be, they hardly suffice to offer a complete explanation of the unusual increase in state and local debts incurred during the decade from 1912 to 1922. Nor can the contention that these debts exaggerate the importance of the increase, because they do not allow for the currency depreciation during the period in question, minimize their significance. Both interest and principal must be paid primarily out of taxes; and to the extent that the general level of prices may fall between the time the debts were contracted and the time they mature, the tax burden of many persons in the community will be increased correspondingly.

Only a rigid policy of governmental supervision and a strict legal limitation of borrowing capacity can remove the apparent temptation to further public borrowing on the part of states and municipalities, which now possess such distinct advantages in competing for funds in the money markets. It does not appear to require much ingenuity on the part of public officials to convince the citizens of a municipality that their public buildings are antiquated and inadequate, that their streets are too narrow to accommodate the increasing volume of traffic, and that their city needs more monuments and artistic public edifices. Laudable as their motives may be, there is always the danger that such improvements will be financed primarily by incurring municipal debts. Reckless borrowing, even for municipal improvements, will entail an increasing burden of taxation on future generations. A severe legal limitation to public borrowing appears the only adequate check on an excessive expansion of public credit for various so-called public improvements.

11. Public Debt Policy.—When a government has once incurred certain interest-bearing debts, the question next presents itself as to the proper policy to pursue in regard to the repayment of such debts.   Some writers have argued in favor of a continuation of the principal of the debt in perpetuity, while others are equally ardent in advocating debt payment.   In the words of J. S. Mill:[1]

The raising of a great extra revenue by any system of taxation necessitates so much expense, vexation, disturbance of the channels of industry and other mischiefs over and above the mere payment of the money wanted by the government, that to get rid of the necessity of such taxation is at all times worth a considerable effort.

On the other hand, it has been claimed that the burdensomeness of a debt depends upon the available resources with which to pay it:

The debt rests upon the resources, and relief from the burden of a debt may be secured either by reducing the debt or by strengthening the resources.[2]

As industry develops, the burden of the debt resting on industry tends to decrease, while large levies on industry for purposes of the repayment of the principal of a public debt would injure the industrial development of a country.

If the public debt payment can be shown to retard the industrial progress of a country, then perhaps it would be more beneficial to the community at large to advocate the nonpayment of the principal.   On the other hand, if it appears that the repayment of public loans does not militate against possible industrial development, then the policy of public debt payment would appear economically sound.

Such an eminent authority on public finance as H. C. Adams[3] contends that "the payment of the principal of debt tends neither to impoverish a nation nor to retard its material development" while "the maintenance of the principal and the constant payment of accruing interest tend to cripple the productive capacity of a people."

We have noted the extent to which preferential treatment is accorded the creditors of various governmental units, by exempting the income derived from their public bonds from certain taxes. Some of these bonds may have passed into the hands of individ-

[1] "Principles of Political Economy," Book V, chap. 7, par. 2.
[2] Cf. ADAMS, H. C., "Science of Finance," p. 556.
[3] Cf. "Op. Cit.," p. 557.

uals possessing large means. The recipients of the income from their tax-exempt securities are able legally to evade the payment of heavy Federal surtaxes on this income. Consequently the burden of taxes to meet governmental obligations, including interest on these tax-exempt securities, must fall more heavily on those who derive their income from other sources. Furthermore, private industry, in order to attract the income now derived from, and invested in, tax-exempt securities must offer higher interest rates, which in turn will be reflected in higher production costs and which will ultimately tend to raise the prices of commodities. Some industries, because of such increased costs, may even be compelled to discontinue production entirely. This is perhaps the strongest argument in favor of a speedy repayment of outstanding public obligations. When the present creditors of the various governmental units are repaid, they will no longer be able to find lucrative public investments. Hence, they will compete with other lenders of funds in the money markets on terms of equality. Because of the increased funds thus made available for private industry, interest rates would probably tend to move downward. This would serve as a stimulus to production and ultimately accrue to the benefit of the whole community.

12. Summary.—Public receipts are derived from a variety of sources, including loans, currency expansion, earnings of public enterprises, sale of public properties, fees, special assessments, and taxes. Borrowing does not constitute a source of public revenues, since loans are public liabilities which must ultimately be repaid, if repaid at all, out of assets in the form of public revenues.

Governments resort to borrowing to finance emergencies, to develop public enterprises, and to make permanent public improvements. During the past century, and particularly since 1914, public debts have increased enormously because of extensive public expenditures for prosecuting wars. Borrowing as a means of financing a war is closely analagous to taxation, if the loans are made within the country and are not repaid by subsequent indemnities collected abroad. Nevertheless, borrowing for war financing possesses certain advantages over taxation, for it provides immediate funds, makes available savings which might not be attached by taxing, makes possible the social appeal, and leaves the time and the manner of payment to the discretion of the lender. On the other hand, extensive borrowing

388   ECONOMIC PROBLEMS OF MODERN LIFE

results in credit inflation with all the incidental hardships to
different classes of society. It may result in the adoption of a
tax system after the war which will tend to increase inequalities
in the distribution of wealth. In view of the experiences of
many countries during and since the World War, a policy of
maximum taxing and minimum borrowing for war financing
appears sound in principle and in practice.

Public borrowing may be in the form of long-term, interest-
bearing, funded obligations; short-term, interest-bearing,
unfunded or unsecured loans; and noninterest-bearing, compulsory loans in the form of credit currency issues.

When governments borrow for purposes of developing productive enterprises, there is no essential difference between public
and private loans made for similar purposes. But when the
proceeds derived from public loans are employed unproductively,
there will be a net loss of consumable wealth to the community.
Moreover, the practice of governmental units in the United States
of issuing tax-exempt securities encourages and makes possible
tax evasion, thus tending to shift a portion of the tax burdens to
those whose incomes are derived from other sources. In view
of this fact a strict legal limitation to further public borrowing
and a rapid repayment of outstanding public obligations appear
to constitute a sound public debt policy for governmental agencies in the United States to pursue in the future.

Collateral Reading

ELY, R. T., "Outlines of Economics," chap. 32.
HAMILTON, W. H., "Current Economic Problems," Nos. 355–358 incl., pp.
    804–810.
HUNTER, M. H., "Outlines of Public Finance," chap. 20.
JENSEN, J. P., "Problems of Public Finance," chap. 30.

References

ADAMS, H. C., "Science of Finance."
Annual Report of the Secretary of the Treasury for 1922.
BOGART, E. L., "Direct and Indirect Costs of the War."
———, "War Costs and their Financing."
Committee on Ways and Means, House of Representatives, Hearings on
    Tax-exempt Securities, etc., H. J. Res. 102, 211, 231 and 232, 1922.
Committee on the Judiciary, United States Senate, Tax-exempt Securities;
    Hearings before a Sub-committee, Sixty-seventh Congress, Fourth Session,
    on H. J. Res. 314, 1923.
DANIELS, W. M., "The Elements of Public Finance."
GRAY, J. M.. "Limitation of Taxing Power on Public Indebtedness."

GOTTLIEB, L. R., "Debts, etc.," *Quarterly Journal of Economics,* November, 1919.
HUNTER, M. H., "Outlines of Public Finance."
LUTZ, H. L., "Public Finance."
PATTERSON, E. M., Supplement to "The New Republic," Nov., 1925.
PIGOU, A. C., "Political Economy of War."
ROBINSON, M. E., "Public Finance."

Questions for Discussion

1. What are the sources of public receipts?
2. Why are public loans not to be construed as sources of public revenue?
3. What are the purposes of public borrowing?
4. Indicate the extent to which loans have been floated to finance wars during the past century.
5. "To finance a war by borrowing is an illusory method of shifting the burden of a war on to future generations." Explain and illustrate.
6. What are the advantages of borrowing over taxing to finance wars?
7. Outline what you would consider a sound policy of war financing.
8. Do you consider the problem of war financing one of historic interest or of future importance?
9. What are the different kinds of loans a government may float to finance public expenditures?
10. What are the reasons for floating different kinds of loans?
11. Outline the general effects of public borrowing, both for productive and for unproductive purposes.
12. What is the significance of issuing tax-exempt securities under existing conditions?
13. What arguments can you advance against Federal tax reduction at present?
14. Outline what you would consider a sound public debt policy for the United States government to pursue.

Topics for Investigation

1. Extent and significance of state and municipal borrowing.
2. The evils of wartime inflation.
3. Public borrowing for either productive or unproductive purposes.
4. Analysis of debt-paying policies of different countries.
5. Public debts and public credit.

CHAPTER XIX

RECEIPTS FROM PUBLIC REVENUES

1. What are Public Revenues?—Public revenues may be defined as those governmental receipts which result in an increase in the aggregate assets of a government without causing an increase in the liabilities. They include receipts from all kinds of taxes, fees, special assessments, fines, forfeits, escheats, highway privileges, interests, rents, donations, gifts, earnings of governmental departments, and net earnings of public service enterprises. They do not include proceeds from the sale of public property or repayments of public investments. These items merely represent a conversion of assets and not an increase in the aggregate public assets. Nor do they include specific receipts to offset specific outlays, such as collection of insurance to be applied to the reconstruction of destroyed property. Again, they do not include refunds of erroneous payments and receipts in error, such as taxes paid by mistake or under protest, which are subsequently refunded. When a government receives taxes under protest, a contingent liability is at once incurred to offset this particular asset. When the government's claim to such receipts is sustained by the courts, they become public revenues subsequently. Finally, as we have noted in the preceding chapter, public revenues do not include public loans, which, in reality, constitute governmental liabilities and not public assets.

2. Classification of Public Revenues.—The commonly accepted classification of public revenues is that developed by Professor Seligman in his "Essays in Taxation."[1] This classification divides public revenues into either gratuitous, contractual or compulsory contributions. Gratuitous contributions, as the term implies, are voluntary public or private gifts, donations or bequests made to a governmental agency, usually for a specifically designated purpose. Contractual revenues are those public receipts derived from various forms of public property and from public service enterprises. They represent specific

[1] *Cf.* Ninth ed., p. 399*ff.*

390

prices, established either by mutual bargaining or by exercising monopoly control, paid by individuals for specific services rendered, or for commodities received. Compulsory contributions, finally, are those payments exacted by public authority by virtue of the "power of eminent domain, of the penal power, or of taxing power."[1] They include expropriations, fines and penalties, fees, special assessments and taxes.

Omitting gratuituous contributions, which are relatively unimportant as sources of revenues of modern governments, we may further analyze the above classification of contractual and compulsory contributions as to purpose. In contractual payments special benefits are the primary consideration, and public welfare is more or less incidental. In the case of taxes, special benefits are incidental, while, on the other hand, general welfare is of primary importance. Between prices paid for specific services and taxes for public purposes, other governmental contributions shade more or less imperceptibly from voluntary to compulsory payments.

3. Historical Development of Public Revenues.—In Chap. XVII the gradual growth of public expenditures with the evolution of our economic, social, and political institutions was traced. As these expenditures increased, old ideas as to methods of raising public revenues were likewise modified by the gradual introduction of new principles.

Public funds to meet public expenditures were derived originally from voluntary gifts bestowed by individuals upon their governments. When such voluntary contributions no longer sufficed to defray the continually increasing expenditures, governments not infrequently besought the people for their support. During the Middle Ages, kings and princes obtained considerable revenues from public domains which were let to their subjects in return for a share of the product yielded by such lands. With the development of private ownership of land, there slowly grew up the custom of transferring title to the occupants on condition that they pay in perpetuity an annual ground rent to the former possessors, who were not infrequently noblemen. But even such contractual contributions did not suffice to meet the increasing public expenditures, particularly those of the past century and a half. The idea of sacrifice on the part of the individual in the interest of the government gradually gained in importance.

[1] *Cf. Op. Cit.* p. 430.

The specific benefits to individuals derived from their contributions to the public coffers became less and less significant. Feeling themselves integral parts of the complex social organism, and realizing the increasing public benefits resulting from ever-extending governmental activities, the citizens of advanced countries gradually developed a sense of public obligation and public responsibility, which caused them to submit to the compulsory levy of direct taxes in one form or another. The recognition of the justice of such taxes is rather modern, and even today we can find many citizens who do not fully recognize their civic duties, and who employ both their own cunning and the shrewdness of others to evade as much as possible their public obligations. Not until this high sense of civic duty is fully developed in a country, do its citizens willingly submit to various kinds of indirect and direct taxes.

4. Gratuitous Contributions.—Donations and gifts, which formed the chief source of public revenues in primitive society, have today become relatively unimportant. Of the aggregate total revenues of the national, state, and local governments in the United States in 1913, gifts and donations were less than one-fifth of 1 per cent, amounting to only $5,689,055. Even today, benevolent individuals occasionally bestow gifts in the form of libraries, museums, art collections, public parks, playgrounds, and the like upon municipalities and states for the benefit of the general public. Such gifts, however, are usually designated for a specific purpose by the donors and cannot be employed to meet general governmental obligations. It is very likely that the progressive rates of the Federal estates tax and state inheritance taxes will continue to induce individuals of large means to perpetuate their memory in various communities by liberal gifts for specific purposes before their death, rather than have a portion of their accumulated wealth flow into the general public coffers after their decease. To the extent that the individual benefactor has provided the community with a source of greater durable benefits than would have resulted if the funds had been expended by public authority, the community has gained. Any such act cannot be judged solely from the standpoint of the motive of the donor, but must be viewed also with reference to public benefit.

Again, gratuituous public services are rendered from time to time by public spirited men, such as the "dollar a year" men who gave their services to the Federal government during the World War. But, in the final analysis, if such services are rendered with a view to obtaining favorable publicity or to acquiring public office, they cease to be gratuitous. Here also the motives prompting the activities of the individuals must ultimately serve as a basis for judging whether their services truly constituted gifts to the government.

Finally, one governmental unit may make donations to another, particularly in times of a great national emergency. Gifts thus bestowed are usually for a specific purpose, to be apportioned by the recipient government or its representatives among its needy subjects. Public gifts, moreover, may take on another form. At some time in the past one nation may have borrowed extensively from another nation to meet certain extraordinary expenditures. If the creditor nation subsequently relieves the debtor nation either in whole or in part of the obligations thus incurred, it has to that extent apparently made a gift to the debtor. If, for example, the United States were to cancel a portion or the whole of the obligations of certain European countries, this would be closely analogous to having made a public gift to these countries. The reason for such action, however, requires careful analysis, for it may be contended that such a seemingly charitable act is prompted by other than purely altruistic motives. The methods of making international payments and the possible effects of such payments upon industrial enterprises within the recipient country should be carefully reviewed in this connection.

Governmental bounties in the form of subventions should not be regarded as gratuitous public contributions. They are revenues, collected by the central authorities, of which a portion is assigned to certain localities. In some American states specific taxes are assessed and collected by the commonwealth, but returned in part to the local governmental units. The aggregate total of the grants and subventions of the national, state and local governments of the United States in 1913 amounted to $78,372,386, or not quite 3 per cent of the combined revenue receipts.

A striking example of subventions is to be found in Germany, where, as a result of the tax reform of 1919–1920, the entire administration and collection of income, turnover, inheritance, and land transfer taxes has been placed in the hands of the

Federal government, which in turn assigns a portion of the revenue to the different provinces and municipalities. Such subventions are really compulsory contributions, collected by one governmental unit, for the benefit of other units.

5. Contractual Contributions from Industrial Sources.— Public revenue from industrial sources, in the broadest sense of the word, includes rents and interest received on public properties and investments, as well as the earnings derived from the sale of the product of public service enterprises. In the Middle Ages, the private domains of kings and noblemen provided the chief source of public revenue, which in many medieval states sufficed to meet the different public expenditures. Subsequently, however, these revenues decreased, as governments gradually relinquished publicly owned wealth to private individuals and adopted a *laissez-faire* policy toward industry in general. During the past fifty years, the governmental policy toward public service enterprises has been undergoing a gradual change. Governmental functions have multiplied rapidly, and in recent years many formerly private enterprises have been undertaken by local governments in the United States. The change in the direction of increased public operation of "public service enterprises" has been even more pronounced in European countries than in the United States. In 1914, the Federal government of the United States initiated the policy of leasing certain public lands to private enterprisers for the purpose of the development of their mineral resources. This principle was further extended in 1920 to include oil and gas lands in Alaska, as well as specific oil and mineral lands in the United States. As yet, the Federal revenues derived from public leaseholds are relatively unimportant.

The general impression still prevails in this country that private operation of public utilities under governmental supervision is to be preferred to public ownership and operation. The arguments for and against the government ownership of public service enterprises bear reviewing in this connection.[1] In general, the tendency toward increasing governmental supervision and regulation of natural monopolies of organization has been very pronounced during the past twenty or thirty years. If this supervision should fail or prove ineffective, there appears to be but one logical sequel, namely, governmental ownership and

[1] See chap. VIII.

operation. It is generally conceded that unrestricted private operation of public service enterprises has proven unsuccessful from the standpoint of the community. Thus far public revenues from public service enterprises are relatively small. In 1913, the aggregate gross earnings of all public service enterprises operated by governmental units in the United States were $393,015,491, or about 14 per cent of the total revenue receipts from all sources.

6. Compulsory Contributions.—(*A*) *Fees and Special Assessments:* Public fees are not specific prices for services accruing primarily to the benefit of the individual. They are, rather, compulsory or semicompulsory payments exacted by the government for specific services rendered in the interest of the public, but conferring a measurable benefit upon the individual making the payment. Special assessments, on the other hand, are compulsory payments made to a public authority by an individual in order to defray the costs of specific property improvements accruing to the benefit of the general public, but paid for by the property owner in proportion to the established valuation of his real estate. It is the boast of many governmental departments that they cost the public nothing, since the fees for specific services which they collect more than cover their total costs. The validity of such an assertion may be seriously questioned. In the final analysis, fees and special assessments resemble taxes levied in accordance with the "specific benefit" principle, rather than in accordance with the "faculty" principle of taxation which will be discussed later.

The primary reason for charging public fees is to regulate the activities of individuals in the interest of the community. In general, it has been found that an individual is willing to pay a fee for the privilege of carrying on a particular activity. Wherever the value of such a privilege to the individual can be approximately estimated, it is charged to him rather than paid for out of the general revenue fund. The Federal government of the United States derives revenues in the form of fees from the issue of passports, letters patent, consular services, and the like, while states and municipalities obtain fees for many kinds of licenses and permits.

As noted above, special assessments are based on the benefit the individual derives from improvements to his property. They should not be confused with special taxes which are levied to be expended for a particular purpose, such as poor taxes or school taxes. Assessments differ, moreover, from fees in that they are usually nonrecurrent payments, levied against property rather than against the person benefited. Although the aggregate total of fees and special assessments collected by states and municipalities in the United States in recent years has shown a material increase, their ratio to the combined revenue receipts has not appreciably altered. In 1915, the gross earnings of the general governmental departments and receipts from special assessments of all the states in the United States amounted to 11.5 per cent of the aggregate revenue receipts, and in 1919 to 13 per cent. Again, the corresponding percentages for municipalities of over 30,000 population in the United States were 10.7 per cent in 1910 and 10 per cent in 1918.

(B) *Taxes:* The combined revenue receipts of all governmental units in the United States from the different sources enumerated above form but a minor portion of the aggregate total revenue receipts. The major portion is derived from either direct or indirect taxes.

A tax may be defined as a compulsory contribution exacted for public purposes by a governmental agency, according to some general rule, without conferring any special benefit upon the payer. An analysis of this definition will indicate the difference between a tax and a fee on the one hand, and a tax and a special assessment on the other. In the first place, a tax is a compulsory payment, and in the second place, no specific benefit accrues to the taxpayer. As noted above, a tax presupposes a highly developed sense of social ethics and civic obligation on the part of those who submit to such a compulsory levy by a governmental agency.

Taxes may be either indirect or direct. An indirect tax is one which is collected either from the manufacturer or the importer of an article, but which is intended to be shifted to the ultimate consumer by adding approximately the amount of the tax to the selling price. The payer generally pays the tax without being conscious of its imposition. A direct tax, on the other hand, is one which is levied against either individual property or income, and which is intended to be collected from those who possess the property or receive the income. The individual is thus made conscious of the fact that he is paying the tax. Unless the tax payer recognizes his civic obligation, he is going to resort to all possible means of evading the obligation or shifting it to someone else.

Direct taxes, in the form of property and income taxes, have grown considerably in relative importance to indirect taxes in the United States during the past century. In 1791, the Federal government of the United States derived all of its revenues to meet the total expenditures chargeable against ordinary revenues from indirect taxes in the form of customs duties. Not until 1863 did the Federal government obtain any revenues from direct taxes. During the Civil War and post-Civil War periods, these taxes still constituted but a minor source of public revenue receipts. In 1922, on the other hand, Federal income and profits taxes totalled $2,086,918,645, while the combined income from customs and miscellaneous internal revenues (fees, prices, and indirect taxes) amounted to $1,478,784,556.

7. Standards of Justice in Taxation.—When our sense of public responsibility has been developed to the point where we consent to the imposition of taxes by governmental agencies, the question of a just basis for such taxes becomes of primary importance. In olden times, when private property, except in land, had not yet been very extensively developed, and the inequalities in the distribution of the material wealth of various communities were not so pronounced as at present, the problem of equitable taxation was relatively simple. A capitation or poll tax was considered a just tax from the standpoint of the legal authority imposing the levy. Poll taxes were employed by all the American colonies at one time or another. At present, thirty-eight states in the United States still have poll-tax provisions in their con-stitutions or statutes.[1] These taxes are the only existing survival of levies against the person of the taxpayer, all other levies being against either property or occupations. With the rapidly increasing wealth of nations since the Industrial Revolution, the growing inequalities in the distribution of this wealth, the growth in population, the ever larger development of centers of popula-tion, the increasing interdependence and growing complexity of modern society in general, and the resultant increasing impor-tance of governmental functions, requiring larger and larger public expenditures; with all these factors, the problem of equitable taxation has become exceedingly complex. Many diverse opinions have been expressed by writers from time to time as to

[1] *Cf. Bulletin of National Tax Association*, November, 1923, p. 46*ff.*

the just basis of taxation. Some have gone so far as to deny entirely the right of governments to take private property by compulsory levies. They seem to forget that they are secured in their possession of property by the will of the people, expressed through the government, and that it is the governmental authority as such which decides what shall be private property and to what extent it shall be privately enjoyed.

At the same time, our sense of justice requires that the power which a governmental agency exercises over private property shall be based on principles of equality and uniformity. This idea has been incorporated in the Constitution of the United States, which provides that "all duties, imports and excises shall be uniform throughout the United States," but even more significant, that "no capitation or other direct tax shall be laid, unless in proportion to the census or enumeration hereinbefore directed to be taken." Similar provisions are contained in practically all the constitutions of the states of the United States. The importance of the principle that taxes shall be equal and uniform becomes sufficiently obvious when we consider the possibilities of political corruption which would exist if one section of the country or a group of individuals could induce legislators to discriminate in their favor in levying certain specific taxes. The application of this principle of equality and uniformity in the administration of equitable taxation, however, has left much to be desired. Let us see whether the rigid application of this principle to present-day conditions would in reality imply just and equitable taxation.

The inequalities in the distribution of wealth and income existing in most modern industrial countries would make an equal and uniform tax imposed on a per capita basis rather inequitable, for it would in reality impose a relatively greater burden upon the poor than upon the rich. In this connection, it is well to recall the important economic principle of diminishing utility. It is generally conceded that a ten-dollar tax, imposed upon an individual with an income of one thousand dollars a year, involves a relatively greater sacrifice of want satisfaction than a similar payment made by an individual having an income of ten thousand dollars a year. The realization of this fact has resulted in giving legislatures considerable latitude in exempting certain property and income from taxes, so that their owners will not be unjustly burdened by the imposition of the tax. Strict justice, moreover, does not make possible the rigid application of the principle of equality and uniformity at present. We have noted in Chap. VI that at times public monopolies are created for either sumptuary or regulative purposes. In such cases revenues are a secondary consideration, the primary purpose being to regulate, and perhaps suppress entirely, certain socially harmful institutions.

There is still another reason why the rigid application of the principle of uniformity and equality of taxes is manifestly unjust today. Certain old and established taxes based on this principle, although conceded to be inequitable, are permitted to continue in existence, since they have become firmly intrenched in our social and fiscal systems. Consequently, the unequal burden which they impose is not apparent to the taxpayer. It has frequently been asserted that an old-established tax is no tax at all. However, to plead contentment with existing inequitable conditions of taxation by way of justification of such conditions is in reality contending that whatever is, is right. We are living today in a dynamic society, in which social and economic conditions are constantly changing. With these changing conditions, our standards of justice are likewise being modified from time to time.

Since the principle of equality and uniformity of taxation no longer conforms to our concept of justice, because of the manifold changes during the past century and a half, a new principle of justice was developed, which became generally accepted by the American courts in the course of the nineteenth century. This principle was based on the maxim that taxes should be apportioned and paid according to the specific benefits derived. In general, it is the basis on which certain public charges, such as prices, fees, special assessments, and the like, are fixed by legislative bodies today. We have noted before, however, that by far the major portion of public revenue is expended at present to gratify collective, immaterial desires, or to promote the general welfare. It is impossible to determine the extent to which a particular individual benefits by such public expenditures. Wherever the specific benefit can be approximated or estimated, it appears to be a justifiable policy to apply the "benefit" principle of taxation. But at best, even if we accept this principle, it can be applied to only a very limited number of payments for public services rendered by governmental agencies today. In view of this fact, authorities are generally agreed that taxes, in order to be just and equitable, should be apportioned according to the individual's ability to pay. This so-called "faculty" principle of taxation is regarded as perhaps the soundest basis of taxation. But even if we should accept this principle, the problem of equitable taxation is by no means solved. Many puzzling questions as to how ability to pay shall be measured must be decided.

What constitutes ability to pay? Shall it be measured in terms of income or in terms of property? Shall it be measured in terms of production or in terms of consumption? The answers to these and many similar questions suggest the real difficulties of the practical application of the "faculty" principle. If we are going to make income the basis for our judgment of capacity to pay, we must decide on a definition of income. Shall we differentiate between "earned" and "unearned" income? If we are going to regard property as the basis, we must bear in mind that all forms of property do not possess the same degree of productivity. If we are going to consider consumption the basis, we must make note of the differences in the standards of living of various social classes.

Even though the "faculty" principle appears to satisfy our sense of justice, the countless problems involved in a practical application of the principle are apparent. It must remain an ideal of justice toward which we should perhaps aspire. No matter what rule for measuring tax-paying ability we adopt at present, we will discover sooner or later that it is only approximately accurate. It is doubtful whether any rigid measure of ability to pay can ever be discovered. Although we may express the measure objectively or quantitatively, the subjective or qualitative concept cannot be accurately measured. The former may be evaluated either in terms of monetary units or in terms of units of product; the latter, however, is a problem of subjective valuation. Two individuals with precisely the same amount of property, possessing the same degree of productiveness, having the same gross income, spending and saving the same amounts annually, and paying the same tax quantitatively, may yet be affected very differently by such tax payments. At best, we can approximate ability to pay only by external evidences of such ability. The attempt to test ability to pay in terms of the sacrifice made in the payment of a tax would probably be valid if it could be accurately applied, but no practical method appears to have been devised for applying such a test.

8. Proportional versus Progressive Taxation.—Having adopted a concrete objective measure of ability to pay, we are next confronted with the question: Does ability to pay increase in direct proportion to the measure of that ability, and if not, less rapidly or more rapidly? In the middle of the last century it was believed by certain economists, notably by John Stuart Mill, that capacity to pay taxes increased in direct proportion to income. In other words, the burden of a 1 per cent tax paid on an income of two thousand dollars, after allowing a minimum of income necessary for physical sustenance to be exempt, would be equal to a similar tax rate levied and collected on an income of two hundred thousand dollars. Opinions have changed since the days of John Stuart Mill, however, and it is now held by many authorities that, in order to arrive at an approximate equality of sacrifice, the rate of taxes should increase as the measure of ability to pay increases. This is known as progressive taxation. The justification for progressive rather than directly proportional taxation lies in the fact that as wealth increases, the ease of producing or acquiring more wealth increases faster than at a proportionate rate, and that the utility of economic goods to an individual normally decreases as he consumes more of such goods. "It is the first thousand that comes hardest" is an expression with which practically everyone is familiar. As long as decided inequalities in the distribution of wealth continue to exist, the justice of progressive taxation can scarcely be questioned, although the rate of progression will probably continue to be a cause of controversy in the future, even as it has been in the past.

9. Incidence and Shifting of Taxes.—The incidence of a tax is the place where the burden of the tax finally rests, while the shifting of a tax signifies the removal of the burden of the tax from where it was originally placed. As noted before, certain indirect taxes, in the form of customs duties and excise taxes, are usually collected from either importers or manufacturers, with the expectation that they will be shifted by the payer to someone else. The word "expectation" is used advisedly, for it is not always true that the business man will be able to add the amount of the tax to his selling price without noting a decided decrease in his own profits. The nature of the demand for the product upon which the specific tax is placed will in part determine to what extent the manufacturer or importer will be able to pass on the tax to the ultimate consumer. Since, in general, the demand for so-called essentials tends to be relatively less elastic than for nonessentials or luxuries, the possibility of dealers shifting a specific tax per unit on necessaries is more likely than on comforts and luxuries. Hence the poor man bears a relatively greater burden in indirect taxation than does the rich man, the taxes on whose articles of consumption are more easily shifted.

In the long run, however, if it is found that the net returns to the enterpriser are reduced by the tax because it cannot be readily shifted, capital will not be likely to flow into the industry in question until it has recovered sufficiently to show a return approximately equal to that on similar investments in other industries. The gradual adjustment of supply will, in consequence, ultimately result in shifting the burden of the tax to the consumers. The mobility of labor and capital will be the chief factors in determining the duration of time necessary to bring about the requisite readjustment in industry.

10. What is a "Good" Tax?—From the point of view of the individual who does not recognize his civic obligations no tax which affects his pocketbook is "good." But assuming the necessary prerequisites, namely, a sense of public duty and of social responsibility, a tax which cannot be evaded, which cannot be shifted, which is levied in accordance with ability to pay and which is convenient of payment, may be regarded a "good" tax from the viewpoint of the individual taxpayer. From the standpoint of society, a tax which does not unduly burden legitimate industrial enterprise, which does not make discriminations among various enterprises except for sumptuary purposes, which will tend to decrease rather than to increase inequalities in the distribution of wealth, and the disbursement of which will result in greater collective benefits than if expended individually—such a tax has much to be said in its favor. Finally, from the point of view of the government making the levy, that tax may be considered "good" which is definite in amount, economical to collect, certain as to time of payment, and productive of revenue. Any tax which meets these requisites, and which satisfies our sense of justice from whichever point of view we may judge it, possesses all the necessary attributes of a "good" tax. In the following chapters certain Federal, state and local taxes will be considered in the light of these general observations.

11. Summary.—Public revenues are governmental receipts resulting in an increase in the aggregate assets of a government without causing an increase in its liabilities. They include taxes, fees, gifts, earnings of governmental departments and of public enterprises, but they do not include refunds of erroneous payments, receipts in error, and public loans.

Public revenues may be classified either as gratuitous, contractual, or compulsory contributions. Public funds to meet public expenditures were originally derived primarily from gratuituous contributions. With the growing complexity of society and the ever-increasing governmental functions, a sense of civic obligation was gradually developed, which made possible the exacting of compulsory contributions by governmental agencies. The "specific benefit" principle of taxation was later stressed, but, because of its limited applicability and the increasing inequalities in the distribution of wealth, the "faculty" principle was finally evolved as the most equitable test of tax paying ability. It is now commonly conceded that ability to pay, measured in terms of property or of income, increases more rapidly than the measure of such ability to pay increases. This principle is the basis of progressive taxation.

If a tax is collected from one individual but ultimately falls on someone else, it is said to be shifted. Not all indirect taxes are necessarily shifted immediately and entirely to the consumer. Over a short period of time, the nature of the demand will be the chief determining factor of the extent to which the tax can be shifted. In the long run, however, changes in the nature of supply will result in shifting the tax to the ultimate consumer.

A "good" tax should be judged not merely from the point of view of the individual taxpayer, but also from the point of view of the community and the government levying the tax.

Collateral Reading

ELY, R. T., "Outlines of Economics," chap. 33.
FETTER, F. A., "Modern Economic Problems," chap. 17.
HUNTER, M. H., "Outlines of Public Finance," chap. 4.

References

BASTABLE, C. F., "Public Finance."
Bulletin of the National Tax Association, November, 1923.
HASTINGS, LYON, "Principles of Taxation."
PECK, H. W., "Taxation and Welfare."
ROBINSON, M. E., "Public Finance."

Rosewater, Victor, "Special Assessments, a Study of Municipal Finance."
Seligman, E. R. A., "Essays in Taxation."
———, "Progressive Taxation in Theory and Practice."
———, "The Shifting and Incidence of Taxation."
Shirras, G. F., "The Science of Public Finance."
Stamp, Sir Josiah, "The Fundamental Principles of Taxation in the Light
    of Modern Development."
Weston, S. F., "Principles of Justice in Taxation."

Questions for Discussion

1. What is meant by public revenues?

2. How are public revenues commonly classified?

3. Explain what is meant by gratuitous, contractual, and compulsory contributions.

4. Trace the historical development of public revenues.

5. Give illustrations of gratuitous contributions to our government.

6. Are the services of "dollar a year" men gratuitous contributions to the government? Give reasons for your answer.

7. What is the nature of governmental subventions and subsidies?

8. Give illustrations of contractual contributions to the government.

9. Distinguish between fees and special assessments.

10. What principle of taxation underlies the charging of fees and special assessments?

11. Explain what is meant by taxes.

12. Distinguish between direct and indirect taxes.

13. What is our present concept of justice in taxation?

14. Show how our concept of justice in taxation has changed during the past century.

15. What, in your opinion, constitutes tax-paying ability?

16. Distinguish between proportional and progressive taxation.

17. Define and illustrate what is meant by incidence and shifting of taxes.

18. Enumerate the features of a "good" tax.

Topics for Investigation

1. Self-supporting governmental departments.

2. Fees and special assessments as sources of federal, state, and local revenues.

3. Financing the construction of public highways.

4. The tendency toward direct rather than indirect taxation.

5. Inductive study of the incidence of certain specific excise taxes.

CHAPTER XX

FEDERAL TAX REVENUES

1. Federal Tax Revenues.—Until the beginning of the present century, Federal taxes were derived chiefly from indirect levies in the form of custom and excise duties. In the last chapter were noted the constitutional limitations to the imposition of direct taxes by the Federal government of the United States prior to 1913. In view of these limitations, Congress imposed direct taxes "apportioned among the several states . . . according to their respective numbers" only five times in the history of the national government before 1900. Two million dollars were apportioned directly in 1798; three million dollars in 1813; six million dollars in 1815; three million dollars in 1816; and twenty million dollars in 1861. Direct Federal taxes were the exception rather than the rule prior to the World War.

In 1913, however, the Sixteenth Amendment to the Federal Constitution was ratified by the necessary three-fourths of the states of the Union. This amendment provided that:

Congress shall have power to lay and collect taxes on incomes from whatever source derived without apportionment among the several states, and without regard to any census enumeration.

It is interesting to note that in spite of this constitutional provision giving Congress power to tax incomes "from whatever source derived" the Supreme Court of the United States has intimated from time to time that Congress may not impose a tax on incomes derived from interest on state and municipal bonds. Until a further constitutional amendment is passed by Congress and ratified by the states, making possible the taxing of income derived from such bonds, the phrase, "from whatever source derived" will continue to have certain definite limitations to its applicability.

2. Customs Duties.—Prior to the imposition of the corporation profits tax in 1911 and the individual income tax in 1913, custom duties were more productive of Federal revenue than the so-called "internal revenue" duties. Before 1860, custom receipts were frequently in excess of the total ordinary Federal expenditures. During the ten years from 1902 to 1911, customs yielded an annual average of 53 per cent of the tax receipts of the Federal government, as compared with 47 per cent yielded by the internal revenue taxes. The revenue receipts from duties on imports for the fiscal year ending June 30, 1925, on the other hand, were but 21 per cent of the total tax revenues of the Federal government.

In general, the relative importance of custom receipts to total Federal receipts from direct and indirect taxes has decreased during the past century and a half. Import duties, moreover, have shown considerable fluctuation from time to time, varying not merely with general industrial conditions within the country, but also with prospects of either war or peace and of possible changes in tariff legislation. At best, custom duties offer but a comparatively uncertain source of Federal revenue, since they are affected by so many disturbing influences. For example, in times of a great national crisis, such as a war, when governmental expenditures ordinarily increase, revenue from customs will tend to decrease rather than to increase, because of the disruption of normal peace-time trade. This fact is well reflected in the statistics[1] of custom receipts of the Federal government from 1850 to 1924. In 1861, custom receipts dropped from $39,582,126, as compared with $53,187,512 the preceding year. Not since 1849 had receipts from import duties been so low. Again, in 1898, at the time of the Spanish American War, custom receipts decreased from $176,554,127 the preceding year to $149,575,062, while in 1918 custom receipts dropped to $182,758,989 from $225,962,393 in 1917.

The wars of foreign nations, as well as those in which our nation participates, affect Federal receipts derived from import duties. The effect on our trade of the outbreak of the World War is reflected in the decreased import duties collected in 1914 as compared with 1913, the figures for the respective years being $292,-320,014 and $318,891,396. As pointed out above, tariff revisions may also cause fluctuations in receipts from customs. The fact that custom revenues tend to decrease at the very time when additional funds are needed to meet urgent public requirements, and that they are relatively uncertain because of the disturbing

[1] Cf. Annual Report of the Secretary of the Treasury, 1924, p. 388ff.

political influences to which they are exposed, offsets, to a large extent, the good features of custom duties as sources of Federal revenue.

The common impression still prevails that custom duties are largely borne by the foreigners from whom we buy. The line of reasoning, leading to this conclusion, runs somewhat as follows. A tax is imposed on an imported product. If the price to the domestic consumer is increased by the amount of the tax, the domestic selling price may be raised to the point where it will be profitable to produce the commodity at home and thus crowd out the foreign competitor, unless he assumes the burden of the customs duty. The problem of the incidence of an import duty, however, cannot be so easily dismissed. It may be true that over a relatively short period of time the seller or producer of the commodity may be compelled to bear either the major portion or all of the duty imposed on his product, because of the nature of the demand for the commodity in question. But in the long run, as we have previously observed, the inevitable readjustments of conditions of supply will tend to shift the burden of customs duties, even as internal excise duties are ultimately shifted, to the consumers.

As noted in Chap. XVI, when duties are imposed on foreign products imported into the United States for the purpose of restricting such importation, it is obvious that they cannot be productive of revenue if they fulfill their full protective purpose. A tariff which is high enough to be prohibitive can yield no revenue. Consequently, a so-called "protective tariff" may not logically be regarded as a part of the revenue system of a country. In general, we may conclude that between certain points, the larger the amount of actual protection to domestic industries, the smaller the resultant revenue to the home government, and the greater the loss to, or the burden on, the domestic consumer. From the point of view of public revenue, therefore, our present tariff system is open to the criticism that the income it affords to the government is out of proportion to the burden it imposes on the taxpayer in the form of higher prices of commodities.

Custom duties for fiscal purposes are open to objections not merely because they are uncertain and because it is difficult to ascertain the incidence of such duties, but also because they can be evaded, in whole or in part, either by smuggling or by misrepresentation. Moreover, as compared with internal revenues they are uneconomical taxes to collect. For the fiscal year 1924 the total cost of collecting $100 of various kinds of custom duties was $2.58, while the total cost of collecting internal revenue taxes was but $1.24 for every $100 collected.[1] Finally, customs duties are not levied in accordance with the principle of ability to pay. To the extent that they are placed on essential commodities or necessities they impose a disproportionately heavy burden on individuals with small incomes and so fail to satisfy our sense of justice in taxation.

In spite of these many objections, customs duties will in all probability continue to be an important part of the Federal revenue system in the future, although perhaps relatively less important than in the past. As sources of public revenue they possess the virtue of high productivity under normal conditions, as well as of convenience of payment. These factors apparently impress legislators sufficiently to advocate their retention as a part of the Federal revenue system.

3. History of the Federal Income Tax.—The first bill providing a Federal income tax in the United States was passed by Congress July 1, 1861. It levied a 3 per cent tax on all monetary incomes above eight hundred dollars. The amount of exemption was subsequently reduced to six hundred dollars and a slightly graduated scale adopted. The revenue derived from this tax rose from $2,741,858 in 1863 to $72,982,159 in 1866, after which it gradually decreased until 1877. The original tax law of 1861 expired in 1870, was reenacted for an additional period of two years, and then discontinued. While effective this income tax yielded nearly 25 per cent of the total internal revenue of the Federal government. The income tax of 1861 was attacked almost immediately on constitutional grounds; it was held that it was a direct tax not duly "apportioned" as provided in the Constitution of the United States. But in 1880 the Supreme Court of the United States decided that this tax was not a direct tax within the meaning of the constitution, and so declared it constitutional.[2]

The next attempt to levy a Federal income tax was made in 1894. The tariff law of that year provided for a Federal income tax in addition to various other sources of revenue. The constitutionality of the law was again questioned, and this time

[1] *Cf. Annual Report of the United States Treasury*, 1924, pp. 419 and 761.

[2] *Cf. Springer vs. United States*, 102 U. S. 586.

the Supreme Court reversed the decision on the Civil War income tax, holding that the tax, in general, was a direct tax and must, therefore, be apportioned according to population. In view of this decision of the Supreme Court of the United States, it became increasingly apparent that a direct Federal income tax could be made possible only by a constitutional amendment. The agitation for such an amendment began in 1909 and continued until the requisite three-fourths of the states finally ratified it in 1913. But in spite of this amendment, the constitutionality of that portion of the Federal Revenue Act of 1913 providing for an income tax was contested in the courts. It was contended that the progressive feature of the income tax, classifying taxpayers according to their wealth, was unwarranted, unjust, and unreasonable. The decision[1] of the Supreme Court, however, upheld the law in every respect.

Thus, the Federal income tax, after a half century of attack, criticism, and protest became an established institution and was incorporated in the Federal revenue system of the United States. For the fiscal year ending June 30, 1925, nearly 50 per cent of the total Federal revenue from taxes was derived from individual income and corporation profits taxes.[2]

4. Provisions of the Federal Revenue Act of 1926 Pertaining to Personal Incomes. (*A*) *The Tax Rate.*—As compared with the personal income tax provisions of the Federal revenue acts passed by Congress since 1918, the Revenue Act of 1926 reduced the normal and surtax rates on individual incomes to their lowest levels since the World War. The following table, taken from compilations by actuaries of the Treasury Department shows how personal income taxes (including both normal and surtaxes) have been reduced since 1918.

[1] *Cf. Bushaber vs. Union Pacific Railroad*, 240 U. S. 1.
[2] *Cf. Annual Report of the Treasurer of the United States*, 1925, p. 1.

TAXES ON SPECIFIED NET INCOMES UP TO $100,000 (FOR MARRIED MEN WITHOUT DEPENDENTS)

Net incomes	Tax under Act of 1918	Tax under Act of 1921	Tax under Act of 1924	Tax under Act of 1926	1926 tax as per cent of 1918 tax
$ 3,000	$ 60	$ 20	$ 7.50	$ 00.00	0.00
4,000	120	60	22.50	5.63	4.69
5,000	180	100	37.80	16.88	9.37
6,000	250	160	52.50	28.13	11.25
8,000	530	340	105.00	56.25	10.61
10,000	830	520	165.00	101.25	11.91
15,000	1,670	1,060	515.00	311.25	18.64
20,000	2,630	1,720	975.00	618.75	23.53
30,000	4,930	3,520	2,275.00	1,778.75	36.08
40,000	7,730	5,840	3,995.00	3,198.75	41.38
50,000	11,030	8,640	6,095.00	4,878.75	44.23
60,000	14,830	11,940	8,635.00	6,798.75	45.84
70,000	19,130	15,740	11,535.00	8,958.75	46.83
80,000	23,930	20,040	14,835.00	11,258.75	47.04
90,000	29,230	24,840	18,495.00	13,658.75	46.73
100,000	35,030	30,140	22,575.00	16,058.75	45.84

The Federal Revenue Act of 1926 provides for a reduction of the normal tax rates from 2 to 1½ per cent on the first $4,000 of net taxable income; from 4 to 3 per cent on the next $4,000; and from 6 to 5 per cent on the remainder of the net taxable income. Surtaxes, which under the Revenue Act of 1924 progressed up to 40 per cent of the net income in excess of $500,000, are scaled down to a maximum of 20 per cent on net incomes in excess of $100,000. Under the Revenue Act of 1924, net incomes in excess of $100,000 and not exceeding $200,000 were subject to a surtax rate of 37 per cent. Thus, a maximum surtax rate, which under the 1924 Revenue Act pertained only to net taxable incomes exceeding $500,000, now applies to all net taxable incomes above $100,000, although the rate has been halved. Consequently, persons with net taxable incomes of $1,000,000, who under the Revenue Act of 1924 were required to pay approximately 43 per cent of their net income to the Federal government in the form of normal and surtaxes, under the present revenue act must pay only 24 per cent of this income. This represents a reduction of no less than 43 per cent of Federal income taxes for a specified tax period on personal incomes of

$1,000,000. On the other hand, the corresponding reductions on net incomes between $30,000 and $60,000 are only about 20 per cent. It may, of course, be contended that heretofore persons with relatively smaller incomes were not bearing their proportionate share of the Federal tax burden. But a comparison between the surtax rates in the Revenue Act of 1924 and those in the Act of 1926 shows that the reduction of rates of Federal taxes on personal incomes very definitely favor persons of large means. These reductions in rates of surtaxes appear somewhat at variance with the "faculty" principle of taxation.

Not only have normal and surtax rates been reduced under the Revenue Act of 1926, as compared with those provided in Federal tax laws since 1918, but the amount of personal exemption has also been increased. Single persons may claim an exemption of $1,500 (formerly $1,000) and married persons, living with husband or wife, are allowed $3,500 personal exemption, (formerly $2,500). In addition, a personal credit of $400 may be claimed by the taxpayer for each dependent (children under eighteen years of age and others depending for their chief support upon the taxpayer). It has been estimated that as a result of the increase in personal exemptions about 2,300,000 individuals, who formerly paid Federal income taxes, are now relieved of such taxes. Relief from taxes and tax reductions are always popular with the average tax payer. The fact that the Federal Revenue Act of 1926 reduced personal income taxes "all along the line" has, in most circles, forestalled adverse criticism of the lower surtax rates, which favor primarily persons with large incomes.

(B) *Distinction between "Earned" and "Unearned" Income.*— The Federal Revenue Act of 1924 was the first Federal tax law which attempted to differentiate between "earned" and "unearned" incomes for purposes of taxation. The theoretical basis for drawing this distinction is the principle of "equality of sacrifice." Theoretically, it requires an effort to acquire an "earned" income, while "unearned" incomes are assumed to have been obtained by their recipients without effort on their part. The theoretical justification for distinguishing between "earned" and "unearned" incomes for purposes of taxation can scarcely be questioned, but the practical application of the principle involves difficulties. What is "earned" income as distinct from "unearned" income? The Revenue Act of 1924[1] defines

[1] Section 209, 1.

"earned" income to mean "wages, salaries, professional fees, and other amounts received as compensation for personal services actually rendered, . . . If the taxpayer's net income is not more than $5,000, his entire net income shall be considered to be earned net income, and if his net income is more than $5,000, his earned net income shall not be considered to be less than $5,000." The same clause is contained in the Revenue Act of 1926, with the further provision that in no case shall earned net income be considered to be more than $20,000 (in the 1924 Revenue Act this maximum was $10,000).

The theoretical distinction between "earned" and "unearned" income cannot be claimed to be the practical basis for the differentiation in the Federal revenue law between these two classes of incomes. For tax purposes, all net incomes of $5,000 or less, regardless of source, are considered as having been earned, and no net incomes exceeding $20,000 are regarded as earned incomes. Thus, the distinction between "earned" incomes and "unearned" incomes, made in the present income tax law, is applied in a very arbitrary manner. Not until incomes for tax purposes are definitely classified with reference to their origin or source, (such as incomes derived from labor services, from capital investments, from land, from gifts, and the like), as is done in the income tax laws of various European countries, notably Great Britain and Germany, can an equitable distinction be drawn between "earned" and "unearned" incomes for purposes of taxation.

(C) *Concept of Net Taxable Income.*—The present Federal income tax law provides that all citizens of the United States and all persons residing in the United States, whose gross incomes are $5,000 or over, regardless of the amount of their net income or whose net incomes are $1,500 (or over) if single, or $3,500 (or over) if married and living with husband or wife, shall make returns of their incomes with the collector of Internal Revenue, not later than the fifteenth of March of each year. To arrive at net taxable income for tax purposes, certain items, such as interest paid on personal loans, taxes paid other than Federal income taxes, losses of property by fire, storm, shipwreck, theft not compensated for by insurance, uncollectible debts and contributions or gifts made within the taxable year to organized religious, charitable, scientific, literary or educational institutions are deductible from gross income. The reason for allowing these deductions is to arrive at the net money income of the taxpayer, representing his increased net claim to the social product realized during a definite tax period.

It is this net money income which constitutes the taxpayer's taxable income. In order to relieve the recipients of small taxable incomes of the burden of direct Federal taxation, specific personal exemptions are allowed, before arriving at the net income subject to the Federal income tax.

5. Corporation Income Tax Legislation.—Not only have individual net incomes been subject to Federal income taxes since 1913, but corporate incomes have also been taxed. As early as 1909, an "excise tax" on corporations, measured by net corporate profits, was imposed by the Federal government. This tax yielded on an average of $32,000,000 annually while in force.

When the individual income tax law was passed in 1913, the corporation income tax, in the form of a tax on net corporate profits, was incorporated in the law. In March, 1917, the corporation income tax law was expanded to include a tax on so-called "excess profits" of corporations, and on Oct. 3, 1917, was superseded by the War Revenue Act, which levied war excess profits taxes on incomes not only of corporations, but also of individuals and of partnerships. As war fiscal measures, the war profits and excess profits taxes were very successful. The combined yield of corporate income and excess profits taxes in the calendar year 1917 was nearly three billion dollars, and in 1918 over four billion dollars. The various war profits and excess profits taxes were repealed in January, 1921, but net corporate incomes of business corporations were subjected to a uniform annual rate of $12\frac{1}{2}$ per cent, which was increased to $13\frac{1}{2}$ per cent under the Revenue Act of 1926.

In the Federal income tax legislation enacted since 1913, there appears to be an attempt made to treat corporations, partnerships, and individuals alike. The legal interpretation that a corporation functions as a "natural person," is retained in the Federal income tax law. Thus, the term "person" is defined in the Revenue Act of 1926[1] to mean "an individual, a trust or estate, a partnership, or a corporation." However, in the sense in which the concept income is applicable to individuals it is impossible to apply it to corporations without considerable confusion of thought. Individuals have net monetary incomes which they can employ either to purchase present enjoyments or gratifica-

[1] *Cf.* Section 2.

tions, or save for the future.   Corporations, on the other hand, are legal entities, creations of the state, ultimately owned by individuals, who derive incomes from them; and as such artificial legal creations, the psychological significance of income to individuals, *a flow of commodities or services to gratify human desires*, is inapplicable to them.   Corporations have receipts, expenditures, profits, and losses, the title to which is ultimately vested in individuals, as is evidenced by the securities they hold.   Specific exemptions and progressive rates of taxation, levied on "net incomes" of corporations, have no relationship in principle to similar provisions as to individual net incomes.   One corporation, having net profits in any one year of one hundred thousand dollars, may be owned by one or two individuals of large means.   Another, with precisely the same net profits for the same taxing period, may be owned by several hundred individuals of moderate means.   To allow the same exemptions and impose the same rates of taxes on both "net corporate incomes" is unjust.   This inequity is only in part offset by the graduated scale of surtaxes on personal incomes, and with every further reduction in surtax rates becomes more pronounced.

Certain practical difficulties in the administration of a corporation profits or income tax must also be borne in mind.   How is the net profit or net income of a corporation to be determined? If based on invested capital, how is the amount of invested capital to be ascertained?   No uniformity in accounting systems exists at present, which would make possible an accurate comparison of "net incomes" of different enterprises for tax purposes.   The tax on net earnings of corporations has been characterized as follows:[1]

To avoid serious inequality and evasion the tax on net earnings would require for administration a thorough examination into the accounts of every corporation taxed, together with strict rules how these accounts should be kept . . .   It would be a continual source of irritation between the corporation and the taxing officials . . . The practical difficulties in the way of imposing a tax on net earnings seem overwhelming.

The economic consequences of heavy taxes on corporate earnings should also be noted.   It has been estimated that possibly

[1] *Cf.* The *Report* of the Special Commission on Taxation of Corporations, State of Connecticut, 1913.

40 per cent of the annual capital formation in the United States results from the direct reinvestment of corporate earnings. To the extent that these earnings, rather than personal incomes, are absorbed by taxes, they are not directly available for reinvestment in private corporate enterprises. The net loss in production resulting from such curtailment of capital formation may cause considerable hardship to certain classes of consumers. In view of both theoretical and practical objections to taxes on "net earnings" of corporations, it is debatable whether they will form a permanent part of the Federal revenue system. From the point of view of the government, they have been very productive, but they are inequitable, for they impose an unequal burden on industrial enterprise. They can, moreover, be evaded by an undue increase of many items of expenditures, salaries, reserves for depreciation, concealed investments and the like. As stated above, the income tax has been introduced as a permanent feature of our Federal tax system. We should now strive to establish it on sound economic principles and further clarify the concept of income in its application to tax legislation.

6. The Federal Estates Tax.—A Federal estates tax was first adopted in 1916. Under the Revenue Law of 1921, it is levied by the Federal government upon the transfer of property at the death of the owner. It differs essentially from an inheritance tax, as popularly understood, since it is levied against the decedent's undivided estate, regardless of the amount of individual inheritances or the relationship of the beneficiaries. In 1923, forty-six of the states of the Union had enacted inheritance tax legislation. These inheritance taxes are commonly based on the separate legacies, and the rates usually differentiate between several classes of heirs. The Federal estates tax, on the other hand, applies to the entire decedent's estate, after allowing for certain deductions, such as funeral expenses, administration claims, public bequests, and an exemption of $50,000. Under the Revenue Act of 1926, a progressive tax is levied on the remaining net estate, ranging from 1 per cent on a net valuation of $50,000 to 20 per cent on a net estate valuation in excess of $10,000,000.

Since its adoption in 1916, the Federal estates tax has shown considerable productiveness, as is indicated in the following statistics:

YIELD OF FEDERAL ESTATES TAX[1]

Year	Yield
1917	$ 6,076,575
1918	47,452,879
1919	82,029,983
1920	103,635,563
1921	154,043,260
1922	139,418,846
1923	126,705,206
1924	102,966,761

A Federal tax on inheritance was adopted as a war measure at the time of the Civil War, but it yielded relatively little revenue. The maximum return was reached in 1870, when $3,091,825.50 was collected. In 1872, the Federal inheritance tax was discontinued, but it was revived in 1899 and continued until 1908. During this interval the maximum yield, that of 1901, was but slightly in excess of five million dollars.

In view of the often voiced dissatisfaction with the high progressive rates of the Federal estates tax, Congress reduced these rates very materially under the Revenue Act of 1926. The common arguments advanced in favor of a reduction or an abandonment of the Federal estates tax are to the effect that high progressive rates on large estates tend to destroy individual initiative and thrift, and so result in a net loss to the community. It is also contended that such rates are intended to equalize the distribution of wealth, and so savor of socialism. Finally, it is held that the estates tax is objectionable because it is a tax levied on capital and not on income. These popular arguments against a Federal estates tax, however, cannot be supported by actual facts.[2]

Most modern governments have included estates taxes, death duties or inheritance taxes of one type or another in their fiscal programs. The general tendency appears to be in the direction of increasing rather than decreasing these taxes, even though

[1] *Cf. Annual Report of the United States Treasury*, 1924, p. 403.

[2] A convincing refutation of these arguments is contained in a study of Federal taxes made by Ernest M. Patterson, in the special taxation supplement to *The New Republic*, Nov. 4, 1925, p. 26f.

there may be a temporary reaction to high progressive rates. As tax measures, estates taxes embody practically all the features of a "good" tax enumerated in the last chapter. From the standpoint of the taxpayer they are burdenless and cannot easily be evaded. They are levied according to the faculty principle of taxation. From the point of view of the government imposing them they are open to the one objection that they are not certain as to time and amount. They are economical to collect, and from the point of view of the general public, possess the merits of tending to decrease inequalities in the distribution of wealth and of not being a burden on industry, unless the rates are such that the lump sum payment of the taxes will constitute an actual drain on industrial capital. To avoid the possibility of imposing undue hardships on an estate, the Revenue Act of 1926 provides that the Commissioner of Internal Revenue may extend the time of payment "not to exceed five years from the due date."[1]

7. Federal Excise Taxes.—Excise taxes are taxes levied on commodities in some stage of production before they reach the consumer. Before the Federal income tax was introduced, excise taxes formed the chief source of internal revenue of the Federal government. These taxes are sometimes referred to as indirect taxes on consumption. Although levied on commodities in various stages of production, they are intended to be shifted to the ultimate consumer. Whether they can actually be shifted, either in whole or in part, will depend upon the effect that the addition of the tax to the selling price of the taxed commodity will have upon demand and supply. In general, it is true that an excise tax will ultimately fall on the consumer.

In the early days of excise duties attempts were frequently made to levy a uniform rate on all classes of commodities, in the belief that such duties would result in an equal distribution of the tax burden. In our present roundabout system of production, involving many stages in the transition from raw materials to finished products, the administrative difficulties of levying uniform taxes on all classes of commodities seem almost insurmountable. On the other hand, because of the present inequalities in the distribution of wealth and income, uniform rates on all classes of commodities would result in a disproportionately heavy burden of taxation being imposed on the consumers having small means, if all classes of commodities were taxed uniformly.

[1] *Cf.* Sec. 305, b.

Excise duties may be employed for several purposes. In the first place, they may be used primarily for fiscal purposes to counteract the effects of certain custom duties. If a government wishes to impose an import duty on a specific commodity for fiscal purposes and at the same time to preserve competitive conditions at home and abroad, it will impose a corresponding duty on the domestic product. Otherwise, the import duty would afford a degree of protection to the home producer, and so defeat the fiscal purpose of the duty. Secondly, import duties may be imposed for sumptuary purposes. It is often socially desirable to limit the consumption of certain commodities considered harmful to the consumer. Whenever excise duties are levied, either for sumptuary or for regulative purposes, the fiscal aspects of such duties are of secondary importance. Familiar illustrations of commodities taxed primarily for sumptuary purposes are intoxicating liquors, tobacco, narcotic drugs and playing cards. The Federal revenues derived from duties on spirits and fermented liquors since the passage of the Volstead Act have shown a very decided decrease, while the duties collected on tobacco show a gradual increase, as is indicated in the following tables:

SOURCES OF INTERNAL REVENUE[1]

Fiscal year	Spirits	Fermented liquors	Tobacco	Special taxes on manufactures and products
1918	$317,553,687.33	$126,285,857.65	$156,188,659.90	$ 36,570,478.37
1919	365,211,252.26	117,839,602.21	206,003,091.84	75,598,257.17
1920	97,905,275.71	41,965,874.09	295,809,355.44	216,230,346.67
1921	82,598,065.01	25,363.82	255,219,385.49	177,802,191.37
1922	45,563.350.47	46,086.00	270,759,384.44	143,942,311.65
1923	30,354,006.88	4,078.75	309,015,492.98	163,981,350.30
1924	27,580,380.64	5,327.73	325,638,931.14	177,531,749.14

Special taxes on manufactures and products include a large variety of excise taxes imposed under the Revenue Acts of 1918, 1921 and 1924, most of which are repealed under the Revenue Act of 1926.

These excise taxes possess certain administrative virtues, for, as can be seen from the above tables, they are productive of revenue. Moreover, they are economical to collect, certain in amount, and payable in such small amounts that the burden which

[1] Cf. Annual Report of the Secretary of the Treasury, 1924, p. 402f.

they impose is not felt by the average taxpayer. But they are objectionable on the ground that they are not levied in accordance with ability to pay and that when imposed in the manner in which many of the specific sales taxes were imposed during the World War, they can be widely evaded. Any impost which cannot be defined precisely and administered equitably is objectionable. Furthermore, excise duties, if imposed for a short period of time upon specific commodities, are objectionable to the producers of the commodities in question. They impose an unjust burden upon the producer, who may have to bear the major portion of the duty before the supply will be readjusted so as to shift the burden to the ultimate consumer. Finally, excise duties are objectionable because the incidence of the tax is difficult to ascertain, and it may impose unequal burdens upon different classes of income.

8. Suggested Federal Sales Tax.—In view of the complexity of the present Federal income tax and the difficulty of administering it equitably, because it can be evaded in whole or in part, a general sales tax or a turnover tax has been advocated from time to time to take its place. Some have suggested a general and uniform tax on the sale of all commodities, while others would confine the tax to the sales of commodities just prior to their reaching the ultimate consumers. Many advantages are claimed for a general sales tax. In the first place, it is believed that it would simplify the present complex Federal revenue system with its many direct and indirect taxes. Second, it is contended that it would be paid by everyone, but in such small amounts that the burden would not be felt. In the third place, the proponents of this tax hold that it would be simple and economical to administer. Fourth, it would yield a regular, constant, and certain flow of revenue. Finally, it is believed that it would abolish the harmful features of many of the present special sales taxes, which often savor of class taxation.

Most of these alleged advantages, however, are administrative, and fail to justify a general sales tax from the viewpoint of the individual taxpayer and the general public. Let us note some of the more important objections. First, the general sales tax is unjust, because it is not levied in accordance with the principle of ability to pay. Second, it is grossly discriminatory, for in so far as the tax cannot be shifted, because of the nature of the demand for a commodity, it is distributed according to gross income among producers, which is no measure of taxpaying ability. Third, it gives a bounty to large integrated industries, to the disadvantage of small industrial units. It will thus encourage vertical and horizontal combinations in industry, and so crowd out the small competitive producers. Finally, the burden of the tax will ultimately be shifted to the consumer, and so fall most heavily on the mass of population having small and moderate incomes.

A careful survey of the arguments for and against a general sales tax warrants the conclusion that the objections to such a tax far outweigh its possible administrative advantages. It is a debatable question whether any one tax should be made the basis of Federal revenues. With the increasing complexity of our economic organization, it is becoming more and more difficult to devise any one or even several taxes which will reach all those who have the ability to pay and which will be productive of the requisite Federal revenue. Moreover, the task of uniting into one equitable tax system all the taxes imposed by the several political divisions of the government of the United States is exceedingly complex. The discussion of this problem will be deferred until the chief state and local taxes have been reviewed.

9. Summary.—Prior to 1913, most of the Federal tax revenues were derived from indirect taxes in the form of custom duties and excise taxes. With the adoption of the Sixteenth Amendment, giving Congress the power to levy taxes on incomes without apportionment among the several states, direct income taxes have assumed increasing importance as a part of the Federal revenue system.

Customs duties are objectionable as fiscal measures, because they are rather uncertain and tend to decrease at the very time when more Federal revenue is needed. They are subject to disturbing political and economic influences from within and without the country. They possess the disadvantages of all indirect taxes in that the incidence of the duties cannot be easily ascertained. A protective tariff cannot logically constitute a part of the fiscal program of a country, for the tariff it yields is out of proportion to the burden it imposes on the domestic consumer. In spite of the several objections to custom duties, they continue to form an important source of Federal revenue, and will no doubt be included in future fiscal programs of the Federal government.

The Federal income tax, after a checkered career of over a half a century, was incorporated in the Federal revenue system in 1913 by the passage of the Sixteenth Amendment. As constituted today, the Federal income tax levies a progressive rate of taxes on individual net incomes. The latter are determined by making definite deductions from gross income for payments of interest on borrowed money, depreciation of capital assets used in the conduct of business, bad debts and losses of various kinds. An attempt is made in the present income tax law to differentiate between "earned" and "unearned" incomes for purposes of taxation, but the distinction is an arbitrary one, since all net taxable incomes up to five thousand dollars, from whatever source derived, are considered earned incomes. The chief objection to the Federal income tax, as constituted at present, is the fact that it can be evaded, both legally and illegally. Corporation income taxes not only are fallacious in theory, but also offer definite practical administrative problems, since the concept of "net corporate income" or "net corporate profit" is very flexible and lacks precision. But corporation income and profits taxes, levied by the Federal government in recent years, have been very productive of revenue, even though they do not conform to our concept of equitable taxation.

As fiscal measures, the Federal estates tax possesses practically all the virtues of a good tax, although it has the one weakness of being indefinite as to the times when the revenue will be forthcoming from this source.

Federal excise taxes are used for both fiscal and sumptuary purposes. They are usually easy to collect, productive of revenue, and in view of the small amounts collected on each unit of the commodity subject to the tax, they are practically burdenless. It is this last feature of excise taxes which has been emphasized by the proponents of a general, small, uniform sales tax, levied on all classes of commodities. But the chief objection to the general sales tax is that it imposes an unequal burden upon the consumers possessing small incomes, and so does not satisfy our sense of justice in taxation. This objection outweighs any administrative and fiscal advantages which may be claimed for a general sales tax.

Collateral Readings

ELY, R. T., "Outlines of Economics," chap. 34.
FETTER, F. A., "Modern Economic Problems," chap. 19.
TAUSSIG, F. W., "Principles of Economics," vol. II, chap. 69.

References

ADAMS, H. C., "Science of Finance."
BULLOCK, C. J., "Selected Readings in Public Finance."

422   ECONOMIC PROBLEMS OF MODERN LIFE

Commissioner of Corporations, *Reports on the Taxation of Corporations.*
Congressional Record, *Debates and Discussions* of proposed revision of
    Revenue Laws, 1925 and 1926.
HEWETT, W. W., "The Definition of Income and Its Application to Federal
    Taxation."
HOLMES, J. E., "Federal Taxes."
HUNTER, M. H., "Outlines of Public Finance."
JENSEN, G. P., "Problems of Public Finance."
MELLON, A. W., "Taxation, the Nation's Business."
ROSSMORE, E. E., "Federal Corporate Income Taxes."
SELIGMAN, E. R. A., "The Income Tax."
United States Treasury Report, 1924 and *Annual Report of the Commissioner
    of Internal Revenue,* 1923.

Questions for Discussion

1. What were the chief sources of Federal revenue prior to the twentieth
century?
2. What are the objections to custom duties as a source of revenue?
3. Who pays the duties on imported products?   On whom does the burden of the tax fall?   Illustrate with a specific example.
4. Trace the history of the Federal income tax prior to 1913.
5. Outline the chief features of the present income tax law pertaining to
individual incomes.
6. What distinction is drawn in the present income tax law between
"earned" and "unearned" income?   Do you consider this a valid distinction?
7. Explain how net taxable income is determined.
8. Distinguish between "net taxable income" and "net income subject to
tax."
9. What are the theoretical objections to corporation income taxes?
10. Enumerate the practical difficulties in applying a concept of income
to corporation receipts.
11. Justify the levying of Federal estates taxes.
12. What are some of the objections which have been raised to the Federal
estates tax?
13. Explain what is meant by excise taxes and point out the purposes for
which they may be employed.
14. Give the arguments for a general sales tax.
15. Give the arguments against a general sales tax.

Topics for Investigation

1. Analysis of changes in the definition of income in Federal income tax
legislation enacted since 1913.
2. Development of state income taxes in the United States.
3. Classification of incomes with reference to source, for purposes of
taxation.
4. Methods of preventing tax evasion.

CHAPTER XXI

STATE AND LOCAL TAXATION

1. General Property Tax.—The general property tax is a tax levied at theoretically uniform and equal rates upon the established valuation of practically all forms of real and personal property in a taxing district. It is the most important tax collected in the United States today, providing three-fourths of the tax revenue of the state and local governments. In 1913, the general property tax amounted to 38 per cent of the total revenue receipts of the states, 76 per cent of the revenues of the counties and 60 per cent of the revenues of incorporated towns. In 1917, the percentage distribution of revenue receipts of all states was as follows:

SOURCES OF REVENUE OF STATES[1]

	Per cent
Property taxes.....	53.1
Special property taxes....................................	2.6
Poll taxes...	0.4
Business and non-business licenses........................	22.3
Special assessments and special charges for outlays..........	0.6
Fines, forfeits, and escheats..............................	0.4
Subventions, grants, donations, and pension assessments......	2.1
Earnings of general departments...........................	12.0
Highway privileges, rents, and interest.....................	6.0
Earnings of public service enterprises......................	0.5
	100.0

In the words of Professor Seligman: "There is perhaps no single feature of our modern tax system that is commonly thought to be more thoroughly American than the general property tax."[2] Nevertheless, for reasons which will be considered presently, there is no tax that has evoked more adverse criticism in recent years than this very tax.

[1] *Cf.* Financial Statistics of States, 1917, p. 71.
[2] *Cf.* "Essays in Taxation," 8th ed., p. 19.

2. Development of the General Property Tax.—Direct property taxes in the form of taxes on land were imposed in ancient Greece and Rome. As other forms of property were developed, the property tax was extended to include them, as well as land, as part of the base. Thus, the concept of a *general* property tax gradually evolved. This evolution of the general property tax out of an earlier tax on land can be traced in most countries. Early English taxes were primarily land taxes, and as new forms of material wealth developed, they were included in the concept of taxable property. The same process can be observed in the early history of continental European countries.

The American Colonies introduced a tax on property at a comparatively early date in their history. In 1654, Peter Stuyvesant, of the Colony of New York, succeeded in having an "honest and fair tax" placed on "land, houses or lots, and milch cows or draft oxen." Under English rule the principle of assessing every person in proportion to his aggregate property became the commonly accepted principle of taxation in the colonies. Various kinds of property, both real and personal, have in the past been considered evidences of tax-paying ability in practically every state and local community of the Union. Even today, as noted above, the general property tax holds the place of primary importance as a source of state and local tax revenues.

3. Analysis of the General Property Tax.—In primitive agricultural communities property was mostly in land. Hence, the amount of land owned was regarded as an approximate indication of ability to pay taxes. But the profound economic changes of the past century and a half have modified very considerably the earlier belief that property, and especially property in land, is an accurate index of ability to bear tax burdens.

What are some of the significant changes that have affected our concept of property as a basis of taxation? In the first place, the ownership of, or legal title to, property has been largely separated from the actual possession of wealth in modern industrial society. Second, this legal ownership, particularly in corporate property, has been widely diffused. Third, different classes and kinds of property have developed different degrees of productivity. Fourth, not all types of property are easily discoverable for purposes of assessment. Finally, many persons derive their incomes from sources other than the ownership or possession of property. In view of these changes, the concept of property as indicative of tax-paying ability has become untenable. Many forms of property have evaded the general property tax entirely; others have been inequitably assessed. Consequently, the practice of making the general property tax a tax on real estate, which can neither hide nor run away, has been adopted by most local governments. Professor Seligman says:[1]

History thus ever teaches the same lesson. As soon as the idea of direct taxation has forced itself into recognition it assumes the practical shape of the land tax. This soon develops into the general property tax which long remains the index of ability to pay. But as soon as the mass of property splits up, the property tax becomes an anachronism. The various kinds of personalty escape, until finally the general property tax completes the cycle of its development and reverts to its original form of the real property tax.

Let us analyze a little more closely the chief defects of the general property tax. One of the outstanding objections to the tax is the inequity of assessment of property. As a rule, a final tax rate is established on the assessor's valuation of the property in a taxing district. If all property were uniformly and equitably assessed, a tax on such a valuation would conform, in general, to the principle of uniformity in taxation. Most tax laws of states and municipalities provide that property shall be assessed at its "fair cash value." For example, the constitution of the state of Ohio provides[2] that:

Laws shall be passed, taxing by a uniform rule, moneys, credits, investments in bonds, stocks, joint stock companies, or otherwise, and also all real and personal property, according to its real value in money.

How is this "real value in money" to be ascertained? In actual practice, as a rule, no uniform methods or standards of valuation appear to be employed by assessors of properties. It is indeed a debatable question whether any uniform, standardized method of evaluating all forms of property can be employed. Some assessors regard sales price as an accurate indication of "true value in money," but others arrive at the valuation by capitalizing realized net money income. Still others trust to their judgment, based on experience, while some merely guess at the valuation of properties. The employing of definite, uniform methods for

[1] *Cf.* "Essays in Taxation," 8th ed. p. 56.
[2] Art. XII.

determining the "true value in money" of definite kinds of property is a comparatively recent practice. Official reports reveal the fact that properties in various taxing districts have been assessed at from 25 per cent of their "real value" to over 100 per cent. A uniform rate of taxes based on such inequitable assessments must inevitably result in injustice to the taxpayer. In some cases, boards of equalization or revision of taxes are appointed to correct this evil. Nevertheless, inequitable assessments continue. Even though property were equitably assessed in one taxing district but not in another, injustice would result from apportioning taxes among several taxing districts, based on such property valuations.

A second defect of the general property tax lies in the fact that it places an undue burden of taxes upon real property, primarily in the form of land and permanent improvements on land, while many forms of personal property are allowed to escape taxation in whole or in part. Inasmuch as personal property, roughly identified with movable objects more closely related to personal use than to land, is largely held in cities, the consequence is a tendency towards shifting a disproportionate portion of the tax burden to rural districts.

Third, the incentive to dishonesty and perjury is given by the general property tax, especially in so far as personal property is concerned. Wherever attempts have been made to require taxpayers to declare their personal property under oath, the inducements to perjury have become very pronounced. Reports of the state and local tax commissions abound in such statements as the following:[1]

The existing system is productive of the gravest injustice; under its sanction, grievous wrongs are inflicted upon those least able to bear them: these laws are made the cover and excuse for the grossest oppression and injustice; above all and beyond all, they produce in the community a widespread demoralization; they induce perjury; they invite concealment. The present system is a school of evasion and dishonesty.

A fourth objection to the general property tax is found in the fact that it frequently results in double taxation. Double taxation is levying two taxes upon the same base, either by the same or by different governmental agencies. If all property were equally subjected to the burden of two taxes, the injustice of

[1] *Cf. Report* of Special Committee on Taxation of the Cleveland Chamber of Commerce, 1895, p. 10.

double taxation would not be so pronounced.   But when two taxes are imposed upon one class of property while another bears but one tax or possibly escapes taxation entirely, the inequitability of a general property tax becomes apparent.   If, for example, a tax is imposed on the plant and equipment of a corporation, and another tax on the evidences of ownership (certificates of stock) of the corporation, we have clearly a case of double taxation on the same base.   Again, when securities are taxed by one jurisdiction, while the actual wealth represented by these securities is taxed by another jurisdiction, double taxation also results.   The twofold use of the concept of property is apparent in much of our tax legislation.   At law, stocks, bonds, promissory notes, mortgages, and similar evidences of ownership are regarded as intangible property, while material objects are spoken of as tangible property.   Thus, the term property is commonly applied to both concepts.

It is obviously unjust to tax both debtor and creditor, the one on his property possession (material wealth), the other on the evidence of the debt.   If a person, having purchased a house and lot for ten thousand dollars, of which amount he borrowed seven thousand dollars on a mortgage, pays a real estate tax on the ten-thousand-dollar valuation of his dwelling, while the mortgagee pays a personal property tax on his evidence of the claim against the real estate for seven thousand dollars, a tax is collected on a valuation of seventeen thousand dollars, where in reality only ten thousand dollars worth of real estate exists.   If, on the other hand, debt deduction were permitted, what would prevent an individual from mortgaging the value of his entire estate to some ficticious "friend" in a far-away locality, and thus escape the entire property tax?   It is a relatively simple matter to create fictitious debts against real estate.   Corporations, which have issued bonds to the extent of the face value of their outstanding capital stock, could possibly escape one half of their general property tax, if debt deduction were allowed.

So long as land and other property were owned in fee simple they could, of course, be taxed only once, and that to the owner . . . In the early and simple organization, all the rights of property were characteristically vested in the user.   Today these various rights in property have become widely diffused and hopelessly entangled for the tax administrator.[1]

[1] *Cf.* JENSEN, "Public Finance," p. 246*f*.

Lastly, the general property tax is often regressive, *i.e.* the rate decreases as the base increases. A small amount of property will usually be in the form of visible realty or personalty, which cannot easily escape the eye of the honest assessor. But as property, in the legal sense of the word, accumulates, it takes on more and more intangible forms, which can be easily concealed. Professor Seligman[1] says:

If we sum up all these inherent defects, it will be no exaggeration to say that the general property tax in the United States is a dismal failure . . . *Practically*, the general property tax as usually administered is beyond all doubt one of the worst taxes known in the civilized world. Because of its attempt to tax intangible as well as tangible things, it sins against the cardinal rules of uniformity, of equality and of universality of taxation . . . It is the cause of such crying injustice that its alteration or its abolition must become the battle cry of every statesman and reformer.[1]

If we accept this opinion we may well ask, why is the general property tax still tolerated on our statute books? Several reasons may be cited for its continuation to the present day. In the first place, the resources of the United States have been such that the tax burdens resulting from the collection of taxes have not imposed a particular hardship upon the people in general. Second, the value of land has increased so rapidly that the burden of the tax on real estate has been largely offset by the increment in land values, while, as has been noted above, an increasing amount of personal property has successfully evaded the tax. Again, competition for industries in different states has from time to time resulted in giving preferential treatment for tax purposes to certain classes of property, and so relieved various enterprises from the burden of the tax. From the administrative point of view, the tax has been retained, since it offers a fruitful source of revenue and is relatively easy to administer. Finally, the general property tax has become an established institution in many parts of the United States, and it is often contended that an old-established tax is no tax at all. This contention, however, does not justify the retention of a tax, which, in its present form, is unsound in theory and unfair in practice.

4. Suggested Reforms of the General Property Tax.— Inasmuch as perhaps three-fourths of the general property tax in the United States today resolves itself into a tax on real estate, a

---

[1] *Cf.* "Essays in Taxation," 8th ed. p. 31 and p. 62.

tax on this form of property, equitably administered, should prove an acceptable substitute for the general property tax. The personal property tax should be abolished, since it is usually impossible to locate such property for purposes of assessment. Again, the problem of assessment of real estate for tax purposes should be taken out of the hands of political appointees and placed under the jurisdiction of those who have qualified for the office of assessor by passing rigorous civil service examinations.

Furthermore, agencies for review and equalization of taxes should be established on the merit system, and not, as is frequently the case today, on the basis of political affiliation. In assessing real estate a careful distinction should be made between land, as such, and improvements on land. In this connection it will be well to review the basic principles underlying the valuation of land and of producible goods. The confusion resulting from applying both the legal and the economic concepts of property to the general property tax should be removed by distinguishing carefully between actual physical property (economic wealth), and property rights or interests. The two concepts cannot be maintained without continuing the present ambiguity in general property tax legislation. A tax on the net profits of corporations and on net personal incomes might be employed as a substitute for the present personal property tax, with its impossible categories of different types of intangible property. In this connection it is interesting to note that to date fourteen states of the Union have adopted personal income taxes, in one form or another, as part of their fiscal programs. The general observations made in the preceding chapter, with reference to the Federal personal income tax law, are also applicable to state income tax legislation.

In the final analysis, the assumption that property measures taxpaying ability and that all property may be regarded alike for purposes of taxation is unsound. But the tax on real estate has become an established institution in most communities, and to advocate its entire abolition would perhaps be construed as somewhat radical. The above recommendations, if carried out more widely in all the states, would not remove entirely, but would decrease very materially, the manifest injustices of the present general property tax.

5. Suggested Tax on Land Values.—When the general property tax is once abandoned, a modified property tax, if adopted, will be one which is levied on selected types of property, either in the legal or in the economic sense. The tax on real estate, suggested above in lieu of the general property tax, is in reality a special property tax.

The proposal has been made from time to time and adopted by some communities in recent years, of "untaxing" the value of improvements on land and levying a progressive rate, graduated according to the increase in land values, upon land. The theoretical justification of this proposal runs as follows: Land is the free gift of nature, the heritage of mankind. Its value is a social product, resulting from the increase of population and prosperity and usually not from any direct contribution of the landlord. The individual, as such, is not responsible for differences in land values, nor for increases in land values. Consequently, the appropriation of this socially created value for the benefit of the community, would not be an imposition on human labor and on industrial activity. Improvements on land, on the other hand, are the result of human labor, and a tax on them is a definite burden to the taxpayer. It should be the desire of every social reformer to untax as much as possible the product of human labor and to impose taxes where they would be burdenless. Moreover, a tax on land values, or on the economic rent of land, cannot be shifted, but it must be borne by the landlord. In general, it is contended that any reward received by an individual, which is not necessary to move him to economic activity, constitutes an economic surplus. Economic rent is such a surplus, and a tax on this surplus would not, on that account, decrease economic activities and diminish the supply of economic goods. A tax on land values, therefore, cannot be shifted.

Furthermore, since the tax on land values cannot be shifted, a permanent tax on such values would decrease the capital value of land. If a tract of land were to yield an annual rental of one thousand dollars, the capitalized value of this income, let us say at 5 per cent, would be twenty thousand dollars. If a ten per cent tax were imposed on the income from this tract of land, the net income to the owner of the land from his possession would be but nine hundred dollars, and the capitalized value of the present income at the assumed rate of five per cent would have decreased promptly to eighteen thousand dollars because of this tax.

Different types of land value taxes may be adopted. In the first place, a definite rate of taxation may be imposed on the present economic rent of land, but not great enough to absorb the entire income from land. As land values increase, the revenues derived from the tax would likewise increase, but not all of the increase in land values would be consumed by taxation. Second, the future increment in land values may be taxed away. Thus, the landlord would retain his claim on the present capital value of his land, but not on the anticipated future increases in land values. Finally, the full economic rent may be taxed away, thus destroying entirely the value of the legal claim which individuals now have to landed property. Private property in land would thus be modified. It is this latter proposal which is the basis of the "single tax" doctrine, as formulated by Henry George in his famous work "Progress and Poverty."

6. The Single Tax.—The single tax, as expounded by Henry George and his disciples, is not merely a tax measure, but a plan for social reform. It is based on the fundamental premise that the use of land is a natural right which cannot be alienated. Everyone has an equal right to the products of the land with everyone else. Man, as an individual, has a right only to those things which he has produced. Since everyone has an equal right to land, the rights of the landlord's title to land need not be respected. While these landlords continue in possession of land and exact tribute from the rest of mankind, poverty with all its accompanying evils, will continue. To remedy these ills, the use of land must be made free. To accomplish this result, land values should be appropriated by society. The landowner has no claim to these products of social rather than individual efforts. The taxing away of the annual rental value of land, as we have noted above, would do away with private property in land. It is contended that the values thus appropriated would suffice to meet all the ordinary requirements of governments. No taxes levied on the product of human labor would be necessary. Hence, the name "single tax."

7. Objections to the Single Tax.—The single tax, as generally understood, assumes an untenable theory of property rights. According to the "single tax" doctrines, an individual has a natural right to the fruits of his labor, but not to the gifts of nature. Can anyone determine how much of the value of a brick house is the fruit of labor and how much is the gift of nature? Is it possible to differentiate between the fruits of labor and the gifts of nature in the crops of a farm, yielded after cultivating and fertilizing the soil, sowing the seed and harvesting the crop, not to mention the utilization of farm implements?

The public requirements of two communities, even though exactly the same in size, differ considerably. One community may develop rapidly, the other slowly, but the revenues derived from the single tax on land values would not necessarily keep pace with the growth of the communities. Furthermore, any single tax is undesirable as the sole source of all public revenue. The single tax would also be inflexible, since it could not be increased to meet urgent public requirements in times of a national emergency. It would also involve the wholesale confiscation of land. Finally, it would be difficult to administer, since it is practically impossible always to distinguish between capital invested in permanent improvements on land and unimproved lands. To appropriate the entire income from improvements on land would be to impose a tax in part on the fruits of human labor. Because of these obvious weaknesses of the "single tax," it is doubtful whether it will ever meet with popular approval in the United States. Nevertheless, the partial taxation of the unearned increment from land is well developed as a program of fiscal and social reform. The taxation of land values has been advocated as a supplement to, rather than as a substitute for, other forms of taxation. But, this cannot be considered a "single tax."

8. State Inheritance Taxes.—The first state inheritance tax in the United States was adopted by Pennsylvania in 1826. Since then other states have from time to time passed inheritance tax laws, until today forty-six states in the Union derive a portion of their revenue from inheritance taxes. All of these laws have certain basic features in common. In the first place, they are not "estates" taxes, such as the Federal estates tax, discussed in the preceding chapter, since they are taxes based on separate legacies and not on the estate as a whole. Secondly, legacies to direct heirs, such as parents, wife, husband, or children of the legator are usually taxed at a lower rate than those to collateral heirs. For example, the New York inheritance tax law imposes a rate of 1 to 4 per cent on net bequests to direct heirs, (the rate varying with the size of the bequest). The corresponding rates on bequests to nonrelatives are 5 to 8 per cent. In some states, legacies to direct heirs are exempt entirely from the inheritance tax. Such is the case in Maryland and Texas.

Furthermore, a minimum exemption is usually allowed. As a rule, gifts to religious, educational, and charitable institutions are not taxed. Finally, rates are generally progressive, increasing with the size of the bequest and the remoteness of the relationship.

On what grounds can we justify high progressive tax rates on collateral inheritances? It is contended that, from the point of view of the beneficiary, an inheritance tax is burdenless, since whatever he receives is so much "unearned" income to him. Again, from the point of view of the testator, the desire to leave a large estate to distant relatives or friends plays an unimportant role in gratifying his acquisitive tendencies. Tax or no tax on collateral inheritances, he would in all probability be inclined to save and accumulate wealth just the same. The incentive to produce and to save is not destroyed by such a tax.

There are many people who question the right of the state to levy heavy taxes on inheritances, contending that such taxation constitutes a confiscation of private property. They seem to confuse the right to possess property and enjoy the benefits of property during life with the right to transfer property at the time of death. The latter right is essentially modern. We do not have to go far back into history to discover that property left at the time of death reverted to the state or to the ruler as a matter of course.

When the owner of property dies, his ownership ceases. The disposition of the property subsequently becomes a problem of decided social significance. No one has an absolute right to the property, although most modern states safeguard the rights of certain direct heirs in the estates of the deceased, "but always under definite limitations designed to promote the general well being."[1] The deceased cannot be permitted to determine what shall be done with the property, regardless of the interest of the living. It does not appear unjust for the state to assume the right to a share in the property which it has safeguarded during the lifetime of the deceased, to be employed for the benefit of the whole community. The share thus appropriated by the state is neither a burden on the deceased, nor does it impose a burden on the heirs, since it is not the product of their labors.

The argument is frequently advanced that too high rates of inheritance taxes will discourage the accumulation of property.

[1] *Cf.* SEAGER, "Practical Problems in Economics," p. 541.

The validity of this argument can be accepted only with qualifications. If the rates of inheritance taxes are moderate and a reasonable amount is exempt to assure a continuation of the accustomed standard of living to the direct heirs of the testator, it is doubtful whether progressive rates will appreciably retard the accumulations of further wealth and impair the industrial efficiency of an individual. Only excessive rates or double and perhaps multiple taxation of the same property will tend to discourage the accumulation of property.

One of the outstanding weaknesses of inheritance and estates tax legislation in the United States today is the fact that the inheritance tax laws are not uniform. They lack uniformity not only in respect to rates, but also in respect to the bases on which the taxes are levied. Some states levy the inheritance tax at the domicile of the decedent, others impose the tax upon the situs of the physical property, while still others impose the tax on evidences of ownership. "Suppose an individual dies in state A, who was a citizen of state B, owned one hundred thousand dollars worth of bonds of a corporation chartered in state C, the actual property of which was in state D, while the bonds were in the safety vault in state E. The inheritance tax law of A taxes the property of every decedent of the state, B that of every citizen, C the bonds of corporations chartered within the state, D the property where located, and E the situs of the bonds."[1] In addition, the Federal government takes its share of the property. A hypothetical case may be worked out according to which the combined state inheritance taxes and the Federal estates tax, as provided in existing laws, would theoretically absorb over 100 per cent of the value of the estate. It is obvious that such chaotic conditions should be remedied. Uniform inheritance taxes, levied on a common base, can be secured only by cooperation among the various states. If the individual states mutually agreed to abolish their present inheritance taxes and allowed the Federal government to tax estates uniformly, the latter returning a certain percentage of the taxes thus collected to the individual states, the outstanding objections to present inheritance taxes would probably be removed.

Furthermore, to remove the possible discouragement to the accumulation of wealth, the rates could be made to vary not only with the degree of relationship and the size of the estate, but also

[1] *Cf.* HUNTER, "Outlines of Public Finance," p. 327*f.*

with the number of times the property exchanged hands through inheritance. In other words, the rate might be made "progressive in time," increasing each time the property passed from testator to beneficiary, until after several generations the original estate would finally pass entirely into the hands of the state. It has been suggested that such a scheme would not discourage the accumulation of wealth so much as do many of the present inheritance taxes. The real problem is to obtain the consent of the states to any such proposal, and to devise a practical basis for administering such a tax and for redistributing the revenue thus collected.

As fiscal measures, inheritance taxes possess practically all the qualities of a good form of taxation. Nevertheless, as was pointed out in discussing the Federal estates tax, they are open to the objection that they are uncertain as to time and indefinite as to the amount of revenue yielded.

9. Special Corporation Taxes.—Most states impose special taxes on different kinds of corporations, in addition to subjecting corporate property to some form of general property tax. These special taxes are justified on the grounds that they are a return for the special privileges extended to the corporations by the state. The "benefit" principle rather than the "faculty" principle of taxation applies to so-called franchise taxes or incorporation taxes. Either the privilege to come into existence or the privilege to perform certain specific functions is taxed. The former tax is usually spoken of as an incorporation tax or incorporation fee, and the latter a franchise tax. When special privileges, such as the use of public highways by public service corporations, are taxed, the taxes thus imposed are referred to as special franchise taxes.

Corporations are artificial creations of the state, owned by the stockholders. On what basis shall these creatures of the state be taxed? Shall they be taxed uniformly, regardless of size, or shall they be subjected to taxes according to the amount of their capitalization? If the latter basis is adopted, how is the capitalization to be ascertained? Most large corporations are engaged in interstate activities. Which state is to have jurisdiction over the corporation for purposes of taxation? A corporation is chartered under the laws of state A, transacts the major portion of its business in states B and C, and is owned by stockholders, largely residing in state D, who have mortgaged their property to bond holders living in state E.   What amount of a "franchise" tax on this corporation should be collected by each one of the five states?   Again, to what extent shall corporations be taxed by local authorities in the districts where their material wealth is located?   These are but a few of the manifold complexities arising from an attempt to impose franchise taxes by the individual states and local governments on miscellaneous corporations. How can they be overcome?   No general agreement exists today among economists and legal authorities as to a solution of the problem.

The general tendency in modern governments appears to be in the direction of increased centralization of governmental control. Taxation is no longer a purely local problem, particularly in so far as it affects corporations.   The integration of industry into units extending their activities far beyond local and state borders, even beyond national boundaries, has to a large extent destroyed the possibility of equitably taxing any one industry by a local government.   "The plan of levying a general state tax and distributing a part of the proceeds to the counties or municipalities contains a fruitful idea," says Professor Seligman.   With the possible Federal chartering or licensing of corporations, the possibility of a Federal corporation franchise tax, based on either corporate profits or invested capital, carefully ascertained by scientific assessment of property, may become a reality in the future.   Such a Federal franchise tax might then be redistributed among the states, either according to population or according to relative importance of the corporations to various localities.

The logical plan for the immediate future, however, is to tax corporations on their receipts, or on a valuation equal to the stock and bonds, for state purposes; and to tax them on their real property for local purposes, with the understanding that in the case of public-service corporations this local real-estate tax should be subject to central assessment in accordance with the unit rule.   The question of the division of the yield of the corporation tax may safely be left to a consideration of the particular needs in each individual case, after the principle has first been applied to the other state-wide taxes.[1]

10. A National System of Taxes.—We have noted in the preceding pages the chief Federal, state, and local taxes.   The criticism has frequently been voiced that there is no uniformity among the different taxes imposed by the different political

[1] *Cf.* SELIGMAN, "Essays in Taxation," 9th ed. p. 314.

divisions of the country. Each political unit appears to levy that tax which offers possibilities of yielding revenue and is relatively easy to collect. Some states levy a variety of taxes, others but a few; some stress indirect taxes, other favor direct taxation. Some consider property as the best measure of tax-paying ability; others regard money income as the most equitable criterion. Some believe in retaining old-established taxes, no matter how inequitable at present; others revise old tax laws and make them conform more nearly to changing economic conditions. How can order be brought out of such chaos and a unified tax system be developed? Certain recommendations may be made in this connection.

1. A sufficiently large variety of taxes should be employed so as to be able to reach the tax paying ability derived from practically all conceivable sources. A "single tax," no matter on what base it might be levied, would probably not reach all classes of income.

2. Specific sources of revenue should be assigned to the several political units making up the United States. This is essential to prevent double and multiple taxation.

3. The principle of progression in taxation should be extended only to the point where it will not destroy initiative or encourage evasion. It is incompatible for instance, to make evasion possible, by investing in tax-exempt securities, and at the same time to levy high progressive rates on large incomes.

4. The general property tax should be abolished and a real estate tax, based on accurate scientific assessments, should be substituted.

5. Tangible wealth and property interests should be clearly differentiated in tax legislation, to avoid the ambiguity resulting from a confusion of the two concepts.

6. Taxes should be levied as far as possible where the burden will be relatively insignificant, and where the possibility of shifting will be reduced to a minimum. For this purpose direct rather than indirect taxes should be encouraged, in spite of the many administrative advantages of indirect taxes.

7. Corporation taxes, in the form of franchise taxes of various kinds, should either be abolished or be made uniform throughout the states, assessed by state authorities, and certain shares duly distributed among the local taxing districts.

8. Property taxes, levied on impersonal wealth, should be supplemented by such personal taxes as the income and inheritance taxes.

9. Greater cooperation among the several states and the Federal government with a view to developing greater justice in taxation cannot be too strongly recommended. A Federal Tax commission, charged with standardizing and systematizing Federal, state, and local taxes with the active cooperation of the state tax commissions, could undoubtedly accomplish beneficial results, if not made a political tool. Any such suggestion will very likely meet with the objection of the staunch New Englander who remarked:

We believe in local self-government. We manage our own affairs. And we resent any outside interference with our cherished historical institutions.

One fact cannot be repeated too often, namely, that we are living in a dynamic world. In our onward movement certain traditional institutions become antiquated and rather out of place in a world of action, where he who stands still is but retarding the progress of civilization. The problem of equitable taxation is no longer a local problem, but has attained national importance. It can be treated adequately only by approaching it from the viewpoint of the nation as a whole.

11. Summary.—The general property tax is a tax levied upon practically all forms of real and personal property. It forms the chief source of state and local tax revenue today. It developed out of the earlier land tax, but was made to include other forms of property as they developed. It is defective because it is inequitably assessed; it places an undue burden on real property; it gives an incentive to false statements as to various types of property; it leads to double taxation and is regressive. In spite of these objections, it is retained by practically all of the states, because it is productive of revenue, and because it has become an established institution. Certain reforms of the general property tax may be suggested. It should be modified into a tax levied on real estate to the exclusion of personal property. Assessments should be made by assessors appointed on merit. Separate valuation of land and of improvements on land should be made. An interpretation of the concept of property should be adopted which avoids ambiguity. Some have suggested a tax on land values, contending that such a tax would be burdenless because the value of land is a social product, and not the productive contribution of the individual landlord. The "single tax" is suggested as a means of obtaining all necessary revenue for ordinary governmental expenditures from a tax on land values, appropriating the economic rent of land for public use, and thereby destroying private property in land. Such a program is theoretically unsound, because it is based on a wrong concept of natural rights. It is practically inexpedient, because it would result in a wholesale confiscation of property in land.

State inheritance taxes, although possessing most features of a good form of taxation, are objectionable because they lack uniformity in the individual states, and because they result in double and multiple taxation. The Federal administration of inheritance taxes would probably remove many of the outstanding objections to these taxes as administered at present. Corporation taxes, in the form of franchise taxes, likewise lack uniformity in the different states. Because the activities of most large corporations extend beyond the state borders, the problem of equitable and uniform taxation is becoming increasingly difficult. It may ultimately require Federal administration for its solution. A national tax system, intended to develop greater uniformity in taxation in the separate states, and greater cooperation between the states and the Federal Government, appears to be the crying need of the day. The problem of taxation is no longer a purely local one, but has now attained national significance.

Collateral Reading

FETTER, F. A., "Modern Economic Problems," chap. 18.
MARSHALL, L. C., WRIGHT, C. W., and FIELD, J. A., "Materials for the Study of Elementary Economics," chap. 19, Nos. 254 and 256.
SEAGER, H. R., "Practical Problems in Economics," chap. 28.
TAUSSIG, F. W., "Principles of Economics," vol. II chap. 70.
WILLIAMSON, T. R., "Readings in Economics," chap. 32.

References

ADAMS, H. C., "Science of Finance."
Annals of the American Academy of Political and Social Science, vol. LVIII, No. 147 and vol. XCV, No. 184.
BASTABLE, C. F., "Public Finance."
GRICE, J. W., "National and Local Taxation."
Johns Hopkins University *Studies* in Historical and Political Science. Series XVIII, "Studies in State Taxation."
POLLOCK, W. W., and SCHOLZ, K. W. H., "The Science and Practice of Urban Land Valuation."
POST, L. F., "The Taxation of Land Values."

Proceedings of the National Tax Association, *Report* on Model State and
   Local Tax System, 1919, pp. 401–470.
Report of Commission of Corporations on System of Taxing Corporations.
SELIGMAN, E. R. A., "Essays in Taxation."
WEST, MAX, "The Inheritance Tax."

Questions for Discussion

1. What is meant by the general property tax?
2. Illustrate the importance of the general property tax in the United
States today.
3. Trace the development of the general property tax.
4. Point out the chief objections to the general property tax.
5. Why is the general property tax retained as a source of public revenue?
6. Suggest certain reforms of the general property tax.
7. Justify a tax on land values as a substitute for the general property
tax.
8. What is meant by the "single tax" as expounded by Henry George?
9. What are the objections to the "single tax?"
10. Distinguish between estates and inheritance taxes.
11. How can you justify progressive rates of inheritance taxes?
12. What is the chief practical obstacle in the way of levying state
inheritance taxes equitably?
13. What is the nature of the various special corporation taxes levied by
the states?
14. Enumerate the practical difficulties in the way of levying such corporation taxes.
15. "The general tendency in modern government appears to be in the
direction of increased centralization of governmental control." Explain.
16. Outline a program for a national system of taxes.

Topics for Investigation

1. Standardized methods of real estate assessments for purposes of
taxation.
2. Distribution of the real estate tax burden in different localities, between
urban and rural population.
3. General property tax evasion and how to prevent it.
4. Development of direct taxation in various states.
5. How may uniformity in state inheritance tax laws be achieved?
6. Federal subsidies and subventions to states.
7. The concept of property in tax legislation.

PART FIVE
PROBLEMS OF LABOR AND INDUSTRIAL UNREST

CHAPTER XXII

ECONOMIC INEQUALITY AND POVERTY

1. Industrial Unrest.—Social unrest is a characteristic of a dynamic society. On the other hand, static societies, like those of medieval Europe and China several centuries ago, suffer from maladjustments of which they are not fully conscious. Social unrest arises from a consciousness of certain maladjustments and a desire to eliminate them. Social adjustment is the securing of greater harmony within the social organism and a better economic adaptation to the physical environment. Intellectual progress and the process of invention permit constantly better adjustments. The process of adjustment may be either evolutionary or revolutionary, according to whether the process is relatively slow or rapid. The forces of social unrest may express themselves in either peaceful or violent forms.

One cause of social unrest is the existence of glaring economic inequalities. Large fortunes and inadequate wages persist side by side. Although economic progress has made for superior adaptations and consequently for higher standards of living, a persistent problem of poverty still exists. Moreover, the Industrial Revolution has created other economic maladjustments, such as child labor and the industrial exploitation of women. The extreme specialization of modern industry and the resulting interdependence of our economic life have created unemployment. The use of machinery has increased industrial accidents and the susceptibility of workers to fatigue. Hence, we have the problems of safety and health in industry, as well as the necessity for social insurance. Modern capitalism has meant the decline of craftsmanship and the loss of ownership of the instruments of production by the workers. This dependence of the workers has resulted in the growth of labor organizations, and collective bargaining has injected itself into the wage system. The conflict of interests between labor and capital results in such economic maladjustments as strikes and boycotts. The

443

promotion of industrial peace is conditioned by the cooperation of workers and employers and the development of the copartnership ideal in industry.

The development of popular education and democratic ideals has made for a greater sensitivity to economic maladjustments. Hence, social unrest exists to an extent never known before. It is to be feared only if it remains inarticulate and finally expresses itself in a violent attempt at adjustment. The French and the Russian Revolutions indicate the danger. Progress is made through conscious evolution and orderly adjustment, rather than through the blind efforts of mob leaders to remove economic burdens from the backs of the masses. Social unrest in America has reflected itself in a variety of ways, such as in humanitarian legislation, in the organization of labor, and in such critical schools of thought as Socialism.

2. Poverty and Pauperism.—Revolution and social unrest have had their seeds in poverty and economic inequality. Poverty is one of the oldest and most persistent of all economic and social maladjustments. The prophets of the Old Testament indicted the rich for the oppression of the poor, and modern statesmen are still striving to formulate plans of internal reform for an amelioration of society. Any study of economic problems must include a consideration of the subject of poverty. Although a discussion of social debtor groups, that is, of defectives, delinquents, and dependents, is within the scope of sociology, the economist must analyze standards of living and the causes of poverty which are resident in our economic environment. We leave to the sociologist the treatment of individual cases of dependency.

It is necessary that we define our terms at the outset. That class in society with the smallest income, and consequently with the lowest standard of living, is usually referred to as the poor. The advance of civilization has increased the total real income of society and generally raised standards of living. The prosperous classes of modern nations live in a state of luxury undreamed of by princes and kings of the Middle Ages. In like manner, the poor of today enjoy comforts which were not possessed by earlier societies. The poor, in the sense of the lowest income class, have persisted because our social order is divided into economic groups. Unless society can be modeled upon some communistic plan, the poor, in this comparative sense, we shall always have with us. The elimination of the poor, in the sense of the lowest income group, is as impossible as the elimination of the last train coach which is frequently the victim of train wrecks. On the other hand, the term poverty may be used in a less comparative sense to refer to those individuals or families whose incomes are so small and whose standards of living are consequently so low that neither health nor working efficiency can be maintained. Although standards of living as well as incomes are comparative, it is possible at any given time to determine minimum standards of normal living. Thus, the social pathologist regards poverty as a social disease, and the poor as abnormal members of society. The poor, in this latter sense of the word, we need not always have with us.

The pauper group, in contradistinction to the poor, includes those individuals in almshouses and those families in their own homes, who require financial assistance from charitable organizations. They constitute a part of the social debtor group, because pauperism is essentially a state of dependency. Poverty and pauperism are not synonymous, however; those individuals who live below the poverty line, but who are too proud to ask for help, should not be referred to as paupers. There is a strong tendency, however, for the poor to become paupers. Indeed, poverty has sometimes been compared to a narrow and treacherous footpath around the morass of pauperism.

3. Standards of Living.—Any attempt to classify standards of living is bound to be rather arbitrary and artificial. Nevertheless, numerous studies of family budgets attempt to define and distinguish different types of standards of living. The pauper-poverty standard of living represents a condition barely above dependency. There is no sharp line between it and the social debtor classes. There is also a minimum of subsistence level, which implies merely an animal existence with just enough to satisfy the chief physical wants. The latter is rather a theoretical concept to which economists have sometimes resorted. Above these two standards is the standard of minimum health and comfort. It implies an income sufficient to maintain health and working efficiency, with some provision for comforts and social insurance. It is the first division above the poverty group. Finally, there is what has been named a standard of health and decency. It has also been termed a normal standard of living.

The United States Bureau of Labor Statistics prepared a quantity budget for the use of Congress in readjusting salaries in 1919. A number of previous attempts had been made to draw up a minimum standard of living and to express it in terms of money. The quantity budget estimates the amounts of food, shelter, clothing, and miscellaneous commodities and services necessary for the maintenance of a desired standard of living. The cost budget expresses the same items in monetary terms.

4. Minimum Standard of Living.—Since the family is the unit of consumption, standards of living involve an analysis of family budgets. The study of the United States Bureau of Labor Statistics in 1918–1919 was based on a family of five.[1] The requirements of a minimum quantity standard of living may be summarized as follows: A sufficiency of nourishing food, with special reference to the health of the children; housing in low-rent neighborhoods with the minimum number of rooms consistent with health and decency; the upkeep of household equipment; clothing of substantial quality, but with slight regard for fashion; miscellaneous provisions for such items as car fare, insurance, medical attention, modest contributions to church and fraternal organizations, and limited expenditure for amusement.

The following table expresses a similar standard of living in monetary units. It is interesting to note the relative budgetary

MINIMUM STANDARD OF LIVING FOR A FAMILY OF FIVE[2]

Items	December, 1914		Per cent increase in cost (1914–1919)	December, 1919	
	Amount	Per cent		Amount	Per cent
Food	$ 430	43.0	91	$ 821	42.0
Clothing	130	13.0	198	387	19.8
Rent	180	18.0	25	225	11.5
Fuel and light	50	5.0	52	76	3.9
Furniture	50	5.0	175	138	7.1
Miscellaneous	160	16.0	95	307	15.7
Total	$1,000	100.0	95	$1,954	100.0

[1] To be exact, of 4.9 persons, or the equivalent of 3.3 adults.
[2] *Monthly Labor Review* of July, 1920, p. 3.

importance of the various items and also to see how the increase in prices from 1914 to 1919 caused an increased expenditure for the same commodities and services. It will be seen that in 1919 it took $1,954 to purchase the same amount of commodities as could be purchased in 1914 for $1,000.

5. Extent of Poverty.—The extent of poverty is difficult to determine, for there are no absolute standards by which we can measure deviations from the normal. Poverty is a chronic as well as an acute problem. Although varying in intensity from time to time, it never entirely disappears. Again, it displays itself in a more concentrated form in the cities than in the country, and in the winter months than in the summer. Charles Booth made the first great investigation on the subject and published his findings in "Darkest London." Rowntree[1] undertook a similar investigation for the city of York. In these two English cities the estimated proportions of individuals living in poverty were 30.7 per cent and 27.8 per cent, respectively. As a result of a similar investigation in our own country, Robert Hunter estimated that the proportion of poverty in our large cities and industrial centers rarely fell below 25 per cent. Although the poverty rate may be smaller in the rural sections of our country, recent investigations have shown that this is doubtful. For society at large, the expression the "submerged tenth" is no exaggeration of the extent of poverty.

The extent of pauperism is equally difficult to determine. The almshouse often shelters such different groups as the aged, the infirm, the feeble-minded, and the shiftless. Moreover, its records of admission and dismissal are carelessly kept. In 1920, the United States Census placed the number of dependents in our various institutions at somewhat less than a million. This estimate, of course, ignores the much larger army of dependents who are cared for by what is known as outdoor relief, that is, by charity outside the almshouse. The total number of paupers and semidependents is surely several millions.

Although monetary estimates of a minimum standard of living for a family of five have varied greatly from time to time

---

[1] *Cf.* BOWLEY, A. L., and HOGG, M. H., "Livelihood and Poverty" (1914) and "Has Poverty Diminished?" (1925). The earlier study showed that 12.6 per cent of the cases studied had an income insufficient to maintain the minimum standard prescribed by Rowntree, but the later study showed only 3.6 or 6.5 per cent below that standard.

with increases in the general price level, most studies of this problem testify to the chronic character of inadequate wages and the persistence of poverty. In the last section was quoted the minimum standard estimate of the United States Bureau of Labor Statistics of 1914. Professor Hollander's statement for the same year is more conservative:

that in order to maintain a decent standard of living in the United States for a family of five an annual income of $600 to $700 is insufficient; that $700 to $800 requires exceptional management and escape from extraordinary disbursements consequent upon illness or death; and that $825 permits the maintenance of a fairly proper standard.[1]

Nevertheless, at that time, the Pennsylvania Department of Labor and Industry reported that the annual earnings of industrial workers in that state averaged $720. Many of these workers were heads of families and some of them were earning even less than this small average. They were living below the minimum standard of living, and in a condition of poverty. Lauck and Sydenstricker concluded from their investigations in 1915 that four-fifths of the family heads in the working population of the United States received less than $800 a year.

We have seen from the figures of the Bureau of Labor Statistics that the cost of living doubled between 1914 and 1919. It is the general concensus of opinion that wage increases in general lagged behind the increase in prices. In 1919, for illustration, the State Industrial Commission of New York estimated that the full-time earnings of factory workers in that state averaged less than $1,500. This wage is considerably below the minimum standard of living estimate for that time. Although there seems to have been a recent tendency of real wages in an upward direction, the problems of poverty and inadequate standards of living still persist.

6. Objective Causes of Poverty.—The older attitude toward poverty was similar to that toward war. Poverty had always existed and would continue to exist so long as the world endured. Almsgiving has always been regarded as a religious duty and the profession of begging is of ancient origin. Philanthropy is necessary for the alleviation of temporary distress, but the elimination of the causes of poverty is far better. The same scientific spirit which has reduced the amount of small-pox, yellow fever,

---

[1] *Cf.* HOLLANDER, J. H., "The Abolition of Poverty," p. 9.

and other physical diseases is now attacking the social disease of poverty.

A number of social reformers made the error of assuming that poverty had but one cause, although they have not all found the same factor. Malthus believed that poverty was due to the pressure of population upon food supply. Karl Marx found its explanation in the ownership of the instruments of production by a capitalistic class and the resulting dependence of the "proletariat" upon the "bourgeoisie." Socialism was therefore his remedy. To Henry George, poverty was the result of an individual rather than a social absorption of economic rent from land. In "Progress and Poverty" he points to single tax and the elimination of the landlord as his answer to the problem of poverty.

There is no single cause of poverty. This social problem is a complex of causes which reside in both the individual and his environment. Although low wages are causes of poverty, there are numerous other causes. Moreover, low wages are a result as well as a cause of poverty. Again, the answer of low wages is inadequate, for the student immediately seeks the answer to the problem of low wages, only to be confronted by problems of population, immigration, productive efficiency of labor, and a host of other questions. Our object is not to give the cause of poverty, nor even a number of causes, but merely to show the complexity of the problem and to indicate a possible method of approach to the various groups of contributory causes. The familiar division into individual and environmental causes is helpful, but it should be remembered that these are reciprocal, not mutually exclusive. This distinction represents merely different ways of classifying the same causal phenomena. Thus, ill health may be a personal cause of poverty, but ill health in turn may be the result of an unsanitary environment.

Although the physiography and natural resources of a nation condition its prosperity, human effort can improve the environment or make a better adaptation to it. Certain countries are poor by nature, but others are poor because of the failure to use adequately their abundant natural resources. By the use of improved methods of production and better economic organization, western nations have made a superior adjustment to their environment than that in the Orient, where dire poverty exists. Active adaptation and technological progress enable a dynamic society to keep ahead of the Malthusian spectre of a static society.   National prosperity is an underlying condition for the amelioration of poverty.   National prosperity depends upon a favorable natural environment and an intelligent adaptation of it.

But national prosperity in itself does not eliminate poverty. In this country, in spite of our large national prosperity, serious economic inequalities prevent an equitable distribution of the national income throughout all economic groups.   The total income for many families is insufficient to maintain decent standards of living.   Unemployment is another economic malad-justment, which reduces still further the meagre earnings of many workers and creates poverty.   Cycles of business depression and seasonal unemployment are attended by an enormous rise in the poverty rate and in the appeals to relief organizations. Strikes and lockouts have similar effects.   That changes in indus-try may produce temporary hardship is well illustrated by the Industrial Revolution.   A bad system of land tenure, such as that which existed in England during the time of the enclosure movement, is productive of poverty.   The rapid industrializa-tion of the United States increased our susceptibility to economic maladjustments which are productive of poverty.   Before this economic transition there was an abundant supply of free land in the West.   The problem of poverty in America can almost be said to date from the extinction of the frontier.

The social environment is also productive of poverty.   Low standards of living are causes as well as results of poverty. Unsanitary living conditions may result in the sickness and death of the bread winner.   Large families and the inability to give these numerous children proper educational advantages perpetu-ate the problem of low wages in the lower income groups.   The tendency of population to grow from the bottom more rapidly than from the top is a cause of poverty and economic inequality. Unrestricted immigration is injurious to the American worker, if it tends to lower wages and standards of living.   The social environment of city slums is as dangerous to social ideals as to physical health.   The degeneracy of family life is accompanied by the absence of economic ideals of thrift and steady industry. Social workers have discovered that the restoration of a healthy family life is essential to the restoration of economic independ-ence.   Unwise philanthropy, rather than the scientific relief measures of organized charity, is also productive of poverty.

As long as indiscriminate giving to professional mendicants flourishes, begging will be as profitable as working. The education of normal as well as of subnormal individuals should include among other ideals that of economic independence. Lack of industrial training and vocational guidance in our schools has been another contributory cause of poverty and crime. Until comparatively recent times it was difficult for a boy to receive training in a trade at public expense, unless he committed a crime and was sent to some reformatory. Statistics show a higher percentage of illiteracy and general ignorance among both paupers and criminals.

Defects in the political as well as in the economic and social environment produce poverty. Political corruption prevents the passage of desirable legislation or the adequate enforcement of existing laws. The ward boss, rather than organized charity, may give coal and food to the voter who is out of work, but the citizen whose vote is purchased so easily is sacrificing ultimate social welfare for his own immediate advantages. Legislation is no panacea for all social ills, and far more is necessary than wise laws and their proper enforcement. Nevertheless, they form an essential part of any scheme of social reform. The attitude toward government is changing and its sphere of activity is widening. The introduction of the factory system and the growing interdependence of all members of society have made labor legislation imperative. The former attitude of *laissez-faire* has been abandoned, and the government has actively interfered in the matter of working standards and living conditions. It has attempted to regulate such matters as hours and wages and to prevent the exploitation of women and children. It has sought to eliminate causes of poverty and to raise subnormal standards of living by such devices as minimum wage laws and social insurance.

7. Economic Ideal of Prosperity.—Prosperity is the opposite extreme to poverty, although both terms are relative. Prosperity may be defined as an abundance of commodities and of services. National welfare consists of many other things besides great national wealth, just as individual welfare consists of many other things beside an abundance of economic goods. Health, education, patriotism, spiritual ideals, and a multitude of other things might be mentioned. Nevertheless, national prosperity is one element in national welfare, just as a minimum of individual wealth is necessary to individual well being.

It should be remembered that prosperity is an economic ideal in the same way that democracy is a political ideal. Economic progress constantly advances the goal of national prosperity and permits higher standards of living to be enjoyed by all members of society. In spite of increased national prosperity and higher standards of living, a dynamic society will continue to strive for still higher levels of material well being.

It is generally conceded that America is a prosperous nation. Today she is the chief creditor of the world. Nature has been very bountiful to the United States, and our physical environment is rich in natural resources. Climate and soil are rich and diversified. Excellent waterways and rich mineral resources exist in abundance. In spite of considerable waste it may be said that America's adaptation to her physical environment has been fairly satisfactory. Our inventive genius and capacity for industrial organization are famous. The intelligence and skill of our workers are probably as great as anywhere else in the world. Although productivity per acre is higher in those countries which practise a more intensive cultivation of the land, productivity per man is higher in America than in most other countries of the world.

In spite of our seeming prosperity a number of economic maladjustments exist which mar our national welfare and limit our national prosperity. Individual prosperity and national prosperity are not synonymous. In a land of plenty, a surprisingly large number of families live in poverty. The scientific method takes nothing for granted and attempts to ascertain the causes of such a situation. It also seeks to determine the size of the national income and its actual distribution. Is it adequate in total size, and is it distributed in such a fashion that a decent standard of living may be enjoyed by all workers and their families? What is the basis in fact for our assumption of national prosperity and how may it be increased? What groups in society chiefly enjoy this prosperity? What is the extent of economic inequality and what are its causes and effects?

8. Achievement of National Prosperity.—Both increased national prosperity and increased individual prosperity are dependent on increasing the national income. Higher standards of living are conditioned by increased production, as well as by a more equitable distribution of the wealth produced. Anything which tends to increase the national income tends to raise real wages. Labor is bound to share to some extent in increased national prosperity and to suffer from any decrease in the national income. If a conflict of interests between individuals representing different factors in production results in such tacit or open industrial warfare that production suffers, the national income will be correspondingly reduced. Unfortunately most attempts of the workers to raise wages have centered solely about the distribution of wealth and the problem of economic inequality. It is sometimes forgotten that greater national prosperity requires increased production.

The national income may be increased in a variety of ways. In the first place, since increased production is contingent on improved economic and social organization, the cooperation of labor and capital is imperative. Limitation of output, unemployment, and strikes reduce the size of the national income. Again, increased production is dependent on an increase in acquired knowledge, by progress in the arts and by the process of invention and discovery. The conservation of natural resources is necessary for the national prosperity of future generations. Eugenic reform is also necessary for an improvement in the quality of our population and for the elimination of social debtor classes. In the last place, popular education is necessary for industrial training and for the cultivation of higher economic and social ideals. National prosperity is decreased by the existence of a leisure class of idle rich on the one hand, and a social debtor class of defectives, delinquents, and dependents on the other hand. Both extremes are outside the great working population of economic producers to whose efforts national prosperity owes its existence.

9. Nature and Size of the National Income.—The national income may be regarded as the flow of commodities and services produced by a nation within a given period of time. Wealth, on the other hand, represents the stock of goods in existence at any given time. Thus, the total material economic wealth of the United States in 1916 was valued by the Department of Commerce at about two hundred and twenty-eight billion dollars. The national income for the same year was estimated by the National Bureau of Economic Research to be about forty billion dollars.

"Our national wealth in material assets in 1922 was 321 billion dollars. This includes real property, live stock, machinery, agricultural and mining products, and manufactured products of all sorts."[1]

A number of factors must be considered in any estimate of the national wealth and income. A considerable portion of the national wealth and income finds its way into the hands of the government in the form of taxes and public goods. Governmental receipts or credits are turned into such things as battleships, roads, and schools. An increasing portion of the national wealth and income goes into collective consumption, which is represented by public goods and governmental services. This was discussed in Chap. XVII on Public Expenditures. Another portion of the national income goes into the formation of intermediate wealth or capital that is to be used in further production. Unless due allowance is made for the replacement fund of industry, duplication in calculation will occur and the national income will be exaggerated.

Moreover, real income must be distinguished from money income. Any evaluation of the national wealth or income over a period of years must be refined by taking into consideration the changes in the general price level. The increase in wealth or income, as expressed in dollars, may be apparent rather than actual. The real income is a flow of commodities and services for which money has been a medium of exchange and a fluctuating standard of value. It is obvious that this stream of the national income divides itself into branches of different sizes. To some families it brings automobiles, fine clothes, and various luxuries, whereas to other families it brings merely the bare necessaries of life.

The size of the national income of the United States was a matter of conjecture until rather recently. Individuals imagined that it was increasing, and speculated as to its adequacy. Within the past few years, however, the National Bureau of Economic Research has completed an exhaustive and scientific analysis of the income of the United States.[2] This estimate is as follows:

[1] Cf. DUBLIN, L. I., "Economics of World Health," Harper's Magazine, Nov., 1926.

[2] See also TAUSSIG, F. W., "The Interallied Debts," Atlantic Monthly, March, 1927. In this article Professor Taussig estimates that the national income in 1925 was about ninety billion dollars.

NATIONAL INCOME OF THE UNITED STATES[1]

1909..................	$27,100,000,000	1916	$39,200,000,000
1910..................	28,400,000,000	1917	48,500,000,000
1911..................	29,000,000,000	1918	56,000,000,000
1912..................	30,600,000,000	1919	67,254,000,000
1913..................	32,000,000,000	1920	74,158,000,000
1914..................	31,600,000,000	1921	62,736,000,000
1915..................	32,700,000,000		

Prosperity, like poverty, is a relative term. The determination of national prosperity therefore involves a comparison with other countries as well as with former years. Such comparisons will show that the national income of the United States is relatively large as compared with those of other nations, and that it is increasing in size.

A COMPARISON OF NATIONAL INCOMES IN 1914, JUST BEFORE THE WORLD WAR[2]

Nation	Total national income	Per capita income
United States..........................	$33,200,000,000	$335
United Kingdom.......................	10,950,000,000	243
Germany..............................	10,460,000,000	146
France................................	7,300,000,000	185
Italy..................................	3,890,000,000	112
Austria-Hungary.......................	5,350,000,000	102
Spain..................................	1,120,000,000	54
Australia..............................	1,260,000,000	263
Canada................................	1,460,000,000	195
Japan.................................	1,580,000,000	29

10. Adequacy of the National Income.—The adequacy of the national income is difficult to determine. The proper approach to such a problem is to divide the national income for a given year by the population figures and to compare the result with estimates of a minimum standard of living for that year. These

[1] *Cf.* "Income of the United States 1900–1919," vol. I, p. 143, and "Income of the United States, 1919, 1920, and 1921," p. 32. The above figures will not correspond to those in the first reference, because they are the revised estimates of the National Bureau of Economic Research which was issued in 1925.

[2] Summary of the estimates of various foreign writers compiled by Sir Josiah Stamp and adapted by National Bureau of Economic Research, "Income of the United States, 1909–1919," p. 85.

are generally expressed in terms of a family of five, and due allowance for this fact should be made in comparing them with per capita estimates of income. Before reaching any conclusions as to the increase or decrease of the per capita income, moreover, the rise or fall of the general price level must be considered, that is, per capita money income must be distinguished from per capita real income.

PER CAPITA MONEY INCOME OF UNITED STATES[1]

1909	$299	1914	$320	1919	$640
1910	307	1915	326	1920	697
1911	309	1916	385	1921	579
1912	321	1917	470		
1913	329	1918	537		

If one takes the above estimates of per capita money incomes and multiplies each by five, the per family income will be found to vary from about fifteen hundred dollars in 1909 to almost thirty-five hundred dollars in 1920. The per family estimates of income will be found considerably higher than the minimum estimates of standards of living for the corresponding years. We may say, not only that our real national income has been increasing more rapidly than our population, but also that it is now sufficiently large to permit a minimum standard of living to be had by all the families of the United States. Although the equal division of the national income would raise all families out of the poverty group, it would not be large enough to permit many luxuries or to allow a great extension of leisure time. The Utopian dreams of certain visionaries that an equal division of the national income would permit all individuals to live in comparative luxury and idleness is not borne out by the statistics of national income. Hence, prosperity is conditioned by increased production, as well as by more equitable distribution.

Although the equal division of the national income would temporarily eliminate poverty and guarantee to each family a minimum standard of living, it does not follow that such a policy would produce permanent social benefits. We are confronted with the possibly serious consequences of a modification in the institution of private property. The right to acquire wealth and to bequeath it to one's children has been a powerful stimulus toward increased production. The removal of this

[1] Revised estimate of National Bureau of Economic Research.

right through rash changes in the distribution of wealth, which savor of confiscation, might result in such a future decrease of the national income that it would become too small to permit the maintenance of existing standards of living. Economic inequalities, however, which are enormous in amount, and which are not based on the productive contributions of various members of our economic society are an important cause of social unrest. Let us now see how our national wealth and income are actually divided among the people of the United States.

11. Division of the National Wealth and Income.—The distribution of the national wealth of the United States has been studied by an analysis of the estates of decedents in Massachusetts and Wisconsin.[1] The population was divided roughly into three groups, the poor, the middle class, and the rich. The poor were those individuals who possessed little or no property. The line was drawn arbitrarily at estates of one thousand dollars. The poor were found to constitute 65 per cent of the total number, but to own only 5 per cent of the total wealth. The average value of their estates was slightly less than four hundred dollars. The middle class was defined as those leaving estates of from one to forty thousand dollars. The middle class was in turn subdivided into a lower and an upper middle class. The estates of the lower middle class varied from one thousand to two thousand dollars. The average estate was about fifteen hundred dollars. Although the lower middle class comprised 15 per cent of the total number of individuals, they possessed only 4 or 5 per cent of the total wealth. Thus, the poorest 80 per cent of the inhabitants of these two states during this particular period apparently owned less than 10 per cent of the total wealth. The upper middle class was defined to include those individuals leaving estates valued at from two thousand to forty thousand dollars. The average estate in this group was about nine thousand dollars. The upper middle class represented 18 per cent of the total population, but owned about 33 per cent of the total wealth. Rich individuals were defined as those leaving estates in excess of forty thousand dollars. The average estate for this rich group was one hundred and fifty thousand dollars. The rich comprised but 2 per cent of the total population, but they owned almost 60 per cent of the total wealth.

[1] *Cf.* KING, W. I., "Wealth and Income of the People of the United States."

The National Bureau of Economic Research studied carefully the distribution of the national income for 1918. The income tax returns for that year were of invaluable assistance, but the investigators were forced to supplement this information by original investigation among those individuals whose wages were too small to necessitate the filing of any income-tax returns. The results for 1918 are as follows:

INCOME OF THE PEOPLE OF THE UNITED STATES[1]

Income class, dollars	Number of persons	Per-centage	Amount of income	Per-centage
Under 0*...............	200,000	.5	$ 125,000,000	.2
0–500	1,827,554	4.9	685,287,806	1.2
500–1,000...............	12,530,670	33.4	9,818,678,617	16.9
1,000–1,500............	12,498,120	33.3	15,295,790,534	26.4
1,500–2,000............	5,222,067	13.9	8,917,648,335	15.4
2,000–3,000............	3,065,024	8.2	7,314,412,994	12.6
3,000–5,000............	1,383,167	3.7	5,174,090,777	8.9
5,000–10,000...........	587,824	1.6	3,937,183,313	6.8
10,000–25,000..........	192,062	.5	2,808,290,063	4.9
25,000–50,000..........	41,119	.1	1,398,785,687	2.4
50,000–100,000.........	14,011	.04	951,529,576	1.6
100,000–200,000........	4,945	.01	671,565,821	1.2
200,000–500,000........	1,976	.005	570,019,200	.98
500,000–1,000,000......	369	.001	220,120,399	.38
1,000,000 and over.....	152	.0004	316,319,219	.55
Totals...............	$37,569,060	100	$57,954,722,341	100

* This group represents those who reported net losses for the year 1918.

This study of income reveals in a very striking fashion the existence of glaring economic inequalities. Although the general price level has altered and the economic position of numerous individuals has changed, there is little reason for supposing that these figures for 1918 are not typical and that the problem of economic inequality is less now than formerly.

In 1918, over fourteen million people, representing almost 40 per cent of those individuals receiving incomes, received incomes of less than one thousand dollars; and over thirty-two million individuals, representing about 86 per cent of the total income receivers, received incomes of less than two thousand dollars

[1] From tables on pp. 136 and 137 of the "Income of the United States." Vol. 1.

a year. At the same time, one hundred and fifty-two individuals received incomes of one million dollars or more a year, and over seven thousand individuals received incomes of over one hundred thousand dollars a year. It would appear that the most prosperous 1 per cent of our population were receiving 14 per cent of the national income; the most prosperous 5 per cent were receiving nearly 26 per cent of the national income; the most prosperous 10 per cent were receiving nearly 35 per cent of the national income; and the most prosperous 20 per cent of the population were receiving about 47 per cent of the total national income.

These findings indicate that our national income, although fairly large and increasing in size, is divided among the people of the United States in a very unequal manner. The maintenance of comfortable standards of living is a problem of distribution as well as one of production. Individual prosperity and national welfare are conditioned not only by the existence of an adequate national income, but also by a more equitable distribution of the national income.

12. Causes of Economic Inequality.—An analysis of the causes of economic inequality brings us face to face with the biological and psychological problem of human differences, with the social problems of population and standards of living, and finally with the economic problem of distribution. As this is not a text on economic principles, we shall not attempt to sketch the law of variable proportions nor the theory of marginal productivity. The division of society into numerous noncompeting groups is very evident even in democratic America. The tendency of population to increase more rapidly in the lower income groups than in the higher income groups has created what has been termed the social pyramid. Within each labor group, the relative supply and demand forces affecting wages are very different.

Competition between these groups and the passage from one group to another is rendered difficult by differences in individual ability, education, skill, and training. Human differences will always persist because of the biological principle of variation. Equality of opportunity merely means that each individual in society be permitted to find his own level, that is, to advance along the lines of and to the limits of his particular abilities. A flat economic equality of wealth and income is not equality of opportunity. The latter would not eliminate economic competition, but merely regulate it. Equality of opportunity would recognize inherent individual differences, but would seek to eliminate social handicaps and those artificial advantages which the inheritance of large fortunes brings.

Certain causes of the concentration of wealth have been common to various countries, and to many different periods. American economic life during the Civil War and that of England during the Industrial Revolution possess certain points of similarity. A striking comparison between modern America and ancient Rome is also possible. Economic expansion was accompanied in both cases by growing inequalities in wealth. Such comparisons are interesting, although not scientific, because history never repeats itself in exactly the same way.

Forces[1] which have been stressed as making for economic inequality in America are monetary legislation, methods of taxation, and methods of railroad construction and finance. Unwise monetary legislation has sometimes caused inflation, which in turn has led to rising prices. Rising prices make possible profiteering on the part of a few, while the great masses of people are suffering from the increased cost of living. The use of indirect rather than direct taxes, the failure to use the principle of progression in taxation, and the reluctance to tax inheritances and large estates have favored the development of economic inequalities. We have noted the great governmental subsidies given to the railroads and the capitalization of franchises as sources of private profit. Nevertheless, it should be remembered that the railroad was originally regarded as a very speculative industry. Indeed, new industries, if successful, are generally accompanied by the growth of large fortunes. This is illustrated by the recent development of the automobile and the motion picture industry. Perhaps this incentive has been necessary to attract capital into new ventures which are characteristic of a dynamic society. Among the additional causes of the concentration of wealth may be mentioned[2] the unearned increment of land, especially in cities; the trust movement; war, with its inflation of the currency; war-time industries and high profits; the development of trustee devices, which permit the existence of the "dead hand" and the continued concentration of wealth; and, finally, economic inertia.

[1] Cf. SPAHR, C. B., "The Present Distribution of Wealth in the United States."

[2] Cf. ELY, R. T., "Evolution of Industrial Society," Chap. 14.

On the other hand, there are a number of forces which make for the diffusion of wealth.[1]   Among them are education for the masses; the public control of corporations; changes in taxation, such as progressive income and inheritance taxes; the development of the idea of property as a social trust; profit sharing and cooperation; sound currency with the reduction of inflation; public ownership or at least regulation of public utilities; labor organizations; miscellaneous institutions in the interest of the economically weaker elements of the community; and saving institutions and insurance, particularly social insurance.

Such lists of causes of economic concentration and of methods for the greater diffusion of wealth are neither final nor complete. The student should regard them merely as a starting point for his own thinking on the subject.

13. Effects of Economic Inequality.—There are a number of reasons why greater equality of income is desirable.   These may be classified as economic, social, political, and philosophical.

Economic production is determined by demand rather than by desire.   Economic demand may be defined as desire which is accompanied by sufficient purchasing power to make itself effective.   If incomes were evenly distributed throughout society, it might then be said with truth that production is determined by the wants of consumers.   Glaring economic inequalities, however, make it profitable for producers to satisfy the slightest whim of the wealthy and to ignore the pressing needs of the poor. During a recent famine in China that country exported eggs to America.   The desire for this food was greater in China, but the demand was greater in America.   Within a nation the same situation exists.   Pleasure yachts may be produced at a time when there is a serious housing shortage.   The quantitative distribution of the national income determines its qualitative character.   Hence, many individuals who are not socialists accept the economic ideal of the production of necessities for all before luxuries for a few.   Although this ideal requires the reduction of economic inequality, it does not imply a flat equality, nor the collective ownership of the instruments of production.   It is socialistic, but not socialism.   The more equal distribution of purchasing power will result in an increase of total consumption utilities without an increase in the total income, because necessities possess greater want-satisfying power than luxuries.   There-

[1] *Ibid.*

fore, a greater equality of income would increase total consumption utilities.

The demand for necessities is relatively stable and can be anticipated within a slight margin of error. Hence, this change in the character of the stream of national income would lessen some of the wastes of our present economic system. Expensive changes in fashion might be reduced, and a misdirection of production rendered less likely. Furthermore, a much more equitable distribution might result in increased rather than decreased production. Low wages are not synonymous with low labor costs. The poorly paid worker may produce not only less, but also proportionately less than the better paid worker. Wages are higher in America than in Europe, but labor costs are not correspondingly higher. Although inefficiency is a cause of low wages and low standards of living, it is also a result of them.

Great differences in income are productive of social instability, as well as of economic waste. Inadequate wages result in subnormal standards of living. At the same time, other individuals are indulging in luxurious leisure. Poverty and riches existing side by side have always been a fruitful cause of social unrest. The palaces at Versailles were erected by peasants who lived in huts. In modern America magnificent stables for horses and kennels for dogs throw their shadows across miserable houses in which numerous human beings exist. Each city has both spacious country clubs and slums, palatial residences and crowded tenements. Economic inequality results in social stratification and the formation of noncompeting economic groups. Equality of opportunity is a far-distant ideal for many individuals in the poorer classes. Social unrest finds a fertile soil in the ranks of poorly paid and irregularly employed workers. If the present economic order offers them no guarantee of a decent standard of living in return for faithful and honest effort, no harm can come to them by revolutionary changes. They become ready listeners to the glowing promises of socialism, radicalism, syndicalism and Bolshevism. On the other hand, steadily employed and adequately paid workers, who are able to own their own small homes and to keep the wolf from the door, form a conservative element within the community.

The chief social effects of economic inequality are poverty and subnormal standards of living. These in turn create other problems, such as those of women and children in industry. Unsani-

tary housing, insufficient food, clothing, and medical attention
are concomitants of low wages, which result in an increased death
rate. Infant mortality is a fairly good barometer of standards
of living. In certain American cities infant mortality rates were
found to vary inversely within certain limits with the size of the
family income. They were found to be twice as great in the
lowest income group as in the income group whose earnings
were considerably higher.

INFANT MORTALITY ACCORDING TO FATHER'S EARNINGS[1]

Earnings	Infant death rate per thousand
Under $450	168
450–549	134
550–649	118
650–849	108
850–1,049	84
1,050–1,249	64
1,250, and over	64

The inadequate wages of the heads of families cast their shadows
over the lives of the children who survive. A large proportion
of the children of pre-school age and of school age are actually
undernourished. Many suffer from remedial physical defects.
The money that is spent for food is often but a fraction of what
should be spent in order to rear a healthy child. Hence, certain
cities have maintained the free distribution of milk or the serving
of hot lunches in their public schools. Free dental and medical
service is also frequently provided. Although ignorance plays a
part in unsanitary conditions of living and ill health, the significance of poverty and low wages cannot be escaped.

Economic inequality may have serious political effects. The
existence of large fortunes may result in a perversion of governmental machinery and a corruption of public officials. The open
or secret miscarriage of justice often results. A great national
income and its flagrantly unequal distribution may convert a

[1] Eight American cities. Compiled from the *Sixth Annual Report* of the
Chief of the United States Children's Bureau, 1918, p. 11.

democracy into a plutocracy.   Such was the situation in ancient Rome.   Goldsmith's famous lines:

> Ill fares the land, to hastening ills a prey,
> Where wealth accumulates and men decay.

are frought with social and political, as well as poetic, meaning.

There are philosophical objections to inequality of income, as well as the economic, social, and political objections advanced. On the basis of abstract justice, why should one individual receive an enormous income and another a pitifully small one?   Let us assume that both are economic producers, and that each contributes to the national income according to his individual ability and opportunity.   Neither one's environment nor one's heredity is of his own making.   Prince and peasant have merely been dropped into different social surroundings.   The fact that one individual is born with an excellent physical constitution or with exceptional mental ability, whereas another individual is born with some physical defect or with feeble-mindedness, is no merit nor fault of his own.   Hence, communists have adopted another slogan, "From each according to his ability and to each according to his needs."   Such a simple analysis of production and distribution affords an excellent ideal, but it is beset with numerous practical difficulties and objections.   If one's income depends on the size of one's family, there is an economic incentive to the production of children rather than of economic goods. The "spawners" rather than the thrifty might inherit the earth.

14. Conspicuous Consumption.—It has been contended that the manner of consumption is as significant as the size and source of one's income.   In his "Gospel of Wealth," Andrew Carnegie developed the idea of great fortunes as public trusts.   His own life was simple and his tastes were frugal.   He returned to society a large portion of his income in the form of free libraries. John D. Rockefeller has likewise donated a large portion of his fortune to educational work and medical research.   It is difficult to overemphasize the social value of such wise donations. Society might never have done these things of its own accord. They represent collective consumption by private initiative. Such philanthropy, however, has been stigmatized as capitalistic feudalism and benevolent despotism.

All individuals, moreover, cannot resist the temptation to extravagance, idleness, and even dissipation, to which great fortunes make them susceptible. Their large incomes may force the productive process into what Ruskin has termed "illth" rather than wealth. Imitation is a powerful force in society and each social group looks longingly at the standard of living of the next higher income group. Sometimes the standard which is set by the so called "social set" is as shallow as it is wasteful. Its purpose may be the mere display of wealth with the consequent inference of superiority. Professor Veblen has termed this the "conspicuous consumption" of the "leisure class." The possession of a given commodity or the consumption of a certain service is not indulged in because of its direct utility to the consumer, but rather because of the social prestige which accompanies it. An individual may not enjoy automobile riding, but may relish the exercise of walking. Nevertheless, the possession of a limousine is an indication of prosperity. Going to the opera may gratify no love of music, but it affords the opportunity to wear expensive gowns, and hence to be considered one of the financial, if not of the cultured, elite. Economic success, which must be demonstrated by ostentatious consumption, gratifies the same human instincts of self-assertion as were formerly gratified by military success on the field of battle. Simplicity and frugality in the consumption of income by the wealthy classes would help in the formation of national ideals of thrift and economy. Poverty, on the one hand, and conspicuous consumption, on the other, call attention to the existence of economic inequalities.

15. Summary.—Social unrest is a characteristic of a dynamic society and arises from the consciousness of certain maladjustments and the desire to eliminate them. Poverty and economic inequality are ancient maladjustments and the source of considerable unrest. Poverty is a condition in which the income is too small to permit a minimum standard of living and the maintenance of health and decency. Pauperism implies dependency or the resort to charity. The older attitude toward poverty was that it was a necessary evil and attention was concentrated on the relief of the poor. The newer or scientific attitude studies the causes of poverty and seeks to eliminate them. The chief objective causes of poverty are to be found in the economic environment, although the social and physical environments are also important. There are numerous individual causes of poverty, but they are often the results of environmental conditions.

Economic society is stratified into a number of social groups. The position of an individual in one of the higher or lower income groups is determined not only by his inherent capacity, but also by his social environment. Although there is a constant passage of individuals from one group to another, there is little economic competition between the workers of these different groups. Their economic qualifications are as different as their social standards. The wages of any type of labor tend to be fixed by its relative supply-and-demand forces. The birth rate in the lower economic groups is considerably higher than that in the higher economic groups. Hence, we speak of the social pyramid.

A standard of living is a qualitative and a quantitative measure of economic consumption. It is a relative rather than an absolute concept, and varies greatly among and within social groups. Standards of living are conditioned by individual desires, individual or family incomes, and by the general price level. Inequality of income results in the enjoyment of luxuries by certain fortunate individuals while others are unable to obtain the bare necessities of life. The family is the usual unit of economic consumption, and family budgets are attempts to balance expenditures against income in order to secure the most economic consumption. A minimum standard of living is one which is sufficient to maintain health and working efficiency. Provision should also be made for saving, insurance, and a certain amount of recreation. Numerous studies of wages and standards of living testify to the inadequacy of the wages of a large portion of our adult male population to support a family with comfort and indeed with decency. The social results are poverty, child labor, subnormal standards of living, and infant mortality. The economic results are industrial inefficiency, discontent, industrial conflict, and radicalism.

Prosperity is the abundance of economic goods. National prosperity is one element in national welfare. It is an economic ideal in the same way that democracy is a political ideal. Poverty may exist in spite of great national prosperity, for individual and national prosperity are quite different. The national income is the flow of commodities and services produced each year. The United States is said to be a prosperous nation because its national income is relatively large. In spite of the confusion due to changing price levels and to increases in the population, the per capita real income of the United States has been increasing. It is highly desirable, however, that the national income be further enlarged by increased production.

Although the national income is sufficiently large to provide a minimum standard of living for all families, it is divided in a very unequal fashion. Large fortunes and poverty exist simultaneously. A relatively small portion of our population own a disproportionately large share of the wealth and receive correspondingly swollen incomes. Glaring inequalities in income result in corresponding differences in standards of living and prevent the production of necessities for all before the production of luxuries for a few. Most large incomes represent property, rather than service incomes in the form of wages or salaries. It does not follow, however, that they should be stigmatized as unearned incomes. The institution of private property with the right to acquire wealth and to bequeath it to one's children has been a powerful motive toward economic progress. Confiscatory legislation may result in a flat economic equality, but it may also decrease production and result in generally lower standards of living. On the other hand, it is desirable that enormous economic inequalities be lessened.

Collateral Reading

ATKINS, W. E., and LASSWELL, H. D., "Labor Attitudes and Problems," chaps. 13, 14, and 15.
BYE, R. T., "Principles of Economics," chaps. 17 and 20.
CARVER, T. N., "Essays in Social Justice," chaps. 6, 7, 12, and 14.
DOUGLAS, P. H., and LAMBERSON, F., "The Movement of Real Wages from 1860 to 1910" in "American Economic Review," Sept., 1921.
EDIE, L. D., "Economics: Principles and Problems," chaps. 19, 20, 21, and 23.
ELY, R. T., "Evolution of Industrial Society," chap. 14.
EPSTEIN, A., "Have American Wages Permitted an American Standard of Living?" in "*Annals* of the American Academy of Political and Social Science," Sept., 1921. (A summary of previous wages and standards.)
FAIRCHILD, F. R., FURNISS, E. S., and BUCK, N. S., Elementary Economics, chap. 41.
KELSEY, C., "Physical Basis of Society," chaps. 6 and 9.
KING, W. I., "Earned and Unearned Income," *Annals* of the American Academy for Political and Social Science, May, 1921.
MARSHALL, L. C., "Readings in Industrial Society," pp. 682–709.
TAUSSIG, F. W., "Principles of Economics," chaps. 47, 51, 53, 54 and 55.
TUGWELL, R. G., MUNRO, T., and STRYKER, R. E., "American Economic Life," chaps. 1 to 5.

References

Devine, E. T., "Misery and Its Causes."
Douglas, P. H., "Wages and the Family."
Gillin, L. J., "Poverty and Dependency."
Hollander, J. H., "The Abolition of Poverty."
Hunter, R., "Poverty."
King W. I., "Wealth and Income of the People of the United States."
Kyrk, H., "Consumption."
National Bureau of Economic Research, "Income of the People of the United States."
Parmelee, M., "Poverty and Social Progress."
Streightoff, F. H., "Standards of Living."
United States Census *Reports.*
United States Bureau of Labor Statistics, *Monthly Labor Review,* and special publications.
Veblen, T., "Theory of the Leisure Class."

Questions for Discussion

1. Why has not economic progress eliminated poverty?
2. Define and distinguish between poverty and pauperism.
3. Show the social significance of the problem of poverty.
4. What is national prosperity? Compare individual prosperity with national welfare.
5. In what ways may national welfare be advanced?
6. What is the basis in fact for the assumption of national prosperity?
7. Show the inequalities in the distribution of the national income and in the ownership of the national wealth.
8. Differentiate between property and service incomes. Is this distinction the same as that between earned and unearned incomes?
9. List some causes of economic inequality.
10. What do you understand by the social pyramid and the stratification of society into noncompeting groups?
11. What do you understand by the social debtor classes and by the leisure class?
12. Illustrate the effects of great economic inequalities.
13. Criticize the slogan of "From each according to his abilities and to each according to his needs."

Topics for Investigation

1. Poverty rates in city and country.
2. The elimination of free land and the problem of poverty in America.
3. The industrialization of the United States and the problem of poverty.
4. Subjective or personal causes of poverty (tabulate from case studies).
5. The analogy between economic competition and the struggle for existence. Does the poverty group represent the unfit?
6. The course of real wages during the World War and afterward.
7. The methods of investigation used by the National Bureau of Economic Research.

CHAPTER XXIII

ECONOMIC INSECURITY AND SOCIAL INSURANCE

The human risks of labor are even more important than the financial risks of enterprises, discussed in Chap. IV. In addition to the problem of economic inequality and the constant menace of inadequate wages and subnormal standards of living, the worker faces the problem of economic insecurity. These human risks of industry include industrial accidents, occupational diseases, dependent old age and unemployment. We shall discuss in turn the causes of these human hazards of industry, how they may be eliminated or lessened, and, finally, the possibilities of social insurance against them.

1. Extent and Causes of Industrial Accidents.—The absence of complete and reliable statistics makes it impossible to state definitely the extent and severity of industrial accidents in the United States. A number of very valuable studies, however, have been made from the available data of the Federal and state governments, as well as from the information of insurance companies. The future development of protective legislation for workers will be accompanied by the compiling of better statistics on the problems of safety and health in industry. The National Safety Council of Chicago estimated that there occurred in 1919 about twenty-three thousand fatal accidents, and five hundred and seventy-five thousand nonfatal accidents, involving four weeks or more of disability, and a grand total of three million accidents of all kinds in all industries in the United States. Since that time there seems to have been an increase rather than a reduction in industrial accidents. Moreover, it will be remembered that these figures refer merely to industrial accidents. If all fatal accidents were included, the total would be several times that of the annual twenty-five thousand deaths in industry. It would seem that the carnage of war can be exceeded by the carnage of peace. The annual industrial casualties in this country are often comparable to those of our troops during the World War. This is the price in human life that America is paying for speed, carelessness, ignorance, and indifference.

469

The immediate and particular causes of industrial accidents vary with individuals, occupations and particular instances. Nevertheless, there are certain groups of causes. These may be classed as mechanical, physiological, and psychological. Industrial accidents originate in the character of modern methods of production and in the failure of the human element in industry. Modern technology makes use of new and powerful forces of nature, such as steam and electricity. The power of destruction in these forces is as great as their power of production. Moreover, industry is now carried on by complicated machinery, rather than by simple tools. The average workman, who is able neither to understand nor to control these machines, confines himself to one simple operation. He is in constant danger from the ignorance or carelessness of thousands of other specialists. The interdependence of modern economic society may be well illustrated in the matter of industrial accidents. The mistake of a railroad switchman, or the carelessness of a fellow miner may result in the killing and maiming of thousands of other individuals. Furthermore, human nature is neither perfect nor automatic. Indeed, it is doubtful if it is entirely fitted for the task placed upon it by modern mechanical industry. The worker cannot adjust himself perfectly to the routine of his task, nor to the continuous and exact motions of the machine. Attention is bound to wander and fatigue to set in. This failure of the human machine to respond quickly and accurately is a contributory cause of industrial accidents.

2. Dangerous Trades and Occupational Diseases.—The risks of the worker include not only his liability to industrial accidents, but also to subtle occupational diseases. Dangerous trades include not only hazardous occupations, but also those which slowly but surely undermine the health of the worker. They result sometimes in specific diseases. Just as it is difficult to prove a certain ailment the result of an industrial accident, so it is sometimes difficult to trace ill health to a specific occupation. Nevertheless, there are certain occupations which may be classified as dangerous because of their physical effects upon the workers. Among them are industries which deal with poisonous substances. The effects may be relatively rapid or slow, and of various degrees of severity. Lead poisoning is a common disease among workers employed in the manufacture of white lead, and in industries where it is commonly handled. The result may be paralysis, insanity, or death at an early age. Several European countries have reduced the mortality in these trades by forbidding such practices as dry rubbing and by insisting upon other precautionary measures. Various other dangerous poisons, such as arsenic, are sometimes used in such industries as the manufactures of dyes, paints, and colors. Workers with phosphorous, used formerly in the manufacture of matches, sometimes contracted a deadly and characteristic disease known as "phossy jaw." This is one of the few dangerous trades against which our Federal government has legislated.

A second source of danger lies in exposure to an excessive amount of dust. The delicate membrane of the lungs may become spotted with foreign particles and lose its power of resistance to tuberculosis and other respiratory diseases. Coal mining is a dangerous occupation for this reason, as well as because of the liability to accident. Precautionary measures, such as screening the coal wet, will help to reduce the amount of dust in the air. An even more dangerous dust is that generated in metal grinding and other industries in which abrasives are used. Similar results may be produced from the fine lint in the air of textile mills. Suction tubes and blowers should be used to draw the contaminated air away from the workers. Where dangerous gases and poisonous fumes are produced, the work should be done under a hood which produces a forced draft. Masks should be used to protect the eyes from the glaring flames of acetyline torches. The management should install such devices and insist on their use by the employees.

A third source of danger lies in sudden changes of temperature and air pressure. Steel workers and those employed near hot furnaces are frequently the victims of pneumonia during the winter months. Workers underground in mines and tunnels sometimes develop a peculiar and characteristic disease due to changes in air pressure.

The reduction of occupational diseases, like the prevention of industrial accidents, calls for concerted action by employees, employers, and the general public. A campaign of education is necessary to overcome ignorance and indifference. Governmental legislation is similarly necessary, but uniformity is difficult because of the differences in state laws. A dangerous trade may merely be driven by law from one state to another. The American Association for Labor Legislation and other bodies have struggled to advance certain standards of safety and health throughout the United States. Legislative action should take the form of abolition or regulation of dangerous practises. Although the former victims of occupational diseases were often excluded from the benefits of workmen's compensation laws, there has been a growing tendency to regard them in the same way as the victims of industrial accidents. They should not be thrown upon the human scrap heap of industry and be forced to resort to charity, but they should be provided for by some sort of social insurance.

3. National Vitality and Health.—The safety-first movement has been paralleled by the public health movement. Although there are important industrial causes of accidents and sickness, both represent the same phase of a general social problem, that of national vitality. The examinations for military service during the World War revealed some alarming facts regarding the physical fitness of the men of our nation. According to a report of the Provost-Marshal General, only 65 per cent of the men between the ages of twenty-one and thirty-one were found fully qualified for military service out of over three million men examined between December, 1917, and September, 1918. Within this limited period of time and of this group of men in the prime of life, over a million were rejected. Later and more complete analyses of this great inventory of the physical fitness of the men of the nation were also far from reassuring. Other approaches to the problem of national vitality have been made through statistics of longevity and sickness. The average span of life has been lengthened appreciably by the progress of the medical sciences and in spite of the increasing hazards of modern life. Nevertheless, personal hygiene and public health measures do not keep pace with the discoveries of medical sciences. Although much is being accomplished, far more could be done by an aroused public opinion, which seeks to apply the teachings of public hygiene.

It has been estimated that the average number of persons who are sick in the United States is continuously about three million, and that nearly one-third of these are within the working period of life. This represents an annual loss in wages of a half billion dollars. If we add to this figure the costs of medical attention, the total economic loss from sickness approximates a round billion dollars a year. The annual economic savings through the prevention of needless deaths, illness, and fatigue probably exceed one and a half billion dollars at present, and may become several times as great.[1]

A more recent study of a half million insured individuals showed that about two per cent were constantly sick, and that the average individual in the United States loses about seven days each year from sickness involving inability to work. This means a loss of two per cent of current production. In round numbers this amounts to more than a billion and a quarter dollars annually. The total cost of the necessary medical care amounts to more than a billion dollars a year additional.[2]

The responsibility for this enormous amount of sickness rests not only with industry, but also with the individual and the community. One of the most significant movements of the day is the public health movement, which seeks to reduce the excessive amount of illness and to lengthen the span of human life. Like the safety-first movement, it should be fostered by the employer, the employee, and the state. Medical, surgical, and dental care should be provided for those individuals who are unable to pay for such professional attention. One of the greatest conservation problems of industry in particular and of society in general is that of human conservation, or the preservation of national vitality and physical fitness. Inasmuch as sickness and poor health are important causes of industrial inefficiency, an expenditure of public funds or corporate earnings in the interest of human conservation might be a wise investment. Moreover, sickness is also an important cause of dependency. Hence, a health program should be supplemented by some sort of sickness insurance for all workers, just as the safety-first movement has been supplemented by workmen's compensation laws.

4. Nature and Amount of Unemployment.—Unemployment may be defined as idleness on the part of the worker which is not due to his own physical, mental, or moral incapacity. It is important that we differentiate between the unemployed and the unemployable. The former are a problem of economics, the latter of sociology. The unemployed, as contrasted with the unemployable, members of society are those workers who are

---

[1] *Cf.* FISHER, IRVING, "National Vitality: Its Wastes and Conservation," pp. 741 and 742.

[2] *Cf.* DUBLIN, L. I., "Economics of World Health," in *Harper's Magazine*, Nov., 1926.

capable of labor, but who are unable to obtain employment, because of some maladjustment in the economic order over which they have little or no control.

Unemployment is enforced idleness, due to some friction in our modern, complex organization of industry. A vacation, on the other hand, is a voluntary cessation of work for the purpose of mental or physical recreation. Irregular employment and underemployment are phases of the general unemployment problem. In the former case, the worker is not steadily employed, and loses a great deal of time from work. For illustration, numerous coal mines do not operate continuously, but only several days in a given week. Underemployment, on the other hand, is irregularity or lack of employment to the extent that the worker is unable to earn wages sufficient to maintain a minimum standard of living. He is reduced to the level of the poverty group, or if he becomes a recipient of charity, to the level of the pauper group. The irregularly employed group gradually merges into the unemployable group.

Studies of the extent of unemployment show that it is a chronic as well as an acute problem of modern economic society. Although the amount of unemployment increases during periods of economic depression, there is a continuous volume of unemployment throughout the entire business cycle. Unemployment is both a temporary and a permanent economic problem which cannot be dismissed lightly.

Because of the great variations of employment among occupations, industries, seasons, and phases of the business cycle, it is difficult to make any general estimate of the volume of unemployment. Unemployment or irregular employment is generally conceded to be much greater in the unskilled than in the skilled trades. Again, the problem is more acute in the winter than in the summer, when agricultural occupations "take in a certain amount of the slack." The problem displays itself more intensely in the city than in the country. There is a general tendency of unemployed or migratory labor to flock to our cities during the winter months, and then to flow out again into the country during the spring and summer. In the meantime, urban demands on charity are taxed to the utmost. During the winter months of any year, the unemployed number several hundred thousand, and, if it be a year of business depression, the total reaches into the millions.

From one million to six million workers, exclusive of farm laborers, were idle continuously between 1902 and 1917, and the average number of unemployed was two and one-half million, or nearly 10 per cent of the laboring population.[1] The economic depression of 1920–1921 resulted in a Federal investigation of the unemployment problem. The United States Bureau of Labor Statistics completed a survey in August, 1921, which showed that the number of unemployed had gone over five and three-quarter millions. The most conservative estimate showed that three and a half millions, or a quarter of our industrial workers, were out of employment in June, 1921.

The Commission on Industrial Relations (1915) estimated that wage earners in the principal manufacturing and mining industries lose on an average from one-fifth to one-fourth of the working time during the normal year. In highly organized trades, from 7 to 20 per cent of all the members of the unions are continuously unemployed. It is perhaps conservative to estimate that 10 per cent of the skilled workers are unemployed in normal times and 20 per cent in years of depression. Among the unskilled workers the proportion of unemployed is far greater, because employment in many unskilled occupations is very irregular at best.

5. Social Costs of Unemployment.—Although the chief burden of unemployment rests on labor, its costs are also felt by the employer and by society in general. To the worker, unemployment means a loss of wages and consequently a lower standard of living. His meagre savings are soon exhausted, and he faces either starvation or charity as alternatives. Moreover, a general wage depression is apt to occur, because discharged labor seeks other fields of employment and tends to cut wages there. Unemployment also has a psychological as well as a material effect, which is equally demoralizing. Irregular employment makes impossible the formation of habits of steady industry and of thrift. It is hard for the unemployed to refrain from drifting with the tide into the great sea of casual labor. It is easy for the idle worker to take the next step to tramp, dependent, or delinquent.

Unemployment is costly to the employer as well as to the employee. Although he may have a greater financial reserve

[1] *Cf.* HART, HORNELL, "Fluctuation in Unemployment in the Cities of the United States from 1902 to 1917."

than the worker, a closed factory pays no dividends. Overhead charges, such as the interest on idle capital, soon eat up past earnings. Moreover, the "laying off" of workers tends to break up the employer's organization, and its general efficiency is lowered when increased output again becomes necessary. Even under normal conditions the continual "hiring and firing" of labor is expensive.

The heavy costs of unemployment to economic society in general are also important. Unemployment creates more unemployment. The majority of consumers are wage earners, and unemployment reduces their purchasing power. Consequently, their effective demand for various economic goods declines and production falls off proportionately. This, in turn, creates more unemployment, and the vicious circle is complete.

The social costs of unemployment may be read in the rates of crime and poverty. A period of industrial depression with consequent loss of employment will increase greatly the demands on public charity. There is also apt to be an increase in petty crimes against property, if not in the more serious crimes against persons. Unemployment among adult male workers may also be a direct or contributory cause of child labor and the entrance of women into industry. The desire to supplement the family income in this crisis may lead to the employment of women and children under sweat-shop conditions. The entire labor market may become "easy." Unemployment breeds discontent, radicalism, and a general spirit of unrest against the existing economic order. Laborers who are able and willing to work but who cannot find employment are easy converts to revolutionary doctrines and actions. On the other hand, regularity of employment and a living wage are the best practical arguments among laborers in defense of the *status quo* of modern industrialism.

6. Causes of Unemployment.—The causes of unemployment, like those of poverty, may be divided into objective or environmental causes, and subjective or personal causes. Among the latter may be mentioned such individualistic, contributory causes as intemperance, crime, indolence, disease, degeneracy, old age, and various physical, mental, and moral defects. We need not stress these factors, however, for they are more important in a causal analysis of the unemployable group than of the unemployed group. Again, subjective and objective causes are in reality merely two different ways of analyzing the same set of factors. As far as the economic problem of unemployment is concerned, these individual cases do not determine the fact of unemployment, but rather its incidence. Personal causes do not determine so much the existence or the amount of unemployment, but rather what individuals will be out of work at any given time.

Objective or environmental causes of unemployment may be grouped as physical, social, economic, and political. Although any such classification is both arbitrary and overlapping, nevertheless it is convenient. Under the physical environment may be mentioned such causes of unemployment as floods, earthquakes, storms, and droughts. Climatic diseases, such as malaria and hook-worm, may explain an apparent shiftlessness and indolence among the laboring population. Under the social environment may be noted such direct or contributory causes of unemployment as acquisitive standards of success and the presence of unsocial ideals among a so-called "leisure class." Under the political environment may be mentioned such factors as a corrupt or inefficient governmental machinery. Political chicanery may prevent an intelligent and aroused public opinion from expressing itself in legislative reform upon the subject of unemployment.

The most important causes of unemployment, however, are to be found in our economic environment. Any survey of the problem would be incomplete without some mention of the following factors: changes in methods of production, changes in the demands of consumers, seasonal occupations, the business cycle, industrial conflict rather than cooperation, changes in the tariff and international trade conditions. Strikes have been found to constitute a relatively small proportion of unemployment. Perhaps the most outstanding of these economic causes of unemployment are the changes in methods of production, the seasonal aspect of many industries, and the business cycle.

The seasonal aspect of many industries may be due to either physical or social causes. The seasonal character of agriculture, lumbering, canning, and construction work is due to climatic reasons. The slack and busy seasons in department stores and tailoring establishments are partially due to such social institutions as Christmas giving and Easter clothing displays. It will be remembered that in Chap. IV we differentiated between technological and marketing risks of industry. Changes in the demands of consumers represent a marketing risk which often causes unemployment to workers as well as financial losses to employers. The invention of machinery and other changes in methods of production represent technological risks. Labor has often opposed the introduction of machinery because it was thought to lessen the "lump of labor." Although a machine may displace particular workers, it does not lessen the total amount of employment. The lowered price of the machine-made article permits purchasers to spend what they save on this article for something else. Hence, a new or an increased demand for labor is created elsewhere. The introduction of machinery, like the entrance of women and children into industry, results merely in a shifting of men from one occupation to another. Although it does not lessen the total amount of employment, it may divert labor from those occupations in which employment is fairly steady into those occupations in which employment is more irregular. The invention of machinery makes production more roundabout and specialized; hence, employment is apt to be more irregular in those industries in which it is used.

7. Maladjustments in Labor Supply and Demand Equilibrium. Unemployment in the strict sense of the word could hardly have existed in a simple undifferentiated economic society. Industrial evolution, however, has generally been from the simple to the complex, and from an undifferentiated to a highly specialized economy. Today, few people satisfy directly by their own labor a given economic want. We consume daily the products of thousands of different specialized workers, whom we have never seen. Likewise, we limit the scope of our own labor to the production of one economic good, or rather to one particular phase of its production. This great cooperation of specialists is made possible only by a similar development of a very intricate mechanism of exchange. Division of labor has made possible the production of more goods, cheaper goods, and perhaps better goods, but it is fraught with certain grave dangers, one of which is that of unemployment. As long as this delicate machinery of specialized production and exchange works smoothly, all is well; but if friction occurs in some one part, the whole mechanism suffers. A Swiss watch is a better timepiece than a sun dial, but it gets out of repair more easily. Standards of living are higher today than before the Industrial Revolution and the poor man's table has on it delicacies from all parts of the world. Nevertheless, this very interdependence of our modern economic world makes it a veritable economic house of cards. A strike among the coal miners of Pennsylvania may force New England textile mills to close temporarily, and a drought in Argentina may put London dock hands out of work. The bobbed hair fad in the United States meant unemployment to 16,000 women hairnet makers in Chefoo, China. American tariffs and German reparations may decidedly affect the unemployment problem in England. We have passed from a local to a national economy and from a national to an international economy.

In Chap. II we saw that there is not only division of labor among individuals and geographical areas, but also division of labor spread over long periods of time. Modern economic production is not only specialized, but also roundabout and capitalistic. Labor was formerly applied directly to natural resources for the production of some finished consumption good. Today, labor first spends itself on the production of capital, and then later by its aid on the production of the desired consumption good. Capitalistic or roundabout production is far more effective than the direct method, but it is more susceptible of misdirection. In the latter case, great economic and human loss results. Between the raw materials of production and the finished article, many stages interpose. The wool on the sheep's backs may be sheared next year, carded several years hence, woven into cloth still further in the future, and not made into clothing until the next generation. In other words, production is not only capitalistic and roundabout, but it is carried on in anticipation of demand rather than in response to demand. This necessary condition enhances the possibility of error and the probability of change. Although general overproduction is impossible, it is possible to have misdirected production and the production of more goods than can be sold at a reasonable profit. The results are economic depression and unemployment. Because modern production is spread out over a long period of time, the original wants of consumers may change in the meantime. The demand, in anticipation of which production has been carried on, may vanish.

Most of this may be summed up by saying that unemployment arises from a disturbance of the equilibrium between the demand for and the supply of labor. Of course, labor creates its own demand for its own products. Producers are consumers and most consumers are producers. It is true that in the long run the demand and supply of labor must balance. But this economic principle, like any other scientific law, merely states a tendency. Modern industrial society is dynamic and not static. There are numerous opposing forces and obstacles. At any given moment there is not apt to be a perfect balance between the demand for and the supply of labor. Although the total supply and demand forces of labor balance in the long run, there are apt to be unbalanced industries, unbalanced localities, and unbalanced periods of production and consumption. Hence, the maladjustment of unemployment will show itself, now here and now there, but always somewhere.

8. Reduction of Unemployment by Private Enterprise.— Philanthropy affords merely temporary relief for the unemployed, and charity is a poor substitute for the "right to a job." Although relief measures of a wholesome sort should be utilized during an unemployment crisis, an effort should be made to reduce the volume of both acute and chronic unemployment to an irreducible minimum. A scientific attack on unemployment, like that on poverty, must begin with a causal analysis. Our brief survey of some of the chief economic causes of unemployment suggests measures for their elimination or amelioration.

The reduction of sudden changes of fashion would eliminate some of the irregularities in industry which result in overtime on the one hand and unemployment on the other. Popular education of men and women on this subject might do some good. Anything which helps to stabilize demand helps to reduce unemployment. In general, the demand for necessities is more stable than the demand for luxuries. Hence, the old slogan of "necessities for all before luxuries for the few" has a corollary on unemployment. Economic production in accordance with this social maxim, however, will remain only an ideal so long as glaring inequalities in incomes exist. Effective demand, it will be remembered, is composed not only of desire but also of purchasing power.

The growth of large business combinations and the decline of fierce competition tends to reduce fluctuations in the demand for labor. Monopoly price has the advantage of being relatively stable. Moreover, with the expansion of the business unit, the opportunities to correlate different industries is increased.

There is not the same tendency for each industry to create its own labor reserve of workers who are utilized in busy seasons but unemployed in slack times. The seasonal aspect of many industries cannot be eliminated, as it is determined not by our economy, but rather by physiography and weather influences. Nevertheless, much can be done toward the dovetailing of seasonal occupations. The combination of coal and ice dealer permits an employer to keep his corps of workers throughout the year. They can deliver ice in summer and coal in winter. In other cases, the correlation of industries may reduce unemployment, but not the migratory character of the labor. An illustration is farming in summer and autumn, lumbering in winter, and construction work in spring.

Irregularity of employment in many industries can be reduced by manufacturing for stock, that is, in anticipation of demand. Such a procedure involves greater risk on the part of the producer, because it intensifies the risk due to possible changes in the wants of consumers. It is safer for the employer to pass on a portion of this risk to his employees in the form of overtime in rush seasons and unemployment during slack seasons. Much could be done, however, by a mutual agreement on the part of manufacturers for the standardization of styles sufficiently far in advance. In the case of staple articles, it is possible to manufacture for stock far more than is done at present. By offering special discounts to pre-season purchases, risks and financial outlays might be reduced. It has been a common practise of coal dealers to sell coal at lower rates in the spring and summer months. If the householder will store coal in his own cellar during the summer months, he will help to stabilize production in the anthracite mines.

The reduction of employment due to general business depression brings us face to face with the problem of the business cycle. This in turn involves problems of money, credit, banking, and price levels. Without reviewing any of these, we may merely say that any economic reforms, such as the stabilized dollar, for illustration, which tend to eliminate or reduce business depressions tend automatically to reduce unemployment.

The invention of machinery and other technological changes will probably continue in the future as they have in the past. Indeed, economic progress is apt to be accelerated. A dynamic society will face a constant problem of adjustment. It is hoped, however, that technological advances will be accompanied by increased social control over industry, and that the adjustments will be conscious adaptations in the light of ethical considerations, with social welfare rather than private gain as the final goal. The scrapping of human machinery cannot be viewed with the same complacency in the future as in the past. The scientific management of a generation ago is being supplemented by the new science of personnel administration. An effective personnel department can do much to eliminate unemployment and labor turnover.

Educational as well as economic reform is necessary. It is possible that we have gone too far in the matter of extreme specialization. There is a dearth of the general all-around mechanic. It is costly to have children and young people in blind alley jobs rather than in industrial or commercial schools. Vocational guidance is now capturing our public school system. A number of educators, moreover, are insisting on general industrial or commercial education rather than on specific trade schools. It is hoped that education within and without the schools will increase not only the skill, but also the mobility of our future wage earners. This will enable them to shift more readily from one occupation to another. Industrial opportunity lies with the adaptable or the "double-barreled" man. It has even been suggested that an individual learn two allied trades instead of one specialized occupation.

9. Public Employment Bureaus and Public Employment.— Employment agencies cannot reduce unemployment by creating work, but they can aid in bringing together the jobless man and the manless job. They can reduce the aimless wandering from place to place of men out of work. Although private employment agencies conducted for profit have been operated for many decades, public employment bureaus represent a new function of government. The first European nation to develop a coordinated system of labor exchanges was Great Britain. The Labor Exchanges Act of 1909 authorized the Board of Trade to establish such bureaus. Administrative divisions were created and a labor exchange located in every important town. Close communication was maintained with the central office in London. In 1917, there was created a Ministry of Labor, which assumed charge of the system. The local offices function largely by means of advisory committees consisting of an equal representation of employers, employees, and the general public. The administrative machinery is correlated with that for unemployment insurance. Transportation charges are advanced to workers in order to get them to places of employment. Steps in the same direction of public employment bureaus have been taken by Germany, Denmark, and other European countries.

Most American states have passed statutes to regulate private employment agencies, for numerous evils and considerable corruption existed among them. Many states have also provided their own public employment bureaus, some of which are fairly successful. An attempt to eliminate by state law private employment agencies was held to be unconstitutional. During the World War, the Federal government inaugurated a nation-wide system of labor exchanges, which functioned with remarkable success until its appropriations were cut in the wave of post-war economy.

The relief of the unemployed by utilizing them on public works is an old economic device. It was tried shortly after the Revolution of 1848 in France, and was widely heralded as an application of the public work shops idea of the socialist Louis Blanc. As a matter of fact, it was nothing more than an attempt to meet an unemployment crisis by occupying the men at public construction work.

During the panic of 1908, several American cities used public improvement work as a means of alleviating unemployment. In the same year the Socialist party wrote this principle into its party platform. In 1909 the English Parliament passed a "development bill" with this object in mind. An Idaho law of 1915 required county commissioners to provide emergency employment upon public highways or elsewhere. In 1921 the state of California passed a law which provided for the extension of public works of the state during periods of extraordinary unemployment caused by temporary industrial depression.

Public employment during periods of industrial depression not only gives jobs to those out of work, but it also has a stimulating influence upon other industries. Thus, to employ men upon the construction of roads and buildings is also to create a demand for stone, cement, and structural steel. The indirect influence of public employment upon unemployment is as great as its direct influence. Society is the gainer, not only because of lessened demands upon charity, but also because of the economic savings resulting from having the work done in periods of low prices.

Unfortunately, many governments follow the example of private business. They spend and expand in periods of prosperity, and they retrench in periods of depression when tax payers feel poor. The result is an accentuation of the business cycle instead of a moderation of it.   Another mistake of the past has been the failure to plan ahead for municipal, state, and Federal projects. American cities have not, as a rule, had their future development planned in advance.   They have just grown.   It is not surprising that the employment on public improvements of those out of work has not been very efficiently utilized in the past from a civic point of view.   Nevertheless, such public employment has alleviated temporary distress.   The enormous amount of public improvements which take place yearly can be seen by a glance at Federal and state budgets or by totalling recent bond issues of American cities.   Although a certain portion of these public improvements is needed immediately, a large proportion can be deferred to the near future and used as an employment reserve for years of depression.

10. Social Insurance.—Early economists, as well as conscientious statesmen, held that workmen should provide for themselves against the various risks of industry.   They stressed individual thrift and pointed to personal savings as the ultimate reserve in cases of emergency.   Moreover, the higher wages paid in dangerous trades or in those in which employment was less regular were regarded as a natural compensation for the greater risks incurred by the workers in those occupations.   It has been found, however, that many workmen are financially unable to make sufficient provision for the event of serious accident, protracted illness, long unemployment, or old age.   Indeed, the risks of industry are often the greatest among those groups which are the least able to bear them.   The result is a final resort to public or private charity for many families in severe emergencies.

On the other hand, it might be possible by relatively small but regular contributions from all healthy and employed workers to pay benefits to individual workers or their families in times of distress.   This is the fundamental principle of insurance, namely, the removal of the financial incidence of some great loss from the particular individuals affected and its diffusion throughout the entire group.   It substitutes a small but certain premium for a large but uncertain financial loss.   If property insurance premiums are regarded as legitimiate costs of production, why should not social insurance make the products of dangerous trades more expensive? Thus, the worker bears the human risk, but passes the financial risk on to the consuming public in the form of higher prices. Social insurance is the application of the basic principle of life or property insurance to the human risks of industry. It cannot compensate an individual for the loss of an arm, except merely in the sense that it can pay him for the loss of earning power which the accident represents.

Although insurance against numerous risks of industry is provided by private insurance companies, by labor unions, and by various fraternal organizations, social insurance represents collective or group action. It implies not only the element of coercion, but also governmental regulation and subsidy. Because of the inability or the reluctance of workers to insure themselves against the various risks of industry, the state has been forced to intervene. Governmental action has been justified not only for humanitarian reasons, but also because social insurance has been regarded as more economic than charity. The premiums may come from the wages of the employees, from the profits of the employer, from the public treasury or from a combination of two or more of these sources. If the worker makes some contribution, it may be called insurance. If it is freely provided by the state, it represents a pension or a dole rather than insurance. The various types of social insurance are determined by the various types of industrial risks. Thus, we have compensation for industrial accidents, sickness insurance, old age pensions, and unemployment insurance.

11. Principles of Compensation.—In both Great Britain and America before the passage of workmen's compensation laws, the only redress of the injured workman was under the common law or various employers' liability acts. The burden of proof was on the victim of an industrial accident, who was forced to bring suit in court for damages against his employer. Litigation was uncertain, slow, and expensive. Lawyers known as "ambulance chasers" took promising cases, paid all legal expenses and divided the damages with the injured worker. It was held that the worker assumed the natural risks of the occupation when he took dangerous employment. If the accident was the result of the negligence of the worker himself or even of "a fellow servant," the employer was not liable. Damages might be awarded only in the event that the employer had not exercised due care in the management of the plant. Direct or contributory negligence on the part of the employer was difficult to prove. Moreover, there was little consistency in the awards of various judges. The damages awarded to injured workers varied greatly in amount for similar cases.

The principle of workmen's compensation laws is quite different. The worker is not forced to go into the courts and to bear the expense and delay of litigation. Moreover, an attempt is made to standardize the awards according to some graduated scale, which takes into consideration the seriousness of the injury and the former earning power of the worker. The question of responsibility for the accident does not enter. It is assumed that the worker will not deliberately injure himself in order to collect damages. The compensation for the victims of industrial accidents is regarded as a legitimate expense of production, which the employer can pass on to society in the form of higher prices. The insurance premiums which the employer is forced to pay are a reflection of the hazards of the occupation. Any reduction in the latter will be reflected in lower insurance rates. Hence, it has been found that the passage of workmen's compensation laws throughout the United States and elsewhere has given a tremendous incentive to the safety-first movement in industry. Industrial accidents are made expensive, and the employer is forced to accept his responsibility.

12. Workmen's Compensation Laws.—Industrial accident insurance is one form of social insurance which is now common throughout the United States. Although the general rule today it developed later than in Europe. Uniformity is lacking, however, because this legislation falls within the province of the individual states. Moreover, early workmen's compensation laws were held to be unconstitutional. Although there had been earlier laws in both Maryland and Montana, the first important workmen's compensation law was passed in 1910 in New York. Like its predecessors, it was declared unconstitutional, and held by the courts to represent the taking of property without due process of law. A constitutional amendment was adopted in New York, and another compensation law passed in 1914. Meanwhile, the state of Washington had passed in 1911 a workmen's compensation law. Although contested in the courts, the legal verdict in the state of Washington was the opposite of that rendered by the New York court, and the law was held to be constitutional. Within the next decade almost all the states and territories of the Union passed such legislation. The Supreme Court of the United States has held that workmen's compensation laws passed by the individual states are not violations of the Fourteenth Amendment of the Federal Constitution. As yet several southern states and the District of Columbia (except for Federal employees) have failed to pass such legislation. There is no Federal law on this subject, for such a national law would probably require an amendment similar to the proposed child labor amendment. There is, however, a Federal compensation law for workers engaged in interstate commerce.

The British workmen's compensation law was the model for most American commonwealths. It has been contended that the state-fund system of Norway is cheaper and more reliable than the British system of direct payment by the employer with optional insurance on his part in private companies. For large industrial states, mutual associations of employers under government regulation have certain advantages. This is the German system, but it has made little headway in the United States.

Not only the form of administration, but also the inclusiveness and the scale of payments of workmen's compensation laws vary greatly from state to state. Domestics and farm laborers are generally excluded. In some cases the victims of occupational diseases are not permitted to share the benefits of workmen's compensation laws. In the absence of uniform legislation, the upward standardization of benefits paid by various state compensation laws would be helpful. These are generally based on the wages of the worker, and the percentages vary with the seriousness of the injury. Most states have fixed maximums of from ten to twenty dollars a week. In many states there is a further time limit during which such benefits may be paid, at the expiration of which period even the totally disabled worker is denied further financial aid.

Workmen's compensation acts represent a distinct advance over employers' liability laws. Apparently the former type of social insurance has established itself in the United States. It is still necessary to secure such legislation in several of our states, however, as well as to raise standards generally to certain uniform levels. Numerous excluded groups, such as the victims of occupational diseases, should be included. In many states the scale of benefits should be raised and the waiting period shortened. State-fund systems are generally regarded as superior to private insurance companies for the administration of workmen's compensation laws.

13. Health Insurance.—Germany began its national system of compulsory sickness insurance with the law of 1883. As subsequently amended, this applied to all wage earners receiving two thousand marks a year or less. Just before the outbreak of the World War, over two-thirds of all individuals gainfully employed were included within its provisions. Employers were forced to purchase insurance stamps, equivalent to the necessary premiums and to see that they were regularly attached to the cards which all insured workers carried. Employers paid one-third of the costs of these stamps and deducted the other two-thirds from the workers' wages. The administration of this sickness insurance was placed in the hands of sick benefit associations, composed of employers, employees, and disinterested citizens, under the supervision of the Imperial Insurance office. Benefits were both medical and financial. They included free medical attendance, or admission to a hospital when necessary, free medicines, and such appliances as spectacles and artificial limbs. Half wages were paid after the third day of sickness and continued during the period of absence from work until a maximum of twenty-six weeks was reached. Funeral and maternity benefits, as well as pensions for widows and orphans, were included. German statistics showed that there was an average of eight days of illness for every person insured. Moreover, there seemed to be an increased proportion of sickness with the application of sickness insurance. On the other hand, there was a decided decrease in the death rate and in pauperism.

The experience of Germany induced Great Britain to utilize the weapon of social insurance in her war against poverty. The Workmen's Compensation Act of 1897 was followed by the National Insurance Act of 1911. Sickness insurance was added to the existing industrial accident insurance. Under this law every worker receiving less than one hundred and sixty pounds a year was required to be insured against illness. A system of stamps and cards was used, and the premiums were paid jointly by the employers and the employees. The responsibility for the enforcement of the law rested with the employers, who were required to see that the workers possessed insurance cards and that the proper stamps were regularly affixed. The worker originally paid three or four pence a week and the employer contributed almost an equal share, whereas in Germany the employer paid only one-third of the premium. Flat sums were specified in the British law for both premiums and benefits, as contrasted with certain percentages of the wages, as in Germany. Hence, it has been necessary for Great Britain to amend the original act and to increase the benefits as the general price level rose.

The benefits of the British system of sickness insurance were closely modeled after those of Germany and included free medical attention as well as financial assistance. The Health Insurance Act of 1911 was amended a number of times and greatly modified in 1920. All manual workers between the ages of sixteen and seventy were now included, as well as non-manual workers whose annual earnings were less than two hundred and fifty pounds a year. The male employee paid five pence a week, and the employer a similar amount. The government also subsidized the scheme by adding a sum equivalent to about one-fourth of the total. The insured male worker, certified by a physician as incapable of employment because of ill health, received fifteen shillings a week after an initial waiting period of three days. After twenty-six weeks of illness, this weekly benefit was reduced one-half but continued until the worker was able to resume his employment. The system is administered by a number of approved nonprofit-making societies under the supervision of the Ministry of Health. The worker may choose a commercial company, a trade union, or a friendly benefit society for the purpose of sickness insurance.

Although health insurance has passed the experimental stage in Europe, it has not found popular support in the United States. In spite of the enormous social and economic burden of sickness, this form of social insurance has not been adopted as yet by any of the states. Sporadic attempts at this type of legislation have been made, but they have been viewed as paternalistic. More-over, they have been viewed as difficult of administration and easy of abuse. Malingering, or the feigning of sickness, might occur in spite of certification by medical officers. The advocates of sickness insurance point out that sick benefits are decidedly less than the wages received, and that there is an initial exemption period of several days. The administrative problem is lessened by the elimination of minor ailments and short absences from the scheme of sickness insurance. Although the present outlook is not very promising, the future development of the public health movement in this country may be accompanied by compulsory sickness insurance.

14. Old Age Pensions.—In addition to the risk of accident and illness, the worker is confronted with the possibility of a dependent old age. Instead of the comforts which should surround the declining years of life, the aged employee is faced with loss of employment and a possible reliance on charity. Benevolent employers and certain large corporations have developed pension systems on their own initiative and for their own workers. National, state, and local governments have also generally performed this service for their aged employees. A number of fraternal societies and a few trade unions also pay old age benefits. There are, of course, private companies which pay annuities to those individuals who have insured themselves. Compulsory old age insurance, however, was unknown until Germany again took the lead in this form of social insurance in 1889. Employers were required to see that every employee over sixteen years of age had an old age card and that stamps covering the required premiums were regularly affixed thereto. The employer bought these stamps from the government and then gave the employee his stamp each week, paying half the cost himself and taking the other half from the employee's wages. The premiums were small, and the annuities correspondingly meagre. Consequently, the government added a subsidy to them.

Inasmuch as the worker paid a portion of the premium, the German system represents old age insurance rather than old age pensions. Denmark met the same problem in 1891 by a national system of gratuitous old age pensions. Great Britain also adopted the latter scheme after considerable study. Under the Old Age Pension Law of 1908, every wage earner of seventy years of age or over, who had lived in that country for the previous twenty years, whose total yearly income from other sources did not exceed thirty-one pounds and ten shillings, and who had been an industrious worker, might receive an old age pension from the state. The benefits varied from one to five shillings a week. This act was amended in 1919 and the maximum increased from five to ten shillings a week. Moreover, the pension was extended to all workers whose total income from other sources was less than forty-nine pounds, seventeen shillings and six pence. There are over a million persons at present in Great Britain who receive governmental old age pensions, and the majority of these are women.

Old age pensions are very common in the United States, but they are generally administered by private concerns for their own employees. They are usually contributory but subsidized insurance, rather than gratuitous pensions. The national government has compulsory and contributory old age insurance for its employees. The same is true of teachers and other employees of various states. There is, however, no national system of old age pensions which applies universally to all workers. Although several states have made attempts at this form of social insurance, little general progress has been made. The laws of Arizona and Pennsylvania have been held to be unconstitutional. The Pennsylvania law of 1923, which was modeled after the British Old Age Pension Law, was held by the courts of that state to violate a provision of the state constitution, which forbade the giving of gratuitous pensions to any individuals except those who had rendered military service.

The relative necessity and justice of old age pensions as compared with sickness insurance are difficult questions. The number of individuals affected by the former is undoubtedly less than the number affected by the latter. There is also less chance of abuse in the case of old age pensions. The administrative difficulty is almost as great, however, unless the system of gratuitous pensions is adopted. Old age pensions are preferable to charitable relief from the points of view of both society and the individual. They are more economical as well as more humane than the maintenance of the aged in almshouses.

15. Invalidity and Mothers' Pensions.—Invalidity insurance represents the payment of pensions to those who are incapacitated by some physical infirmity other than that of old age. The loss of sight or hearing may prevent an individual from remaining self-supporting. Such invalidity may not be the result of an industrial accident and may extend beyond the provisions or time limits of sickness insurance. In order to prevent the baneful effects of charity, the state might well pension such unfortunate members of society in proportion to their loss of earning capacity. Invalidity insurance merely pleads for the extension of the prin-

ciple of compensation, which developed first in industrial accidents. Thus, certain communities have provided that the blind
who are attempting to earn a living, and who are not recipients of
charity or of workmen's compensation, shall receive a stipend
from the public treasury.

Mothers' pensions are gratuitous payments by the state to
the needy widows and orphans of wage earners. Such pensions
are very small in amount and are restricted to those who have
practically no other means of support. The aim is to substitute
a pension system for charity, to lessen infant mortality, and to
prevent young children from growing up in homes of poverty
or orphan institutions. This is one form of social insurance
in which the United States has taken the lead. At the present
time, about forty states have enacted some kind of mothers'
pension laws. They are also in operation in several European
countries and in New Zealand.

16. Unemployment Insurance.—Unemployment insurance is
one of the most debatable forms of social insurance. It is the
most difficult to administer because of the ease of simulating
unemployment. Opponents of unemployment insurance have
stigmatized it as "Cæsar's bread," and as analogous to the free
distribution of grain in the Roman Empire, which produced
such dire social results. It is contended that unemployment
insurance will increase rather than decrease idleness. If men
are paid when they are out of work, they will be relieved of the
necessity of looking for work and will remain in idleness. The
friends of unemployment insurance reply that the amount which
is paid to the worker who is unemployed is less than his regular
wage, and that it is not sufficient to relieve him of the necessity
of seeking employment. Moreover, unemployment insurance
should be carefully correlated with a system of national labor
exchanges. Those who are receiving unemployment insurance
are listed with the public unemployment office and are offered
work when it can be found. Refusal to accept such work means
a loss of unemployment insurance.

Unemployment insurance has two objects—the relief of the
unemployed and the reduction of unemployment. It will be
remembered that unemployment in its strict economic sense
refers to enforced idleness on the part of the worker due to
objective causes in the industrial system. Consequently,
unemployment insurance attempts to alleviate the sufferings of

the worker due to circumstances beyond his control. To a certain extent, any scheme of unemployment insurance performs this object.

In the second place, unemployment insurance usually seeks to reduce the total volume of unemployment in the same way that workmen's compensation laws seek to reduce the volume of industrial accidents. This second aim of unemployment insurance will be accomplished only if the system is carefully planned and administered. Otherwise, unemployment insurance fails in this important objective and may even increase rather than decrease unemployment. Scientific unemployment insurance must be carefully distinguished from a "dole" system. The latter consists of an indiscriminate distribution of funds to individuals out of work. Scientific unemployment insurance assumes that the volume of unemployment in various trades is carefully studied and the relative risks of unemployment mathematically computed. Hence unemployment, like industrial accidents, becomes an insurable risk. The premium which is paid by employer and employee in any occupation depends not only on the wage received or the total wages paid, but also on the risk of unemployment in that particular occupation. Hence, there is an incentive to employers to reduce slack and busy seasons and to spread the volume of unemployment as evenly as possible throughout the year. Scientific unemployment insurance seeks to lessen the labor reserve and the number of casual workers. If no attempt were made to require premiums in proportion to the dangers of the occupation, workmen's compensation laws would not have succeeded in reducing the volume of industrial accidents. So-called unemployment insurance has sometimes operated as an equal drain on all employers and the general public, without putting the financial burden upon the backs of irregular occupations.

Although no nation had attempted unemployment insurance before the passage of the British National Insurance Act of 1911, several European cities had done so. Perhaps the most famous plan was that of the Belgian city of Ghent, commonly referred to as the "Ghent system." The most significant feature of this plan was that it was administered by the local trade unions. Indeed, this form of public unemployment insurance was little more than a municipal subsidy to the existing trade union unemployment dues and benefits. This municipal contribution was justified on the ground that it relieved the drain on local charities and avoided their demoralizing effects on individual character. The administration of this unemployment insurance by the labor unions, which contributed substantially to the fund, lessened the abuses by individual members.

17. British Unemployment Insurance Experience.—The British government has had the greatest experience with national unemployment insurance. In 1911, this type of social insurance, as well as sickness insurance, was added to the existing workmen's compensation laws and old age pensions. The National Insurance Act of 1911 provided for a system of unemployment insurance in certain trades and for approximately two million wage earners. It was correlated with the previously established public labor exchanges. The administration of this unemployment insurance was somewhat similar to that of the sickness insurance established at the same time. The employer was required to see that every worker included in the act possessed an unemployment card and that each week he affixed a five-penny stamp to it. These stamps were purchased from the post office and half the costs were borne by the employer and the other half deducted from the wages of the workers. Benefits of seven shillings a week for a maximum of fifteen weeks were paid those workers who could not obtain work from the public employment offices. It was hoped that public unemployment insurance would stimulate rather than eliminate unemployment benefits on the part of trade unions.

The National Insurance Act has been subsequently amended a number of times. In the years which followed the war, the disturbance of international trade and the cessation of war industries created the most serious unemployment problem in the history of Great Britain. Consequently, the provisions of unemployment insurance were changed to meet the existing emergency. A new act was passed in 1920 and amended in 1921. The original provisions of the law were changed in many respects. The number of workers included, the scale of premiums paid, and benefits received have steadily increased. At the present time, about twelve million workers are covered by unemployment insurance, of whom over three million are women. The original premium of a few pennies per week has been increased to almost a shilling for employees and for employers per each employee. Benefits have been similarly increased from seven shillings to

almost a pound.   In 1924, for illustration, each male worker
paid eighteen cents a week and the employer twenty cents
a week for each worker on his payroll.   At that date, the weekly
unemployment benefit amounted to $3.75 for a man, with
$1.20 additional if he had a dependent wife, and with a shilling
extra (twenty-four cents) for each dependent child.   The
benefits to unemployed female workers were considerably less.
The time limit has been increased to twenty-six weeks[1] within a
given year with the possibility of still further extension.   Furthermore, it has been necessary for the state to subsidize the process.
Appropriations from the public treasury amounted to one-fourth
of the joint contributions of employers and employees.   Furthermore, an amendment of 1922 provided that if these funds were
insufficient to meet the necessary unemployment benefits, they
might be still further increased by additional subsidies from
the government.

The British unemployment system is under considerable criticism at home and abroad.   The labor leaders contend that the
benefits are inadequate and seek still further increases.   Manufacturers contend that the differences between unemployment
benefits and regular wages are not sufficient to induce men to
work.   The present law increases rather than decreases the
amount of unemployment.   The chief difficulty seems to be that
no distinction is drawn between various occupations and that
there is no attempt to base the unemployment premiums on
predetermined unemployment risks.   Partly because of this
fact and partly because of the large drain on the public treasury,
the present system has been said to represent an industrial
pension system or a "dole" rather than scientific unemployment insurance.   The present character of unemployment
insurance in Great Britain must be explained in terms of the post-
war industrial crisis.   Whether future years of economic recovery
will change or will eliminate the present unemployment insurance
remains to be seen.   Most students of the problem feel that it
cannot continue indefinitely in its present status without serious
national injury.

There has been little tendency to imitate the British experiment
in unemployment insurance, although Italy passed a similar
act in 1920.   Within the United States there has been some
agitation in favor of scientific unemployment insurance.   Upon

[1] This brought it into conformity with the time limit of sickness insurance.

two occasions an unemployment insurance bill was presented before the legislature of Wisconsin, although at the present time no state possesses such a law. A number of trade unions have endeavored to provide unemployment benefits. Furthermore, certain socially minded employers have attempted not only to reduce unemployment, but also to establish a scheme of unemployment insurance for their own workers. Illustrations are the Dennison Company and the Delaware and Hudson Railroad. Moreover, certain firms have attempted to meet the situation by the payment of what are known as dismissal wages. If the employee is discharged through no fault of his own, but merely because of lack of work, he receives a bonus at the time of his separation from the services of his employer.

18. Summary.—Industrial accidents and occupational diseases represent a serious form of human waste in industry. The national vitality is also impaired by the tremendous amount of general sickness, which can be reduced by modern hygienic measures. The economic losses, as well as the individual costs, create a serious problem of human conservation. The statement of the problem suggests methods of approach. The safety-first and health-in-industry movements seek to reduce the human costs of industry to an irreducible minimum. The cooperation of the employee, the employer, and the state is necessary for the realization of this ideal. Remedial, as well as preventive measures, are also necessary. Provision must be made for the victims of the hazards of modern industry. These include medical or surgical care and educational or rehabilitation work, in order that the injured worker may become economically independent so far as possible. Financial assistance in the form of social insurance is also necessary.

Unemployment is enforced idleness on the part of the workers. The unemployed are to be distinguished from the unemployable. The unemployment problem displays itself most acutely in the city, in the winter months, and in periods of economic depression. Although varying in intensity, there is a permanent problem of unemployment. This is due primarily to a lack of perfect and continuous adjustment in the demand for and the supply of various kinds of labor. This arises from the complexity of modern industrial society, which is characterized by extreme specialization, the use of machinery, and the capitalistic or roundabout method of production. Specific causes of unemployment are

changes in methods of production, changes in the wants of consumers, seasonal occupations, the business cycle, industrial
conflicts, and changes in the tariff and international trade.   The
labor reserve is a human reservoir from which industry draws
its workers whenever necessary.   The organization of modern
industry results not only in the existence of a large number of
irregularly employed workers, but also in the existence of a
considerable body of migratory labor.   The alleviation of unemployment by philanthropy is merely a temporary expedient.   A
scientific approach to the problem necessitates a removal of the
chief causes so far as possible.   The deferring of public works
until a period of economic depression will help both directly
and indirectly the problem of unemployment.   Although public
employment offices cannot create employment, they can help to
adjust the existing supply of labor to the existing demands for
it.   They can serve as effective clearing houses and eliminate
some evils of the present system of private labor exchanges.
Unemployment insurance is a final resort for the irreducible
minimum of unemployment.

The common generalization that the employer assumes the
risks of industry is not entirely true.   Although he may assume
important financial risks for the capital invested, which may
justify the existence of profits, the worker bears many of the
so-called human risks of industry.   There is no guarantee to
labor of a living wage or of regular employment.   In addition
to the constant hazard of occupational accidents or sickness,
there is the spectre of a dependent old age.   For the financial
compensation of those individuals who are the victims of the
hazards of modern economic organization, social insurance has
been developed.   This is an application of the principles of
insurance to the human risks of industry, the financial incidence
of which is diffused throughout society in general.   Although
often voluntarily undertaken by private corporations and by
trade unions, social insurance implies the element of compulsion
and governmental supervision.   State subsidy is also justified
because of the reduction in the number of appeals to public and
private charity.

Workmen's compensation laws provide for the remuneration
of victims of industrial accidents in proportion to their loss of
earning power.   They are a distinct advance over the older
employers' liability acts, because the employee is no longer

obliged to bring suit, nor to prove the direct responsibility of the employer. Although compulsory sickness insurance has developed in Europe upon a wide scale, it is almost unknown in America. Dependent old age may be avoided by either old age pensions, as in Great Britain, or by old age insurance, as in Germany. Neither has made much progress in America. Perhaps the most debatable type of social insurance is that of unemployment insurance. Great Britain is the chief illustration of this national experiment. The theoretical fear of paternalism, on the one hand, and the practical fear of abuse, on the other hand, have militated against the extension in America of other forms of social insurance except that against industrial accidents. Mothers' pensions to dependent widows are common in many states, but the limited appropriations available restrict their extension to all deserving cases. Invalidity insurance seeks to apply the principle of compensation to the victims of nonindustrial accidents and sickness.

Collateral Reading

ATKINS, W. E., and LASSWELL, H. D., "Labor Attitudes and Problems," chaps. 11 and 12.
CARLTON, F. T., "History and Problems of Organized Labor," chaps. 11 and 17.
COMMONS, J. R., "Trade Unionism and Labor Problems," part 1.
COMMONS, J. R., and ANDREWS, J. B., "Principles of Labor Legislation," chaps. 6, 7 and 8.
FAIRCHILD, F. R., FURNISS, E. S., and BUCK, N. S., "Elementary Economics," chap. 51.
FETTER, F. A., "Modern Economic Problems," chap. 23.
FURNISS, E. S., "Labor Problems," chaps. 2, 3, and 7.
HAMILTON, W., "Current Economic Problems," pp. 554–586.
SEAGER, H. R., "Principles of Economics," chap. 32.
WATKINS, G. S., "Introduction to a Study of Labor Problems," chaps. 10, 11, and 26.

References

American Association for Labor Legislation, *Quarterly Review.*
BEVERIDGE, W. H., "Unemployment, a Problem of Industry."
BLANCHARD, R. H., "Liability and Compensation Insurance."
DAWSON, W. H., "Social Insurance in Germany, 1883–1911."
EASTMAN, C., "Work-accidents and the Law."
EPSTEIN, A., "Facing Old Age: A Study of Old Age Dependency in the United States and Old Age Pensions."
Federated Engineering Societies, "Waste in Industry."
FISHER, I., "National Vitality, Its Wastes and Conservation."

FRANKEL, L. K., and DAWSON, M. M., "Workingmen's Insurance in Europe."

FRANKEL L. K., and FLEISHER, A., "The Human Factor in Industry."

GIBBON, L. G., "Unemployment Insurance."

HART, H., "Fluctuations in Unemployment in Cities of the United States, 1902-1917."

KELLOR, F., "Out of Work."

LESCHIER, D. D., "The Labor Market."

National Industrial Conference Board, 1921. "The Unemployment Problem."

RUBINOW, I. M., "Social Insurance."

SEAGER, H. R., "Social Insurance."

THOMPSON, W. G., "The Occupational Diseases."

United States Bureau of Labor Statistics, *Bulletins* 207, 249, 183, 195, 157, and 206.

United States Commission on Industrial Relations, *Report* of 1916.

United States Report of President's Conference on Unemployment in 1921.

WOODBURY, R. M., "Social Insurance."

Questions for Discussion

1. Show the significance of the problem of industrial accidents.

2. What are some typical dangerous trades and why?

3. Outline some of the chief sources of danger in industry.

4. Show the significance of the problem of national sickness.

5. Compare workmen's compensation laws with employers' liability acts.

6. Define social insurance. What are its essentials?

7. Make out a case in favor of compulsory health insurance in the United States. Point out the objections.

8. Show the different methods of administering workmen's compensation.

9. Compare old age insurance with old age pensions.

10. Compare the necessity and dangers of sickness insurance with those of old age insurance.

11. Make out a case in favor of unemployment insurance. Indicate objections.

12. What are the essentials of scientific unemployment insurance?

13. Define unemployment.

14. Differentiate between the unemployed and the unemployable.

15. Explain what is meant by the incidence of unemployment.

16. Differentiate between unemployment as an acute problem and unemployment as a chronic problem of industry.

17. Outline the social costs of unemployment.

18. Outline causes of unemployment in the physical, social, and political environment.

19. Explain unemployment as a maladjustment in the demand for and the supply of labor.

20. Outline concrete causes of unemployment in our economic organization.

21. Suggest remedies in each case.

22. Show reasons for the existence of migratory labor and the dangers of this situation.

23. Discuss public improvements as a scientific measure for the problem of unemployment.

24. What are some advantages and disadvantages of public employment bureaus?

Topics for Investigation

1. The exhaustion of free land and the problem of unemployment in America.
2. Unemployment and the business cycle.
3. The dovetailing of seasonal industries.
4. The machine and the problem of unemployment.
5. Unemployment and changing fashions.
6. The reduction of the labor reserve for unskilled labor.
7. Public employment bureaus in America.
8. Public employment bureaus in Europe.
9. Unemployment and the demands upon charity.
10. Public workshops in France during the Revolution of 1848.
11. The post-war unemployment problem of Great Britain.
12. The reduction of mine accidents.
13. The rehabilitation of industrial cripples.
14. Merits and defects of the workmen's compensation law of your state.
15. British unemployment insurance since the war.
16. Germany, the pioneer in social insurance.
17. Mothers' pensions in the United States.

CHAPTER XXIV

HUMAN CONSERVATION AND LABOR LEGISLATION

1. Social Problems of Industry and Federal Legislation.— In addition to the maladjustment of inadequate wages and subnormal standards of living, we have seen that workers are subjected to such risks of industry as industrial accidents, occupational diseases, dependent old age, and unemployment. Social insurance is designed to lessen poverty and the economic insecurity of workers. Other maladjustments of industry include child labor, the exploitation of women, the sweat shop, and excessive hours of work. In this chapter we shall consider these problems of human conservation and continue our story of labor legislation. We shall see that the state has interfered in the matter of child labor, women in industry, and excessive hours of toil. Governmental regulation, however, has been undertaken by the individual states rather than by the Federal government. Hence, the same absence of uniformity that characterized laws of social insurance is also characteristic of child labor laws, minimum wage laws, and laws for the regulation of hours and working conditions.

The United States is a Federal government with a written constitution. Congress possesses only those powers which are specifically given to it in the Constitution. All residual rights and powers are vested in the several states. The small but important provision in the Constitution which gives to Congress the power to regulate interstate commerce has been the legal rock on which has developed Federal control of the railroads and Federal regulation of the trusts. The progress of social and humanitarian legislation in the United States has been retarded by the fact that these matters fall largely within the jurisdiction of the individual states. Labor legislation, with which this section of the text deals, is essentially state legislation; hence, uniformity is well nigh impossible. It is possible for strict legislation within one state to cause an industry or industries to seek refuge across the state boundaries. This threat has often been

501

sufficient to defeat within a given state the passage of a reform bill. Federal legislation is the only method of securing uniformity, and in most cases Federal legislation requires a constitutional amendment. Such is the case with the problem of child labor.

The early amendments to the constitution, which are known as the Bill of Rights, were designed to preserve the individual liberties of our citizens against the encroachment of the Federal government. Thus the Fifth Amendment provides that Congress shall not deprive a citizen of life, liberty, or property without due process of law. The Fourteenth Amendment, which was designed to give the Negro rights of citizenship, provides that no state shall pass a law depriving any citizen of the same rights of life, liberty, and property without due process of law. As the right of property has been held by the courts to include freedom of contract, it is difficult for either the national government or any state to pass a law abridging the contractual freedom of any citizen. It has been held that certain labor laws interfere with this legal right of freedom of contract; hence, these constitutional protections have sometimes meant that the actual economic freedom of the worker has been sacrificed to his theoretical legal rights.

The police power of the state has been called on to justify the passing of social legislation which seems to encroach on individual liberty. The police power of the state is its right to pass legislation or to enforce executive mandates when the common needs of the group require that individual liberty be sacrificed to the safety, health, or welfare of the group. All of these legal considerations present themselves in a study of labor legislation. There seem to be special reasons for the interference of the state in the case of women and children. For years men have had the ballot and have been organized into unions to press their claims. Women and children have been less successful in fighting their industrial battles and have been subjected to tremendous exploitation. It is a legal fiction to speak of the freedom of contract of a child or of any other relatively helpless party to the contract. Hence, the state has been forced to resort to child labor laws and to such expedients as minimum wage laws for women. The police power of the state has also been successfully utilized to justify the passage of labor legislation concerning general working conditions and hours of labor. On the other hand, the passage of laws regulating wages, especially the wages of adult male workers, has generally been viewed by the courts as a violation of freedom of contract and as an unwarranted extension of the police power of the state.

2. Problem of Child Labor.—Child labor has been defined as the work of children under conditions that interfere with the physical development, education, and opportunities for recreation which children require. It is the working of children at unfit ages, for unreasonable hours or under unhealthful conditions.

The factory system in America produced social problems similar to those of England. With the development of the textile industries in New England, the evils of women and children in industry made their appearance. Idleness had no part in Puritan traditions, and a century ago it was regarded as philanthropic to give work to women and children in the new factories. Alexander Hamilton and other early protectionists made use of this argument in their plea for the establishment of industries in America. The opening of our mines, however, was not attended by such horrors as prevailed in England a century ago. The industrialization of the United States did not take place until a full half century later than in England, whose experience may have had some influence in shaping public opinion in this country. The beginning of manufacturing in this country, however, found children under sixteen years of age working twelve, thirteen, and even fourteen hours a day. The situation improved gradually because of remedial legislation. Nevertheless, the improvement was sporadic, for the United States, unlike Great Britain, is a Federal government and the matter of child labor legislation is within the province of individual states. With the recent growth of an industrial South, evils of child labor have appeared in this new manufacturing section. Again, much cotton is picked by both women and children, for this problem is agricultural as well as industrial.

The problem of child labor today is no longer an English or an American problem. It has become a world problem. The United States, Germany, and more recently Japan have become industrialized. Moreover, cotton factories and other manufacturing industries are springing up in India, Egypt, and China, as well as in many of the smaller states of Europe. Very often there is neither legislation nor an enlightened public opinion to interfere with the exploitation of the human as well as the natural resources of these countries. Recent observers in the Orient report that child labor conditions there may be found to parallel those in England a century ago.

3. Extent of Occupations, and Earnings of Children.—For many reasons it is extremely difficult to estimate the amount of child labor. The number of children reported legally at work varies greatly from the number of children actually at work. The problem is also complicated by the existence of part-time work and the varying age definitions of children. According to the census of 1900, there were one and three quarters million children, and according to the census of 1910 almost two million children, between the ages of ten and fifteen years, who were gainfully employed. Of this number about one-third were working girls. The conclusion of the World War in 1918 and the absorption of several million men into industry resulted in a considerable decrease in the volume of child labor. It was probably accelerated by the economic depression of 1920. Nevertheless, the census for 1920 showed over one million children from ten to sixteen years of age at work in factories, canneries, agriculture, mining, and other industries of the United States. Nearly four hundred thousand of these million working children were between the ages of ten and fourteen years. The somewhat smaller number of children reported as gainfully employed by the census of 1920 was due to the existence at that date of a Federal child labor law which was later declared unconstitutional, as well as to the general economic depression of that year.

All studies of child labor reveal the fact that the earnings of children are pitifully small. Except for the war period, former averages were from three to five dollars a week. This seems hardly sufficient to supplement the family income to any great extent, nor to warrant the loss of educational opportunity which it involves.

The character of child labor can be seen by a study of the occupations in which it plays a considerable part. It may be said that children enter almost any industry, from which they are not excluded by law, and in which their unskilled labor and limited physical strength can be exploited. Their occupations may be divided into three great groups: manufacturing, mercantile, and agricultural. Children of the cities are found in great numbers in department stores and mills, where employment certificates are generally required. On the other hand, children do a considerable amount of labor of which there is no record.

Some of this is legal, but much of it is illegal. Industrial home-work or the sweat shop claims many children who are unable to obtain employment certificates to work in factories. The number of children in agriculture and in many other occupations is far greater than the recorded number of those gainfully employed.

4. Causes and Effects of Child Labor.—The minute subdivision of labor which accompanied the introduction of machinery lessened the need for craftsmen and skilled laborers. Little strength or intelligence is required to feed and attend many machines in the modern factory, which labor can consequently be performed by children. Moreover, such labor is plentiful and cheap. An indifferent public opinion is a second factor. Although cheap goods sometimes take a fearful toll in the health and welfare of the workers, sweated goods can easily be sold. Organizations, such as Consumers' Leagues, have inaugurated a campaign of popular education to inform the public of the social cost of certain commodities. It maintains an honor list of firms whose working conditions are satisfactory and which therefore warrant public patronage. A third factor in the problem of child labor is the necessity for self-support. Poverty is a cause which demands the child's wages to supplement the family income. In the fourth place may be mentioned an unsatisfactory school system. The child may be glad to leave school as soon as it is permitted to do so by the compulsory school law. School discipline is necessary, but it may be found irksome. The subjects taught may be neither practical nor interesting. The modern school, however, is providing a curriculum sufficiently diversified to appeal to the needs and capabilities of various groups of children.

The effects of child labor may be viewed from three angles: first, the effects on the child; second, the effects on society; and third, the effects on industry. The physical effects of child labor are frequently unfortunate. Childhood is the period of physical growth which requires an abundance of fresh air, freedom, and activity. The monotony of repeated operations of the same character is a poor substitute for the self-expression of play and the intellectual training of the school. Again, the moral atmosphere of the working child is often bad. At best, child labor is apt to stunt the physical, intellectual, and moral growth of the individual child. In the second place, must be mentioned the injurious effects on society. Child labor tends to break up the family life by removing the child from his normal place in the home. The young wage earner may become independent of parental authority. At best, his opportunity to rise out of a blind-alley job is limited, and he gradually becomes accustomed to low wages and low standards of living. It must be remembered that the present army of child workers will become the fathers and mothers of the next generation. In the last place, must be considered the effects of child labor on industry. In the long run, child labor is not always the cheapest from either the economic or the social point of view. It lowers the efficiency of the worker, because a dollar earned before the age of fourteen years must be subtracted several fold from later earning capacity. Moreover, the labor of children is wasteful and dangerous. Their inefficiency is a frequent source of both human and economic loss. In general, little can be said to justify the existence of child labor in any enlightened community.

5. Child Labor Legislation.—The first attempt at child labor legislation in this country was made in Massachusetts, in 1836, when a law was passed providing for the instruction of children employed in factories. It is significant that the motive was education, rather than health and recreation. In 1842, the working day for children under twelve years of age in Massachusetts was limited to ten hours a day. A number of states had child labor laws on their statute books by the time of the Civil War. For the most part, however, these laws were unenforceable. There was generally no effective system of factory inspection, and only "wilful" violations were punished. After the Civil War, however, the state of Massachusetts again took the lead in the child labor laws of 1866 and 1867. Manufacturing industries were forbidden to employ any children under ten years of age, and children from ten to fifteen years could not be employed for more than sixty hours a week. An adequate system of inspection was provided, as well as penalties for violations of the law. A minimum of schooling was also required.

The real impetus for the legal protection of child workers did not develop until the opening of the present century. In 1903, Illinois introduced the eight-hour-day for children under sixteen years of age, and set a new standard for future child labor legislation. A National Child Labor Committee was organized in 1904, which urged reform and suggested model laws for enactment.

Although each of the states now has some sort of law on the subject of child labor, they vary greatly in their provisions. Most state laws agree in the legal minimum age definition of fourteen years, but they vary as to hours of work, occupations, and certain important exemptions. There are at present as many child labor laws as there are individual states. Massachusetts, Illinois, Ohio, and New York, for illustration, have comparatively good child labor laws. Pennsylvania in 1915 passed an act which decidedly improved the situation in that state. On the other hand, children are still legally permitted to work ten hours a day in a number of states, and even longer in North Carolina and South Carolina. A half-dozen states still permit the employment at night of children under sixteen years of age. A happy omen for the future is found in the creation of a Federal Child Labor Bureau and the still more recent proposal of a Federal child labor amendment. The development of compulsory school attendance laws is also making great inroads on the evils of child labor.

In spite of the absence of uniformity in the laws of various states, it is generally agreed that there are certain fundamentals in all satisfactory child labor laws. Various welfare bodies have attempted to standardize these essential requirements and to draft model but flexible child labor laws. Adequate legislation must not only be precise in its language, but it must also provide effective machinery for the enforcement of its various provisions. A salaried corps of inspectors should be created with power to prosecute violations of the law. While many employers seek to cooperate in enforcing the laws, others have been guilty of evasion.

It is generally agreed that a model child labor law should cover certain well-defined points. The maximum working day should be one of eight hours. Night work should be prohibited and a closing hour fixed. The minimum age at which a child should be permitted to work should be fourteen. Some states still have a limit of twelve years of age and certain southern states make a further exception in the case of the children of pauper parents. Children employed between the ages of fourteen and sixteen years should have duly signed working papers. The state laws on child labor should be correlated with those on compulsory education. No children should be permitted to enter dangerous trades, and these should be carefully specified in the law.

As there are constitutional obstacles to the passage of a Federal child labor law,[1] the only legal redress for the problem lies in the passage of a constitutional amendment. Public sentiment finally crystallized to such an extent that in 1924 a child labor amendment was drawn up and passed by both houses of Congress with the necessary two-thirds vote. Arkansas was the first state to ratify the proposed twentieth amendment and it was hoped that three-fourths of the states of the Union also would soon give their consent. Strong opposition developed, however, and a number of states rejected this Federal amendment. Thus Massachusetts, the home of child labor legislation, refused its ratification of the proposed twentieth amendment.

It should be remembered that this child labor amendment is only an enabling measure, by virtue of which the Federal Congress may, if it so desires, pass a child labor law. Although it limits the authority of the individual states in this regard, it does not prevent them from passing additional laws on the subject of child labor. It is quite unlikely that any child labor law which might be passed by Congress would be extreme in its provisions. It is merely hoped to standardize child labor legislation and to provide a legal "dead line," in the sense of a minimum standard for conditions of child labor throughout the country. Child labor laws of many progressive states would continue to be in advance of these minimum requirements.

The text of the first two sections of the proposed child labor amendment reads as follows:

Section 1. The Congress shall have power to limit, regulate, and prohibit the labor of persons under eighteen years of age.

Section 2. The power of the several States is unimpaired by this article except that the operation of State laws shall be suspended to the extent necessary to give effect to legislation enacted by the Congress.

It does not follow from these provisions that a Federal child labor law would select the outside age limit of eighteen years.

6. Women in Industry.—The problem of women in industry is not new, because woman has always been an important factor

---

[1] In 1916 a Federal Child Labor Law was passed, which prohibited the shipment in inter-state commerce of the products of child labor; but the law was declared unconstitutional in 1918. The Revenue Act of 1918, approved 1919, provided for an excise tax of ten per cent on the products of child labor. This law was also declared unconstitutional by the Supreme Court in 1922.

in economic production. The early development of the arts, such as the manufacturing of pottery and the weaving of textiles, was largely woman's share in primitive culture. The new feature is the employment of women outside the home as operators of power machinery. When the Industrial Revolution brought an end to manufacturing by hand under the former domestic system, women as well as children became workers under the new factory system. The economic causes of woman's entrance into industry are often the same as those affecting children, and the social consequences are somewhat similar. For physical reasons the efficiency of women in certain industries is not so high as that of men, although in other kinds of work she may surpass him. Again, her health and vitality are more seriously impaired by the strain of industry than are those of man.

From the standpoint of society, the effects of the employment of women may be unfortunate, especially in the case of mothers forced to leave small children. A function of the family is that of socialization, or the preparation of children for their larger life in society. This cannot be accomplished in a family which is impaired by the absence of its mother or children in industry. However, mature women cannot be denied their right to economic independence and self-support, for this movement is but a part of the larger field of political and social equality into which women have entered. Nevertheless, it is necessary to protect them in the exercise of their new freedom. Therefore, laws have been passed to regulate the industries into which women may enter, so that their surroundings may be healthful and sanitary. The wages of women, like those of children, have often been pitifully small, for both groups have generally been unorganized and in an unfortunate bargaining position. The police power of the state has been used to justify legislation in behalf of both women and children, because of their peculiarly helpless position and because of the unfortunate social consequences of their industrial exploitation. There exists, however, as great a discrepancy in the laws of the different states as to the working conditions of women as on the subject of child labor. Moreover, the courts have also declared unconstitutional many laws designed to protect both women and children in industry.

The growing number of women in industry can be seen from the following figures from the United States Census reports. It gives the number of women gainfully employed and their ratio to the total number of females over ten years of age in the general population.

WOMEN IN INDUSTRY

	Number of women gainfully employed	Percentage of total female population over ten years of age
1880	2,647,000	15
1890	4,005,000	17
1900	5,319,000	19
1910	8,076,000	23
1920	8,500,000	21

Not only has the number of women in industry increased, but also their ratio to the total number of women and to the total number of all individuals gainfully employed.

The entrance of women into industry and commerce raises the question as to what extent, if at all, they are displacing men. It may be said that women, in general, have been employed in addition to men rather than instead of men. The spending of the wages that women receive creates a demand for labor elsewhere. Women may eliminate men from a particular occupation, but their employment does not lessen the total "lump of labor." It must be remembered that women and children were producers under the domestic system. The Industrial Revolution merely changed the location and the character of their work. Women constitute a fairly elastic labor reserve. They enter industry in periods of expansion, but withdraw or are forced out in periods of economic depression.

7. Occupations of Women.—There has been a great change in the character of the occupations of women, as well as an increase in the number of women in industry. The qualitative aspect of the problem is just as interesting as the quantitative. The occupations of women may be grouped under the five following great divisions: (1) domestic service, (2) agriculture, (3) industry, (4) commerce and business, and (5) professional life. Domestic service employs a large number of women, larger perhaps than statistics would seem to indicate. Moreover, it has been exempt from many laws dealing with women in industry. Although domestic service was one of the first occupations open

to women, it has become relatively less important. American women have not engaged in agriculture in the same way that European peasants have; nevertheless a large amount of fruit, berries, and cotton is picked by female labor.

It is in the last three groups of occupations, however, that the great change has come. With the advent of the Industrial Revolution, women, like children, went to work in the factories. This is the problem of woman in industry in the strict meaning of the expression. Of more recent years, however, the problem has broadened considerably. Women have invaded commerce, business, and the professions. They have been motivated by other reasons than economic pressure to increase the family income. The only profession formerly open to women was that of teaching. The great universities, however, have now begun to open their doors to women who desire to study law, medicine, and the new profession of social service. A generation or two ago women were scarcely seen in the mercantile pursuits, but now they are taking the places of men as clerks, stenographers, and saleswomen. Since the age of marriage has advanced, women have utilized such positions to provide themselves a means of support until they enter upon the oldest and noblest of all professions—that of home-making. There has also been a growing tendency to retain the position after marriage. Many women desire economic independence secured through a professional or a business career. In most cases, however, women are simply loaned to industry.

8. Working Conditions and Hours.—The problem of hours and working conditions is even more important with women and children than with adult men. Woman's work is not so apt to be finished when she leaves the factory or the office. Moreover, she is more susceptible of fatigue than is man. For these reasons as well as because of the greater possibility of exploitation, the law has been more ready to limit the employment hours of women than those of adult male workers. As we shall soon see, these laws vary greatly in different states. Although the legal eight-hour day for women has been introduced in several states, the nine- and ten-hour day frequently prevails. Social and biological reasons make desirable the eight-hour day and the six-day week for women in industry. Nevertheless, excessive hours, overtime employment, and night work are very common among women workers. They are employed frequently in open or secret defiance of existing statutes. The United States Women in Industry Service in 1918 made a study of the working conditions of over twelve thousand women workers in Indiana. The result showed that 30 per cent of these women had a working day of ten hours or more. This was normal and did not include overtime. An industrial survey of almost nineteen thousand women workers in Virginia in 1919 showed that 46 per cent of those studied were working ten hours or more per day.[1]

The general working conditions of women are as important as the number of hours that they are employed. Conditions in this respect are also far from satisfactory. The Women in Industry Service of the United States Department of Labor in 1918 drew up certain standards for women in industry which were subsequently endorsed by the United States War Labor Policies Board. It gave us a well-formulated set of standards concerning the employment of women. The eight-hour day and the forty-eight-hour week were specified and home work was proscribed. The cooperation of workers and employers was sought for the maintenance of existing laws and the passage of better laws. Desirable working conditions were also insisted upon and specific recommendations made. Although working conditions vary in different industries and places of occupation, there are surely some common standards of decency and comfort. Seats and rest rooms should be provided for women workers, as well as sanitary toilets and wash rooms.

9. Low Wages of Women.—It is a matter of common knowledge that the wages of women as well as the wages of children are often very small. It has frequently been true that women have received less money than men for the same work. The Federal Census of Manufacturers in 1905 indicated that 18 per cent of women employees over fifteen years of age were receiving under four dollars a week, 50 per cent under six dollars a week, and almost 80 per cent under eight dollars a week. Professor Persons made a study of the income of women wage-earners in 1915 in the United States and found that 75 per cent of them were receiving less than eight dollars a week and that these small wages were often still further reduced by unemployment and time lost through sickness. He further pointed out that the average wage for male workers at about the same time was four dollars a week higher, or 50 per cent more than for

[1] Cf. the Monthly Labor Review, August, 1920, pp. 99 and 100.

women.[1] Even today, the wages of many women are insufficient to support themselves, and hopelessly inadequate for the support of a family. On the other hand, they may be sufficient for "pin money" or to help supplement the family income.

The low wages paid to women workers are the result of a number of causes. The United States Commission on Industrial Relations (*Report* of 1916) in its final conclusions puts the matter somewhat as follows: The low wages paid to men have made it imperative that women enter industry in order to help support the family. There is also a tendency of employers to substitute women for men because they will accept lower wages and are less likely to protest against undesirable conditions. Finally, the introduction of improved machinery makes exceptional skill and strength unnecessary. The causes of the low wages paid women have been outlined as follows by Professor Watkins: (1) nature of the positions, dexterity required but no great skill; (2) inferior physical strength of women; (3) their relative immobility; (4) their comparatively lower cost of subsistence; (5) frequent dependence upon other members of the family; (6) indifference to the acquisition of adequate industrial training and experience; (7) lack of organization; (8) greater cost of employing women due to the numerous legal restrictions; (9) lack of appreciation of their own services; (10) lack of demand because of the crowding of women workers into a relatively few industries; (11) tradition or custom; (12) political weakness until the recent acquisition of the franchise.[2]

10. The Sweat Shop.—An important phase of the problem of women in industry is the sweat shop. Although sweated trades are frequently those in which women are employed, the problem is not exclusively such. Old men, young children, and the infirm of both sexes and all ages are also represented here. It may be said that the sweating system exists wherever there is an abundant supply of labor helplessly dependent upon unscrupulous employers. It is merely an extreme form of economic exploitation. Although machinery is sometimes used, the sweat shop is not a part of the factory system. Indeed, one of its most characteristic features is that the work is not done in large supervised factories, but in the homes of the sweaters or in the

[1] *Cf.* "Women's Work and Wages in the United States" in "Quarterly Journal of Economics" Feb., 1915, p. 232.

[2] *Cf.* WATKINS, G. S., "Introduction to a Study of Labor Problems," p. 156.

rooms of the workers. For this reason some students of the problem have regarded the sweat shop as a modern survival of the domestic system of manufacturing which antedated the Industrial Revolution and the factory system. The fact that it is industrial home work makes supervision and regulation difficult.

Although there are many sweated industries, such as the manufacture of cigars and artificial flowers, the clothing industry is a good illustration. The system existed in practically all our large cities where there was a plentiful supply of cheap, immigrant labor. Before the development of any organization among the garment workers, the sweat shop flourished in the Russian Jewish section of New York City. The essence of the system is the farming out to competing contractors of material cut for garments which, in turn, is distributed among the individual workers to be sewn up into finished garments. The cutting of the cloth is generally done under the direct supervision of the manufacturer, and the pieces when tied into bundles are delivered to the contractors, who have agreed to make them up at so much per garment. The contractor or "sweater" may furnish a room, the "sweat shop," and have the work done there under his supervision, or he may distribute the garments among the workers to be finished in their own homes. In either case there is a complete absence of collective bargaining, and the sweater makes a wage agreement with the individual worker. The sweater's profit lies in the margin of difference between the contract price and the wage cost of each garment.

The causes of the sweat shop evil are those common to the employment of women and children. The work is simple in character, and the chief requirement of the labor is cheapness. The competition for industrial home work among certain unfortunate groups in society reduces its remuneration to a mere pittance. What is "pin money" to one woman may be subsistence to the widowed and aged. The infirm, the crippled, and the whole group of partially employable may be utilized by the sweater in busy seasons. The seasonal aspect of many industries is also partially responsible for the sweat shop. Large manufacturers hesitate to install capital which cannot be used continuously. The small establishment or the sweat shop may be utilized to take care of a temporary increase in demand. Again, the existence of large groups of isolated or ignorant labor, such as the immigrants in our large cities, facilitates the development of the sweat shop.

The social results of this economic situation are unfortunate. Wages are not only low, but also unequal for the same amount of work. Self-interest impels the sweater to drive the hardest possible bargain with every worker, and he is in a position to take advantage of their individual misfortunes or ignorance. During the Spanish-American War, for illustration, a quantity of standard army trousers was manufactured under this system. The result was that within the city of Philadelphia the piece wages paid to the workers in different shops varied from thirty-five to seventy-five cents a garment. Other results of the sweating system are long hours of work and irregular employment. During a busy season such as Easter, garment workers toil far into the night, in spite of the fact that they may have had scant employment in the previous weeks. Finally, the conditions of work under the sweating system are generally miserable. The wearers of fashionable, tailored to measure clothing are usually ignorant of the surroundings in which their garments were finished. Conditions of employment in many sweat shops are dangerous, not only to the workers, but also to consumers and the general public. As the work is located in the homes of the sweater or in the rooms of the workers, adequate factory inspection is impossible.

The very nature of the sweat shop makes remedial legislation difficult. The attempt has been made to require licenses for all premises on which the sweating trades are conducted. This offers the possibility of inspection. In the interest of public health and safety, the police power of the state may invade the homes of its citizens. Under the licensing system, contractors are held responsible for the work done in unlicensed premises. A large corps of inspectors is necessary to make such legislation effective. Moreover, it seeks to remedy only the working conditions, for it cannot affect the evils of low wages and long hours. These have been attacked by other legislation for women, such as minimum wage laws. The sweat shop has been more susceptible of attack by organized labor than by state legislation. Low wages in sweat shops mean low wages in factories. Organized labor has been consistent in its efforts to eliminate rather than to ameliorate the sweat shop. The Amalgamated Clothing Workers and the International Ladies' Garment Workers have included prohibitions against industrial home work in their joint agreements.

11. Protective Legislation for Women.—Child labor legislation has been paralleled by the development of protective legislation for women workers. Because women as well as children were employed on a considerable scale in the manufacture of textiles, these industries were among the first to be regulated by the states in which they flourished. In the wave of humanitarianism which swept the country just before the Civil War, the organized women workers of New Hampshire secured the ten-hour law of 1847. Other New England and Middle Atlantic States followed, but the movement came to naught because the laws specified that the ten-hour day prevail "in the absence of an express contract requiring greater time." Employers took advantage of this loophole and made the signing of a blanket contract a condition of employment. It is important that all protective legislation be carefully worded, for the existence of any "joker" in the text of the law may nullify its purpose.

Effective legislation for women did not appear until a decade or two after the Civil War. We may date the era of protective legislation for women from the passage of the Massachusetts law of 1874, which limited the number of hours of employment of women to ten daily and sixty weekly. As only "wilful" violations could be punished, however, this law did not really accomplish its purpose until 1879, when it was amended. Similar laws were passed by other states in the closing years of the nineteenth century. It was contended that these laws interfered with an individual's right of freedom of contract. In 1908, a crisis was passed, when the United States Supreme Court upheld the constitutionality of the Oregon ten-hour law for women workers, and viewed it as a legitimate exercise of the police power of the state. The effects of this legal victory were powerful and immediate. The Superior Court of Illinois reversed its decision of a decade before and declared that a law of that state, which limited the number of hours that women might be employed in certain industries, was not class legislation and therefore not unconstitutional. In 1915, an eight-hour law for women was similarly sustained in the state of California. Apparently a national victory had been won.

In only a few states today are there no legal restrictions as to the number of hours that a woman may be employed. In some states the eight-hour day is specified, in others the nine-hour day, and in still others the ten-hour day. In some states the maximum number of hours is expressed on a weekly basis and varies from forty-eight to sixty hours per week. In other states there is a combination of the daily and weekly basis. In many instances the maximum number of hours is prescribed for only certain classes of industries, as, for illustration, manufacturing or certain specified manufacturing industries. In most states an exception to the law is made in the case of women employed in agriculture or domestic service. The laws of a number of states absolutely forbid the employment of women in dangerous and unhealthy occupations, such as mining. In many states the employment of women at night is either forbidden or limited. The tendency has been to eliminate or to reduce overtime on the part of women workers by a legal insistence on excessive rates of pay for these hours of work. In order to eliminate the sweat shop, a number of states have legislated against industrial home work for certain industries, except for members of the immediate family who live on the premises. Working conditions for women are even more a matter of legislation than working conditions for men. Some of the recommendations of the Women in Industry Bureau of the Department of Labor have crystallized into legislation. Proper sanitation, ventilation, and fire protection require, however, not only adequate laws, but also adequate factory inspections. Some states have passed laws against the employment of women for several weeks before and after child-birth.

12. Minimum Wage Legislation.—The minimum wage law represents still another attempt at the legal protection of women in industry. Its avowed purpose is to secure a living wage and to prevent any employment at less than this minimum level. Although sometimes applied to adult male workers, the scope of minimum wage laws in this country is generally limited to women workers. They developed as a weapon of last resort against the sweated industries.

Minimum wage laws may be either general in their application or limited to particular groups of workers in specific occupations. They may either prescribe a flat rate of pay as a minimum or proscribe the paying of wages less than sufficient to maintain a minimum standard of living. In the latter case there must be some provision in the law for the creation of a permanent administrative board to determine from time to time what constitutes a minimum standard of living and, hence, a minimum wage. The constantly changing price level, local differences in costs of living, and variations in wage schedules make the latter type of minimum wage law preferable to the former. The expression of a minimum wage in terms of a constantly changing price level is very difficult.

Minimum wage laws, like many other experiments in labor legislation, originated in Australasia. The conciliation boards of New Zealand, established in 1894 for the compulsory arbitration of industrial disputes, were authorized to prevent sweating by the grant of power to fix a minimum wage within the sweated industries. In 1896, in Victoria, Australia, the first independent minimum wage law was passed. This was also an attempt to regulate the sweated industries. Administrative power was vested in specifically created boards, composed of an equal number of employers and employees under the chairmanship of a nonpartisan umpire acceptable to both sides. By 1900, the experiment was regarded as so successful that its application was broadened from the six specified sweated industries to nearly all the important industries of the province. In the first decade of the twentieth century, other Australian states enacted similar legislation.

Great Britain enacted in 1909 the Trade Boards Act for the regulation of certain specific trades which were regarded as sweated industries. The jurisdiction of the boards was gradually extended in 1912, 1913, and 1919 to include men as well as women, skilled as well as unskilled workers, and agricultural as well as industrial labor. Minimum wage legislation in some form has also spread to the continent of Europe, to Canada, and to South America.

In the United States, Massachusetts in 1912 was the first state to pass a minimum wage law. The act provided for the creation of an administrative board to determine what should constitute a minimum wage, but the prescribed minimum wage was not mandatory. The law relied for the enforcement of its minimum standard on the weapons of publicity and public opinion. In this respect it has been remarkably effective. Eight other American states enacted similar legislation the next year, and before the World War, the movement was well on its way in this country. In 1918, the Federal Congress passed a minimum wage law for the District of Columbia. Minimum wage laws in American states have invariably been limited in their application to women and unorganized workers in the sweated trades. Whether there will be an expansion similar to that which took place abroad remains to be seen. For a number of years the attitude of organized labor in America was frankly hostile to the extension of minimum wage legislation to all adult male workers.

The constitutionality of minimum wage laws in this country is still controversial. Legislative regulations concerning hours and working conditions have been viewed by the Courts in general as a legitimate extension of the police power of the State. This question has been fairly definitely settled on the basis of the injurious effects of long hours and unhealthy surroundings on the physical well-being of the workers. On the other hand, the right of the state to interfere in the matter of wages is still an unsettled question. Minimum wage laws have been fought in the courts as class legislation and as an unwarranted interference with the constitutional right of freedom of contract. The Supreme Court of the United States, in 1917, refused to set aside a decision of the Superior Court of Oregon in favor of the minimum wage law of that state. Following this verdict of the Supreme Court of the United States, the Superior Courts of a number of states refused to declare unconstitutional the minimum wage laws of their respective states. The legal status of minimum wage laws seemed fairly well established when events suddenly took a different turn. In April, 1923, the United States Supreme Court declared unconstitutional the District of Columbia mandatory wage board law. It was held to be an unwarranted interference with the constitutional guarantee of freedom of contract. This important decision implied the invalidity of other mandatory minimum wage laws in various states throughout the Union. A storm of protest was aroused, some of which later crystallized into a movement for an amendment of the Constitution to limit the powers of the Supreme Court.

13. The Long Day.—Although states have passed laws regulating the hours of work of women and children, they have been reluctant to do so for adult male employees. In the case of the latter, hours of work have been reduced and the wages raised by collective bargaining, rather than by state legislation. In the general absence of legislation on the subject, the length of the working day for men in this country has varied from place to place, from industry to industry and from time to time, according to the strength of organized labor.

The invention of power machinery has made it possible to increase production and to decrease the hours of work. The gains of the Industrial Revolution, however, were not immediately realized by the workers in the form of a shorter working day. The gradual development of collective bargaining has lessened the possibility of exploitation in the form of excessive hours of work. This can be seen in the gradual decrease in the average working day.[1]

HOURS OF LABOR IN MECHANICAL AND MANUFACTURING ESTABLISHMENTS

Year	Average work day, hours	Year	Average work day, hours
1840	11.4	1890	10.0
1850	11.5	1900	9.8
1860	11.0	1910	9.25
1870	10.5	1920	9.00
1880	10.3		

The 1909 Census of Manufactures showed, concerning the six and one half million employees covered in its survey, that 76 per cent were working nine or ten hours a day. The Census for 1914 showed that 25 per cent of the seven million workers included in its study were working for ten hours or more per day. During the World War considerable progress was made toward the eight-hour day in the skilled trades and toward the nine- or ten-hour day in the unskilled occupations. The Census for 1919 showed that of the nine million workers employed in manufacturing, almost half were employed in establishments where the eight-hour day prevailed. This compares very favorably with the 12 per cent shown for the group in the Census of 1914. The figures for 1919 also showed that in the manufacturing industries only 35 per cent of the employees were working fifty-four hours or more per week, and only 12 per cent for sixty hours or more per week. During the business depression which followed two years after the war, many of these gains were lost. Many employers lapsed back from the eight-hour day to the ten-hour day, and

[1] The averages for the decades of the nineteenth century are those given by ADAMS and SUMNER, "Labor Problems," p. 518, and those for the twentieth century are those of the United States Bureau of Labor Statistics.

from the ten-hour day to still longer hours of employment. One of the worst features of the entire situation was the existence of the twelve-hour shift and the seven-day week in the steel industry. The blast furnaces require continuous operation, and in the past they have often been worked by two shifts instead of three. Moreover, in making the change from the day shift to the night shift, workers were commonly required to remain continuously on duty for twenty-four hours.

The United States Commission on Industrial Relations began an investigation which lasted several years and published its final report in 1916. Some of its conclusions are significant and well worth repeating here.

1. The physical well being, mental development, and recreational needs of every class of population demand that under normal circumstances, the working day should not exceed eight hours.

2. A large percentage of the workmen in manufactures, transportation, and mining work more than eight hours a day. This is in marked contrast to the condition of those whose economic position enables them to define the length of their own working day.

3. Practical experience has shown that the reduction of the working hours is in the interest not only of the worker and of the community, but of the employer.

4. The regulation by legal enactment of working hours of adult workmen is not generally practical nor desirable except for public employees.

It is suggested that the Commission recommend in the so-called continuous occupations, other than the movement of trains, requiring work both day and night for six or seven days per week, the state and the Federal government should directly intervene, so that the working hours should not exceed eight hours per day nor extend to more than six days per week.[1]

Little can be said to justify the existence of excessive hours of employment in an enlightened community. Among the most conspicuous social effects are loss of health, rest, recreation, and the absence of the necessary leisure time for educational opportunities, for social pleasure and domestic duties. From an economic point of view excessive hours of work represent a serious maladjustment. It is hard to reconcile the ten-, eleven- or twelve-hour day with the simultaneous existence of unemployment. Among the important effects of excessive hours of work are those relating to the efficiency of the worker and to

[1] *Report of Commission on Industrial Relations,* vol. I, p. 69.

the volume of output. It is true that hours of work may be shortened to such an extent that there will be a decline in production which will reflect itself in lower real wages for the worker. On the other hand, it has been shown that a curtailment of the hours of labor within reasonable limits has not resulted in a proportionate increase in labor costs. In some cases the shorter working day has acted as so great an economic stimulus that no loss in production has occurred.[1]

Opponents of the shorter working day predicted dire results, such as a serious decrease in productive capacity, an increase in labor costs and hence a general rise in prices, a loss of world markets, and finally unfortunate effects upon the workers themselves, such as idling, intemperance, and other forms of dissipation. Few of these have come to pass with a general shortening of the working day. Studies of night work, Sunday labor, and other forms of overtime employment seem to indicate that they are very questionable expedients and should be used only in emergencies. The increase in leisure time has not been abused by most workers. Indeed, many students of the problem have agreed that dissipation is often a violent mental reaction to excessive hours of continuous and monotonous toil. A decrease in the length of the working day and an increase in leisure time seems to result in more wholesome forms of recreation.

14. Eight-hour Day.—Public opinion and the law in the United States have generally been unwilling to limit freedom of contract in the case of adult male workers, although willing to interfere in behalf of women and children. The eight-hour day is still hardly more than an ideal for the great mass of laborers. For the unskilled and unorganized workers the ten-hour day prevails in most cases. Among the skilled and organized workers the eight-hour day is the rule.

Alleged attempts to shorten the working day frequently have been movements to secure increased wages. Thus, we must distinguish between the eight-hour day and the basic eight-hour day. The latter does not prevent an employee from working

[1] The British Munition Workers' Committee showed that a reduction of from seven to twenty hours per week in no cases resulted in more than an insignificant reduction of the total output, while on the average it produced a substantial increase. The Illinois Industrial Survey of the hours and health of women workers in 1918 discovered that the reduction of the weekly hours of work from fifty-five and fifty-four to forty-eight hours resulted not in a decrease of production, but in an increase.

more than eight hours, but it merely provides that hours of work in excess of that amount shall be construed as overtime, which is paid for at higher rates. The Adamson Act of 1916 for railroad employees was of this character.

Students of the problem have questioned the desirability of fixing some definite number of hours as the proper and universal working day. Conditions vary greatly in different industries, and, indeed, among different tasks within the same industry. This is another reason for the reluctance of the government to interfere in the regulation of hours.

Shortly after the Civil War several states made legislative attempts at the eight-hour day, but these laws were either not enforced or not enforceable. The movement was continued, however, by various labor organizations. It was felt that voluntary agreements were better than general legislation. With the development of the American Federation of Labor the eight-hour day became one of its great objectives. Public opinion has also become rather sympathetic toward the movement for a shorter working day in many occupations. It is felt that:

"Eight hours for work, eight hours for play,
Eight hours for sleep, make up the full day."

In Europe, progress toward the eight-hour day has been made by both organized labor and governmental legislation on the subject. In Great Britain, the miners have now secured a seven-hour day and are agitating for a six-hour day. At present, however, a reactionary force is at work. The mine operators are contending that a return to the eight-hour day is essential to an economic operation of the coal mines. British hours of labor in the ordinary working week in the principal industries are now from forty-four to forty-eight hours a week. Countries of continental Europe have followed the example of Great Britain in introducing laws upon the eight-hour day. Although there has been a reaction in certain quarters, the movement is also well under way in France, Germany, and Scandinavia.

15. Welfare Work in Industry.—Welfare work has been commonly defined to include all those services which an employer may render to his working people over and above the payment of wages. It is a far cry from the welfare work of a modern industrial establishment to the factory conditions of a

ECONOMIC PROBLEMS OF MODERN LIFE

century ago. During the past generation the concept of the functions of the employer has widened far beyond the matter of economic production. He is regarded as having social as well as economic responsibilities. The stimulus to welfare work first came from the employment of large numbers of women and children within the factory and the large mercantile establishment. Although it has since spread to other workers, organized labor has not taken a very sympathetic attitude toward such a program. It has been stigmatized as "capitalistic feudalism" and "benevolent despotism," which merely increases the dependence of the employees upon the employer. The workers often resent attempts to influence the way in which they spend their leisure time. It is further charged that welfare work is sometimes used as a substitute for higher wages. Organized labor has insisted that the workers be given a greater share in the product of their labor and that they be permitted to spend it as they see fit. Paternalistic schemes of the employers reduce the workers from the high level of free men and women to that of "wards of capitalism." In the last place, it is contended that elaborate welfare schemes have sometimes been inaugurated not for humanitarian reasons, but merely for the purpose of advertising the products of the employer.

The advocates of welfare work point out in reply that low standards of living among many workers' families are due not only to low wages, but also to the fact that their wages are not spent economically. Higher standards of living are conditioned not only by more efficient production, but also by more efficient consumption. In the second place, welfare schemes can give to the workers the benefits of large-scale production and wholesale purchases. In theory at least, the company store or the company home should give the employees a better product for the same money. Only in rare cases is there any compulsion exerted upon the worker to buy at the company store or to live in a company house. The latter is necessary only where the plant is located in some new section on the frontier of industry. In most cases the workers are free to choose for themselves. In welfare programs it is highly desirable that committees of the workers administer as far as possible the details of the scheme. Moreover, such programs should be developed gradually and expanded only as rapidly as the sentiment among the workers seems to warrant. If wisely and democratically administered, welfare work should not develop antagonism among the employees; on the contrary it should breed contentment and loyalty to the "corporation with a soul."

The various welfare schemes which have been developed include housing, recreation, education, health, safety, and thrift projects. They are sometimes directly under the control of the personnel department, sometimes directly under the supervision of the employer, and sometimes administered by joint committees representing both the employer and the employees. They are sometimes accompanied by schemes for profit sharing and for industrial representation or the joint control of industry.

16. Summary.—Among the maladjustments of the Industrial Revolution are the problems of child labor and women in industry. In the absence of collective bargaining the sweat shop is apt to develop. Because of the danger of exploitation, the state is constrained to pass legislation in behalf of women and children in industry. Such legislation is within the sphere of the individual states, although at the present time a Federal child labor amendment is possible. In the case of both women and children, hours of work are frequently excessive and earnings very meager. Conditions of employment are often far from satisfactory. While we may desire the elimination of child labor for both economic and social reasons, the right of women to economic independence cannot be denied. The entrance of women into industry has been greatly accelerated in the present century and they have been constantly entering new fields of economic endeavor. The minimum wage law has been developed as a legislative weapon against the sweat shop and against the employment of women at wages too low for the maintenance of a minimum standard of living. Under a recent decision of the United States Supreme Court the constitutionality of mandatory minimum wage laws in the United States is questionable.

Long hours of work as well as inadequate wages have been a frequent cause of industrial unrest. Often wages have been lowest where hours of work were the longest. Social welfare demands wages sufficient to maintain decent standards of living and a working day which will permit sufficient time for recreation. Although the eight-hour day prevails in many skilled trades, the ten-hour day is the rule in the unskilled occupations. Often hours of work are still longer, and there is no provision for one day of rest in seven. Excessive hours of work on the part of some workers and unemployment on the part of others constitute a serious challenge to our present industrial system. Progress in the United States toward the eight-hour day for all workers (not merely for women and children) has been achieved by organized labor rather than by state legislation. The same may be said of wage increases. Wage boards and minimum wage laws in this country are primarily for women workers.

Machinery and minute specialization make modern industrial conditions extremely monotonous and fatiguing. Progressive employers are paying considerable attention to the health, comfort, and safety of their employees. Numerous large concerns have entered upon extensive welfare programs which extend far beyond the confines of their plants. Although criticized as paternalistic rather than democratic, and as selfish rather than humanitarian, they have often succeeded in raising the standards of living of particular groups of workers. These welfare projects include housing, recreational and educational programs, as well as social service work and schemes for economic betterment. The new ideal in industry is the reconciliation of industrial efficiency with the welfare of the individual worker.

Collateral Reading

ADAMS, T. S., and SUMNER, H., "Labor Problems," chaps. 2 and 4.
ATKINS, W. E., and LASWELL, H. D., "Labor Attitudes and Problems," pp. 481-483.
BLUM, S., "Labor Economics," chaps. 2, 3 and 4.
CARLTON, F. T., "History and Problems of Organized Labor," chaps. 13, 14 and 15.
COMMONS, J. R., and ANDREWS, J. B., "Principles of Labor Legislation," chaps. 4 and 5.
FAIRCHILD, F. R., FURNISS, E. S., and BUCK, N. S., "Elementary Economics," chap. 52.
FURNISS, E. S., "Labor Problems," chaps. 5 and 6.
HAMILTON, W., "Current Economic Problems," pp. 591-612.
SEAGER, H. R., "Principles of Economics," chap. 30.
United States Commission on Industrial Relations Report of 1916, pp. 255-261.
WATKINS, G. S., "Introduction to the Study of Labor Problems," chaps. 8, 9, and 25.

References

ABBOTT, E., "Women in Industry."
American Labor Legislation Review, quarterly.
ANDREWS, I. O., and HOBBS, M. A., "Economic Effects of War upon Women and Children of Great Britain."
ANDREWS, I. O., "Mininum Wage Legislation."

ANDREWS, J. B., "Labor Problems and Labor Legislation."
BROWN, R. G., "Minimum Wage."
COMMONS, J. R., and others. "History of Labor in the United States."
COMAN, K., "Industrial History of the United States."
GOLDMARK, J., "Fatigue and Efficiency."
KELLY, FLORENCE, "Some Ethical Gains through Legislation."
Massachusetts Commission on Minimum Wage Boards, 1912.
Massachusetts Minimum Wage Commission, *Annual Reports.*
National Child Labor Committee publications.
Report of Committee of British War Cabinet upon Women in Industry, 1919.
Report of Illinois Industrial Survey on Hours and Health of Women Workers, 1919.
SPARGO, J., "Bitter Cry of Children."
United States Bureau of Labor Statistics, *Monthly Labor Review.*
United States Children's Bureau publications, particularly *Bulletins* 60, 74, and 79.
United States Commission on Industrial Relations, *Report* of 1916.
United States Women in Industry Service publications.

Questions for Discussion

1. What was the theory of *laissez-faire*, and how did it oppose the passage of child labor legislation?

2. Is child labor a local, a national, or an international problem?

3. Is it essentially an industrial problem?

4. Outline causes of child labor.

5. Outline effects.

6. What are some essential points in a model child labor bill?

7. Does the proposed child labor amendment prohibit the employment of children under eighteen years?

8. Show the increasing number of occupations of women.

9. What are some of the causes of the low wages paid to women?

10. What are some essentials of the sweating system?

11. How can the evils of sweating be overcome?

12. Show the arguments for and against minimum wage laws.

13. Discuss the constitutionality of minimum wage laws.

14. Show the similarities of the problems of child labor and of women in industry.

Topics for Investigation

1. Early English conditions of child labor and of women in industry.

2. Legislative reform in England during the first part of the nineteenth century.

3. Child labor today in the cotton mills of the Orient.

4. The American constitution and child labor legislation.

5. Child labor and the industrial South.

6. The child labor laws of your own state.

7. Effects of the World War upon the problem of women in industry.

8. "Equal pay for equal work."

9. Mininum wage legislation in Australasia.

10. Recent minimum wage legislation in Europe.

CHAPTER XXV

COLLECTIVE BARGAINING AND LABOR ORGANIZATIONS

1. Wage System.—The development of the wage system was contingent on the evolution of specialization, and it was further complicated by the capitalistic method of production. Although the wage system antedated the Industrial Revolution, it was not until then that division of labor took its modern form and capital assumed its present importance. The factory system replaced the domestic system and power machinery the skilled craftsman. There came into existence a group of machine owners, and a group of machine operators who had lost control of their instruments of production. The Industrial Revolution produced a line of cleavage between capitalist and laborer and a new type of class consciousness. These factors have colored the modern concept of the wage system.

The term "wage system" is difficult of exact definition. It is essential, however, that we note some of its chief characteristics. The wage system implies the existence of the enterpriser, individual initiative, and the institution of private property. The enterpriser determines the course of production, brings together the various factors in production, and accepts the financial responsibility of his economic venture. As production is roundabout and in anticipation of demand, the enterpriser must own or borrow the capital from which he makes advances to the workers in the form of wages. He directs the economic process, and in a measure both insures and advances to labor its part of the final product in the form of wages. The enterpriser's reward in the form of competitive profits is relatively uncertain, although often large. The tendency of losses to balance profits is sometimes overlooked by labor leaders, who appreciate the economic insecurity of the workers but not that of the employer. The wage system involves the ownership of the instruments of production by a capitalistic class. It does not follow, however, that the employee is completely dependent on the employer as to wages, hours, and conditions of work. The organization of labor has developed in response to the present wage system.

2. Nature and Origin of Collective Bargaining.—The term "collective bargaining" is likewise a very indefinite expression. It may be defined as group, rather than individual, competition and agreements between organized associations rather than isolated individuals. Like the wage system, collective bargaining antedated the Industrial Revolution, but acquired with it a new form and a new importance.

It should be remembered that the term "collective bargaining" may be used in a political and social as well as in an economic sense. Moreover, it must be remembered that collective bargaining has been used by capitalists as well as by workers, and by employers as well as by employees. Organized labor has attempted to inject such concepts as the closed shop and the walking delegate into the general expression of collective bargaining. It seems best, however, that these issues should be discussed upon their own merits, although labor leaders regard them as essential to effective collective bargaining. It is very easy to agree upon the existence of, and indeed, the necessity for collective bargaining. But to interpret collective bargaining in terms of various practises and institutions is very difficult. The labor delegation withdrew from President Wilson's post-war conference between labor and capital, because the conference refused to include in its definition of collective bargaining certain things demanded by labor, although willing to agree on the general principle of collective bargaining.

Collective bargaining may be traced as far back as the medieval charters which the townspeople received from a local duke or a distant king. These charters were essentially collective contracts containing certain privileges. Moreover, the medieval guilds practised collective bargaining and had mutual understandings among their members as to output, prices, quality, and working conditions. Interesting comparisons may be drawn between medieval craft guilds and modern trade unions. Essential differences, however, lay in the absence of power machinery, the factory system, and large-scale production. In an age of craftsmanship and production by hand tools, the apprentice strove to become a master worker. Considerable skill but only a small amount of wealth were necessary. Master and apprentice worked side by side in the same shop and the relationship was personal and even paternal. There was no class or craft consciousness of laborer as against capitalist, because of the relative unimportance of capital.

With the expansion of foreign markets, charters were granted to merchant adventurers for distant enterprises. Great trading companies came to replace the medieval merchant guilds. Gradually there was developed the principle of limited liability and the modern corporation took its present form. However, collective action on the part of capitalists did not stop with the formation of the business corporation. Monopoly is the final extreme of collective action on the part of both labor and capital. It has often been contended, however, that governmental hostility toward the collective action of capitalists was not expressed until the final stage of monopoly was reached. On the other hand, labor's early attempts at collective bargaining were regarded as conspiracy and bitterly opposed by both employers and governments.

3. Emergence of Trade Unionism in England.—The prevalent economic philosophy of England during the opening years of the nineteenth century was that of *laissez-faire* or nonintervention. The classical economists contended that wages were limited by the supply of capital available for the employment of labor. Any arbitrary interference with the result of these forces of supply and demand was a futile and unwarranted attempt to raise wages beyond a certain natural rate. Accordingly, trade unions were viewed with disdain by economists and with opposition by the government. Indeed, they were conspiracies under both the common and the statute laws. Several centuries earlier the Statute of Apprentices had attempted to fix wages by governmental authority. After the decline of Mercantilism or the National System under the vigorous attacks of Adam Smith, a series of statutes, known as the Combination Acts, was passed by the English Parliament. These were designed to prevent either employers or employees from combining to raise the prices of their products or services. A new group of capitalists, who had supplanted in control the old landed aristocracy, legislated specifically against all agreements among workers to raise wages, to lessen hours of work, or to improve conditions of employment. Justices of the peace were empowered to sentence to two months' imprisonment members of any such combination. Under these acts a number of labor leaders were deported from the country and sent to the convict colony in Australia.

Statutes expressly forbidding labor unions were repealed in 1824, and in 1825 an act was passed which gave legal recognition to collective bargaining. It was not until a full half century later, however, that trade unions acquired full legal sanction with the passage of the Trade Union Acts between 1871 and 1875. In the Conspiracy and Protection of Property Act of 1875 it was declared that no act in connection with a trade dispute, which was not criminal if committed by an individual, should be viewed as conspiracy when committed by two or more persons acting in combination. This law has been regarded as the Magna Charta of British trade unions, which now enjoy a greater freedom from restraint than those in most other countries. This legal principle of immunity from the charge of conspiracy has not been generally established in the United States, where some activities, which are legitimate when done by individuals, are questionable when done collectively. In 1906, Great Britain passed a Trades Dispute Act which considerably relieved organizations of both employers and employees from liability for suits for damages for acts committed in connection with trade union disputes. Such immunity does not prevail in the United States.

4. Early Labor Organizations in America.—Colonial America was largely agricultural and the labor supply was augmented on a large scale by slaves and indentured servants. Manufacturing did not establish itself until about the time of the War of 1812. Nevertheless, there were numerous craft organizations of skilled workers in many of our larger towns and cities. It was not until after the first quarter of the nineteenth century, however, that organizations of labor became significant in our national life. The modern trade union or association of allied and organized crafts of workmen may perhaps be said to have originated with the "Mechanics' Union of Trade Associations" in Philadelphia in 1827. Similar organizations were formed in other cities and the movement was reflected in the development of local labor parties in a number of states. A National Trades Union was organized, which held its first annual convention in 1834. Carpenters, cordwainers, printers, and other skilled mechanics were organized into national trade unions. Early organizations of labor expressed themselves vigorously against imprisonment for debt, convict labor, and sweat shops, and in favor of the ten-hour day, free schools, and mechanics lien laws. The early trade unionist movement in America, however, lost its identity in the general uplift and humanitarian movements of the antebellum period. It was a time of reformers and anti-slavery agitators, and the air was full of Utopian schemes such as that of Brook Farm.

The great industrial development which followed the Civil War was accompanied by a reorganization of labor on a vaster scale than was ever before known in America. Every large city had its trades assembly composed of all organized crafts. In 1866, the National Labor Union was formed, which held annual conventions for the following six years. The Noble Order of the Knights of Labor was founded by a tailor in Philadelphia on Thanksgiving Day, 1869. At first, it was a secret organization with a rather elaborate ritual. This was soon abandoned and the movement spread from the garment workers to those of other trades. Moreover, it ceased to be a local organization, and its ideal became that of an amalgamation of all workers into one great industrial organization. For a decade or two the Knights of Labor were a powerful force in our national life, but its zenith was reached in 1886, when the membership amounted to over a half million workers. The original policy of the Knights of Labor was to discourage strikes and boycotts. It aimed to rely on political action rather than on economic weapons. Through cooperative means and a campaign of education it hoped to abolish the evils of the wage system and to substitute a cooperative commonwealth. The governmental machinery of the Knights of Labor was very highly centralized, and when internal dissensions arose among the local trade unions, its membership and influence gradually waned. It is now merely an historical landmark in the evolution of labor organization in the United States.

5. Growth of the American Federation of Labor.—The American Federation of Labor was first organized in 1881, but it was reorganized under its present name in 1886. It began as a reaction against the idealistic and centralized labor unionism of the Knights of Labor and in favor of the more practical objectives and independent organization of trade unionism. The later disintegration of that once powerful organization discouraged political activity on the part of organized labor and encouraged reliance on its own weapons of collective bargaining. Out of these circumstances, and with these policies in mind, the American Federation of Labor was born. At the time of its inception, the affiliated national unions possessed a total membership of a quarter of a million workers. The American Federation of Labor was overshadowed by the Knights of Labor and it grew very slowly in the first decade of its existence. In the last two or three years of the nineteenth century, however, its membership began to increase very rapidly, and at the close of the century it had developed from a quarter to a half million members. In 1902, the million mark was passed, and during the next decade the total membership doubled. This increase in numbers was very irregular and varied with periods of prosperity and depression.

The World War and the two years of inflation which followed it was another period of rapid growth, during which time the membership of two millions in 1914 doubled to a membership of four millions in 1920. The period of economic depression in 1921 reduced the membership of the American Federation of Labor from well over four millions to considerably under that figure. Exact estimates of its numerical strength are very difficult. Trade unions often have upon their lists members who are not in good standing, as their payments of dues have lapsed. Moreover, the membership of trade unions within the American Federation of Labor is constantly changing. Secessions and new affiliations are very common. Among the prominent trade unions outside the American Federation of Labor are the Amalgamated Clothing Workers of America, the American Textile Workers, and the various railroad brotherhoods of engineers, conductors, firemen, and trainmen. In spite of the great membership of trade unions, both within and without the American Federation of Labor, it is a minority as contrasted with unorganized labor. Not only are the professional and salaried workers unorganized, but also agricultural workers, domestic servants and the great mass of unskilled labor. In estimating the strength of the American Federation of Labor, the common practice of labor leaders is to base their percentages on the total number of skilled workers rather than on the total number of all persons gainfully employed. The American Federation of Labor has never made any great appeal to unskilled labor, and today the great majority of workers in America are unorganized.

The table on page 534 will show the growth and present strength of trade unionism in the United States. In Germany, in 1922, there were twelve and a half million trade unionists and in Great Britain five and a half million trade unionists.[1]   When judged by absolute numbers and especially by the ratio of trade union membership to the total population or to the total number of adult male workers, the strength of trade unionism in many other industrial countries is greater than in the United States.

TRADE UNION MEMBERSHIP IN THE UNITED STATES[2]

	Total wage earners	Trade union membership	Per cent organized
1920...............	26,080,689	4,881,200	18.7
1910...............	22,406,714	2,101,502	9.4

	Total wage earners excluding agriculture	Trade union membership	Per cent organized
1920...............	23,480,077	4,881,200	20.8
1910...............	19,262,941	2,101,502	10.9

6. Organization of American Federation of Labor.—The American Federation of Labor is a loose affiliation of slightly over a hundred national and international trade unions representing thousands of local unions.   The late Samuel Gompers, when president of the American Federation of Labor, defined it as follows:

The American Federation of Labor is "a federation of organizations, each of which has its own government, determined by its own needs and requirements, the result of the experiences of the members of the organization.   The right to self-government was recognized in the beginning and it has been reaffirmed and adhered to as consistently as possible. The Federation has no powers except those which are authorized and conceded by the organizations which compose it.   These powers are enumerated in its written constitution and the definite direction of conventions."[3]

The local trade union is to the American Federation of Labor what the cell is to a biological structure.   The local union is the basic unit of this economic organism.   With this as the starting

[1] Cf. WOLMAN, L., "Growth of American Trade Unions," p. 65.
[2] Ibid. p. 85.
[3] Cf. GOMPERS, S., "The American Labor Movement," p. 7.

point the process of federation may be vertical, horizontal, or both. The locals are required to join the national union in their trade. Sometimes there are also state and international trade unions. In the absence of a national trade Union, a local organization may be directly affiliated with the American Federation of Labor. In such a case it is termed a Federal trade local.

If the number of workers in any one craft is too small to form a local for that particular trade, they may ignore craft lines and organize as a Federal labor union. Any detailed study of the organization of the American Federation of Labor is impossible in this text, but it is important that the student observe behind its great complexity of structure the variety of organization and the freedom of action.

Strong national trade unions maintain experienced organizers, create their own locals and issue charters. They sometimes render financial assistance to their struggling locals, but at other times discipline and even suspend them for going counter to the general policy of the national trade union and the American Federation of Labor. The annual convention of the American Federation of Labor is important. Here officers are elected, problems discussed, and policies formulated. Each national trade union is represented by one delegate for each four thousand paid-up members or fraction thereof. One delegate each is also allowed for state federations, city centrals, Federal labor unions, and Federal trade locals. Numerous fraternal organizations are also represented. There is elected annually an Executive Council, consisting of a president, numerous vice-presidents, a secretary, and a treasurer. It is this executive council which carries on the work of the American Federation of Labor from one annual convention to another. Permanent headquarters are maintained in Washington from the revenue derived from a per capita assessment of the membership of affiliated bodies.

7. Industrial Workers of the World.—The Industrial Workers of the World, as contrasted with the American Federation of Labor, is an industrial rather than a trade union. Its aims and practices, as well as its organization, afford a striking contrast to the more conservative American Federation of Labor. It represents revolutionary rather than evolutionary unionism. The organization known as the Industrial Workers of the World emerged in 1905 at Chicago as a merger of such radical

groups as the Socialist Labor party, the American Labor Union and the Western Federation of Miners.[1] Bitterly opposed to the utilitarian aims and the conservative methods of trade unionism, the promoters of this new labor organization sought the union of workers by industries rather than by crafts, and cherished the hope of final amalgamation into one big union. Whereas the American Federation of Labor accepts capitalism, and indeed the wage system, the Industrial Workers of the World seek the destruction of the present economic and political order.

In 1908, differences developed as to their course of action, and the Industrial Workers of the World split into two groups which were known as the Chicago and the Detroit branches. In 1915, the latter became known as the Workers' International Industrial Union. This group has socialism as its objective and favors political as well as industrial action. It may be classified as a type of socialism. The Industrial Workers of the World, that is, the Chicago branch, since the secession of the Detroit branch, has been syndicalistic rather than socialistic.

Syndicat is the French word meaning union. The Industrial Workers of the World in America, syndicalism in France, and Bolshevism in Russia are different national aspects of the same world movement. Private property rights and the state, as we understand it, are condemned. The ideal is an industrial commonwealth of free associations of workers like the Russian union of soviets. The Industrial Workers of the World repudiate the political action of the Socialists on the one hand and the collective bargaining of the trade unions on the other. They seek direct industrial action by means of a general strike of all workers simultaneously. The doctrine of class struggle is taught, and the solidarity of all workers is sought for the overthrow of capitalism. Direct industrial action includes not only the general strike, but also sabotage. The American phrase "dropping a wrench in the works" is the equivalent of sabotage. Sabotage sometimes takes the peaceful form of "soldiering on the job," but often expresses itself in violent forms. If the demands of the workers are not met, they may secretly destroy the machinery or goods of the employer. It is almost impossible to discover the malefactor, although great financial loss may result. If sabotage is practised rather than a strike declared, the workers do not suffer

[1] This organization later withdrew and joined the American Federation of Labor.

the loss of employment and wages which a strike generally necessitates.

Because of the radical aims and the violent means used to accomplish them, the Industrial Workers of the World is a much feared and hated organization. However, it is less powerful numerically than is sometimes supposed. Its paid-up membership just before the World War was only fourteen thousand, although at that time there were a hundred thousand membership cards which had been issued to various workers. Just before America's entrance into the War, the paid-up membership of the Industrial Workers of the World was probably sixty thousand. Hence, it would seem to have been on the increase. During the War a vigorous policy of suppression was carried on by the government. Whether the result was to increase or decrease the membership of the Industrial Workers of the World is difficult to determine. A policy of secrecy was adopted and a resort to underground methods of activity was made by this and many similar radical organizations. At best, it would be far more difficult to get authoritative figures for the membership of the Industrial Workers of the World, than for the American Federation of Labor. The Industrial Workers of the World represents a very variable and unsteady group of workers. It is largely composed of floaters or migrants and of casual workers. Even within the group itself, there is little solidarity or unity of thought and action. It seems hardly likely that the Industrial Workers of the World will assume the leadership of the American labor movement, even though their numbers should increase. In spite of certain apparent radical tendencies, the labor movement in this country still seems craft conscious rather than class conscious, practical rather than Utopian, and individualistic rather than collectivist.

8. Types of Labor Organizations.—Labor organizations are associations of workmen for the purpose of improving their economic and social conditions. They may be classified either according to their form of organization or according to their functions. From the former point of view, it may be said that there are three structural types of labor organizations; (1) labor unions, (2) trade unions, and (3) industrial unions. The significance of labor unions, in the strict sense of the term, is chiefly historical, and the Knights of Labor may be taken as the best illustration of this type of labor organization. All classes of wage earners are admitted into the labor union; indeed, employers and professional men have sometimes been included. Labor unions are usually humanitarian and idealistic, and they embrace most of the earlier labor movements in this country. Instead of the strike and boycott, reliance was placed upon education, social reform, cooperation, and political activity.

The trade union is essentially an association of the workers of one given craft. Although there may be federations of trade unions, each individual trade union preserves its own independent organization and autonomy of action. It is essentially utilitarian in its purposes, and exists primarily for the purpose of collective bargaining among the members of the trade union. Reliance is placed on the strike and other economic weapons rather than on political action. The United Brotherhood of Carpenters and most member organizations of the American Federation of Labor are illustrations of this type of labor organization.

The industrial union, unlike the trade union, cuts across craft lines. It seeks to unite all the workers within a given industry into a coherent and centrally controlled organization. Class consciousness and group solidarity are stressed rather than trade unionism. Unskilled as well as skilled workers are admitted. Although the United Mine Workers' Union is associated with the American Federation of Labor, the former organization is an industrial and not a trade union. All the workers in the mine, no matter of what occupation or degree of skill, may be members. The Industrial Workers of the World is the greatest industrial union in America. It ignores craft lines and seeks the amalgamation of all workers.

Organizations of labor have been classified by their functions as follows: (1) business unionism, (2) friendly or uplift unionism, (3) revolutionary unionism, and (4) predatory unionism.[1] It will be seen that the results of these two different classifications are somewhat similar. Business unionism is another way of expressing the bread-and-butter aims of trade unions. Immediate and local issues such as increased wages for a given group of workers are stressed. Friendly or uplift unionism is also comparatively conservative. As illustrated by most labor unions, in the strict sense of the word, it is more general in its appeal and more idealistic in its aims than business or trade unionism.

[1] *Cf.* Hoxie, R. F., "Trade Unionism in the United States," pp. 45–50.

Revolutionary unionism, as illustrated by the Industrial Workers of the World, stresses class consciousness and calls upon all workers to unite in an attempt to overthrow private capitalism and to escape from the wage system. Revolutionary unionism consists of various socialistic groups, as well as of those who would establish a syndicalist commonwealth by industrial methods and action. Predatory unionism is "business unionism gone wrong." Like the political machine in a number of our cities, it is corrupt and boss ridden. Without definite aims, its course of action is expediency and opportunism. It has sometimes been characterized by violence and terrorism, as in the case of the bridge and structural iron workers and some of the Chicago building trades.

9. Legal Status of Trade Unions.—The serious development of labor organizations in America, as well as of our industries, came at a later date than in England. Although many of labor's weapons have been fought in the courts, American trade unions did not have to go through such a great pioneer struggle for existence here as did those in England. At the present time, however, trade unions are probably less free of legal restriction here than are those in Great Britain. Although the development of labor organizations was not opposed, many of their activities have been held to be illegal violations of the constitutional rights guaranteed individual citizens. The laws of our different states vary greatly on the subject of collective bargaining and on the methods which may be employed by organized labor. Although certain weapons of organized labor have been held to be illegal under the Sherman Anti-trust Act of 1890, trade unions themselves have not been generally indicted as combinations in restraint of trade. The Clayton Act of 1914 specifically stated that they were not to be so regarded. This American Magna Charta of labor affirmed that labor was not a commodity, and attempted to strengthen the weapons of collective bargaining and to restrict the counter weapon of injunction. As we shall see later, judicial decisions concerning many provisions of this Federal law have not justified the high hopes of labor leaders concerning it.

The legal status of labor organizations is assured, but it is not well defined. Unions are generally organized and considered as voluntary associations of workers. Most states authorize the incorporation of labor organizations, and the Federal government has likewise legalized the incorporation of national unions. This right of incorporation, however, has rarely been utilized by trade unions. Labor leaders generally oppose incorporation on the grounds that their funds can easily be attached after an unfavorable legal verdict. Moreover, incorporated trade unions can be more seriously affected by court injunctions. Employers, on the contrary, have advocated the incorporation of labor organizations, as a measure which would facilitate suits for breach of contract. Thus labor's responsibility would be increased. At the present time, however, it is possible for an unincorporated union to be sued in the courts and a verdict sustained. In the Danbury Hatters' case of 1908, for illustration, an unincorporated union was adjudged guilty of being a combination in restraint of trade because of the boycott which it maintained against the Loewe Hat Company. Its members were fined 300 thousand dollars under the provisions of the Sherman Act. Hence, labor leaders sought Federal legislation which was subsequently achieved in the Clayton Act.

10. Functions of Labor Organizations.—Collective bargaining is the answer of the workers to their real or fancied helplessness under the wage system and modern captalism. Its chief object is to raise or to maintain the existing wages and standards of living of labor. Closely associated with this aim is the desire for a shorter working day. Indeed, these two primary objectives have frequently been identified by workers. The following slogan of the American Federation of Labor is typical:

> Whether you work by the piece or work by the day,
> Decreasing the hours increases the pay.

The securing of these two aims may be regarded as the primary objects of collective bargaining. Their attainment is conditioned by the strength of organized labor. Hence, another primary function of labor unions is the maintenance of the right of collective bargaining. They seek to strengthen their own organizations and to eliminate any practices which sap this power of collective bargaining.

Labor organizations have secondary functions of considerable importance. Trade unions are often mutual benefit associations and provide for their members out of their own dues. They sometimes maintain unemployment, accident, sickness, and life insurance for their own group. They also serve as employment bureaus and seek to find work for their members. In the third place, some trade unions perform educational work. Periodicals are published and educational as well as business meetings are held. Thus, the garment workers maintain evening classes and even college courses for their members. Their annual almanac possesses artistic, literary, and educational value as well as utilitarian objectives. A social as well as a group consciousness is bound to develop from such a program. A fourth function may be described as recreational. The local labor organization may become a civic and social center for the workers and their families. In a large town or city a number of local unions may have their headquarters in one building, which may develop many of the features of a club house.

Labor organizations were at first primarily concerned about wages, hours, and the right of collective bargaining. They were singularly indifferent to general working conditions. We have seen that it was state legislation rather than trade unionism which attacked such maladjustments as dangerous trades, child labor, and unsanitary living conditions. Of recent years, however, labor organizations have become vitally interested in these broader problems. Moreover, they have become interested not only in a greater participation by workers in the product of industry, but also in the control of industry. Revolutionary unionism proposes the elimination of the enterpriser, capitalism, and the wage system. Conservative unionism, however, is merely pleading for the co-partnership concept of labor in industry.

11. Collective Bargaining and Wages.—Collective bargaining on the part of labor is the result of the disadvantages of the individual worker in bargaining about his wage. The economic concept of a competitive wage is affected by the fact that the two parties to the wage contract possess different bargaining power. Among the chief disadvantages of the individual worker in making a wage bargain are the following: Labor is a service and therefore similar to a perishable commodity. Time spent in finding employment is a loss of working hours and hence of wages. The proffered wage may be lower than the competitive rate for a given type of labor, but its refusal means unemployment. Loss of wages to the worker is also more serious than loss of profits to the employer. The worker has no great surplus of past savings from which he may draw. Another disadvantage of the unorganized worker is the superior knowledge of the employers as to general conditions of employment. A third disadvantage lies in the worker's ignorance and immobility. He does not know where to go in order to better his conditions. Moreover, it is not easy for the worker and his family to move from place to place under the lure of a slight wage differential. A final disadvantage is the frequent existence of understandings among employers of labor as to wages and conditions of employment. A gentleman's agreement may prevent them from competing actively for workers and thus forcing wages up to the competitive level. Associations of employers are reluctant about "spoiling" the labor market. Collective bargaining among employers has been very successful.

How far labor organizations can succeed in raising the wages of labor in general is a controversial point of economics. It is quite evident that a trade union of sufficient power can restrict the number of its members by a restriction of apprentices. By the use of such monopoly power as the closed shop with the closed union, a labor organization can definitely limit the supply of its services and hence raise its price or wages. By so doing, however, it raises the price of its product, and hence increases costs of living for other workers. The money wages of the latter must be advanced if their real wages are to be kept intact. Hence, it is contended that the whole movement is that of a vicious circle. Prices and money wages go up for all workers, but not in the same proportion. It has been contended that any increase of real wages within a given labor group benefits the organized workers at the expense of the unorganized.

Economic theorists question the ability of trade unions to raise the general level of real wages above the competitive wage level for a given group of labor, as fixed by the forces of supply and demand for that type of labor. It does not follow, however, that trade unions are futile. Intelligent labor leaders justify their activities on the ground that they are necessary to secure this economic rate of wages for the workers, and to prevent employers from taking advantage of their ignorance or helplessness by giving them wages below this rate.

A review of various wage theories is merely suggested to the student at this time, as it is beyond the scope of this text. Labor leaders are apt to stigmatize such a theory as the marginal productivity analysis as a mere "commodity theory of labor."

Nevertheless, how else can one approach the problem of wages except through an analysis of the relative supply and demand forces within the various labor groups in society? The dislike of a given theory is no proof of its falsity. Economic theorists, on the other hand, will do well to consider how far the force of competition has free play in fixing the prices of service and commodities. A strong labor union may be a virtual monopoly. The relative bargaining power of any labor group must be considered, as well as the relative supply and demand forces for its services.

In conclusion, let us turn to the argument from experience. It is true that the development of trade unionism since the Industrial Revolution has been accompanied by an increase not only of money wages, but also of real wages, and of the wages of labor in general and of organized labor in particular. This relationship may not necessarily be a casual one, and the greater wages of labor today may be ascribed to other things, such as modern technology and an increased control over the forces of nature. Nevertheless, without the development of labor organization and collective bargaining, it is very likely that labor might not have got so large a share. Today, the economic tug of war is contested between participants of more nearly equal bargaining power.

The situation may be summed up as follows:[1]

The chief effects of the system of collective bargaining are (1) it tends to level time wages; (2) to increase the average wage; (3) to establish a minimum wage and to transfer competitive pressure among workers from wages to efficiency and skill. "The standard rate" fixed by unions through the use of collective bargaining is a minimum or rate a "living wage."

Thus, collective bargaining has a leveling effect upon wages, irrespective of whether or not it raises them. It is contended by some that this leveling process works an injustice upon the skilled and efficient worker. On the other hand, it is true that the union rate is apt to be higher than the competitive rate established by individual bargaining. Thus, the leveling process is one of leveling upward, rather than one of leveling downward.

12. Restriction of Output and Limitation of Apprentices.— Because of the fatiguing nature of modern industry, organized

[1] *Cf.* CARLTON, F. T., "History and Problems of Organized Labor," p. 130.

labor has not only demanded a shorter working day, but has also made recourse to limitation of output. This has been defended as a counter weapon to the employer's attempt to speed up the workers. Machinery may be geared deliberately to such a speed that the worker is continuously taxed to his greatest exertions. Moreover, pace setting is often done by encouraging certain employees to set a fast pace. Other workers on the same machine or the same job are urged to similar production under the threat of discharge or a cut in wages. The most flagrant abuses of this system are found in the sweated industries. Organized labor has retaliated by deliberately limiting the number of units of production within a given unit of time. Thus, the laying of a certain number of bricks and no more may be considered a fair day's work by the union workers. Unorganized laborers soon come to tacit agreements among themselves to prevent a new worker from "killing the job."

Restriction of output has been regarded as a leveling down process, as compared with the leveling up process of pace setting. The capacity of the poor worker rather than that of good workers is chosen as the standard of output. The workers have two objects in mind. The first aim of restriction of output is to prevent the impairment of the health and strength of the workers. The second aim is less justifiable, for it arises from the economic fallacy of making work. It is thought that the rapid worker is lessening too quickly the total amount of employment. The introduction of machinery is similarly opposed on the grounds that it lessens the "lump of labor." The restriction of output, however, only apparently creates additional employment. Although at any given time and within any given occupation the amount of work is definitely limited, the attempt to make work is a selfish and short-sighted policy. Limitation of output tends to raise prices and hence to lower the real wages of other workers. In general, we may say that both excessive speeding on the part of employers and arbitrary limitation of output on the part of employees are mistaken social policies. Human capacities differ so greatly that any fixed pace, like any fixed wage, may work injustice.

Neither the limitation of apprentices nor the restriction of output are new. The medieval guildsmen practised both. However, in an age of craftsmanship the time of apprenticeship was a period of trade instruction under the personal supervision of a master worker. The advent of the machine meant the replacement of the skilled worker by the unskilled or the semi-skilled worker in many occupations. Today, the period of apprenticeship is sometimes a mere fiction. Employers and their foremen have little time, ability, or inclination to teach boys a trade. The term "apprenticeship" in many occupations has become a mere unit of classification between the older and better paid workers and the new workers. The helper has replaced the apprentice where the machine has displaced the craftsman.

Limitation of apprentices is defended on two grounds: first, the improvement in the character of the work; and second, the raising of wages. In spite of the prevalence of the machine, a number of occupations and trades are still performed by hand and require both skill and training. Boys cannot effectively learn a trade if there are too many apprentices to every skilled journeyman. Where organized labor is sufficiently strong to express itself on this point, a certain ratio of apprentices to journeymen is insisted upon. If a high quality of workmanship is the desired objective, a relatively long period of apprenticeship is necessary. Although organized labor has been more insistent on a limitation of apprentices than on a longer period of apprenticeship, the highly skilled trades have contended that a fairly long period of apprenticeship is essential in learning a trade. Trade schools have been viewed with suspicion for this reason.

The limitation of output creates a scarcity of a given commodity or service and hence raises its price. In this way it may raise the wages of labor per unit of product. A limitation of apprentices creates an artificial scarcity of a given type of labor and hence raises its price or the wages of labor in that occupation. If a limitation of apprentices is accompanied by the closed shop, a monopoly of labor is created. Organized labor has also feared that trade schools may create too great a supply of skilled workers. For this reason rather than from a fear of deterioration in the quality of the work, organized labor has insisted on a practical apprenticeship in the trades rather than a mere trade-school preparation.

13. Open and Closed Shop.—The open shop is one in which both union and nonunion men may be employed. The closed shop is one in which only union men may be employed. It must be remembered, however, that there are shops which are closed to union men, that is, in which the employer will openly or secretly employ only nonunion men. Certain employers have professed to maintain the open shop, but a close inspection revealed that union men were either not employed at all or were dismissed in preference to nonunion men. The open shop which is free from any discrimination against union men is very rare. This is one of the strongest arguments for the closed shop.

The closed shop may be operated by either the open or the closed union. In the closed shop with the open union, the employer may hire whom he pleases, but if he employs a nonunion man, the latter must join the union before he begins work. In the closed shop with the closed union, the employer may employ only men who are already members of unions. The power of the employers to discharge a workman is limited as well as their power to hire him. The causes of the discharge must be passed upon by the union official, or the other workers will walk out. On the other hand, efficient workers who lose their standing in the union must be discharged.

In some cases the employer actually performs some of the administrative work of the union. This is known as the "check-off" system. Employers maintain records and deduct the union dues and fines from the wages of their workers. These are subsequently turned over to the union officials. The "check-off" system is very common in the organized bituminous coal fields, where it works with remarkably little friction in administrative detail.

The closed shop with the closed union is a labor monopoly which is difficult to defend. It is an autocracy of labor which discriminates against capable workers who are not members of the union, entrance into which is sometimes difficult. The anti-union shop is also discriminatory, in that it forces workers to give up their right to union membership. There are some anti-union shops in which the employee is not only solicitous about the well-being of his employees, but is also willing to treat with them. On the other hand, many nonunion shops are openly or secretly hostile to the very principle of collective bargaining. In some cases a resort to the spy system is made by employers in order to eliminate any union organizers or sympathizers.

Employee representation may be achieved in nonunion shops through what are known as company unions, that is, organizations of workers employed in particular plants. It is doubtful whether employee representation through company unions should be classified as collective bargaining, because many powerful weapons of organized labor are sacrificed. The American Federation of Labor has bitterly opposed company unions. "Walking delegates," or union organizers who are not employees, have been regarded as essential to effective collective bargaining. The fear of discharge makes an employee timid about pressing the claims of the workers, and the lure of promotion or special favors may tempt him to sell out to his employer.

Since the period of the World War, associations of manufacturers and other employers' organizations have begun a national campaign in behalf of the open shop. Organized labor has been equally insistent upon the closed shop. The literature of both sides has been propagandist rather than unbiased, and emotional rather than scientific. Any economic problem has its two sides, and its advantages as well as its disadvantages. The advocates of the open shop indict the closed shop with being "un-American," monopolistic, and unfair to both the employer and unorganized labor. It is sometimes charged that the public welfare is endangered by the closed shop, which is classified with various forms of radicalism and often regarded a cause of many existing economic ills. Employers contend that the closed shop prevents them from running their own business without outside interference. All workers are reduced to the dead level of mediocrity under union control as to output, wages, and working conditions. The unorganized workers are deprived of their "constitutional right of freedom of contract" to sell their labor as they see fit. The general public suffers in the form of high prices.

Organized labor replies that the open shop exists in name only and that most open shops are in reality antiunion shops. The movement in favor of the open shop is merely a disguised movement against organized labor. It is held that effective collective bargaining is dependent upon the closed shop, and that without collective bargaining the exploitation of the worker would result. Moreover, the closed shop with the open union is democratic and not monopolistic. It is also strange that great monopolies of capital should dare to raise the charge of monopoly against the closed shop. If modern large-scale business finds it necessary to standardize the quality of its product as well as its prices, why should not organized labor do the same for its services? Many advocates of the closed shop justify the coercion upon unorganized labor to join unions. The nonunion man who works beside a union man receives the benefits of collective bargaining in wages, hours, and working conditions. Why should he not be compelled to join the union and to assume some of the burden when he shares the benefits? In the last place, no employer has an absolute right to run his business without interference. The employee, as well as the employer, and the laborer as well as the capitalist, must share in the determination of conditions of industry. Industrial absolutism must give way to industrial democracy.

14. Summary.—Economic maladjustments may be attacked with either economic or political weapons. Economic progress may be achieved by state legislation, by collective bargaining, and by the individual efforts of socially minded employers. The study of labor legislation and labor organization is supplementary, for economic maladjustments may be attacked by the state from without or by the workers from within industrial society.

The disadvantages of the individual workers under the present wage system gave rise to modern collective bargaining. The century following the Industrial Revolution witnessed the growth of various kinds of labor organizations. Their principal objectives were the raising of wages and the shortening of hours, rather than the improvement of general working conditions. State legislation rather than organized labor has attacked such problems as dangerous trades and unsanitary working conditions. On the other hand, the state has generally refused to interfere in the matter of wages and sometimes in the matter of hours in the case of adult, male workers.

Early trade unions in Great Britain were regarded as conspiracies and punished as such. At the present time, however, they enjoy a singular freedom from legal restriction within that nation. Within the United States, labor organizations are no longer viewed as conspiracies, but their legal status is uncertain. The present legal battle centers about certain weapons of collective bargaining and the practices of labor organizations rather than about their right to exist. Although generally organized as voluntary associations, they are sometimes incorporated.

Labor organizations may be classified according to their type of organization, *e.g.* industrial unions or trade unions; or according to their functions and methods, *e.g.* conservative or revolutionary unions. The significance of the Knights of Labor is merely historical. The American Federation of Labor and the

Industrial Workers of the World are the two important organizations of labor at the present time within the United States. The American Federation of Labor relies upon the strike, the boycott, and other methods of collective bargaining, but the Industrial Workers of the World advocate the general strike and sabotage. The former accepts the present industrial system, but the latter seeks to overthrow modern capitalism. Although the American Federation of Labor numbers several millions, a larger portion of the workers of the country are unorganized. Illustrations are unskilled labor, agricultural workers, and children.

Trade unions can raise the wages of their own members by such monopoly practices as the limitation of apprentices. This creates an artificial scarcity in the supply of a given type of service and hence raises its price. Restriction of output is an attempt to increase the volume of employment, but it merely raises prices and lowers real wages. Collective bargaining has often raised money wages rather than real wages, and the wages of organized groups at the expense of unorganized groups. On the other hand, it has limited the competition between various workers and prevented exploitation by unscrupulous employers. It may be viewed as an attempt to standardize the labor commodity and to balance the competitive power of the two parties to the labor contract.

Collateral Reading

ATKINS, W. E., and LASSWELL, H. D., "Labor Attitude and Problems," chaps. 16 and 17.

BLUM, S., "Labor Economics," chaps. 5, 13, 14, 15 and 18.

CARLTON, F. T., "History and Problems of Organized Labor," chaps. 1 to 6.

COMMONS. J. R., "Trade Unionism and Labor Problems," Second Series, chaps. 24 to 29 incl.

FAIRCHILD, F. R., FURNISS, E. S., and BUCK, N. S., "Elementary Economics," chap. 53.

FURNISS, E. S., "Labor Problems," chaps. 8–11.

GROAT, G. G., "Organized Labor in America," chaps. 1 to 8 incl. and 16, 17, 19 and 20.

HAMILTON, W., "Current Economic Problems," pp. 615–650 and pp. 677–686.

WATKINS, G. S., "Introduction to a Study of Labor Problems," chaps. 6, 15, and 16.

WRIGHT, S. D., "Industrial Evolution of the United States," chaps. 19 and 20.

References

BEARD, M., "A Short History of the American Labor Movement."

BRISSENDEN, P. F., "History of the I. W. W."

BROOKS, J. G., "American Syndicalism: the I. W. W."
COMMONS, J. R., "History of Labor in the United States."
ELY, R. T., "The Labor Movement in America."
FITCH, J. A. "Causes of Industrial Unrest."
GOMPERS, S., "The American Labor Movement."
HOLLANDER, J. H., "Studies in American Trade Unionism."
HOXIE, R. F., "Trade Unionism in the United States."
MITCHELL, J., "Organized Labor."
PERLMAN, S., "History of Trade Unions in United States."
POWDERLY, T. V., "Thirty Years of Labor."
TANNENBAUM, F., "The Labor Movement."
United States Industrial Commission *Reports*, 1901 and 1902.
WEBB, SIDNEY, and BEATRICE, "History of Trade Unionism."

Questions for Discussion

1. How and why were early trade unions opposed in England?
2. Are labor organizations combinations in restraint of trade?
3. Outline the different classifications of labor organizations.
4. Contrast the American Federation of Labor with the Industrial Workers of the World with regard to organization, weapons and objectives.
5. Can it be fairly said that the American Federation of Labor represents the workers of the nation?
6. What do you understand by the wage system?
7. How did the Industrial Revolution affect the status of labor?
8. What do you understand by collective bargaining?
9. Indicate the disadvantages of the individual worker in bargaining.
10. Differentiate between the primary and secondary functions of trade unions. Illustrate.

Topics for Investigation

1. Effects of labor organizations upon wages.
2. Theories of wages.
3. Fraternal and benefit features of trade unions.
4. The early struggle for existence of trade unions.
5. The labor movement in America before the Civil War.
6. Trade unions outside the American Federation of Labor.
7. The organization and constitution of some trade union with which you are familiar.
8. Its relationship with other such organizations.
9. The Industrial Workers of the World and the World War.

CHAPTER XXVI

INDUSTRIAL CONFLICT AND THE PROMOTION OF INDUSTRIAL PEACE

1. Nature of Strikes.—The United States Bureau of Labor has defined a strike as "a concerted withdrawal from work by a part or all of the employees of an establishment, or several establishments, to enforce a demand on the part of the employees." The counter weapon of the employer is the lockout. Both are manifestations of industrial unrest and represent conflict rather than cooperation. The causes of strikes and lock-outs are similar, and the result is the same, namely, a cessation of work. In the former case, the initiative lies with the employees, and in the latter case with the employer. Initiative, however, means very little, for employers can create conditions which result in strikes and employees can create conditions which result in lock-outs. A scientific analysis of the causes of both international and industrial warfare requires more knowledge than merely which party to the conflict fired the first gun.

Strikes may be either positive or negative. They are said to be positive if the workers are making demands for improved conditions of labor, but negative when they are merely striving to maintain existing standards. They are similarly classified as attack strikes and defense strikes. Strikes may be classified according to their extent, as well as according to their purpose. There may be local, national, or international strikes. Local strikes are those which are confined to a particular plant or to plants in a single occupation or within a limited area. National strikes affect an entire industry and are operative throughout the country. Illustrations are coal and railroad strikes. International strikes are relatively rare, although the effects of any large strike may be international. A general strike involves the cessation of work in all industries. The sympathetic strike is a cessation of work by employees in other industries than the one in which the strike originates. It is apt to be unsuccessful and it is rarely used by the trade unions belonging to the American Federation of Labor. Fellow workers in other industries can cooperate with the strikers more effectively as consumers than as producers. A sympathetic boycott is generally more practical than a sympathetic strike.

2. Development and Extent.—The forerunners of modern strikes were the slave insurrections of ancient Rome and the peasants' revolts of medieval Europe. Strikes are as old as the wage system itself; we can find references to them in the chronicles of the fourteenth, fifteenth, and sixteenth centuries. The first recorded strike in America was that of the journeymen bakers of New York City, in 1741, for increased wages. The bakers were tried and convicted of conspiracy, but no record remains of a sentence passed upon them. Other sporadic illustrations of local strikes may be found in the closing years of the eighteenth century and the opening years of the nineteenth century. During the period of rising prices before the panic of 1837, a relatively large number of strikes occurred. It was not until after the Civil War, however, that the problem assumed a national aspect. The first great labor dispute in the United States was the railway strike of 1877. Although the chief disturbance was centered about Pittsburg, riots were common elsewhere. Interstate commerce was crippled and considerable property was destroyed. A resort was finally made to the state militia.

Prior to 1881, statistics as to industrial disputes were very incomplete. From 1881 to 1905, however, the Bureau of Labor attempted to compile information as to strikes and lockouts. During this quarter of a century there occurred 36,757 strikes and 1,546 lockouts. The average length of strikes was twenty-five days and of lockouts about eighty-five days. Approximately two hundred thousand establishments and seven million workers were involved. Nearly half of these strikes occurred in the great industrial states of Pennsylvania, New York, and Illinois, and more than half if we include Ohio and Massachusetts. Peak years were 1894, the year of the Pullman strike, and 1902, the year of the anthracite coal strike. The period of the World War produced a great increase in the number of strikes. From 1916 to 1921, inclusive, there took place almost twenty thousand strikes and over six hundred lockouts.

It is controversial as to whether industrial disputes are more common in periods of economic prosperity than in periods of depression. In the former case strikes are probably more numerous, but in the latter case they are apt to be serious and protracted. Strikes are symptoms of industrial unrest, which is most acute in periods of economic readjustment.

The success of a strike is very difficult to measure. There are indirect results as well as direct results. Moreover, any resultant gains must be balanced against the losses sustained during the strike. There is a definite connection between the strength of labor organization and the success of strikes. Strikes called in the absence of effective organization almost invariably fail. Strikes are generally more successful in periods of prosperity than in periods of depression.

3. Causes of Strikes.—Industrial conflicts, like international conflicts, have a number of causes. They are frequently so blended together that it is difficult to isolate a single cause and to distinguish between immediate and remote causes. Some leading causes of industrial unrest have been indicated in our discussion of the objectives of organized labor. The chief causes of strikes are demands for increased wages, for a reduction in the number of hours, and for a recognition of the union and union rules. Although still the chief cause of industrial disputes, the wage rate seems to have declined in relative importance as compared with purely union causes of strikes.

The growing strength of organized labor is making the strike a more formidable weapon of collective bargaining. The statistics of strikes give little ground for the feeling that they are on the decrease. The number of employees and establishments affected, as well as the number of strikes, seems to be on the increase. On the other hand, the percentage of successful strikes seems to be decreasing. This may be due to an increasing centralization of control over capital. Not only are strikes becoming of greater importance to both labor and capital, but also to the general public. Recent strikes or threats to strike in key industries, such as the coal mines and the railroads, have made the problem one of great national importance. Causes of strikes must be studied and an attempt made to avert them, as well as to regulate the conduct of strikes by the elimination of flagrantly unsocial practices.

4. Economic and Social Losses.—Attempts to determine the cost of industrial conflicts are as varied as attempts to estimate the cost of the World War. The Bureau of Labor estimated that the total loss due to strikes and lockouts during the twenty years from 1881 to 1900 was almost a half billion dollars.[1]   This is a large lump sum, but it becomes very small when divided among the large number of people concerned or spread out over these twenty years on a weekly basis.   The workman has probably spent less than 1 per cent of his income on strikes, or probably less than one day per year per adult working man.[2]   When compared with the total volume of unemployment, the unemployment due to strikes and lockouts is relatively small.   Moreover, when strikes and lockouts take place in slack seasons or in periods of economic depression, the resulting unemployment is not due entirely to these industrial conflicts.

The indirect losses of industrial conflicts are larger than the direct losses, and the social costs greater than the economic costs.   Violence often accompanies strikes and lockouts.   Conservative labor leaders deplore the use of violence, which frequently acts as a boomerang and alienates public sympathy. Revolutionary unionism, on the other hand, condones the use of open or secret force.   Strikes of well-organized unions of skilled workers are less apt to be accompanied by violence than are those of poorly organized and unskilled workers.   A large portion of the disorder which accompanies strikes can be ascribed neither to the employers nor to the striking employees.   It is the work of various restless elements in the community which have no regard for law and order and which care little for either human or property rights.   The attempt of an employer to keep his plant in operation often converts peaceful strikes into scenes of violence.   This was the situation at Herrin, Illinois, where it was necessary to proclaim martial law.   Although strikers have sometimes asserted that troops are employed in order to break strikes and to weaken labor organizations, such measures become necessary when the local civil authorities are no longer able to cope with the situation.   In times of grave disorder Federal aid can be requested, for the Constitution provides that a republican form of government shall be guaranteed to the individual states.   Industrial conflict may not only result in a destruction of life and property, but it may endanger for a time the very existence of a democratic form of government.

[1] Cf. "Monthly Labor Review," Sept., 1920, p. 189.
[2] Cf. MITCHELL, J., "Organized Labor," pp. 309–310.

5. Legality of Strikes.—The legality of trade unions and the right of labor to organize are merely historical questions. Nevertheless, many methods of collective bargaining are of doubtful legality. The strike as a collective cessation of work is recognized as legal, where the aim is an improvement in the condition of the employees. On the other hand, where the primary purpose of the strike is the injuring of the employer or of nonunion workers, it is generally regarded as illegal. The intent of a strike like that of a boycott must be considered. Moreover, a strike is also to be condemned when the elements of coercion or intimidation are present.

The laws on the legality of strikes, as well as their judicial interpretation, vary greatly from state to state. Strikes were forbidden in all basic industries in Kansas when the compulsory arbitration of industrial disputes was in vogue. On the other hand, strikes are legalized by the laws of California. The problem here is not so much one of the legality of a given strike, but of the methods used in conducting it. The law merely insists on the absence of violence. The legality of a strike depends on the industry, as well as on the state in which it occurs. There is a growing feeling against strikes of public employees. The strike of the Boston policemen in 1919 was universally condemned. A strike of railroad employees endangers the industrial life of the nation and causes untold suffering. It would seem that the essential nature of an occupation must limit the power to utilize the strike, rather than merely to increase its potential effectiveness as a weapon of collective bargaining for a particular group of workers.

6. Picketing.—Although a strike may be legal, the methods used in conducting it may be illegal. Violence and unlawful measures may be resorted to in order to terrorize the employer and the employees who remain at work. Danger arises when the employer endeavors to keep his plant running by filling the vacant places of the strikers with nonunion workers. Individuals make a living by keeping on hand groups of laborers who may be rushed from place to place to act as strike breakers. These industrial mercenaries are composed of the unskilled and casual laborers, including chiefly the ignorant, the reckless, and the indifferent elements in the laboring population. Organized labor has attached the stigma of the word "scab" to strike breakers. They are hated more intensely than the employers themselves, to whom they are regarded as having sold out. Strike breakers are viewed as taking bread out of the mouths of labor, and they must frequently work under the protection of the guns of plant guards.

The term "picketing" is used to designate attempts of strikers to persuade the employees remaining at work to join the strike. Pickets are placed a short distance from the entrances and exits of the plant, and they attempt to dissuade the workers from continuing work. Picketing may develop from peaceful persuasion to threats of violence and intimidation. Picketing may extend from the borders of the plant into the homes of the workers. The "scab" may find it difficult to buy food and he may be subjected to numerous other annoyances. He may find his home damaged by some unseen hand or an unexpected missle thrown at his head. The danger lies not so much in picketing itself as in the violence growing out of it.

The Trades Disputes Act of 1906 legalized peaceful picketing in Great Britain. In the United States peaceful picketing was regarded as legal. This view was confirmed by the Clayton Act of 1914. On the other hand, intimidation and coercion have been condemned. Peaceful picketing without these attendant evils is very rare. Consequently, the courts have found it necessary to define what picketing may include. In December, 1921, Chief Justice Taft gave out the most complete statement yet issued by the Supreme Court of the United States upon the subject of picketing. It was pointed out that there are limits beyond which even persuasion may not go without violating the rights of others. "Persistence, importunity, following and dogging become unjustifiable annoyance and obstruction which is likely to savor of intimidation." The number of pickets that might be stationed at each point of ingress or egress was limited to one. A worker must be approached singly and not by a group in order for the element of coercion to be absent. "Appeals shall not be abusive, libelous, or threatening." This decision of Chief Justice Taft was viewed by organized labor as destroying the effectiveness of picketing.

The laws and judicial decisions of the individual states on picketing are as varied as those on the subject of strikes. In California, where neither strikes nor boycotts are violations of the state law, the courts have condemned the entire practice of picketing as intimidation. Several other states have also passed laws which make picketing illegal. The theory behind such legislation and judicial decision is that peaceful picketing is impossible.

7. Boycotts.—A boycott is an organized refusal of a number of persons to purchase goods from an individual or corporate producer. It has sometimes been used by the public at large as a protest against high prices and monopolies. It has been commonly used by groups of workers and trade unions to bring a recalcitrant employer to terms by checking his sales and profits. The boycott, as contrasted with the union label, is a negative rather than a positive weapon of organized labor.

The primary boycott is a refusal by the employees to buy articles produced by a firm which in their judgment is unfair to union labor. The secondary or compound boycott is one which involves other people who are not directly interested in the particular labor dispute. When the members of a given union seek to extend the boycott from their own membership to the general public and to persuade or coerce a third party into refusing to buy the product of the obnoxious firm, the primary boycott becomes a secondary boycott. The boycott tends to expand, if it is to become an effective weapon in industrial disputes.

The ultimate success of a boycott, like the success of a strike, depends on both the strength of the particular union and the general solidarity of all organized labor. Both may involve thousands of disinterested individuals and cause great suffering, injustice, and financial loss. In a recent street-car strike, for illustration, storekeepers were advised not to sell to various individuals who patronized the cars during the strike. The boycott and the strike went on simultaneously. In strong labor communities stores have been forced to discontinue the keeping in stock of products of boycotted companies. Not to comply with this temporary interdict of organized labor meant the loss of general patronage.

Although the legal status of the boycott is somewhat controversial, it is more definitely fixed than many other practises of organized labor. Under the common law, the legality of the boycott, like the legality of the strike, depends on its intent. In the absence of any Federal legislation on the subject, there came into existence a number of conflicting state laws. The courts have consistently ruled that boycotts are illegal if there exists a deliberate attempt to injure any one. It has been held that boycotts in order to be effective necessitate the coercion of third parties, and that they are therefore conspiracies which limit the constitutional guarantees to citizens of life, liberty, and property. It has been pointed out that there is a difference between an individual who refuses to patronize a given firm and a group of individuals who organize to accomplish this object collectively. The power to harm is greater and the element of conspiracy is present. If free from malicious intent, violence, or threats of violence, and if free from the attempt to coerce third parties, the boycott has generally been viewed as legal. Such a boycott is as rare as "civilized warfare."

The secondary boycott has generally been viewed by the courts as illegal. The passage of the Sherman Act of 1890 meant that boycotts might be considered to be combinations in restraint of trade. Boycotts have also been viewed as an interference with the Federal interstate commerce regulations. The Clayton Act of 1914 declared that labor unions should not be viewed as violations of the Sherman Act, although the right of injunction remains against threatened damage by a violation of the anti-trust laws. Boycotts are permitted if conducted by peaceful and lawful methods. Recent court decisions, however, have continued to hold the secondary boycott illegal, and the Clayton Act has not materially changed the legal status of this weapon of organized labor.

8. Injunctions.—Just as the boycott is a weapon of employees in industrial disputes, so the injunction is usually a weapon of the employer. Organized labor has fought not only for the extension of the boycott, but also for the restriction of the injunction. An injunction is an order from a court in equity to various individuals to do or to cease from doing certain particular things. The judge issues the order, and determines whether it has been disobeyed. Any one who violates such a court order is guilty of contempt of court and can be summarily punished without jury trial or a recourse to cumbersome judicial routine. The injunction is naturally an emergency measure, and it is designed to prevent irreparable injury to persons or property until a final determination of right can be made. Of recent years, this legal weapon has become a rather common resort in industrial disputes. Moreover, instead of specifying certain particular acts, "blanket" injunctions have frequently been issued.

Among the most famous uses of the injunction in labor disputes was the Debs case in connection with the railroad strike of 1894. The general public suffered greatly from interference with interstate commerce and the delay of the mails. An injunction was issued against all persons from interfering with interstate commerce and the transportation of the mails. Disobedience of this order was punished as contempt of court, in spite of the fact that under existing Federal statutes interference with the mail was already specified as a crime. Another important instance of the use of the injunction was the Buck Stove and Range Company case, in which three high officials of the American Federation of Labor—Samuel Gompers, John Mitchell and Frank Morrison—were sentenced to imprisonment for disobeying the order of the court.

Organized labor has objected to "blanket" injunctions and to their issuance when no emergency justifies the sacrifice of due process of law. The objections to the injunction, or rather to the abuse of the injunction, are as follows: in the first place, it leads to a sacrifice of the constitutional guarantees of freedom of speech and freedom of the press. In the second place, it is contended that full publicity as to working conditions is desirable and that the injunction is often used to suppress the full facts. Has not a person or a combination of persons the right to make public the fact that a given plant pays low wages, works long hours, or opposes the closed shop? If an individual's business is injured, the intent is not personal or malicious, but merely the general improvement of working conditions.

The Clayton Act of 1914 attempted to remedy some of the abuses of the injunction. It provided that injunctions, issued by the Federal courts, should not prohibit the stoppage of work, peaceful picketing, and the refusal to patronize. Moreover, a jury trial was to be allowed in contempt of court cases where the offense was indictable as a crime. It was further provided that no preliminary injunction should be served without notice to the opposite party, nor any restraining order issued without similar notice, unless it was evident that immediate and irreparable injury would result. Recent judicial decisions seem to show, however, that the Clayton Act has not restricted the injunction any more than it has extended the boycott. It applies merely to the Federal courts and not to the state courts. State legislation, however, has also attempted to limit injunctions and to prevent their abuse.   An anti-injunction law was passed in 1913 by the state of Arizona, but it was declared unconstitutional by the Supreme Court of the United States in 1921.

9. Methods of Adjusting Industrial Disputes.—The *laissez-faire* philosophy of government was possible so long as competition prevailed, industries were small in size, and workers were unorganized.   The development of modern capitalism and concentrated control, on the one hand, and the evolution of labor organization, on the other hand, made such an economic philosophy no longer tenable.   The rise of collective bargaining has meant the growth of strong organizations of employers and employees.   The economic and social costs of modern industrial conflicts are so great that the general public can no longer remain a mere spectator or a silent partner.   Today, the social control of industry is crystallizing into new and varied forms.   Industrial peace, like international peace, is seeking articulation in some practical forms, as well as in mere idealistic expressions.   The chief methods for the settlement of industrial differences are trade agreements, conciliation, mediation, and arbitration.

Trade agreements are compacts as to wages, hours, recognition of the union and general conditions of employment, which are made between an employer or an association of employers and the employees.   The agreement is generally reached at a joint conference and has a specific time limit, at the end of which a new conference is held for the purpose of drawing up a new trade agreement or reaffirming an old one.   Trade agreements are moral rather than legal compacts, since there is no governmental machinery for their enforcement.   Moreover, they are primarily agreements between employers and organized employees, in which the general public or the state has no representatives.

The term "conciliation" should be used for the settlement of industrial disputes without the interference of a third party. Trade agreements are normal and regular, but conciliation implies the existence of a crisis or of the failure to reach an agreement. Mediation is the presence of an outside person or a nonpartisan body for the facilitation of industrial peace.   Conciliation and mediation are similar in that neither is compulsory.   Both parties must first agree as to the acceptance or to the subsequent election of the award.   The mediator has been termed a "confidential advisor" and an "industrial diplomat."   His chief function is to help the two sides come to an agreement of their own accord, rather than to render an award or decision of his own making.

Industrial arbitration, on the other hand, is judicial rather than diplomatic. Arbitration means the existence of a person, board, or court for the purpose of making an investigation and submitting a decision. Arbitration may be either compulsory or voluntary, and the acceptance of the award may likewise be either compulsory or voluntary. Reliance is sometimes placed upon publicity rather than upon legal compulsion. Compulsory arbitration with the voluntary acceptance of the award merely means compulsory investigation.

10. Relative Advantages of Various Methods of Governmental Action.—The various attempts of governments to adjust industrial disputes may be grouped as mediation, voluntary arbitration, compulsory investigation, and compulsory arbitration. Great Britain, the Federal government of the United States, and most individual states of the Union have utilized mediation and voluntary arbitration. Compulsory investigation has been tried in Canada and Colorado. Compulsory arbitration has been used in Australasia and Kansas. What are the relative advantages and disadvantages of these different methods?

The chief advantage of mediation is that it permits the disputants to solve their own problems. A common understanding and voluntary agreement between the two parties is better than some award imposed by an outside body of arbitration. A governmental commission of mediation accomplished a great forward step in merely bringing together the two disputants. A discussion of the mutual differences develops a knowledge of "the other fellow's point of view." A sympathetic understanding of mutual differences may develop a way out of the difficulty or a possible compromise.

Arbitration and mediation are different stages rather than different methods. After mediation has been tried unsuccessfully, the two parties may agree to submit their differences to an impartial board of arbitration. Voluntary arbitration of industrial disputes, like that of international disputes, is far superior to the costly methods of fighting them out. It is alleged, however, that an outside board of arbitration cannot be familiar with existing conditions and with the problems at issue. In order to obviate this disadvantage, representatives of both employers and employees are sometimes placed on the board of arbitration in addition to representatives of the general public. In such a tri-part body, however, the votes of the first two groups are assured in advance, and the real decision rests as before with the representatives of the public. The award of such a non-partisan board of arbitration is apt to be a compromise which is pleasing to neither party. The resulting peace may be only temporary.

Compulsory investigation means an impartial study of the causes of an industrial dispute. More light without more heat, is the slogan. A public statement of the findings will rest the case with the great jury of public opinion. The temporary suspension of the right to strike, which is necessarily involved, may result not merely in the postponement of industrial warfare, but often in its elimination.

The advocates of compulsory arbitration point out that mediation, voluntary arbitration, and compulsory investigation minimize industrial conflicts, but they do not entirely eliminate them. Compulsory arbitration is defended as a final resort because of the tremendous economic and social losses involved in industrial conflicts. Moreover, the complexity and interdependent character of our modern civilization means that strikes, lockouts, boycotts, and other weapons of industrial warfare injure countless individuals who are not parties to the disputes. In the final analysis, the case for compulsory arbitration rests on the public welfare which is jeopardized by industrial conflicts.

There are numerous arguments against this drastic step of compulsory arbitration. The existence of a powerful board of arbitration, whose award is compulsory, implies the existence of certain standards of justice in accordance with which the judgment is rendered. The determination of a "fair" wage is even more difficult than the determination of a minimum wage. The change from reliance on natural economic forces to dependence on political machinery has been termed the entering wedge of socialism. It is regarded as destructive of such pillars of modern capitalism as economic competition and individual enterprise. Boards of compulsory arbitration have been viewed as price-fixing bodies for the labor commodity. The judicial method of using precedents makes difficult the development of the concept of a progressive wage. Organized labor has also attacked compulsory arbitration because of the resulting limitations on the weapons of collective bargaining. The right of labor to strike is sacrificed. Moreover, the reasons for the existence of trade unionism are lessened, as they no longer exercise their primary weapons or functions. Again, the enforcement of unpopular decisions is difficult, for individuals cannot be compelled to work against their will. Most of the verdicts of courts of compulsory arbitration in both Australasia and Kansas have been favorable to labor. Nevertheless, the cry of favoritism or prejudice has been raised by both sides. Ultra conservatism, on the one hand, or radicalism, on the other, is charged by the defeated litigant. Finally, the legality or constitutionality of compulsory arbitration is a serious question in the United States. It would seem that judicial opinion might sanction it in public utilities and in basic industries, but would oppose it as a general principle capable of universal application.

11. Compulsory Arbitration in Practice.—New Zealand led in this field when it passed a law in 1894 which made strikes and lockouts misdemeanors. The system of administration was later built up around what were known as industrial unions. Any fifteen or more employees, any three or more individual employers, or an incorporated company might constitute such an organization. Existing trade unions were frankly recognized as parts of the system. There are state officials known as commissioners of conciliation who seek to mediate in industrial disputes. When the efforts of the commissioner are futile, he organizes a council of conciliation by asking each side to appoint the same number of assessors to serve with him upon this board. This council suggests compromises and attempts to adjust differences.

In case of failure to reach an acceptable solution, an appeal is made to the court of arbitration, which is an important governmental tribunal. Its presiding officer is a judge of the Supreme Court, and the governor appoints in addition one member to represent the employers and one to represent the employees. These two appointees are selected from the industrial unions of employers and of organized labor. This court of three members has full powers of investigation and there is no appeal from its decision. The time limit of the award, which is carefully specified, is generally three years. This award may also be applied to all similar workers in a given industry and in a given locality. Strikes or lockouts for the purpose of changing the conditions specified in the judicial award are illegal and punishable by heavy fines. The New Zealand experiment was imitated in Western Australia and New South Wales. In 1904, a Federal compulsory arbitration law was passed for industries under Federal jurisdiction. South Australia and Queensland likewise later adopted compulsory arbitration.

The state of Kansas in 1920 introduced compulsory arbitration in industrial disputes. In New Zealand, strikes are illegal for registered unions, but in Kansas they were illegal for vital industries which seriously affected the public interest. The scope of compulsory arbitration was somewhat differently determined. The Kansas law specified public utilities and industries producing such necessities as fuel, clothing, and food. Indeed, the law grew out of a serious coal strike. The Kansas Court of Industrial Relations consisted of three judges appointed by the governor on the approval of the state senate. This body for industrial arbitration was unique in that it contained representatives from neither employers nor employees. The familiar tri-part composition was entirely absent and the court was nonpartisan. In spite of its judicial character, the functions of the Industrial Relations Court were largely administrative. It was given the powers which were previously held by the Public Utilities Commission and later those of the Industrial Welfare Commission and the Department of Labor.

In cases of industrial disputes the court could investigate on its own initiative or on a request from either party or from a group of citizens. As a result of its findings it could issue an order as to hours, wages, or general working conditions. For a defiance of its orders, the court could bring suit in the Supreme Court of Kansas. Fines and imprisonment could be imposed, and several mine leaders were actually sentenced. The court was empowered to operate an industry during a labor crisis, if conditions seemed to warrant this measure. Although the right of labor to organization and to collective bargaining was not denied, the law prohibited strikes, lockouts, picketing, boycotts, and other weapons of industrial conflicts. Although individuals might quit work themselves, they could not induce other workers to do so collectively in vital public industries.

The Kansas Court of Industrial Relations attracted tremendous interest throughout the United States as the first American experiment in compulsory arbitration. Organized labor consistently opposed the project. Within the state of Kansas, the

Industrial Relations Court became a political issue in the fall election of 1922. The Democratic party, which represented the opposition, was victorious at the polls and soon began to strip the court of its powers. It later abolished the Court and transferred its power to a public utilities commission. In 1923, the Supreme Court of the United States had declared unconstitutional the application of the act to the meat-packing industry. Another similar decision in 1925 undermined compulsory arbitration by declaring it unconstitutional wherever its effect was "to compel owners and employees to continue the business on lines not of their own making."

12. Compulsory Investigation.—The Canadian Industrial Disputes Act of 1907 made strikes and lockouts unlawful until the causes of the disputes had been investigated by a governmental body appointed for that purpose and full publicity had been given to the results of its investigation. This law was applicable to all public utilities and mines. Moreover, thirty days' notice must be given in advance of any change or organized demand for a change in wages or hours. Thus, an opportunity is given to either party to apply to the Department of Labor for a board of conciliation and investigation. This is a tri-part body of three members. Strikes and lockouts are forbidden prior to the publication of the findings of this body and penalties imposed for any such offenses. The postponement of the opening of industrial conflict gives an opportunity for both mediation and investigation. The aim is to prevent strikes rather than to settle them. Unlike compulsory arbitration, this law does not make illegal these weapons of collective bargaining, but merely restricts their use. A recent decision by Lord Haldane held the Canadian Industrial Disputes Act to be a violation of the British North American Act, which is the constitution of the Dominion of Canada.

The Colorado Industrial Commission Act of 1915 is similar to the Canadian Industrial Disputes Act. It provides for compulsory investigation and makes strikes and lockouts illegal in the interim. The Industrial Commission has the further power of making an award, but its acceptance is not compulsory. Thirty days' notice must be given before employers can make changes in conditions of employment, or before the workers can call a strike. This act is applicable to all large industries. Agriculture, domestic service, and very small establishments employing less than four workers are exempt.

13. Trade Agreements.—The development of governmental machinery for the adjustment of industrial disputes has been paralleled by the organization of similar institutions on the part of organized labor and associations of employers. Both the state and the Federal governments have been acquiring a new function, namely, the development of better industrial relations. Even more significant, however, has been the gradual evolution of parliamentary, judicial, and diplomatic machinery for the functioning of collective bargaining directly between employees and employers, and for the settlement of industrial disputes by the parties themselves. Within the political state, but often apart from it, numerous experiments in industrial democracy are being tried. Trade agreements, industrial representation, and profit sharing are some of its chief manifestations.

Trade agreements are collective bargains between representatives of organized labor and associations of employers. A compact is made concerning wages, hours, and conditions of employment in a particular industry, which is to hold good until another joint conference takes place. Trade agreements are practical rather than idealistic. They do not often represent attempts to harmonize the general interests of labor and capital, but rather attempts frankly to face existing differences in a given industry. The alignment of interests is clear cut, and there is no participation of the public.

The usual parliamentary filibustering, higgling, and political chicanery are present on both sides. After both labor and capital have been forced to show their hands and to play their trump cards, a heated discussion takes place. Either of two things results—a compromise, which is largely determined by relative bargaining power, or a declaration of war. Loss of profits, on the one side, and loss of wages, on the other, are the sinister shadows which hover over the discussion. In order to prevent industrial warfare, each side generally yields on certain points and hopes that conditions will be more favorable at the next conference. The general public watches from a distance this economic volcano, which is never extinct but merely temporarily quiet. However, the trade agreements of the well-organized and better-paid industries are fairly well kept. On the other hand, there is generally no legal weapon for their enforcement.

The repeated failures of joint conferences to make successful trade agreements is interpreted as a failure to function successfully as devices for securing industrial peace. Trade agreements are common in the coal-mining industry but they have not succeeded in eliminating strikes although they may reduce them. Moreover, the absence of representatives of the public from trade agreements is feared by some students of the problem. Representatives of the consumers are not present to oppose an agreement for higher wages and for necessarily higher prices of the commodity produced. Trade agreements may promote harmony within an industry, but the public may be forced to pay the bill. Nevertheless, contented workers are more effective producers, and freedom from labor troubles is a business asset. Trade agreements, accompanied by provisions for voluntary arbitration, are common in the clothing industry. The Hart, Schaffner and Marx agreement is a notable illustration of effective machinery for the elimination and settlement of industrial disputes.

14. Industrial Representation.—Industrial representation is the participation of workers in the control of their working conditions. It is representative government in industry. This new economic ideal is reflected in such institutions as shop committees, works councils, and industrial councils. The first organization is confined to one department of a plant and the second organization includes the entire factory. District industrial councils are regional, but national industrial councils are Federal rather than local. All of these different units, however, are similar in that they include representatives of both employees and employers. Their primary reason for existence is the reduction of industrial unrest. The aim is not merely the settlement of industrial disputes, but also their elimination. These parliaments of industry are designed to serve as peaceful channels for the rubbing away of friction points between capital and labor. They may serve as agencies of education in the points of view of the opposite side. Better mutual understandings will promote industrial good will and efficiency. Although sometimes prompted by practical and even selfish motives, they are generally the expression of the new democratic ideal in industry.

Although industrial representation is old, it received a new stimulus during the World War. Experiments have been tried in America and in other countries, but the most elaborate plans have been worked out in Great Britain. The Reconstruction

Committee Subcommittee on Relations between Employers and Employees, which is generally termed the "Whitley Committee," made its famous report in 1917. It sought to attack the causes of industrial unrest and to continue the economic cooperation which the war had engendered. Participation in the control of industry seemed more fundamental than schemes of profit sharing. The "Whitley Committee" therefore recommended national joint industrial councils, district industrial councils and works councils in all possible industries. Great flexibility of organization was desired because of the divergent character of different industries. The Industrial Councils Division of the Ministry of Labor was created for the purpose of assisting in the formation of these industrial councils. Practical applications of this scheme have been made in Great Britain, and the movement has also spread to the continent of Europe. The machinery of existing trade unions has been utilized to a considerable extent.

Industrial representation exists in America, but not on the same scale as in Great Britain. Moreover, it has developed apart from the organized labor movement. The impetus in this country has come from neither the government nor from trade unions, but rather from individual employers, who have voluntarily introduced schemes of industrial representation among their own workmen. These various attempts at employee representation have been prompted by broad humanitarian motives, by the practical desire to develop industrial good will as a business asset, or by efforts to capture the control of the labor movement. They form a part of the general story of labor management rather than of industrial conciliation.

Justly or unjustly, organized labor has looked askance at "company unions," and has insisted that labor must work out its own salvation by means of its own organization and its own weapons of collective bargaining. In 1919, the American Federation of Labor formally expressed its objections to "company unions" or plant systems of collective bargaining and industrial representation. The charges of unfair elections and intimidation of representatives were made. It was further contended that the company representatives attempted to divert the attention of the workers from the real objects of collective bargaining into such items as "safety-first" movements and educational programs for increased efficiency and greater production. Again, "company unions" were regarded as lacking in power and in danger of becoming subservient implements of employers' associations. Behind all these arguments, there was the great fear that the whole organized labor movement would be weakened.

Many employers are also opposed to industrial representation, but for different reasons. They insist on their individual right to run their own business in their own way, and resent the attempt of employees to dictate or to pry into what they consider their own affairs. Other employers are sympathetic toward a participation by the workers in the control of industry, but they are skeptical of the ability of labor to do this in an intelligent fashion. The success of industrial representation is dependent on intelligent labor leadership, as well as on the sympathy and vision of the employer. Great precautions should be taken in the introduction of any such scheme. Many have failed because they were applied without any previous attempt to create a sentiment in favor of them among the workers. Sudden liberty may spell license to the irresponsible laborer.

15. Profit Sharing.—Greater participation in the product of industry, as well as in the control of industry, is another aim of the labor movement. The promotion of industrial peace has found expression in profit sharing as well as in industrial representation. Although labor has attempted through collective bargaining to increase the share of the national income which goes to wages, it has been unable or unwilling to participate in the financial risks of industry. Although demands for increased wages have emanated from the workers, schemes of profit sharing have generally come from employers.

Profit sharing may be defined as a method of industrial remuneration by which the employee receives in addition to his regular wage a definite share, fixed in advance, of the profits of the business. Thus, profit sharing does not eliminate the wage system, but exists with it as an extra financial inducement to increased production or to decreased waste. In addition to these objectives, it has been utilized as a means of reducing labor turnover. Profit sharing has been the experiment of certain socially minded employers for the reduction of industrial unrest as well as for the promotion of efficiency. On the other hand, it has also been introduced for advertising purposes and for strengthening "company unions" at the expense of trade unionism.

Profit sharing may exist in many different forms, which fall into three general groups. In the first place, it may take the form of a cash distribution of profits. At the expiration of a definite period of time profits are computed in a manner previously decided upon, and then distributed to the workers as cash bonuses. In the second place, profit sharing may take the form of a distribution of shares of stock in the company. In the third place, profit sharing may take the form of pensions, annuities or other types of deferred savings.

Profit sharing schemes may also be classified according to the degree that they approximate true profit sharing. So-called profit-sharing schemes are often merely the payment of a bonus in times of prosperity without any real effort to make this bonus conform to a definite share of net profits. Again, profit sharing must be distinguished from gain sharing. Profit sharing treats the workers as a group or as a number of groups. The total profit is divided among the total number of workers according to some measure of increased production or decreased waste. It makes no effort to determine what contribution to profits has been made by the individual worker and to reward him accordingly. Gain sharing, however, has this objective. As under a system of piece work, the individual worker is rewarded according to his individual productivity. Although the worker may be paid by the time rather than by the piece rate, his individual productivity is measured in gain sharing. Any excess beyond a previously determined fair rate is correspondingly rewarded out of the profits of the firm.

The earliest form of profit sharing was the sliding scale. It usually provided for a basic wage below which wages might not fall. As the market price of the product increased, profits were paid to employees according to some prearranged scale. The assumption was that profits varied roughly with prices. Many early schemes of profit sharing have been abandoned. The most recent aspect of the profit sharing movement is the attempt of employers to induce their employees to become stockholders in the concern by giving them the privilege of buying shares of stock upon favorable terms. Employee ownership of stock has been encouraged by the United States Steel Corporation, the Atlantic Refining Company and other large corporations. The Philadelphia Rapid Transit Company, under Mitten management, has provided not only for employee representation, but also for profit sharing and the ownership of stock by employees.

16. Industrial Democracy.—The worker as a citizen enjoys the right of suffrage, although the political machine sometimes distorts this theoretical democracy into practical corruption and absolutism. The citizen as a worker generally has no such right to participate in the formation of the policy of the industry in which he labors. Very often he is a mere cog in the machinery.

Just as political absolutism has given way to political democracy, so industrial absolutism is also apparently on the wane. It is a far cry back to the absolute monarchy of Louis XIV, who was able to say "I am the state." It is also a far cry back to a generation ago in America, when an officer of a New York street railroad company refused arbitration with his employees upon the grounds that they were his servants, whose duty it was to do his bidding so long as they were in his employ. The absence of political democracy results in revolutions for which the ballot box is a preventive. The absence of industrial democracy results in economic unrest which is expressed in strikes and other forms of industrial warfare, rather than in peaceful manifestations.

It should be remembered, however, that democracy is an ideal, and that there is no such thing as absolute democracy. Industrial, as well as political democracy, is a progressive concept whose pathway is strewn with fantastic experiments, failures, and hypocrisy, as well as with practical achievements. "Benevolent despots in industry" and "capitalistic feudalism" seem to be passing off the stage in favor of the new economic ideal of the copartnership of labor. Such a situation, however, is conditioned by the spread of public education among the masses and by the development of broad and intelligent leadership in industry.

17. Summary.—The concentration of capital has been accompanied by an organization of labor, and associations of employers are matched by those of employees. While employers insist on the open shop, labor insists that the closed shop and the walking delegate are essential to effective collective bargaining. The use of the union label is a positive attempt and the use of the boycott is a negative attempt to organize the workers as consumers. Counter weapons of the employer are the blacklist and the injunction. Strikes and lockouts are symptoms of industrial unrest and represent militant aspects of collective bargaining. The resulting economic loss and the tendency toward violence demand that society scientifically attack the causes of industrial unrest and that industrial conflict be superseded by industrial cooperation between capital and labor.

The prevention of industrial disputes is even better than their settlement. In order to avoid the serious economic and social consequences of industrial warfare, arising out of the conflict of interest between employers and employees, various plans have been tried for the promotion of industrial peace. Mediation and voluntary arbitration have been used by the Federal government in interstate commerce and in other national industries, such as mining. Individual states have instituted boards of mediation and voluntary arbitration. Mediation is diplomatic and represents the attempt of an outside party to help the disputants solve their own problems. Arbitration, however, is essentially judicial and necessitates a verdict from an arbitration board. Most arbitration boards are tri-part bodies, consisting of representatives of the employees, of the employers, and of the public. In Australasia and Kansas the experiment of compulsory arbitration has been tried. In Canada and Colorado compulsory investigation has been utilized. The promotion of better industrial relations is a new function of modern government.

For the elimination of strikes and lockouts, organized labor has made trade agreements with associations of employers. Representatives of the public do not participate in these industrial armistices. Trade agreements rely on moral support rather than on legal compulsion for their enforcement. Industrial representation may be expressed through trade union organizations or through company unions. Workers are seeking participation in the control of industry as well as a share in its profits. Shop committees, works councils, and national industrial councils have been developed for the prevention of industrial disputes as well as for their settlement. Industrial representation, somewhat comparable to political representation, seems to be in the process of evolution. The American and French Revolutions were forward steps in political and social democracy, but the twentieth century may see the development of greater industrial democracy.

Collateral Reading

ATKINS, W. E., and LASSWELL, H. D., "Labor Attitudes and Problems,"
    chaps., 18, 20, and 26.
BLUM, S. "Labor Economics," chaps. 6, 11, 12, 16 and 17.

CARLTON, F. T., "History and Problems of Organized Labor," chaps. 6, 7, 8, and 10.

COMMONS, J. R., "Trade Unionism and Labor Problems," second series, chaps. 19 to 23 incl., 30 to 37 incl., and 39 to 41 incl.

COMMONS, J. R., and ANDREWS, J. B., "Principles of Labor Legislation," chap. 3.

EDIE, L. D., "Economics; Principles and Problems," chap. 38.

ELY, R. T., "Outlines of Economics," chap. 23.

FAIRCHILD, F. R., FURNISS, E. S., and BUCK, N. S., "Elementary Economics," chaps. 54 and 55.

FURNISS, E. S., "Labor Problems," chaps. 12 to 15.

GROAT, G. G., "Organized Labor in America," chaps. 10–15 and chap. 18.

HAMILTON, W., "Current Economic Problems," pp. 638–666.

KING, W. L. M., "Industry and Humanity," chaps. 10 and 11.

SEAGER, H. R., "Principles of Economics," chaps. 29 and 31.

TAUSSIG, F. W., "Principles of Economics," chap. 59.

WATKINS, G. S., "Introduction to a Study of Labor Problems," chaps. 14, 18, 19, and 21.

WEBB, SIDNEY, and BEATRICE, "Industrial Democracy," part 2, chaps. 2 and 3.

WRIGHT, C. D., "Industrial Evolution of the United States," chaps. 25 and 26.

References

American Federation of Labor, History, Encyclopedia, and Reference Book.

BAKER, R. S., "The New Industrial Unrest."

BARNETT, G. E., and McCABE, D. A., "Mediation, Investigation, and Arbitration in Industrial Disputes."

BROADHEAD, H., "State Regulation of Labor and Labor Disputes in New Zealand."

BURTON, E. R., "Employee Representation."

CARVER, T. N., "Present Economic Revolution in the United States."

CLARK, V. S., "The Labor Movement in Australasia; a Study in Social Democracy."

COHEN, J. H., "Law and Order in Industry; Five Years' Experience."

COLE, G. D. H., "Labor in the Commonwealth."

COOKE, F. H., "The Law of Combinations, Monopolies, and Labor Unions."

CROWTHERS, S., "Why Men Strike."

EMMETT, B., "Profit Sharing in the United States," *Bulletin* 203 U. S. Bureau of Loan Statistics.

GILMAN, N. P., "Methods of Industrial Peace."

——, "Profit Sharing between Employer and Employee and a Dividend to Labor."

GOMPERS, S., "Labor and the Employer."

GOODRICH, C. L., "The Frontier of Control."

GROAT, G. G., "Attitude of American Courts in Labor Cases."

HEILMAN, R. E. "Profit Sharing."

HOLLANDER, J. H., and BARNETT, G. E., "Studies in American Trade Unionism."

LAIDLER, H., "Boycotts and the Labor Struggle."

MARTIN, W. A., "A Treatise on the Law of Labor Unions."

MITCHELL, J., "Organized Labor."

OLDS, M., "The High Cost of Strikes."

MOTE, C. H., "Industrial Arbitration."

National Industrial Conference Board's Research Report No. 29, "Profit Sharing by American Employees."

PIGOU, A. C., "Principles and Methods of Industrial Peace."

SUFFERN, A. E., "Conciliation and Arbitration in the Coal Industry."

THOMPSON, L. A., "Profit Sharing and Labor Copartnership, A List of Recent References." *Monthly Labor Review* April, 1923.

United States Bureau of Labor Statistics, *Bulletins* 60, 98, 124, 133, 144, 145, 191, 198, 233, 237, 255.

Report of the Industrial Commission of 1902, vol. 17, pp. 325–546.

Questions for Discussion

1. Differentiate between the primary and the secondary boycott.
2. Discuss the legality of boycotts.
3. What is an injunction?   Defend its use.
4. How may injunctions be abused?
5. Discuss the legality of strikes.
6. Discuss the legality of picketing.
7. Compare the economic and social costs of industrial disputes.
8. Differentiate between mediation and conciliation and between mediation and arbitration.
9. Contrast the relative advantages and disadvantages of mediation and voluntary arbitration.
10. Show the objectives and limitations of compulsory investigation.
11. Explain the methods used in Canada and Colorado.
12. Justify or criticize compulsory arbitration.
13. Outline briefly the methods used in Kansas and New Zealand.
14. What are some of the distinctive features of trade agreements?
15. What do you understand by industrial democracy?
16. Is it both practical and desirable?   Why or why not?

Topics for Investigation

1. Causes of strikes and their changing character.
2. Functions and duties of walking delegates.
3. Effects of the Clayton Act of 1914 upon collective bargaining.
4. The sympathetic strike and the general strike.
5. The railway strikes of 1877 and 1894.
6. The anthracite coal strike of 1902.
7. Governmental machinery for better industrial relations in your own state.
8. The promotion of industrial peace during the War.
9. President Wilson's First and Second Industrial Conferences.
10. The success of compulsory arbitration in Australasia.
11. The history of the Kansas Court of Industrial Relations.

12. The success of compulsory investigation in Canada and Colorado.

13. Compulsory arbitration and organized labor.

14. Works councils and industrial councils in Great Britain.

15. Trade agreements in the coal mines.

16. Prevention and settlement of industrial disputes in the clothing industries.

CHAPTER XXVII

SOCIALISM AND ECONOMIC RADICALISM

1. Nature of Socialism.—There are so many different types of socialism that it is difficult to define the movement with any exactness. Only a broad definition is possible. The common essential in all true schools of socialism is the substitution of collective ownership and control of industry for individual initiative and the present competitive system. The profits motive is to be eliminated or reduced in favor of the social service motive. A democratic organization of the workers is to succeed industrial absolutism. Moreover, socialism involves some fundamental changes in the institution of private property. Although permitting property rights in a certain amount of consumption goods, socialism attacks private property rights in land and capital. The cooperative movement would eliminate the individual enterpriser and the single-tax movement the landlord, but socialism would eliminate the capitalist also. It differs from communism in that the latter refuses to recognize any property rights whatsoever. Socialism seeks to eliminate property incomes from such sources as inheritance, rent, interest, and profits. Wages would be the only form of income and all incomes would be earned incomes. Socialists differ among themselves on the question of equality or inequality of wages. They generally regard the salaries of brain workers, as well as the wages of manual laborers, as earned incomes.

There are many programs of social reform which are socialistic but which are not socialism, because they do not involve the collective ownership and operation of industry. The defeat of such measures is sometimes accomplished by the use of invective rather than reason. The specter of socialism is paraded through the legislative halls with deadly effect. Moreover, socialism is often confused with other relatively radical movements which are not socialism. We have seen that socialism is not communism. Again, socialism is entirely different from anarchism ,although the two movements are sometimes regarded

576

as identical. Anarchism seeks the reduction of governmental functions and the elimination of the political state. This may be done by evolutionary as well as by revolutionary methods. State socialism, on the other hand, seeks the increase of governmental functions, for it proposes that the state own and operate all industries. Socialism does not propose the elimination of religion, the church or the institution of the family. It is true that certain early socialists were atheists and proposed to substitute a kind of promiscuity for the monogamous family. These radical religious and social proposals, however, have nothing to do with the economic creed of socialism. There are Christian socialists and agnostic capitalists. It might be argued with equal falsity that all socialists are Christians and that all capitalists are agnostics.

2. Socialists' Indictment of Capitalism.—Socialists usually begin their arguments with a criticism of the present economic system, rather than with a statement of the proposals of socialism. To a mind in which a burning consciousness of the evils of modern capitalism has been aroused, the promises of socialism stand out in bright relief. Remedial measures and other alternatives are slighted, and socialism in general or a certain type of socialism in particular is stressed as the one way of economic salvation.

The first indictment made by the socialists is that the present competitive system is wasteful. There is an unnecessary duplication of material equipment and human effort. Thus, the railroads developed as competitive enterprises under individual initiative. The result is the present struggle to develop integrated systems and to bring order out of chaos. Would it not have been better for the state or some other central agency to have directed the railroad development of the country? The tendency toward monopoly can easily be seen in other industries. Our economic development has been from small-scale production to large-scale production with all the advantages of the latter. The present tendency seems to be toward large-scale management and monopoly. As private monopoly is unthinkable, governmental ownership is necessary.

The advantages of monopoly result from the greater utilization of the advantages of large-scale production and management with the consequent elimination of the wastes of competition. They can be seen in the meat-packing and steel industries, as well as in public utilities. There are advantages in administration and distribution, as well as in production. Cross freights can be eliminated and the goods shipped from the nearest point to the consumer. Witness the economies of a large mail-order house such as Sears, Roebuck and Company. On the other hand, note the lost effort which results when numerous milk wagons and bread boys cover the same route to the discomfort of the sleeping millions of our large cities. Compare this situation with the distribution of the mail by a centralized governmental authority.

In a somewhat similar fashion, selling expenses can be reduced and the enormous wastes of competitive advertising eliminated by large-scale management. It is thus contended that under socialism ugly billboards would no longer shriek the merits of "X" kidney pills as compared with "Y" kidney pills, or "A" shaving cream as compared with "B" shaving cream. In the last place, it is generally agreed that a monopoly price is more stable than a competitive price. That the present competitive system does not work smoothly is attested by the business cycle with its constantly recurring periods of depression. Socialists claim that under the control of numerous individual enterprisers rather than under some central governmental agency there will always be misdirected production and economic crises.

Another indictment of the present economic system is the existing inequality of wealth and income. We have seen how unequally the national income is distributed among the people of the United States. At the present time the nation possesses several thousand millionaires and several million paupers. Conspicuous consumption exists on the one hand and dire poverty on the other. Socialists point out that if all incomes were earned and all property incomes were eliminated, such economic inequality would be reduced.

The socialist also criticizes the profits motive which directs production under our present system. Economic demand rather than social welfare is the indicator which production now follows. Inequalities in income make possible the production of luxuries for some before necessities for all. Moreover, the quality and character of economic goods also suffer. It is profitable to produce shoddy cloth, to adulterate food, and to make things which are injurious to their users but which have a ready market. "Illth" rather than wealth is the result. The method of production is also important. Goods are made in ugly factories, which belch out clouds of smoke into the air we breathe, and which pour streams of refuse into the water which is used for drinking water by towns farther down the river. Public health and aesthetic values are threatened by this spirit of gain. The conservation of natural resources is impossible in a competitive society.

Although human nature is social as well as individualistic, the sordid profits motive has developed our acquisitive traits and inhibited our cooperative efforts. The esteem of one's fellows, or social recognition, is desired by every member of society. The valor of the soldier and the research of the scientist are rewarded by the laurel wreath rather than by pecuniary compensation. To certain groups at all times and to all groups at certain critical times, the social service spirit transcends the profits motive. Could such a spirit not be extended to normal industrial life? The profits motive has dominated our economic order and expressed success in terms of the dollar mark. Social recognition rather than the accumulation of fortunes might have proven an equally adequate reward for those great captains of industry who have led the army of economic progress.

In the last place, socialism indicts the present system as productive of human as well as of economic wastes. Not only does the profits motive lower the social plane of competition and degrade human nature, but it is also responsible for certain economic maladjustments, many of which have been discussed in earlier chapters. Child labor, unemployment, dangerous trades, and occupational diseases are laid by socialists at the door of modern capitalism. In spite of the fact that labor is the source of all wealth the wages of many workers are inadequate to maintain decent standards of living. Because the instruments of production are owned by a propertied class, labor is exploited and does not receive its full product.

3. Proposals of Socialism.—The very definition of socialism gives its first and fundamental proposal, that of collective ownership and operation of the instruments of production. Some socialists would apply collective owernship to all the instruments of production and would permit individual ownership only of the worker's own home, clothing, and personal effects. More conservative socialists, however, would apply collective ownership only to the basic industries. Between these two extremes there are many compromise positions. Most socialists would permit the farmer to claim as much land as one man could culti-vate. He could not rent any excess amount to some other indi-vidual, nor could he hire a laborer to till his land for him. In these cases the wage system or the landlord would be reintroduced. Although the individual tradesman might be permitted in cer-tain businesses which are by nature small scale, all large stores and manufacturing plants would be collective enterprises.

The change from individual to collective ownership of industry involves a process of confiscation to which many people object. The socialist replies that the landlord and capitalist have already confiscated for themselves the free gifts of nature and the products of labor of all workers. Socialism is therefore not confiscation, but recovery. Moreover, the old argument of confiscation opposes all social reform. The abolition of human slavery involved the confiscation of the property of the poor widow who owned but a single slave. In order to avoid the charge of confiscation, a socialistic state might purchase private industries from their present owners by exchanging corporate stocks and bonds for the governmental bonds of the new social-istic state. In this manner collective ownership of industry might be established without confiscation. However, inequality of wealth would persist. Unless these government bonds were to become worthless, interest must be paid upon them. This would constitute a form of property income repugnant to all true socialists.

Socialism proposes the elimination of all forms of income except wages. Although earned income is the only type of income which socialists recognize, this includes the rewards of brain as well as of brawn. Moreover, it does not follow that all incomes should be the same. Although some socialists insist on a flat equality of income, others propose an income dependent on the size of the family, that is, in proportion to needs rather than economic productivity. Most socialists, however, recognize the necessity for a moderate wage differential in proportion to economic productivity, or at least in proportion to individual effort. If all workers received the same wage irrespective of their economic productivity, there would be a dangerous tendency toward idle-ness or "soldiering on the job." To apportion income according to the size of the family would be to accentuate the Malthusian tendency and to reward biologic productivity rather than eco-nomic productivity. The exact method of determining wages under socialism is a matter of considerable controversy. There would probably be a minimum wage in order to prevent any individuals from living below a decent standard of living. Above this line wages would vary according to the subjective sacrifices or the objective productivity of the workers. There would be no enormous wages or property incomes of any sort.

Commodity money might be used under socialism, although there would be no private banks or bankers. Socialism does not necessarily involve an abandonment of the gold standard or of ordinary credit currency. On the other hand, wages might be paid in labor checks, which in turn could be used for the purchase of goods from government stores. Under the present competitive system the prices of goods and the wages of labor are determined in the open market by the forces of supply and demand. Under socialism price as a controlling and organizing factor would not play its present rôle. Socialism does not necessitate the elimination of a price system, although it would considerably modify it. It might be necessary for some central agency to determine the productivity or sacrifice of a given worker in order to fix his wages. It might also be necessary to fix the price of a given commodity in terms of the amount of labor which it represents. It is difficult to conceive of any governmental agency qualified to perform such a task or of any method by which this might accurately be done.

In the fourth place, socialism proposes to substitute an industrial democracy for an industrial absolutism. Control by the workers through some form of industrial representation is regarded as essential. This factor in socialism was overlooked by many early state socialists. They proposed to substitute governmental ownership and operation for individual initiative in industry, but they failed to provide any method for the democratization of industry. State socialism with its centralized governmental bureaus failed to give the workers a voice in the control of industry. Hence, guild socialism developed its ideal of the self-governing workshop.

There are a number of other miscellaneous proposals of socialists, which, although not a part of socialism in the strict sense of the word, are generally associated with it. Thus, socialists propose certain educational reforms. Children would be prevented from leaving school at an early age and going to work. Educational opportunity would be extended in all directions.

The government rather than benevolent individuals would be the builder of museums and art galleries. The state would become the patron of the arts and sciences. Community centers, parks and playgrounds, as well as supervised theaters, would be provided for the recreation of all citizens of the socialistic state. Health and safety in industry, as well as improved housing and better living conditions, would be promoted. Municipal tenements would take the place of slums. Public hospitals would be open to all, and most physicians would be governmental officers. Social insurance is not socialism, but the latter generally includes the former. A socialistic state would provide not only workmen's compensation for industrial accidents, but also sickness insurance, unemployment insurance and old age pensions.

4. Theories of Karl Marx.—The "Communist Manifesto," published in 1848, the year of the political Revolution, is the practical handbook of socialism and contains its various proposals. It was compiled by Karl Marx and Friedrich Engels as the party platform of early socialism. "Das Kapital," a later work of Marx, contains an elaborate exposition of the economic theories of Marxian socialism. Karl Marx was a German Jew who was exiled from his native land and who accomplished most of his writing in London. "Das Kapital" has been regarded as "the Bible of Socialism." It is to socialists what Henry George's "Progress and Poverty" is to single taxers. This monumental work is fundamental to all theories of socialism, whether of Marxian or of dissenting schools. Marxian socialism is also known as scientific socialism. Some of the leading principles of Marx must be outlined in any discussion of socialistic theory. These included the economic interpretation of history, the concentration of capitalistic control, the exploitation of the proletariat or the theory of surplus value, the overproduction theory of industrial crises, and the doctrine of class struggle.

Karl Marx's economic interpretation of history, in brief, is that the economic environment is the determining factor in civilization. In other words, our political life, our social institutions and even our religious and moral ideas are vitally affected by our economic environment. Consequently, the Industrial Revolution was of profound significance. The invention of power machinery and the introduction of the factory system have influenced not only our economic life, but also our cultural institutions. The result is a crass materialism and an identification of wealth with welfare.

The invention of power machinery and the introduction of the factory system result inevitably in the substitution of large-scale production for small-scale production. The craftsman and the small independent producer will gradually disappear. Indeed, the middle class or bourgeoisie will ultimately cease to exist. There is a growing concentration in the control of industry. The socialists point to the modern trust as proof of the truth of this economic doctrine of concentration. While the capitalist is increasing in power and wealth, the workers are suffering from ever-increasing poverty and misery.

The exploitation of the proletariat, *i.e.* the workers who have been dispossessed of their instruments of production, is closely connected with Karl Marx's labor theory of value. Socialists contend that the value of any commodity depends upon the quantity of socially necessary labor contained in it. The productivity of capital unaided by labor is denied, and labor is regarded as the primary or ultimate source of all wealth. Capital itself is merely stored up labor. Inasmuch as interest, rent and other forms of property income are recognized today, the worker does not receive all the wealth which he produces. A surplus value, or the difference between the wages of the worker and the value of his product, is appropriated by the capitalist. Hence the laborer is exploited.

Another principle of Marxian socialism is that of overproduction as the cause of industrial crises. Because of the existing inequality of wealth, the poorer classes in society cannot buy enough. On the other hand, the wealthy groups have an income in excess of their needs and are forced to invest a large share of it in productive enterprises. The result is a further increase in production until more consumption goods are in existence than can be disposed of at existing prices. The result is an economic depression or a halting of the processes of industry until consumption again catches up with production. The socialists point to our regularly recurring economic crises as proof of this doctrine of overproduction. They contend that crises are inevitable under modern capitalism, and that they are becoming steadily worse. As they will finally become intolerable, capitalism carries within itself the seeds of its own destruction.

A final principle of Marxian socialism is that of class struggle along economic lines. History has told us the story of the struggles between masters and slaves and between lords and serfs. The Industrial Revolution created an irremovable and ever-widening gulf between capitalists and proletariat. Scientific socialism does not preach revolution, but regards it as inevitable. As the middle class disappears, the conflict of interests between the two extremes in society will become more intense. The dispossessed proletariat will finally rise in their might. By sheer power of numbers they will take possession of the instruments of production and operate them collectively. The wage slavery of modern industrialism will then be eliminated.

5. Criticism of Marxism.—This mere outline of the underlying principles of Marxian socialism is too brief to state them thoroughly and with sufficient qualifications. One of the weakest points in scientific socialism is its labor theory of value. If we admit that labor is the ultimate source of all wealth and that capital itself is the product of labor, we are still compelled to point out that roundabout production, or labor aided by capital, is more productive than labor unaided or directly applied. The socialist himself will admit the superior productivity of capitalistic labor, but demands the collective ownership and operation of the capital. Labor as a measure of value is even more difficult to defend than labor as the source of all value. Marx assumes homogeneous units of labor, the number of which would determine the value of a coat or a book. This abstraction is impractical as a measure of the costs of production. The labor theory of value also minimizes the factor of demand, as influenced by the divergent desires of consumers. Of what value is the product of a given number of labor units, if no one has any desire for it? Marx merely assumes that the good is socially desirable and does not provide for varying degrees of utility.

The Marxian concept of overproduction needs considerable refinement. Although there may be misdirected production or general overproduction in the sense of more goods than can be disposed of at current prices, unqualified general overproduction is impossible in the sense that there are more goods produced than can be consumed. On the other hand, the socialist is probably correct in his contention that greater equality of income would have a stabilizing effect on industry by increasing the effective demands of the workers. Although this factor is of great importance, an explanation of crises, however, must take other things into account, such as sound currency and changes in price levels.

Although we are forced to admit the growing concentration in industry, it does not follow that the middle class is disappearing or that society may be divided arbitrarily into two great hostile groups of exploiting capitalists and exploited proletariat. Today, the stock of many great corporations is held by thousands of small stockholders. Again, the laboring class is materially better off now than at the time when Karl Marx wrote "Das Kapital." Indeed, it is a debatable matter as to whether it is relatively worse off. In spite of the inadequacy of the wages of a large portion of our laboring population, the long-run tendency of real wages has been upward. Moreover, the growth of labor organizations and industrial representation has given the workers a greater participation in the control of industry as well as a greater share in its product.

6. Early Schools of Socialism.—Although the socialists are united in their indictment of modern capitalism and in their proposal to substitute collective ownership and operation of the instruments of production for individual enterprise and private property rights, they differ widely among themselves as to other proposals and as to the methods by which the main objective of socialism is to be accomplished. Hence, it will be necessary to outline some different schools of socialism.

Socialistic or communistic Utopias are as old as Plato's "Republic." The term "Utopian socialism," however, is generally restricted to a small group of writers who lived in the closing years of the eighteenth century and the opening years of the nineteenth century. These include Saint Simon, Fourier, and Proudhon in France, and Robert Owen in England. They dreamed of an ideal society in which voluntary cooperation would replace competition and coercion. The movement expressed itself in numerous communistic societies, such as New Harmony in Indiana, and Brook Farm in New England.

As a reaction against Utopian socialism, scientific or Marxian socialism appeared in Germany about the middle of the last century. State socialism has been regarded as a practical application of scientific or Marxian socialism. It may be said to date from the Congress of Eisenach in 1872. State socialism has also been termed "socialism of the chair" because of the advocacy of its doctrines by certain German professors of economics. It magnifies the importance of the state as the fundamental social institution and proposes to extend governmental

functions to industry.   State socialism favors the governmental
ownership and operation of basic industries.   It has also reflected
itself in protective labor legislation and social insurance.   After
an unsuccessful campaign against this "spectre of Europe,"
Bismarck appropriated a number of the proposals of state
socialism and put them into effect in Germany.

As a reaction against the fantastic and atheistic character of
some of the proposals of early Utopian socialists, Christian
socialism emerged.   It developed in England under the leadership
of F. D. Maurice, J. M. Ludlow, and of Charles Kingsley, who
expressed his convictions in the novel entitled "Alton Locke."
It stressed the immoral rather than the uneconomic character
of our present industrial system.   It preached the gospel of the
brotherhood of man and the dignity of labor.   The first great
socialist was He who enunciated the great commandment that
man should love his neighbor as himself.   Christian socialism
spent itself in humanitarian legislation and in the development
of higher ideals in industry.   It sought to carry the Golden Rule
into economic society.

While scientific or Marxian socialism is revolutionary, Fabian
socialism is evolutionary.   The Fabian Society of London was
organized in 1884 by a small group of English intellectuals.   The
name is supposed to have been derived from the Roman general,
Fabius cunctator, or the delayer.   The abandonment of his
waiting policy in the campaign against Hannibal, the Carthagin-
ian general, brought disaster to the Roman republic.   In a
similar manner popular education is regarded by Fabians as a
necessary preparation for socialism.   It would be unfortunate
for it to come to pass before the great mass of citizens were ready
for it.   Fabian socialism teaches that socialism is to come by the
gradual process of peaceful change rather than by the method of
bloody revolution.   It points out that monopolies are becoming
more and more prevalent and that governmental regulation is
constantly widening.   It is but a step from regulation to socialization, and Fabian socialists propose the gradual nationalization
of all important industries.   Thus, socialism will come almost
unconsciously.[1]   Fabian socialists include such brilliant writers
as H. G. Wells, Bernard Shaw, and Sidney and Beatrice Webb.

[1] Tawney, the keen critic of modern industrial society, characterized the
Fabian socialists as those who pray, "Give us Socialism, Oh Lord, but not in
our time."

Of recent years, however, Fabian socialism in England has declined in favor of guild socialism.

7. Guild Socialism.—Guild socialism is a still more recent cult of socialism. It may be regarded as a hybrid of socialistic theory and trade union machinery. It developed in England, where G. D. H. Cole has been one of its chief exponents. It may be regarded as a reaction against the centralized bureaucracy of state socialism. Guild socialists claim that the factory system has robbed the worker of his independence, and that the machine process has stifled the joy of workmanship. Like John Ruskin and William Morris, they have idealized the craftsmanship of the medieval guilds and have revolted against the modern standardization of the worker and his product. The guild socialist's cry is for self-government in industry. This could not be accomplished under state socialism, which necessitates the autocratic control of industry by cabinet ministers or state departments of industry. Thus, the state socialism of Germany has been regarded as stifling the initiative and creative efforts of the individual worker. Guild socialism would use the administrative machinery of modern trade unions, but in some mysterious way it would breathe into them the spirit of the medieval craftsman. It is not a revolt against the machine process itself, however, such as Ruskin and Morris voiced in their writings, or as Ghandi preached in India.

Under guild socialism foremen are to be elected by the workers, and there are to be shop committees and works councils. A national guild congress is to represent the workers of the various industries in some such way as the American Federation of Labor represents the different groups of workers in the United States. Professional and clerical groups, however, would also be represented. Thus, there would be guilds of physicians and teachers, as well as guilds of carpenters and miners. Guild socialism proposes an industrial as well as a territorial representation, and an economic as well as a political democracy. A dual concept of the state is involved. Sidney and Beatrice Webb in a recent book entitled, "A New Constitution for the Socialistic Commonwealth of Great Britain," propose to retain the monarchy and also the present House of Commons as representative of the consumers of the United Kingdom. Their radical proposal is the abolition of the useless House of Lords and its replacement by a new national body to represent national organizations of producers. Sovereignty is divided between the Guild Congress and the House of Commons.

8. Syndicalism.—Syndicalism is sometimes incorrectly classified as a radical type of socialism. Most syndicalists accept the socialistic indictment of capitalism and the leading theories of Karl Marx. However, they favor economic rather than political action. Syndicalism, as we have seen, may also be regarded as a revolutionary type of labor organization, which favors industrial unions rather than trade unions and direct action rather than collective bargaining. It seeks the overthrow of capitalism rather than higher wages and improved working conditions.

Syndicalism proposes one big union of all workers and repudiates the present political state. It ignores the political activities of numerous socialistic groups which look toward a gradual nationalization of industry. Syndicalists advocate the general strike and condone the weapon of sabotage. They accept the Marxian principle of class struggle and eagerly await the economic revolution of the workers of the world. The new industrial state is to function through local bodies of workers and their national representatives. Syndicalism differs from guild socialism in that it is revolutionary rather than evolutionary. Moreover, it does not propose industrial representation in addition to political representation, but rather in lieu of it. Control is to be in the hands of the workers who are numerically the strongest group. It has already been indicated that there is much in common among the Industrial Workers of the World in the United States, syndicalism in France and Italy and Bolshevism in Russia.

9. Sovietism and Bolshevism.—In the strict sense of the word sovietism is merely industrial representation, rather than political or territorial representation. If sovietism were fairly applied, all economic groups would be represented in an industrial parliament in proportion to their numerical strength. However, such has not been the case in Russia. Certain economic groups, such as the brainworkers and the farmers, were either excluded or unfairly represented. The word "Bolshevist" merely means majority. Nevertheless, it happened in Russia that the Bolshevists were not the majority, but rather a very active minority which succeeded in gaining control. It is often the case in revolutions that small groups succeed in dominating the entire situation. It is too early as yet to say much of the Russian situation, and an accurate description of this momentous experiment is rendered difficult because of active propaganda both for and against Bolshevism. When its complete history is written at some future date, the truth will be found to be somewhere between the two extremes of current public opinion.

The leader of the Russian Revolution, Nikolai Lenin, outlined four different stages in its progress: (1) capitalism, (2) dictatorship of the proletariat by revolution, (3) socialism, and (4) communism. Thus, socialism was regarded as a mere step toward ultimate communism. With the progress of the Russian Revolution the large estates of the former landed aristocracy were divided among the peasants. The nationalization of the land was found to be impractical. All industries, however, were taken over by the state and managed by the Supreme Economic Council with its various production departments. There was a Commissariat of Labor which directed the labor supply and was empowered to conscript workers. The unemployed were to receive the wages of unskilled labor and a system of public labor exchanges was organized. The state fixed the prices of goods produced and arranged a graduated scale of wages depending upon skill and technical knowledge. Because of the embargo of foreign nations, Russia found it difficult to obtain capital and other necessaries for the health and industry of the nation. Food for the industrial population of the cities was requisitioned of the agricultural workers, who were paid in the worthless Russian currency. Great suffering resulted from the breakdown of existing systems of exchange and transportation. The chaotic condition of Russian industry finally resulted in a number of concessions to capitalism and a partial return of private enterprise. The present economic situation of Russia is more comparable to a modified form of state socialism than to pure communism and sovietism.

The much-heralded failure of the Bolshevistic experiment in Russia is often cited as an illustration of the impossibility of socialism. It must be pointed out that the Russian experiment neither proves nor disproves the success of socialism. Indeed, Bolshevism is more of an experiment in communism than socialism. Moreover, a revolutionary period is hardly a fair test of any movement. Social, educational, religious and political changes were going on simultaneously with economic changes. It is doubtful how well a capitalistic government would have succeeded under the burden placed upon it. Demagogues competed with statesmen for control and immediate expediency triumphed over ultimate aims. The open hostility of foreign nations colored the character of the Russian Revolution, just as a century before a similar situation had changed the character of the French Revolution.

10. International Progress of Socialism.—A sketch of the development of socialism is difficult because of the existence of many different types and movements. The strength of socialism has been dissipated by the secession of still more radical elements, such as the communists and the syndicalists. The World War and the Russian Revolution divided the socialists still further. A proper appraisal of their strength must include such an allied movement as that of the British Labor Party. In the last place, the indirect achievements of socialism are perhaps of more importance than its direct achievements. Thus, socialism has often reflected itself as the voice of protest against existing evils and in favor of socialistic legislation, such as social insurance, progressive income, inheritance taxes, and the public ownership of utilities. Any appraisal of the strength of socialism must include not only its allied movements, but also its indirect influences. At the present time, however, socialism is not merely the economic philosophy of a small group of visionary idealists, but the practical political conviction of a large number of statesmen and voters. There are one or more socialist parties in every important nation.

Socialism has been an international rather than a national movement. Hence, it calls upon the workers of all nations to stop capitalistic warfare and to unite in a new war against capitalism itself. The first such international appeal was the Communist Manifesto issued in 1848. An International Workingmen's Association was held in 1864, which developed into what was known as the First International. It endured eight years, but was finally disrupted by a schism between the Marxian socialists and the communist anarchists under the leadership of the Russian radical, Bakunin. The Second International was inaugurated in Paris in 1889 as a direct movement against militarism. The triumph of nationalism during the World War meant the end of this Second International. The Third or Communist International was organized in Moscow in 1919. It is a direct reaction against political and evolutionary socialism. A product of Russian Bolshevism, it seeks to spread to other lands the system of soviets or workingmen's associations. Conservative socialists have refused to affiliate themselves with the Third International.

11. State Socialism in Europe.—The earliest development of socialism took place in Germany, and the chief stronghold of state socialism is still on the continent of Europe. The Social Democrats of Germany were the first important political party to organize on a collectivist platform. They professed adherence to Marxian principles and attempted to bring about state socialism. Expediency, however, dictated a resort to evolutionary rather than revolutionary progress. Practical political experience also caused a resort to constitutional methods rather than to violence. Although Bismarck and Emperor William I attempted to stifle the socialist movement in Germany, it grew steadily in numbers and political importance. In spite of the government's refusal to reapportion seats in the Prussian Assembly in accordance with changes in population, the number of socialist deputies increased. At the close of the last century the Social Democrat party throughout the German Empire polled two million votes, and just before the World War five million votes, which represented the largest popular vote of all parties. Although the socialist deputies had previously refused to vote for military expenditures, they were submerged during the War. In Germany, as elsewhere, nationalism triumphed over socialism. A crisis was finally reached in the last year of the War, when the socialists directed the republican revolution of 1918. The late President Ebert, a conservative socialist, headed the new coalition government of Germany. The Spartacan revolt was the work of a group of radicals, who were communists rather than socialists.

Like most continental countries, and unlike England and the United States, Germany has many political parties rather than two chief ones. Coalition governments are common in Germany and France. In the German parliamentary elections of 1920 and 1924 the Social Democrat party polled eleven million and seven million votes, respectively. It is still the largest single political party in Germany. In spite of a nationalistic reaction which crystallized in the election of President von Hindenburg in 1925, the socialists still hold the balance of power. In the presidential election of April, 1925, the Social Democrats received a popular vote of almost eight million out of a total of twenty-seven million votes. At the same election, the communists received about two million votes.   Foreign affairs, reparations and currency problems have diverted the attention of German statesmen from programs of socialization.   Socialists have been attacked by nationalists on the one extreme and communists on the other.   Nevertheless, German socialists have attempted to further their already highly developed program of public ownership and operation.   This socialization of industries is perhaps even more important in German municipal life than in her national industries.

Most of the new republics of Central Europe are also in the control of socialists, and a mild form of state socialism predominates.   Such is the situation in Austria.   Under the leadership of Bela Kun, Hungary experienced six months of communism and sovietism.   Although the nationalization of industry and agricultural land was effected, a conservative reaction soon triumphed.   In Czechoslovakia a progressive republican government has been in control since 1920, and the Social Democrats maintain a large portion of the total number of seats in the assembly.   Most countries in central Europe are now republics with various programs of state socialism.   However, although the socialists seem to hold the balance of power, nationalism and nationalistic parties are important.   There are also powerful undercurrents of radicalism and communism.   However, the westward spread of sovietism has apparently been checked.

In France, there are a number of socialist factions, which range all the way from conservative and constitutional state socialism to radical syndicalism.   We have seen that syndicalists repudiate the political activities of socialists and would rely on such economic weapons as direct action.   As syndicalists propose the elimination of the present political state, they border on anarchism. Syndicalists, communists and other radical groups have been the source of considerable embarassment to many French ministries which have risen and fallen with bewildering rapidity in recent years.   The socialist vote in France increased from the formation of the Third Republic in 1870 to the outbreak of the World War in 1914.   Numerous socialists held cabinet positions in the various coalition governments.   During the World War nationalism triumphed over socialism in France as it did in Germany.   After the Armistice, however, socialists increased in power, and in 1925 they were in control of the Chamber of Deputies.

The Socialist party has been very strong in Belgium, where the election of 1925 gave them a larger vote than that of any other party. There are also strong Socialist parties in other small countries of Europe, such as Holland and the nations of Scandinavia and the Balkans. Socialism developed to such proportions in Italy, that a nationalistic reaction in the form of Fascism occurred. The dictatorship of Mussolini perverted parliamentary government and violated the constitutional rights of freedom of speech and freedom of the press. A military dictatorship also exists in Spain and in other countries of Europe.

12. British Labor Party.—The British Labor party is a complex of trade union machinery and socialistic principles. Its policy is opportunistic, but constitutional. It savors more of Fabian and guild socialism than of Marxian or state socialism. The program of the British Labor party includes the nationalization of the railroads, mines, and other large industries, as well as the socialization of extensive private holdings of land. Strict governmental regulation is proposed for what industries are left to individual enterprise. The reduction of economic inequality is sought through progressive income and inheritance taxes. Strong belief in social insurance is maintained and opposition is expressed to any reduction in its scopes and benefits.

The significance of trade unionism in British political life may be illustrated by the fact that in 1920 trade unions possessed a membership of over eight millions. Unlike American trade unionism, British trade unionism has expressed itself politically. The British Labor party is a powerful factor in national politics. During the last generation it has grown more rapidly and more consistently than any other party in Great Britain or in any other great democracy. In 1906, it polled a popular vote of a third of a million and had twenty-nine representatives in Parliament; in 1910, a half million popular votes and forty-two representatives; in 1918, over two million popular votes and seventy representatives; in 1922, four million popular votes and one hundred and forty-four representatives; in 1924, four and a half million popular votes and one hundred and ninety-two representatives; and in 1925, five and a half million popular votes but only one hundred and fifty-one representatives in Parliament. In 1924, there were three strong political parties in England, the Conservatives, the Liberals, and the Labor party. The Labor party had become the strongest single party, although it represented but a minority of the total number of voters. Consequently, it was called upon to form the ministry in 1924. Ramsay MacDonald, as leader of the Labor party, became prime minister of England. In a later election of the same year, however, the Labor party lost its control of the government, in spite of the fact that it polled more votes than ever before. The numerical plurality of the Conservative party, which triumphed at the polls, is to be explained by the fact that several million Liberals voted as Conservatives in order to defeat the Labor party. Great Britain returned to its former two-party system by the reduction of the Liberal party to one of minor importance.

13. Socialism in United States.—The majority of the labor group in America have been opposed to the formation of a separate political party. At the present time, however, there are a Socialist party and a Socialist Labor party in the United States. Although neither of these has attained much numerical strength, the socialist vote has increased. The late Eugene V. Debs, when a socialist candidate for President, received almost a million votes in one of the presidential elections. In 1919, the Socialist party in America was split into three parts, the Conservative right wing remaining in the Socialist party, the ultra-radical left wing forming the Communist party, and the central group forming the Communist Labor party. Both of the latter organizations became affiliated with the Moscow International. Unlike the socialists, they despaired of political action and gradual legislative reform. Because of their advocacy of direct action, they should be classified as syndicalists rather than as socialists. In December, 1921, an attempt was made to amalgamate these groups into the United Communist party.

Governmental hostility during the war and the years which followed forced a policy of secrecy. It drove a number of radical movements under ground. Although there has never been a strong national Socialist party in the United States, the socialists have been sufficiently strong in certain communities to elect representatives to the state legislatures. Socialist assemblymen who were recently elected to the New York legislature were refused admission at first by the other members, upon the mere ground that they were socialists. This action was a direct challenge to representative government in America. In Milwaukee a socialist mayor has been elected several times, and a socialist Congressman, Victor Berger, has been sent to the national Congress.

14. Some Criticisms of Socialism.—Students of economic problems may accept the socialistic indictment of our present industrial system without accepting socialism as the best way out of the situation. Moreover, they may accept the ideals of socialism without believing that socialism will successfully bring them to pass. One cannot but admit the economic and human wastes of the present industrial system. One cannot but admire the attempt to substitute social service for the profits motive. It is necessary, however, to raise constantly the practical question as to whether such a scheme will work. Although socialism may gradually improve human nature, we live in an acquisitive society. Although it is dangerous to speak in terms of instincts, self-interest does seem to be a powerful inherent force.

In most individuals, however, there is an inherent or acquired desire to win social recognition. It is possible and desirable that this be expressed in some other way than in the mere accumulation of wealth. It is doubtful, however, if individuals will exert themselves so strenuously for the good of society as for their own individual welfare and that of their immediate group. Socialists reply that they do not propose to eliminate the material rewards of industry, but merely to reduce them. Moreover, social prestige through economic advancement is as great an incentive as material rewards. Although there might be little differences in wages, most individuals would prefer to be executives rather than common laborers. Hence, they will exert themselves to greater efforts because of a desire for leadership.

Private property would be seriously altered by the elimination of the rights of inheritance and private ownership of producers' goods. The right of an individual to own and to bequeath wealth has been a powerful motive toward economic progress. Individual initiative rather than collective enterprise has shaped production.

Not only is the economic motive toward production under socialism rather weak, but there are also obvious administrative objections. We have indicated that the determination of wages and prices would be a difficult task in the absence of competition. Moreover, the determination of the course of production would also be far from easy. It would involve a greater standardization of human wants than exists at present. Although distasteful to certain individuals, who glory in a great variety of economic goods, it need not result in a drab uniformity. Greater standardization would certainly produce an enormous economy of material and effort. Moreover, it is quite likely that collective consumption would be increased at the expense of individual consumption. Public art galleries would supplant private collections and public parks private estates.

If production is no longer in the hands of individual enterprisers who seek to make profits by anticipating the wants of individual consumers, who will be empowered to direct industry and to shape the course of economic production? Competition with its selective power in producing leaders will have been removed. It is contended that socialism is merely an attempt to substitute political competition for economic competition, and that the latter is far more efficient than the former. But the average individual considers more carefully how he spends his money than how he votes. Our political democracy is far from efficient, and socialism substitutes the successful politican for the successful business man as the director of our industrial system.[1]

Has our trial of governmental operation of certain public utilities been sufficiently successful to warrant the universal extension of this system? The direction of the great army of workers would be as difficult as the selection of leaders. Who would be clerks and who would be ditch diggers? Psychological tests and vocational education have not progressed sufficiently far for educational leaders and government employment experts to place men properly in industry. Moreover, such a selection would be far from democratic. Socialism, however, might provide sufficient competition for all individuals to find their own level in economic society. Although admitting biological differences in individuals, socialism would seek to provide equality of opportunity. Moreover, it might provide shorter hours of work in the more disagreeable tasks and higher pay for those occupations which are viewed with social disdain. At present, higher pay and shorter hours characterize the more pleasant and dignified occupations.

There are numerous arguments against socialism which are rather weak. It is contended that socialism would prevent the payment of interest upon capital, because of its elimination of property incomes. As capital is the result of saving and as saving involves abstinence, the abolition of interest as a form of property income would decrease savings and prevent the further accumula-

[1] CARVER, T. N., "Essays in Social Justice," chap. 9.

tion of capital. The socialist replies that capital as well as land would be owned collectively and that saving would be done collectively rather than individually. The state would produce capital goods as well as consumption goods. It would systematically set aside a replacement fund for industry.

15. Summary.—Although there are many different kinds of socialism, their common characteristic is the collective ownership and operation of the instruments of production, rather than a reliance upon individual enterprise and competition. A considerable change in the institution of private property is involved, for the inheritance of large estates and the existence of property rather than service incomes would be prevented. Socialism is not communism, although certain thinkers have regarded the former as a step toward the latter. Socialism is not anarchism, for the former magnifies the state and the latter seeks to eliminate it.

The most complete statement of the theories of socialism is to be found in "Das Kapital," by Karl Marx. He developed the economic interpretation of history, the belief in the concentration of industry and the elimination of the middle class, the theory of overproduction as the cause of industrial crises, the doctrine of class struggle and the exploitation of the proletariat and the labor theory of value. Marxian socialism is also known as scientific socialism. It is deterministic, for it regards the revolution of the workers and the ultimate triumph of socialism as inevitable. Fabian socialism is evolutionary rather than revolutionary. State socialism seeks the government operation of industry and proposes the nationalization, rather than the regulation of basic industries. Guild socialism is a reaction against the bureaucracy of state socialism and proposes self-government in industry. It is an idealization of trade unionism and seeks the development of works councils and national guild congresses of the workers. Syndicalism is economic rather than political, and it proposes direct action of the workers rather than legislative progress toward the nationalization of industries.

Socialists criticize the present economic system upon numerous grounds. They contend that competition is wasteful. Large-scale production is more efficient than small-scale production and results in many savings in production and marketing. There seems to be a natural trend in industry toward the final step of monopoly. Therefore, socialists propose the substitution of collective monopolies for private monopolies. The profits motive is selfish and results in numerous economic maladjustments under our present system of individual enterprise. There are human wastes, as well as material wastes which would be eliminated if production were carried on in the interests of social welfare. Moreover, glaring inequalities in income would be impossible and a greater equality of opportunity would be permitted.

It must be admitted that the socialists' indictment of the present economic system is sound. It does not follow, however, that socialism would remedy those faults which it so keenly discloses. Nor does it follow that we should scrap the present economic system and build anew, rather than merely strive to eliminate existing maladjustments. The institution of private property has been an important factor in economic progress, and the sordid profits motive has stimulated individual enterprise to greater economic production. Whether the social service motive would be as effective is doubtful. Again, numerous administrative problems would confront the new socialist state, such as the wise selection of leaders, the determination of wages and prices, and the direction of the productive forces of industrial society. For these and other reasons many individuals who accept the ideals of socialism reject socialism as a practical solution of our economic problems. They are socialistic, but not socialists. Many of the greatest results of socialism have been indirect rather than direct results.

Collateral Reading

ATKINS, W. E., and LASSWELL, H. D., "Labor Attitudes and Problems," chap. 22.
BLOOMFIELD, D., "Modern Industrial Movements," pp. 153–169 and 243–373.
BLUM, S., "Economics of Labor," chaps. 19, 20, and 21.
CARVER, T. N., "Principles of Political Economy," chaps. 45–49.
———, "Essays in Social Justice," chap. 9.
EDIE, L. D., "Economics Principles and Problems," chap. 37.
FAIRCHILD, F. R., FURNISS, E. S., and BUCK, N. S., "Elementary Economics," chap. 56.
FETTER, F. A., "Modern Economic Problems," chap. 31.
GIDE, C., and RIST, C., "A History of Economic Doctrines," Book II, chaps. 1, 2, and 3; Book IV, chaps. 2 and 3.
HAMILTON, W., "Current Economic Problems," pp. 847–899.
HOBSON, J. A., "The Industrial System," chap. 14.
Report of the British Labor Party on Bolshevism in Russia.

Seager, H. R., "Principles of Economics," chap. 33.
Taussig, F. W., "Principles of Economics," chaps. 66 and 67.
Tugwell, R. G., Munro, T., and Stryker, R. E., "American Economic Life," chaps. 34 and 35.
Watkins, G. S., "Introduction to a Study of Labor Problems," chap. 24.
Williamson, T. R., "Readings in Economics," chaps. 19, 23, 24, 25, and 26.

References

Beer, M., "History of British Socialism."
Bernstein, E., "Evolutionary Socialism."
Boucke, F., "The Limits of Socialism."
Brailsford, H. N., "Russian Workers' Republic."
Brasol, B. L., "Socialism *vs.* Civilization."
Brissenden, P. F., "The I. W. W."
Brooks, J. G., "American Syndicalism, the I. W. W."
Cole, G. D. H., "The World of Labour."
———, "Guild Socialism."
———, "Guild Socialism Restated."
———, "Social Theory."
———, "Self-government in Industry."
Commons, J. R., "The Webb's Constitution," *American Economic Review*, March, 1921 pp. 82–90.
Ely, R. T., "Socialism and Social Reform."
Estey, J. A., "Revolutionary Syndicalism in Europe."
Farbman, M. S., "Bolshevism in Retreat."
Field, G. C., "Guild Socialism."
Herley, J. H., "Syndicalism."
Hillquit, M., "Socialism in Theory and Practise."
———, "History of Socialism in the United States."
———, "From Marx to Lenin."
Hobson, S., "National Guilds."
Hughes, T. J., "State Socialism after the War."
Jaures, J. L., "Studies in Socialism."
Kirkup, T., "History of Socialism."
Kropotkin, P., "Conquest of Bread."
Laidler, H., "Socialism in Thought and Action."
LeRossignol, J. E., "What is Socialism?"
Lewis, A. D., "Syndicalism and the General Strike."
MacDonald, J. R., "Social Unrest."
———, "Socialism."
Mallock, W. H., "A Critical Examination of Socialism."
Marx, K., "Capital."
Marx, K., and Engels, F., "Communist Manifesto."
Pasvolsky, L., "The Economics of Communism."
Reckitt, M. B., and Bechhofer, C. E., "The Meaning of National Guilds."
Russell, B., "Proposed Roads to Freedom."
Sellers, R. W., "The Next Step in Democracy."
Shaw, B., "Fabian Essays."
Skelton, O. D., "Socialism: a Critical Analysis."

SOREL, G., "Reflections on Violence."
SPARGO, J., "Syndicalism, Industrialism, and Socialism."
SPARGO, J., and ARNER, G. L., "Elements of Socialism."
TAWNEY, R. H., "The Acquisitive Society."
WALLING, W. E., and LAIDLER, H. W., "State Socialism, pro and con."
WEBB, SIDNEY, and BEATRICE, "A Constitution for the Socialist Common wealth of Great Britain."
————, "Decay of Capitalist Civilization."
WEBB, S., "Socialism and Individualism."
WELLS, H. G., "New Worlds for Old."
WITHERS, H., "The Case for Capitalism."

Questions for Discussion

1. What do you understand by the term socialism?
2. In what ways might one be socialistic without being a socialist?
3. Differentiate between (1) socialism and anarchism, (2) socialism and communism, and (3) socialism and syndicalism.
4. State five tenets of Karl Marx.
5. Criticize each of these in turn.
6. Upon what grounds do the socialists criticize modern capitalism?
7. Which of these criticisms seem sound to you and why?
8. If one accepts the socialist's indictment of modern capitalism must one also accept socialism?   Why or why not?
9. Contrast revolutionary with evolutionary socialism.
10. Outline some of the leading schools of socialism.
11. Contrast state socialism with guild socialism.
12. What changes would guild socialism involve in the nature of the state?
13. Distinguish between the ideals of socialism and the practical possibilities of socialism.
14. What administrative difficulties do you see in the way of socialism?
15. Do you believe that the profits motive can be eliminated?
16. Should competition be eliminated or regulated?   Why?   How?
17. Distinguish between regulation and nationalization.

Topics for Investigation

1. The progress of socialism in Germany before 1914.
2. Socialism in Germany since the Revolution.
3. Socialism in France.
4. Socialism and international warfare.
5. Socialism and the British Labor party.
6. Bolshevism and private property.
7. Concessions to capitalism in Russia.
8. The socialist movement in the United States.
9. Syndicalism in France and Italy.
10. The First, Second, and Third Internationals.

INDEX

A

Achievement of national prosperity, 452

Ad valorem duties, 334

Adams, H. C., 371, 386

S. R., quoted, 280

Adamson Eight-hour Act, 208

Adequacy, of gold standard, 243

of national income, 455

Adequate working capital, 106

Adjustment of interally debts, 327

Advance contracts, price uncertainties and, 70

Advantages, of corporations over partnerships, 90

of monopoly, 139

of public ownership, 180

of sales tax, 419

Agreements, debt funding, 323

informal, 128

Aldrich Plan, 257

Aldrich-Vreeland Act, 256

Allocation of transportation charges, 217

"Alton Locke," 586

Aluminum Company of America, 346

American Can Company, 137

Cotton Oil Trust, 132

Steel and Wire Company, 140

Sugar Refining Company, 127, 135, 151

Telephone and Telegraph Company, 111

Tobacco Company, 127, 129, 135, 149, 151

American Federation of Labor, 20, 532

growth of, 532

organization of, 534

Anarchism, 576

Anti-trust Act, Sherman, 147

Antwerp Bourse, 48

Applied economics, 5

Apprentices, limitation of, 543

Arbitrage, speculation and, 71

Arbitration, compulsory, 561

voluntary, 561

Arguments for protection, 335 *ff*

Armour and Company, 129

Assessments, inequity in, 425

special, 395

Assets, current, 104

defined, 99

Atchison, Topeka and Santa Fé, 190

Atlantic Coast Line Company, 133, 190

Refining Company, 29, 152

B

Babson Statistical Agency, 69

Balance sheet, international, 300

Baltimore and Ohio Railroad, 186, 189, 200

Bank currency, development of, 230

simplification of, 266

Banking, problems of, 248 *ff*

Banks, investment, function of, 250

Bargaining, collective, 528

Bela Kun, 592

Benefits of foreign investments, 321

Berger, Victor, 594

Bills of exchange, 297

origin of, 297

Bimetallism, illustrated, 228

Bland-Allison Act, 229

"Blanket" injunctions, 559

"Blue Sky" laws, 93

Bolshevism, 588

Bonds, classified, 102

Bonds, coupon, 102
  defined, 102
  registered, 102
Booth, Charles, 447
Borrowing, advantages of, over
    taxing, 375
  disadvantages of, 376
  public receipts from, 371 *ff*
  versus taxing to finance wars, 374
Boston and Maine Railroad, 189
Boycott, 557
  primary, 557
  secondary, 557
Bradstreet Company, 65, 69
British, American Tobacco Com-
    pany, 129
  Labor party, 592
  North American Act, 556
  unemployment insurance, 494
Brook Farm, 585
Buck Stove and Range Company,
    559
"Bucket shops," 57
Budget control of public expendi-
    tures, 367
Bureau of corporations, 154
Business, corporations, 88 *ff*
  crises in the United States, 271
  cycle and price levels, 276
  cycles, 271
    characteristics of, 273
    explanation of, 277
    natural phenomena theories of, 277
    nature of, 271
    phases of, 273
    private control of, 283
    problem of, 271 *ff*
    public control of, 283
    unequal distribution theories
      of, 281
  depressions, remedying effects of,
    282
  operation, cycle of, 104
  organization, 109
Buying on margin, 57

C

California   Cooperative   Fruit
  Growers' Association, 42

Canadian Industrial Disputes Act,
    565
Capital, defined, 26
  fixed, 103
  goods, defined, 27
  new, flotations, 325
  owned and borrowed, 101
  sources of, 98
  working, 103
Capitalism, defined, 26
  socialists' indictment of, 577
Capitalization of franchises, 174
  theories of business cycles, 281
Carnegie, Andrew, 29, 140
Cartwright, Edmond, 11
Carver, T. N., 281
Causes of child labor, 505
  of economic inequality, 459
  for growth of public expenditures,
    362
  of industrial accidents, 469
  of poverty, 448
  of strikes, 553
  of unemployment, 476
Census of Manufacturers, 187
Central Pacific Railroad, 186, 188
Characteristics of business cycles,
    273
  of economic life, 25
  of money, 225
  of public utilities, 171
Chicago Board of Trade, 47, 49, 69
  Burlington, and Quincy, 190, 200
  Indianapolis,   and   Louisville
      Railroad, 134
  Milwaukee, and St. Paul, 190
Child labor, causes of, 505
  effects of, 505
  extent of, 504
  legislation, 506
  problem of, 503
Class struggle, 583
Classification, of public revenues,
    390
  of warehouse certificates, 51
Clay, Henry, 339
Clayton Act, 157, 539, 559
  effects of, on railroads, 206
Closed shop, 545

610 ECONOMIC PROBLEMS OF MODERN LIFE

Occupations, of women, 510
Old Age, Pension Law, 490
  pensions, 490
Open shop, 545
Organization, of American Federation
    of Labor, 534
  of corporation, 96
  of Federal reserve system, 257
  of New York Stock Exchange, 53
Organizations, labor, 528 *ff*
Organizing factor, price as, 45
Origin, and development of economic problem, 7
  of bills of exchange, 297
  of collective bargaining, 529
Overcapitalization, 109, 137
Overproduction, as cause of industrial crises, 583
  theories of business cycles, 278
Owen, Robert, 585
Ownership, municipal, 170

P

Page, Thomas Walter, 340
Panama Canal Act, 206
Par, of exchange, 301
  purchasing power, 305
Patent pool, 130
Patents, 168
Pauperism, poverty and, 444
Payment of foreign debts to United
    States, 317
Payments, economic, 325
  legal, 325
  of old indebtedness, 325
Payne-Aldrich Tariff Act, 334
Pennsylvania Railroad, 111, 133,
    189, 200
Pensions, invalidity, 491
  mothers', 491
  old age, 490
Personal incomes in Federal Revenue
    Act of 1926, 409
Persons, Warren M., 277
Phases of business cycle, 273
Philadelphia, and Reading Railroad,
    133, 189
  Gas Works, 178

Philadelphia, Rapid Transit Company, 178
  Union Traction Company, 174
Physical cause theories of business
    cycles, 277
Picketing, 555
Plato's "Republic," 585
Points, gold, 303
Political science, economies and, 4
Pool, patent, 130
Pools, 128
Post-war inflation, 263
Poverty, 443 *ff*
  and pauperism, 444
  extent of, 447
  objective causes of, 448
Powers of Federal Reserve Board,
    258
Price, 33
  as organizing factor, 45
  defined, 226
  levels and business cycle, 276
  uncertainties, 70
Prices, control over, 164
  monopoly, 135
  problems of, 225 *ff*
  rising, and economic prosperity,
    284 *ff*
Principle of uniformity in taxation,
    399
Principles, of compensation, 485
  of Railroad Transportation, 210
Private, control of business cycles,
    283
  enterprise, reduction of unemployment by, 480
  expenditures, differences between
    public and, 356
  property, institution of, 35
Problem, economic, 6
  of business cycle, 271 *ff*
  of child labor, 503
  of city government, 179
  of money, 225 *ff*
  of monopoly, 117 *ff*
  of protective tariff, 332 *ff*
Problems, of banking, 248 *ff*
  of prices, 225
  of public finance, 353 *ff*